WORLD TRADE ORGANIZATION

Dispute Settlement Reports

2000
Volume VII

Pages 3041-3537

CAMBRIDGE
UNIVERSITY PRESS

PUBLISHED BY THE PRESS SYNDICATE OF THE UNIVERSITY OF CAMBRIDGE
The Pitt Building, Trumpington Street, Cambridge, United Kingdom

CAMBRIDGE UNIVERSITY PRESS
The Edinburgh Building, Cambridge CB2 2RU, UK
40 West 20th Street, New York, NY 10011–4211, USA
477 Williamstown Road, Port Melbourne, VIC 3207, Australia
Ruiz de Alarcón 13, 28014 Madrid, Spain
Dock House, The Waterfront, Cape Town 8001, South Africa

http://www.cambridge.org

Printed in the United Kingdom at the University Press, Cambridge

French edition and Spanish edition paperbacks of this title are both available directly from WTO Publications, World Trade Organization, Centre William Rappard, 154 rue de Lausanne, CH-1211 Geneva 21, Switzerland http://www.wto.org

ISBN 0 521 82353 8 hardback

THE WTO DISPUTE SETTLEMENT REPORTS

The *Dispute Settlement Reports* of the World Trade Organization (the "WTO") include panel and Appellate Body reports, as well as arbitration awards, in disputes concerning the rights and obligations of WTO Members under the provisions of the *Marrakesh Agreement Establishing the World Trade Organization*. The *Dispute Settlement Reports* are available in English, French and Spanish. Starting with 1999, the first volume of each year contains a cumulative index of published disputes.

This volume may be cited as DSR 2000:VII

TABLE OF CONTENTS

Page

CANADA - CERTAIN MEASURES AFFECTING THE AUTOMOTIVE INDUSTRY

Report of the Panel

WT/DS139/R
WT/DS142/R

Adopted by the Dispute Settlement Body on 19 June 2000 as Modified by the Appellate Body Report

TABLE OF CONTENTS

TABLES

FIGURES

I. PROCEDURAL HISTORY

1.1 This proceeding has been initiated by two complaining parties, Japan and the European Communities.

A. *Consultations*

1.2 In a communication dated 3 July 1998 (WT/DS139/1), Japan requested consultations with Canada in accordance with Article 4 of the Understanding on Rules and Procedures Governing the Settlement of Disputes (DSU), pursuant to Article XXIII of the General Agreement on Tariffs and Trade 1994 (GATT), Article 8 of the Agreement on Trade-Related Investment Measures (TRIMs Agreement) (to the extent that Article 8 invokes Article XXIII of GATT 1994), Articles 4 and 30 of the Agreement on Subsidies and Countervailing Measures (SCM Agreement) (to the extent that Article 30 refers to Article XXIII of GATT 1994), and Article XXIII:1 of the General Agreement on Trade and Services (GATS), with respect to certain Canadian measures affecting the automotive industry. Japan and Canada held consultations in Geneva on 27 August 1998, but these consultations did not result in a resolution of the dispute.

1.3 In a communication dated 17 August 1998 (WT/DS142/1), the European Communities requested consultations with Canada pursuant to Article 4 of the DSU, Article XXIII:1 of GATT 1994, Article 8 of the TRIMs Agreement, Articles 4 and 30 of the SCM Agreement, and Article XXIII:1 of the GATS, concerning certain measures affecting the automotive sector. The European Communities and Canada held consultations on 21 September and 13 November 1998, but these consultations did not result in a resolution of the dispute.

1.4 On 12 November 1998 Japan (WT/DS139/2) and on 14 January 1999 the European Communities (WT/DS142/2) each requested the establishment of a panel pursuant to Articles 4.7 and 6 of the DSU.

B. *Establishment and Composition of the Panel*

1.5 At its meeting on 1 February 1999, the DSB established a Panel pursuant to the requests by Japan and the European Communities. The DSB agreed, pursuant to Article 9.1 of the DSU, that a single panel should examine both complaints.

1.6 At that meeting, the parties to the dispute agreed that the Panel should have standard terms of reference provided for in Article 7.1 of the DSU. The terms of reference of the Panel are the following:

> "To examine, in the light of the relevant provisions of the covered agreements cited by Japan and the European Communities in documents WT/DS139/2 and WT/DS142/2 respectively, the matter referred to the DSB by Japan and the European Communities in those documents and to make such findings as will assist the DSB in making the recommendations or in giving the rulings provided for in those agreements".

1.7 On 15 March 1999, the European Communities and Japan jointly requested the Director-General, pursuant to Article 8.7 of the DSU, to determine the composition of the Panel. The Director-General accordingly determined the composition of the Panel (WT/DS139 and 142/3) as follows:

Chairman:	Mr. Ronald Saborío Soto
Members:	Mr. Timothy Groser
	Mr. Rudolf Ramsauer

1.8 India, Korea and the United States reserved their third-party rights in the dispute.

C. *Panel Proceedings*

1.9 The Panel met with the parties on 14 and 15 June 1999 and on 13 and 14 July 1999. The Panel held a third-party session on 15 June 1999.

II. BACKGROUND

2.1 This dispute concerns Canadian measures which accord to certain motor-vehicle manufacturers established in Canada the right to import motor vehicles with an exemption from the generally applicable customs duty.

2.2 To qualify for the exemption, an eligible manufacturer's local production of motor vehicles (including in certain cases the production of parts) must achieve a minimum amount of Canadian value added (CVA), and its local production must maintain a minimum ratio ("production-to-sales" ratio) with respect to its sales of motor vehicles in Canada.

A. *The Auto Pact*

2.3 The measures at issue in this case stem from the Agreement Concerning Automotive Products Between the Government of Canada and the Government of the United States (the "Auto Pact"), a treaty between Canada and the United States concluded in January 1965. Under the Auto Pact, Canada agreed to accord duty-free treatment to vehicles and original equipment manufacturing parts[1] of the United States[2], provided the importer met the definition of a motor vehicles "manufacturer" under the terms of the Auto Pact. An Auto Pact manufacturer must have produced in Canada, during the base year (1963-64), motor vehicles of the class it is importing, and (i) must have maintained a ratio of the sales value of its local production of vehicles of that class to the vehicles of that class sold in Canada of a prescribed minimum, and (ii) must have achieved a minimum amount of CVA in its local production of motor vehicles (including in certain cases the production of parts therefor).[3] The

[1] Excluding tires and tubes.

[2] Article II(a) of the Auto Pact.

[3] Para. 2 of Annex A of the Auto Pact defines a manufacturer as one that:

"(i) produced vehicles of that class in Canada in each of the four consecutive three months' periods in the base year, and

(ii) produced vehicles of that class in Canada in the period of twelve months ending on the 31st day of July in which the importation is made,

(A) the ratio of the net sales value of which to the net sales value of all vehicles of that class sold for consumption in Canada by the manufacturer in that period is equal to or higher than the

Auto Pact also provided that Canada could designate a manufacturer not meeting the base year criterion to import duty-free motor vehicles and original equipment manufacturing parts.[4]

1. Letters from Auto Pact Manufacturer Beneficiaries to Industry Canada

2.4 Prior to the conclusion of the Auto Pact, the Canadian Government requested from the Auto Pact manufacturers certain Letters specifying how each company viewed its operations in relation to the Auto Pact. While the Letters were not released publicly, those of General Motors of Canada, Ltd., Ford Motor Company of Canada, Ltd., Chrysler Canada, Ltd., and American Motors[5] were made public in hearings of the US Congress on the Automotive Products Trade Act, 1965 (the US implementing legislation for the Auto Pact).

2.5 The Letters address similar issues, and some of them are framed in similar and, in parts, identical language. The complainants contend that these Letters contain additional CVA requirements and constitute binding undertakings. The respondent contends that the Letters are not binding, that they contain no such requirements, and that the only evidence on the record indicates that the Letters are not binding. The parties' arguments relating to the status of these Letters are found in Section V (Factual Arguments of the Parties) and in Section VI (Legal Arguments of the Parties).

2. GATT Working Party Examination of the Auto Pact

2.6 In March 1965 a GATT Working Party was established to examine the Auto Pact.[6] The Working Party found that the US application of the Auto Pact would violate the GATT:

> "It was the general consensus of the Working Party that, if the United States implemented the Agreement in the manner proposed, United States action would be clearly inconsistent with Article I and it would be necessary for the United States Government to seek a waiver from its GATT obligations."[7]

2.7 The United States sought and obtained a waiver under Article XXV:5.[8] In November 1996 that waiver was renewed at the request of the United States[9], until

---

ratio of the net sales value of all vehicles of that class produced in Canada by the manufacturer in the base year to the net sales value of all vehicles of that class sold for consumption in Canada by the manufacturer in the base year, and is not in any case lower than seventy-five to one hundred; and

(B) the Canadian value added of which is equal to or greater than the Canadian value added of all vehicles of that class produced in Canada by the manufacturer in the base year."

[4] Para. 3 of Annex A of the Auto Pact.

[5] American Motors was acquired by Chrysler in 1987.

[6] Report of the *Working Party on Canada - US Agreement on Automotive Products*, submitted to the Council of Representatives 19 November 1965, BISD 13S/112 (hereinafter Report of the *Working Party on Canada - US Agreement on Automotive Products*).

[7] Ibid., para. 17.

[8] Ibid., para. 15; Decision of the Contracting Parties of 20 December 1965 granting the waiver requested by the United States, BISD 14S/37.

[9] G/L/103.

1 January 1998[10], when the duties on imports of Canadian automotive products were fully eliminated in accordance with the provisions of the North American Free Trade Agreement (NAFTA).

2.8 When the Working Party went on to examine the relationship between Canada's Auto Pact obligations and the GATT, members noted that, in his introductory remarks, "the representative of Canada had stressed that his Government was implementing the Agreement on a most-favoured-nation basis and was extending to all contracting parties the same tariff benefits, on the same terms, as it had undertaken to grant the United States under the Agreement."[11] Although some members questioned whether Canada's application of the Auto Pact was compatible with GATT Articles I and III[12], there was no consensus in the Working Party on whether or not Canada was in violation of its GATT commitments.

B. The Canada - United States Free Trade Agreement (CUSFTA)

2.9 Trade in automotive products was also affected by the Canada - United States Free Trade Agreement (CUSFTA)[13], which entered into force 1 January 1989. The CUSFTA provided for the elimination of duties on automotive products by 1 January 1998, so long as the products qualified under CUSFTA origin rules.

2.10 The CUSFTA also changed the Auto Pact provisions which had allowed the Canadian Government to designate additional manufacturers to benefit from the duty exemption.[14] It did so by limiting eligibility for the import duty exemption to firms falling into one of three categories:[15] (i) Auto Pact manufacturers; (ii) manufacturers designated by the Canadian Government as beneficiaries prior to the signing of the CUSFTA; and (iii) other firms which were expected to be designated by the Canadian Government by the 1989 model year.[16] In other words, the CUSFTA had the effect of closing the list of those entitled to import duty free, after a grace period for certain potential new entrants, so that the only way a company outside those categories might be authorized to import duty free pursuant to this programme would be by acquiring control of, or being acquired by, a beneficiary.[17]

---

[10] Decision adopted by the General Council at is meeting of 7, 8 and 13 November 1996, WT/L/198.

[11] Report of the *Working Party on Canada - US Agreement on Automotive Products*, *supra* note 6, para. 20.

[12] Ibid., paras. 21 and 22.

[13] Exhibits EC-12 and JPN-33.

[14] Auto Pact, Annex A, para. 3.

[15] Annex to Article 1002.1 of the CUSFTA.

[16] The last category was added in order to allow CAMI, a joint venture between General Motors and Suzuki which did not begin production until 1989, to benefit also from the Tariff Exemption.

[17] A note in the Annex to Article 1002.1 of the CUSFTA states that the duty exemption shall cease being granted if, as a result of the acquisition of control over a recipient, "the fundamental nature, scope or size of the business of the recipient is significantly altered". This provision has been reproduced in the MVTO 1998, Schedule, Part 1, para. 4. See footnote 24.

C. *The North American Free Trade Agreement (NAFTA)*

2.11 The CUSFTA was suspended with the 1 January 1994 entry into force of the NAFTA, an agreement notified to the GATT as an Article XXIV free-trade area involving Canada, Mexico and the United States.

2.12 The NAFTA allows Canada to maintain the import duty exemption subject to the conditions stipulated in the CUSFTA, including those relating to Auto Pact manufacturer eligibility.

2.13 Under the NAFTA, Mexican trucks now enter Canada duty free, while other vehicles are currently subject to duties of 1.3 per cent (passenger cars) and 2.4 per cent (heavy trucks and buses), so long as these products meet the NAFTA origin rules. All such vehicles imported from Mexico will enter duty free after 1 January 2003. Under the NAFTA, all US automotive products meeting NAFTA origin rules have entered Canada duty free since 1 January 1998.

2.14 The European Communities stipulates that, although not themselves in dispute, the CUSFTA and the NAFTA are directly relevant for this dispute.[18] Japan contends that the agreements amplified and exacerbated the discriminatory effects of the measures[19], but it does not include them in its list of measures that it is challenging in this proceeding.[20]

D. *Canada's Domestic Measures*

2.15 The provisions relating to Auto Pact manufacturers were given effect domestically in Canada through the Motor Vehicles Tariff Order (MVTO) 1965[21], known as the MVTO, and the Tariff Item 950 Regulations [22], which specified the terms under which duty free entry would be permitted. These instruments were replaced by the MVTO 1988[23] and later the MVTO 1998[24], which preserved the essential elements of the earlier legal instruments. The MVTO 1998 is the measure in effect today.

2.16 In line with the Auto Pact provisions allowing Canada to designate additional manufacturers as eligible to import duty free, beginning in 1965 the Government of Canada extended eligibility for the import duty exemption by granting Special Remission Orders (SROs)[25] to individual manufacturers that had not met the original conditions of the MVTO 1965 and its successors.

---

18 See para. 5.5.

19 See paras. 5.139 and 5.144.

20 See para. 5.2.

21 P.C. 1965-99, of 16 January 1965 (Exhibit EC-5 and JPN-25).

22 P.C. 1965-100, of 16 January 1965 (Exhibit EC-5).

23 P.C. 1987-2733, of 31 December 1987 (Exhibits JPN-32), amended in P.C. 1988-2872, of 30 December 1988 (Exhibit EC-4).

24 Exhibits EC-3 and JPN-4. The MVTO 1998 is an Order-in-Council passed by the Governor General in Council, on the recommendation of the Minister of Finance. The enabling authority is found in subsections 14 (2) and 16 (2) of Canada's Customs Tariff. The MVTO 1998 is administered by the Minister of National Revenue.

25 Special Remission Orders are regulations adopted under authority of the Financial Administration Act, R.S.C. 1985, c. F-11, s. 23 (Exhibit JPN-3). The MVTO 1965 required companies to have produced motor vehicles in all quarters of the base year, which was defined as the 12-month period from 1 August 1963 to 31 July 1964. Any manufacturer which had not met this requirement was thus effectively prevented from qualifying for the import duty exemption.

2.17 Whereas the Auto Pact calls for Canada to extend to certain manufacturers the right to import duty-free vehicles and original equipment manufacturing parts from the United States[26], the MVTO 1965 accorded the manufacturers the right with respect to "goods imported into Canada on or after 18 January 1965 from any country entitled to the benefit of the British Preferential Tariff or Most-Favoured Nation Tariff...".[27] Similarly, the import duty exemptions provided in the MVTO 1998 and current SROs apply to imports from any country entitled to Canada's MFN rate.

2.18 The MVTO 1998 and current SROs also provide a tariff exemption for the importation of certain parts and components for use as original equipment in the manufacture of motor vehicles. That exemption is not at issue in this dispute.[28]

1. The MVTO 1998

2.19 The MVTO 1998 provides an import duty exemption for the importation of automobiles[29], specified commercial vehicles[30], and buses.[31] (Throughout this Report, the terms "automobile", "specified commercial vehicle" and "bus" are used with the same meaning as in the MVTO 1998, and the term "motor vehicle" is used to designate collectively "automobiles", "specified commercial vehicles" and "buses".)

2.20 The beneficiaries of the MVTO 1998 are the same as the beneficiaries of the Auto Pact, i.e. those manufacturers of a given class of motor vehicles which produced vehicles of that class during each of the four consecutive quarters of the base year.

2.21 A list of beneficiaries of the MVTO 1998 is contained in the Appendix to Memorandum D-10-16-3, issued by the Ministry of National Revenue on 10 April 1995.[32] That Appendix lists a total of 33 firms, of which 4 are identified as manufacturers of automobiles, 7 as manufacturers of buses and 27 as manufacturers of specified commercial vehicles.

---

26 Article II(a) of the Auto Pact.

27 MVTO 1965, para. 1 (Exhibits EC-5 and JPN-25).

28 The tariff rate for imports of all original equipment parts was reduced to zero in 1996, irrespective of the status of the importer. See the Memorandum D10-15-21 (Exhibit EC-10).

29 The MVTO 1998 defines the term "automobile" as "four-wheeled passenger motor vehicle having a seating capacity for not more than 10 persons, but does not include an ambulance or a hearse." It includes headings HS 87.02 or 87.03. Schedule, Part 1, 1(1).

30 The MVTO 1998 defines the term "specified commercial vehicle" as "a truck, an ambulance or a hearse, or a chassis therefor, but does not include any of the following vehicles or chassis therefor, namely, a bus, an electric trackless trolley bus, a fire truck, an amphibious vehicle, a tracked or a half-tracked vehicle, a golf or invalid cart, a straddle carrier or motor vehicle designed primarily for off-highway use, or any machine or other article to be mounted on or attached to a truck, an ambulance or a hearse or a chassis therefor for purposes other than for loading or unloading the vehicle." It includes headings HS 87.01, 87.03 or 87.05 and chassis therefor of heading HS 87.06. Schedule, Part 1, 1(1).

31 The MVTO 1998 defines the term "bus" as "a passenger motor vehicle having a seating capacity for more than 10 persons or a chassis therefor, but does not include any of the following vehicles or their chassis, namely, an electric trackless trolley bus, an amphibious vehicle, a tracked or half-tracked vehicle or a motor vehicle designed primarily for off-highway use." It includes heading HS 87.02 and chassis therefor of heading HS 87.06. Schedule, Part 1, 1(1).

32 Exhibits JPN-7 and EC-9.

2.22 The four manufacturers of automobiles listed in Memorandum D-10-16-3 are Chrysler Canada Ltd.[33], Ford Motor Company of Canada Ltd., General Motors of Canada Ltd., and Volvo (Canada) Ltd.[34]

2.23 The granting of the import duty exemption provided for in the MVTO 1998 is subject to the same type of CVA and ratio requirements as those stipulated in the Auto Pact. Specifically, the schedule to the MVTO 1998 defines a manufacturer as "a manufacturer of a class of vehicles" who:

> "(a) produced vehicles of that class in Canada in each of the four consecutive quarters of the base year; and
>
> (b) produced vehicles of a class in Canada in the 12-month period ending on July 31 in which the importation is made where
>
> > (i) the ratio of the net sales value of the vehicles produced to the net sales value of all vehicles of that class sold for consumption in Canada by the manufacturer in that period is equal to or higher than the ratio of the net sales value of all vehicles of that class produced in Canada by the manufacturer in the base year to the net sales value of all vehicles of that class sold for consumption in Canada by the manufacturer in the base year, and is not in any case lower than 75 to 100, and
> >
> > (ii) the Canadian value added is equal to or greater than the Canadian value added in respect of all vehicles of that class produced in Canada by the manufacturer in the base year."

2.24 The requirements are different for each MVTO 1998 beneficiary, depending on its level of CVA, production and sales during the base year.

2.25 A document published by Industry Canada, a department of the Federal Government of Canada,[35] indicates that the ratio requirements applicable to the MVTO 1998 beneficiaries are, "as a general rule", 95 to 100 for automobiles[36], at least 75 to 100 for specified commercial vehicles, and at least 75 to 100 for buses. That same document states that the CVA requirements have been rendered "insignificant" by inflation.

---

33 In May 1998, Daimler-Benz and Chrysler agreed to merge their businesses. DaimlerChrysler Canada Inc. (formerly Chrysler Canada, Ltd.) is now a wholly-owned subsidiary of Daimler Chrysler Corp. (formerly Chrysler Corporation), which in turn is a wholly owned subsidiary of Daimler Chrysler AG, a holding company incorporated in Germany which also controls Daimler-Benz AG. Chrysler Canada Ltd. now imports motor vehicles of the Mercedes brand under the MVTO 1998.

34 Volvo (Canada) Ltd. ceased the assembly of automobiles in Canada as of December 1998. Accordingly, it has apparently lost the right to import automobiles duty free under the Auto Pact as from 1 August 1999, the next model year. However, Ford Motor Corporation is purchasing the automotive division of Volvo AB and, therefore, can continue to import Volvo automobiles under the Duty Waiver.

35 "Canada-US Automotive Products Agreement (Auto Pact Background)", Industry Canada, 10 June 1998 (Exhibit EC-20).

36 Reflecting base-year CVA levels.

2.26 The MVTO 1998 lays down detailed rules for the calculation of the CVA.[37] In accordance with those rules, the cost items to be counted as CVA are, broadly speaking, the following:

- the cost of parts produced in Canada and of materials of Canadian origin that are incorporated in the motor vehicles;
- direct labour costs incurred in Canada;
- manufacturing overheads incurred in Canada;
- general and administrative expenses incurred in Canada that are attributable to the production of motor vehicles;
- depreciation in respect of machinery and permanent plant equipment located in Canada that is attributable to the production of motor vehicles; and
- a capital cost allowance for land and buildings in Canada that are used in the production of motor vehicles.

2.27 The same rules are applicable for calculating the CVA contained in original equipment parts for motor vehicles.[38]

2.28 The MVTO 1998 requires the beneficiaries to submit, each model year prior to their first importation, a declaration to the Minister of National Revenue, in which they declare that they will comply with the CVA and ratio requirements that model year.[39] The beneficiaries are also to submit to that Minister and to the Minister of Industry "reports that may reasonably be required by those Ministers respecting the production and sale of vehicles by the manufacturer".[40]

2.29 A manufacturer beneficiary not meeting the CVA or ratio requirements stipulated in the MVTO 1998 in any model year as to a class of motor vehicles is liable for the payment of the applicable customs duties on all imports of motor vehicles of that class made during that year. However, only duty-free imports are included in the ratio calculation. Therefore, an importer that is at risk of not meeting its production-to-sales ratio is entitled to start paying duty on any additional imports to be made without having to pay duties on what has already been imported. A manufacturer beneficiary which fails to meet the requirements in any given year does not lose the status of manufacturer beneficiary and may still qualify for the duty exemption in successive model years.

2.30 (For further discussion on administration and enforcement, see Factual Arguments of the Parties, Section V.)

2. *Special Remission Orders*

2.31 An administrative memorandum of Revenue Canada lists 63 firms as SRO beneficiaries[41] of which 2 are identified as manufacturers of automobiles, 5 as manu-

---

[37] MVTO 1998, Schedule, Part 1, 1(1), definition of "Canadian Value Added" , letter (a).

[38] Ibid., letter (b).

[39] Ibid., Part 1, 2 (a). The form of the declaration is set out in MVTO 1998, Schedule, Part 2.

[40] Ibid., Part 1, 2 (b). Samples of the reporting documents are provided as Exhibit EC-14.

[41] Memorandum D-10-16-2 lists the SROs for every company still manufacturing, but it does not include companies that are still in existence but no longer manufacturing. The orders for those com-

facturers of buses and 59 as manufacturers of specified commercial vehicles. The two manufacturers of automobiles are CAMI Automotive Inc. (a joint venture between Suzuki Motors Corp., of Japan, and General Motors Corp., of the United States) and Intermeccanica International Inc., an artisanal manufacturer of hand-built replicas of famous cars.[42]

2.32 All SROs contain a CVA requirement and a manufacturing requirement (i.e. production-to-sales ratio requirement). The definitions of both requirements under the SROs are the same as the definitions under the MVTO 1998, though the specific levels of CVA and the ratios required vary. Because the SROs were granted after the conclusion of the Canada - US Auto Pact, different base years, or initial periods, were assigned to each SRO beneficiary.

2.33 Regarding CVA requirements, typically the SROs issued before 1984 stipulate that, during an initial period of one to two years, the CVA of the motor vehicles produced in Canada by the beneficiaries should be at least 40 per cent of their cost of production. Thereafter, the CVA should be at least the same (in dollar terms) as in the last 12 months of the initial period. Nevertheless, those SROs provide that if in any subsequent year the cost of production falls below the level of the initial period, the CVA (in dollar terms) could also be less, but in no case less than 40 per cent of the cost of production in that year. In contrast, the SROs issued from 1984 onwards provide, as a general rule, that the CVA of the motor vehicles produced in Canada by the beneficiaries (and in some cases, of the original equipment parts and components) shall be no less than 40 per cent of the cost of sales of the vehicles sold in Canada, with no reference to the values of an initial period. By way of exception, the SRO granted to CAMI[43] prescribes that the CVA of the motor vehicles and original equipment parts produced in Canada by CAMI must represent at least 60 per cent of the cost of sales of the vehicles sold in Canada by CAMI.

2.34 Regarding the production-to-sales ratio requirement, the SROs issued before 1977 set the minimum ratio at 75 to 100. Since then, almost all SROs have a ratio set at 100 to 100. In other words, the sales value of the vehicles produced in Canada by the SRO beneficiaries must be at least equal to the sales value of all the vehicles sold by them in Canada.

2.35 In terms of administration, the SROs lay down reporting obligations similar to those stipulated in the MVTO 1998 (described above), with similar consequences for a company failing to meet the requirements. As with the MVTO 1998, SRO beneficiaries at risk of not meeting their ratio requirements are entitled to start paying duty on any additional imports without having to pay duty on what has already been imported. (See also Factual Arguments of the Parties, Section V.)

panies remain in force, but they are not in use. (Canada's response to Question 37 from the Panel). See Exhibits EC-8 and JPN-8. Copies of all the SROs listed in the Appendix to the Memorandum appear in Exhibits EC-6 and JPN-6. A table summarising the content of the SROs appears in Exhibit EC-7, and a summary of SRO conditions and evolution over time is contained in Exhibit JPN-28.

[42] See Exhibit EC-21.

[43] P.C. 1988-2910, of 30 December 1988 (Exhibit JPN-6).

III. FINDINGS AND RECOMMENDATIONS REQUESTED BY THE PARTIES

A. *Japan's Request for Findings and Recommendations*

3.1 **Japan** requests that the Panel make the following findings and recommendations:

(i) the Duty Waiver[44] is inconsistent with Article I:1 of the GATT 1994 and Articles II and XVII of the GATS;

(ii) the Duty Waiver, by virtue of the domestic content requirement, is inconsistent with Article III:4 of the GATT 1994, Article 2.1 of the TRIMs Agreement, Articles 3.1(b) and 3.2 of the SCM Agreement, and Article XVII of the GATS; and

(iii) the Duty Waiver, by virtue of the manufacturing requirement, is inconsistent with Articles 3.1(a) and 3.2 of the SCM Agreement.[45]

3.2 Finally, Japan requests that the Panel recommend that the Government of Canada bring itself into conformity with its obligations under the GATT 1994, the TRIMs Agreement and the GATS. With respect to the inconsistencies with Articles 3.1 and 3.2 of the SCM Agreement, the Government of Japan respectfully requests that the Panel recommend that the Government of Canada withdraw the prohibited subsidy "without delay" in accordance with Article 4.7 of the SCM Agreement.

B. *The European Communities' Request for Findings and Recommendations*

3.3 The **European Communities** requests that the Panel make the following findings and recommendations:

- the CVA requirements are inconsistent with GATT Article III:4 in that they afford less favourable treatment to imported parts and materials for the manufacture of motor vehicles and parts therefor than to domestic like goods;
- the Ratio requirements are inconsistent with GATT Article III:4 in that they afford less favourable treatment to imported motor vehicles than to domestic like products with respect to their internal sale in Canada;
- the Tariff Exemption[46] is inconsistent with GATT Article I:1 because it provides an advantage to imports of automobiles originating in the

---

44 Japan uses the term "Duty Waiver" collectively to refer to the MVTO 1998, the SROs, related statutory and administrative instruments, and the Letters. See also Section V.A.1.

45 The manufacturing requirement would also be inconsistent with Article III:4 of the GATT 1994 and Article 2.1 of the TRIMs Agreement.

46 The European Communities uses the term "Tariff Exemption" collectively to refer to (i) the tariff exemption for the importation of motor vehicles, as well as the CVA requirements and production-to-sale "ratio" requirements attached thereto, contained in the Auto Pact, as supplemented by the Letters, and in the MVTO 1998; and (ii) the tariff exemptions for the importation of motor vehicles, and the CVA requirements and "ratio" requirements attached thereto, provided for in the SROs. See also Section V.A.1.

United States and Mexico *vis-à-vis* imports of like products originating in other Members;

- the CVA requirements and the ratio requirements are TRIMs prohibited by Article 2.1 of the Agreement on TRIMs;
- the Tariff Exemption is a subsidy contingent upon export performance as well as upon the use of domestic over imported goods, which is therefore prohibited by Article 3 of the SCM Agreement;
- the CVA requirements are inconsistent with GATS Article XVII because they afford more favourable treatment to Canadian services used in the manufacture of motor vehicles and parts therefor than to like services of other Members; and
- the Tariff Exemption is inconsistent with GATS Article II because it accords more favourable treatment to US suppliers of wholesale trade services for automobiles than to like service suppliers of other Members.

3.4 The European Communities further requests the Panel to find that, by committing the above violations, Canada has nullified and impaired benefits accruing to the European Communities under the cited Agreements.

3.5 The European Communities also requests the Panel to recommend that Canada bring the measures into conformity with its obligations under the GATT, the TRIMs Agreement and the GATS.

3.6 Finally, the European Communities requests the Panel to recommend, pursuant to Article 4.7 of the SCM Agreement, that Canada withdraw the subsidy without delay and to specify in its recommendation the time period within which the subsidy must be withdrawn.

C. Canada's Request for Findings and Recommendations

3.7 **Canada** requests that the Panel make the following findings and recommendations:

3.8 Neither Japan nor the European Communities has demonstrated that the measures at issue violate Canada's WTO obligations. More particularly:

- They have failed to show that the measures violate Article I of the GATT 1994: there is no discrimination against products based on national origin;
- They have failed to show that the measures violate Article III of the GATT: they do not have any effect on the competitive position of imported parts and vehicles in the Canadian market;
- They have failed to show that the measures violate the TRIMS Agreement: the measures are not investment measures, they are not trade-related, they do not violate Article III of the GATT 1994 and in any event they are not included on the Illustrative List;
- They have failed to show that the measures violate the SCM Agreement: they are not a subsidy contingent upon export performance or upon the use of domestic over foreign goods;

- They have failed to show that insofar as the measures accord duty-free treatment they violate the GATS: the measures do not affect services and in any event there is no discrimination against foreign wholesale service suppliers or in favour of service suppliers of certain countries, nor is there any evidence that the companies identified by the claimants compete with each other, or in the case of Article XVII, that Canada has made a relevant commitment; and
- They have failed to show that insofar as the measures contain a CVA requirement they violate Canada's commitments under the GATS: the measures do not discriminate against foreign service suppliers.

3.9 In the light of the foregoing, Canada requests that the claims of Japan and the European Communities be dismissed.

IV. REQUEST FOR PRELIMINARY RULING

A. *Japan's Argument Giving Rise to Canada's Request for a Preliminary Ruling*

4.1 **Japan** argues as follows:

4.2 Despite the fact that the Government of Japan does not discuss in detail the inconsistency of the manufacturing requirement with Article III:4 of the GATT 1994 or Article 2.1 of the TRIMs Agreement in its arguments to the same extent as was discussed in its Request for the Establishment of a Panel (WT/DS139/2), the Government of Japan reserves its right to elaborate during the course of the panel deliberation on these claims already contained in the said request.

4.3 In discussing how an eligible manufacturer can meet the conditions for the import duty exemption, Japan notes the following:

> "...this manufacturing requirement (the production-to-sales ratio) would be inconsistent with Article III:4 of the GATT 1994, because the manufacturing requirement requires the Auto Pact Manufacturers to increase production of motor vehicles in Canada and this in turn would lead to increased sales of such domestic motor vehicles in the Canadian market beyond the level of sales that would have occurred in the absence of this requirement, thereby upsetting the balance of conditions of competition for sales of like imported motor vehicles. In this regard, the manufacturing requirement would 'affect' the internal sale, purchase or use of products within the meaning of Article III:4 of the GATT 1994."[47]

B. *Canada's Request for a Preliminary Ruling*

4.4 **Canada** responds as follows:

4.5 Japan purports to reserve the "right to elaborate during the course of the panel deliberation" on its claims regarding the alleged inconsistency of "the manufacturing

[47] See footnote 397.

requirement with Article III:4 of the GATT 1994 or Article 2.1 of the TRIMS Agreement." Canada objects to this reservation and requests this Panel to rule as a preliminary matter that it is not open for Japan or the European Communities to proceed as Japan has proposed to do. As this Panel is well aware, the fundamental tenet of due process requires that the responding party must know the case it is to meet. To permit Japan to develop its claims only when it chooses to do so would necessarily prejudice Canada's ability to defend itself in this action, and would risk offending the basic principle of fairness enshrined in the maxim *audi alteram partem.*[48] WTO panels and the Appellate Body have made it abundantly clear that procedural fairness requires that the complaining party set out its case at the commencement of proceedings and it is not open to it to eke out its claims incrementally during the various stages of the case.[49]

4.6 Prior to its first substantive meeting with the parties, the Panel invited Japan and the European Communities to file a response to Canada's request. Japan responded by reiterating its right to elaborate its claims at a later time; the European Communities did not file a response.

C. *The Panel's Decision*

4.7 On 14 June 1999 at the first substantive meeting with the parties, the Chairman read out the following decision by the **Panel**:

4.8 The Panel recalls that Japan has stated the following:

> "Despite the fact that the Government of Japan does not discuss in detail the inconsistency of the manufacturing requirement with Article III:4 of the GATT 1994 or Article 2.1 of the TRIMS Agreement in its arguments to the same extent as was discussed in its Request for the Establishment of a Panel (WT/DS139/2), the Government of Japan reserves its right to elaborate during the course of the panel deliberation on these claims already contained in the said request".

4.9 The Panel further recalls Canada's objection to this reservation by Japan and Canada's request to the Panel "to rule as a preliminary matter that it is not open for Japan or the European Communities to proceed as Japan has proposed to do".

4.10 Having carefully considered this matter, including the arguments of each of the parties to the dispute, the Panel has come to the following conclusions:

4.11 First, the Panel does not consider that this is a situation where, as argued by Canada, the complaining party is permitted "to eke out its claims incrementally during the various stages of the case". In making this argument, Canada refers to the Appellate Body decision in *European Communities - Regime for the Importation, Sale and Distribution of Bananas* (EC - *Bananas III). However, the situation here is unlike that in *EC - Bananas III*, where the Appellate Body stated that "Article 6.2 of the DSU requires that the *claims*, but not the *arguments*, must all be specified sufficiently in the request for the establishment of a panel in order to allow the defending

---

48 Let the other side be heard.

49 Appellate Body Report on *European Communities - Regime for the Importation, Sale and Distribution of Bananas*, adopted on 25 September 1997, WT/DS27/AB/R (hereinafter Appellate Body Report on *EC - Bananas III*), DSR 1997:II, 591, paras. 127-128, 143.

party and any third parties to know the legal basis of the complaint" (WT/DS27/AB/R, para. 143). In the case before us there is no Article 6.2 issue of specificity of the measures identified in the panel request. Japan in this dispute has not attempted to reserve a right to present a new claim at a later stage of the proceedings; rather, it appears that Japan has simply indicated that it may wish to further elaborate its arguments as to claims already set out in the panel request and in its initial arguments. As such, the Panel does not consider, at this stage, that Canada is likely to be prejudiced in its ability to defend itself in this action.[50]

4.12 Second, to the extent any issue of procedural fairness should arise, for example, as to the right of rebuttal by Canada should Japan wait until a later stage of these proceedings to develop its arguments as to its GATT Article III:4 and TRIMS Article 2.1 claims with respect to the "manufacturing requirement" (production-to-sales ratio requirement), the Panel will ensure such procedural fairness by providing Canada with adequate opportunity to respond to any such further elaboration by Japan of its arguments under these claims.

4.13 Third, in addition to ensuring procedural fairness, it is of course necessary to set a cut-off date beyond which no new argumentation as to the claims in issue may be accepted, except upon a showing of good cause. In the instant case, the Panel considers that no new argumentation should be introduced beyond the second panel meeting with the parties, except in response to any questions posed by the Panel or otherwise upon a showing of good cause.

V. FACTUAL ARGUMENTS OF THE PARTIES

A. *The Measures at Issue*

1. *Terminology and Clarification of Claims*

(a) Japan's Framing of the Measures at Issue

5.1 In setting out the measures at issue, **Japan** indicates the following:

5.2 Canada implements and applies the Duty Waiver through domestic legislation, regulations, statutory instruments, departmental memoranda and administrative practices. More specifically, Canada implements the Duty Waiver pursuant to: (i) section 115 of the Customs Tariff and section 23 of the Financial Administration Act[51]; (ii) the Motor Vehicles Tariff Order, 1998 (MVTO 1998)[52]; (iii) letters of undertaking signed by individual manufacturers upon the demand of the Government of Canada[53]; (iv) Special Remission Orders (SROs) providing for the remission of cus-

[50] See the Appellate Body Report on *EC - Bananas III*, *supra* note 49, para. 141, where the Appellate Body states that, in its view, "there is a significant difference between the *claims* identified in the request for the establishment of a panel, which establish the panel's terms of reference under Article 7 of the DSU, and the *arguments* supporting those claims, which are set out and progressively clarified in the first written submissions, the rebuttal submissions and the first and second panel meetings with the parties".

[51] Exhibit JPN-3.

[52] Ibid.-4.

[53] Exhibit JPN-5.

toms duties on motor vehicles imported by specified manufacturers[54]; (v) departmental memoranda relating to the MVTO 1998 and the SROs[55]; and (vi) implementing measures taken thereunder. The Government of Canada also exercises administrative discretion regarding certain aspects of the Duty Waiver.[56] In Japan's arguments, the term "Auto Pact Manufacturers" means those companies that are qualified to import motor vehicles duty free under the Duty Waiver MVTO 1998 or its predecessors, or SROs. The term "Non-Auto Pact Manufacturers" mean those companies that are not Auto Pact Manufacturers.

(b) The European Communities' Framing of the Measures at Issue

5.3 In setting out the measures at issue, the **European Communities** indicates the following:

5.4 The measures in dispute are contained in:

- the Agreement Concerning Automotive Products between the Government of Canada and the Government of the United States of America, done at Johnson City on 16 January 1965 (the "Auto Pact")[57];
- the so-called Letters of Undertaking submitted by certain manufacturers of motor vehicles to the Government of Canada in connection with the Auto Pact (the "Letters of Undertaking")[58]:
- the Motor Vehicles Tariff Order, *1998* (the "MVTO 1998")[59];
- the Special Remission Orders providing for a remission of customs duties on imports of motor vehicles issued to certain manufacturers of motor vehicles not covered by the Auto Pact and the MVTO 1998 (the SROs)[60]; and
- the D-Memoranda issued by the Minister of National Revenue for the administration of the above measures, and other implementing measure.[61]

5.5 In addition, although not themselves in dispute, the following are directly relevant for this case:

- the Canada-United States Free Trade Agreement, signed on 2 January 1988 (the CUFSTA)[62]; and
- the North American Free Trade Agreement, signed on 17 December 1992 by the Governments of Canada, Mexico and the United States (the NAFTA).[63]

---

54 Ibid.-6.

55 Ibid.-7 and JPN-8. Departmental Memoranda (D-Memoranda) set out the administrative procedures followed by Revenue Canada in the administration of various statutes and regulations.

56 For example, on 3 December 1998, the Government of Canada exercised administrative discretion to grant the remission of MFN duties on imports made by PACCAR Inc. notwithstanding the fact that this eligible importer did not meet the applicable Auto Pact conditions (Exhibit JPN-9).

57 Exhibit EC-1.

58 Ibid. -2.

59 Ibid. -3.

60 Ibid. -6. A Table summarising the requirements of the SROs is provided as Exhibit EC-7.

61 Ibid. -8, -9 and -10.

62 Copies of the relevant provisions are supplied as Exhibit EC-12.

63 Ibid. -13.

5.6 The measures complained of by the European Communities are the following:

- the Tariff Exemption for the importation of motor vehicles, as well as the CVA requirements and production-to-sale "ratio" requirements attached thereto, contained in the Auto Pact, as supplemented by the Letters of Undertaking, and in the MVTO 1998; and
- the Tariff Exemptions for the importation of motor vehicles, and the CVA requirements and "ratio" requirements attached thereto, provided for in the SROs.

5.7 Hereinafter, both types of exemptions will be referred to collectively as the "Tariff Exemption". In turn, the various CVA requirements and ratio requirements attached to the Tariff Exemption will be designated as the "CVA requirements" and the "ratio requirements", respectively. Finally, those manufacturers of motor vehicles which qualify for the Tariff Exemption will be referred to as the "beneficiaries".

(c) Canada's Response to the Complainants' Framing of the Measures At Issue

5.8 With respect to the way the complainants set out the measures at issue, **Canada** responds as follows:

5.9 Both Japan and the European Communities have adopted in their arguments the use of a single term to refer to the measures at issue. Japan refers throughout its arguments to "the Duty Waiver", while the European Communities uses the term "the Tariff Exemption". The Panel is asked to rule that "the Duty Waiver" or "the Tariff Exemption" violates Canada's obligations under the WTO. The complainants' strategy appears to be to combine all manner of items together (be they current measures, repealed provisions, private letters, international agreements, or administrative memoranda) in the hope that this mixture will be enough to constitute a WTO violation. In other words, the complainants recognise that they cannot make out a violation for each of the measures they seek to challenge. So they created a "single" measure, a combination of elements, to try to meet their burden.

5.10 This strategy is misleading and cannot succeed. For there are a number of measures that have been challenged[64], and to succeed in their claims, Japan and the European Communities must prove that each of them is inconsistent with Canada's WTO obligations.

5.11 A ruling on "the Duty Waiver" or "the Tariff Exemption" would have no meaning in law, as neither is a measure subject to challenge under the WTO. In fact, the measures at issue are as follows:

- the Motor Vehicles Tariff Order, 1998 (MVTO 1998)[65]; and
- each of the current Special Remission Orders (SROs).[66]

---

[64] See *Request for the Establishment of a Panel by Japan*, WT/DS/139/2, 13 November 1998; *Request for the Establishment of a Panel by the European Communities*, WT/DS142/2, 14 January 1999.

[65] SOR/98-43 (Exhibits EC-3 and JPN-4).

[66] See Exhibits EC-6 and JPN-6.

5.12 The complainants have also raised other matters, but they cannot properly be described as measures. They include the Auto Pact, Revenue Canada memoranda, letters written in 1965 by certain vehicle manufacturers to the then Canadian Minister of Industry, as well as certain provisions of the CUSFTA and of the NAFTA.

Canada's Figure 1

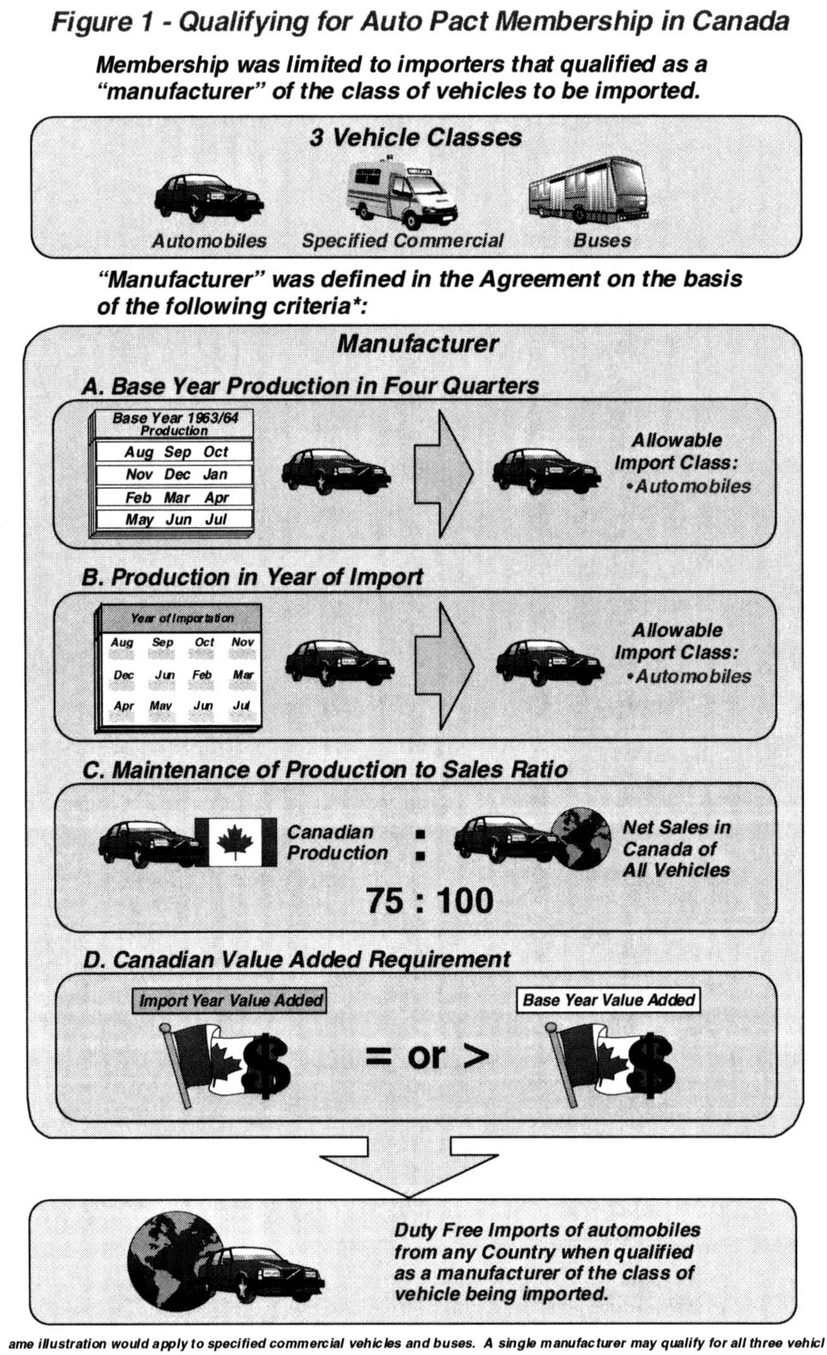

(d) Japan's Follow-Up to Canada's Response

5.13 Following up on Canada's response to the complainants' framing of the measures at issue, **Japan** adds:

5.14 The Duty Waiver is comprised of a "benefit" in the form of a duty exemption that is contingent on three conditions: (i) an eligibility requirement implemented in the form of an eligibility restriction; (ii) a domestic content requirement implemented in the form of a Canadian value-added (CVA) requirement; and (iii) a manufacturing requirement implemented in the form of a production-to-sales ratio.

5.15 The term "Duty Waiver" is used to simplify the Government of Japan's arguments regarding this series of complex measures.

5.16 It is the position of the Government of Japan that the three classes of instruments (i.e. measures) that implement the Duty Waiver — the MVTO 1998, the letters of undertaking and the SROs—are inconsistent with the obligations of the Government of Canada under the above-noted WTO Agreements. The Government of Japan recognizes that it has the burden to present a *prima facie* case of WTO-inconsistency with respect to the MVTO 1998, the letters of undertaking and the SROs. Given that the characteristics that give rise to the WTO-inconsistencies are identical or very similar in these three classes of instruments, the arguments that apply to the instruments are identical or very similar. To the extent that the arguments differ, the differences have been expressly addressed in the Government of Japan's arguments and are further elaborated upon below.

(e) The EC's Follow-Up to Canada's Response

5.17 Following up on Canada's response to the complainants' framing of the measures at issue, the **European Communities** adds:

5.18 At several points Canada has referred to CAMI as being the only "relevant" SRO beneficiary. In response to a request from the European Communities to clarify those statements, Canada has answered the following:

> " ... the EC raised specific allegations only with respect to the Canadian Big Three and Volvo as MVTO beneficiaries and the two SRO automobile manufacturers, namely CAMI Automotive Inc. and Intermeccanica ... Canada, as the defending party, is not required to rebut the contents of the EC's Panel request, but only the evidence presented to the Panel ...".[67]

5.19 The above assertions are incorrect. The EC's claims under GATT Article I and GATS Article II are limited in scope to imports of automobiles and to the provision of wholesale distribution services for automobiles, respectively. The only SROs concerned by those two claims are the SROs issued to CAMI and Intermeccanica, which are the only two SROs beneficiaries authorised to import automobiles duty free.

5.20 In contrast, the claims submitted by the European Communities under GATT Article III:4 and GATS Article XVII, as well as the EC's claims under the TRIMs

[67] Canada's response to Question 1 from the EC.

Agreement and the SCM Agreement, cover not only the category of "automobiles", but also the other two categories of "motor vehicles", i.e. "buses" and "specified commercial vehicles". Those claims concern *all* the SROs currently in force (a total of 63, according to the list appended to Memorandum D-10-16-2)[68], and not just the SROs issued to CAMI and to Intermeccanica.

5.21 The scope of the EC's claims is stated clearly in the EC's Panel request and in its argumentation. Contrary to Canada's assertions, the European Communities has provided evidence with respect to all the SROs. The European Communities attached a copy of Memorandum D-10-16-2, which contains a complete list of the SROs in force.[69] Furthermore, the European Communities has supplied to the Panel copies of all those SROs[70], as well as a table summarising their contents.[71]

5.22 In response to a question from Japan, Canada has disclosed the name of seven vehicle manufacturers currently utilising SROs to import vehicles other than automobiles.[72] To avoid any possible misunderstanding, the European Communities would like to recall that its claims in this dispute are not limited to those SROs that are currently being "utilised" by their beneficiaries. They cover all SROs in force, whether or not they have been "utilised" recently.

5.23 If an SRO beneficiary which is not currently "utilising" its SRO decided to do so as from the next model year, the Canadian Government would be legally obliged to accord to that beneficiary duty-free treatment, provided that it meets the conditions stipulated in its SRO. Thus, the SROs constitute "mandatory legislation" which, in accordance with settled case law, may be subject to dispute settlement even in those cases where they are not currently being "utilised".[73]

2. *Letters*

(a) Japan's Arguments Concerning the Letters

5.24 With respect to the Letters (noted above in paras. 2.4 and 2.5), **Japan** argues as follows (with arguments also appearing in Section VI, Legal Arguments of the Parties):

5.25 At the time the Auto Pact was being negotiated, the Government of Canada obtained from a number of Auto Pact Manufacturers additional commitments to meet higher domestic content requirements than specified under the Canada-US Auto Pact. These commitments were set out in company-specific letters of undertaking. Upon the demand of the Government of Canada, General Motors, Ford, Chrysler and American Motors undertook commitments that exceeded those in the MVTO 1965.

---

[68] Exhibit EC-8.

[69] Ibid. -8.

[70] Ibid. -6.

[71] Ibid. -7.

[72] Canada's response to Question 4 from Japan. It is unclear whether, in addition to the seven beneficiaries identified by Canada, there are other beneficiaries which have not given permission to the Canadian Government to disclose their names.

[73] See, e.g., the Panel Report on *United States - Taxes on Petroleum and Certain Imported Substances*, adopted on 17 June 1987, BISD 34S/136 (hereinafter Panel Report on *US - Petroleum*), paras. 5.2.1-5.2.2.

A report of the United States Senate noted that the terms of the letters of undertaking provided for a continuing commitment to increase CVA by a minimum percentage in every year.[74] The report also noted that the manufacturers considered the letters to be binding and even continued to report their compliance every year to the Government of Canada.[75] The language of the letters indicates they are actually binding.[76]

5.26 Based on a review of such letters that became publicly available in the United States in 1965, the producers in question have made a commitment beyond the requirements of the MVTO to increase the Canadian value added in the production of vehicles and parts by 60 per cent of the increase in their Canadian sales of automobiles and by 50 per cent of the increase in their Canadian sales of commercial vehicles. Furthermore, the major manufacturers undertook to increase CVA in the production of vehicles and original equipment parts by CDN$260 million from 1964 to the end of the 1968 model year.[77]

5.27 These commitments were undertaken at the request of the Government of Canada as a prerequisite for qualifying under the Duty Waiver. Under the terms of the letters, the commitment to increase CVA by a minimum percentage each year does not expire.

5.28 These undertakings have not been published in any official instrument of the Government of Canada. The number of letters of undertaking that have been signed and whether those letters have been amended over time is not publicly known.

(b) The EC's Arguments Concerning the Letters

5.29 With respect to the Letters, the **European Communities** argues as follows (with arguments also appearing in Section VI, Legal Arguments of the Parties):

---

[74] Exhibit JPN-27, p. 27.

[75] Ibid.

[76] Exhibit JPN-5 presents Letters of Undertaking from General Motors Canada (GM), Ford Canada (Ford), Chrysler Canada (Chrysler) and American Motors Canada (AMC):

> *GM* - GM's letter indicates that the right to import motor vehicles duty-free is conditional on the fulfilment of two requirements not mentioned in the MVTO:
>
> (i) an increase of the CVA by an amount equal to 60 per cent of market growth (para. 3); and
>
> (ii) an increase in the annual CVA by the end of the model year 1968 (see para. 4, which states that, for GM, the increase is CDN $121 million. See also p. 35, where GM's president reports to the Minister: "You have requested that we should increase CVA ...").
>
> In the last part of the letter, GM's president mentions the difficulties that will be encountered by GM in attaining the objectives on time, but undertakes that the company will reorganize its production facilities in Canada in order to meet the requirement and undertakes studies in that connection.
>
> *Ford* - After stating that Ford undertakes to reach such an amount of CVA in order to "meet the objectives of the Agreement," Ford's president mentions that the company will report to the Minister its plans to fulfill its obligations under the letter.
>
> *Chrysler and AMC* - These two letters incorporate language similar to that noted above in the Ford letter.

[77] United States Senate, Committee on Finance, Data Relating to H.R. 9042 Automotive Products Trade Act of 1965 (US Government Printing Office: 1965), 59 (Exhibit JPN-39).

5.30 Prior to the conclusion of the Auto Pact, and as a condition for signing it, the Canadian Government requested and obtained from the beneficiaries certain additional commitments regarding their CVA, over and above the requirements imposed by the Auto Pact.

5.31 Those additional commitments are contained in so-called "Letters of Undertaking", which were submitted by each beneficiary to the Canadian Minister of Industry a few days before the signature of the Auto Pact.

5.32 The contents of the Letters of Undertaking were kept secret by both Governments at the time of the conclusion of the Auto Pact. Nevertheless, the Letters of Undertaking sent by the Canadian subsidiaries of the US "Big Four" (i.e. GM, Ford, Chrysler and American Motors)[78] were eventually made public in the course of the debate by the US Congress of the Automotive Products Trade Act, 1965. While it is generally believed that other beneficiaries of the Auto Pact (e.g., Volvo) were also requested to submit Letters of Undertaking by the Canadian Government, those letters have never been disclosed to the public.

5.33 The terms of the Letters of Undertaking were negotiated by the Big Four with the Canadian Ministry of Industry. Their wording is very similar, and in some cases identical.[79] In essence, they impose upon each beneficiary two additional commitments:

(A) to increase in each model year the dollar value of CVA in the production of motor vehicles of a class, and of original equipment parts therefor, by a certain percentage of the annual "growth in the market" for the motor vehicles of that class. For automobiles, that percentage is 60 per cent, and for specified commercial vehicles and buses 50 per cent; and

(B) to increase the dollar value of CVA in the production of motor vehicles, and original equipment therefor, by a certain stated amount, over and above the amount achieved in the base year, and that achieved pursuant to commitment (A), during the model year.[80]

5.34 For purposes of the first commitment, "growth in the market" is defined as the difference between the cost to each beneficiary of the vehicles of the class concerned during the preceding model year and the cost to the beneficiary of the vehicles of the same class sold during the current model year.

5.35 The second commitment, like the requirement to maintain the CVA of the base year laid down in the Auto Pact, has been eroded over the years by inflation. As a result, the required CVA now approaches 60 per cent (in the case of automobiles) or 50 per cent (in the case of specified commercial vehicles and buses) of the beneficiary's cost of sales.

---

[78] American Motors was acquired by Chrysler in 1987.

[79] Compare, for example, the Letters of Undertaking submitted by Chrysler Canada, Ltd. and American Motors, Ltd. This strongly suggests that all Letters of Undertaking were drafted after a model provided by the Canadian Government.

[80] For the "Big Four", the required increase in CVA totalled C$239 million. The individual requirements were C$121 million for General Motors, C$74.2 million for Ford, C$33 million for Chrysler and C$11.2 million for American Motors.

5.36 For purposes of both commitments, the calculation of CVA includes, in addition to the CVA of vehicles produced and sold in Canada, the CVA of vehicles and original equipment parts produced in Canada and exported from Canada by the beneficiary or purchased by foreign affiliates of the beneficiary from independent Canadian vendors.[81]

5.37 The Letters of Undertaking also contain some reporting and auditing provisions[82] intended to allow the Canadian authorities to verify that the beneficiaries meet the additional CVA commitments.

5.38 The CVA requirements of the Letters of Undertaking differ from those contained in the MVTO 1998 and the SROs in that failure to comply with them in a given model year does not result in the obligation for the beneficiary to pay customs duties on the imports made during that year.

5.39 This does not, however, mean that the commitments contained in the Letters of Undertaking are merely "voluntary". It is obvious that those commitments do not, as such, advance the commercial interests of the beneficiaries.[83] They were exacted by Canada from the beneficiaries as a condition for signing the Auto Pact. The beneficiaries, therefore, have assumed that, were they to infringe the commitments, the Canadian Government would respond by withdrawing the tariff benefits.[84] In practice, that implicit sanction appears to have been sufficient and instances of non-compliance have remained exceptional.[85]

(c) Canada's Response to the Complainants' Arguments Concerning the Letters

5.40 In response to the complainants' arguments regarding the Letters, **Canada** responds as follows (with arguments also appearing in Section VI, Legal Arguments of the Parties):

5.41 Japan and the European Communities both have mischaracterized letters sent to the Canadian Minister of Industry contemporaneously with the negotiation and signature of the Auto Pact, and have included them in their respective "single meas-

81 See e.g., the Letter of Undertaking submitted by Ford Motor Co. of Canada, Ltd, p. 2, sub-para. (ii).

82 For example, the letter sent by Ford Motor Co. of Canada, Ltd. reads as follows:

"The Ford Motor Co. of Canada Ltd., also agrees to report to the Minister of Industry every three months beginning April 1 1965, such information as the Ministry of Industry requires pertaining to progress achieved by our company as well as plans to fulfil our obligations under this letter. In addition, Ford Motor Co. of Canada Ltd. understands that the Government will conduct an audit each year with respect to the matters described in this letter".

83 The Letters of Undertaking submitted by General Motors of Canada, Ltd and Ford Motor Co. of Canada, Ltd. discuss at length the problems encountered by those companies in order to achieve the goals set by the Canadian Government.

84 Note that the Auto Pact would not be an effective obstacle to such withdrawal of benefits. Indeed, the Auto Pact gives to each party the right to terminate the agreement, subject only to giving one year notice (Auto Pact, Article VII).

85 According to Canada's Ministry of Industry, the Letters of Undertaking "while not being binding, typically have been meet". See Canada - US Automotive Products Agreement (Auto Pact Background) Industry Canada, 10 June 1998 (Exhibit EC-20).

ures" they have invented solely for the purpose of these proceedings.[86] The complainants in this case would have the Panel regard the letters as legally binding and enforceable, presumably so that they can be considered measures subject to WTO disciplines. However, the letters have not been implemented through any Canadian law or regulation, and they are not legally binding.

5.42 Both Japan and the European Communities have characterized certain letters as "requirements". The European Communities in particular has claimed the letters were required of the manufacturers as a condition of Canada's signing the Auto Pact, and that the beneficiaries have assumed that a failure to meet them would result in Canada withdrawing the "Tariff Exemption". These arguments have no basis in fact.

5.43 These letters are not legally binding under Canadian law. They are not contracts, because they do not meet the Canadian legal requirements of contract formation. They are not statutory instruments, because they were not passed by the legislature, or by the executive under the authority of the legislature. Had the Canadian Government intended to make the letters binding, it could certainly have done so. It did not. Consequently, the letters have no legal status and no legal effect.

5.44 Moreover, those arguments have no basis in law. Because the letters have no legal status they are not covered by meaning of "laws, regulations and requirements" as used in Article III:4.

5.45 The question of duty-free eligibility in any given year is determined exclusively by the requirements in the MVTO 1998.[87] By law, these are the only grounds under which duty remission can be denied. The European Communities has provided no legal basis under which Canada could withdraw benefits for a failure to meet commitments under the letters.[88] This is because there is none. Should a manufacturer fail to meet the voluntary undertakings in its letter, the Canadian Government would lack the legal authority to deny duty-free eligibility. Indeed, the D-Memorandum submitted by the European Communities and Japan demonstrates clearly that Revenue Canada does not review whether MVTO companies have met their commitments under the letters.[89]

(d) Japan's Rebuttal to Canada's Response

5.46 As a rebuttal to Canada's response regarding the Letters, **Japan** argues the following:

5.47 The Government of Canada takes the position that the letters of undertaking are not "measures" that can be subject to WTO discipline on the basis that the letters

---

[86] Japan claimed the letters were provided at the "demand" of the Canadian Government, but it offered no proof of its claim. The Europeans have alleged that signature of the letters was a condition precedent to signing the Auto Pact, although it has filed nothing in support of this contention and relies instead on speculation: "it is generally believed" that other Auto Pact beneficiaries submitted letters.

[87] MVTO 1998, s. 2.

[88] The European Communities did suggest that Canada could simply withdraw from the Auto Pact, but the suggestion is without merit. Such an action would be so inimical to Canada's interests that it would never be contemplated, as the MVTO beneficiaries are well aware.

[89] See Exhibits EC-9 and JPN-7 (Memorandum D-10-16-3). The remaining memoranda are filed as Exhibit CDA-7. In no case do the memoranda state that Revenue Canada will verify anything other than whether MVTO requirements have been met.

are not binding on the signatory manufacturers and are not "requirements" within the meaning of Article III of the GATT 1994.[90] Clearly, this is not the case. The signatories of the letters viewed them as binding, the letters contain audit and reporting requirements, and there is no expiry date on the letters. It is irrelevant that the letters have not been expressly implemented in Canadian law or regulation and that the MVTO 1998 and SROs do not provide for sanctions in the event that the commitments in the letters are not complied with. The MVTO 1998 and the SROs are "Orders in Council" which are statutory instruments that can be revoked or amended by the Government of Canada should it be inclined to do so. Accordingly, the letters of undertaking are clearly enforceable as the Government of Canada can revoke the relevant instruments if their conditions are not met. There is no doubt that they are measures to which the disciplines of the WTO apply.

5.48 The Government of Canada's position that the letters of undertaking are not binding on their signatories is contradicted by statements of the Chief Executive Officers of two of the signatories.

5.49 On 17 November 1997, Mr. G.Y. Landry, then Chairman, President and CEO of Chrysler Canada Ltd., made the following statement to the Rotary Club of Windsor:

> "In exchange for exemption from Canadian customs duties, each Auto Pact member must ensure that it meets a one to one production to sales ratio (one vehicle produced in Canada for each one sold in Canada."
>
> "In addition, each member must meet a 60 per cent Canadian value added commitment. The 60 per cent of the value of automobiles sold in Canada by the "Auto Pact" members, has resulted in a significant purchase of vehicle parts produced in Canada."[91]

5.50 On 16 October 1997, Ms. Bobbie Gaunt, then President and CEO of the Ford Motor Company, made the following statement to the Empire Club of Canada:

> "Ford, Chrysler and GM signed commitments that we would produce at least one vehicle in Canada for each vehicle sold here, and that we would achieve a Canadian Value Added content of at least 60 per cent. We have exceeded those obligations by a country mile.[92]"

5.51 These statements, made independently by the highest officials of two of the MVTO 1998 recipients, are prima facie evidence that the CVA that is applicable to Ford, Chrysler and GM is 60 per cent. This, in turn, is prima facie evidence that the letters of undertaking are binding and operative.

5.52 Accordingly, the Government of Japan maintains its position that the Letters of Undertaking are requirements within the meaning of Article III of the GATT 1994. It also takes the position that the Letters of Undertaking constitute "measures" that are clearly subject to the WTO disciplines identified in its challenge.

---

[90] See Canada's responses to Questions 4 and 16 from the Panel.

[91] Remarks of G. Yves Landry to the 71st International Day, Rotary Club of Windsor, 17 November 1997, Caboto Club, Windsor Ontario (Exhibit JPN-46).

[92] Remarks by Bobbie Gaunt, President and Chief Executive Officer, Ford Motor Company of Canada, Limited, to the Empire Club of Canada, 16 October 1997, Toronto (Exhibit JPN-47).

(e) The EC's Rebuttal to Canada's Response

5.53 As a rebuttal to Canada's response regarding the Letters, the **European Communities** argues the following:

5.54 As a preliminary matter it is necessary to address a threshold issue raised by Canada which concerns several of the claims made by the European Communities: whether the CVA requirements contained in the Letters of Undertaking submitted by certain manufacturers in connection with the Auto Pact are "measures" subject to dispute settlement.

5.55 Canada's argument with respect to this issue is not entirely clear. On the one hand, Canada contends that the European Communities and Japan have not proven their allegations that the Letters of Undertaking were submitted at the request of the Canadian Government. This would suggest that Canada's position is that the Letters of Undertaking are "private acts" not attributable to the Canadian Government. On the other hand, Canada argues that the Letters of Undertaking are not "legally binding". This in turn would seem to imply an admission that the Letters of Undertaking are acts of the Canadian Government, but nevertheless lack the necessary attributes to qualify as "measures" subject to dispute settlement.

(i) The Letters of Undertaking are attributable to the Canadian Government

5.56 As recalled by the Panel Report on *Japan - Measures affecting Consumer Photographic Film and Paper*[93], past GATT practice confirms that formally "private" acts may nevertheless be deemed Governmental action subject to dispute settlement, provided that there is sufficient involvement of the Government.

5.57 The involvement of the Canadian Government in the Letters of Undertaking is indisputable and makes Canada's contention that the Letters of Undertaking are "private" acts of the Auto Pact beneficiaries untenable.

5.58 First, the Letters themselves state expressly that they are submitted in response to a previous request from the Canadian Government. The Letter submitted by General Motors is particularly candid in this regard. It contains statements such as the following:

> "... this letter is in response to your request for a statement with respect to the proposed agreement ...".[94]
>
> and
>
> "...you have requested that we should increase Canadian value added in our products by $121 million between 1964 and the end of the model year 1968, as outlined under condition (4). Also you have requested that the amount should be further increased to the extent required under condition (3) stated above...".[95]

---

[93] Panel Report on *Japan - Measures Affecting Consumer Photographic Film and Paper*, adopted on 22 April 1998, WT/DS44/R (hereinafter Panel Report on *Japan - Film*), DSR 1998:VI, 1179, para. 10.56.

[94] Letters of Undertaking of General Motors of Canada Ltd., para. 1 (Exhibit EC-2).

[95] Ibid., para. 10.

5.59 Second, the commitments included in the Letters of Undertaking do not, as such, advance the commercial interests of the beneficiaries. Why would the beneficiaries have submitted the Letters of Undertaking, unless they had been pressed to do so by the Canadian Government? In fact, some of the Letters discuss at length the difficulties encountered by the beneficiaries in order to meet the objectives assigned by the Canadian Government.[96]

5.60 Third, all the beneficiaries gave the same commitments. Furthermore, the wording of the Letters of Undertaking is very similar, and in some cases identical.[97] This "coincidence" suggests that all the Letters of Undertaking were drafted after a common model provided by Canada's Ministry of Industry.

5.61 Lastly, when the Automotive Products Trade Act of 1965[98] was debated by the US Congress, chief executives of the US Big Four and Government officials testified that the Letters of Undertaking had been negotiated with the Canadian Ministry of Industry and that their submission was regarded by Canada as a condition *sine qua non* for signing the Auto Pact.

5.62 For example, according to the Executive Vice-President of General Motors:

> "The Canadian Government asked us to write them a letter stating our understanding of the provisions of the agreement as it was finally determined and to ask for our endorsement of the principles to the extent that we did understand them and assigned to us an objective whereby, over the 4 years that are involved in this agreement, we would undertake to increase our Canadian production or our Canadian value."[99]

5.63 Equally explicit was the Vice-President of Chrysler with respect to the link between the Letters and the Auto Pact established by the Canadian Government:

> "The agreement was entered into by Canada only after Canada received assurances from the Canadian vehicle manufacturers which were designed to protect and stimulate Canada's much smaller and less developed manufacturing industry."[100]

5.64 The accounts of the industry were corroborated by officials of the US Government. Thus, the Assistant Secretary of State for Economic Affairs testified that:

> "... It ought to be a matter of record that there have been such conversations between the Canadian Government and each of the Canadian automobile manufacturers, and that the results of those conversations - that is, the letters of assurance, or statements of intentions, are an im-

---

96 See, e.g., the Letters of Undertaking of General Motors of Canada Ltd., where that company complains that the CVA objectives assigned by the Canadian Government are "extremely ambitious" (Exhibit EC-2, para. 10 ff.).

97 Compare, for example, the Letters of Undertaking submitted by Chrysler Canada, Ltd., and American Motors (Canada) Ltd. (both in Exhibit EC-2).

98 Exhibit EC-11.

99 US Congress, Hearings before the Committee on Ways and Means, House of Representatives, 89th Congress, First Session, H.R. 6960, p. 148 (Exhibit EC-22).

100 Ibid., p. 157.

portant part of this agreement as a whole from the Canadian standpoint."[101]

5.65 Further details are provided by the testimony of the Deputy Assistant Secretary for Trade Policy:

> "... We knew during the course of the negotiations that went on for many, many months that the Minister of Industry of Canada was holding conversations with the automobile manufacturing companies in Canada in respect of their intentions as to production under the differing conditions of the prospective agreement ...
>
> "... It took the Canadian Government some time to formulate what was in the letters but I would say [that we became aware of the terms of the letters] in the winter certainly of 1964.
>
> "... I imagine that during the separate conversations that the companies had with the Minister of Industry, that the discussion was perhaps a common one, and perhaps the Minister of Industry drafted a proposed letter that he discussed with each of them that had identical language in it, and that these letters were taken by the Canadian companies and modified to suit their particular circumstances and returned to the Ministry with a lot of common language remaining.[102]"

5.66 As already explained by the European Communities, the US Government and the Big Four tried unsuccessfully to keep secret the Letters of Undertakings. Their concern proved to be justified. When the Letters were eventually disclosed to the US Congress, they were heavily criticised by many congressmen who feared that the additional CVA requirements would cause a serious prejudice to the US parts industry.[103] That led to the insertion in the Automotive Products Trade Act of 1965 of a special provision requiring the President to report to Congress any subsequent undertakings. The wording of that provision evidences that the US Congress entertained no doubts with respect to the true nature of the Letters of Undertaking. It reads as follows:

> "Whenever the President finds that any manufacturer has *entered into any undertaking, by reason of governmental action,* to increase the Canadian value added ... he shall report such finding ... The President shall also report whether such undertaking is additional to *undertakings agreed to in letters of undertaking* submitted by such manufacturer before the date of enactment of this Act."[104] (*emphasis added*)

---

[101] US Congress Hearing before a subcommittee of the Committee of Foreign Relations, US Senate, 89th Congress, 1st Session., 10 February 1965, p. 23 (Exhibit EC-22).

[102] US Congress, Hearing before the Committee on Finance, US Senate, 89th Congress, 1st Session, H.R. 9042, pp. 151-152 (Exhibit EC-22).

[103] See e.g., the Statement by Hon. John Brademas, Representative of Indiana, in US Congress, Hearings before the Committee on Ways and Means, House of Representatives, 89th Congress, First Session, H.R. 6960, p. 196 ff (Exhibit EC-22).

[104] Section 205(a) (Exhibit EC-11).

5.67 The Letters of Undertaking envisaged that the Canadian Government and the beneficiaries would enter into new "discussions" before the end of model year 1968.[105] The Big Four testified to the US Congress that those discussions did in fact take place in due course and that the Canadian Government requested them to sign new undertakings.[106] All of them declared to have refused Canada's request. By way of example, Chrysler testified the following:

> "Chrysler Canada Ltd. has informed us of their discussions with representatives of the Canadian Government. The Department of Industry, Trade and Commerce of Canada has a long standing practice of regular meetings with representatives of the Canadian Motor Vehicles Manufacturers' Association, including Chrysler Canada Ltd. For approximately a year these meetings have centred around a review of the progress in achieving the commitments made in 1965 and the Canadian's Government strong desire for additional undertakings for the years after 1968 ... The Canadian Government requested that Chrysler Canada Ltd., sign a new undertaking to achieve Canadian value added of 75 per cent by model year 1971 and 80 per cent by model year 1974. Chrysler Canada Ltd. supplied Chrysler Corp. with a draft copy of that letter and has informed us of a number of telephone conversations and meetings between various ranking Canadian Government officials and top executives of Chrysler Canada, Ltd. ... Chrysler Canada Ltd., has informed us that they have not agreed to any additional undertakings with the Government of Canada, either by letter or verbally...".[107]

5.68 Although Chrysler did not agree to sign a new undertaking, the above account serves to illustrate the extent of the Canadian Government's involvement in the submission of the Letters of Undertaking in 1965.

5.69 In its reply to a question from the Panel, Canada has eventually admitted that the Letters of Undertaking were submitted at the request from the Canadian Government. Further, Canada even concedes now that the Canadian Government itself drafted the model for the Letters of Undertakings. Nevertheless, Canada pretends that the Canadian Government was not seeking any additional commitments from the beneficiaries:

> "At the conclusion of the Auto Pact the Canadian Government sought assurance from the affected companies that they understood the new system. It provided them with a draft letter outlining what the requirements would be under the pact, and what it hoped would be achieved as a result. The companies were free to modify the letter in any way they chose - for example the letter from General Motors of

[105] All the four Letters of Undertaking conclude with the following para.: "I understand that before the end of model year 1968 we will need to discuss together the prospects for the Canadian automotive industry and our company's program."

[106] US Congress, Hearing before the Committee on Finance, US Senate, 19th Congress, 2nd Session, pp. 82 ff (Exhibit EC-22).

[107] Ibid., pp. 87 ff.

> Canada Ltd. is different in both form and substance from the others, and in no way affected that company's MVTO status".[108]

5.70 It is simply not true that the Canadian Government was merely seeking the assurance from the Auto Pact beneficiaries that they "understood the new system". The above transcribed passage of the Letter of Undertaking submitted by General Motors proves that the Canadian Government requested something more substantial from the beneficiaries:

> "... You have requested that we should increase Canadian value added in our products by $121 million between 1964 and the end of the model year 1968, as outlined under condition (4). Also you have requested that the amount should be further increased to the extent required under condition (3) stated above ...".[109]

5.71 So does the testimony by the Executive Vice-President of General Motors:

> "The Canadian Government asked us to write them a letter stating our understanding of the provisions of the agreement ... *and assigned to us an objective whereby, over the 4 years that are involved in this agreement, we would undertake to increase our Canadian production or our Canadian value".[110] (emphasis added)*

5.72 Moreover, it is disingenuous to pretend that the companies "were free to modify the letter in any way they chose". The testimony given by US Government officials to the US Congress refers to lengthy negotiations between the Canadian Government and the beneficiaries.[111] Also, if the beneficiaries had been truly "free to modify the letters", why did all of them eventually give identical commitments? Further, why did the beneficiaries give any CVA commitments at all, since it is obvious that those commitments go against their own interest?

---

108 Canada's response to Question 17 from the Panel.

109 Exhibit EC-2.

110 US Congress, Hearings before the Committee on Ways and Means, House of Representatives, 89th Congress, First Session, H.R. 6960, p.148 (Exhibit EC-22).

111 See above para. 5.63.

(ii) The Letters of Undertaking are binding

5.73 As to the argument that the Letters of Undertaking are not "legally binding", it must be recalled at the outset that by now it is well established that "non-binding" acts, such as Government recommendations or guidance, may constitute "measures" subject to dispute settlement.[112]

5.74 This issue, however, does not even arise in the case at hand. Contrary to Canada's assertions, the Letters of Undertaking are not mere "statements of what was hoped to be achieved under Canada's implementation of the Auto Pact system".[113]

5.75 The Letters state in unequivocal fashion that the beneficiaries "*undertake*" to meet the CVA requirements.[114] According to a standard dictionary definition[115], "*to undertake*" means "*to agree to do*", "*to give a promise or pledge*", "*to guarantee*", "*to contract*", "*to make oneself responsible for*"...

5.76 Furthermore, at several points the Letters refer to the additional CVA commitments as "*obligations under this letter*"[116] and as "*conditions*".[117] Thus, the wording of the Letters of Undertaking leaves no doubt as to the fact that they purport to impose binding obligations upon the beneficiaries, rather than stating simple "hopes".

(iii) The Letters of Undertaking are enforceable

5.77 The mere fact that there is no sanction explicitly attached to the violation of the Letters does not mean that they are not "enforceable". As testified by executives of the Big Four before the US Congress, the Canadian Government made it clear to them that the submission of the Letters was a necessary condition for the conclusion of the Auto Pact.[118]

5.78 The existence of a link between the submission of the Letters and the conclusion of the Auto Pact is acknowledged in the Letters themselves. By way of example, a letter submitted by Ford together with its Letter of Undertaking states unambiguously that:

> "Our undertakings are, of course, conditional upon the execution of that agreement, upon the adoption of an order in council, and regulations substantially in the form of drafts that you have already delivered

[112] See e.g., the Panel Report on *Japan - Film, supra* note 93, para 10.49: "... moreover, we also consider it conceivable ... that even non-binding, hortatory wording in a government statement of policy could have a similar effect on private actors to a legally binding measure ...". See also the Panel Report on *Japan - Trade in Semiconductors*, adopted on 4 May 1988, BISD 35S/116 (hereinafter Panel Report on *Japan - Semiconductors*), para 117: "The Panel considered that the complex of measures exhibited the rationale as well as the essential elements of a formal system of export control. The only distinction in this case was the absence of formal legal legally binding obligations ... However, the Panel concluded that this amounted to a difference in form rather than substance because the measures were operated in a manner equivalent to mandatory requirements ...".

[113] Canada's response to Question 17 from the Panel.

[114] See e.g., the Letter of Undertaking of Ford Motor Co. of Canada, Ltd., para. 6 (Exhibit EC-2).

[115] Webster's New World Dictionary, Third College Edition.

[116] See e.g., the Letter of Undertaking of Ford Motor Co. of Canada Ltd., para. 9 (Exhibit EC-2)

[117] See eg., the Letter of Undertaking of General Motors of Canada Ltd., para. 4 (Exhibit EC-2).

[118] See above para. 5.62.

to us, and upon an acceptable response in respect of the enclosed supplementary letter."[119]

5.79 Given that link, the beneficiaries have assumed that, were they to disregard the commitments contained in the Letters, the Canadian Government would withdraw the Tariff Exemption. The Canadian Government could do so simply by repealing or amending the MVTO 1998. There is nothing, either in the MVTO 1998, or in any other provision of Canadian law, that could prevent the Canadian Government from taking that action.

5.80 In particular, the Auto Pact would not constitute an obstacle for withdrawing the Tariff Exemption, because it can be denounced by either party subject only to one year notice.[120]

5.81 Canada has asserted that withdrawing from the Auto Pact "would be so inimical to Canada's interests that it would never be contemplated, as the MVTO beneficiaries are well aware".

5.82 That statement, however, is hardly credible. The Auto Pact no longer provides any benefit to Canadian exports of motor vehicles to the United States. Indeed, the United States is no longer enforcing the Auto Pact provisions. Moreover, according to Canada, the only "real" benefit enjoyed by the Auto Pact manufacturers consists of the possibility to import duty-free motor vehicles from third countries other than the United States. Yet that benefit does not flow from the Auto Pact, which only requires Canada to grant duty-free treatment to imports from the United States. It is a benefit provided by Canada on a purely unilateral basis under the MVTO 1998 and the SROs.

(iv) The Canadian Government monitors compliance with the Letters of Undertaking

5.83 The existence of elaborate reporting and auditing procedures constitutes an additional indication that the Letters of Undertaking are treated as binding by both parties.

5.84 Those procedures were expressly foreseen in the Letters of Undertaking. For example, the Letter of Undertaking submitted by Ford contains the following provision:

> "Ford Motor Co. of Canada Ltd. also agrees to report to the Minister of Industry every 3 months beginning April 1 1965, such information as the Minister of Industry requires pertaining to progress achieved by our company as well as plans to fulfil our obligations under this letter. In addition Ford Motor Co. of Canada Ltd. understands that the Gov-

[119] Letter of Ford Motor Co. of Canada, Ltd., dated 4 January 1965, para. 4 (Exhibit EC-2).

[120] See Article VII of the auto Pact (Exhibit EC-1). Moreover, according to Canada, the Auto Pact is not self-executing, which presumably means that the beneficiaries would have no remedy under Canadian law in case that the Canadian Government decided to withdraw the Tariff Exemption (see Canada's response to Question 2 from the EC).

ernment will conduct an audit each year with respect to the matters described in this letter".[121]

5.85 Canada has argued that the D-Memoranda demonstrate that Revenue Canada does not review whether MVTO companies have met their commitments under the Letters of Undertaking, but only whether they have complied with their MVTO commitments.

5.86 This argument is disingenuous. The specimens of reporting documents included in Exhibit EC-14 evidence that the type of information collected by Revenue Canada from the beneficiaries of the MVTO 1998 makes it possible for the Canadian authorities to ascertain compliance also with the requirements contained in the Letters of Undertaking.

5.87 In fact, given that according to Canada the CVA requirements contained in the MVTO "have long been insignificant"[122], it may be suspected that the only reason why those requirements continue to be enforced is precisely in order to obtain the necessary information to enforce the CVA requirements contained in the Letters of Undertaking.

(v) The CVA requirements in the Letters of Undertaking are complied with in practice

5.88 In a document entitled "Auto Pact Background" found on Canada Industry's website it is stated that the Letters of Undertaking "while not being binding typically have been met".[123]

5.89 This confirms that compliance with the Letters of Undertaking is actually ascertained by the Canadian Government. It confirms also that, despite Canada's protestations, the Letters continue to have "current practical significance"[124] and are treated as binding by both the Government and the beneficiaries.

(f) Response by Canada to the Complainants' Rebuttals

5.90 **Canada** responds as follows (with arguments also appearing in sections relating to specific claims):

5.91 The complainants have argued that the letters also violate Article III:4. That Article states that it applies to all "laws, regulations and requirements". Japan and the European Communities have not attempted to argue that the letters are laws or regulations because clearly they are not. They are not found in any legal instrument. The only question is whether the letters are requirements.[125]

---

[121] Letter of Undertaking of Ford Motor Co. of Canada, Ltd., para. 8 (Exhibit EC-2). Identical statements are contained in the Letters of Undertaking of Chrysler Canada Ltd., para. 6, and of American Motors (Canada) Ltd., para. 6 (both in Exhibit EC-2).

[122] See para. 6.271, below.

[123] Exhibit EC-2.

[124] Canada's response to Question 17 from the Panel.

[125] Canada, in its answer to Question 4 from the Panel, has already set out its views on the interpretation of the terms "measures" and "laws, regulations and requirements". In Canada's view, the terms do not have the same meaning, with measure being the broader term. It is thus only necessary to determine whether the letters are "requirements". If so, they are necessarily measures. Conversely, a finding that the letters are "measures" would not be determinative. It would still be necessary to

5.92 The European Communities and Japan bear the burden of proving that the additional letters are requirements, a burden they cannot meet. The test for whether the CVA amounts in the letters are "requirements" is found in the Panel Reports in *Canada - Administration of the Foreign Investment Review Act*[126] and *EEC - Regulation on Imports of Parts and Components*.[127] The *Canada - FIRA* panel found that voluntarily submitted undertakings could be "requirements" within the meaning of Article III:4. However, the panel explicitly noted that the undertakings at issue in *Canada - FIRA* were not complied with voluntarily. Once they were submitted, the undertakings formed part of the legally enforceable regime applying to the investment. There was, in short, a sanction for failing to comply with the requirements. This fact was central to the panel's reasoning.[128]

5.93 The Panel on *EEC - Parts and Components* distinguished between "requirements" that a company is legally bound to carry out (the *Canada - FIRA* situation) and "requirements" that a company voluntarily accepts in order to obtain an advantage. It nevertheless found that both were "requirements" within the meaning of Article III:4, but only to the extent that the requirements were conditions precedent to obtaining a benefit.[129]

5.94 The letters are not requirements under these tests. They are not part of the legally enforceable regime applying to the MVTO. Should a beneficiary fail to meet the CVA amounts in its letter, it would still qualify for its duty-free privileges. Japan's own evidence has made it clear that this is the case.[130] Indeed, should a beneficiary refuse to provide the information that would be necessary to determine whether it had met the amounts, it would still qualify. Moreover, just as there is no sanction for failing to meet the amounts in the letters, there is no reward for doing so. No additional benefits accrue to companies that honour the letters. Companies are not bound to carry out their terms, nor do they do so voluntarily in order to obtain a benefit. The letters are thus not requirements. They are completely unrelated to a company's ability to import duty free under the MVTO.

5.95 Canada has made public its position that the letters are not requirements. Indeed, Japan has filed as evidence a public statement from Industry Canada that explicitly describes the letters as non-binding.[131] Canada has made the same statement repeatedly in the proceedings before this Panel; it should be noted that Canada makes all of its WTO submissions public upon request. These very submissions are thus also public statements that the letters are not binding and cannot be enforced.

5.96 The European Communities has made much of the wording of the letters, which it claims is mandatory. In fact, the wording varies and is at most ambiguous - the word "undertake" can mean to commit oneself formally, but it can also mean to

---

determine whether the letters are "requirements", or to find that the two terms have identical meanings.

[126] Panel Report on *Canada - Administration of the Foreign Investment Review Act*, adopted on 7 February 1984, BISD 30S/140 (hereinafter Panel Report on *Canada - FIRA*).

[127] Panel Report on *EEC - Regulation of Imports of Parts and Components*, adopted on 16 May 1990, BISD 37S/132 (hereinafter Panel Report on *EEC - Parts and Components*).

[128] Panel Report on *Canada - FIRA* , *supra* note 126, para. 5.4.

[129] Panel Report on *EEC - Parts and Components*, *supra* note 127, para. 5.21.

[130] Exhibit JPN-27, p. 63.

[131] Exhibit JPN-38, p. 38-1.

take on a task.[132] Where there is no sanction and no reward, even the most strongly worded private undertaking cannot be considered a requirement under Article III:4.

5.97 To date, the complainants' other evidence has focused on the questions of whether the Canadian government was involved in the preparation of the letters, whether the manufacturers were required to submit letters as a *sine qua non* of Canada's signing the Auto Pact, and whether the beneficiaries believed themselves bound by the letters. The evidence provided is at best ambiguous, and does not demonstrate that the letters were ever requirements.[133]

5.98 The European Communities has also claimed that the letters are enforceable on the theory that nothing in Canadian law prevents Canada from repealing or amending the MVTO. This argument is a fundamental misstatement of WTO law. The WTO agreements do not apply to actions that Members *could* take. They apply to actions that Members have *taken*. The letters are not requirements because they are not enforceable and offer no rewards; whether the Canadian government has the constitutional authority to convert them into requirements is irrelevant.

5.99 That the letters are not requirements is clear from what would happen in the event that Canada had to implement a finding that they violate Article III:4. The Canadian government would not have to take any action in order to comply with the finding. It would not have to repeal the letters because it never passed them in the first place - there is nothing to repeal. It would not have to repudiate them, because it has already been made clear that neither the government nor the companies affected regard themselves as bound by them. It would not have to stop enforcing them, because it does not do so.

5.100 Virtually all of the evidence the complaining parties have supplied relates to the time when the letters were written, thirty-five years ago. All of this evidence is irrelevant. Regardless of the past status of the letters, they are not requirements today, and will not become requirements in the future. Even prior to the complaining parties bringing this case, Canada had publicly stated that the letters were not binding.[134] The complainants themselves have cited the statement, and have never rebutted it. Canada has also stopped making any effort to verify whether companies achieved the amounts contained in the letters. Canada has now repeatedly made it

---

[132] See, e.g., The New Shorter Oxford English Dictionary on Historical Principles, definition 4(a) (vol. 2 [Oxford: Clarendon Press, 1993], p. 3476, Exhibit CDA-13), and Merriam-Webster's Collegiate Dictionary, definition 1 (10th ed. [Markham: Thomas Allen, 1993], p. 1289 (Exhibit CDA-14).

[133] For example, Exhibit EC-22, p. 11 contains the following statement from an official of General Motors Corp. of the United States: "I can speak for General Motors and I can say that *there have been no secret agreements, there have been no negotiations*. The Canadian Government asked us to write them a letter stating our understanding of the provisions of the agreement as it was finally determined and to ask for our endorsement of the principles to the extent that we did understand them and assigned to us an *objective* whereby, over the 4 years that are involved in this agreement, we would undertake to increase our Canadian production or our Canadian value." (*emphasis added*) United States-Canada Automotive Products Agreement: Hearings before the House Comm. on Ways and Means on H.R. 6960 "The Automotive Products Trade Act of 1965", 89th Cong., 1st Sess. (1965), p. 148 (testimony of James M. Roche, Executive Vice President, General Motors Corp.). This statement agrees exactly with Canada's explanation of the facts provided in response to Question 17 from the Panel.

[134] Exhibit JPN-38 and Exhibit EC-20.

clear that it does not regard the letters as binding. If the executives of the beneficiary companies were ever in any doubt on this point, they no longer are.

5.101 Regardless of whether the letters have ever been thought binding, they have never been enforceable. Japan has now joined the European Communities in claiming that the letters could be enforced by repealing or amending the MVTO, and even withdrawing from the Auto Pact if necessary. This argument is a fundamental misstatement of WTO law. The WTO agreements do not apply to measures that Members could take. They apply to measures that Members have taken.

5.102 In any event, Canada would never - indeed, could never - have withdrawn from the Auto Pact. First, it would punish every MVTO and SRO company, not just the non-compliant one. Second, from 1965 until 1998, when NAFTA duty phase-outs for the United States reached zero, duty-free access to the American market depended on the Auto Pact. There was never any possibility that Canada would withdraw from it under those circumstances.

5.103 For these reasons, Canada submits that the letters of undertaking do not create requirements within the meaning of GATT Article III:4. They therefore cannot give rise to a violation of that Article.

(g) The European Communities' Follow-Up to Canada's Response

5.104 As a follow-up to Canada's response, the **European Communities** argues as follows (with arguments also appearing in sections relating to specific claims):

5.105 Canada appears to have recognised that the position that the Letters of Undertaking are not "measures" is untenable. Thus, in its response to the complainant's rebuttals, Canada limits itself to argue that the Letters of Undertaking are not "laws, regulations and requirements". By way of justification, Canada explains in a footnote that since the term "measure" is "broader" than the term "requirement", it is only necessary for the Panel to determine whether the Letters are requirements.

5.106 The European Communities disagrees. Even assuming that the term "measure" was indeed "broader", the European Communities has submitted claims with respect to the CVA requirements not only under GATT Article III:4 and Article 2.1 of the TRIMs Agreement, but also under GATS Article XVII and Article 3.1(b) of the SCM Agreement. Neither of those two provisions refers to "requirements". Therefore, a finding that the Letters are not "requirements", would not dispense the Panel from ascertaining whether they are "measures".

5.107 Canada's defence relies on an extremely narrow interpretation of the term "requirement". In essence, Canada argues that the Letters are not "requirements" because they are not "legally enforceable", either through sanctions or through rewards explicitly attached to them.

5.108 That interpretation, however, is not compelled by the ordinary meaning of the term "requirement". "Required" and "legally enforceable" are not synonyms. The existence of a explicit legal sanction furnishes the proof that something is a "requirement", but is not an inherent element.

5.109 The Letters of Undertaking contain "requirements" because they are drafted in mandatory terms and are regarded as binding by the Canadian Government and by the beneficiaries, as evidenced by the fact that compliance is regularly verified and that in practice the beneficiaries do comply with the terms of the Letters.

5.110 The statement found in Industry Canada's website to the effect that the Letters "while non-binding, typically have been met"[135] cannot be taken as evidence that the Canadian Government does not regard the Letters as "binding". That statement is not addressed to the beneficiaries, but to the general public. The Canadian Government does not need to post statements in the internet in order to convey to the beneficiaries its views on the nature of the Letters. In any event, Canada Industry uses the term "binding" in the narrow sense of "legally enforceable". In the same paragraph, Canada Industry also refers to the terms of the Letters as something the beneficiaries "undertook" and as "conditions".

5.111 For similar reasons, the statements made by the Canadian Government in these proceedings cannot be taken as evidence that it does not regard the Letters as binding or that it has repudiated them. The Big Three understand perfectly well that Canada is forced to make those arguments in order to preserve the Tariff Exemption for their benefit.

5.112 Canada claims that its interpretation of the term "requirement" is derived from *Canada - FIRA*[136] and *EEC - Parts and Components*[137] Those reports, however, in no way suggest that the panels purported to formulate, or that they were applying a set of generally applicable criteria.

5.113 In any event, the Letters of Undertaking fit within the same pattern as the measures at issue in *EEC - Parts and Components*. As explained by Canada, in that case the Panel found that the undertakings to increase local content given by the subsidiaries of certain Japanese companies were "requirements" because they were a "condition precedent to obtaining a benefit". The same is true of the Letters of Undertaking. The Canadian Government would not have concluded the Auto Pact if the Big Three had not submitted the Letters of Undertaking.

5.114 The only difference between the two cases is that the EC antidumping regulations envisaged that, if the undertakings were breached or withdrawn, the EC Commission could (but was not obliged to) re-institute proceedings and eventually impose anti-circumvention duties.[138] The MVTO does not envisage expressly the possibility to impose sanctions. That does not mean, however, that the Letters are unenforceable. Given the linkage between the conclusion of the Auto Pact and the submission of the Letters established by the Canadian Government, there has always been a tacit understanding between the parties that if the beneficiaries failed to comply with the Letters, the Canadian Government would withdraw the tariff benefits.

5.115 In one of the supplemental questions put by the Panel, the Panel has asked Canada whether any of the manufacturers operating under the MVTO have indicated in their annual reports that they have gone above the CVA requirements of the MVTO.[139]

5.116 The answer is that there is no need for the beneficiaries to do so. The samples of reporting forms included in Exhibit EC-14 show that the MVTO beneficiaries are required to report, among other things, the total CVA amount in the relevant period,

---

135 Exhibit EC-20.

136 Panel Report on *Canada - FIRA* , *supra* note 126.

137 Panel Report on *EEC - Parts and Components*, *supra* note 127.

138 Ibid., para 5.20.

139 Question 40 from the Panel.

as well as the net sales value of the vehicles sold in Canada during the same period. Those two amounts allow the Canadian Government to verify, by making a very simple calculation, whether the Big Three comply with the CVA requirements in the Letters. The Big Three know that. And the Canadian Government knows that the Big Three know.

3. *The Auto Pact, the CUSFTA and the NAFTA*

(a) Japan's Arguments Regarding the Auto Pact, the CUSFTA and the NAFTA

5.117 Regarding the Auto Pact, the CUSFTA and the NAFTA, **Japan** argues as follows (with additional arguments contained in sections relating to specific claims):

(i) From the outset, the Canada-US Auto Pact was designed to be discriminatory in nature

5.118 In the early 1960s, the Government of Canada was concerned that its automotive policies were insufficient to stimulate growth in the Canadian automotive industry. To address its concern, a new duty rebate program was initiated in 1963 for automotive parts. Exports of automotive parts to the United States soared and an US radiator producer responded by initiating a countervailing duty action. The Governments of Canada and the United States then began negotiations to resolve the matter. The result of these negotiations was the Canada-US Auto Pact.

5.119 On 16 January 1965, the Governments of Canada and the United States signed the Canada-US Auto Pact, a sectoral agreement applicable to trade in automotive goods.[140] The parties agreed that if certain conditions were met, automobiles and original equipment parts would be traded between the two countries on a duty-free basis.[141] In other words, the Canada-US Auto Pact originally was designed to accord benefits and competitive advantages only to North American automobile manufacturers, their distributors and their products, given the fact that no manufacturer (other than American Motors, Chrysler, Ford, General Motors, Studebaker and Volvo)[142] had made substantial investments in Canada at that time.

5.120 The Governments of Canada and the United States used different criteria to determine eligibility for such duty-free treatment. In the case of the United States, automotive products from Canada would qualify if they were "products of Canada" meeting certain rules of origin".[143]

5.121 On the Canadian side, in order for the products to qualify for duty-free treatment they had to be imported by motor vehicle manufacturers that met certain conditions, *inter alia,* specified domestic content and manufacturing requirements.[144] Also,

---

[140] The Canada-US Auto Pact provisionally entered into force on 16 January 1965.

[141] Article II of the Canada-US Auto Pact reflects the agreement on duty-free trade, and Annexes A and B thereto describe the covered products (Exhibit JPN-1).

[142] Volvo was the only original Member of the Canada-US Auto Pact that was not a North American-owned manufacturer.

[143] Annex B of the Canada-US Auto Pact (Exhibit JPN-1).

[144] Annex A of the Canada-US Auto Pact. A vehicle manufacturer was defined as a manufacturer of automobiles, buses or certain commercial vehicles, that produced such vehicles in Canada in the

Canada reserved the right to designate manufacturers not meeting the specified conditions as entitled to the benefit of duty-free treatment.[145] The Government of Canada's approach was motivated by the Government's objective that a certain share of the North American industry would remain in Canada as motor vehicle manufacturers restructured their operations.[146]

5.122 In March 1965, a GATT 1947 Working Party initiated a review of the terms of the Canada-US Auto Pact.[147] Since the United States' implementation of the Canada-US Auto Pact would confer duty-free status only on parts and motor vehicles originating in Canada, it was considered to be a clear violation of Article I of the GATT 1947. Thus, the United States requested and eventually obtained a GATT 1947 waiver.[148]

5.123 While the United States recognized that its commitments under the Canada-US Auto Pact constituted a clear violation of Article I of the GATT 1947 and thus sought and obtained a waiver, the Government of Canada did not request a waiver. According to the Canadian representative appearing before the Working Party, the Canada-US Auto Pact would be implemented on a most-favoured-nation basis, and the benefits of the Agreement would be extended on the same terms to all contracting parties. According to the Canadian representative, Paragraph 3 of Annex A of the Canada-US Auto Pact, which contained the Government of Canada's obligations, provided that automobile producers who met the same conditions as the intended Auto Pact Manufacturers would qualify for t he same treatment.[149] According to the Canadian representative, this position illustrated the open-ended character of the Canada-US Auto Pact.[150] However, as discussed below, the open-ended nature of the Canada-US Auto Pact was fundamentally changed in 1989 when the list of eligible importers was frozen. This action crystallized the discriminatory nature of the Canadian regime.

5.124 At the time of the 1965 GATT Working Party, several contracting parties challenged the Government of Canada's view. In particular, they noted that the Agreement introduced *de facto* differentiation between those third country producers which had production facilities in Canada and those which did not.[151] Moreover, one Member of the Working Party referred to the possibility of "like products imported

---

1963-1964 base year. In addition, such manufacturers had to maintain, in each subsequent year: (i) an equal or higher ratio of the net sales value of the vehicles they produced to the net sales value of all vehicles they sold in Canada (production-to-sales ratio) than the ratio that they maintained in the base year, or seventy-five to one hundred, whichever was greater; and (ii) the same or greater Canadian value added (CVA) to the vehicles they produced in Canada in the base year (Exhibit JPN-1).

[145] Annex A of the Canada-US Auto Pact, para. 3 (Exhibit JPN-l).

[146] J.R. Johnson, "The Effect of the Canada-US Free Trade Agreement on the Auto Pact" in M.A. Molot, ed., Driving Continentally: National Policies and the North American Auto Industry (Ottawa: Carleton University Press, 1993) 256 (Exhibit JPN-23).

[147] Report of the *Working Party on Canada - US Agreement on Automotive Products*, adopted on 25 March 1965, BISD 13S/112.

[148] The waiver, which had been extended under the WTO, expired on 1 January 1998 (Exhibit JPN-24).

[149] Exhibit JPN-1.

[150] Report of the *Working Party on the Auto Pact, supra* note 147, 114, para 10.

[151] Ibid., 119, para. 27.

by different classes of importers being charged different rates of duty and inquired whether this would not result in discrimination between sources of supply" contrary to Article I of the GATT 1947.[152] Members of the Working Party inquired as to the criteria that would be applied to new producers wishing to qualify as manufacturers. The representative of Canada replied that "it was not the intention of his Government to discriminate either against or in favour of new producers of any nationality".[153] The Working Party did not reach a conclusion with regard to the GATT-consistency of the Government of Canada's implementation measures of the Canada-US Auto Pact.

(ii) From 1965 to 1969, Canada implemented a discriminatory scheme through the Canada-US Auto Pact

5.125 The Government of Canada initially implemented its obligations under the Canada-US Auto Pact through the Motor Vehicles Tariff Order 1965 (MVTO 1965) and the Tariff Item 950 Regulations (950 Regulations) which set out the declarative and reporting requirements for eligible importers.[154] The Government of Canada established conditions in the MVTO 1965 that, if met, would entitle a manufacturer to import automotive goods duty free from any country benefiting from MFN or British Preferential Tariff Treatment.[155] With respect to the eligibility condition, the MVTO 1965 applied only to those producers who operated in the 1963-1964 base year.[156] Given the definition of "base year", the MVTO 1965 applied only to six automobile producers (American Motors, Chrysler, Ford, General Motors, Studebaker and Volvo) and a number of specified commercial vehicle and bus producers. Thus, the benefits of the Duty Waiver were limited to those eligible importers, foreign manufacturers that had relationships with those importers, products of such foreign manufacturers, eligible importers' wholesale trade services, and, indirectly, to suppliers of certain domestic products and services to those eligible importers.

5.126 Because manufacturers that had not operated during the 1963-1964 base year were not eligible to receive the Duty Waiver's benefits under the MVTO 1965, the Government of Canada issued company-specific SROs for other manufacturers requesting equivalent status where certain conditions were met.[157] The criteria for determining initial eligibility for SRO status were unclear and appear arbitrary as the Government of Canada reserved the right under the Canada-US Auto Pact to designate manufacturers as entitled to the Duty Waiver and as there is no mentioning of the criteria that might be applied for such designations.[158] According to a United States Senate report, the Government of Canada required the establishment of production facilities and the fulfilment of conditions similar to the production-to-sales

[152] Report of the *Working Party on the Auto Pact, supra* note 147, 117, para 21, and 119, para. 27.
[153] Ibid., 114, para. 10.
[154] Exhibit JPN-25.
[155] Section 2 of the Schedule to the MVTO 1965 (Exhibit JPN-25).
[156] Ibid., at subsection 2(1).
[157] A list of SROs that were still in force in 1998 is set out in Exhibit JPN-26.
[158] Canada-US Auto Pact, Annex A, Section 3 (Exhibit JPN -1).

ratio and the Canadian value added (CVA) requirement before an SRO would be issued.[159]

5.127 The express conditions for duty-free importation of automotive products under the SROs were similar to those under the MVTO 1965 and the 950 Regulations. All SROs provided for a manufacturing requirement and the CVA requirement, although the level that had to be reached could differ from those applying to manufacturers that qualified under the MVTO 1965.[160] Manufacturers that qualified under an SRO were granted a benefit equivalent to those companies that qualified under the MVTO 1965.[161]

(iii) The Canadian motor vehicle industry benefited substantially from the Canada-US Auto Pact preferences

5.128 The adoption of the Canada-US Auto Pact favoured the development of the Canadian motor vehicle industry. Before 1965, the Canadian motor vehicle industry, as with most other national automotive industries, was organized on a national basis. The market was supplied by locally based, foreign-owned producers and import penetration was minimal as high tariff barriers insulated the market.[162] Following the conclusion of the Canada-US Auto Pact, the Canadian automotive industry rapidly transformed from an industry geared towards the supply of a small domestic market to the sixth-leading producer in the world.[163] The industry expanded primarily due to the conditions for obtaining duty-free treatment under the Canada-US Auto Pact, which emphasize Canadian production of finished motor vehicles.

5.129 By providing for the liberalisation of imports in motor vehicles and automotive parts between Canada and the United States, the Canada-US Auto Pact encouraged the mainly foreign-owned producers located in Canada to rationalise their production. The main automotive producers concentrated the production of specific models in specific plants to take advantage of cost savings through economies of scale and to ship finished products from each plant, wherever located, to all regional markets in Canada and the United States.

5.130 The implication of Canada's automotive sector was that a number of plants would produce a narrower range of models but these would be destined for both the domestic and American markets. Other models would be imported into Canada from

---

159 United States Senate, Committee on Finance, United States International Trade Commission Report on the United States-Canada Automotive Agreement: Its History, Terms and Impact (Washington: US Government Printing Office, 1976), at p. 25 (Exhibit JPN-27).

160 Exhibit JPN-28 summarizes the SRO conditions and their evolution over time.

161 *Memorandum D10-16-2*, Revenue Canada, 22 May 1998, s. 1 (Exhibit JPN-8).

162 J. Holmes, "From Three Industries to One; Towards an Integrated North American Automobile Industry", in M.A. Molot, ed., Driving Continentally; National Policies and the North American Auto Industry (Ottawa: Carleton University Press, 1993) at 25 (Exhibit JPN-23).

163 Industry Canada's web site shows that the US, Japan, Germany, France and South Korea preceded Canada in 1997, "Motor Vehicle Production by Major Producing Country (Thousands of Units)": http://strategis.ic.gc.ca/SSG/am01178e.html, document published 23 November 1998, date accessed: 1 February 1999.

United States or other plants to complete the product lines available to consumers.[164] Auto Pact Manufacturers were allowed under the Government of Canada's tariff regime to decide which models were to be imported into Canada with the benefit of the Duty Waiver, and the country of origin of those models. However, as discussed in arguments appearing in paragraphs 5.238 - 5.240 and 5.264 - 5.269, due to the global integration of the motor vehicle manufacturing industry, most imports have been from overseas manufacturers that are affiliates or related companies of the eligible importers. Thus, as expected by one Member of the GATT 1947 Working Party that reviewed the terms of the Canada-US Auto Pact, the Duty Waiver indeed resulted in "discrimination between sources of supply".

(iv) The Government of Canada's administration of the Canada-US Auto Pact from the 1970s to the 1990s crystallized the discriminatory aspects of the Duty Waiver

5.131 The manner in which the Government of Canada regulated automotive trade during the 1970s through the 1990s served to exacerbate and crystallize the discriminatory aspects of the Duty Waiver. More specifically, restrictions introduced as a result of the (CUSFTA) and the NAFTA ensured that the motor vehicles, parts and components thereof, wholesale trade services and other services of Japanese manufacturers and suppliers would be denied the benefits of the Duty Waiver.

- Recognizing the discriminatory effects of the Duty Waiver, the Government of Canada initially offset the effects by providing certain compensatory programmes

5.132 Acknowledging the adverse discriminatory effects of the Duty Waiver and seeking to attract further foreign investment, the Government of Canada introduced compensatory programmes that, in part, offset those effects. However, these compensatory programmes did not remove the discriminatory aspects of the Duty Waiver. Moreover, they were arguably, in themselves, inconsistent with the Government of Canada's international trade obligations.

5.133 Introduced in the 1970s and 1980s, these compensatory programmes permitted Non-Auto Pact Manufacturers to import motor vehicle products duty free. However, companies that did not manufacture automobiles in Canada could not benefit from these programmes, restricting the compensatory effect of the programmes to a narrow class of importers. Moreover, the compensatory benefits were subject to certain conditions.

5.134 The compensatory nature of these programmes and the fact that they were intended to permit Non-Auto Pact Manufacturers to compete with Auto Pact Manufacturers is confirmed by a former Canadian Ambassador for Trade Negotiations and the Deputy Chief Negotiator for the CUSFTA. In his recent book, Mr. Gordon Ritchie states that the programmes in question were negotiated to enable Japanese and

[164] This concept is sometimes referred to as the "decoupling" of domestic sales from national production.

Korean manufacturers "to compete with American companies until they could qualify under the Auto Pact".[165]

5.135 Over this period, the Government of Canada issued duty remission orders to Non-Auto Pact Manufacturers. The first type of remission orders applied to export of parts (export-based remission orders).[166] The second type of remission orders were based on production (production-based remission orders).[167]

5.136 The production-based remission orders resembled the MVTO 1965 and its successors and the Special Remission Orders in that they contained similar performance requirements. Given the relatively high MFN rates on automobiles at the time, the production-based remission orders were significant for the participating companies.

5.137 In addition to the export and production-based remission orders, the general Inward Processing Remission Programme provided companies with certain relief from the payment of customs duties on parts they used in their Canadian production of automobiles. The Government of Canada exempted payment of customs duties on imported parts used in Canadian production and exported to third countries (in practice, the most important third country was the United States).

5.138 In 1988, Canada amended the Customs Tariff - the federal statute that provided legislative authority for the MVTO 1965.[168] As a result, Canada revoked the MVTO 1965 and issued a new order, the Motor Vehicles Tariff Order, 1988 (MVTO 1988), to reflect the legislative changes.[169] The MVTO 1988 replaced and consolidated both the MVTO 1965 and Tariff Item 95000 (Entry of Motor Vehicles) Regulations.[170] It preserved the essential elements of the MVTO 1965 and the Tariff Item 95000 (Entry of Motor Vehicles) Regulations.

---

165 Ritchie, Gordon, Wrestling with the Elephant, the Inside Story of the Canada-US Trade Wars (Toronto; MacFarlane, Walter & Ross; 1997) at p. 112 (Exhibit JPN-29).

166 Individual remission orders were revoked in 1975 and were replaced by the Automobile Components Remission Order (SI/75-58). In 1985, the Automobile Components Remission Order was revoked (SI/85-48). Then, throughout the 1980s, Canada issued a series of company-specific remission orders (Exhibit JPN-30).

167 The companies that qualified for production-based remission orders were Honda, Toyota, and Hyundai (Honda Remission Order, 1988, SI/89-15; Toyota Remission Order, *1988*, SI/89-14; Hyundai Remission Order, *1988-2*, SI/89-16) (Exhibit JPN-31).

168 Customs Tariff, R.S.C. 1985, c.41 (3rd Supp.). The Regulatory Impact Analysis Statement for the MVTO 1988 states that the Government of Canada's adoption of the Harmonized Commodity Description and Coding System (HS) required the passage of new Customs Tariff legislation. As a result of this legislative change, certain orders made pursuant to the Customs Tariff (e.g., MVTO 1965) had to be amended to reflect the new tariff classification system (SOR/88-71, Canada Gazette Part II, Vol. 122, No. 2, 615 at 623) (Exhibit JPN-32).

169 Exhibit JPN-32.

170 The original Tariff Item 950 Regulations were renamed Tariff Item 95000 (Entry of Motor Vehicles) Regulations upon the 1978 consolidation of Canadian regulations, C.R.C. 1978, c.480.

- The discriminatory effects of the Duty Waiver were amplified by the CUSFTA through the introduction of an eligibility restriction and the elimination of the compensatory programmes

5.139 On 1 January 1989, the CUSFTA entered into force. The Agreement amplified the discriminatory effects of the Duty Waiver. New restrictions imposed as a result of the CUSFTA had a profound adverse effect on the compensating benefits that the Japanese and other Non-Auto Pact Manufacturers in Canada had been receiving under the duty remission programmes described above. According to Gordon Ritchie, the Government of Canada's Deputy Chief Negotiator for the CUSFTA, these restrictions were imposed at the insistence of the United States:

> "The Americans made it abundantly clear that they were not prepared under any circumstances to have these companies enjoy the Auto Pact benefits, even if it meant terminating the pact itself."[171]

5.140 Accordingly, the Governments of the United States and Canada agreed in CUSFTA Article 1002 that waivers of customs duties could not be extended to any recipient *other than* those listed in Part One of Annex 1002.1 to the CUSFTA.[172] That Annex listed all existing companies with "Auto Pact Manufacturer status" in Canada. The effect of CUSFTA Article 1002, therefore, was to prohibit new applicants from qualifying for Auto Pact Manufacturer status. In short, the list of Auto Pact Manufacturers was frozen. As a result, contrary to statements made by the Government of Canada's representative before the GATT 1947 Working Party, eligibility for the Duty Waiver could no longer be extended to new manufacturers. Since 1 January 1989, new manufacturers, including Japanese manufacturers, have been barred forever from enjoying the benefit of the Duty Waiver.

5.141 The eligibility restriction was implemented in the Canadian automotive regulatory framework by virtue of an amendment to the MVTO 1988.[173] Specifically, a definition of eligible "recipients", which refers to the manufacturers listed in Part I of Annex 1002.1 to Chapter 10 of the CUSFTA (the "Tier I" companies, as discussed below) was added. The amendment also stipulated that no customs duties would be removed in the case of a manufacturer who did not qualify prior to 1 January 1988, as a manufacturer of a class of vehicles under the MVTO 1965, as that Order read on 31 December 1987.[174] Thus, one of the major conditions for the enjoyment of the Duty Waiver is that the relevant manufacturers are included on this list.

5.142 Consequently, in addition to eliminating preferential duty programmes previously available to Non-Auto Pact Manufacturers, the CUSFTA created two classes of motor vehicle manufacturers. The first class, known as "Tier I" companies, consists of General Motors, Ford, Chrysler, Volvo, CAMI, Intermeccanica and the companies that are eligible for Auto Pact Manufacturer status under MVTO 1998 and SROs.[175]

---

171 Exhibit JPN-29, at 112.

172 CUSFTA, Annex 1002.1 (Exhibit JPN-33).

173 Motor Vehicles Tariff Order, 1988, Amendment, SOR/89-48 (Exhibit JPN -35).

174 In the case of CAMI Automotive Inc. (CAMI), an extension was granted so that it could qualify for the 1989 model year. It later qualified and its SRO is still in effect. Sections 1 and 3 of the Schedule to the MVTO 1998 set out the same restrictions.

175 See D-Memoranda D10-16-3 and D10-16-2 for a list of companies that qualify (Exhibits JPN-7 and 8).

These companies have full Auto Pact Manufacturer status, which permits them to import automobiles and parts duty free so long as they meet the specified performance requirements.

5.143 The second class, known as "Tier II" companies, consists of Toyota, Honda and others. As a result of the restrictions introduced by the CUSFTA (and, as discussed below, the NAFTA), these companies can never attain Tier I status.[176] Of course, other manufacturers in the world having no manufacturing facilities in Canada have no possibility to enjoy such Tier I status and the associated benefits.

The NAFTA reaffirmed the discriminatory aspects of the CUSFTA

5.144 On 1 January 1994, the NAFTA entered into force.[177] Like the CUSFTA, it contained extensive provisions dealing with trade and investment in the automotive sector.[178] In addition to the general restriction on duty waiver programmes[179], it stated that both the Governments of Canada and the United States could maintain the Canada-US Auto Pact as modified by the CUSFTA.[180]

Preferential trade and MFN trade

5.145 For the purposes of this dispute, one must distinguish between preferential trade under the CUSFTA and NAFTA and MFN trade that takes place outside the scope of the preferential trade under those Agreements.[181] As discussed below, *bilateral* duty-free trade in motor vehicles between Canada and the United States now takes place exclusively under the terms of the NAFTA since the Canada-US Auto Pact is no longer operative in the United States.[182]

5.146 In some cases where the NAFTA rules of origin are not met, the Duty Waiver is available with respect to Canada-US trade. However, this applies only to imports into Canada. Imports into the United States do not benefit from similar treatment.

5.147 Accordingly, the Duty Waiver applies mostly to MFN trade between Canada and other countries. Thus, to the extent that the two regional trade agreements amplified and maintained the Duty Waiver's discrimination, the rights and obligations of WTO Members have been adversely affected.

---

[176] Section 1 of Article 1002 of the CUSFTA provides that neither Party to the Agreement shall extend a duty waiver to anyone but those recipients listed in Annex 1002.1. Part One of Annex 1002.1 lists those companies that qualified for Auto Pact Manufacturer status; no Japanese companies are included on this list. Sections 2 and 3 of Article 1002 provide specific termination dates for the previously enjoyed export-based and production-based waivers of customs duties.

[177] In Canada, the date on which the legislation implementing the NAFTA became effective was fixed by regulation at 1 January 1994 (Order Fixing January 1, 1994, as the Date of the Coming into Force of the Act, except Section 177, SI/94-1, Canada Gazette Part II, Vol. 128, No. 1, 604.)

[178] Annex 300-A, Article 403, and Annex 401 of the NAFTA (Exhibit JPN-36).

[179] Sections 1 and 2 of Article 304 of the NAFTA (Exhibit JPN-36).

[180] Sections 1-3, Appendix 300-A.1, NAFTA, (Exhibit JPN-36).

[181] The scope of preferential trade under the Agreements is defined by their respective rules of origin.

[182] Until 31 December 1997, the motor vehicle trade under the Duty Waiver prevailed over the trade under the terms of the NAFTA, since a 0.9 per cent duty had been imposed on NAFTA imports.

The MVTO 1998 is directed solely at protecting Canada's domestic industry

5.148 On 1 January 1998, the United States' GATT 1947 waiver (that had been continued under the WTO Agreement) expired.[183] After that date, Canadian motor vehicle products entered the United States duty free solely under the terms of the NAFTA. In other words, the Canada-US Auto Pact became inoperative with respect to imports into the United States.[184]

5.149 Also in December 1997, the federal Customs Tariff was once again amended and a new Order in Council, the MVTO 1998, was enacted and entered into force on 1 January 1998.[185] The MVTO 1998 contains the technical changes required to ensure consistency with the terminology and structure of the amended Customs Tariff, consolidates the MVTO 1988 and includes amendments thereto. The conditions required in order to benefit from the Duty Waiver remain the same.

5.150 On 10 June 1998, the Government of Canada released a report on the Canadian automotive industry.[186] In that report, it determined that the discriminatory duty treatment would be maintained and "decided against any unilateral changes to the MFN vehicle duty at this time".[187]

5.151 Thus, after 1 January 1998, the Duty Waiver was no longer related to the implementation of the Canada-US Auto Pact. Rather, it was aimed solely at protecting Canada's domestic motor vehicle industry; Canada's parts, components and materials industries; and certain suppliers of wholesale trade and other services.

(b) The EC's Arguments Regarding the Auto Pact, the CUSFTA and the NAFTA

5.152 Regarding the Auto Pact, the CUSFTA and the NAFTA, the **European Communities** argues as follows (with additional arguments contained in Section VI, Legal Arguments of the Parties):

---

183 Exhibit JPN-24.

184 Also in 1994, as apparent concessions to Non-Auto Pact Manufacturers, the Government of Canada reduced the MFN duty rates on original equipment parts for manufacturers of automobiles to zero for certain goods and 2.5 per cent for others (Customs Duties Reduction or Removal Order, 1988, amendment, SOR/94-18). As of 1 January 1996, the Government of Canada eliminated the MFN duties on "[p]arts, accessories and articles, excluding tires and tubes, for use in the manufacture of original equipment parts for passenger automobiles, trucks or buses, or for use as original equipment in the manufacture of such vehicles or chassis thereof." (Customs Duties Reduction or Removal Order, 1988, amendment, SOR/96-4. This statutory instrument expired on 31 December 1997.) However, the elimination of the MFN duties was made part of the new Customs Tariff, S.C. 1997, c. 36, under tariff code 9958.

185 Customs Tariff, S.C. 1997, c. 36. Section 213 repealed the previous version of the Customs Tariff (R.S.C. 1985, c.41 (3rd Supp.)).

186 Industry Canada, The Automotive Competitiveness Review: A Report on the Canadian Automotive Industry (Ottawa: Industry Canada, 1998) (Exhibit JPN-2).

187 Ibid., p. 29.

(i) The Auto Pact

- Antecedents

5.153 The measures in dispute stem from the Auto Pact concluded in January 1965 by the Governments of the United States and of Canada. The Auto Pact purported to resolve the trade frictions caused by Canada's persistent efforts to build and maintain a local automotive industry.

5.154 Prior to 1965, Canada sought to achieve that objective through the application of high import duties on motor vehicles[188] and parts therefor[189], together with a system of tariff exemptions, whereby the manufacturers of motor vehicles established in Canada could import duty free original equipment parts[190], provided that they met a minimum "Commonwealth"[191] content requirement[192].

5.155 While those measures permitted the development of a local automotive industry (albeit one dominated by US firms[193]), they led to costly inefficiencies[194]. In fact, those measures encouraged foreign manufacturers to assemble locally a very large range of models. Since the size of the Canadian market was relatively small, each model had to be produced in short runs, with the ensuing loss of economies of scale. As a result, unit production costs, and hence prices to Canadian consumers, were higher than in the United States and other producing countries.

5.156 Concern about that situation, as well as about Canada's growing deficit in trade in automotive products with the United States, prompted the adoption in 1963 of a so-called "full-duty remission plan" designed to stimulate exports of automotive products.[195] Under that plan, qualified manufacturers[196] of motor vehicles could earn a remission of duties on imports of motor vehicles and original equipment parts to the extent that they increased the Canadian content of its exports of automotive products over that achieved in a base period.

5.157 The full-duty remission scheme gave rise to protests by the US parts industry and, eventually, to the filing of a petition requesting the imposition of countervailing

[188] The applicable duty on imports of complete cars was 17.5 per cent.

[189] The applicable import duty was up to 25 per cent.

[190] This incentive applied only with respect to parts and components of a kind not manufactured in Canada.

[191] In practice, imports of inputs from other members of the British Commonwealth were negligible, so that this requirement amounted effectively to a Canadian content requirement.

[192] From 40 per cent to 60 per cent of the ex-factory cost of the motor vehicles assembled in Canada, depending on the size of the manufacturer.

[193] Over 90 per cent of the automobiles sold in Canada were assembled by firms owned in part or in whole by US companies.

[194] The Canadian industry prior to 1965 has been described as a "high-cost duplication in miniature of the United States' automotive industry". Carl. E. Beige, The Canada-US Automotive Agreement: an evaluation, The Canadian-American Committee, 1970, p. 11.

[195] P.C. 1963-1/1544, of 22 October 1963. The Plan was based on the recommendations of a one-man Royal Commission appointed by the Canadian Government in 1960, the "Bladen Commission", and was preceded by the introduction of a so-called "pilot plan" on 31 October 1962 (P.C. 1962-1/1536). Under the pilot plan, the duties paid by qualified manufacturers on imports of automatic transmissions and stripped engines were remitted to the extent that the Canadian content of automobile parts exported by the manufacturer exceeded that of the base period.

[196] Qualified manufacturers were those producing in Canada at least 40 per cent of their sales.

duties. However, fears of retaliation, together with the desire to avoid a confrontation with a major ally, led the US authorities to opt for a negotiated solution. The result of those negotiations was the Auto Pact.

5.158 The Auto Pact is an asymmetrical agreement that imposes different obligations on each of the two signatories.

- Obligations of the United States

5.159 The United States agreed under the Auto Pact to provide duty-free treatment for imports of certain classes of motor vehicles, as well as of original equipment parts therefore.[197]

5.160 That exemption applies to imports of Canadian products exclusively.[198] Furthermore, the Auto Pact required that any materials from third countries incorporated into those products should not exceed 50 per cent of their appraised customs value when imported into the United States.[199] Subsequently, that requirement was replaced by the origin rules laid down first in the CUSFTA, and then in the NAFTA.

5.161 As from 1 January 1998, all Canadian automotive products can be imported duty free into the United States under the NAFTA, provided that they satisfy the relevant origin rules of that agreement. Since, as explained below, imports under the Auto Pact into the United States also have to comply with the NAFTA origin rules, the US side of the Auto Pact has become redundant. Indeed, the European Communities understands that the United States effectively discontinued the administration of the Auto Pact as of 1 January 1998.

- Obligations of Canada

5.162 For its part, Canada agreed to provide duty-free treatment to imports of certain classes of motors vehicles (namely, "automobiles", "specified commercial vehicles" and "buses"[200]), as well as of original equipment parts therefor, but only when those imports were made by certain designated manufacturers of motor vehicles established in Canada.[201]

5.163 Specifically, the Auto Pact reserves the right to import duty free a given class of motor vehicles to those manufacturers which produced motor vehicles of that class in Canada during the so-called "base year", which is defined as the period commencing on 1 August 1963 and ending on 31 July 1964.[202]

5.164 In addition, those manufacturers must comply, on an annual basis and for each "class" of vehicles concerned, with the following CVA and Ratio conditions.[203]

---

[197] Auto Pact, Article II (b). Note that the US Government did not agree to provide duty-free treatment but rather to "seek enactment" by the US Congress of the necessary legislation. That legislation is contained in the Automotive Products Trade Act, 1965, Public Law 89-23, of 21 October 1965 (Exhibit EC-11).

[198] Auto Pact, Article II (b).

[199] Ibid., Annex B, para. 3.

[200] These categories are defined in the Auto Pact, Annex B, paras. 2(1), 2(3) and 2(7). Those definitions have been refined in the MVTO 1998.

[201] Auto Pact, Article II (a).

[202] Ibid., Annex 2(2).

[203] Ibid., Annex A, para. 2(5).

(A) the ratio of the net sales value of the motor vehicles produced in Canada to the net sales value of all vehicles sold for consumption in Canada must be equal to or higher than the corresponding ratio in the base year, and in no case lower than 75 to 100; and

(B) the total CVA (in dollar terms) of the motor vehicles produced in Canada during that period must be at least equal to the CVA of the base year.

5.165 Canada reserved expressly the right in the Auto Pact to accord similar duty-free treatment to other manufacturers which did not meet the above conditions.[204] Prior to 1989, Canada exercised that right in order to extend, by means of SROs, similar tariff benefits to other manufacturers which established themselves in Canada after the base year. However, as discussed below, Canada renounced that right in the CUFSTA, which contains a provision freezing definitively the list of beneficiaries of the Tariff Exemption as of 1 July.

5.166 By its own terms, the Auto Pact applies only to imports of US products.[205] But, as will be explained below, Canada has extended unilaterally the same treatment to imports originating in all other countries entitled to MFN treatment.

5.167 As from 1 January 1998, all US automotive products which meet the NAFTA origin rules can be imported duty free into Canada under the NAFTA.[206] By contrast, duties on imports of automotive products from Mexico will not be fully eliminated under the NAFTA until 1 January 2003. This does not, however, mean that the Auto Pact benefits have become redundant also with respect to US imports into Canada. In the first place, unlike imports of Canadian products into the United States, US imports into Canada do not have to comply with the NAFTA origin rules in order to qualify for the Auto Pact benefits.[207] Moreover, even in those cases where US products have sufficient "North American content" to meet the relevant NAFTA origin rules, the Auto Pact beneficiaries can avoid the complex paperwork required for proving that origin by importing the products under the Auto Pact instead of under the NAFTA.

- Status of the Auto Pact in the GATT/WTO

5.168 The Auto Pact was examined by a GATT Working Party established in March 1965.[208] During the discussions, the United States were led to admit that its obligations under the Auto Pact were inconsistent with GATT Article I:1.[209] Subsequently, the United States requested a waiver under Article XXV:5, which was granted.[210] In

---

[204] Auto Pact, Annex A, para. 3.

[205] Ibid., Article II (a).

[206] By contrast, duties on imports of automotive products from Mexico will not be fully eliminated under the NAFTA until 1 January 2003.

[207] Under the CUSFTA, motor vehicles and most automotive parts had to contain at least 50 per cent Canadian/US value. The required percentage of "North American" value under the NAFTA is currently 56.5 per cent. It will be increased to 62.5 per cent as from 1 January 2002.

[208] Report of the *Working Party on Canada - US Agreement on Automotive Products, supra* note 6.

[209] Ibid., para. 15.

[210] See ibid. and the Decision of the CONTRACTING PARTIES of 20 December 1965 granting the waiver requested by the United States, BISD 13S/37.

November 1996 that waiver was renewed, at the request of the United States[211], until 1 January 1998[212], the date on which the duties on imports of Canadian automotive products were fully eliminated in accordance with the provisions of the NAFTA.

5.169 In contrast, Canada took the position that its obligations under the Auto Pact were fully consistent with the GATT, even though some members of the Working Party questioned their compatibility with Articles I and III of GATT.[213] As a result, unlike the United States, Canada did not request a waiver. In an attempt to allay the concerns expressed within the Working Party, Canada gave assurances that the benefits provided in the Auto Pact would be extended to imports of all sources on the same terms.[214] Canada also gave assurances that the Auto Pact would not lead to discrimination against new entrants[215] [216] Yet, as explained below, the provisions of the CUSFTA forced Canada to break those assurances.

(ii) The CUSFTA

5.170 The CUSFTA provides for the elimination of all import duties on trade in automotive products between the United States and Canada by 1 January 1998. Nevertheless, the abolition of import duties applies only with respect to imports of "originating" products, i.e. of products which meet the preferential origin rules contained in the CUFSTA.

5.171 The CUSFTA made two important changes to the operation of the Auto Pact.

5.172 First, whereas the Auto Pact had permitted Canada to grant similar tariff benefits to other manufacturers which did not qualify for the Auto Pact benefits, the CUFSTA includes a provision excluding expressly that possibility.

5.173 Specifically, Article 1002.1 of the CUFSTA provides that Canada shall not grant any waiver from import duties on automotive products which is contingent upon the fulfilment by the recipient of performance requirements to any firm which is not included in the Annex to that provision.[217]

5.174 The Annex to Article 1002.1 then lists three categories of firms: (1) the beneficiaries of the Auto Pact; (2) the beneficiaries of SROs issued before the signature of the CUFTSA which accord benefits similar to those of the Auto Pact; and 3) other

---

[211] G/L/103.

[212] Decision adopted by the General Council at is meeting of 7, 8 and 13 November 1996, WT/L/198.

[213] Report of the *Working Party on Canada - US Agreement on Automotive Products, supra* note 6, paras. 21 and 22.

[214] Ibid., para. 20.

[215] According to the Report of the *Working Party on Canada - US Agreement on Automotive Products, supra* note 6, para. 10: "The representative of Canada emphasised that the Agreement placed no impediment in the way of companies wishing to start production in Canada. It was not the intention of his Government to discriminate either against or in favour of new producers of any nationality. The criteria which would be applied in the case of a new producer wishing to participate in the programme could not be identical with the criteria for existing producers (because there would be no production during the base period) but the terms of admission would have to be consistent with these criteria".

[216] Both types of assurances were confirmed by Canada during the subsequent discussion by another Working Party of the request for a waiver made by the United States. See the Report of the *Working Party on Canada - US Agreement on Automotive Products, supra* note 6, para. 15.

[217] Exhibit EC-12.

firms which "may be reasonably expected" to qualify for one such SRO by the 1989 model year.[218] The last category was added in order to allow CAMI, a joint venture between General Motors and Suzuki which did not begin production until 1989, to benefit also from the Tariff Exemption.

5.175 Article 1002.1 of the CUFSTA had thus the effect of freezing the list of recipients of the Tariff Exemption as of 31 July 1989. The only possible way in which a company not listed in the Annex to Article 1002.1 may benefit from the Tariff Exemption is by acquiring the control of a listed recipient. Nevertheless, even that possibility is restricted by a note in that Annex, which states that the Tariff Exemption shall cease being granted if, as a result of the acquisition of control over a recipient, "the fundamental nature, scope or size of the business of the recipient is significantly altered".[219]

5.176 Article 1002.1 was included in the CUFSTA at the request of the United States, and has the clear purpose of reserving the Tariff Exemption for the subsidiaries of US companies. More particularly, Article 1002.1 was directed against the Japanese companies Honda and Toyota, which had built up manufacturing plants in Canada shortly before the conclusion of the CUFSTA and, but for Article 1002.1, could have qualified for an SRO granting the Tariff Exemption within a few years.[220]

5.177 The second change introduced by the CUFSTA concerns the origin rules applicable to imports of Canadian products into the United States under the Auto Pact. Pursuant to the CUFSTA[221], those imports must comply with the relevant CUFSTA origin rules, instead of the requirements laid down in Annex B of the Auto Pact. By contrast, the CUFSTA origin rules do not apply to imports of US products into Canada under the Auto Pact.[222]

(iii) The NAFTA

5.178 Effective 1 January 1994, the CUFSTA was replaced by the NAFTA. The NAFTA authorises expressly Canada to maintain the Tariff Exemption subject to the conditions stipulated in the CUFSTA, including in particular Article 1002.1 and the Annex to that provision.[223]

5.179 The only change introduced by NAFTA with regard to the operation of the Auto Pact concerns the origin rules applicable to imports into the United States. Pursuant to the NAFTA, those imports became subject to the relevant NAFTA origin rules, in place of the CUFSTA origin rules.[224]

---

218 Ibid.

219 This provision has been reproduced in the MVTO 1998, Schedule, Part 1, para. 3. The obvious purpose of this clause was to prevent that a major EC or Japanese manufacturer could gain Auto Pact benefits through the acquisition of control of Volvo (Canada) Inc.

220 Honda's plant in Allison, Ontario, with a capacity of 120.000 units, was opened in 1986, whereas Toyota's Plant in Cambridge, Ontario, with a capacity of 85.000 units, was opened in 1988.

221 CUFSTA, Article 1005.1 (a). (Exhibit EC-12).

222 Ibid.1 (b) (Exhibit EC-12).

223 NAFTA, Annex 300-A; and Appendix 300-A.1., paras. 1 and 2 (Exhibit EC-13).

224 Ibid.

(c) Canada's Response to the Complainants' Arguments Regarding the Auto Pact, the CUSFTA and the NAFTA

5.180 Regarding the complainants' arguments on the Auto Pact, the CUSFTA and the NAFTA, **Canada** responds as follows (with additional arguments contained in Section VI, Legal Arguments of the Parties):

5.181 Japan and the European Communities both have referred in their arguments to the CUSFTA[225] and the NAFTA.[226] The European Communities stated in its arguments that the CUSFTA and the NAFTA are "not themselves in dispute" but that they are "directly relevant for this case", complaining that the United States and Mexico fare better than other WTO Members do in motor vehicle trade with Canada. Japan claimed that the CUSFTA "amplified the discriminatory effects of the Duty Waiver" and that the NAFTA "reaffirmed the discriminatory aspects of the CUSFTA."

5.182 In fact, these free-trade agreements are of no relevance to this dispute. The CUSFTA created a free-trade area composed of Canada and the United States and in doing so provided for duty-free automotive trade between Canada and the United States, provided that certain requirements were met. The CUSFTA was suspended when the NAFTA came into force, and as such has no relevance for any country, much less the complainants. The NAFTA continued this regime, and expanded the free-trade area to include Mexico with the result that Mexican trucks now enter Canada duty free, and other vehicles are currently subject to nominal duties of 1.3 per cent (passenger cars) and 2.4 per cent (heavy trucks and buses). All NAFTA originating vehicles imported from Mexico will enter duty free after 1 January 2003.

5.183 The NAFTA provides for a free-trade area in accordance with Article XXIV of the GATT 1994. Canada is at liberty to accord to the United States and Mexico treatment more favourable than it does to other WTO Members. Indeed, it may even treat its NAFTA partners better than that Agreement requires it to do. By virtue of Article XXIV, such favourable treatment can have no bearing on the treatment Canada accords to other WTO Members, and the complaints of discrimination levied by Japan and the European Communities in this dispute have no basis in law.

(i) Application of the Auto Pact in the United States

5.184 As outlined in the arguments of Japan and the European Communities, the application of the Auto Pact in the United States stood in sharp contrast to its application in Canada. Essentially, goods could enter the United States duty free only if they contained sufficient Canadian content. In other words, the United States implemented the Auto Pact on a discriminatory basis, rather than on a non-discriminatory basis. *Figure 3* illustrates the contrast between the Canadian and US application of the Auto Pact: imports into Canada are origin-neutral while imports into the United States are based on Canadian origin.

---

[225] Free Trade Agreement between the Government of Canada and the Government of the United States of America , CTS 1989/3. See relevant sections at Exhibits EC-12 and JPN-33.

[226] See relevant sections at Exhibits EC-13 and JPN-36.

Canada's Figure 3

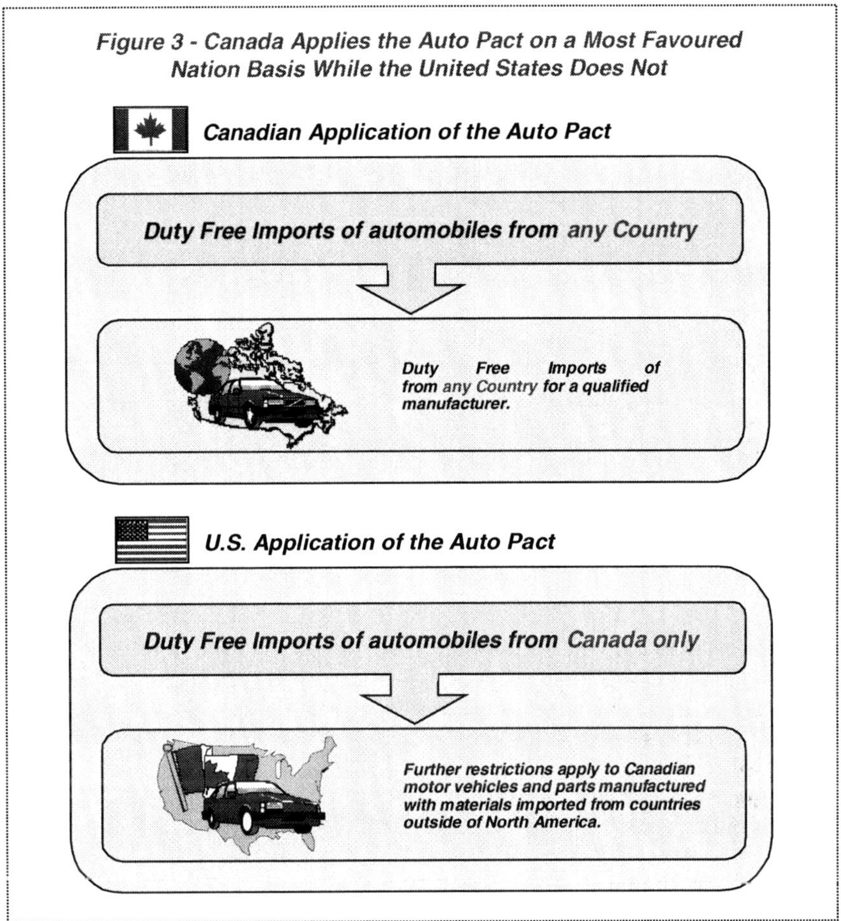

(ii) The United States required a GATT waiver for the Auto Pact; Canada did not

5.185 In 1965, prior to the implementation of the Auto Pact, a GATT Working Party was established to determine its consistency with the GATT.[227] The Working Party found that the US application of the Auto Pact violated the GATT:

> "It was the general consensus of the Working Party that, if the United States implemented the Agreement in the manner proposed, United States action would be clearly inconsistent with Article I and it would

[227] Report of the *Working Party on Canada - US Agreement on Automotive Products, supra* note 6, para. 31.

be necessary for the United States Government to seek a waiver from its GATT obligations".[228]

5.186 Consequently, the United States sought and received a waiver.[229] This is significant because, while the United States failed to pass GATT scrutiny, Canada's implementation of the Auto Pact was not similarly faulted and therefore Canada was not required to obtain a waiver.[230] The complainants in this case make much of the fact that Canada did not receive a waiver. But Canada was not required to do so. Canada would have done so had the Working Party required it. The fact is, it did not.

5.187 Canada does not contest that the measures favour certain manufacturers in Canada over others. Eligible manufacturers may import vehicles from outside the NAFTA Area duty free. Manufacturers that had not qualified as manufacturers as of 27 October 1989, when the list of eligible manufacturers was closed, may not import vehicles from outside the NAFTA area duty free. The WTO does not forbid such differentiation between manufacturers. The complainants have tried to suggest that it does by stretching existing rules and quoting selectively from panel opinions. But there is no such prohibition, and Canada's measures are perfectly consistent with WTO rules.

(d) Japan's Rebuttal to Canada's Response

5.188 As a rebuttal to Canada's response to factual arguments regarding NAFTA, **Japan** argues as follows:

5.189 The Government of Japan would like to bring to the Panel's attention the fact that the Duty Waiver affects two categories of non-preferential (i.e. MFN) trade. First, the Duty Waiver is applied to imports of motor vehicles that originate in the territories of certain WTO Members that are not Parties to the NAFTA. Second, the Duty Waiver is applied to imports of certain motor vehicles that originate in the territories of WTO Members that are also Parties to the NAFTA (i.e. the United States and Mexico).

5.190 In this second category of MFN trade, the Duty Waiver is applied to those motor vehicles that do not meet the strict NAFTA rules of origin which qualify goods for preferential duty treatment under that Agreement. The Duty Waiver is also ap-

---

228 Ibid., para. 17.

229 The waiver expired on 1 January 1998. This expiry has not affected the duty-free entry of Canadian
origin automotive products, which now enter the United States under the NAFTA.

230 See also Report of the *Working Party on Canada - US Agreement on Automotive Products, supra* note 6, para. 13, indicating that a group of Members stated that Canada had already extended Auto Pact advantages immediately and conditionally as required by Article I of the GATT: Members of the Working Party noted that Article V of the Agreement which lays down that "access to the Canadian and United States markets provided for in this Agreement may by agreement be accorded on similar terms to other countries" does not require that similar access "be accorded immediately and unconditionally to like products originating in or destined for the territories of all other contracting parties" in the terms of Article I of the GATT. They however observed that, *as the Government of Canada had unilaterally extended duty-free treatment for the products described in Annex A to all contracting parties,* Article V would, in practice, have significance only with respect to the extension of access to the United States. (*emphasis added*)

plied in instances where the applicable NAFTA rule of origin is met but the applicable NAFTA duty has not yet been reduced to zero.

5.191 In recent years, imports from the United States and Mexico have benefited to a great extent from the Duty Waiver. As noted earlier, automobiles originating from these two countries can still be imported into Canada by Auto Pact Manufacturers duty free under the Auto Pact which is not a free-trade agreement. As shown in Exhibit JPN-37-3, the Government of Canada exempted automobiles imported from the United States from the customs duty of 0.9 per cent in 1997 that otherwise would have had to be paid, even if such automobiles complied with the NAFTA origin rules. The total exempted amount of customs duty was over CD$88 million. Further, the Government of Canada also exempted automobiles imported from Mexico from the 2.0 per cent customs duty in 1997 that would otherwise be applicable even if the automobiles complied with the NAFTA origin rules. The total exempted amount of customs duty was CD$21 million. As a result, importers of Japanese automobiles paid over CD$142 million customs duties, while importers of US automobiles and Mexican automobiles paid only about CD$637,000 and CD$12,000 respectively. This comparison demonstrates the magnitude of the customs duties paid and is a clear indication of their potential effect on competitive conditions between goods imported from Japan and those from other countries.

4. *Measures Relating to Administration*

(a) Japan's Account of Canada's Administration of the Import Duty Exemption

5.192 Concerning measures relating to the administration of the Duty Waiver, Japan contends the following:

(i) MVTO 1998 and the Letters of Undertaking

- Eligibility for the Duty Waiver is restricted to certain manufacturers

5.193 The eligibility requirement for the Duty Waiver is contained in the definition of "manufacturer" provided in subsection 1(1) of the Schedule to the MVTO 1998. Paragraph (a) of this definition provides that a manufacturer first must have produced in Canada vehicles of the class for which it seeks the Duty Waiver in each of the four consecutive quarters of the base year.[231] The base year is defined as the 12-month period from 1 August 1963 to 31 July 1964.[232]

5.194 Therefore, to meet this requirement, a manufacturer of motor vehicles must have had production facilities in Canada before 1965, when the Canada-US Auto Pact came into force. The list of manufacturers that continue to qualify for the Duty Waiver under the MVTO 1998 appears in the Annex to Revenue Canada's Memorandum D10-16-3.[233] According to this list, the only importers considered to be manufacturers of automobiles under the MVTO 1998 are subsidiaries of General

231 MVTO 1998 (Exhibit JPN-4).

232 Definition of "base year", subsection 1(1) of the Schedule to the MVTO 1998 (Exhibit JPN-4).

233 Exhibit JPN-7.

Motors, Ford, Chrysler and Volvo as these companies had production facilities in Canada during the base year.

5.195 Although eligibility for importers under the MVTO 1998 has been frozen, there is a narrow exception under which an importer who also is a "manufacturer" may achieve Auto Pact Manufacturer status. Under subsection 1(5) of the Schedule to the MVTO 1998, a manufacturer may designate another person as a person associated with the manufacturer for the production of motor vehicles in Canada. For the purposes of the Duty Waiver, Revenue Canada will consider this associated person to be the same person.[234] Thus, this exception was introduced for the convenience of existing Auto Pact Manufacturers and not for newcomers. It is meaningless to Non-Auto Pact Manufacturers including Japanese automobile manufacturers.

5.196 Nevertheless, the products of a Non-Auto Pact Manufacturer may obtain the benefit of the Duty Waiver where the manufacturer acquires a recipient, that is, a manufacturer listed in Part One of Annex 1002.1 of the CUSFTA.[235] However, the manufacturer must meet the requirements of section 4 of the Schedule to the MVTO 1998.

5.197 Section 4 of the Schedule to the MVTO 1998 provides as follows:

> "4. A recipient is not entitled to a reduced rate of customs duty in respect of vehicles referred to in section 2 if
>
> (a) effective control of the conduct and operation of the recipient's business or substantial ownership of its assets is acquired, directly or indirectly, by a person who manufactures vehicles and is not a recipient; and
>
> (b) after that person's acquisition of effective control or substantial ownership of the assets of the recipient's business, the fundamental nature, scope or size of the business is significantly altered from the business as it had been carried on by the recipient immediately before the acquisition."

5.198 Thus, two conditions must be met to enable the acquired company to maintain its Auto Pact Manufacturer status. With respect to the first condition, the transaction must be such that effective control of the company or substantial ownership of its assets is transferred to a manufacturer that does not qualify under the Duty Waiver programme. The second condition relates to whether the fundamental nature, scope and size of the business of the recipient have been significantly altered. The MVTO 1998 does not define the term "recipient's business" although section 4 requires that the change of ownership must significantly alter the business "as it had been carried on by the recipient immediately before the acquisition".

5.199 Consequently, pursuant to section 4 of the Schedule to the MVTO 1998, the imports of a Non-Auto Pact Manufacturer may become eligible for the Duty Waiver only when the manufacturer acquires a recipient without altering significantly "the fundamental nature, scope and size" of the recipient's business. In the event of a take-

---

[234] The list of these associated persons is in the Annex to Revenue Canada's Memorandum D10-16-3 (Exhibit JPN-7).

[235] The manufacturers contained in that list have qualified for Auto Pact Manufacturer status under the MVTO 1998 or under an SRO before 1 January 1988 (Exhibit JPN-33).

over or acquisition of assets, the new owner effectively must continue the recipient's business as it existed before the acquisition.

5.200 This means that, except through the substantial acquisition of Canadian subsidiaries of General Motors, Ford or Chrysler, Japanese automobile manufacturers cannot become eligible for the Duty Waiver. Accordingly, the acquisition method does not provide a meaningful opportunity to gain access to the Duty Waiver.

- Manufacturing and CVA requirements

5.201 An Auto Pact Manufacturer may benefit from the Duty Waiver if it fulfils two performance requirements: (i) a manufacturing requirement; and (ii) a CVA requirement.

- Manufacturing requirement

5.202 The manufacturing requirement is contained in the definition of "manufacturer" found at subsection 1(1) of the Schedule to the MVTO 1998. In simple terms, the value of motor vehicles produced by an Auto Pact Manufacturer in Canada must be in proportion to the value of motor vehicles it sells in a given year. The ratio of production-to-sales for each year must be equal to or higher than that manufacturer's ratio achieved in the base year, without being lower than 75 to 100. This ratio consists of the net sales value of vehicles of a given class produced in Canada in a given year over the net sales value of all vehicles of that class sold for consumption in Canada in that year.

5.203 While the actual production-to-sales ratios are not publicly available, according to Industry Canada, the production-to-sales ratio for cars must be at least 95 to 100.[236]

5.204 The operation of the manufacturing requirement is best illustrated in an example. Assuming that the production-to-sales ratio is 80 to 100 and an Auto Pact Manufacturer produces in Canada and sells in Canada motor vehicles for a value of $1,000,000, it can import into Canada motor vehicles valued up to $250,000. The ratio of 80 to 100 is maintained in that situation as it has produced $1,000,000 worth of vehicles and has sold a total value of $1,250,000 ($1,000,000 + $250,000).[237]

5.205 In practice, the application of the manufacturing requirement means that a certain value of motor vehicles must be exported by Auto Pact Manufacturers.

5.206 In the case of Auto Pact Manufacturers qualifying under the MVTO 1998, the production-to-sales ratio provides that an Auto Pact Manufacturer must maintain in a given year a ratio of the "net sales value of the vehicles produced by the company" to the "net sales value of all vehicles of that class sold for consumption in Canada" that is equal to or higher than the ratio obtained in the base year and in no case less than

[236] Exhibit JPN-38. The Government of Canada is aware of the ratio for each Auto Pact Manufacturer since it receives declarations and reports from each Auto Pact Manufacturer. Schedule to the MVTO 1998, Sections 2.(a), (b). Exhibit JPN-4.

[237] The simplest case is where the production to sales ratio is 100 to 100. In that case, for every imported motor vehicle sold in Canada, an Auto Pact Manufacturer must produce a motor vehicle or vehicles of equal net sales value in Canada, which eventually must be exported.

75 to 100.[238] For most of the Auto Pact Manufacturers qualifying under an SRO, the specified ratio is 100 to 100.[239]

5.207 With respect to the situation where the production-to-sales ratio is 100 to 100, the pressure to export, which arises from the application of the production-to-sales ratio, can be illustrated as follows:

(i) Where an Auto Pact Manufacturer imports motor vehicles and sells them in Canada, it increases the net sales value of the vehicles "sold for consumption in Canada"[240];

(ii) The Auto Pact Manufacturer must increase the net sales value of the vehicles it produces in Canada in order to comply with the ratio;

(iii) But if the vehicles so produced by the Auto Pact Manufacturer are sold for consumption in Canada, those sales would only increase the net sales value of the vehicles for the Manufacturer, thereby widening the disparity between the net sales value and the net production value; and

(iv) Thus, the only way for the Auto Pact Manufacturer to maintain its compliance with its production-to-sales ratio is to export the vehicles it produces.[241]

5.208 Where the production-to-sales ratio is less than 100 to 100, the requirement to export also arises. An example can be illustrated for a case where an Auto Pact Manufacturer has been operating under a production-to-sales ratio of 75 to 100 (the lowest possible ratio) as follows:

(i) Where an Auto Pact Manufacturer imports motor vehicles and sells them in Canada, it increases the net sales value of the vehicles "sold for consumption in Canada";

---

[238] Mathematically, this ratio can be represented as follows: $P_X/S_X \geq P_1/S_1$ where P_X = value of cars produced in year X_1; S_X = value of cars sold in year X_1; P_1 = value of cars produced in year 1 (i.e. the base year); and S_1= value of cars sold in year 1 (i.e. the base year).

[239] For a number of Auto Pact Manufacturers, the production-to-sales ratio is based on the production and sales figures achieved in the base year. For SROs issued since 1977, the production-to-sales ratio is set at 100 to 100. See Exhibit JPN-28 for a summary of the SROs' condition and their evolution.

[240] Vehicles sold for consumption in Canada includes imported vehicles sold for consumption in Canada where the customs duty on those vehicles has been removed: Subsection 1(4) of the Schedule to the MVTO 1998 only excludes from the calculation of vehicles sold for consumption in Canada those imports for which the customs duty is *not* removed. *A contrario*, where the duty is removed such import sales are included in the calculation. (Exhibit JPN-4).

[241] In other words, any increase in production that is sold in Canada will affect to the same extent both elements of the ratio. The value of sales of motor vehicles (S) consists of products manufactured in Canada that are sold in Canada (D) and products manufactured abroad that are sold in Canada (I). The value of motor vehicles produced consists of those vehicles that are sold in Canada (D) and those that are exported (E). Mathematically, these relationships can be shown as: $S_X = D_X + I_X$ and $P_X = D_X + E_X$. To solve: $P_X/S_X = (D_X + E_X) / (D_X + I_X)$. If $P_X/S_X \geq 1$, then $P_X \geq S_X$. Replacing these values in the equation we obtain $D_X + E_X \geq D_X + I_X$. Therefore, $E_X \geq I_X$.

(ii) The Auto Pact Manufacturer must increase the net sales value of the vehicles it produces in Canada in order to comply with the ratio;

(iii) As is the case in the example shown in para. 5.207, if the vehicles so produced by the Auto Pact Manufacturer are sold for consumption in Canada, those sales would only increase the net sales value of the vehicles for the Manufacturer, thereby widening the disparity between the net sales value and the net production value;

(iv) Thus, the only way for the Auto Pact Manufacturer to maintain its compliance with its production-to-sales ratio is to export the vehicles it produces, but a lesser degree of production-to-sales requirement imposes a lesser degree of pressure in comparison with the case exemplified in para 109.[242]

- CVA requirement

5.209 The MVTO 1998 describes this domestic content requirement as follows:

> "the Canadian value added is equal to or greater than the Canadian value added in respect of all vehicles of that class produced in Canada by the manufacturer in the base year."[243]

5.210 In other words, the Canadian value added (CVA) for vehicles of a specified class must be equal to or greater than the CVA for the base year.

5.211 The MVTO 1998 lists a broad range of expenses that are included in the calculation of CVA.[244]

5.212 With respect to trade in goods, the definition of CVA identifies a number of categories of expenses that are particularly relevant to this dispute. (See Section II, Background.)

5.213 As discussed in Exhibits JPN-15 through 19, the full range of motor vehicle parts, components and materials are available both within Canada and outside of Canada. The CVA requirement clearly favours domestic parts, components and materials over imported competing products.

5.214 With respect to trade in services, the elements included in the definition of CVA are costs that are reasonably attributable to the production of the vehicles such as the cost of maintenance and repair work executed in Canada on machinery and equipment used for the production process, the cost of engineering services, experimental work and product development work executed in Canada, and administrative and general expenses incurred in Canada.[245]

5.215 These services are available both within Canada and outside of Canada. The domestic content requirement in the CVA clearly favours such services supplied in Canada over competing services supplied outside Canada.

---

242 For example, applying the formula set out in footnote 241 in a case where the ratio is 75 to 100, instead of $E_x \geq I_x$, the formula will be $E_x \geq I_x - 1/3P_x$.

243 See para. (b)(ii) of the definition of "manufacturer " in Subsection 1(1) of the Schedule to the MVTO 1998 (Exhibit JPN-4).

244 Ibid., definition of "Canadian value added".

245 Ibid.

5.216 The domestic content targets that must be met by each manufacturer in order to qualify for the Duty Waiver depend on the figures that were attained in the base year. These figures are not publicly available, although the Government of Canada would be aware of these figures from declarations and reports from Auto Pact Manufacturers.[246]

(ii) Special Remission Orders (SROs)

5.217 Beginning in 1965, the Government of Canada extended eligibility for the Duty Waiver by granting SROs to individual manufacturers that had not met the original conditions of the MVTO 1965 and its successors.[247] At present, 83 manufacturers continue to qualify for the Duty Waiver under a company-specific SRO granted prior to 1 January 1989. Among the 83 manufacturers, only two are producers of automobiles (i.e. CAMI and Intermeccanica). A list of the SROs that are currently in force and the manufacturers that are benefiting from them is set out in Exhibit JPN-26.

- Eligibility requirement to obtain an SRO

5.218 A manufacturer may no longer obtain a new SRO if it did not meet the qualifying requirements before 1 January 1988. As a result of the above noted restrictions introduced in the CUSFTA, the Government of Canada cannot grant the Duty Waiver to any company other than those already listed in Annex 1002.1 of the CUSFTA.

- Manufacturing and CVA requirements

5.219 Although the conditions may vary according to the time period in which the SROs were granted, all SROs contain the CVA requirement and a manufacturing requirement (i.e. production-to-sales ratio). The definitions of both requirements under the SROs are the same as the definitions under the MVTO 1998. Because the SROs were granted after the adoption of the Canada-US Auto Pact, different base years had to be applied to each manufacturer in order to establish the amounts on which the domestic content and manufacturing requirements would be based.

5.220 The SROs that were granted through 1976 set the minimum production-to-sales ratio at 75 to 100. Since 1977, almost all SROs set the production-to-sales ratio at one to one. Until 1984, the CVA requirement was the amount of CVA achieved in the specified base year. The only limitation was that the base year level of CVA had to be at least 40 per cent of the cost of sales. Since 1984, the CVA requirement for a given year has been expressed as a percentage of the cost of sales achieved in the year for which the Duty Waiver is claimed. There is no reference to the values for the

---

[246] Auto Pact Manufacturers must report periodically to the Government of Canada, Section 2(a) and (b) of the Schedule to the MVTO1998.

[247] Special Remission Orders are regulations adopted under authority of the Financial Administration Act, R.S.C. 1985, c. F-11. s. 23 (Exhibit JPN-3). The MVTO 1965 required companies to have produced motor vehicles in all quarters of the base year, which was defined as the 12-month period from 1 August 1963 to 31 July 1964. Any manufacturer which had not met this requirement was thus effectively prevented from qualifying for the Duty Waiver.

base year. Hence, over the years, the manufacturing and CVA requirements attached to the SROs have become more onerous.[248]

(iii) Declarations and Reports

5.221 To maintain the Duty Waiver, each Auto Pact Manufacturer is required under the MVTO 1998 to send to the Minister of Revenue Canada a declaration before importing the first vehicles during a given period. This declaration must be sent before any 12-month period ending on 31 July.[249] Failure to submit the declaration would result in the loss of the Duty Waiver status for imports during the affected year.

5.222 In addition, the MVTO 1998 provides that every Auto Pact Manufacturer who imports vehicles under the Duty Waiver must submit any reports that may be reasonably required by the Minister of Revenue Canada and the Minister of Industry regarding the production and sale of vehicles by the Auto Pact Manufacturer.[250] Auto Pact Manufacturers that qualified for the Duty Waiver under a company-specific SRO also are required under the SRO to submit reports to show that they have complied with the conditions of their order for each period.[251]

5.223 Further filing requirements are provided in Revenue Canada's Memorandum D10-16-3 to show compliance with the MVTO 1998.[252] A series of reports must be submitted to the Minister of Revenue Canada and to the Minister of Industry by 1 November of each year.

5.224 Based on the reports supplied by the Auto Pact Manufacturer, officials of Revenue Canada determine if the Auto Pact Manufacturer has complied with the conditions of the MVTO 1998 or company-specific SRO. If the Auto Pact Manufacturer has complied with all the conditions, no duties are assessed on motor vehicle imports for the preceding year. If the Auto Pact Manufacturer does not comply with the conditions, duties are assessed on the previous year's imports. There are no provisions in the MVTO 1998 or the D-Memoranda providing for a Auto Pact Manufacturer to lose its Auto Pact Manufacturer status following the failure to meet the performance requirements for a given year. If the Auto Pact Manufacturer meets the criteria in the following year, it appears that the MFN duty is waived on that year's imports.

5.225 Discretion plays a role in the administration of the measure. There is evidence that some Auto Pact Manufacturers are entitled to the remission of import duties even though they failed to meet the performance requirements. One notable example is Paccar Inc.[253]

---

[248] Exhibit JPN-28 provides a comparative table of the conditions included in the various SROs according to the time period in which they were granted.

[249] Section 2, para. (a), of the Schedule to the MVTO 1998 (Exhibit JPN-4).

[250] Ibid., para. (b).

[251] Memorandum D-10-16-2, Revenue Canada, section 8 (Exhibit JPN-8). This requirement also appears in a number of SROs, starting with the Truck Equipment Remission Order, SI/72-38 (Exhibit JPN-6).

[252] See Memorandum D-10-16-3 (Exhibit JPN-7).

[253] PACCAR Inc. Remission Order, 1998, SOR/98-585, 2 December 1998, Canada Gazette Part II, Vol. 132, No 26, 3174 (Exhibit JPN-9). In addition, Volvo did not satisfy the production-to-sales

(b) The EC's Account of Canada's Administration of the Import Duty Exemption

5.226 Concerning measures relating to the administration of the Tariff Exemption, the **European Communities** contends the following:

5.227 Each model year the beneficiaries must submit, before they make the first importation, a signed declaration to the Minister of National Revenue, in which they undertake to comply with the CVA and ratio requirements stipulated in the MVTO 1998 during that model year.[254]

5.228 In addition, the beneficiaries must submit periodical reports containing information regarding production costs, output and sales.[255] That information allows the Canadian authorities to ascertain compliance not only with the requirements of the MVTO 1998 but also with the additional commitments contained in the Letters of Undertaking. The reports are audited after the close of each model year by Revenue Canada.

5.229 Any manufacturer that fails to meet the CVA or ratio requirements stipulated in the MVTO 1998 in any model year as to a class of motor vehicles is liable for the payment of the applicable customs duties on all imports of motor vehicles of that class made during that year. Nevertheless, the manufacturer concerned does not lose the status of Auto Pact beneficiary and may still qualify for the Tariff Exemption in successive model years.

5.230 The SROs lay down reporting obligations similar to those stipulated in the MVTO 1998.

5.231 The consequences in case that a beneficiary fails to meet the CVA and ratio requirements prescribed in its SRO are the same as in the case of violation of the requirements imposed by the MVTO 1998.

(c) Canada's Response to the Complainant's Arguments Regarding Administration of the Import Duty Exemption

5.232 With respect to the complainants' arguments on measures relating to the administration of the Duty Waiver, **Canada** responds as follows:

5.233 Japan and the European Communities refer to the D-Memoranda.[256] These documents explain the conditions under which vehicle manufacturers may qualify for the duty remission, and note that vehicle producers are required to submit reports demonstrating compliance with the conditions set out in the MVTO.

5.234 Japan has furnished evidence that the Big Three plus Volvo (Canada) Ltd. have consistently exceeded their 1964 ratio requirements (based on aggregate performance of all four manufacturers).[257] Indeed they generally operate far in excess of

---

ratio in 1997 (Exhibit JPN-40). However, Volvo could import vehicles duty-free (Exhibit 37-1). This is another example of abusive use of its discretion on the part of the Government of Canada.

[254] MVTO 1998, Schedule, Part 1, 2 (a). The form of the declaration is set out in MVTO 1998, Schedule, Part 2.

[255] Ibid., 2 (b). Samples of the reporting documents are provided as Exhibit EC-14.

[256] See examples filed by the EC and Japan in Exhibits EC-8/JPN-8, EC-9/JPN-7 and EC-10.

[257] Exhibit JPN-27, p. 27-40.

their individual ratios. It should be noted, however, that no additional benefits accrue to manufacturers that operate above their required ratio.

5.235 Both Japan and the European Communities have acknowledged that the CVA requirement imposed by the MVTO is of no consequence today.[258] This is aptly illustrated in *Figure 2*.[259]

[258] Exhibit EC-18 p. 54; see also United States International Trade Commission Report on the United States - Canadian Automotive Agreement: Its History, Terms, and Impact in the Ninth Annual Report of the President to the Congress on the Operation of the Automobile Products Trade Act of 1965, US Senate Committee on Finance, January 1976. That report, filed by Japan as Exhibit JPN-27, indicates at page 27-40 that the CVA "is of minor importance today" ... "due to effects of inflation and the growth in the Canadian market." (See also pp. 27-35, 27-59). The CVA is even less significant today, some 23 years after the preparation of that Report.

[259] For supporting evidence, see Exhibit CDA-2.

Canada's Figure 2

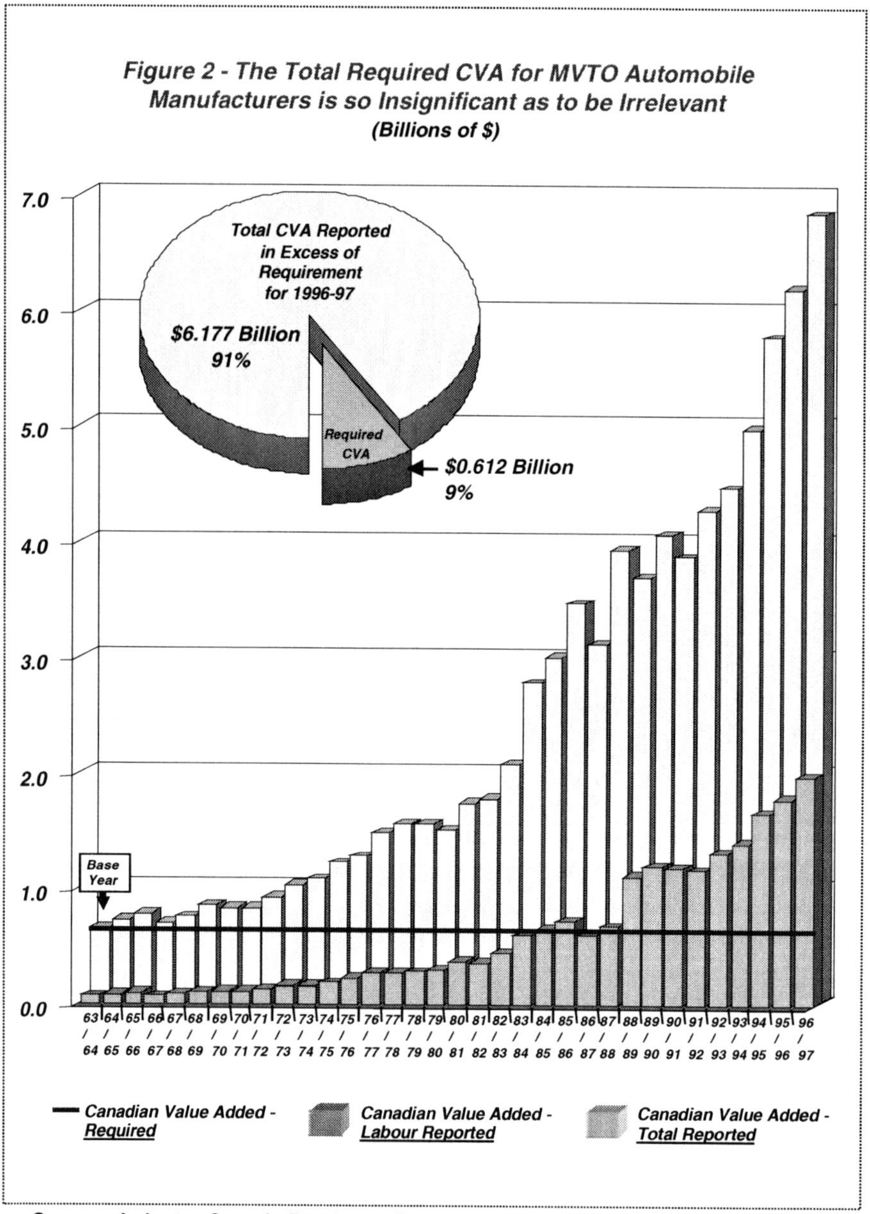

Source: Industry Canada Database. Complete data for 1997/98 is not available.

5.236 *Figure 2* illustrates that the total required Canadian value added was fixed for the Big Three automobile manufacturers plus Volvo (Canada) at roughly $612 million in the base year (1963-64). It remains the same today, some thirty-five years later. In model year 1996-97, the last year for which complete data is available, the reported aggregate CVA for the Big Three plus Volvo (Canada) was about $7 billion[260], or more than 11 times greater that the required level. As illustrated in *Figure 2*, labour costs alone have enabled the Big Three plus Volvo (Canada) to meet or exceed their aggregate CVA requirement consistently since 1988.

B. Structure of the Automotive Industry

1. Japan's Arguments on the Structure of the Motor Vehicles Industry

5.237 Regarding the structure of the motor vehicles industry, **Japan** argues as follows:

(a) The Integration of the Global Automobile Industry And its Implications for the Structure of the Canadian Industry

5.238 The global automobile industry is dominated by a limited number of transnational automobile manufacturers. These manufacturers include: (i) Japanese companies such as Honda Motor Co. Ltd. (Honda) and Toyota Motor Corporation (Toyota); (ii) North American companies such as Ford Motor Company (Ford) and General Motors Corporation (General Motors); (iii) European companies such as Bayerische Motor Werke AG (BMW); Volkswagen AG (Volkswagen); and Volvo AB (Volvo); and (iv) a new transcontinental company, DaimlerChrysler AG (DaimlerChrysler), formed by the merger of Chrysler Corporation and Daimler Benz AG.

5.239 These transnational companies have integrated their production and distribution operations over several different countries to increase their efficiency and rationalize their production. In particular, they control subsidiaries that have been mandated to manufacture specific models at specific plants located in various countries. The models produced at these plants can be shipped to domestic and export markets. As a result, motor vehicles produced at each plant are destined for many different markets. This permits the manufacturers to offer a broad range of models to consumers located in many different markets while maintaining economies of scale. The complex corporate relationships and the resulting patterns of sourcing in the Canadian market are documented in Exhibits JPN-10 and JPN-11.

5.240 To complete their product lines, some manufacturers also have contracted with non-subsidiaries or have acquired equity interests in other manufacturers for the purpose of selling specific models. For example, as documented in Exhibit JPN-10, General Motors has a 50 per cent equity stake in Saab (Sweden), a 37.5 per cent stake in Isuzu (Japan), a 50 per cent stake in CAMI (the other 50 per cent is owned

[260] Note that the *reported* amount is significantly less than the actual amount. This is because none of the Big Three companies goes to the trouble of calculating every dollar of Canadian value added, given that they exceed the requirements by such a wide margin.

by Suzuki) and wholly owns Opel (Germany). Until recently Ford had a 10 per cent equity stake in Kia (South Korea), and wholly owns Jaguar. Commercial relationships such as these allow the leading manufacturers to distribute more models and occupy new market segments without having to build new production facilities.

(b) Implications for the Structure of the Canadian Industry

5.241 This process of global integration has influenced the structure of the motor vehicle industry in Canada. Specifically, a number of these transnational manufacturers own Canadian subsidiaries that produce, distribute and sell their full range of products.

5.242 The Canadian light vehicle sector, which includes passenger cars and light-duty trucks, is dominated by a few foreign-owned subsidiaries that are fully integrated in the global operations of their parent corporations. The only Canadian-owned manufacturer of automobiles which is eligible for the Duty Waiver is Intermeccanica International Inc. (Intermeccanica), a small manufacturer of specialty automobiles.[261]

5.243 There are two general categories of Canadian subsidiaries of transnational automobile manufacturers - those that manufacture and distribute motor vehicles in Canada and those that only distribute imported automobiles in Canada.

5.244 The following table lists the companies included in the first category:

Japan's Table 1

Canadian Subsidiary	**Parent Company and Ownership**
Chrysler Canada Ltd. (Chrysler Canada)	100 per cent owned by Chrysler Corporation (a United States-owned corporation)[262]
Ford Motor Company of Canada Ltd. (Ford Canada)	100 per cent owned by Ford Motor Company (a United States-owned company)
General Motors of Canada Ltd.(GM Canada)	100 per cent owned by General Motors Corp. (a United States-owned corporation)
Volvo Canada Limited (Volvo Canada)	100 per cent owned by Volvo Canada Holdings, which is owned by Volvo AB.[263] (a Swedish-owned corporation)

[261] Exhibit JPN-12.

[262] The effect of the creation of DaimlerChrysler on the legal ownership of Chrysler Canada is unclear.

[263] Ford Motor Corporation has announced that it is purchasing the automotive division of Volvo AB.

Canadian Subsidiary	Parent Company and Ownership
CAMI Automotive Inc. (CAMI)	50 per cent owned by General Motors Corporation (a United States-owned corporation) and 50 per cent owned by Suzuki Motor Corporation (a Japanese-owned corporation)
Toyota Motor Manufacturing Canada Inc. (Toyota Manufacturing Canada)	100 per cent owned by Toyota Motor Corporation (a Japanese-owned corporation)
Honda Canada Inc. (Honda Canada)	50.14 per cent owned by Honda Motor Company (a Japanese-owned company) and 49.86 per cent owned by American Honda Motor Company (a United States company that is 100 per cent owned by Honda Motor Company)

5.245 These subsidiaries produce particular models determined by their respective parent corporation(s). Such subsidiaries then distribute these automobiles in the Canadian domestic and export markets. With the exception of Toyota Manufacturing Canada, such subsidiaries also distribute imported models in Canada.

5.246 The following table lists certain companies included in the second category of subsidiaries - i.e. those companies that only distribute imported automobiles in Canada with the exception of Toyota Canada Inc. which distribute imported as well as domestic automobiles manufactured by Toyota Manufacturing Canada:

Japan's Table 2

Canadian Subsidiary	Parent Company and Ownership
Toyota Canada Inc. (Toyota Canada)	50 per cent owned by Toyota Motor Corporation and 50 per cent owned by Mitsui & Company Ltd. (a Japanese-owned corporation)
Nissan Canada Inc. (Nissan Canada)	38.3 per cent owned by Nissan Motor Co., Ltd. (a Japanese-owned company) and 61.7 per cent owned by Nissan North America Inc. (a United States company that is 100 per cent owned by Nissan Motor Co.)
Mazda Canada Inc. (Mazda Canada)	60 per cent owned by Mazda Motor Corporation (a Japanese-owned corporation) and 40 per cent owned by Itochu Corporation (also a Japanese-owned company)
Suzuki Canada Inc. (Suzuki Canada)	100 per cent owned by Suzuki Motor Corporation of Japan
Subaru Canada Inc. (Subaru Canada)	100 per cent owned by Fuji Heavy Industries, Ltd. of Japan
BMW Canada Inc.	BMW AG
Volkswagen Canada Inc.	Volkswagen AG

(c) Production and Importation of Like Motor Vehicles

(i) Canadian production of automobiles

5.247 The companies that manufacture automobiles in Canada are identified above in Japan's Table 1. Exhibit JPN-13 identifies the Canadian manufacturing facilities of these companies and the automobile models produced at each facility.

5.248 Competition in the Canadian automobile market takes place within specific market segments which are comprised of competing models of automobiles. Exhibit JPN-11 outlines the market segments relevant to the Canadian market.

5.249 Based on the information in Exhibit JPN-11, the following table classifies the automobiles produced in Canada in 1996 by applicable Canadian market segment[264]:

Japan's Table 3

Market Segment	**Company, Model (1996)**
Subcompact	GM Firefly/Metro Suzuki Swift Honda Civic HB
Compact	Toyota Corolla Honda Acura EL Honda Civic Sedan/Coupe
Small Sporty	GM Firebird GM Camaro
Intermediate	GM Regal W GM Monte Carlo Chrysler Intrepid Chrysler Eagle Vision Chrysler Concorde
Full-size	GM Bonneville H Ford Grand Marquis Ford Crown Victoria Chrysler New Yorker LH
Luxury	Volvo 850
Compact Sport Utility	GM Tracker/Sun Runner Suzuki Sidekick
Compact Van	Chrysler Town & Country Chrysler Voyager/Caravan Ford Windstar
Full Size Pickup	Ford F150 Light Duty GM C/K 1500 Light Duty
Full Size Van	Chrysler B150 Ram Van/Wagon

[264] The market segmentation used in the following charts is generally accepted in the Canadian market by consumers. This is confirmed in Exhibit JPN-14 which consists of copies of the magazine Wheel sold in the Canadian market.

(ii) Importation of automobiles

5.250 Broad ranges of models of automobiles are imported into Canada by manufacturer/distributors and distributors. Exhibit JPN-11 lists the automobiles imported into Canada and identifies these automobiles by importer. The following table classifies the imported automobiles from outside North America by importer in 1996 and by applicable Canadian market segment:

Japan's Table 4

Market Segment	Company, Model (1996)
Subcompact	**Chrysler** Eagle Summit (Japan) Colt 100/200 (Japan) **Ford** Aspire (Korea) **Hyundai** Accent (Korea) Excel (Korea) **Lada** Lada (Russia) **Subaru** Justy (Japan) **Toyota** Tercel (Japan) **Mazda** 323 HB (Japan)
Compact	**Subaru** Impreza (Japan) **Suzuki** Esteem (Japan) **Mazda** 323 Protégé (Japan) **Hyundai** Elantra (Korea) **Honda** Civic (Japan) **Toyota** Corolla (Japan)
Small Sporty	**Chrysler** Stealth (Japan) **Volkswagen** Corrado (Germany) Audi Coupe/Quattro (Germany) **Toyota** Paseo (Japan) Celica (Japan) **Nissan** 240SX (Japan) **Mazda** MX-5/Miata (Japan) MX-3/Precidia (Japan) **Hyundai** Scoupe (Korea) Tiburon (Korea)

Market Segment	Company, Model (1996)
	Honda Acura Integra (Japan) Prelude (Japan) Del Sol (Japan)
Intermediate	**Volkswagen** Passat (Germany) **Nissan** Maxima (Germany) **Hyundai** Sonata (Korea) **Toyota** Camry (Japan)
Small Luxury	**GM** Cadillac Catera (Germany) Saab 900 (Sweden) **Honda** Acura TL (Japan) **Mazda** Millenia (Japan) 929 (Japan) **Nissan** Infiniti G20 (Japan) Infiniti I30 (Japan) **Toyota** Lexus ES250/300 (Japan) **Mercedes** 190GAS/C-Class (Germany) **Volkswagen** Audi 90 (Germany)
Luxury	**GM** Saab 9000 (Sweden) **Ford** Jaguar Sedans (UK) **BMW** 5-Series (Germany) 7-Series (Germany) **Honda** Acura Legend/RL (Japan) **Nissan** Infiniti J30 (Japan) Infiniti Q45 (Japan) **Toyota** Lexus GS300 (Japan) Lexus LS400 (Japan) **Volkswagen** Audi 100/200 (Germany) Audi A8 (Germany) **Volvo** 960's (Belgium or Sweden) 940's (Belgium or Sweden) **Mercedes** S Class (Germany) 300E/400E/Eclass (Germany)
Luxury Sport	**Ford** Jaguar Sports Coupe (UK)

Market Segment	Company, Model (1996)
	Volkswagen Porsche (Germany) **Toyota** Lexus SC400 (Japan) Supra(Japan) **Subaru** SVX (Japan) **Nissan** 300ZX (Japan) **Mazda** RX7 (Japan) **Honda** Acura NSX (Japan) **BMW** 6/8 Series (Germany)
Compact Pickup	**Toyota** T100 4x2 (Japan) T100 4x4 (Japan)
Compact Sport Utility	**GM** Isuzu Trooper II (Japan) **Lada** Niva (Russia) **Land Rover** Discovery (UK) Defender 90 (UK) **Nissan** Pathfinder (Japan) Infiniti QX4 (Japan) **Toyota** RAV4 (Japan) 4 Runner (Japan)
Compact Van	**Chrysler** Summit Wagon (Japan) **Mazda** MPV (Japan) **Nissan** Axcess (Japan) **Honda** Odyssey (Japan) **Volkswagen** Bus/Transporter (Germany) Camper (Germany) Eurovan (Germany)
Full Size Sport Utility	**Land Rover** Range Rover (UK) **Toyota** Lexus LX450 (Japan) Land Cruiser (Japan)

5.251 Reading Japan's Table 4 in conjunction with Japan's Table 3, it is clear that imported automobiles compete in every market segment in which there is domestic automobile production in Canada.

5.252 It is also clear from Japan's Table 4 that there are competitions among imported automobiles within each market segment.

(d) Production and Importation of Like Parts, Components and Materials Used in the Manufacture of Automobiles

(i) Canadian production of parts, components and materials

5.253 Canada has a substantial automotive parts and components industry that produces a full range of parts and components. These products include body parts, stampings, trim, instrument panels, controls, engine components and drive train components. Exhibit JPN-15 provides a comprehensive description of the Canadian automotive parts and components industry.

5.254 Canada also produces a full range of materials used in automobile production, such as steel, plastics, glass, rubber and lubricants. Exhibits JPN-16 and JPN-17 document the producers of some of these materials.

(ii) Like imported parts, components and materials

5.255 Most developed economies with automotive manufacturing industry have significant automotive parts, components and materials industries. Exhibit JPN-18 lists major companies in Japan that manufacture automotive parts and components. Exhibit JPN-19 lists some of Japan's industries that produce materials that can be used in the production of automobiles.

5.256 It is clear from a comparison of Exhibits JPN-15 through 19 that comparable and competitive automotive parts, components and materials are available from outside of Canada.

(e) Supply and Consumption of Like Services

(i) Wholesale trade services

5.257 As noted above, the transnational automobile manufacturers distribute imported automobiles in Canada through distribution streams established by their Canadian subsidiaries. Typically, the Canadian subsidiary is responsible for importing the automobile, complying with customs formalities including the payment of customs duties where applicable and distributing the automobiles to dealerships.

5.258 Each of the major global automobile manufacturers has its own distribution network in Canada. The respective numbers of dealers of such manufacturers are shown in the table in Exhibit JPN-20.

5.259 No substantial differences can be found in their business activities, irrespective of the nationality of the manufacturer.

5.260 Further, as documented in Exhibits JPN-10 and 11, each of the automobile distributors in Canada imports automobiles from foreign manufacturers with which it has an equity relationship or with which its parent company is in a contractual relationship such as a joint venture agreement.

(ii) Services related to the production of automobiles

5.261 Broad ranges of services are used by motor vehicle manufacturers in the production of motor vehicles. These services include the following:

Repair and Maintenance Services

- Technical advice and other related services regarding the manner or method of the repair and maintenance of machinery and equipment used in the production of motor vehicles.

Engineering Services

- Technical advice and other related services for the facilitation of the manufacturing process in motor vehicle factories.

General Services

- Accounting and data processing services through telecommunication networks.
- Software implementation services.
- Services for optimal administration of inventories.
- Management consulting services.

5.262 These services are available from service suppliers located in Canada and around the world.

(iii) The bus and commercial motor vehicle industry in Canada

5.263 Most of the importers who qualify for the Duty Waiver are also manufacturers of buses or specified commercial vehicles. The Canadian production of buses and specified commercial motor vehicles is documented in Exhibits JPN-21 and 22.

(f) The Discriminatory Effects of the Duty Waiver

5.264 As a result of the regulation of automotive trade in Canada, some imports enter Canada under the Duty Waiver while competing imports do not qualify for the Duty Waiver. Japan's Table 5 presents data on imports of these two categories of automobiles: (i) imports that enter Canada under the Duty Waiver; and (ii) competing imports that enter Canada but do not qualify for the Duty Waiver.

Japan's Table 5

Imported Models That Are Imported Duty Free under the Duty Waiver		**Competing Imported Models That Are Not Eligible for the Duty Waiver**	
Segment **Importer** Model (Country of origin)	Unit sales of imported motor vehicles (1996)	*Segment* **Importer** Model (Country of origin)	Unit sales of imported motor vehicles (1996)

Imported Models That Are Imported Duty Free under the Duty Waiver		**Competing Imported Models That Are Not Eligible for the Duty Waiver**	
Segment **Importer** Model (Country of origin)	Unit sales of imported motor vehicles (1996)	*Segment* **Importer** Model (Country of origin)	Unit sales of imported motor vehicles (1996)
Subcompact			
Ford		**Hyundai**	
Aspire (Korea)	2,309	Accent (Korea)	2
Chrysler		Excel (Korea)	10,540
Eagle Summit (Japan)	290	**Lada**	
Colt 100/200 (Japan)	891	Lada (Russia)	981
		Subaru	
		Justy (Japan)	88
		Toyota	
		Tercel (Japan)	11,502
		Mazda	
		33 HB (Japan)	124
Small Luxury			
GM		**Honda**	
Cadillac Catera (Germany)	96	Acura TL (Japan)	1,569
Saab 900 (Sweden)	1,031	**Mazda**	
		Millenia (Japan)	403
		929 (Japan)	8
		Mercedes	
		190GAS/C-Class	1,929
		Nissan	
		Infiniti G20 (Japan)	164
		Infiniti I30 (Japan)	742
		Toyota	
		Lexus ES250/300 (Japan)	1,208
		Volkswagen	
		Audi 90 (Germany)	1,347
Luxury			
GM		**BMW**	
Saab 9000 (Sweden)	275	5-Series (Germany)	996
Ford		7-Series (Germany)	449
Jaguar Sedans (UK)	859	**Honda**	
Volvo		Acura Legend/RL (Japan)	938
960's (Belgium or Sweden)	539	**Mercedes**	
940's (Belgium or Sweden)	46	S Class (Germany)	761
		300E/400E/E Class (Germany)	2,013
		Nissan	
		Infiniti J30 (Japan)	96
		Infiniti Q45 (Japan)	138
		Toyota	
		Lexus GS300 (Japan)	38
		Lexus LS400 (Japan)	464
		Volkswagen	
		Audi 100/200 (Germany)	359
		Audi A8 (Germany)	31

Imported Models That Are Imported Duty Free under the Duty Waiver		Competing Imported Models That Are Not Eligible for the Duty Waiver	
Segment **Importer** Model (Country of origin)	Unit sales of imported motor vehicles (1996)	*Segment* **Importer** Model (Country of origin)	Unit sales of imported motor vehicles (1996)
Luxury Sport		**Volkswagen**	
Ford		Porsche (Germany)	373
Jaguar Sports Coupe (UK)	192	**Toyota**	
		Lexus SC400 (Japan)	100
		Supra (Japan)	7
		Subaru	
		SVX (Japan)	63
		Nissan	
		300ZX	45
		Mazda	
		RX7	328
		Honda	
		Acura NSX	16
		BMW	
		6/8 Series	16

Source: The Canadian Association of Japanese Automobile Dealers (Exhibit JPN-11)

5.265 This table shows that the Duty Waiver discriminates between imported automobiles that are imported duty free under the Duty Waiver and their competing imported automobiles. This is most apparent in the case of Swedish, Belgian and Japanese imported automobiles. Almost all imported Swedish automobiles (i.e. Saab and Volvo) and Belgian automobiles (i.e. Volvo) benefited from the Duty Waiver while none of the competing imported Japanese automobiles (*Acura*, *Infiniti* and *Lexus*) were eligible for the Duty Waiver.

5.266 Moreover, as a result of the global integration described above, imports of each manufacturer or distributor into Canada always will originate from a single, specific source and not from a variety of sources. This characteristic, which is documented in Exhibit JPN-11, has important implications for the effect of the Duty Waiver. First, the countries from which motor vehicles can be imported under the Duty Waiver are restricted: they are limited to countries where Auto Pact Manufacturers have affiliates or related companies. Second, the competitive balance is tilted in favour of motor vehicles originating in this restricted class of countries compared to competing motor vehicles originating in other countries.

5.267 Canadian import statistics on the percentage of motor vehicles that benefit from the Duty Waiver for each country of origin clearly illustrate the discrimination that is inherent in the Duty Waiver. Depending on the country of origin, the volume of imports that benefit from the Duty Waiver ranges from close to 100 per cent to zero per cent, as is illustrated in the following table:

Japan's Table 6

Country of Origin	Duty Free Import Sales Quantity (1997)	Imports Quantity (1997)	Duty Free Percentage
Sweden	1,776	1,851	95.95%
Belgium	4,746	5,047	94.04%
United Kingdom	1,020	2,275	44.84%
Germany	1,560	21,256	7.34%
(EC total)	9,102	30,629	29.72%
South Korea	972	19,956	4.87%
Japan	4,502	153,349	2.94%
Other countries	0	826	0%

Note: The figures in the above table do not include imports from the United States and Mexico.
Source: Ward's Automotive Year Book 1998, Statistics Canada (Exhibit JPN-37).

5.268 The competitive advantage that accrues from the Duty Waiver is clearly significant. It can affect all aspects of an importer's and wholesale trade services supplier's operations including pricing, marketing, earnings and the establishment of distribution networks.

5.269 The discriminatory effects of the Duty Waiver on trade in goods (motor vehicles, parts and components, materials) and services (wholesale trade services and other services related to the production of motor vehicles) are discussed in detail in the arguments presented.

2. *Canada's Response to Certain Arguments Regarding the Structure of the Motor Vehicles Industry*

5.270 With respect to information presented in Japan's Table 5, **Canada** responds as follows (with additional arguments contained in sections relating to specific claims):

5.271 Japan's Table 5, according to Japan, is intended to demonstrate "that the Duty Waiver discriminates between imported automobiles that are imported duty free under the Duty Waiver [i.e. those from Sweden and Belgium] and their competing imported automobiles that are not imported duty free [i.e. those from Japan]". The Panel should note that Table 5 uses only 1996 data, and features a number of models that are either no longer produced or no longer available in Canada.[265] In addition, some models listed in the source document cited by Japan (Exhibit JPN-11) are not included in Table 5, presumably because if they had been, Japan would have had to acknowledge several competing Japanese-origin automobiles that enter duty free. [266]

5.272 As the facts before this Panel demonstrate, Canada's measures do not restrict benefits to any particular vehicle, and beneficiary manufacturers may import from

[265] See Exhibit CDA-5 for the models listed in Table 5 that are no longer in production or sold in Canada.

[266] For 1996 there are: Suzuki Esteem (1291 vehicles), Chrysler Stealth (20 vehicles), Honda/Acura CL series (1226 vehicles), Toyota Avalon (2163 vehicles), General Motors Isuzu Trooper II (261 vehicles), Chrysler Summit Wagon (98 vehicles). But see footnote 267.

anywhere in the world. Which Member's products benefit at any given time depends entirely on the commercial decisions made by the manufacturers. The tariff regime, however, is completely neutral as to nationality.

3. *Japan's Rebuttal to Canada's Response*

5.273 As a rebuttal to Canada's comments in response to Japan's Table 5, **Japan** argues as follows (with additional arguments contained in sections relating to specific claims):

5.274 With respect to Japan's Table 5, the Government of Canada argues that the Table includes models of automobiles that are no longer manufactured and, therefore, no longer imported into Canada. However, it is industry practice for automobile manufacturers to regularly renew their line of car models and change model names in certain market segments. In the case of Japanese cars, models are renewed approximately every four years. As examples of such practices, the names of the Audi 90 and Hyundai Excel were changed to Audi A4 and Hyundai Accent, respectively, when recent model changes occurred. Both automobiles continue to be imported into Canada under their new names.

5.275 Notwithstanding the above-noted qualification to Table 5, the Table provides concrete examples of imports and sales in Canada in the 1996 model year, and can be relied on to illustrate the discrimination that is inherent in the Duty Waiver. The Table documents the "less favourable" treatment that was accorded to certain automobiles imported from certain countries as a result of the application of the Duty Waiver in the past. Irrespective of the fact that certain models listed in the Table might no longer be imported and sold in Canada, the inherent discrimination still exists.

5.276 At the present time, automobiles originating in the territories of certain WTO Members are imported into Canada duty free while like automobiles originating in the territories of other WTO Members, including Japan, do not benefit from this advantage when imported into the Canadian marketplace. These discriminatory effects are also confirmed by the evidence submitted by the Government of Canada. Exhibit CDA-6 demonstrates that, in 1998, the following automobiles listed under the small luxury and luxury car market segment were imported duty free under the Duty Waiver and sold in Canada:

Model	***Origin***
Saab 9-3	Sweden
Saab 9-6	Sweden
Saab 900	Sweden
Saab 9000	Sweden
Volvo 90	Sweden
Volvo S70 V70	Sweden
Jaguar XJ6	United Kingdom
Jaguar XJ5	United Kingdom
Catera	Germany

5.277 All like automobiles imported from Japan and sold in Canada in 1998 were subject to the applicable MFN duty. According to Exhibit JPN-37, these are:

Model	***Origin***
Acura TL, Legend	Japan (Honda)
Lexus ES300, LS400, GS300/400	Japan (Toyota)
Infiniti G20, I30, Q45, J30	Japan (Nissan)

5.278 Thus, imports of automobiles from Japan and from other countries continue and will continue to be subject to the 6.1 per cent MFN duty while like automobiles originating in the territories of other WTO Members continue and will continue to be imported duty free. This is due to the fact that, as Canada admitted, Auto Pact Manufacturers only import and distribute automobiles from certain specific sources.

5.279 In fact, the evidence on the record demonstrates that capital relationships between Auto Pact Manufacturers and other entities are decisive in the determination of the country of origin of duty-free imports. For example, automobiles listed in Exhibit CDA-6 that have been imported by Chrysler Canada and GM Canada were manufactured by the following foreign manufacturers:

Importers	**Models**	**Manufacturers**
Chrysler	Colt (Dodge) Stealth RAM 50	Mitsubishi
GM	Metro, Storm/Spectrum, Asuna, Sunfire	Suzuki
GM	Tiltmaster	Isuzu
GM	Lemans	Daewoo

5.280 It is a well-known fact that Chrysler held a 24 per cent (maximum) stake in Mitsubishi Motors from 1971 to July 1993. Further, GM is a stakeholder of both Suzuki and Isuzu. GM also owned a 50 per cent equity interest in Daewoo until October 1992.

5.281 As appears from Exhibit CDA-6, Chrysler continued to import and sell Mitsubishi automobiles until mid-1996 and GM ceased to import and sell Daewoo automobiles in 1992. The phasing-out of imports by Chrysler after the termination of the capital relationship and the immediate close of imports of Daewoo automobiles after the termination of the capital relationships indicate that such relationships determine the Auto Pact Manufacturers' source of imports. Although Chrysler continued to sell imported Mitsubishi cars, the number of which had been decreasing during such a phase-out period, this period should be considered as the transition period which Chrysler needs to gradually change its line of products by maintaining its dealers networks.

5.282 Hence, contrary to the allegations of the Government of Canada, the evidence before this Panel makes it clear that, at any given time, the benefits of the Duty Waiver are restricted to particular imported automobiles originating from particular countries. Such benefits are not granted to all like automobiles originating in the territories of all WTO Members.

5.283 The Government of Canada also argues that some models listed in the source document cited by Japan are not included in Japan's Table 5. However, the Government of Japan wants to point out to the Panel that the CAJAD report (Exhibit JPN-11) that was used to construct Table 5 is not completely accurate.[267]

5.284 In the light of the above, Canada's statement that an "examination of the complete data leads to a result that stands in marked contrast to the theory espoused by the Japanese" is not supported by the facts. Automobiles of Japanese origin are clearly denied an advantage that is granted to like automobiles originating in the territories of other WTO Members.

5.285 The Government of Canada stated that over 82 per cent of imports subject to the minimum 6.1 per cent MFN duty came from Japan. This consideration is irrelevant. What is relevant is the fact that more than 97 per cent of imports of Japanese cars to Canada have been subject to the MFN duty and are being forced to compete with cars imported duty free from a few other WTO Members. The 181,000 motor vehicles referred to by the Government of Canada are motor vehicles imported from countries located outside of North America. However, 540,000 additional motor vehicles a year have been imported duty free from the US and Mexico under the Duty Waiver regime. As admitted by Canada, imports from Mexico are subject to certain reduced duties under the NAFTA but those duties have been fully exempted, as a consequence of the Duty Waiver. The argument of the Government of Canada in this respect in no way justifies the inconsistency of the Duty Waiver with the WTO Agreements. (Exhibit JPN-37.)

5.286 Further, Canada's *Figure 4* does not contain data regarding duty-free imports from Mexico and the United States. If the Government of Canada refers to the aggregate volume of duty-free imports under the MVTO 1998 and the SROs, it should also refer to the imports from Mexico and the United States thereunder and *Figure 4* should be revised accordingly. Of course, since 1998, the majority of imports of automobiles from the US are no longer subject to any customs duty under NAFTA; thus, they should be deleted from *Figure 4* beginning with the 1998 year only when they meet strict NAFTA origin rules and importers declares the satisfaction with such rules at the customs office by submitting certifications. The figure, revised to include the data of the duty-free imports from the United States and Mexico, is as follows:

[267] The data contained in the Ward's Automotive Yearbook (Exhibit JPN-37-4) indicates that two models listed in footnote 266 were manufactured in the United States by affiliates of Toyota and Honda. These are the Toyota Avalon and the Acura CL. Thus, such models were not imported from Japan as suggested by Canada. As for the other automobiles listed by Canada, they do not fall under the same market segments as those automobile models listed in Table 5 that are not eligible for the Duty Waiver. Accordingly, they were not included in the Table.

Japan's Table 7

Duty-free Imports of Automobiles to Canada (Including Imports from the US and Mexico) (Numbers)							
Origin	US	Mexico	Japan	Sweden/ Belgium	UK	Others (Germany and Korea)	Total
1998	277,188	19,375	5,878	5,538	1,293	1,853	311,125
1997	308,140	52,319	4,566	2,837	1,020	2,532	371,414
1996	255,403	6,420	4,856	4,263	1,051	2,405	274,398
1995	244,800	4,403	8,036	8,368	948	4,646	271,201
1994	326,107	32,156	23,537	7,812	713	3,647	393,972
1993	261,596	42,497	50,064	5,814	630	5,765	366,366
1992	283,086	50,348	52,953	4,059	581	12,788	403,815
1991	368,209	47,073	41,180	4,499	727	6,930	468,618

Source: Imports from Mexico to Canada; AMIA Statistic
Others; Ward's Autoinfo Bank

1. Imports from the United States and Mexico only includes the automobiles imported by Big 3.
2. Imports from Mexico in 1991-1993 includes the commercial vehicles.

Japan's Table 8

Duty-free Imports of Automobiles to Canada (Including Imports from the US and Mexico (Percentage)							
Origin	US	Mexico	Japan	Sweden/ Belgium	UK	Others (Germany and Korea)	Total
1998	89.1	6.2	1.9	1.8	0.4	0.6	100
1997	83	14.1	1.2	0.8	0.3	0.7	100.1
1996	93.1	2.3	1.8	1.6	0.4	0.9	100.1
1995	90.3	1.6	3	3.1	0.3	1.7	100
1994	82.8	8.2	6	2	0.2	0.9	100.1
1993	71.4	11.6	13.7	1.6	0.2	1.6	100.1
1992	70.1	12.5	13.1	1	0.1	3.2	100
1991	78.6	10	8.8	1	0.2	1.5	100.1

5.287 (*Additional arguments relating to the structure of the industry are found in Section VI, Legal Arguments of the Parties.*)

VI. LEGAL ARGUMENTS OF THE PARTIES

A. *Article I of the GATT*

1. *Arguments of Japan*

6.1 **Japan** argues as follows:

6.2 The Duty Waiver is inconsistent with Canada's MFN obligation under Article I:1 of the GATT 1994 because the advantage, i.e. removal of customs duty, is not accorded immediately and unconditionally to like products originating in the territories of all other Members.

6.3 Article I:1 of the GATT 1994 provides that:

> "With respect to customs duties and charges of any kind imposed on or in connection with importation or exportation or imposed on the international transfer of payments for imports or exports, and with respect to the method of levying such duties and charges, and with respect to all rules and formalities in connection with importation and exportation, and with respect to all matters referred to in paragraphs 2 and 4 of Article III, any advantage, favour, privilege or immunity granted by any [Member] to any product originating in or destined for any other country shall be accorded immediately and unconditionally to the like product originating in or destined for the territories of all other [Members]."

6.4 To assess whether there is any inconsistency with Article I:1 of the GATT 1994, one must answer the following questions:

(i) Does the Duty Waiver relate to a customs duty within the meaning of Article I:1 of the GATT 1994?

(ii) Is the Duty Waiver an advantage within the meaning of Article I:1 of the GATT 1994?

(iii) Are the products at issue "like" products?

(iv) Has the advantage accorded to the products originating in particular WTO Members been accorded "immediately and unconditionally" to all like products originating in the territories of all other WTO Members?

(a) The Duty Waiver Relates to a Customs Duty Within the Meaning of Article I:1 of the GATT 1994

6.5 The Duty Waiver relates to the 6.1 per cent MFN duty and is, therefore, within the scope of Article I:1 of the GATT 1994.

(b) The Duty Waiver is an Advantage Within the Meaning of Article I:1 of the GATT 1994

6.6 Article I:1 applies to "*any* advantage" granted to products originating in any country. The plain meaning of "advantage" is "a beneficial feature; a favourable circumstance", or, in simple terms, a "benefit".[268] The term "advantage" has been interpreted broadly both under the GATT 1947 and the GATT 1994.[269]

6.7 The Duty Waiver grants a benefit to certain imported motor vehicles because such motor vehicles are exempt from an otherwise applicable customs duty.[270] Accordingly, it is an "advantage" within the meaning of Article I:1 of the GATT 1994.

(c) The Products at Issue are "Like" Products

6.8 The determination of whether products are "like" must be assessed on a case-by-case basis in the light of all relevant facts and circumstances. Relevant factors include physical characteristics, end-uses, consumer tastes and habits, and price.[271]

6.9 In this case, the Duty Waiver covers the full range of motor vehicles imported into Canada.[272] It does not distinguish between motor vehicles based on physical characteristics, end-uses, consumer tastes and habits or price. With the Duty Waiver in place, Canada applies a higher import duty to Non-Auto Pact Manufacturers' imports than it does to identical Auto Pact Manufacturers' imports. Accordingly, the motor vehicles to which the Duty Waiver applies and those to which it does not apply are *per se* "like" products.[273] This reasoning applies to all types of motor vehicles (i.e. automobiles, buses and specified commercial vehicles).

---

[268] The Concise Oxford Dictionary of Current English, 8th Edition (Clarendon Press: Oxford, 1990) (Exhibit JPN-41).

[269] The Appellate Body made this observation in its report on *EC - Bananas III*, *supra* note 49, para. 206, when referring to the interpretation of the term by the Panel Report on *United States - Denial of Most-Favoured-Nation Treatment as to Non-Rubber Footwear from Brazil*, adopted on 12 June 1992, BISD 39S/128 (hereinafter Panel Report on *US - Non-Rubber Footwear*), para. 6.9. See also Panel Reports on *European Communities - Regime for the Importation, Sale and Distribution of Bananas*, adopted as modified by the Appellate Body on 25 September 1997, DSR 1997:II, 803, Complaint by Ecuador - WT/DS27/R/ECU, Complaint by Guatemala - WT/DS27/R/GTM, Complaint by Honduras - WT/DS27/R/HND, Complaint by Mexico - WT/DS27/R/MEX, Complaint by the United States - WT/DS27/R/USA, 22 May 1997 (hereinafter Panel Reports on *EC - Bananas III (ECU/GTM/HND/MEX/USA)* [The reports of each of the complaining parties in the dispute have identical para. and footnote numbering. In the Findings section of each report, however, certain para. and footnote numbers are not used.], (USA) para. 7.221.

[270] In its Report on *Indonesia - Certain Measures Affecting the Automobile Industry*, adopted on 23 July 1998, WT/DS54/R, WT/DS55/R, WT/DS59/R & WT/DS64/R (hereinafter Panel Report on *Indonesia - Autos*), DSR 1998:VI, 2201, para. 14.139, the Panel found that customs duty benefits (i.e. duty reductions) were "advantages" under Article I:1 of the GATT 1994.

[271] Appellate Body Report on *Japan - Taxes on Alcoholic Beverages*, adopted on 1 November 1996, WT/DS8/AB/R, WT/DS10/AB/R & WT/DS11/AB/R (hereinafter Appellate Body Report on *Japan - Alcoholic Beverages*), DSR 1996:I, 97, at 112. These criteria, which were addressed by the Appellate Body in the context of Article III of the GATT 1994, were applied to the like products analysis under Article I of the GATT 1994 by the Panel in *Indonesia - Autos*, *supra* note 270, para. 14.141.

[272] There are limited exclusions from the scope of coverage that are not relevant to these proceedings. For example, subsection 1(1) of the Schedule to the MVTO 1998 defines "automobile" to exclude "an ambulance or a hearse", "bus" to exclude "electric trackless trolley bus, an amphibious vehicle, a tracked or half tracked vehicle or a motor vehicle defined primarily for off-highway use", and "specified commercial vehicle" to exclude "a bus, an electric trackless trolley bus, a fire truck, an amphibious vehicle, a tracked or half-tracked vehicle, a golf or invalid cart, a straddle carrier or motor vehicle designed primarily for off-highway use".

[273] Panel Report on *Indonesia - Autos, supra* note 270, para. 14.141; Panel Report on *US - Non-Rubber Footwear*, *supra* note 269, para. 6.12.

6.10 Exhibit JPN-11 and Japan's Tables 3, 4, and 5 categorise automobiles imported into Canada into applicable market segments.[274] They demonstrate that both Auto Pact Manufacturers and Non-Auto Pact Manufacturers import "like" automobiles.[275]

(d) The Advantage is Not Accorded Immediately and Unconditionally to Like Products Originating in All WTO Members

6.11 The advantage must be accorded "immediately and unconditionally" to the like products originating in the territories of all WTO Members under Article I:1 of the GATT 1994. The plain meaning of "unconditional" is "not subject to conditions".[276]

6.12 In this case, the Government of Canada accords the advantages of the Duty Waiver only to the motor vehicles imported by the Auto Pact Manufacturers in accordance with the many conditions or requirements described in Japan's factual argumentation. The advantage that accrues from the Duty Waiver is conditional upon the several criteria not related to the imported products themselves. Such criteria include, among others, (i) whether motor vehicles were imported by the Auto Pact Manufacturers and (ii) whether the Auto Pact Manufacturers have satisfied the CVA and manufacturing requirements.

6.13 The panel on *Indonesia - Autos* made clear that under Article I:1 of the GATT 1994, any advantage "cannot be made conditional on any criteria not related to the imported product itself".[277]

6.14 This interpretation is further confirmed by the *Belgian Family Allowances* Panel Canada quoted, which states that "the Belgian legislation would have to be amended insofar as it ... made the granting of the exemption dependent on certain conditions."

6.15 The reference by the *Indonesia - Autos* Panel to "the imported product itself" in articulating this interpretation is rational. To the extent that such conditions or

---

274 In the context of automobiles, the Panel in *Indonesia - Autos* included market segment classification as part of its like products analysis. Panel Report on *Indonesia - Autos, supra* note 270, paras. 14.110 and 14.111.

275 Japan has indicated that the CAJAD report used in constructing Table 5 (Exhibit JPN-11) is not completely accurate. See *supra* para. 5.283 and notes 266 and 267.

276 The Concise Oxford Dictionary, 238 (Exhibit JPN-41). In *Indonesia - Autos*, the Panel found that this requirement means that an advantage cannot be made conditional on any criteria that are not related to the imported product itself, *see supra* note 270, para. 14.143. See also Panel Report on *Belgian Family Allowances*, adopted on 7 November 1952, BISD 1S/59 (hereinafter Panel Report on *Belgian Family Allowances*) and Report of the *Working Party on the Accession of Hungary*, adopted on 30 July 1973, BISD 20S/34 (hereinafter Report of the *Working Party on the Accession of Hungary*).

277 Panel Report on *Indonesia - Autos, supra* note 270, para. 14.143. Further, the Panel in *Indonesia - Autos* stated as follows: "For the reasons discussed above, we consider that the June 1996 car programme which introduced discrimination between imports in the allocation of tax and customs duty benefits based on various conditions and other criteria not related to the imports themselves and the February 1996 car programme which also introduce discrimination between imports in the allocation of customs duty benefits based on various conditions and other criteria not related to the imports themselves, are inconsistent with the provisions of Article I of GATT." (para.14.147).

criteria are related to the physical product in question, they could permit a distinction between products on the basis that they are not "like". Where products are not "like", discrimination in the sense of GATT Article I cannot arise.

6.16 Thus, Canada has failed to accord the advantage "immediately and unconditionally" to the like products originating in the territories of all WTO Members and the Duty Waiver is inconsistent with Canada's MFN obligation under Article I:1 of the GATT 1994.

(e) The Advantage Accorded to the Products Originating in Particular WTO Members Has Not Been Accorded to Like Products Originating in the Territories of All WTO Members

6.17 By virtue of its eligibility restriction, the Duty Waiver discriminates in practice by according an advantage to motor vehicles from certain countries while effectively denying the same advantage to like motor vehicles originating in the territories of other WTO Members.

6.18 Although, ostensibly, the Auto Pact Manufacturers are permitted to import motor vehicles of any national origin, in practice they have chosen and will continue to choose to import the products of particular companies from particular countries, in consideration of their previous history of transactions, the capital relationships as shown in Exhibit JPN-10, and the nationality of companies investing in the Auto Pact Manufacturers. For example, the MFN duty would be imposed upon motor vehicles imported from Japan by such companies as Toyota Canada and Honda Canada, while the majority of motor vehicles entitled to duty waiver are of particular national origin, and are produced by the Big Three, Volvo or those manufacturers that have capital relationships with the Big Three (such as Saab, Opel and Jaguar).

6.19 This means that the eligibility restriction and other conditions attached to the Duty Waiver effectively limit access to the advantage to certain Members having the companies with which Auto Pact Manufacturers have certain commercial relationships.

6.20 Furthermore, the discriminatory nature of the Duty Waiver was strengthened due to the fact that the list of eligible importers (i.e. Auto Pact Manufacturers) has been frozen since 1 January 1989. This regime explicitly narrows the origins from which motor vehicles can be imported under the Duty Waiver.

6.21 This discrimination is evidenced in the general import statistics discussed in Japan's Table 6. These statistics demonstrate that while approximately 100 per cent of imports from certain countries qualify for the Duty Waiver, this is not the case for imports from other countries.

6.22 Japan's Tables 9 and 10 document two examples wherein imported automobiles originating in the territory of a WTO Member benefit from the Duty Waiver while imports of "like" automobiles originating in the territory of another WTO Member do not benefit.

6.23 General Motors imports from Sweden the *Saab 900* and *Saab 9000*, luxury automobiles manufactured by Saab.[278] These automobiles are imported into Canada duty free under the Duty Waiver and sold in the Canadian market.
6.24 Japanese manufacturers produce like automobiles that are imported into Canada for sale in the Canadian market. These are shown in the right-hand column of the following table.

Japan's Table 9

Models Imported Under the Duty Waiver	Like Automobiles Produced by Japanese Manufacturers That Are Imported into Canada Without the Duty Waiver
Small Luxury **GM** Saab 900 (Sweden)	 **Honda** Acura TL (Japan) **Mazda** Millennia (Japan) 929 (Japan) **Nissan** Infiniti G20 (Japan) Infiniti I30 (Japan) **Toyota** Lexus ES250/300 (Japan)
Luxury **GM** Saab 9000 (Sweden)	 Honda Acura Legend/RL (Japan) **Nissan** Infiniti J30 (Japan) Infiniti Q45 (Japan) **Toyota** Lexus GS300 (Japan) Lexus LS400 (Japan) Infiniti Q45 (Japan) **Toyota** Lexus GS300 (Japan) Lexus LS400 (Japan)

6.25 None of these automobiles, which comprise all of the "like" automobiles produced in Japan and exported to Canada, have been imported into Canada under the Duty Waiver. Consequently, the MFN duty has been applied to date.
6.26 Volvo Canada (soon to be part of Ford) imports from Belgium or Sweden *Volvo 960's* and *940's* model automobiles. These automobiles are imported into Canada duty free under the Duty Waiver and sold in the Canadian market.
6.27 Japanese manufacturers produce like automobiles that are imported into Canada for sale in the Canadian market. These are shown in the right-hand column of the following table.

[278] According to publicly available information from Saab's web site, General Motors owns 50 per cent of Saab's shares (stock).

Japan's Table 10

Models Imported Under the Duty Waiver	Like Automobiles Produced by Japanese Manufacturers That Are Imported into Canada Without the Duty Waiver
Luxury **Volvo** 960's (Belgium or Sweden) 940's (Belgium or Sweden)	**Honda** Acura Legend/RL (Japan) **Nissan** Infiniti J30 (Japan) Infiniti Q45(Japan) **Toyota** Lexus GS300 (Japan) Lexus LS400 (Japan)

6.28 None of these automobiles, which comprise all of the "like" automobiles produced in Japan and exported to Canada, have been imported into Canada under the Duty Waiver. Consequently, the MFN duty has been applied to date.

6.29 The effect of this discrimination is clearly reflected in Canada's import statistics. During 1997, nearly 100 per cent of the imports of *almost all* automobiles from Sweden or Belgium entered Canada duty free under the Duty Waiver.[279] This compares to zero per cent of imports of the above-noted like and thus competing automobiles imported from Japan. Based on the foregoing, it is clear that the advantage that accrues from the Duty Waiver has in practice not been accorded to like products originating in all WTO Members.

6.30 The foregoing reasoning applies equally to imports of all motor vehicles (i.e. automobiles, buses and specified commercial vehicles) whenever like motor vehicles are imported under the Duty Waiver, even where there have never been explicit examples as shown above due to the absence of such import to date in those market segments.[280]

6.31 In this manner, the fact that the Duty Waiver is available only to the Auto Pact Manufacturers has brought about the effect of denying duty-free access to the Canadian market to exports from any origin other than from a limited group of WTO Members. As a corollary to the argument laid down in the Appellate Body in *EC - Bananas III*[281], the Duty Waiver is inconsistent with the MFN principle in Article I:1 of the GATT 1994.

---

[279] See Table 6.

[280] See Panel Report on *United States - Section 337 of the Tariff Act of 1930*, adopted on 7 November 1989, BISD 36S/345 (hereinafter Panel Report on *US - Section 337*), para. 5.13, and Appellate Body Report on *Korea - Taxes on Alcoholic Beverages*, adopted on 17 February 1999, WT/DS/75/AB/R & WT/DS84/AB/R (hereinafter Appellate Body Report on *Korea - Alcoholic Beverages*), DSR 1999:I, 3, at 28-32. See also Panel Report on *Canada - Certain Measures Concerning Periodicals*, adopted on 30 July 1997, WT/DS31/R (hereinafter *Panel Report on Canada - Periodicals*), DSR 1997:I, 481, para. 5.23, as confirmed by the Appellate Body Report, adopted on 30 July 1997, WT/DS31/AB/R (hereinafter Appellate Body Report on *Canada - Periodicals*), DSR 1997:I, 449, at 466.

[281] Appellate Body Report on *EC - Bananas III, supra* note 49, para. 232.

2. *Arguments of the European Communities*

6.32 The European Communities argues as follows:

6.33 GATT Article I:1 provides in pertinent part that:

"With respect to customs duties and charges of any kind imposed on or in connection with importation ... any advantage, favour, privilege or immunity granted by any contracting party to any product originating in ... any other country shall be accorded immediately and unconditionally to the like product originating in ... the territories of all other contracting parties."

6.34 As shown below, the Tariff Exemption is inconsistent with GATT Article I:1 in that *de facto* it provides an advantage to imports of automobiles originating in the United States and Mexico *vis-à-vis* imports of like products originating in other Members.

(a) The Measures Confer an "Advantage" Covered by Article I:1

6.35 GATT Article I:1 applies, *inter alia*, to any advantage granted by a Member "with respect to customs duties...". The Tariff Exemption is, therefore, an "advantage" covered by GATT Article I:1.

(b) The Automobiles Imported by the Beneficiaries Are "Like" the Automobiles Imported by Non-Beneficiaries

6.36 The Tariff Exemption is not based on the characteristics of the automobiles imported by the beneficiaries. Imports by non-beneficiaries would not qualify for the tariff exemption even if the automobiles imported by them were identical in all respects to those imported by the beneficiaries.

(c) The Tariff Exemption Benefits Mainly Imports from the United States and Mexico

6.37 Article I:1 of GATT does not prohibit only measures that discriminate formally, or *de jure*, according to the country of origin of the imported goods. As recalled by the Appellate Body in *EC - Bananas III*, Article I:1 of the GATT has also been applied, in past practice, to measures involving *de facto* discrimination[282].

6.38 On its face, the Tariff Exemption is non-discriminatory, as it applies equally with respect to all imports of automobiles by the beneficiaries, irrespective of their country of origin. In reality, however, since the main beneficiaries of the Tariff Exemption are subsidiaries of US companies with large manufacturing facilities in the

[282] Appellate Body Report on *EC - Bananas III*, *supra* note 49, paras. 231-232. As examples of that practice, the Appellate Body referred to the Panel Reports on *Spain - Tariff Treatment of Unroasted Coffee*, adopted on 11 June 1981, BISD 28S/102 (hereinafter Panel Report on *Spain - Unroasted Coffee*); Panel Report on *European Economic Communities - Imports of Beef from Canada*, adopted on 10 March 1981, BISD 28S/92 (hereinafter Panel Report on *EEC - Beef from Canada*); and Panel Report on *Japan - Tariff on Imports of Spruce-Pine-Fir (SPF) Dimension Lumber*, adopted on 19 July 1989, BISD 36S/167 (hereinafter Panel Report on *Japan - SPF Lumber*).

United States and in Mexico, the Tariff Exemption benefits almost exclusively to imports of automobiles originating in those two Members.

6.39 As shown in the EC's Table 1, in 1997 imports of automobiles originating in the United States and Mexico accounted for 97 per cent of imports under the Tariff Exemption. That share is not the result of commercial factors, as evidenced by the fact that, in contrast, imports from the United States and Mexico accounted for under 80 per cent of all imports of automobiles into Canada.

6.40 Moreover, as set out in the EC's Table 2, whereas in 1997 the vast majority of imports from Mexico and the United States benefited from the Tariff Exemption, most imports from other sources were subject to customs duties.

EC's Table 1

Imports of automobiles by country of export - 1997
(million C$)

	All imports	Share of All imports	Auto Pact* imports	Share of Auto Pact* imports
USA	12,526	70.68%	10,498	88.23%
Mexico	1,459	8.23%	1,071	9.00%
USA + Mexico	13,985	78.91%	11,569	97.23%
Japan	2,492	14.06%	0.2	0.02%
Europe	898	5.07%	164	1.38%
Other countries	363	2.04%	162	1.36%

* Includes imports under the MVTO 1998 and the SROs
Source: 1997 Automotive Trade Report, Industry Canada, Tables 2 and 3 (Exhibit EC-15).

EC's Table 2

Ratio of Auto-Pact imports to All imports of automobiles - 1997

	All imports (million C$) (A)	Auto Pact* imports (million C$) (B)	Ratio of Auto Pact imports* (B) to All imports (A)
USA	12,526	10,498	83.81%
Mexico	1,459	1,071	73.41%
USA + Mexico	13,985	11,596	82.91%
Japan	2,492	0.2	0.01%
Europe	898	164	18.26%
Japan + Europe	3,390	164.2	4.84%
Total	17,720	11,898	67.14%

* Includes imports under the MVTO 1998 and the SROs
Source: 1997 Automotive Trade Report, Industry Canada, Tables 2 and 3 (Exhibit EC-15).

3. *Canada's Response*

6.41 **Canada** responds as follows:

(a) The Complainants Have Failed to Meet their Burden of Proof

6.42 The complainants appear to believe that this Panel could find for them on the basis of mere assertions that Canada is in breach of its WTO obligations. This is wishful thinking; there can be no doubt that the complaining parties bear the burden of proving their claims against Canada. This is well established in WTO law, notably by the Appellate Body in the leading case on this issue, *United States - Measure Affecting Imports of Woven Wool Shirts and Blouses from India:*[283]

> ... we find it difficult, indeed, to see how any system of judicial settlement could work if it incorporated the proposition that the mere assertion of a claim might amount to proof. ... [I]t is a generally-accepted canon of evidence ... that the burden of proof rests upon the party, whether complaining or defending, who asserts the affirmative of a particular claim or defence.[284]

6.43 The Appellate Body has further explained that the complaining party must:

> ... *put forward evidence and legal arguments* sufficient to demonstrate that action by [the defending party] is inconsistent with the obligations assumed [under the WTO]. ... Then, ...the onus shifts to the defending party] to bring forward evidence and arguments to disprove the claim.[285] (*emphasis added*)

6.44 The complainants' submissions fall well short of this legal and evidentiary obligation. As Canada will show, neither of the complainants has been able to demonstrate a prima facie case with respect to any of their claims, which is not surprising because those claims are not sustainable. What is surprising and disturbing, however, is that in many instances, no attempt is even made to do so. The Appellate Body has stated clearly that it is not sufficient for a complainant to shift the burden simply by referring to a measure and asserting that it contravenes a WTO rule.[286] To say something is so does not make it so. Moreover, filing copies of excerpts from a directory of Canadian automotive parts manufacturers, a handbook listing Japanese automotive parts and components manufacturers, web sites of companies that manufacture goods used in the production of automobiles, and lists of vehicle models, while perhaps of interest to automobile manufacturers, does not by any measure constitute proof of any allegations made by the Japanese who have filed them,[287] or indeed of anything at all relevant to this dispute.

(b) The MVTO and the SROs Provide MFN Treatment for Products

6.45 The complainants each allege, albeit for different reasons, that Canada's implementation of its Auto Pact obligations is inconsistent with its MFN obligations with respect to trade in goods under Article I:1 of the GATT 1994. Their respective

---

[283] Appellate Body Report on *United States - Measure Affecting Imports of Woven Wool Shirts and Blouses*, adopted on 23 May 1997, WT/DS33/AB/R (hereinafter Appellate Body Report on *US - Wool Shirts*), DSR 1997:I, 323, 333 *et seq.*

[284] Ibid., p. 14.

[285] Appellate Body Report on *India - Patent Protection for Pharmaceutical and Agricultural Chemical Products*, adopted 16 January 1998, WT/DS50/AB/R (hereinafter Appellate Body Report on *India - Pharmaceuticals*), DSR 1998:I, 9, paras. 73-74. See also Panel Report on *Argentina - Measures Affecting Imports of Footwear, Textiles, Apparel and Other Items*, adopted 22 April 1998, WT/DS56/R (hereinafter Panel Report on *Argentina - Footwear*), DSR 1998:III, 1033, paras. 6.34-6.40.

[286] Appellate Body Report on *US - Wool Shirts*, *supra* note 283, p. 14.

[287] Exhibits JPN-13 through JPN-19.

contentions misinterpret and misapply Article I. As a matter of fact and of law, Canada's tariff regime applicable to automotive products is fully consistent with the letter and spirit of Article I. Moreover, if any advantage is accorded to Canada's NAFTA partners, this would be perfectly legitimate because the NAFTA creates a free-trade area within the meaning of Article XXIV of GATT 1994.

6.46 Article I:1 provides:

> "With respect to customs duties and charges of any kind imposed on or in connection with importation or exportation or imposed on the international transfer of payments for imports or exports, and with respect to the method of levying such duties and charges, and with respect to all rules and formalities in connection with importation and exportation, and with respect to all matters referred to in paragraphs 2 and 4 of Article III, any advantage, favour, privilege or immunity granted by any contracting party to any product originating in or destined for any other country shall be accorded immediately and unconditionally to the like product originating in or destined for the territories of all other contracting parties."

6.47 Article I by its terms forbids discrimination based on *origin* of the *product.* It refers to an advantage granted to a product "originating in or destined for any other country" and such advantage must be accorded to "the like product originating in or destined for" any other Member country. Advantages granted to the products of one Member must be granted to like products of any other Member. That the treatment relates to *products* is clear from the text of the Article, and it is confirmed by the negotiating history.[288] Moreover, it has been recognized by a recent WTO Panel.[289] A Member may therefore legitimately treat *products* differently, so long as the distinction in treatment is based on criteria other than *national origin.* Thus distinctions based on activities of importing manufacturers do not offend Article I.

6.48 The complaining parties can therefore make their prima facie case only by demonstrating that like products receive differential treatment because of their national origin. They have not met this burden, nor can they, since Canada's measures do not differentiate in any way on the basis of national origin.

(i) The complainants concede there is no *de jure* violation of Canada's MFN obligation

6.49 Both Japan and the European Communities concede that the MVTO and SROs provide for MFN treatment on their face. Japan states: "Ostensibly, the Auto Pact manufacturers are permitted to import motor vehicles of any national origin..." The European Communities is equally categorical: "On its face, the Tariff Exemption is non-discriminatory, as it applies equally with respect to all imports of automobiles

---

[288] The word "product" was deliberately chosen to limit the scope of Article I to goods and to exclude intangible questions such as the rights of business people. See J. Jackson, World Trade and the Law of GATT (Charlottesville: The Michie Company, 1969), p. 57 (Exhibit CDA-3). See also UN Document EPCT/C.II/3, p. 14 (Exhibit CDA-4).

[289] Panel Reports on *EC - Bananas III, supra* note 269, para. 7.239. The Appellate Body did not modify this finding. See Appellate Body Report on *EC - Bananas III, supra* note 49, para. 207.

by the beneficiaries, irrespective of their country of origin." The MVTO 1998 provides explicitly for MFN treatment. Vehicles are entitled to the remission "on condition that the goods are imported into Canada on or after January 18, 1965 from any country entitled to the Most-Favoured-Nation Tariff ...".[290] Moreover, none of the SROs limits the sources from which vehicles may be imported duty free.

(ii) The complainants' contention that there is *de facto* violation of Canada's MFN obligation cannot be sustained

6.50 GATT and WTO cases demonstrate that to prove a *de facto* violation of Article I, claimants must prove that a criterion that is neutral on its face is in fact able to be met only by products of a particular origin or origins, such that national origin determines the tariff treatment the product receives.[291] The simple fact is that MVTO and SRO duty remissions have been and are still applied to products from a number of sources, including notably the complaining parties. There is no incentive to source from any particular country.

6.51 Japan and the European Communities have attempted to use trade statistics to demonstrate that the products of some countries receive a disproportionate share of the duty-free benefit. The allegation of the European Communities is that an illegal advantage is granted *de facto* to US and Mexican products. The Japanese claim is that the MVTO and SROs grant a *de facto* advantage to Swedish and Belgian products without extending it to Japanese products. The fact that the complainants' allegations are so markedly different suggests that neither theory has any basis in fact.

6.52 First, the EC's allegation, even if true, cannot assist the European Communities in this case. This is because any advantage that may be accorded to the United States or Mexico, Canada's NAFTA free-trade partners, would in any event be exempted from Article I disciplines by virtue of Article XXIV of the GATT 1994. Indeed, should Canada decide to accord to the United States and Mexico treatment more favourable than it is required to do under the NAFTA, the European Communities can have no legitimate complaint. Canada is free to go beyond its commitments to its NAFTA partners, just as European Communities member States may extend to each other more favourable treatment than the Treaty of Rome requires.

6.53 In contrast to the European Communities, Japan recognised that it has no legitimate complaint under Article I as regards treatment of the United States and Mexico. Indeed, Japan correctly reached the conclusion that the real benefits from the MVTO and the SROs flow to products imported from countries *other* than the United States and Mexico. Japan provided data indicating that vehicles from Sweden, Belgium, the United Kingdom, Germany, South Korea and Japan enjoy duty-free access to the Canadian market.

6.54 Japan's Tables 5 and 6 purport to show that sales of imported Japanese automobiles are disadvantaged as compared to Belgian and Swedish automobiles. Quite apart from the factual errors in both tables, neither proves the Japanese theory.

---

290 Schedule to the MVTO 1998, *supra* note 10, Part 1, s. 2.

291 See, e.g., Panel Report on *EEC - Beef from Canada*, *supra* note 282, paras. 4.2-4.3

6.55 As Japan said, Japan's Table 5 is intended to demonstrate "that the Duty Waiver discriminates between imported automobiles that are imported duty free under the Duty Waiver [i.e. those from Sweden and Belgium] and their competing imported automobiles that are not imported duty free [i.e. those from Japan]". The Panel should note that Table 5 uses only 1996 data, and features a number of models that are either no longer produced or no longer available in Canada.[292] In addition, some models listed in the source document cited by Japan (Exhibit JPN-11) are not included in Table 5, presumably because if they had been, Japan would have had to acknowledge several competing Japanese-origin automobiles that enter duty free. [293]

6.56 Japan's Table 6 uses only 1997 data, although data for previous and subsequent years are available. An examination of the complete data leads to a result that stands in marked contrast to the theory espoused by the Japanese. In fact, the data demonstrate that Japanese-origin MVTO and SRO import sales in 1995, 1996 and 1998 were about equal to those from Sweden and Belgium.[294] In any event, it is far from clear that statistics like those found in Table 6 bear any relevance to the establishment of an MFN violation. Certainly Japan has not explained how they prove *de jure* or *de facto* discrimination in favour of or against goods of a particular national origin. But even if it is assumed, for the sake of argument, that they do show this, the comparison that Japan undertakes using these statistics is misguided. The proper comparison is not to compare the total duty-free import sales from one country to the total import sales from that country, and then compare all of the resulting percentages. In other words, it is not useful to compare total duty-free import sales from Sweden to total import sales from Sweden, and then compare the resulting percentage to another country's percentage.

6.57 A more instructive comparison would be to contrast the total duty-free import sales from one country against the total duty-free import sales from other countries. Take Sweden again as an example. Japan's evidence in Japan's Table 6 indicates that in 1997, there were 1,776 duty-free import sales of vehicles from Sweden. In the same year, there were 4,502 from Japan. In fact, of the six countries of origin shown, Japan is second only to Belgium, which had 244 more than Japan. According to Japan's evidence, of the roughly 15,000 total duty-free import sales in 1997, just under 31 per cent were of Japanese origin.

6.58 In the early 1990s, Japanese-origin vehicles enjoyed a commanding lead over the European models. *Figure 4* illustrates that Japanese-origin vehicles have had great success in the Canadian market and have benefited from the duty waiver that they now seek to challenge.[295] It also confirms the Japanese argument that Sweden and Belgium have fared well under the MVTO and SRO duty waiver regime. Finally,

---

[292] See Exhibit CDA-5 for the models listed in Table 5 that are no longer in production or sold in Canada.

[293] For 1996 there are: Suzuki Esteem (1291 vehicles), Chrysler Stealth (20 vehicles), Honda/Acura CL series (1226 vehicles), Toyota Avalon (2163 vehicles), General Motors Isuzu Trooper II (261 vehicles), Chrysler Summit Wagon (98 vehicles).

[294] Note that the source cited by Japan erroneously indicates that all Volvos imported into Canada are of Swedish origin (Exhibit JPN-37). However, Japan correctly states in its submission that the Volvos originate in Belgium and Sweden. Some Volvos from Belgium are shipped to Sweden for onward shipment to Canada.

[295] For supporting evidence, see Exhibit CDA-6.

it underlines that single year data are not representative and should not be relied upon to support theories of discrimination, since they tell only part of the story.

Canada's Figure 4

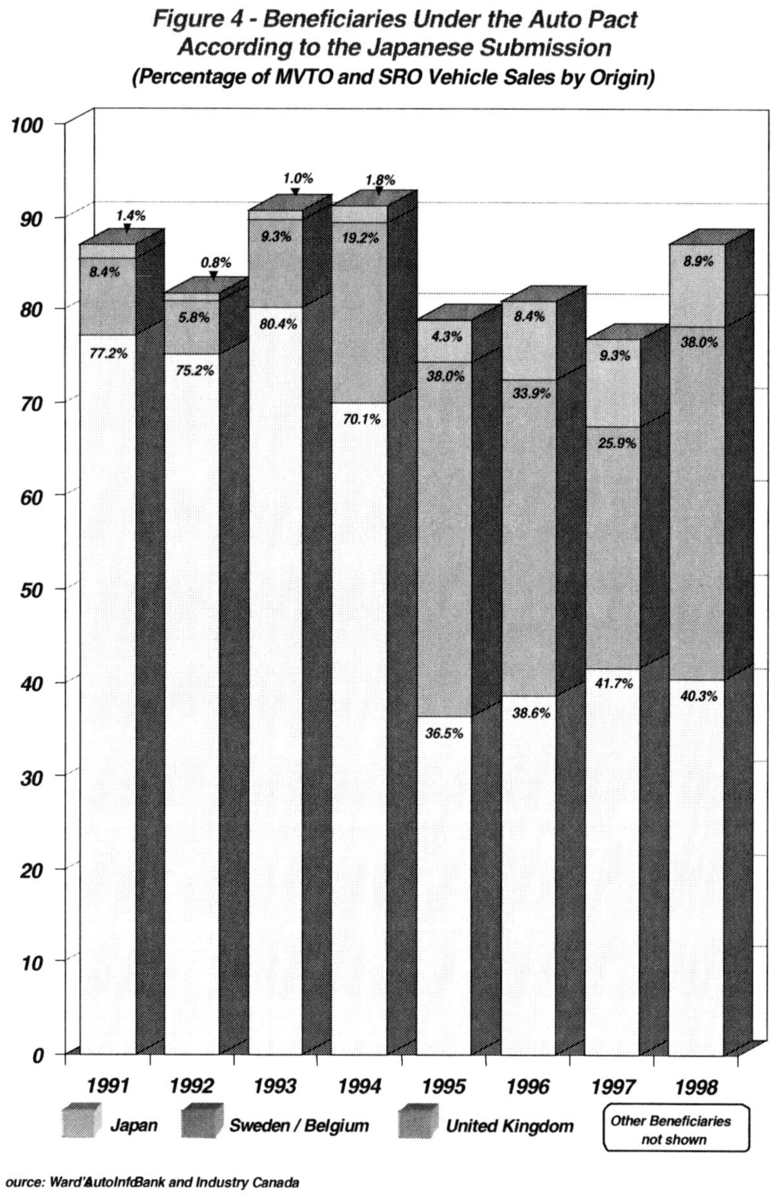

1.

6.59 In any event, the important question is not how many Japanese and European vehicles qualify for MFN treatment; it is whether they qualify under the same terms as the products of all other WTO Members. The short answer is that they do.

(iii) The complainants' contentions that the MVTO and SROs do not extend MFN treatment unconditionally are without merit

6.60 The European Communities argues that Canada's measures are discriminatory because the importers are almost exclusively subsidiaries of United States companies with large manufacturing interests in the United States and Mexico. But the European Communities has no legitimate complaint in this regard because, as mentioned above, Canada has formed a free-trade area with the United States and Mexico and advantages accorded by Canada to products of these countries are exempt under Article XXIV of GATT 1994.

6.61 Japan appears to argue that the mere fact that duty-free importers are likely to have preferred sources of supply is itself enough to mean that duty-free treatment has not been extended on an MFN basis. Where the identity of duty-free importers is limited, according to Japan, the discrimination is "strengthened". And Japan posits that a simple limitation on the identity of importers "explicitly narrows the origins from which motor vehicles can be imported under the Duty Waiver." The "regime" to which Japan refers has no such effect, whether explicitly, implicitly or otherwise, and Japan has no basis in law or in fact for making this claim. Indeed, measures such as import-licensing regimes, tariff-rate quotas and end-use requirements that provide advantages all have the effect of limiting the number of eligible importers and are nonetheless perfectly consistent with WTO obligations. There is no basis whatsoever under the GATT 1994 or any other WTO Agreement for a claim that the private commercial relationships of importers entitled to an advantage can, by themselves, form the basis for a violation of Article I:1 of GATT 1994.

6.62 Japan has raised the argument that the MVTO and SROs do not extend "unconditional" MFN treatment because manufacturers must meet certain conditions in order to qualify for duty-free importation. The argument is based on one passage in a single, unappealed, WTO case: *Indonesia - Certain Measures Affecting the Automobile Industry*.[296] GATT and WTO cases have made it abundantly clear that Article I prohibits treatment that discriminates between like products on the basis of nationality.[297] Thus, the proper test of whether the imposition of a condition or criterion infringes Article I is whether that condition or criterion is both (a) insufficient to afford a basis to distinguish the products as not "like", *and* (b) of a nature that results in discriminatory import treatment on the basis of the national origin of the product. The MVTO and the SROs contain no such conditions.

---

[296] Panel Report on *Indonesia - Autos, supra* note 270.

[297] Panel Report on *Belgian Family Allowances, supra* note 276; Panel Report on *EEC - Beef from Canada, supra* note 282.

(iv) In summary, the Japanese and EC claims under Article I must fail

6.63 Having failed to demonstrate that Canada has granted an illegal advantage to the products of any country or countries, the Japanese and EC claims under Article I:1 must fail. The MVTO and the SROs provide no advantages, *de jure* or de facto, to the products of any country or group of countries, although products of the United States and Mexico may enjoy more favourable treatment as a result of a free-trade agreement. The irony is that this challenge has been brought by the Members whose products are currently the principal beneficiaries of the MVTO and SROs.

6.64 As the facts before this Panel demonstrate, Canada's measures do not restrict benefits to any particular vehicle, and beneficiary manufacturers may import from anywhere in the world. Which Member's products benefit at any given time depends entirely on the commercial decisions made by the manufacturers. The tariff regime, however, is completely neutral as to nationality.

4. *Rebuttal Arguments by Japan*

6.65 **Japan** rebuts as follows:

6.66 With respect to Article I of the GATT 1994, the Government of Canada incorrectly states that "[i]n contrast to the EC, Japan recognized that it has no legitimate complaint under Article I as regards treatment of the United States and Mexico". The Government of Japan has expressly recognized the preferential aspects of the Duty Waiver in the context of Canada-US and Canada-Mexico trade and supports the position of the European Communities on this issue.[298]

6.67 As discussed in the above argumentation by the Government of Japan, the Duty Waiver is inconsistent with Article I:1 of the GATT 1994 because there is an advantage granted to certain motor vehicles originating in various countries, and that advantage is not granted immediately and unconditionally to "like" motor vehicles originating in the territories of certain WTO Members.

6.68 The Government of Canada does not expressly contest that: the Duty Waiver (made up of its constituent instruments) is a measure within the scope of Article I:1; there is an advantage that is granted within the meaning of Article I:1; the products at issue are "like"[299]; and Article I:1 prohibits measures involving de facto discrimination.

6.69 Instead, Canada relies on an incorrect interpretation and application of Article I:1. More specifically, the Government of Canada:

- narrows the scope of the legal obligation in Article I:1;

---

[298] *Supra* paras. 5.145- 5.147. See also *supra* paras. 5.189 - 5.191.

[299] Although the Government of Canada states that: "filing … lists of vehicle models ... does not by any measure constitute proof of any allegations…", Canada has not actually contested "likeness". Moreover, the evidence referred to by the Government of Canada in this statement does in fact constitute prima facie evidence that the automobiles imported by Auto Pact Manufacturers and Non-Auto Pact Manufacturers are "like". Canada has not produced any evidence to rebut this prima facie evidence. The evidence in question is referred to in Japan's Tables 4, 5 and 7 (as modified in Japan's rebuttal to Canada's response to certain arguments regarding the structure of the motor vehicle industry, Section V.B.3).

- incorrectly asserts that where imports originating in one or more WTO Members receive the advantage, this is somehow indicative of MFN-consistency;
- erroneously suggests that receipt of the advantage results from private commercial relationships not from the application of Government measures; and
- misstates the legal interpretation of unconditional MFN treatment.

6.70 The Government of Canada has suggested that the mere fact that the Government of Japan and the European Communities have decided to advance different examples of the discriminatory effect of the Duty Waiver somehow means that the Government of Japan's position regarding the violation of Article I:1 is not consistent with the EC's approach. To the contrary, the fact that there are so many different ways to illustrate the discriminatory effect of the Duty Waiver serves to highlight the inconsistency with Article I:1.

6.71 Like the European Communities, the Government of Japan is of the view that the *de facto* discrimination can also occur with respect to imports of motor vehicles from the United States and Mexico. The Duty Waiver is still applied to those motor vehicles that do not meet the strict NAFTA rules of origin. In the case of imports from Mexico, since the applicable NAFTA duty has not been yet reduced to zero, the Duty Waiver is still used even in cases where the applicable rule of origin is met.

(a) Correct Interpretation of Article I:1 of the GATT 1994

6.72 The Government of Canada consistently misstates the legal obligation in Article I:1.[300] This may be due, in part, to the fact that the Government of Canada does not appear to have followed the required approach for interpreting the provisions of WTO Agreements.[301] The relevant part of Article I:1 reads as follows:

> "Any advantage ... granted by any contracting party to any product originating in ... any other county shall be accorded immediately and unconditionally to the like product originating in ... the territories of all other contracting parties."

---

[300] From the outset of its defense under Article I:1, where it states that "Article I by its terms forbids discrimination *based on* origin of the product" (emphasis added, emphasis in original deleted), the Government of Canada misstates the obligation therein. Article I:1 does not expressly nor implicitly refer to discrimination *based on* origin of the product.

[301] In accordance with Article 3:2 of the DSU, as interpreted and affirmed many times by the Appellate Body (e.g., Appellate Body Report on *United States - Import Prohibition of Certain Shrimp and Shrimp Products*, adopted on 6 November 1998, WT/DS58/AB/R (hereinafter Appellate Body Report on *United States - Shrimp*)), DSR 1998:VII, 2755, Article I:1 must be interpreted by applying the "customary rules of interpretation of public international law". This requires an interpretation based on the ordinary meaning of the words in Article I:1, read in their context and the light of the object and purpose of the GATT 1994. As stated by the Appellate Body, the interpretative analysis: "... must begin with, and focus upon, the text of the particular provision to be interpreted. It is in the words constituting that provision, read in their context, that the object and purpose of the states parties to the treaty must first be sought."

6.73 Leaving aside for the moment the argument over the words "immediately and unconditionally", the ordinary meaning of the words of Article I:1 in context is clear. Products originating in the territory of a WTO Member must receive any advantage granted by an importing Member to like products of any other country. Thus, an advantage such as a duty waiver that is granted to products imported from one or more countries must be granted to like products originating from all WTO Members.[302] If that advantage is not granted, either expressly on the face of a measure or in effect as a result of the implementation and application of a measure, to the like products of each and every WTO Member[303], the MFN obligation is violated.

6.74 Therefore, Article I:1 prohibits Canada from granting the advantage (i.e. the waiving of the 6.1 per cent tariff) to products (e.g., Volvo and Saab automobiles) imported from certain countries (e.g., Sweden) while at the same time denying that advantage to "like" products (e.g., Honda Acura, Nissan Infiniti and Toyota Lexus automobiles) originating in the territory of all other WTO Members (e.g., Japan).[304]

6.75 The ordinary meaning of the words in context do not support Canada's assertion that WTO Members can discriminate between imported products of different origins as long as the "distinction" in treatment is based on criteria other than national origin or unless "like" products receive "differential" treatment because of their national origin. Canada has offered no textual or contextual justification for its interpretation. Nor does Canada identify any GATT 1947/WTO Panel or WTO Appellate Body Reports that stand for such a proposition.

6.76 If the purpose of Article I:1 is to further one of the fundamental objectives of the GATT 1994 (i.e. to eliminate "discriminatory treatment in international commerce"[305]), surely Article I:1 must apply to situations where a distinction in treatment has the effect of "like" products originating in the territory of a WTO Member not receiving the advantage at issue.[306]

6.77 As is clear from the WTO Panel's analysis in *EC - Bananas III*, if a measure "affects the competitive relationship" between products that originate in any country to the detriment of like products from a WTO Member, that measure violates Article

---

[302] As noted above, Canada does not contest that the waiver of the 6.1 per cent tariff is an advantage granted to products imported from one or more countries. As well, Canada does not contest that the products at issue are "like", and that some like products receive the advantage and others do not.

[303] "All other contracting parties" means each and every WTO Member. The Concise Oxford Dictionary of Current English defines "all" to mean "the entire number of " (Oxford: Clarendon Press, 1995, 33).

[304] It should be noted that, in previous years, certain Volvo products were also imported under the Duty Waiver from Belgium (see Japan's Table 5).

[305] Preamble to the GATT 1994, third para.

[306] The treatment as between imported products should be assured on the objective basis of their "likeness" as products. Otherwise, imported products could be exposed to a highly subjective and variable treatment according to extraneous factors, which could create instability and uncertainty in the conditions of competition as between like imported products. Although this substantive concern was originally raised in respect of GATT Article III:4 (by the Panel in its Report on *United States - Standards for Reformulated and Conventional Gasoline*, DSR 1996:I, 29, adopted as modified by the Appellate Body on 20 May 1996, WT/DS2/R & WT/DS4/R (hereinafter Panel Report on *US - Gasoline*)), DSR 1996:I, 3, and elaborated by the Appellate Body Report on *Japan - Alcoholic Beverages*, *supra* note 271, it seems equally applicable to the complementary non-discrimination provision set out in Article I:1.

I:1.[307] In short, a WTO Member may legitimately treat products differently only if the distinction in treatment does not adversely affect the competitive relationship of imported products originating in a WTO Member in relation to like imported products from other countries.

(b) The Fact that Imports Originating in One or More WTO Members Receive the Advantage is not Indicative of MFN-Consistency

6.78 The Government of Canada appears to argue that the Duty Waiver is consistent with the MFN obligation because it is available to motor vehicles imported from the territories of several WTO Members.

6.79 As is tacitly recognized, although not followed by the Government of Canada, the proper interpretation of Article I:1 mandates a focus on the *products* originating in the territories of Members that are not granted the same advantage. Thus, contrary to the Government of Canada's position, whether imports originating in the territory of one or more WTO Members receive the advantage is not determinative of whether that advantage is granted on a MFN basis.[308]

6.80 To the contrary, Article I:1 should be interpreted to ensure that where the products of *any* country receive an advantage, the like products of *all* WTO Members (not just those of some Members, even if it is a majority of Members) receive that advantage. To the extent that a measure operates so as to exclude certain products of even one WTO Member from receiving such an advantage, there is a violation of Article I:1 of the GATT 1994.

6.81 As demonstrated in the Government of Japan's arguments and confirmed by Canada's own evidence, there is such exclusion in the present case.[309] When imports into Canada of "like" automobiles are examined, certain models from certain countries (e.g., Volvo and Saab automobiles from Sweden) benefit from the Duty Waiver while this preferential treatment is not granted to like automobiles from Japan (e.g., Honda Acura, Nissan Infiniti and Toyota Lexus automobiles).

6.82 The Government of Canada further contends that because *some* automobiles originating in Japan have benefited from the Duty Waiver, the measures are consistent with the MFN obligation. This argument is wholly without merit. As affirmed by the WTO Panel in *EC - Bananas III*, Article I:1 does not permit balancing more favourable treatment in one instance against less favourable in another. Therefore, the

---

[307] Panel Reports on *EC - Bananas III, supra* note 269, para. 7.239. The Appellate Body did not modify this finding. See the Appellate Body Report on *EC - Bananas III, supra* note 49, para. 207, where the Appellate Body tacitly affirms the relevance of conditions of competition by noting that a "competitive advantage" give to certain suppliers over other suppliers (of WTO Members) constitutes an advantage not given to WTO Members contrary to Article I:1.

[308] Even under Canada's erroneous interpretation of Article I:1, there is still a clear breach of Article I:1. Restricting the advantage of the Duty Waiver to automobiles originating in particular countries means that there is a distinction in treatment based on national origin. Whether Canada actually "intended" such a distinction to arise is irrelevant. The relevant consideration is the practical effect of the Duty Waiver.

[309] Exhibit CDA-6.

fact that certain Japanese automobiles may receive the advantage under the Duty Waiver is irrelevant for the purpose of determining if Article I:1 has been violated.

6.83 Moreover, as Canada has conceded, Auto Pact Manufacturers only import and distribute automobiles from certain specific sources. The evidence makes it clear that the advantage of the Duty Waiver is restricted to particular imported automobiles originating from particular countries, and that the advantage is not granted to like automobiles originating in the territories of all WTO Members.

6.84 Therefore, in the light of the proper interpretation of Article I:1 (i.e. that products originating in a WTO Member must receive any advantage that is granted by an importing Member to like products of any other country), there is an obvious breach of Article I:1 on the facts of this case.

6.85 Based on the fact that not all motor vehicles from Japan are denied the advantage of the Duty Waiver, Canada claims that the *de facto* discrimination is not present, while insisting that Article I violation is established only when discrimination is based solely on the country of origin. As the Government of Japan stated in its reply to the Questions of the Panel, the Government of Japan is unaware of any Report recognizing such a narrow interpretation of Article I as is described by Canada, using the language "GATT and WTO cases demonstrate that to prove a *de facto* violation of Article I, claimants must prove that a criterion that is neutral on its face is in fact able to be met only by products of a particular origin or origins, *such that national origin determines the tariff treatment* the product receives." (*emphasis added*)

6.86 The Government of Japan is of the view that such a test has never been established in any panel or Appellate Body report, despite the Government of Canada's assertion. Indeed, the relevant authority directly contradicts Canada's position. In *EEC - Beef from Canada*, the Panel found an EC levy-free tariff rate quota for high-quality grain-fed beef to be inconsistent with Article I:1 of the GATT 1994 because only the US Department of Agriculture was able to issue the requisite certificate of authenticity. On its face, there was no discrimination based on origin.

6.87 However, there, as here, the effect was discriminatory and hence there was a violation of Article I:1. More broadly, accepting Canada's argument would limit the MFN obligation to *de jure* discrimination, for no distinction in treatment could be found to be based on the criterion of national origin unless that criterion was spelled out in the measure at issue. Such a result would be inconsistent with WTO and GATT authority, most recently the declaration by the Appellate Body in *EC - Bananas III* that Article I:1 applies to *de facto*, as well as *de jure* discrimination.[310]

6.88 To judge *de facto* discrimination, the Panel needs only to apply a test that has already been established by the *EEC - Beef from Canada* referred to above. With this test, the MVTO 1998 and SROs are on their face origin neutral as to motor vehicles imported duty free by Auto Pact Manufacturers. However, as demonstrated above by Japan and confirmed by Exhibit CDA-6, the Duty Waiver has "in effect" been granted largely to products originating in Sweden and Belgium and not granted to "like" products originating in the territory of Japan. As Canada admitted, Auto Pact Manufacturers have a strong tendency to import automobiles from certain specific

[310] Appellate Body Report on *EC - Bananas III*, *supra* note 49, para. 232.

sources in certain countries. Such tendency is based on the corporate relationship of Auto Pact Manufacturers with their affiliated Manufacturers.

6.89 The example shown for the Mitsubishi-Chrysler affiliation is a case in point. During the years 1971-1993 the affiliation was in place, Chrysler imported motor vehicles from Mitsubishi. When the relationship ended, so did the imports. Importation of automobiles from parent or affiliated companies makes commercial sense. Given such pattern of trade among manufacturers, the eligibility restriction of the Duty Waiver has the effect of restricting the manufacturers from which the Auto Pact Manufacturers import motor vehicles. As each manufacturer has its own country of establishment, restricting the exporting manufacturers would invariably restrict the countries from which the products originates. Thus, the MVTO 1998 and SROs have the effect of preventing duty-free access of like products from origins other than the particular countries. Therefore, they violate Article I of the GATT 1994. With regard to the data the Government of Japan presented for *de facto* discrimination, Canada claims that Japan's Table 6 is simply unreliable. The Government of Japan in fact has already submitted multi-year data to the same effect in Exhibit JPN-37 which enables the Government of Canada to verify the factual basis of this argument.

6.90 The Government of Canada uses *Figure 4* to paint a misleading picture of the Duty Waiver, disguising the fact that the majority of motor vehicles imported from Japan are not accorded the advantage of Duty Waiver. Canada attempts to emphasize the sheer volume of duty-free imports from Japan while ignoring the far greater volume of imports from US and Mexico. In order to rectify such a distortion, the Government of Japan created the new *Figure 4* presented below, on the same basis as that was used for the original but with the addition of volume of imports from the United States and Mexico.

Japan's New Figure 4

Correction of Figure 4 in the First Submission of the Government of Canada

Correct Figure 4 - Beneficiaries Under the Duty Waiver

(Percentage of MVTO 1998 and SROs Automobiles by Origin)

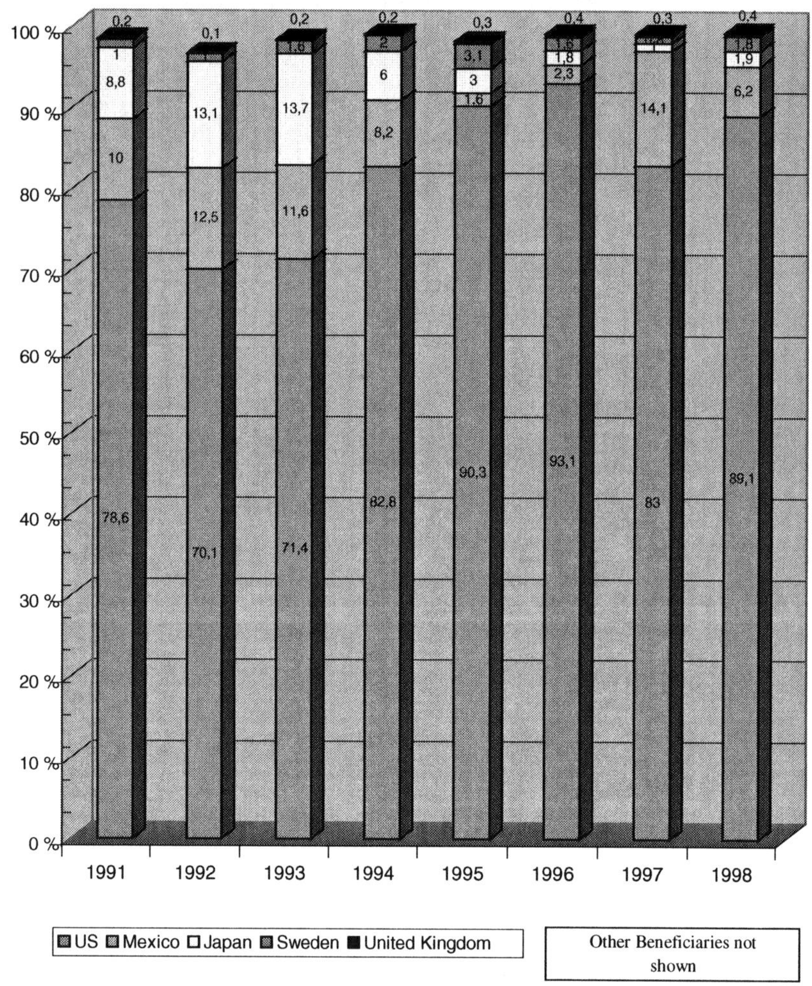

Source: Ward's Automotive Yearbook, Ward's Communications, Ward's Autoinfo Bank, Industry Canada, AMIA

6.91 Although the Government of Canada states that it prepared *Figure 4* based on information provided with Japan's initial argumentation, the data used by the Government of Canada are not the same as those included in Japan's Table 6 or Exhibit JPN-37. The Government of Japan uses the data in Exhibit CDA-6 for the purpose of comparison.

6.92 While the Government of Japan showed in its initial argumentation the duty-free percentage among the total import quantity by each origin, and thus has not needed to include the data on the imports from the United States and Mexico, the Government of Canada used *Figure 4* to show the percentage of duty-free imports by origin among the total imports of Canada. Nevertheless, if the Government of Canada intended to show the percentage by each origin among its total duty-free imports, it should have included figures regarding the imports from the United States and Mexico, because significant amounts of automobiles have been imported from those countries duty free under the MVTO 1998 and SROs and not under the NAFTA.

6.93 Thus, the Government of Canada uses Japan's Table 6 in an incorrect manner.

6.94 Finally, it should be noted that the figure for imports from Mexico in 1991-1993 includes the imports of commercial vehicles (since it is not possible to differentiate them based on the available statistics). Motor vehicles made in Mexico may not be imported duty free into Canada even if they satisfy the NAFTA origin rules because the applicable NAFTA duty has not yet been reduced to zero. Although the automobiles made in the United States and satisfying NAFTA origin rules may be imported duty free since 1998, the figure has been included, because the MVTO 1998 and SROs are measures totally unrelated to the NAFTA.

(c) Receipt of the Advantage Results from the Application of Government Measures not from Private Commercial Relationships

6.95 The Government of Canada also seems to suggest that there is no *de facto* discrimination because whether products receive the advantage under the Duty Waiver depends on private commercial relationships of importers. Such a suggestion seriously misconstrues the Government of Japan's position and arguments in this dispute. The Government of Canada even goes on to assert that "Which Member's products benefit at any given time depends entirely on the commercial decisions made by the manufacturers". In fact the converse is true — which Member's products are granted relief from the 6.1 per cent import tariff actually depends on the regime that the Government of Canada has created, implemented and applied.

6.96 As noted in the Government of Japan's response to Question 4 from the Panel in this dispute, the measures at issue (e.g., the MVTO 1998, the SROs, related statutory and administrative instruments, and the letters of undertaking) are clearly and indisputably governmental measures. It is these measures, collectively referred to as the "Duty Waiver", that are at the core of the Government of Japan's various claims of WTO Agreement violations.

6.97 To the extent that actions taken by private parties play any role in ensuring the discriminatory effects of the Duty Waiver, this is precisely the sort of activity that must be viewed as having "sufficient government involvement" to be deemed governmental.[311] What the Government of Canada has done in implementing the Duty Waiver, however, is to ensure that, given the economic realities of the global automotive industry, discrimination will occur.[312] That is, given the global integration of the automotive industry, each qualified manufacturer imports motor vehicles from a limited number of sources.

6.98 This is confirmed by the undisputed evidence presented by the Government of Japan. Each qualified manufacturer in fact imports motor vehicles only from countries where its parent company, or a company with which it has a capital relationship, has production facilities. "Like" motor vehicles manufactured around the world by their competitors have been prevented from enjoying any possibility of ever qualifying for the Duty Waiver, and will always be excluded from receiving that advantage.

5. *Rebuttal Arguments by the European Communities*

(a) Canada's Interpretation of the Notion of *De Facto* Violation is Unduly Restrictive

6.99 The **European Communities** rebuts as follows:

6.100 Canada concedes that GATT Article I:1 may be applied also to *de facto* violations. Nevertheless, it puts forward an extremely narrow test:

> "GATT and WTO cases demonstrate that to prove a *de facto* violation of Article I, claimants must prove that a criterion that is neutral on its face is in fact able to be met only by products of a particular origin or origins, such that national origin determines the tariff treatment the product receives."

6.101 The test advanced by Canada is unduly restrictive and would make it virtually impossible to prove the existence of *de facto* discrimination. In order to establish a *de facto* violation of GATT Article I:1 it is not necessary to show that "only" imports of a certain origin may benefit from the advantage concerned. Instead, it may be sufficient to show that imports of a certain origin benefit *disproportionately* from that advantage.

6.102 Previous GATT and WTO cases do not support Canada's very narrow interpretation of the notion of *de facto* discrimination. On this point, the European Communities refers the Panel to its response to Question 1 from the Panel.

---

[311] Panel Report on *Japan - Film*, *supra* note 93, para. 10.56.

[312] At a minimum, as Canada acknowledges, the regime permits automobile manufacturers that are direct competitors of Japanese and other national-origin manufacturers to ensure that certain automobiles from certain countries will obtain duty free access into Canada.

(b) The European Communities Has Shown that *De Facto* the Tariff Exemption Provides an Advantage to Imports Originating in the United States and Canada

6.103 The European Communities has shown that the main beneficiaries of the Tariff Exemption are the Canadian subsidiaries of the US Big Three, all of which have large manufacturing facilities in the United States and Mexico. As a result, the Tariff Exemption provides an advantage to imports from those two countries over imports from those countries where the non-beneficiaries of the Tariff Exemption have their main manufacturing facilities.

6.104 The above is demonstrated by the statistics summarised in the EC's Tables 1 and 2 above, which show that the share of US and Mexican imports under the Tariff Exemption (97 per cent in 1997) is larger than their share of total imports (80 per cent in the same year).

6.105 Canada has failed to refute that evidence. Indeed, Canada has not even addressed it in its arguments[313]. During the first meeting with the Panel, the European Communities asked Canada to complete the import data shown in Canada's *Figure 4* with data for imports under the Tariff Exemption from the United States and Mexico. Canada has ignored that request[314]. It is submitted that the Panel should draw appropriate inferences from Canada's unjustified lack of response.

(c) The Advantage Accorded to Automobiles from the United States and Mexico Cannot Be Exempted by GATT Article XXIV

6.106 Canada contends that any advantages granted to Mexico and the United States are "exempted" from Article I by virtue of Article XXIV of GATT.

6.107 That claim, however, is refuted by the very wording of Article XXIV:5, which reads in relevant part as follows:

> "Accordingly, the provisions of this Agreement shall not prevent, the formation of ... a free-trade area ... or the adoption of an interim agreement necessary for the formation of ... a free-trade area"

6.108 There is currently no "free-trade area" between Mexico and Canada. Trade between those two countries, including trade in automotive products, is still subject to customs duties. In the absence of a "free-trade area", the exception in Article XXIV may apply only with respect to the "adoption of an interim agreement necessary for the formation of a free-trade area".

6.109 Even assuming that NAFTA qualified as such an agreement (something which the Panel does not need to decide), the Tariff Exemption is neither part of, nor

---

313 Canada has limited itself to making an unsupported assertion to the effect that the European Communities has not proved its claim of de facto violation of GATT Article I. Ironically, in the same statement, Canada acknowledges the relevance of the type of statistical data supplied by the European Communities.

314 Canada's response to Question 4 from the EC.

required by NAFTA[315]. NAFTA permits, but does not oblige Canada to maintain the Tariff Exemption, which constitutes a derogation from generally applicable NAFTA rules. The decision to maintain the Tariff Exemption is a unilateral decision of Canada, except to the extent that the Tariff Exemption implements the provisions of the Auto Pact[316]. The Auto Pact, however, lacks the trade coverage required by Article XXIV:8(b).

6.110 In response to a question from the Panel, Canada argues that the Tariff Exemption does not constitute a "derogation" from NAFTA[317]. The truth, however, is that but for the provisions contained in paragraphs 1 and 2 of Appendix 300-A.1 of NAFTA[318], which expressly authorise (but do not require) Canada to "maintain" the Tariff Exemption, the continued application by Canada of that measure would be a flagrant violation of NAFTA[319].

6.111 Canada further argues that the parties to an interim free-trade agreement often proceed to the elimination of import duties faster than required by the agreement[320]. That analogy, however, is clearly inapt. In accordance with GATT Article XXIV, the parties to an interim free-trade agreements are "required" to eliminate customs duties at the end of a transitional period. In contrast, NAFTA does not "require" Canada to continue to apply the Tariff Exemption either now or at any time in the future.

6.112 Most transitional periods provided for in NAFTA with respect to trade between Canada and the United States seem to have already expired. It may thus be arguable that a "free-trade area" has been "formed" between Canada and the Unites States. Once again, however, the Panel does not need to reach that issue. Even assuming that a "free-trade area" in accordance with Article XXIV existed between the United States and Canada, the measures in dispute would not be exempted by the terms of that provision.

6.113 Article XXIV:5 does not provide a legal basis for adopting all sorts of measures otherwise incompatible with Article I. Article XXIV:5 merely authorises the "formation of a free-trade area", a notion which is defined in Article XXIV:8 (b). Consequently, only those measures that are inherent in that objective can be exempted by Article XXIV.

6.114 The Tariff Exemption does not fall within that category of measures. It is not necessary for the "formation of a free-trade area". NAFTA already provides for the

[315] Canada admits implicitly in its First Submission that the Auto Pact is neither part, nor required by NAFTA when it argues that NAFTA is "of no relevance to this dispute" and that it may "treat its NAFTA partners better than the Agreement requires it to do".

[316] The Auto Pact only requires Canada to grant duty free treatment to imports from the United States.

[317] Canada's response to Question 8 from the Panel.

[318] Exhibit EC-13.

[319] Annex 300-A, para. 1 of NAFTA (Exhibit EC-13) makes it clear that paras. 1 and 2 of Appendix 300-A.1 are exceptions to the generally applicable NAFTA rules contained in that Annex. It reads as follows: "Each Party shall accord to all existing producers of vehicles in its territory treatment no less favourable than it accords to any new producers of vehicles in its territory under the measures referred to in this Annex, except that this obligation shall not be construed to apply to any differences in treatment specifically provided for in the Appendices in this Annex".

[320] Canada's response to Question 8 from the Panel.

elimination of duties on imports into Canada of motor vehicles originating in Mexico and the United States, as required by Article XXIV:8 (b).

6.115 Furthermore, the Tariff Exemption does not contribute to achieving a greater degree of trade liberalisation, but rather the opposite. The only purpose of the Tariff Exemption is to provide an advantage to the US Big Three, not only *vis-à-vis* foreign manufacturers of motor vehicles, but also *vis-à-vis* the other manufacturers established in the United States[321]. It distorts competition between those manufacturers and, as a result, trade between Canada and the United States, thereby preventing NAFTA from displaying all its potential trade-creating effects.

6.116 Moreover, as noted in one of the Panel's questions[322], the CVA and ratio requirements attached to the Tariff Exemption are "restrictive regulations of commerce" in the meaning of GATT Article XXIV:8 (b). In fact, those requirements afford "less favourable treatment" not only to goods imported from non-members of NAFTA, but also to goods imported from the United States and Mexico.

6.117 For example, the CVA requirements create an incentive to use Canadian parts and materials for the assembly of motor vehicles in Canada instead of like products imported from the United States and Mexico. Those restrictions have not become "moot"[323] simply because the beneficiaries can now import motor vehicles duty free from the United States under NAFTA[324]. For the beneficiaries, it is more advantageous to import motor vehicles under the Tariff Exemption than under NAFTA. As a result, the Tariff Exemption continues to afford less favourable treatment to parts and materials for the assembly of motor vehicles imported from the United States and Mexico.

6.118 Thus, in sum, far from "going beyond NAFTA" (as Canada has asserted), the measures in dispute represent an obstacle to the full achievement of the objectives of NAFTA and, consequently, to the formation of a free-trade area as defined in Article XXIV:8 (b).

6.119 To conclude, it is worth noting that until recently the United States did not share Canada's view that the Auto Pact benefits are exempted by Article XXIV. In fact, as late as 1996 the United States deemed necessary to request a renewal of the

[321] In response to a question from the Panel, Canada claims that the Tariff Exemption does not discriminate against other US manufacturers because the vehicles produced in the United States by those manufacturers may also qualify for duty free treatment under NAFTA (Canada's response to Question 10 from the Panel). However, as discussed in the EC's argumentation above, for the Big Three it is more advantageous to import motor vehicles into Canada under the Tariff Exemption than under NAFTA because they can avoid the application of the NAFTA origin rules. Canada also suggests that the Big Three may import under the Tariff Exemption vehicles produced by other manufacturers in the United States. But, as argued by Canada itself in the context of Article II of GATS, in practice the Big Three are unlikely to import and distribute in Canada motor vehicles produced by other US manufacturers that have their own distribution network in Canada.

[322] Question 11 from the Panel.

[323] Canada's response to Question 11 from the Panel.

[324] As mentioned above, imports from Mexico under NAFTA are still subject to customs duties.

1965 waiver for the Auto Pact, notwithstanding the conclusion in the meantime of CUSFTA and NAFTA[325].

6. *Response by Canada to the Complainants' Rebuttals*

6.120 **Canada** responds as follows:

6.121 The Japanese and EC claims regarding a violation of Article I:1 must fail because they find no support in the facts before the Panel and they do not accord with previous panel and Appellate Body interpretations of the provision.

6.122 Canada maintains that the measures at issue do not violate Article I:1. They are not discriminatory, either *de jure*, which both complainants concede, or *de facto*, because the facts and the law confirm otherwise. The Canadian measures, the MVTO 1998 and the various SROs, permit certain automotive producers to import vehicles duty free from any WTO Member country, provided that the producers meet eligibility criteria to qualify as a Canadian manufacturer. The measures distinguish between manufacturers of vehicles, but make no distinctions among that favour vehicles of any country over those of any other country. There is no advantage that has been granted to the products originating in one country that is not accorded immediately and unconditionally to the like products originating in any other WTO Member country. Hence the measures do not violate Article I:1 of the GATT 1994.

6.123 If it is true, as suggested by Japan, that global integration of the automobile industry is responsible for automotive trade patterns, this does not render the Canadian measures a violation of Article I:1 where no governmental measures limit commercial choices as to origin of goods. No GATT/WTO cases support the proposition that a GATT Article I:1 violation can be based solely on private commercial relationships. If it is true, as suggested by the European Communities, that the majority of vehicles entering Canada duty free are manufactured in the United States or Mexico, this is not *ipso facto* proof of discrimination. Nor would it constitute a violation of Article I:1 of the GATT because Article XXIV of the GATT provides for an exception to MFN obligations for members of free-trade areas, such as the North American Free Trade Area.

(a) The Japanese and EC Interpretations of Article I:1 Are Not Supported by the Facts

6.124 Both complaining parties concede that there is no *de jure* violation of Article I:1 of the GATT. Therefore, the Panel's inquiry regarding Article I relates only to alleged *de facto* violations. The complaining parties' positions differ markedly as to the nature of the *de facto* violation.

6.125 Japan argues that the Canadian measures have the effect of discriminating against Japanese automobiles in favour of automobiles from Belgium and Sweden.[326] Japan also suggests that the Canadian measures are discriminatory and a violation of GATT Article I:1 because they have the effect of limiting imports to the WTO Mem-

[325] The evasive answer given by the United States to a question raised by the European Communities in this connection reveals the US embarrassment before this glaring inconsistency. See US response to Question 3 from the EC, and Section VIII - Third-Party Arguments.

[326] Japan's response to Question 1 from the Panel.

bers that are favoured by certain commercial relationships formed as a result of the global integration of the automotive industry.[327]

6.126 Canada demonstrated above in its response to the claims that the facts do not support Japan's contentions regarding favoured treatment for vehicles of Belgium and Sweden. Canada's *Figure 4* demonstrates that the single year data cited by Japan[328] are of limited value and that when data for the last several years are examined, the evidence is that Japanese-origin vehicles have benefited from the duty-free treatment provided for in Canada's measures to a much greater extent than have vehicles of Belgium, Sweden and several other WTO Member countries. In fact, products from Japan have accounted for a larger share of duty-free import sales in the Canadian market than have products from Sweden and Belgium every year since 1990 except 1995, when Japanese duty-free imports accounted for 1.5 per cent less sales than those of Belgium and Sweden combined.[329]

6.127 Japan's theory of discrimination based on the global integration of the automotive industry is difficult to reconcile with its complaint regarding favouritism toward Belgium and Sweden. But in any event, the argument cannot be sustained. If manufacturers determine the source of vehicle imports on the basis of where they have business affiliations, this would be due entirely to the private business decisions of manufacturers. The Canadian measures have no bearing on these decisions. Discrimination is plainly absent. And in any event, the number of countries implicated in these commercial relationships is quite significant. DaimlerChrysler AG has affiliations in Austria, China, Egypt, India, Japan, Thailand, and the United States. Ford Motor Company has affiliations in Belarus, China, India, Japan, Malaysia, Portugal, Taiwan, South Africa, Sweden, Vietnam and the United Kingdom. And General Motors Corporation has affiliations in Argentina, Australia, China, Ecuador, France, Germany, India, Indonesia, Japan, Kenya, Nigeria, Russia, South Africa, Sweden and the United Kingdom. These relationships involve 24 separate countries.[330]

6.128 It is telling that Japan and the European Communities do not agree on the alleged discriminatory aspects of the Canadian measures. While Japan claims that the measures favour EC countries, the European Communities claims that they favour the United States and Mexico. This suggests that there is no discrimination at all, and like the Japanese claim, the EC's claim of Article I:1 violation must also fail.

6.129 The EC's position has evolved since the commencement of these proceedings. Its most recent elaboration of its position, contained in the response to Question 2 posed by the Panel, indicates that the European Communities:

> "is not arguing that the Tariff Exemption discriminates *de facto* in favour of US and Mexican imports simply because those imports account currently for the majority of imports into Canada ... The EC's complaint is that reserving the Tariff Exemption to the Big US Three has the consequence that the share of US and Mexican imports into

[327] Japan's argumentation and Japan's response to Question 1 from the Panel.

[328] Japan's Table 6.

[329] See also Exhibit CDA-6.

[330] See "Global Joint Ventures and Affiliations for 1999," *Automotive Industries* (AI) website http://www.ai-online.com/stats/globalventure.htm (Exhibit CDA-12). Note that Belarus, China, Russia, Taiwan [Chinese Taipei] and Vietnam are in the process of acceding to the WTO.

> Canada is even larger than it would be if the Tariff Exemption was [sic] available to all importers ... [T]his is demonstrated by the fact that the share of the US and Mexican imports under the Tariff Exemption (97% in 1997) is larger than their share of total imports (80% in the same year).[331]

6.130 How this is evidence of discrimination by Canada is not explained. The European Communities advances this proposition with such assurance as if to suggest that it is a statement of the obvious. But the European Communities offers no analysis for its conclusion. The EC's position may be rejected on this basis alone.

6.131 Had the European Communities provided an objective analysis, it would have demonstrated that in the absence of the measures at issue, all NAFTA-qualifying vehicles would still enter Canada duty free[332] and all non-NAFTA vehicles would enter subject to Canada's MFN duty. The absence of the measures would make no difference to the NAFTA-qualifying vehicles, but it would adversely affect imports from the complaining parties. Indeed, it is likely that in the absence of the measures, the percentage of imports from the United States and Mexico would be even greater than it is with the measures in effect.

6.132 In any event, even if the European Communities were able to substantiate its allegation of discrimination based on a preponderance of automotive trade with the United States and Mexico, this could not result in a finding of a violation of Article I:1. Canada, the United States and Mexico have formed a free-trade area and, therefore, any advantage that may be accorded by Canada to its free-trade partners is exempt from Article I:1 obligations by virtue of Article XXIV of the GATT.

6.133 The European Communities raised several arguments regarding Article XXIV. First, it argues that there is no free-trade area between Mexico and Canada because Canada-Mexico trade is still subject to customs duties and that Article XXIV is unavailable to Canada. The European Communities also suggests that it is "arguable" that a free-trade area has been formed between Canada and the United States, but that Article XXIV would still provide no assistance, though no explanation is offered for this conclusion. The Panel need waste no time on these allegations because they have no basis in law. Article XXIV status is not premised on the total elimination of all duties between the parties to a free-trade agreement. And in any event, the European Communities itself said the Panel does not need to make a determination on the status of the NAFTA.

6.134 Finally, the European Communities was in error when it suggested that the measures in dispute are not part of the NAFTA, but rather derogation therefrom. The NAFTA specifically provides for the measures to continue. Paragraph 1 of NAFTA Appendix 300-A.1 incorporates Article 1001, as well as Articles 1002(1) and (4) of the Canada-United States Free Trade Agreement (CUSFTA) "as they refer to Annex 1002.1, Part One." CUSFTA Annex 1002.1, Part One is the list of recipients exempted from the restrictions imposed by CUSFTA Articles 1002(1) and (4). The

[331] EC's response to Question 2 from the Panel.

[332] With the exception of passenger cars and heavy trucks and buses from Mexico, which are subject to nominal duties; see Canada's argumentation above.

specific reference in NAFTA Appendix 300-A.1 to Annex 1002.1, Part One has the effect of bringing the measures within the NAFTA.[333]

(b) The Japanese and EC Interpretations of Article I:1 Find no Support in the Law

6.135 The complainants concede there is no *de jure* violation with regard to Article I:1. Their claims relate only to *de facto* violations.

6.136 Japan said that "the eligibility restriction *de facto* excludes certain motor vehicles from certain countries from benefiting from the Duty Waiver." It also explains its *de facto* claim in its response to Question 1 of the Panel:

> "the Duty Waiver has been 'in effect' granted largely to products originating in Sweden and Belgium and not so granted to 'like' products originating in the territory of Japan ... MVTO and SROs have the effect of preventing duty-free access of like products from other origins than the particular countries [where Auto Pact manufacturers have business relationships] and thus they constitute a violation of Article I of GATT 1994."[334]

6.137 The European Communities did not elaborate on its *de facto* claim, except in response to Question 1 from the Panel. The European Communities suggests that the test of *de facto* discrimination under Article I:1 of the GATT is "whether the disputed measure results in an allocation of imports among supplying Members which is different from that that would have prevailed in the absence of that measure."[335]

6.138 A survey of the panel and Appellate Body reports that deal with Article I:1 will demonstrate that the theories espoused by Japan and the European Communities regarding the interpretation to be given to Article I:1 find no support in the jurisprudence. It will also demonstrate that the cases support Canada's position regarding the test for *de facto* discrimination, i.e. that the measures in question must result in like products of certain countries being favoured over like products of others.

6.139 In *Belgian Family Allowances*,[336] Norway and Denmark complained about the application by Belgium of its levy of a 7.5 per cent charge on foreign goods purchased by public bodies. Norway and Denmark alleged that Belgium granted an exemption from the levy when these goods originated in a country whose system of family allowances met specific requirements. The Panel found that the Belgian legislation "introduced a discrimination between countries having a given system of family allowances and those which had a different system or no system at all, and made the granting of the exemption dependent on certain conditions."[337] The Panel concluded that "the exemption would have to be granted unconditionally to all other contracting parties"[338] and that "[t]he consistency or otherwise of the system of fam-

333 These provisions are found in Exhibits EC-12 and EC-13.

334 Japan's response to Question 1 from the Panel.

335 Ibid., para. 1.

336 Panel Report on *Belgian Family Allowances, supra* note 276.

337 Ibid., para. 3.

338 Ibid.

ily allowances in force in the territory of a given contracting party with the requirements of the Belgian law would be irrelevant in this respect."[339]

6.140 There is no similarity between the measures contested in that case and those challenged before this Panel. Unlike the Belgian measures that granted exemptions depending upon where the goods originated and what system of family allowances was in place in the country of origin, the Canadian measures impose no conditions that limit the country of origin. Duty-free treatment is accorded based on the activities of the manufacturer, not on the origin of the products being imported, or on any internal systems or measures that may exist in the country of origin. Thus, *Belgian Family Allowances* supports Canada's position regarding what constitutes *de facto* discrimination.

6.141 *European Economic Community - Imports of Beef from Canada*[340] is often cited as the leading case on *de facto* discrimination under Article I:1 of the GATT. Canada cited this case above in support of its test for *de facto* discrimination, namely that it is necessary to "prove that a criterion that is neutral on its face is in fact able to be met only by products of a particular origin, such that national origin determines the tariff treatment the product receives." In that case, the Panel found *de facto* discrimination contrary to Article I:1 because importation of beef was possible *only* upon certification, and certification was possible *only* from a US agency that was mandated to certify *only* US products. The practical result, or *de facto* effect, was that *only* products from the United States could enter the EEC duty free; products from every other Member were necessarily dutiable. The discrimination is plain: the products of one country were favoured over like products of other countries. The Canadian measures at issue stand in marked contrast to those contested in *EEC - Beef from Canada*. In the case before this Panel, importation is based on commercial decisions made by manufacturers. Products need not be certified to enter duty free. They do not have to meet any tests whatsoever. All vehicles may enter Canada duty free from anywhere in the world, without distinction, provided that they are imported by eligible manufacturers. Indeed, the facts before this Panel demonstrate that vehicles entering Canada duty free come from a large number of countries.[341]

6.142 *Spain - Tariff Treatment of Unroasted Coffee*[342] deals primarily with the issue of "like products", but it is also instructive regarding the interpretation to be give to *de facto* discrimination under Article I:1. In that case Brazil complained of *de facto* discrimination because Spain, which had been applying a single tariff rate to all unroasted coffee, created a new tariff regime in which certain types of coffee were subject to much higher duties than other types. Brazil exported almost exclusively types subject to the higher duties while other Latin American countries exported almost exclusively types subject to lower duties. Spain said it instituted the new tariffs without regard for which countries produced mild coffee and which produced other types. The Panel found, however, that the different types of coffee under considera-

---

[339] Ibid. It is interesting to note that the Belgian measures in question limited the tax exemption to purchases only by Belgian public bodies, a condition that was not found inconsistent with Article I:1.

[340] Panel Report on *EEC - Beef from Canada, supra* note 282.

[341] See Canada's *Figure 4* and Exhibit CDA-6.

[342] Panel Report on *Spain - Unroasted Coffee, supra* note 282.

tion were like products and that the different rates of duty resulted in *de facto* discrimination against products of Brazil. As in the case of *Belgian Family Allowances*, the condition or criterion at issue (in this case the type of coffee) did not make the products unlike but did cause discrimination by national origin.[343]

6.143 Both Japan and the European Communities rely on *EC - Bananas III*,[344] although for different reasons, but neither can legitimately claim support for their position from that case either. Japan relies on *EC - Bananas III* as it refers to *EEC - Beef from Canada* discussed earlier.[345] Canada has demonstrated that *EEC - Beef from Canada* supports Canada's position regarding *de facto* discrimination, not the complainants'. The EC's Article I analysis as set out in its response to the Panel's Question 1 relies on paragraphs 7.332-334 and 7.350-351 of *EC - Bananas III*.[346] But its reliance on those findings is inapt. Those paragraphs consider whether certain EC measures are inconsistent with the GATS. The European Communities had introduced a licensing allocation system that favoured operators of predominantly EC (or ACP) nationality, while disfavouring others. The question the *EC - Bananas III* panel (and subsequently the Appellate Body) examined was whether "formally identical" treatment of service suppliers nevertheless resulted in less favourable conditions of competition for like service suppliers of other countries. That test for *de facto* violation of the MFN obligation under the GATS is not found in GATT Article I. GATS Article XVII is framed in terms of "no less favourable treatment," which leads to a comparison of the competitive opportunities open to service suppliers of various nationalities. Article I:1 of the GATT 1994 refers to granting an "advantage, favour, privilege or immunity" immediately and unconditionally to the like products of all WTO Members. The latter has nothing to do with "competitive opportunities," which entails a more far-reaching enquiry. Under the Auto Pact, Canada agreed to permit qualifying manufacturers to import vehicles and other automotive products duty free from the United States. Canada fulfilled its obligations under GATT Article I:1 by extending this "advantage" to products originating from all WTO Members.

6.144 Although the European Communities relies on *EC - Bananas III* to support its Article I:1 *de facto* discrimination theory, it does not refer to the section of that Report that deals specifically with Article I:1. Presumably, this is because the Appellate

---

[343] Panel Report on *Japan - SPF Lumber, supra* note 282, paras. 5.7, 5.14 and 6.1, followed a similar analysis, but came to a different result than the Panel Report on *Spain - Unroasted Coffee, supra* note 282. In the *Japan - SPF Lumber* case, Canada complained that Japan's tariff on certain lumber cut to specified dimensions ("dimension lumber") violated Article I:1 because Canadian exports of SPF dimension lumber to Japan were subject to a customs duty of eight per cent, whereas other comparable types of dimension lumber enjoyed the advantage of a zero tariff duty. Canada claimed it had been subject to *de facto* discrimination because Japan had arranged its tariff classification in such a way that a considerable part of Canadian exports of SPF dimension lumber was subject to the eight per cent duty, whereas comparable types of dimension lumber from the United States were imported duty free. The Panel concluded that reliance by Canada on the concept of dimension lumber was not an appropriate basis for establishing likeness of products under Article I:1, and therefore that there was no Article I:1 violation.

[344] Panel Reports on *EC - Bananas III, supra* note 269, and Appellate Body Report on *EC - Bananas III, supra* note 49.

[345] Japan's response to Question 1 from the Panel.

[346] EC's response to Question 1 from the Panel.

Body analysis in that section supports the Canadian approach to *de facto* discrimination regarding differentiation among like products originating from different Members. It provides no support for the theory advanced by the European Communities.[347]

6.145 Moreover, even if the language and meaning of Article I of the GATT were substantially identical to that of Article II of the GATS, the legal analysis of the *EC - Bananas III* panel would not support the EC position in this dispute. In *EC - Bananas III*, the European Communities had in effect taken licences that were essential to conduct a services business away from one group of service suppliers predominantly owned or controlled by nationals of certain WTO Members. The European Communities re-allocated them by criteria that favoured another group of suppliers that were predominantly nationals of the European Communities or certain other countries. There was evidence that the European Communities intended to achieve this re-allocation among service suppliers. No comparable situation is present here, since, as previously noted, the Canadian measures do not discriminate by origin of vehicles, nor do they establish conditions that would constrain or favour particular origins. Even the commercial choices of Canadian importers demonstrate no preference for products of particular countries outside of the North American free-trade area.

6.146 The Panel on *Indonesia - Autos*[348] also considered Article I:1. The panel quite properly found that Indonesia's measures were *de facto* violations of Article I:1. Korean products were in fact capable of meeting the conditions imposed by Indonesia. All three Indonesian conditions were nominally neutral on their face, but they were inconsistent with Article I:1 because in practice they determined the national origin of the products that could be imported duty free. The panel concluded that the measures, in their application, amounted to differential treatment on the basis of national origin. The difference between the case before this Panel and *Indonesia - Autos* is manifest. In the latter, conditions imposed by the government meant that only Korean cars qualified for special treatment. None of the Canadian measures challenged impose conditions that in law or in practice determine the national origin of imported products. This is evident in the import statistics demonstrating that imports are sourced based on commercial decisions of manufacturers and not based on the national origin of the products.

6.147 The *Indonesia - Autos* case is also of interest for its finding on the relevance of commercial relationships as they impact on the application of ostensibly neutral measures. In *Indonesia - Autos*, the panel considered whether a particular company "had made a deal with [the] exporting company to produce [the] National Car."[349] The existence of the commercial relationship was relevant to the rate of duty applied. However, the "deal" was enshrined in a legal instrument which, by law, defined a particular Korean vehicle as the only vehicle entitled to the duty benefits.[350] In the case before this Panel, commercial relationships may govern the choices companies

347 Appellate Body Report on *EC - Bananas III, supra* note 49, paras. 205-207.
348 Panel Report on *Indonesia - Autos, supra* note 270.
349 Ibid., para. 14.145.
350 Ibid.

make to source imports from particular companies. But these relationships are not enshrined in any Canadian law.

6.148 Finally, it is worth examining *Japan - Film*[351] because the European Communities seeks to use that case to support its test of *de facto* discrimination. The *Japan - Film* panel considered a complaint by the United States of non-violation nullification or impairment under Article XXIII:1(b), and specifically whether measures had had a disparate impact on imported products in their application, thereby upsetting competitive conditions of market access for imported film and paper.

6.149 As it did with the *EC - Bananas III* case, the European Communities seeks to import into Article I a test used for another provision - in this circumstance it is borrowing jurisprudence relating to Article XXIII:1(b). The legal merit of making this analogy is questionable. A claim of non-violation nullification or impairment is necessarily based on non-violation. It is inappropriate, therefore, to use the rationale of *Japan - Film* in support of a theory on violation of Article I:1.

6.150 Japan has raised one further argument under Article I of the GATT. Japan has claimed that the limitation on which manufacturers may qualify to import duty free, together with the CVA and ratio requirements, should be considered to violate the "immediately and unconditionally" clause of Article I. The European Communities has not joined in this claim, but rather has articulated a diametrically opposite view. The European Communities states in its response to Question 3 of the Panel that "the European Communities is not arguing that any condition unrelated to the imported goods is as such contrary to the obligation to provide most favoured national (sic) treatment 'unconditionally' laid down in GATT Article I:1."[352] In any event, Canada has explained in its response to Question 5 of the Panel and in previous arguments that Japan's allegations are based on a misinterpretation of the "immediately and unconditionally" clause.[353]

6.151 Contrary to the Japanese claim and to the *dicta* in the *Indonesia - Autos* Panel Report on which Japan appears to base its claim, there is no prohibition in Article I of origin-neutral terms and conditions on importation that apply to importers as opposed to the products being imported. Were it otherwise, end-use tariff provisions or programmes such as foreign trade zones or duty drawbacks would be inconsistent with Article I because like products attract different rates of duty, even though there is no discrimination based on origin of the product.

6.152 In summary, this review of the relevant panel and Appellate Body reports demonstrates that the jurisprudence, like the evidence, does not support either the Japanese or EC allegations under Article I:1 of the GATT 1994. The complainants cannot meet their burden of proof because the Canadian measures at issue do not discriminate either *de jure* or *de facto* contrary to Article I:1.

7. *Japan's Follow-Up to Canada's Response*

6.153 As a follow-up to Canada's response, **Japan** argues as follows:

---

351 Panel Report on *Japan - Film, supra* note 93.

352 EC's response to Question 3 from the Panel.

353 Canada's response to Question 5 from the Panel.

6.154 Canada asserts in its response to the complainants' rebuttals that "there is no prohibition in Article I of origin-neutral terms and conditions on importation that apply to importers as opposed to the products being imported." This assertion, however, oversimplifies and incorrectly narrows the scope of obligation under Article I of the GATT 1994.

6.155 As is clear in the *EC - Bananas III* Panel Report (paragraph 7.239), Article I covers terms and conditions on importation that apply to the importers. In essence, the Panel declared that Article I concerned both treatment of foreign products originating from different foreign sources and treatment of the suppliers of these products on the basis that the transfer of tariff quota rents actually occurred when bananas originating in certain Members were exported to the European Communities. The measure had the effect of giving certain suppliers a competitive advantage over other suppliers which, in turn, had a discriminatory effect on products originating in different WTO Members.

6.156 Article I of the GATT 1994 covers terms and conditions that are, on their face, origin neutral. This point has been made in past GATT 1947 Panel Reports, including *Spain-Tariff Treatment of Unroasted Coffee.* Moreover, Canada itself acknowledges this in the context of *Indonesia - Autos*, stating at paragraph 6 of its answer to the Question 5 of the Panel, that "all three Indonesian conditions, in spite of their apparent neutrality, were inconsistent with the requirement of Article I:1."

6.157 Following the above assertion, Canada goes on to contend that Article I does not prohibit origin-neutral terms and conditions on imports because there are various measures of this sort consistent with Article I, such as import licensing schemes, tariff quotas, end-use classification, free-trade zones and duty drawbacks. It is wrong, however, to argue that these measures are in themselves consistent with Article I. As is the case with any measure permitted under the WTO, these measures would violate Article I if they either *de jure* or *de facto* fail to abide by the MFN provisions contained in Article I. Thus, this oversimplified contention of Canada has no merit in this case.

6.158 Japan would re-emphasize that the core cause of the inconsistency arises from the fact that the eligibility of the privileged importers has been limited by the governmental measure referred to in its arguments as eligibility restriction, though removal of this restriction alone would not completely cure the WTO inconsistency of the Duty Waiver.

6.159 Canada's statement in its response to the complainants' rebuttals that the scheme permits certain producers to import vehicles duty free from any WTO Member country, "provided that the producers meet eligibility criteria to qualify as a Canadian manufacturer" does not tell the whole story. They not only must be a Canadian manufacturer but also must qualify as an Auto Pact manufacturer satisfying various other conditions such as the CVA requirement.

6.160 The Government of Canada tries to misguide the Panel by taking the position that which Member's products benefit at any given time from the Duty Waiver depends entirely on the commercial decisions made by the manufacturers. However, there is severe limitation by the governmental action on the eligibility of the privileged importers.

6.161 Given the fact admitted by Canada that Auto Pact Manufacturers have strong tendency to import motor vehicles from certain specific sources, the governmental action, i.e. limiting the eligibility of the Auto Pact Manufacturers, inevitably affects the countries of origin of duty free imports. In other words, whether or not the advantage granted by Canada to the motor vehicles from certain Members is accorded to the like products originating in the territories of all other Members, totally depends on the choice made by the Auto Pact Manufacturers. The sources of duty-free imports would be different if the Duty Waiver were available to any potential importer.

6.162 The Government of Canada attempts to portray incorrectly the reality of the Duty Waiver to its advantage with Figure 4 by way of turning a blind eye to the fact that majority of motor vehicles imported from Japan are not accorded the advantage of the Duty Waiver. Canada attempts to emphasize the sheer volume of duty-free imports from Japan while ignoring the far greater volume of imports from the United States and Mexico.

6.163 The Duty Waiver is still available to imports from the United States and Mexico. The Duty Waiver is the only measure through which the duty-free treatment is provided to the imports from Mexico.

6.164 Prior to 1 January 1998 (when the NAFTA duty with regard to imports from the United States to Canada was reduced to zero), the Duty Waiver was the only measure whereby the duty-free treatment was provided to the imports from the United States. After 1 January 1998, the Duty Waiver is available to imports of motor vehicles produced in the United States, whether or not they meet the strict NAFTA rules of origin.

6.165 Canada's *Figure 4* as corrected by Japan demonstrates that the vast majority of duty-free imports come from the United States, Mexico and other countries which host the parent manufacturers of or manufacturers in partnership with the Auto Pact manufacturers.

6.166 The *Spain - Unroasted Coffee* case demonstrated that it is sufficient that Brazil exported to Spain "mainly" the varieties subject to the higher duty rate, in order to establish a violation of Article I. The *EEC - Beef from Canada* case found that the EC's measure had the effect of preventing access of like products from other origin than the United States, and for that reason found the measure to be inconsistent with Article I.

6.167 The statistics referred to above easily meet these criteria, and demonstrate that the advantage of the Duty Waiver is accorded "mainly" to the countries which host the parent manufacturers of or manufacturers in partnership with the Auto Pact manufacturers, and that the Duty Waiver has the effect of preventing access of like products from other countries. In other words, in the given context of the strong tendency of Auto Pact Manufacturers, Canada fails to observe its unconditional MFN obligation under Article I by maintaining a scheme which sets the condition that the duty-free importation of automobiles can only be made by the group whose membership has been limited by the governmental measure.

8. *The European Communities' Follow-Up to Canada's Response*

(a) The Tariff Exemption Provides an Advantage to Imports from the United States and Mexico

6.168 As a follow-up to Canada's response, the **European Communities** argues as follows:

6.169 Canada has argued that "it is likely" that in the absence of the Tariff Exemption, "the percentage of imports from the United States and Mexico would be even greater than it is with the measures in effect".

6.170 Even if true (*quod non*), that would not dispose of the EC's complaint, which is that reserving the Tariff Exemption to the US Big Three has the consequence that the share of US and Mexican imports is greater than it would be if the Tariff Exemption was equally available to *all* importers.[354]

6.171 Implicit in Canada's argument is the suggestion that the Tariff Exemption affords no real advantage to imports from the United States and Mexico by the Big Three, because those imports could in any event enter duty free under NAFTA.

6.172 That suggestion is misleading. In the first place, imports from Mexico will remain subject to import duties until 2003. Second, the only imports from the United States which may enter duty free under NAFTA are those meeting NAFTA's origin rules. This means that, for example, a car manufactured by GM in the United States with 55 per cent "North American" content would not qualify for duty-free treatment under NAFTA. Yet that car would still be a US car under Canada's non-preferential origin rules.

6.173 The best proof that the Tariff Exemption constitutes a genuine advantage is that the Big Three continue to import cars from the United States under the Tariff Exemption, rather than under NAFTA, in spite of the fact that since 1 January 1998 import duties on vehicles originating in the United States have been eliminated under NAFTA.

(b) The Test of *De Facto* Discrimination

6.174 In response to a question from the Panel, the European Communities has explained that in order to establish a *de facto* violation of GATT Article I:1 it is not necessary to show, as claimed by Canada, that "only" imports of a certain origin may benefit from the advantage concerned. Instead, it is sufficient to show that imports of a certain origin benefit disproportionately from that advantage.[355]

6.175 The European Communities cited a number of Panel Reports supporting that test. In its response to the complainants' rebuttals, Canada strives to demonstrate that those reports are irrelevant or say something different from what their ordinary meaning would suggest.

6.176 According to Canada, in *Spain - Unroasted Coffee*[356], the Panel found a violation of Article I:1 because "Brazil exported almost exclusively types subject to the higher duties while other Latin American countries exported almost exclusively types subject to lower duties". That is not, however, what the Panel said. The Panel noted that Brazil exported "mainly" the types subject to the higher duties[357] and said nothing about exports from other Latin American countries. In any event, the test read by Canada into *Spain - Unroasted Coffee* is inconsistent with the test advanced by Canada and would lead to a finding of *de facto* violation also in this case.

[354] See also EC's response to Question 2 from the Panel.

[355] Question 1 from the Panel.

[356] Panel Report on *Spain - Unroasted Coffee, supra* note 282.

[357] Ibid., para. 4.10.

6.177 Canada goes on to argue that the test of *de facto* discrimination applied in *EC - Bananas III* when addressing the claims under GATS Article II is irrelevant here because GATT Article I:1 has "nothing to do with competitive opportunities, which entails a more far-reaching analysis".

6.178 Yet, in the very same case the Appellate Body affirmed the Panel's finding that certain export certificate requirements enforced by the European Communities were inconsistent with GATT Article I:1 precisely because they accorded to banana suppliers of BFA countries a "competitive advantage" over other Latin American suppliers.[358]

6.179 Furthermore, also in *EC - Bananas III*, the Appellate Body relied upon past practice under GATT Article I:1 in order to conclude that GATS Article II applies also to *de facto* discrimination.[359] Surely, the analogy drawn by the Appellate Body would have been inappropriate if, as claimed by Canada, *de facto* discrimination under GATT Article I:1 "had nothing to do" with *de facto* discrimination under GATS Article II.

6.180 Canada argues that the European Communities is ignoring the section of the Appellate Body report on *EC - Bananas III* dealing with Article I:1 of GATT because, it claims, "the Appellate Body analysis in that section supports the Canadian approach to *de facto* discrimination". Yet Canada does not explain how the Appellate Body report supports its approach. That is not surprising, given that the claims addressed by the Appellate Body in that section are claims of *de jure* discrimination and not *of de facto* discrimination.[360] The EC's defence was not that the measures applied equally to all imports, but rather that the differences in treatment among Members did not provide an "advantage".[361]

6.181 Canada also misreads the Panel Report on *Indonesia - Autos*.[362] According to Canada, the Panel "quite properly found that Indonesia's measures were *de facto* violations of Article I:1". The Panel did not say that in the report. Instead, as argued by Japan in this dispute, the Panel wrote in its report that the measures were inconsistent with Article I:1 of GATT because they discriminated among like product based on conditions not related to the imports themselves.[363]

6.182 Canada concludes its review of case law by asserting that *Japan - Film*[364] is not relevant because in that case the Panel considered a non-violation complaint under GATT Article XXIII:1(b). *Japan - Film* is a very long report. The Panel considered a non-violation complaint, but it addressed also a violation complaint under GATT Article III:4.[365] As made clear by the European Communities, its argument alluded to the test applied by the Panel in connection with the claim under Article III:4.[366]

---

358 Appellate Body Report on *EC - Bananas III*, *supra* note 49, para. 207.
359 Ibid., paras. 231-232.
360 Ibid., paras. 205-207.
361 Ibid., paras. 37-39.
362 Panel Report on *Indonesia - Autos*, *supra* note 270.
363 Ibid., para. 14.145 in fine and 14.147.
364 Panel Report on *Japan - Film*, *supra* note 93.
365 See the Panel Report on *Japan - Film*, *supra* note 93, paras. 10.368-10.382.
366 EC's response to Question 1 from the Panel.

(c) The Tariff Exemption Is Not Exempted by GATT Article XXIV

6.183 Canada continues to argue that, even if the Tariff Exemption were inconsistent prima facie with Article I:1 of GATT, it would nevertheless be exempted by GATT Article XXIV. According to Canada:

> "Canada, the United States and Mexico have formed a free-trade area and, therefore, any advantage that may be accorded by Canada to its free-trade partners is exempt from Article I:1 obligations by virtue of Article XXIV of the GATT."

6.184 That statement reflects a gross misunderstanding of the scope and function of Article XXIV. Article XXIV does not say that if two Members form a free-trade area, then trade between them is no longer subject to GATT rules. Rather, Article XXIV stipulates that other GATT provisions shall not prevent two or more Members from forming a free-trade area or from adopting an interim agreement necessary for the formation of a free-trade area.[367]

6.185 Accordingly, the issue before the Panel is whether the Tariff Exemption is necessary for the formation of a free-trade area, as defined in Article XXIV:8 (in the case of US imports) or is part of an interim agreement necessary for the formation of a free-trade area (in the case of imports from Mexico). Although the burden of proof lies with Canada, the European Communities has shown that the Tariff Exemption is neither.

6.186 The Tariff Exemption is not part of, nor required by NAFTA. Canada's assertion to the effect that "NAFTA specifically provides for the measures to continue" is misleading. NAFTA does not require Canada to continue to apply the Tariff Exemption. It merely authorises Canada to "maintain" the Tariff Exemption.[368] The Tariff Exemption is a unilateral measure of Canada, except to the extent that it implements the Auto Pact. The Auto Pact, nevertheless, is a purely sectoral agreement which does not meet the requirements of Article XXIV:8.

6.187 It is also misleading to say that Appendix 300.A.1 "has the effect of bringing the measures within NAFTA". The reason why that provision authorises Canada to maintain the Tariff Exemption is precisely because, otherwise, the Tariff Exemption would have been in violation of NAFTA's generally applicable rules concerning *inter alia* the elimination of customs duties, origin rules, the national treatment of goods[369], the abolition of performance requirements[370], and the national treatment[371] and most-favoured-nation treatment[372] of investors. Thus, contrary to Canada's claims, it is not an error to describe the Tariff Exemption as a "derogation" from NAFTA.

6.188 In addition to not being part of NAFTA, the Tariff Exemption is not necessary for the formation of a free-trade area as defined in Article XXIV:8, something

---

[367] C.f. GATT Article XXIV:5.
[368] Appendix 300-A.1, paras. 1 and 2 (Exhibit EC-13).
[369] C.f. Article 301 of NAFTA.
[370] C.f. Articles 304 and 1106 of NAFTA.
[371] C.f. Article 1102 of NAFTA.
[372] C.f. Article 1103 of NAFTA.

which is already achieved by NAFTA. Furthermore, the Tariff Exemption detracts from the objectives of NAFTA. It discriminates between the Big Three and the other car manufacturers established in Mexico and the United States and, as a result, distorts trade between Canada and its NAFTA partners.

9. *Canada's Follow-Up Response*

6.189 **Canada** responds as follows:

(a) Both Complainants Concede that there is no *De Jure* Violation

6.190 Canada has stated and Japan and the European Communities both concede that there is no *de jure* violation of Canada's obligations under Article I:1 of the GATT 1994. There is no doubt about this aspect of the dispute. The MVTO 1998 states on its face that vehicles are entitled to the duty remission "on condition that the goods are imported into Canada on or after January 18, 1965 from any country entitled to the Most-Favoured-Nation Tariff...".[373] Moreover, none of the SROs limits the sources from which vehicles may be imported duty free.

6.191 Both complainants allege *de facto* violation of Article I:1, although their claims differ markedly on this issue. Neither claim can succeed. First, neither complainant has supported its allegations with evidence proving *de facto* discrimination. Indeed, the facts Canada has presented in rebuttal confirm there is no discrimination. Second, neither complainant finds support for its allegations in the law. Canada's review of the law in its Second Written Submission confirms that the cases support the Canadian interpretation of Article I:1 and debunk the legal theories presented by the complainants.

6.192 Finally, neither complainant succeeds in its attempt to undermine Canada's position regarding the meaning of Article I:1. They have both misstated Canada's position and then proceeded to attack a theory they claim is espoused by Canada. This is because neither complainant can successfully make a valid rebuttal of Canada's true position.

6.193 Canada's position is clear: to prove a *de facto* violation of Article I:1, the claimants must prove that a criterion that is neutral on its face is in fact able to be met only by products of a particular origin or origins, such that national origin determines the tariff treatment the product receives. The GATT and WTO cases that Canada reviewed in its Second Written Submission fully support this position.

(b) Japan's Position on *De Facto* Violation is not Supported by the Facts and it Misinterprets the Law

6.194 Japan has two main arguments regarding *de facto* violation of Article I:1. First, Japan says that Sweden and Belgium are favoured by the tariff measures because virtually all automobile imports from those countries enter Canada duty free. Japan claims that most Japanese imports, by contrast, do not enter duty free. Second, Japan argues that commercial relationships dictate from where vehicles are sourced

[373] SOR/98-43 (Exhibits EC-3 and JPN-4).

and therefore, by limiting the number of importers, the effect of Canada's measures is to limit the WTO Members from which vehicles will be imported into Canada.

6.195 Japan's theory of discrimination is flawed for a number of reasons, the major ones being:

- first, Japan seeks to find discrimination among luxury models but the measures at issue make no distinction among model segments, or indeed any distinctions of any kind;
- second, Japan's theory of what constitutes *de facto* violation of Article I:1 is at odds with all of the relevant panel and Appellate Body reports, each of which Canada reviewed in its response to the complainants' rebuttals; and
- third, Japan has not provided reliable evidence to support its assertions; the data upon which Japan relies are wrong, as Japan itself now admits.

(i) Japan's like products argument is inapt because the Canadian measures do not distinguish on the basis of model segment or on any other basis

6.196 The first major flaw in the Japanese argument regarding Article I:1 is that Japan seeks to prove discrimination by comparing imports of certain "luxury" models from Japan to those of certain "luxury" models from Europe. Specifically, Japan decries the fact that Saabs, Volvos, Jaguars and Cateras from Sweden, the United Kingdom and Germany enter Canada duty free, while "like automobiles" from Japan (such as the Acura, the Infiniti and the Legend) do not. It then dismisses as irrelevant the fact that a large number of other vehicles from Japan receive duty-free treatment Japan is essentially attempting to make a "like products" analysis by distinguishing what it considers to be certain luxury models from all other vehicles, and then comparing imports within that particular group of automobiles.

6.197 The Japanese analysis is inapt. The Canadian measures at issue make no distinction among model segments. The MVTOs and the SROs treat all automobiles identically, regardless of model segment, size, price, origin, or any other distinction. This was not the case in *Indonesia - Autos*[374], where the regulations in issue contained the specifications for the Kia Sephia model. The like products analysis in that case proceeded on the basis of whether the products of other countries were "like" that particular vehicle.

6.198 This case is different. The Saab 900 may be "like" a Honda Acura, and the Suzuki may or may not be "like" the Saab or the Honda. But the MVTO and the SROs make no distinction of any kind among different models of cars on the basis of origin. The Honda will be subjected to the MFN duty if it is not imported by a qualified manufacturer, unless of course it is imported from Honda's US production facilities. The Saab imported from Sweden will be exempt from duty if imported by a qualified manufacturer. But the difference in duty is exclusively the result of the importing company's choice, and not due to the Canadian measures.

---

[374] Panel Report on *Indonesia - Autos, supra* note 270.

6.199 This is not so extraordinary as the complainants contend. Article I:1 does not mean that, unless there is some specific GATT exception, all like products must always bear the same rate of duty. That is clear from the plain language of Article I:1, and it is clear from long-standing GATT practice. The only obligation under Article I:1 is that an advantage accorded to the products of one Member must be accorded to like products of all Members. Tariff rate quotas, end-use requirements, duty drawbacks and foreign trade zones all result in different duties on imported like products. These practices are perfectly acceptable. They are all consistent with Article I, so long as those using such programs to import at lower rates of duty are free to make such imports from any origin. This is true even if the importers' choices result in greater importation from some origins than others.

6.200 Canada recalls the GATT Working Party that examined the Auto Pact. It understood very well - and made no objection to - the fact that the Canadian system would allow only imports by qualified manufacturers to enjoy duty-free treatment, while imports of like products by others would be subject to the MFN duty. By contrast, the Working Party recommended to the United States that it seek a waiver from Article I for its intended preferences - preferences that applied exclusively to products from Canada. As well, in the *Belgian Family Allowances* case[375], the panel found inconsistent with Article I only the condition that limited the origin of products that could qualify for tax-free treatment. The panel had no problem with the other condition that only certain Belgian government entities could enjoy the exemption, while the like imported product would be subject to tax if purchased by any other person or entity in Belgium.

6.201 The lesson from this is clear: the fact that some vehicles enter Canada duty free and that some other vehicles are subject to an MFN duty is not a *per se* violation of Article I:1. As long as there is no distinction or condition in the measures themselves that discriminates based on the origin of the vehicles, differential duty treatment for like products is perfectly consistent with Article I:1. The Canadian measures at issue in this case make no such distinction and are therefore perfectly consistent with Article I:1.

(ii) Japan's de facto arguments are not supported by panel and Appellate Body reports

6.202 The second fundamental problem with Japan's *de facto* discrimination theory is that it is out of step with previous panel and Appellate Body reports dealing with *de facto* violation of Article I:1. Japan contends that Canada's measures fall afoul of Article I:1 because automotive companies tend to import only from their affiliates around the world. Since only certain companies qualify for the duty waiver, and those companies have not chosen to source automobiles from all WTO Members, in Japan's view there is "in effect" a violation of Article I:1. Japan further contends, in its response to Question 2 of the Panel, that even if every manufacturer in Canada qualified for the duty waiver, there would still be an Article I violation because those manufacturers who do not operate in Canada could not import automobiles duty free.

375 Panel Report on *Belgian Family Allowances, supra* note 276.

6.203 The GATT and WTO jurisprudence does not support this position. The purely commercial decisions of private automobile manufacturing companies cannot result in a violation by Canada of its international trade obligations when there is no involvement of the government in these decisions.

6.204 Japan suggests that the companies' decisions have "sufficient government involvement" so as to be "deemed governmental", but it offers no explanation for this point of view. It states only that the Government of Canada has "ensured discrimination" because it has implemented the duty waiver "given the economic realities of the global automotive industry" and given that "each qualified manufacturer imports vehicles from a limited number of sources". The truth is that the measures adopted by the Government of Canada have nothing to say about with the commercial decisions of the importers regarding from where they source their vehicles.

6.205 The MVTO and the SROs set no conditions that limit the origin of products that may be imported duty free. Commercial choices have never been the basis of a finding of *de facto* violation when there was nothing in the government measures that limited those choices. The only case in which commercial choice was argued was *Indonesia - Autos*, but there the regulations had the effect of limiting the choice to one company in one country. Moreover, the contractual obligation in that case was "covered by the authorization of June 1996 with specifications that correspond to those of the Kia car produced only in Korea".[376] Unlike *Indonesia - Autos*, in the case before this Panel the commercial decisions are not carried forward into the government measures.

6.206 There have been few complaints in the past regarding *de facto* violation of Article I:1. The notion of a *de facto* violation of the MFN obligation does not derive from the text of Article I:1 itself, which may explain why panels have not accorded this concept the broad meaning and effect now sought by Japan. As Canada has shown, the cases do not support Japan's reading. But they do confirm Canada's position. *De facto* violations of Article I:1 were found when the measures in dispute had the inherent effect of discriminating by origin of the product.

6.207 Japan cites *EEC - Beef from Canada*[377] in support of its interpretation. But it appears to have misunderstood the Panel Report, which actually supports the Canadian position - not Japan's. In the *EEC - Beef from Canada* case, the measure itself permitted duty-free access provided that the product was certified by one particular agency. That agency was a US government agency, and it was mandated to certify only US beef. The effect of the measure was that there was no possibility for Canadian-origin beef, or any beef other than US-origin beef, to achieve certification and thereby qualify for preferential duty treatment. Only US-origin beef could enter duty free. Thus Canada's criteria for making out a *de facto* case are met: a criterion that is neutral on its face is in fact able to be met only by a product of a particular origin or origins, such that national origin in effect determines the tariff treatment the product receives. In the case before this Panel, there is no similar government condition or criteria that limits the origin of products that may benefit. And there is no *de facto* violation. Automobiles from any WTO Member can gain duty-free access to the Ca-

---

[376] Panel Report on *Indonesia - Autos, supra* note 270, para. 14.145.

[377] *Supra* note 282.

nadian market. And automobiles are in fact imported duty free from around the globe.[378]

6.208 *Indonesia - Autos* also deals with *de facto* violation of Article I:1. The condition established by the regulation had the effect that products of only one country - Korea - could possibly benefit from the duty exemption. In *Spain - Unroasted Coffee*[379], Spain had introduced a distinction between types of coffee that disfavoured types exported by Brazil, but not by most other Latin American countries. These cases, too, support Canada's interpretation.

6.209 *EC - Bananas III*[380] is offered by Japan as support for its theory of Article I *de facto* violation, but Japan has misunderstood the panel's findings. Japan cited the case as authority for the proposition that "a Member may legitimately treat products differently only if the distinction in treatment does not adversely affect the competitive relationship of imported products originating in a WTO Member." What Japan has failed to mention is that the measures in question discriminated explicitly, *de jure*, by origin. To import bananas of certain specified origins (namely BFA countries), an importer had to ensure that an export licence accompanied the bananas. Japan cites paragraph 7.239 of the *EC - Bananas III* Panel Report. But, it neglects to mention the next paragraph of the report, which states:

> "Since the EC accords this advantage to products originating in Colombia, Costa Rica and Nicaragua 'while denying the same advantage to a like product originating in the territories of other [Members], i.e. the Complainants' countries, the requirement to match licences with BFA export certificates as provided for in Article 3 of Regulation 478/95 is inconsistent with Article I:1."[381]

6.210 Clearly the violation of Article I:1 was expressly based on the origin of products. Japan similarly misconstrues the reference to the *EC - Bananas III* Appellate Body Report. Paragraph 207 of the Report, which is cited by Japan, simply upholds what the panel found. It reads in relevant part as follows:

> "The EC export certificate requirement accords BFA banana suppliers, which are initial holders of export certificates, preferential bargaining leverage to extract a share of the quota rents for their fruit exported to the European Communities, and gives them a competitive advantage over other Latin American suppliers. The EC export certificate requirement thus provides an advantage to some members (i.e. the BFA countries) that is not given to other Members. Therefore, we agree with the Panel that the export certificate requirement is inconsistent with Article I:1 of the GATT 1994."[382]

6.211 Thus the *EC - Bananas III* case does not support Japan's argument. In fact, none of the cases supports Japan's theory of *de facto* violation of Article I:1. They all support Canada's interpretation. They confirm that the Canadian measures cannot be

---

[378] See Exhibit CDA-6.

[379] Panel Report on *Spain - Unroasted Coffee, supra* note 282.

[380] Panel Reports on *EC - Bananas III, supra* note 269.

[381] Ibid., para. 7.240.

[382] Appellate Body Report on *EC - Bananas III, supra* note 49.

found to breach Article I:1 without extending the MFN obligation beyond anything panels have subscribed to in the past.

6.212 One final point regarding the Japanese interpretation of Article I:1. It would appear that Japan has abandoned its position regarding the meaning of "immediately and unconditionally" as used in Article I:1 since it does not endorse this argument in its rebuttal argumentation, nor in its follow-up points. Canada refuted this argument noting that "unconditionally" means without conditions that limit origin, such as a conditional MFN requirement based on reciprocity, which was present in early commercial treaties. Canada notes that the European Communities has taken a position in its responses to the Panel's Question 3 that is diametrically opposed to the one advanced by Japan on this issue.

(iii) The data upon which Japan's de facto arguments rest are wrong

6.213 Having looked at the deficiencies in the Japanese legal arguments, Canada turns to the errors in Japan's data and the consequences thereof for the case Japan seeks to make. Canada pointed out earlier that the data Japan offered in support of its claim are incorrect. Japan admitted its errors in its rebuttal argumentation. Japan acknowledged that Canada was correct when it pointed out that Japan's Table 5 included vehicle models no longer produced or available in Canada.

6.214 Canada also pointed out that Japan omitted from Japan's Table 5 certain information found in Exhibit JPN-11. That exhibit was filed by Japan to support Table 5. The information that was omitted included vehicle models that originate in Japan and that enter Canada duty free. Canada assumes the data were omitted because they would have undermined the discrimination theory espoused by Japan. In seeking to rebut Canada's arguments about the omission and the inference to be drawn therefrom, Japan stated that "the Government of Japan wants to point out to the Panel that the CAJAD report (Exhibit JPN-11) that was used to construct Table 5 is not completely accurate". In other words, Japan contests Canada's argument by pointing out that the evidence Canada relied upon, which was provided by Japan, is wrong. The extent of the inaccuracy is not revealed. Japan acknowledges that some model segments were left out, but it does not explain why.

6.215 Canada cannot agree with Japan that despite these errors reliance may still be placed on Japan's Table 5 to support Japan's claim of discrimination, because the very foundation of Japan's discrimination analysis is inaccurate and has crumbled away.

6.216 In any event, even if the data could be relied upon, they do not illustrate the assertions made by Japan. How a list of 1996 vehicles sales (even if accurate) separated into model segments and by dutiable status illustrates discrimination is never explained - neither in the initial argumentation where it first appears, nor in subsequent documents filed by Japan. What the statistics do show is that in 1996, total Japanese-origin imports into Canada far exceeded those of any other country listed (Germany, Korea, Russia and United Kingdom). They also show that total Japanese duty-free imports exceeded those of Germany and the United Kingdom.

6.217 Canada recalls *Figure 4* of its initial response illustrating that Japan is far and away the leading duty-free source of automobiles into Canada, excluding the United States and Mexico.

6.218 Japan seeks to dilute its prominence among the Auto Pact beneficiaries by comparing the volume of its duty-free imports to those of the United States and Mexico. It does this in seeking to rebut Canada's *Figure 4.* But any advantage that may be accorded to the United States and Mexico would be irrelevant because of the North American free-trade area and Article XXIV of the GATT. Canada will return to this matter later in this statement. It is worth noting that Japan appears to have adjusted the factual and legal basis for its claim of *de facto* violation of Article I:1. Japan did not argue that imports from the United States and Mexico were the basis of a *de facto* violation of ArticleI:1. Instead, Japan focussed on imports from Belgium and Sweden. Now, Japan appears to endorse the position espoused by the European Communities that imports from the United States and Mexico receive favourable treatment. It is not clear whether the European Communities shares Japan's objections to alleged favourable treatment of products from Belgium and Sweden.

(c) The EC's Position on *De Facto* Violation is not Supported by the Facts and it Misinterprets the Law

6.219 Like Japan, the European Communities has offered nothing in its rebuttal to counter Canada's defense. The European Communities has repeated its assertions that because most vehicles imported duty free are of US or Mexican origin, this constitutes a *de facto* violation of Article I:1. The European Communities contends that this duty-free treatment does not fall within Article XXIV because it is not required by the terms of the North American Free Trade Agreement, the most important accord forming the free-trade area.

6.220 Regarding the interpretation the European Communities ascribes to Article I:1, Canada notes that the European Communities does not provide a definitive interpretation of *de facto* violation of Article I:1. The European Communities states that "it may be sufficient to show that imports of a certain origin benefit *disproportionately* from that advantage". In its follow-up points, the European Communities said it "is sufficient" to show this. The cases reviewed by Canada in its response to the complainants' rebuttals and in this Statement do not support this interpretation. Nor can this interpretation reasonably be inferred from the ordinary meaning of the words in their context and in the light of their object and purpose. Canada submits therefore that the EC's interpretation of Article I:1 be rejected.

6.221 Regarding the factual arguments the European Communities has alleged with a view to demonstrating that *de facto* the Canadian measures provide an advantage to imports originating in the United States and Mexico, Canada pointed out in its response to the rebuttals that the evidence put forward by the European Communities to prove the alleged advantage was unconvincing. The European Communities offered that in 1997 the share of US and Mexican duty-free automobile imports was larger than their total share of imports - the spread it cited was 97 per cent to 80 per cent. It offered no statistical analysis or other data. More fundamentally, it did not explain how this percentage spread was evidence of discrimination.

6.222 The European Communities has repeated its erroneous description of the NAFTA. Canada will not repeat its refutation of the EC description, because it has already set out the correct information in its Responses to the Questions of the

Panel.[383] Suffice it to say here that the measures do not constitute a derogation from the NAFTA. Rather, they are an integral part of it. This is confirmed in the *Canadian Statement on Implementation*, published in the *Canada Gazette* upon the coming into force of the NAFTA, where it is stated that:

> "The rights and obligations in respect of the Autopact agreed between Canada and the United States under the terms of the FTA *are incorporated into the NAFTA.*"[384] (*emphasis added*)

6.223 The European Communities seeks to raise some doubts about the status of the NAFTA. But there is no doubt. Canada, the United States and Mexico have formed a free-trade area. The fact that a few duties remain to be phased out between Canada and Mexico does not change the nature of the agreement. The European Communities conceded in its follow-up points that there is a free-trade area between Canada and the United States, and at least an interim agreement necessary for the formation of such a free-trade area between Canada and Mexico.

6.224 In any event, these distinctions between free-trade areas or customs unions and interim agreements are not significant for purposes of this dispute. Duty-free treatment on the widest and earliest possible basis is arguably the most fundamental objective of a free-trade area or an interim agreement. Nothing in Article XXIV limits the exemption from Article I to the duty reductions and schedules stipulated in the treaty forming the free-trade area, such as the North American Free Trade Agreement, or a customs union, such as the Treaty of Rome.

6.225 The European Communities provides no explanation for what it means by its unsupported assertion that "only those measures that are inherent" in the objective of forming a free-trade area or required by an agreement forming the free-trade agreement can be exempted by Article XXIV. The EC's interpretation of Article XXIV of the GATT 1994 is manifestly wrong.

6.226 One final word on the EC's interpretation of Article XXIV. The European Communities states that "as noted in one of the Panel's questions, the CVA and ratio requirements attached to the Tariff Exemption are 'restrictive regulations of commerce' in the meaning of Article XXIV:8(b)". The Panel will be aware that the European Communities is misrepresenting the Panel's position. The Panel did not note that the CVA and ratio requirements were "restrictive regulations of commerce". Instead, the Panel asked Canada in Question 11 to clarify how it regards the CVA and ratio requirements given that Article XXIV:8(b) provides that "A free-trade area shall be understood to mean a group of two or more customs territories in which the duties and other restrictive regulations of commerce ... are eliminated...". Canada's response to the Panel's question made it clear that the CVA and the ratio requirements are not restrictive regulations of commerce within the meaning of Article XXIV:8(b). They are qualifications contained in the MVTO and SROs regarding qualifying as a "manufacturer". They do not in any way restrict commerce between Canada, the United States or Mexico. The Panel may wish to note in this regard that

---

[383] See Canada's response to Question 8 from the Panel.

[384] Canada Gazette, Part I, 1 January 1994, p. 92. (Exhibit CDA-23).

the panel in the recent *Turkey - Textiles*[385] case indicated that "there is no agreed definition between Members as to the scope of this concept of 'other regulations of commerce'".[386]

6.227 In sum, should the Panel find that there is an advantage afforded products of the United States and Mexico, this would not result in a violation of Article I:1 of the GATT 1994 because any such violation would be exempted by Article XXIV of the GATT 1994.

B. Article III:4 of the GATT

1. Arguments of Japan

6.228 **Japan** argues as follows:

(a) The CVA Requirement

6.229 By virtue of its CVA requirement, the Duty Waiver is inconsistent with Canada's national treatment obligation under Article III:4 of the GATT 1994. The CVA requirement accords a competitive advantage to domestic motor vehicle parts, components and materials that is not accorded to like imported motor vehicle parts, components and materials.

6.230 The relevant part of Article III:4 of the GATT 1994 provides that:

> "The products of the territory of any [Member] imported into the territory of any other [Member] shall be accorded treatment no less favourable than that accorded to like products of national origin in respect of all laws, regulations and requirements affecting their internal sale, offering for sale, purchase, transportation, distribution or use."

6.231 To demonstrate an inconsistency with Article III:4 of the GATT 1994, a three-part analysis is required:

(i) Is the CVA requirement laws, regulations or requirements affecting the internal sale, offering for sale, purchase or distribution of products?

(ii) Are the affected imported and domestic products "like"?

(iii) By virtue of the CVA requirement, does the Duty Waiver accord less favourable treatment to imported products than to the like domestic products?

6.232 The answer to all three questions is "yes". Accordingly, the Duty Waiver is inconsistent with Article III:4 of the GATT 1994.

---

385 Panel Report on *Turkey - Restrictions on Imports of Textile and Clothing Products*, circulated 31 May 1999, WT/DS34/R [on appeal at time of argumentation] (hereinafter Panel Report on *Turkey - Textiles*).

386 Ibid., para. 9.120.

(i) The CVA requirement is a law, regulation or requirement affecting the internal sale, purchase or use of products

(a) Article III:4 of the GATT 1994 applies to all laws, regulations and requirements affecting a product's internal sale, offering for sale, purchase, transportation, distribution or use. Moreover, it applies both to mandatory laws, regulations and requirements and to requirements that an enterprise voluntarily accepts in order to obtain an advantage.[387]

(b) The CVA requirement is an express condition in the MVTO 1998, the Special Remission Orders, and the letters of undertaking signed by Auto Pact Manufacturers.[388] The MVTO 1998 and the SROs are considered in Canadian law to be statutory instruments.[389] As such, they constitute "regulations" within the meaning of Article III:4 of the GATT 1994. The letters of undertaking were accepted by the Auto Pact Manufacturers in order to obtain the advantage of the Duty Waiver. As such, they constitute "requirements" within the meaning of Article III:4 of the GATT 1994.

(c) These regulations and requirements clearly affect the "internal sale ... purchase ... or us" of products. In this context, the word "affect" has been broadly interpreted so as to cover regulations and requirements that directly govern the conditions of sale *and* those that might adversely modify the conditions of competition between domestic and imported products on the internal market.[390]

(d) As a condition of the Duty Waiver, the CVA requirement in practice requires Auto Pact Manufacturers to purchase and use domestic rather than like imported motor vehicle parts, components and materials or

---

[387] Panel Report on *EEC - Parts and Components, supra* note 127, para. 5.21; Panel Report on *Canada - FIRA , supra* note 126, para. 5.4.

[388] Section 2 of the Schedule to the MVTO 1998 specifies that the reduced rate of customs duties is subject to, *inter alia,* the filing of a declaration by every *manufacturer* who intends to import vehicles and the submission of a report by every *manufacturer* who imports vehicles in respect of which customs duties are removed. The term "manufacturer" is defined in subsection 1(1) of the Schedule to the MVTO 1998 as a "manufacturer of a class of vehicles" who, *inter alia,* "produced vehicles ... where ... the [production-to-sales ratio is complied with] and the Canadian value added is equal to or greater than the Canadian value added in respect of all vehicles of that class produced in Canada by the manufacturer in the base year". Similar language is incorporated in the SROs. The letters of undertaking expressly incorporate the domestic content requirement and provide additional commitments in excess of these requirements. As discussed in the para. 56 of the submission, the manufacturers consider these commitments to be binding and continue to report their compliance to the Government of Canada.

[389] Statutory Instruments Act, R.S.C. 1985, c. S-22, s. 2 (Exhibit JPN-42).

[390] Panel Report on *Italian Discrimination Against Imported Agricultural Machinery,* adopted on 23 October 1958, BISD 7S/60 (hereinafter Panel Report on *Italian Agricultural Machinery*), para. 12. Conditions of competition are adversely affected, for example, where a purchasing requirement "excludes the possibility of purchasing available imported products": Panel Report on *Canada - FIRA , supra* note 126, para. 5.8.

to maintain their purchases and uses of such products at certain levels. In this way, the requirement adversely affects the conditions of competition between such products. Accordingly, the CVA requirement "affects" the internal sale, purchase or use of products within the meaning of Article III:4 of the GATT 1994.

(ii) The affected imported and domestic products are "like"

(a) The determination of whether products are "like" must be assessed on a case-by-case basis in the light of all relevant facts and circumstances. Relevant factors include physical characteristics, end-uses, consumer tastes and habits, or price.[391]

(b) The CVA requirement covers the full range of motor vehicle parts, components and materials and distinguishes between such products solely on the basis of whether they are of domestic or foreign origin. Accordingly, the affected imported and domestic parts, components and materials are *per se* " like".[392]

(c) Exhibits JPN-15 through to 17 document the parts, components, and materials manufactured in Canada and used in the production of motor vehicles. Exhibits JPN-18 and 19 document the availability of like products manufactured outside of Canada.

(iii) The Duty Waiver, by virtue of the CVA requirement, accords less favourable treatment on like imported products

6.233 Article III:4 of the GATT 1994 provides that imported products must receive treatment no less favourable than that accorded to like domestic products. "Treatment no less favourable" means that imported products must be granted competitive opportunities no less favourable than those accorded to domestic products.[393] In this light, Article III of the GATT 1994 protects expectations of "the equal competitive relationship between imported and domestic products".[394]

6.234 By effectively requiring the Auto Pact Manufacturers to purchase and use domestic motor vehicle parts, components and materials, the CVA requirement accords less favourable competitive opportunities to like imported motor vehicle parts, components and materials than those accorded to domestic products. Accordingly, the Duty Waiver, by virtue of the CVA requirement, is inconsistent with the national treatment obligation in Article III:4 of the GATT 1994.[395]

---

[391] Panel Report on *Indonesia - Autos, supra* note 270, paras. 14.110, 14.111 and 14.141.

[392] Ibid., para. 14.141. In the case of automobile parts, in *Indonesia - Autos*, the Panel concluded that parts imported for use in a particular car were like parts imported from the complainants' companies. See also Panel Report on *US - Non-Rubber Footwear, supra* note 269, para. 6.12.

[393] Panel Report on *US - Section 337, supra* note 280.

[394] Appellate Body Report on *Japan - Alcoholic Beverages, supra* note 271, p. 17.

[395] In the Panel Report on *Canada - FIRA , supra* note 126, paras. 5.7-5.11 and 6.3, the Panel found that various undertakings to purchase goods of Canadian origin and undertakings to use Canadian

(b) The Production-to-Sales Ratio

6.235 In order to import motor vehicles duty free under the Duty Waiver, the Auto Pact Manufacturers must comply with another requirement under which the sales value of vehicles produced by a manufacturer in Canada must be equal to or exceed a specified proportion of the sales value of vehicles sold by the manufacturer for consumption in Canada.

6.236 If an Auto Pact Manufacturer wants to increase the value of its motor vehicle imports subject to the Duty Waiver, because of the manufacturing requirement (i.e. production-to-sales ratio) it must increase the value of its production in Canada *and* either: (i) increase its exports of motor vehicles produced in Canada; (ii) increase its domestic sales of motor vehicles produced in Canada; or (iii) do both, in order to meet the specific production-to-sales ratio specified by the Government of Canada. If the manufacturer chooses to sell in Canada additional motor vehicles produced in Canada (i.e. under case (ii) or case (iii)) in meeting this requirement, this would increase the competition for sales of like imported motor vehicles.[396] In this case, this requirement creates a situation in which imported motor vehicles are accorded treatment less favourable than that accorded to motor vehicles produced in Canada.[397]

6.237 It is possible, depending on how the Auto Pact Manufacturers organise their production, for the production-to-sales ratio to also violate GATT Article III. For example, in meeting the ratio, the Auto Pact Manufacturers could organise their production and inventory practices so that certain models of automobiles would be exported while others would be primarily directed at the Canadian market. If the additional production resulting from the manufacturers' attempts to observe the ratio (or that production resulting from the minimum production level maintained by the ratio) is not exported, it has to be sold in the Canadian market. Then, such production could harm competitive opportunities to like imported products. Accordingly, a violation of the national treatment obligation in Article III:4 could occur.

2. *Arguments of the European Communities*

6.238 The **European Communities** argues as follows:

---

sources of suppliers (irrespective of the origin of the goods) violated Article III:4 of the GATT 1994. In its conclusions, the Panel noted that "the purchase requirements under examination ... tend to tip the [competitive] balance in favour of Canadian products, thus coming into conflict with Article III:4".

[396] The increased domestic production that results from the manufacturing requirement also multiplies the discriminatory effect of the CVA requirement. Since the manufacturing requirement results in more motor vehicles being produced that meet the CVA requirement, it increases the market for Canadian motor vehicle parts, components and materials.

[397] Also under the cases (ii) and (iii) in para. 6.236 of this submission, this manufacturing requirement (the production-to-sales ratio) would be inconsistent with Article III:4 of the GATT 1994, because the manufacturing requirement requires the Auto Pact Manufacturers to increase production of motor vehicles in Canada and this in turn would lead to increased sales of such domestic motor vehicles in the Canadian market beyond the level of sales that would have occurred in the absence of this requirement, thereby upsetting the balance of conditions of competition for sales of like imported motor vehicles. In this regard, the manufacturing requirement would "affect" the internal sale, purchase or use of products within the meaning of Article III:4 of the GATT 1994.

6.239 The CVA Requirements are inconsistent with GATT Article III:4 because they afford less favourable treatment to imported parts and materials for use in the manufacture of motor vehicles, or of parts therefor, than to like domestic goods.
6.240 In turn, the ratio requirements are inconsistent with GATT Article III:4 because they provide less favourable treatment to imported motor vehicles than to like motor vehicles manufactured in Canada with respect to their sale in the Canadian market.
6.241 Article III:4 of GATT reads as follows in relevant part:

> "The products of the territory of any contracting party imported into the territory of any other contracting party shall be accorded treatment no less favourable than that accorded to like products of national origin in respect of laws, regulations and requirements affecting their internal sale, offering for sale, purchase, transportation, distribution or use [...]."

6.242 Accordingly, in order to rule on the European Communities claims under GATT Article III:4, the Panel is required to make the following determinations:

- whether the measures at issue are "laws, regulations or requirements";
- whether the measures "affect" the internal sale, offer for sale, purchase, transportation, distribution or use of the products concerned;
- whether domestic products are "like" imported products; and
- whether the measures afford "less favourable treatment" to imported products than to domestic products.

6.243 The above issues will be examined here below separately in connection with each of the two claims raised by the European Communities under GATT Article III:4.

(a) The CVA Requirements

(i) The measures at issue are "laws, regulations or requirements"

The CVA requirements contained in the MVTO 1998 and the SROs

6.244 Both the MVTO 1998 and the SROs are so-called "Orders-in-Council" issued by the Governor General of Canada. Therefore, they are clearly "laws, regulations or requirements" within the meaning of GATT Article III:4.
6.245 The CVA requirements contained in the MVTO 1998 and the SROs are not "compulsory", in the sense that they do not impose upon the beneficiaries an obligation to achieve the relevant CVA level. Failure to do so only entails the obligation to pay the generally applicable customs duties.
6.246 By now, however, it is well-established that GATT Article III:4 applies not only to "compulsory" measures, but also to measures compliance with which is necessary to obtain an advantage. As noted by the Panel on *EEC - Regulation on Imports of Parts and Components*,

> "The comprehensive coverage of 'all laws, regulations or requirements affecting the internal sale, etc.' of imported products suggests that not only requirements which an enterprise is legally bound to carry out ... but also those which an enterprise voluntarily accepts in order to ob-

> tain an advantage from the government constitute 'requirements' within the meaning of that provision."[398]

6.247 Further confirmation is provided by the chapeau of Item 1 of the Illustrative List of prohibited TRIMs annexed to the TRIMS Agreement[399], which states that:

> "TRIMs that are inconsistent with the obligation of national treatment provided for in paragraph 4 of Article III of GATT 1994 include those which are mandatory or enforceable under domestic law or under administrative rulings, or compliance with which is necessary to obtain an advantage ..."

6.248 The "advantage" in question may consist of a benefit in respect of a border measure, such as a tariff exemption. Thus, in *EC -Bananas III*, the Panel found that a requirement to purchase domestic bananas in order to obtain the right to import bananas at a lower duty rate under a tariff quota was a requirement "affecting" the internal purchase of a product within the meaning of GATT Article III:4[400].

6.249 More recently, in *Indonesia - Autos*, the Panel concluded that the granting of a tariff exemption conditional upon compliance with a local content requirement was inconsistent with GATT Article III:4 and violated Article 2 of the TRIMs Agreement[401].

- The CVA commitments contained in the Letters of Undertaking

6.250 On their face, the Letters of Undertaking are "private" acts of the beneficiaries, and not acts of the Canadian Government. It must be recalled, nevertheless, that the submission of the Letters of Undertaking was required by the Canadian Govern-

---

[398] Panel Report on *EEC - Parts and Components, supra* note 127, para. 5.21. The same interpretation underlies the Panel Report on *Italian Agricultural Machinery, supra* note 390, para. 12, where the Panel concluded that an Italian law providing especial credit terms to farmers for the purchase of agricultural machinery conditional upon the purchase by the farmers of Italian machinery was contrary to Article III:4 of GATT.

[399] In its Report on *Indonesia - Autos, supra* note 270, the Panel found that the granting by Indonesia of tax and tariff benefits conditional upon certain local content requirements was inconsistent with GATT Article III:4 and violated Article 2 of the TRIMs Agreement. In reaching that conclusion, the Panel rejected an argument by Indonesia to the effect that the local content requirements were not mandatory. According to the Panel, para. 14.90: "The wording of the Illustrative List of the TRIMs Agreement makes it clear that a simple advantage conditional on the use of domestic goods is considered to be a violation of Article 2 of the TRIMs Agreement even if the local content requirement is not binding as such."

[400] See e.g., Panel Reports on *EC - Bananas III, supra* note 269, paras. 7.179 and 7.180. On appeal, this finding was upheld in the Appellate Body Report on *EC - Bananas III, supra* note 49, paras. 208-211.

[401] In reaching this conclusion, the Panel rejected Indonesia's attempted defence that the measure was a "border" measure not covered by GATT Article III:4: "We do not consider that the matter before us in connection with Indonesia's obligations under the TRIMs Agreement is the customs duty relief as such but rather the internal regulations, i.e. the provisions on purchase and use of domestic products, compliance with which is necessary in order to obtain an advantage, which advantage here is the customs duty relief. The lower duty rates are clearly 'advantages' in the meaning of the chapeau of the Illustrative List to the TRIMs Agreement and as such, we find that the Indonesian measures fall within the scope of the Item 1 of the Illustrative List of the TRIMs." Panel Report on *Indonesia - Autos, supra* note 270.

ment as a condition for signing the Auto Pact. Further, the terms of the Letters of Undertaking were negotiated by each beneficiary with Canada's Ministry of Industry. Thus, there can be no question that the Letters of Undertaking constitute acts attributable to the Canadian Government[402].

6.251 Furthermore, as already explained in the factual part, the CVA commitments contained in the Letters of Undertaking are not "voluntary", even if no specific sanction has been formally attached to their violation. Those commitments were a condition for the conclusion by Canada of the Auto Pact. For that reason, the beneficiaries have assumed that, were they to disregard them, Canada would respond by withdrawing the Tariff Exemption.

6.252 The existence of elaborate reporting and auditing procedures that allow the Canadian authorities to monitor regularly if the beneficiaries comply with the Letters of Undertaking, as well as the fact that in practice non-compliance has remained exceptional constitute additional indications that neither the Canadian Government nor the beneficiaries regard the commitments as "voluntary".

(ii) Domestic goods are "like" the imported goods

6.253 The product distinctions made by the CVA requirements are based exclusively on the country of origin of the products: on the one hand, Canadian made parts and materials, as well as certain non-permanent equipment are always counted as CVA[403]; on the other hand, imported parts, materials and non-permanent equipment are never counted as CVA[404].

6.254 More specifically, the CVA calculation rules provide in relevant part that the following items shall be counted as CVA[405]:

> "(i) the cost of parts *produced in Canada*, and the cost of materials to the extent that they are *of Canadian origin*, that are incorporated in vehicles in the factory of the manufacturer in Canada ...
>
> (iv) the part of the following costs that is reasonably attributable to the production of the vehicles, namely, ...
>
> > (J) the cost of tools, dies, jigs, fixtures and other similar equipment of a non permanent nature that have been *manufactured in Canada*"

402 As recalled by the Panel Report on *Japan - Film, supra* note 93, para. 10.56: "Past GATT cases demonstrate that the fact that an action is taken by private parties does not rule out the possibility that it may be deemed to be governmental if there is sufficient government involvement with it." The Panel based that conclusion on the Panel Report on *Japan - Semiconductors, supra* note 112, and the Panel Report on *EEC - Restrictions on Imports of Dessert Apples*, adopted on 22 June 1989, BISD 36S/93.

403 With the only exception of parts and materials previously exported from Canada. MVTO 1998, Schedule, Part 1, Para. 1(1) definition of "Canadian Added Value", item (a) (i) in fine.

404 With the only exception, subject to certain limitations, of the cost of iron, steel or aluminium parts produced outside Canada from iron, steel or aluminium poured in Canada. Ibid., Item (a)(i) (iii).

405 Ibid., items (a)(i) and (iv)(J).

(*emphasis added*)

6.255 Clearly, however, the mere fact of having "Canadian origin", or of having been "produced" or "manufactured in Canada", is not, as such, apt to confer upon parts, materials and non-permanent equipment any characteristic, property or quality which makes them, by definition, "unlike" any imported goods[406].

(iii) The measures "affect" the internal "use" of the products concerned

6.256 The term "affect" has a broad scope of application. According to the Panel Report on *Italian Agricultural Machinery*:

> The selection of the word 'affecting' would imply ... that the drafters of the Article intended to cover in [Article III:4] not only the laws and regulations which directly governed the conditions of sale and purchase but also any laws or regulations which might adversely modify the conditions of competition between the domestic and imported products on the internal market.[407]

6.257 The CVA requirements "affect" the "internal use" of parts, materials and non-permanent equipment for the manufacture of motor vehicles because they provide a financial incentive for the manufacturers of motor vehicles, and parts therefor, to use domestic parts, materials and non-permanent equipment instead of like imported goods, thereby modifying the conditions of competition between imported and domestic goods.

(iv) Imported goods are afforded "less favourable treatment"

6.258 Using domestic parts, materials and non-permanent equipment makes it easier for the beneficiaries to reach the prescribed level of CVA, and hence to qualify for the Tariff Exemption attached thereto, than using like imported goods.

6.259 Consequently, the beneficiaries will always give preference, all other conditions being equal, to Canadian goods over like imported goods. Thus, the CVA requirements afford "less favourable treatment" to imported goods than to domestic goods.

[406] In its Report on *Indonesia - Autos, supra* note 270, the Panel noted, para. 14.113, that an "... origin-based distinction in respect of internal taxes suffices in itself to violate Article III:2, without the need to demonstrate the existence of actually traded like products".

[407] Panel Report on *Italian Agricultural Machinery, supra* note 390, para. 12. The Appellate Body confirmed this interpretation of the term "affect" in its Report on *EC - Bananas III, supra* note 49, para. 220.

(b) The Ratio Requirements

(i) The measures are "laws, regulations or requirements"

6.260 The test of Article III:4 conformity as articulated above with respect to CVA requirements is equally applicable with respect to the ratio requirements.

(ii) The measures "affect" the internal sale of motor vehicles

6.261 The ratio requirements "affect" the internal sale of motor vehicles because they provide an incentive to limit the sales of imported motor vehicles, thereby modifying the conditions of competition between those vehicles and domestic motor vehicles, the internal sale of which is not subject to any similar restriction.

(iii) Domestic and imported motor vehicles are "like" products

6.262 The product distinctions drawn by the ratio requirements are based exclusively on the origin of the motor vehicles. Again, however, the mere fact that a motor vehicle is manufactured in Canada is not, of itself, apt to confer upon that motor vehicle any characteristic, property or quality which makes it, by definition, "unlike" any imported motor vehicle.

(iv) Imported motor vehicles are afforded "less favourable treatment"

6.263 The ratio requirements prescribe that the total value of all the motor vehicles of each relevant category sold in Canada by a beneficiary must keep a certain proportion with the total sales value of the motor vehicles of the same class manufactured in Canada by that beneficiary.

6.264 Although the ratio requirements place a maximum limit on the total sales value of all motor vehicles, irrespective of their origin, in practice that limit operates so as to restrict exclusively the sales of imported motor vehicles, given that:

- by definition, any increase in the sales value of motor vehicles produced in Canada by the beneficiary will give rise automatically to an identical increase in the value of permitted domestic sales; and
- by contrast, an increase in imports of motor vehicles does not entail any increase in the value of permitted domestic sales.

6.265 Thus, the ratio requirements have the consequence that the beneficiaries cannot, without losing the entitlement to the Tariff Exemption, sell in Canada any imported motor vehicles in excess of a certain amount that is directly related to the sales value of their domestic production of motor vehicles.

6.266 No similar limit is placed upon the internal sales of domestic motor vehicles. The beneficiaries may sell in Canada as many Canadian made motor vehicles as they wish, without forfeiting the Tariff Exemption or any other equivalent advantage. Therefore, the ratio requirements afford "less favourable treatment" to imported motor vehicles than to Canadian motor vehicles with respect to their internal sale in Canada.

3. *Canada's Response*

6.267 **Canada** replies as follows:

(a) Article III:4 Creates a Two-Step Test

6.268 A measure violates Article III:4 only if it fails the two-step test set out in *United States - Standards for Reformulated and Conventional Gasoline.*[408] The measure must be a law, regulation or requirement affecting the internal sale, offering for sale, purchase, transportation, distribution or use of an imported product. And it must provide the imported product treatment that is less favourable than that accorded to the like domestic product. The burden is on the complainants to demonstrate that the MVTO and SROs fail each step of this test. The complainants have failed to make even a prima facie case for a violation of Article III. The reason for this is simple: Canada's measures do not provide any competitive advantage to its domestic products.

(b) The CVA Requirement

(i) The MVTO and SROs do not affect the sale or use of products

6.269 The MVTO and the SROs are laws, regulations or requirements within the meaning of Article III:4. However, they do not affect the "internal sale, offering for sale, purchase, transportation, distribution or use" of products. Neither the production-to-sales ratio nor the Canadian-value-added requirement has any effect on the internal market. Neither influences the parts-sourcing decisions of automobile manufacturers in Canada. Neither affects in any way the sale of imported vehicles in the Canadian market. They exist only to ensure that importers claiming a duty exemption are really manufacturers.

(ii) The CVA provides no advantage to Canadian parts

6.270 The complainants' arguments concerning the CVA suffer from similar factual misunderstandings. They have argued that the CVA is a local-content requirement, affecting the use of products. This argument ignores the ordinary meaning of the CVA's terms, transforming it from a broadly-based value-added requirement to a local-products-content requirement. The key element of CVA in the MVTO and the SROs is labour, not local products, and the labour costs of a Canadian manufacturer will necessarily be Canadian. In fact, Canadian-produced products play no role in determining whether an automobile manufacturer meets its CVA levels.

6.271 The MVTO requires companies to incorporate into each class of vehicle produced in Canada a fixed amount of Canadian value added. Those amounts were set in 1964 and have not been adjusted for inflation or for the growth of the Canadian industry; they have long been insignificant. The SRO amounts are generally ex-

---

[408] Panel Report on *US - Gasoline, supra* note 306, para. 6.5.

pressed as a percentage. Nevertheless, they too can still be met without including Canadian parts.

6.272 Revenue Canada's reviews of the CVA numbers confirm that every automobile manufacturer using the MVTO easily meets the CVA levels required of it, and does so on the basis of labour costs alone.[409] So does CAMI Automotive, Inc., the only SRO automobile manufacturer of significance to this case.[410] Indeed, the manufacturers meet their CVA requirements so easily that it has become standard practice for them not to tally their actual amounts and for Revenue Canada to review only the amounts reported. The CVA is therefore not a consideration in parts-sourcing decisions. Indeed, the MVTO's inclusion of labour - a necessarily Canadian cost - clearly makes parts-sourcing decisions irrelevant. The CVA can thus have no effect on the competitive opportunities of imported as opposed to domestic parts.

6.273 Under the circumstances, it cannot be argued that the MVTO and SROs affect the sale or use of products. The production-to-sales ratio has no effect on the conditions of competition in the Canadian automobile market. The CVA has no effect on product sourcing. Manufacturers make their parts-sourcing decisions on a fully competitive basis; they need not and do not consider their CVA requirements. Rather, these decisions are made in the light of more practical considerations such as the efficiency and price advantage of various sources, and the need to meet NAFTA rules of origin.

6.274 The facts do not support Japan's claim. There is no effective requirement to use Canadian parts in the manufacture of vehicles in Canada. Canada would draw the Panel's attention to *Figure 2* of its written submission, which is attached to this submission. Canada demonstrated with this figure that MVTO manufacturers can meet their CVA requirements on the basis of their labour costs alone. Canada has also stated that CAMI, the only SRO manufacturer relevant to this case, can and does meet its CVA requirement on its labour costs alone. All of these companies could source all of their parts abroad and still qualify for all of their benefits.

6.275 Japan is also mistaken when it claims that the production-to sales ratios exacerbate the effect of the CVA requirements. Japan argues that the ratios increase production, and the increased production results in there being more vehicles produced that meet the CVA requirements. According to Japan, this increases the market for Canadian original equipment parts. Canada has already demonstrated that the ratios do not increase production. For purely commercial reasons, manufacturers are already operating well above their ratios. However, even if the ratios did increase production, that would still not increase the effect of the CVA. On the contrary, increased production *dilutes* the already marginal significance of the CVA requirements. CVA levels set a minimum amount of Canadian value-added in a class of vehicles, not in each vehicle. Thus, the more vehicles are produced, the more readily CVA levels are achieved on labour costs alone, without using any Canadian parts at all. Japan's allegation therefore has no factual basis.

409 See *Figure 2*, comparing CVA amounts required with CVA amounts reported each year. Note that reported amounts are well below actual amounts, since MVTO companies routinely under-report their CVA.

410 Information provided by Revenue Canada and released with the consent of CAMI Automotive, Inc.

6.276 The failings of the EC's arguments are legal rather than factual. The European Communities has presented an argument that is based on a novel but erroneous interpretation of Article III:4, although it has tried to present it as a matter of well-established law. The European Communities claims that the mere inclusion of domestic parts in the definition of "domestic value-added" is enough to create a violation of Article III:4. There is no WTO authority for this argument.

6.277 A number of cases have found local-content requirements to be a violation of GATT Article III:4.[411] In each of these cases, the measures *required* the use of domestic products in order to receive an advantage. These measures accorded treatment more favourable to domestic products than to imported ones. However, the Canadian measures in dispute are not like the measures at issue in previous cases. They are not domestic product requirements - they are value-added requirements. As a matter of both fact and law, MVTO and SRO beneficiaries are not required to use Canadian parts in order to qualify for duty-free importation. They can and do meet CVA requirements without using Canadian parts.

6.278 The European Communities is therefore asking for a broad and unwarranted extension of Article III:4. It argues that a violation is created by the mere inclusion of domestic parts in the concept of domestic value-added. Such an interpretation would free complaining parties from demonstrating that impugned measures have any effects on the conditions of competition between imported and domestic products. This reverses the burden of proof, and is contrary to the well-established principle that complaining parties must demonstrate the truth of their assertions.

(iii) The letters are not laws, regulations or requirements

6.279 Both Japan and the European Communities have characterized certain letters as "requirements". The European Communities in particular has claimed the letters were required of the manufacturers as a condition of Canada's signing the Auto Pact, and that the beneficiaries have assumed that a failure to meet them would result in Canada withdrawing the "Tariff Exemption". These arguments have no basis in fact.

6.280 These letters are not legally binding under Canadian law. They are not contracts, because they do not meet the Canadian legal requirements of contract formation. They are not statutory instruments, because they were not passed by the legislature, or by the executive under the authority of the legislature. Had the Canadian Government intended to make the letters binding, it could certainly have done so. It did not. Consequently, the letters have no legal status and no legal effect.

6.281 Moreover, those arguments have no basis in law. Because the letters have no legal status they are not covered by meaning of "laws, regulations and requirements" as used in Article III:4.

6.282 The question of duty-free eligibility in any given year is determined exclusively by the requirements in the MVTO 1998.[412] By law, these are the only grounds under which duty remission can be denied. The European Communities has provided

[411] See, e.g., Panel Report on *Italian Agricultural Machinery, supra* note 390; Panel Report on *Canada - FIRA, supra* note 126, 30/140; Panel Report on *Indonesia - Autos, supra* note 270.

[412] MVTO 1998.

no legal basis under which Canada could withdraw benefits for a failure to meet commitments under the letters.[413] This is because there is none. Should a manufacturer fail to meet the voluntary undertakings in its letter, the Canadian Government would lack the legal authority to deny duty-free eligibility. Indeed, the D-Memorandum submitted by the European Communities and Japan demonstrates clearly that Revenue Canada does not review whether MVTO companies have met their commitments under the letters.[414]

(c) The Ratio Requirement

6.283 Article III mandates the effective equality of competitive opportunity once products have entered the domestic market.[415] The production-to-sales requirement has no effect on the competitive position of vehicles imported into the Canadian market and therefore does not fall within the scope of Article III:4.

6.284 Japan and the European Communities argue that the ratio requirement affects the sale of imported vehicles. Japan's argument is so abbreviated that it does not even approach the threshold of a prima facie case. Japan argues that a qualified manufacturer must increase its imports in order to increase the value of its MVTO or SRO benefits. According to Japan, however, the ratio requirements prevent such an increase unless it is accompanied by additional domestic production. Japan concludes that if some of this extra production is sold on the domestic market, it must necessarily increase the competition for sales of imported vehicles, thereby violating Article III:4. This argument cannot succeed, since Japan has offered no evidence for its factual assertions, and no authority for its legal interpretations.

6.285 Indeed, Japan is only correct in the first step of its reasoning. A manufacturer must increase its *imports* in order to increase its benefits. Of course, this contradicts the claim that the measures disadvantage imported products. By Japan's own admission, the effect of the measures is to *increase* importation. Having made this admission, Japan must somehow convert an incentive to import into a disadvantage for the products so imported. It does this by claiming that the measures also require an increase in domestic production, and that any such increase necessarily disadvantages imported vehicles.

6.286 The European Communities claims that the ratio imposes a limit on the number of imported vehicles a manufacturer may sell without losing its duty-free entitlements, and therefore creates a disincentive to selling imported vehicles that does not exist for domestic ones.

6.287 Both arguments are based on serious factual misunderstandings. Neither has any basis in law. The Japanese argument, insofar as it has been made at all, appears to rely on the assumption that all MVTO and SRO beneficiaries operate at exactly the

---

[413] The European Communities did suggest that Canada could simply withdraw from the Auto Pact, but the suggestion is without merit. Such an action would be so inimical to Canada's interests that it would never be contemplated, as the MVTO beneficiaries are well aware.

[414] See Exhibits EC-9 and JPN-7 (Memorandum D10-16-3). The remaining memoranda are filed as Exhibit CDA-7. In no case do the memoranda state that Revenue Canada will verify anything other than whether MVTO requirements have been met.

[415] Panel Report on *Italian Agricultural Machinery, supra* note 390, para. 12; Panel Report on *US - Section 337, supra* note 280, para. 5.11.

required ratio. This is not so. The ratio is simply a minimum production requirement for the receipt of duty-free benefits; it is well below real levels of production. All the automobile manufacturers operate far in excess of the required ratios, and can therefore significantly increase their imports sales without increasing production, while still maintaining their ratios. Indeed, they could even decrease production. The requirement therefore does not affect conditions of competition between domestic and imported products.

6.288 Furthermore, it cannot be argued that production levels have reached their current heights by the operation of the MVTO and the SROs. The ratio requirements in these measures set only the minimum ratio of production to sales. The measures provide no benefit whatsoever for production beyond the required ratio. If a manufacturer were only interested in increasing its duty-free importation, it would source abroad as many vehicles as possible, and keep its Canadian production just high enough to meet its ratio.

6.289 The MVTO and SRO manufacturers do not do this. Their Canadian production levels greatly exceed their ratios. This is because production is determined not by ratios but by market considerations such as labour costs and plant efficiency. The level of competition faced by imported vehicles is completely unrelated to the ratio requirements.

6.290 Japan's argument would fail even if it were assumed that future production levels might drop dramatically, such that importation would have to be offset with a new increase in production. Setting aside the great unlikelihood of such an occurrence, the argument remains wrong in law. Neither the GATT nor any other WTO Agreement prohibits measures that increase production levels; there is no authority anywhere for the proposition that a mere increase in domestic production negatively affects the conditions of competition for like imported products.

6.291 Japan cannot simply claim that greater production of domestic vehicles must mean fewer sales of imported ones. WTO law recognizes no such claim. Japan must demonstrate that the impugned measures adversely affect the conditions of competition for imported vehicles. It has failed to do this.

6.292 Even if Japan's assumptions were correct, its argument would still fail, since it is plainly wrong in law. The production-to-sales ratio simply sets the minimum production value required to receive a given level of benefits. This is similar to a production-based subsidy, which requires a certain level of production to receive a certain level of benefits.[416] It is obvious that under such subsidies manufacturers must increase production to increase their benefits. It is equally obvious that the increased production must be either exported, sold in the domestic market, or both. Japan claims the production-to-sales ratio violates Article III because it has precisely these effects. Yet production-based subsidies are not violations of GATT Article III. If Japan's argument were correct, it would render null the entire Section III of the *Subsidies and Countervailing Measures Agreement*, which makes such subsidies actionable rather than prohibited.

[416] Note the ratio does not link benefits to production, in the sense that production beyond the ratio does not increase benefits. MVTO and SRO companies are therefore operating at their current levels for purely commercial reasons.

6.293 The EC's argument too is based on a misconstruction of the facts. Like the Japanese argument, it assumes that manufacturers operate at exactly the required minimum levels. More important, it assumes that manufacturers are faced with an all-or-nothing proposition - they can pay duty either on all imports or on no imports. This is a serious misunderstanding of the Canadian measures. In fact, manufacturers can always ensure that they remain within their MVTO or SRO ratios, regardless of the number of imported vehicles they sell, simply by paying duty on some vehicles. Under the measures, they can deduct from the sales side of their ratio calculation the value of vehicles on which they paid duty.[417] Thus the ratio never creates an incentive to stop selling imported vehicles. If at any point in the model year a manufacturer believes it might exceed its ratio, it can simply begin paying duty. The sales of these duty-paid vehicles would not enter the ratio calculation, and therefore would not affect the duty-free status of previously imported and sold vehicles.

6.294 The European Communities contends that manufacturers would refrain from selling imported vehicles in order to maintain their production-to-sales ratio. However, the ratio requirement applies only to vehicles imported by an MVTO or SRO beneficiary. It cannot under any circumstances affect vehicles imported by another company. The European Communities therefore appears to be arguing that vehicles imported under the MVTO or SRO are at a disadvantage in the Canadian domestic market. It is difficult to understand how this argument can be reconciled with the European Communities' Article 1 argument that these vehicles receive an advantage denied to other imports.

6.295 Indeed, it is difficult to understand the argument. The European Communities is suggesting that a manufacturer would import a vehicle in order to receive the benefit of not paying duty on it, and then refuse to sell it to preserve that benefit. This is an argument at odds with commercial reality. No manufacturer would import vehicles only to withhold them from the market: vehicles are expensive to warehouse, and their market value drops immediately upon the introduction of the next model year. When a manufacturer imports a vehicle, it is quite obviously with the intention of selling it. Indeed, manufacturers typically import only on the basis of projected or confirmed demand. The ratio has no effect on this. A manufacturer can always remain within its ratio by paying the duty on some of its imports, thereby removing that value from the ratio calculation.

6.296 This fact ensures that the production-to-sales ratios cannot limit sales of imported vehicles. They simply set a minimum level of production for any given level of duty-free importation. Importation beyond that level requires the payment of the normally applicable MFN duty. The European argument therefore suffers from the same basic legal flaw as the Japanese one. That is, there is nothing in the GATT or any other WTO Agreement that prohibits Canada from capping duty-free benefits in this way. The European Communities, like Japan, must demonstrate that Canada's measures provide conditions of competition that are less favourable to imported vehicles than to domestic ones. Like Japan, the European Communities has failed to do this.

[417] See, for example, MVTO 1998, Schedule, s. 1(4).

6.297 In Canada's view the EC's argument is a disguised attempt to argue that the production-to-sales ratio acts as a limit on *importation*. As such, the argument would be properly made under Article XI of the GATT 1994, and not under Article III:4. The complaining parties have not done this because the Canadian market is so clearly open to imports. There are no restrictions whatsoever on importation, as the share of imports on the Canadian market - particularly the complainants' imports - demonstrates.[418]

4. *Rebuttal Arguments by Japan*

6.298 **Japan** rebuts as follows:

6.299 The Government of Canada argues that the CVA requirement is not inconsistent with Article III:4 of the GATT 1994 because it has no relevance to the sourcing of parts within Canada and, therefore, has no impact on the competitive opportunities relating to parts sold in the Canadian market. The Government of Canada also argues that the CVA is comprised of a number of cost elements and that, under current circumstances, the CVA requirement can be met by the MVTO 1998 recipients solely on the basis of labour costs.[419]

6.300 Before responding to the Government of Canada's arguments, the Government of Japan wishes to address an evidentiary issue raised by the Government of Canada when it stated:

> "Filing copies of excerpts from a directory of Canadian automotive parts manufacturers, a handbook listing Japanese automotive parts and components manufacturers, web sites of companies that manufacture goods used in the production of automobiles ... does not by any measure constitute proof of any allegations ... "

6.301 The evidence referred to by the Government of Canada in this statement is prima facie evidence that the full range of parts, components and materials used in the manufacture of automobiles are available from Canadian and non-Canadian sources and, therefore, "like" products are affected.[420] It is also prima facie evidence that domestic and imported automobiles are "like".[421] Such evidence is relevant to the "like" products comparison under Article III:4 with respect to the CVA. Most importantly, Canada has not produced any evidence to rebut this prima facie evidence.

6.302 The Government of Canada's arguments fundamentally misconstrue the nature of the discrimination against imported motor vehicles parts, components and materials that is inherent in the CVA requirement.

6.303 It is undisputed that the CVA is, in law, a mandatory condition for obtaining the favourable treatment under the Duty Waiver. It is also clear from the regulatory

---

[418] The evidence filed by the European Communities and Japan shows that almost $2.5 billion worth of Japanese vehicles entered Canada in 1997, together with almost $1 billion worth of vehicles from the European Communities. See p. 8 of Industry Canada, Automotive Trade 1997, filed as Exhibit EC-15 and Exhibit JPN-37-10 (pp. 37-166 in Japan's pagination). See also *Figure 4*.

[419] Ibid., paras. 30-31, 65, 74, and 77.

[420] See Exhibits JPN-15, 16, 17, 18 and 19, paras. 33-36.

[421] Domestic automobiles are identified in Japan's Table 3 and like imported automobiles in Japan's Table 4.

requirements governing the CVA that the cost of imported parts, components and materials can never qualify for inclusion in the CVA. This means that, in law, the cost of imported parts, components and materials is excluded from ever being taken into account in the CVA calculation. Accordingly, since the mandatory CVA stipulates an express legal exclusion of the cost (and therefore the use) of imported, parts, components and materials, it discriminates between domestic and like imported products.

6.304 The foregoing reasoning applies to the CVA irrespective of whether it is incorporated in the MVTO 1998, the letters of undertaking or in the individual SROs. Accordingly, with respect to all three classes of instruments, the CVA requirement discriminates between domestic and imported parts, components and materials, and is, therefore, inconsistent with Article III:4 of the GATT 1994.

6.305 The fact that, under current circumstances, imported, parts, components and materials may not be affected by the CVA requirement is irrelevant to the violation of Article III:4. The Appellate Body has stated that:

> "The broad and fundamental purpose of *Article III* is to avoid protectionism in the application of internal tax and regulatory measures. ... Toward this end, *Article III* obliges Members of the WTO to provide equality of competitive conditions for imported products in relation to domestic products. ... Moreover, it is irrelevant that the "trade effects" of the tax differential between imported and domestic products, as reflected in the volumes of imports, are insignificant or even non-existent; *Article III* protects expectations not of any particular trade volume but rather of the equal competitive relationship between imported and domestic products."[422]

6.306 Thus, Article III:4 protects expectations as to the competitive relationship between domestic and imported products for both current trade and to create predictability for future trade.[423] In applying Article III:4, the practice is to determine whether discrimination exists by examining the distinctions made by the laws, regulations and requirements themselves and on their potential impact rather than on the actual consequences for specific imported products.[424] In short, Article III:4 covers laws, regulations and requirements that do or could adversely modify the conditions of competition between domestic and imported products in a given internal market.[425]

6.307 The foregoing principles have a direct bearing on the Government of Canada's defense that, in the case of the MVTO 1998 recipients, the CVA can be met solely on the basis of labour costs. The fact that, under current circumstances, the CVA requirement may have little or no effect is irrelevant. What is relevant is that the discrimination in the CVA requirement has the potential to modify the conditions of competition between domestic and like imported products. As the current MVTO

[422] Appellate Body Report on *Korea - Alcoholic Beverages, supra* note 280, para. 21 (citing the Appellate Body Report on *Japan - Alcoholic Beverages, supra* note 271, at 110, with references to earlier Panel Reports).

[423] Panel Report on *US - Petroleum, supra* note 73, para. 5.2.2.

[424] Ibid. - *Section 337, supra* note 280, para. 5.13.

[425] Panel Report on *Italian Agricultural Machinery, supra* note 390, paras. 11-13.

1998 recipients consolidate their Canadian manufacturing operations in the future, one or more of the recipients could be placed in a position where it would be forced to use domestic rather than like imported parts, components and materials in order to comply with the CVA requirement. In the view of the Government of Japan, this "potential" adverse effect in the future is why the discrimination in the CVA requirement must be disciplined today.[426]

6.308 The fact that only a small volume of imported parts, components and materials could be affected is also irrelevant to the violation of Article III:4. As reflected in the Appellate Body statement quoted above, Article III:4 protects competitive conditions between domestic and like imported products, it does not protect expectations as to volume.[427]

6.309 Accordingly, the arguments presented by Canada are not persuasive and should be rejected. Clearly, the CVA requirement, whether implemented in the MVTO 1998, the letters of undertaking or the SRO, discriminates against imported parts, components and materials.

5. *Rebuttal Arguments by the European Communities*

6.310 The **European Communities** rebuts as follows:

(a) The CVA Requirement

(i) The actual effects of the CVA requirements are not relevant

6.311 Canada argues that the CVA requirements do not violate GATT Article III:4 because the beneficiaries can easily meet those requirements on the basis of labour costs alone, so that the CVA requirements have "no effect on product sourcing".

6.312 This argument is thoroughly misguided. As established by a long series of Panel Reports and confirmed by the Appellate Body, GATT Article III protects competitive opportunities and not trade flows[428]. Hence, in order to establish a violation of Article III:4 it is not necessary to show that the measure concerned has had any actual effects. The mere possibility that a measure may result in some circumstances

---

426 Just prior to the initiation of the Canada-US negotiations that resulted in the CUSFTA, there was substantial discussion regarding the automotive industry in Canada. The following comment illustrates the potential of adverse effects caused by the CVA: (as noted in Exhibit CDA-2, in 1986 the Big 3 and Volvo labour component of their CVA also exceeded the CVA requirement as it did at the time of this statement). "So called domestic auto manufacturers, those that operate under the rules of the Autopact, have invested heavily in Canada - $12 billion in the last six years. They now assemble two vehicles in Canada for every one they sell in Canada, double the ratio required under the Autopact, Canadian value added is now at 90 per cent minimum. (It must be recognized, however, that these rules apply by company and therefore remain very important incentives for certain firms; and market changes can rapidly reduce current levels)" Windsor Star, "Strong leaders needed to save our auto trade from slow death", Monday, 20 October 1996 (Exhibit JPN-48).

427 Panel Report on *United States - Measures Affecting Alcoholic and Malt Beverages*, adopted on 19 June 1992, BISD 39S/206 (hereinafter Panel Report on *US - Malt Beverages*), para. 5.6 and Panel Report on *US - Petroleum, supra* note 73, para. 5.1.9.

428 See, e.g., the Appellate Body Report on *Japan - Alcoholic Beverages, supra* note 271, at 110 and the Panel Reports cited therein.

in less favourable treatment being afforded to imported products is already sufficient to establish a violation of Article III:4[429].

6.313 The CVA requirements violate GATT Article III:4 because, all other conditions being equal, they provide an incentive for using local parts and materials instead of imported like goods. How effective that incentive turns out to be in practice is not a relevant consideration for the purposes of GATT Article III:4.

(ii) In any event, Canada has not shown that the beneficiaries can meet the CVA requirements without using domestic parts and materials

6.314 In any event, Canada has not proved its assertion that the beneficiaries can meet the CVA requirements on the basis of labour costs alone.

6.315 The table contained in Exhibit CDA-2[430] only shows that *currently* the aggregate labour CVA of the US Big Three and Volvo is sufficient to meet the CVA requirements contained in the Auto Pact and in the MVTO 1998. This does not necessarily mean, however, that it will always be so. The US Big Three may decide to move some production back to the United States or to a lower cost country such as Mexico[431]. In that case, the US Big Three could be forced to use Canadian parts and materials in order to meet the CVA requirements contained in the Auto Pact and the MVTO 1998.

6.316 Furthermore, Exhibit CDA-2 does not prove that the labour CVA of the US Big Three and Volvo is sufficient to meet the more onerous CVA requirements contained in their Letters of Undertaking.

6.317 In the exchange of written questions and replies, the European Communities asked Canada to complete the data shown in Exhibit 2 with the aggregate cost of sales of the producers concerned[432]. The requested data would have enabled the Panel to verify whether the labour CVA of those producers is sufficient to meet the CVA requirements in the Letters of Undertaking. Unfortunately, Canada has refused to provide the information requested on the spurious ground that it is not "relevant" to this dispute[433]. Once again, the Panel should draw appropriate inferences from Canada's lack of a response.

6.318 Nonetheless, the evidence already made available by Canada is sufficient to confirm indirectly that the Big Three cannot meet the CVA requirements in the Letters of Undertaking on the basis of labour CVA alone. Exhibit CDA-2 shows that in

[429] See, e.g., the Panel Report on *EEC - Payments and Subsidies Paid to Processors and Producers of Oilseeds and Related Animal-Feed Proteins*, adopted on 25 January 1990, BISD 37S/86 (hereinafter Panel Report on *EEC - Oilseeds*), where the Panel noted, para. 141: " ... the Panel examined whether a purchase regulation which does not necessarily discriminate against imported products but is capable of doing so is consistent with Article III:4. The Panel noted that the exposure of a particular imported product to a risk of discrimination constitutes, by itself, a form of discrimination. The Panel therefore concluded that purchase regulations creating such a risk must be considered to be according less favourable treatment within the meaning of Article III:4."

[430] Canada's *Figure 2* is based on that Exhibit.

[431] Volvo has already done so. As explained in the EC's arguments, it ceased production of motor vehicles in Canada as of December 1998.

[432] Question 5 from the EC.

[433] Canada's response to Question 5 from the EC.

model year 1996/97 labour CVA accounted for approximately 29 per cent of the total CVA reported by the Big Three and Volvo. In turn, according to the official statistics supplied by Canada during the consultations[434], the total CVA of the major MVTO and SRO beneficiaries accounted in 1996 for 70 per cent of their cost of sales in Canada. Thus, it may be estimated that the labour CVA of the Big Three represents just 20 per cent of their cost of sales in Canada (29 per cent of 70 per cent), i.e. much less than the 50 per cent to 60 per cent required by the Letters of Undertaking.

6.319 Canada has not provided any evidence whatsoever regarding the CVA requirements imposed upon the SRO beneficiaries. Canada limits itself to assert that according to Canada Revenue, CAMI's labour CVA is sufficient to meet its CVA requirements, but provides no supporting evidence. Clearly, that assertion is not sufficient to meet Canada's burden of proof [435].

6.320 In any event, CAMI is not the only SRO beneficiary. According to Canada, eight other beneficiaries are currently utilising their SROs. In response to a question from the Panel, Canada has admitted that four of those eight SRO beneficiaries have not, in recent years, meet their CVA requirements on the basis of labour CVA alone[436].

(iii) The CVA commitments in the Letters of Undertaking are "laws, regulations or requirements" in the meaning of Article III:4

6.321 Canada has argued that the CVA commitments in the Letters of Undertaking are not "laws, regulation or requirements" in the meaning of Article III:4.

6.322 The European Communities considers that those terms are intended to have the same broad coverage as the term "measure" in, for example, GATT Article XI. The national treatment obligation contained in Article III:4 complements the prohibition on import restrictions contained in Article XI[437]. It would be absurd if non-binding border measures that restrict imports were prohibited by Article XI, but then non-binding internal measures that discriminate against imported products were permitted by Article III:4.

---

[434] Statistical Review of the Canadian Automotive Industry, 1997 Edition, Industry Canada, Table 4.7 (Exhibit EC-18).

[435] As noted by the Panel Report on *Indonesia - Autos, supra* note 270, para. 14.235, the parties to a dispute may not invoke the confidentiality of business information as a justification for failing to provide the positive evidence required to prove their assertions.

[436] Canada's response to Question 32 from the Panel.

[437] As noted by the Panel Report on *Italian Agricultural Machinery, supra* note 390, para. 11: "... the intention of the drafters of the Agreement was clearly to treat the imported products in the same way as the like domestic products once they had been cleared through customs. Otherwise indirect protection could be given".

Similarly, the Panel Report on *US - Petroleum, supra* note 73, noted, para. 5.2.2: "... The general prohibition of quantitative restrictions under Article XI... and the national treatment obligation of Article III... have essentially the same rationale, namely to protect expectations of the contracting parties as to the competitive relationship between their products and those of the other contracting parties ..."

6.323 Nevertheless, even if the term "requirement" had to be construed more narrowly than the term "measure", the European Communities submits that, for the reasons explained above, the CVA requirements would still qualify as "requirements".

(b) The Ratio Requirements

6.324 Canada argues that the ratio requirements do no limit sales of imported vehicles by other importers, nor sales of vehicles imported by the beneficiaries outside the Tariff Exemption.

6.325 It is a well established principle, however, that the "no less favourable" treatment requirement of GATT Article III:4 is applicable to each individual case of imported products[438]. Accordingly, the mere fact that sales of vehicles imported outside the Tariff Exemption benefit from the same treatment as sales of domestic products cannot offset the fact that internal sales of vehicles imported within the Tariff Exemption receive less favourable treatment.

6.326 Canada also makes the argument that the ratio requirements are an import measure and should be examined under GATT Article XI, rather than under GATT Article III.

6.327 Yet the distinction between import and internal measures is a formal one and not one based on the effects of the measure. The ratio requirements are internal measures subject to Article III, and not to Article XI, because they do not affect the right to import motor vehicles, but the right to sell them in Canada[439].

6. *Response by Canada to the Complainants' Rebuttals*

6.328 **Canada** responds as follows:

(a) The CVA Requirements

(i) The CVA amounts in the MVTO and SROs do not affect the sale of original equipment manufacturing parts

6.329 Japan and the European Communities have both argued that the CVA amounts in the MVTO and SROs are *per se* violations of Article III:4.[440] As Canada has already stated, the arguments of the European Communities and Japan rest on a characterization of the CVA as a domestic content requirement. The CVA is not a domestic content requirement, it is a value-added requirement. Previous GATT and WTO cases have found violations in measures that required the purchase or use of

---

[438] See e.g., the Panel Report on *US - Section 337, supra* note 280, para. 5.14; and the Panel Report on *US - Gasoline, supra* note 306, para. 6.14.

[439] The Panel Report on *Canada - FIRA* , *supra* note 126, noted, para. 5.14, that: "The Panel shares the view of Canada that the general Agreement distinguishes between measures affecting the 'importation' of products, which are regulated in Article XI:I, and those affecting 'imported products' which are dealt with in Article III. If Article XI:I were interpreted broadly to cover also internal requirements, Article III would be partly superfluous."

[440] Japan had initially argued that the CVA requirements are a de facto requirement to use domestic parts, but appears to have abandoned this line of reasoning.

domestic products in order to receive an advantage.[441] However, there is no GATT or WTO authority to support the proposition that the mere inclusion of local products in a broadly-based value-added requirement is a violation of GATT Article III:4.

6.330 This interpretation of Article III:4 finds support in the text of paragraph 1 to the Illustrative List in the TRIMs Agreement. Paragraph 1 provides examples of TRIMs that are inconsistent with Article III:4 and refers to measures that *require* the use of domestic products.

6.331 Canada demonstrated in its initial response that all the companies for which the complainants raised arguments easily meet their CVA amounts by labour alone. In response, Japan argues that the actual effects of the measure are irrelevant, because the test is whether the measure "might adversely modify the conditions of competition between domestic and imported products on the internal market". As authority, Japan cites two cases: *Italian Discrimination Against Imported Agricultural Machinery*[442] and *United States - Taxes on Petroleum and Certain Imported Substances.*[443]

6.332 The phrase quoted above comes from paragraph 12 of *Italian Agricultural Machinery*. The panel was dealing with Italy's argument that Article III:4 did not apply to its measure, because it did not directly govern the conditions of sale of products. The panel rejected this argument, finding that Article III:4 applies to all measures that "might adversely modify the conditions of competition between the domestic and imported products on the internal market." In other words, this test determines whether Article III:4 applies at all, not whether the measure is a violation. The Italian measure in question provided a benefit only to purchasers of Italian farm equipment. There was thus a real and immediate incentive to favour those products, not a mere potential for it in the future. That is where the panel found the violation of Article III:4.

6.333 The paragraph from *Taxes on Petroleum* cited by Japan says nothing about measures that "might" adversely modify conditions of competition. It stands for the proposition that one cannot justify a higher tax on imported products than like domestic ones (an indisputable violation of Article III:2) on the basis that the measure has a negligible effect on the volume of imports. This finding is irrelevant to this case.

(ii) The CVA requirements do not affect conditions of competition between domestic and imported products

6.334 Japan and the European Communities have claimed that the CVA requirements violate GATT Article III:4. Japan initially argued that the CVA is a *de facto* requirement to use Canadian parts. It has joined the European Communities in arguing that the CVA is a *de jure* violation of Article III:4 because it might, someday, under some potential future circumstances, create the possibility of less favourable

---

[441] See, e.g., Panel Report on *Italian Agricultural Machinery, supra* note 390; Panel Report on *Canada - FIRA* , *supra* note 126; Panel Report on *Indonesia - Autos, supra* note 270.

[442] Panel Report on *Italian Agricultural Machinery, supra* note 390, paras. 11-13.

[443] Panel Report on *US - Petroleum, supra* note 73, para. 5.1.9.

treatment for imported products. If this is indeed the correct test for a violation of Article III:4, it seems unlikely that any measure could ever pass it. It is not surprising then, that none of the cases cited by the complaining parties has made such a finding.

6.335 Both complaining parties have cited a line of cases holding that Article III protects equality of competitive opportunity, not trade flows. This, they argue, frees them from having to demonstrate that the Canadian measures actually have any of the effects they allege. They claim that these and other cases[444] support a test based on the possibility of a future change in circumstances creating the potential for discrimination.

6.336 No Panel Report - and certainly not a single one cited by the complaining parties - has ever found a violation of Article III:4 based on discrimination that might exist after a change in circumstances that could occur at some unspecified time in the future. Japan and the European Communities, as the complaining parties, cannot simply assert that there may be the possibility of discrimination under some potential future circumstances. In every case cited by the complaining parties, the potential for discrimination actually existed under the circumstances present at the time the case was brought. Not a single case contains a finding that the complaining party need only demonstrate the potential for future discrimination given the right change in circumstances. Thus, to succeed, the complaining parties have to demonstrate the current potential for discrimination under present circumstances. They have only tried to demonstrate the future potential under hypothetical circumstances.

6.337 Their evidence is insufficient even for that purpose. Japan's production of a single newspaper article, in which the author speculates that market conditions could one day result in lower production levels, does not constitute evidence.[445] The European Communities suggests that the Big Three might shift production to the United States, or to some other country, just as Volvo (Canada) did. This proves nothing, since companies that cease production in Canada will no longer be eligible for duty-free treatment under the MVTO or SROs, at least until they resume production. Their ability to meet CVA requirements in these circumstances is meaningless.

6.338 The CVA calculations require companies importing vehicles under the MVTO and SROs to achieve a total amount of Canadian value in each class of vehicle they produce. The three classes are automobiles, buses and specified commercial vehicles. Because the requirement operates for a "class" of vehicles, there is no requirement for individual vehicles to contain any Canadian products. Furthermore, "Canadian value" includes labour, factory overhead such as heating and lighting, and depreciation on buildings and equipment. Because of these additional inclusions, it is possible to meet CVA requirements without using Canadian products, even within an entire class of vehicles. Every company importing any class of vehicle under the MVTO meets its CVA requirement on the basis of labour alone. Except for four

[444] *EEC - Oilseeds, supra* note 429, para. 141; Appellate Body Report on *Korea - Alcoholic Beverages, supra* note 280, para. 21; Panel Report on *US - Petroleum, supra* note 73, para. 5.1.9; Panel Report on *US - Section 337, supra* note 280, para. 5.13; Panel Report on *Italian Agricultural Machinery, supra* note 390, para. 12.

[445] Japan's argumentation referring to Exhibit JPN-48.

companies[446], the same is true of companies importing vehicles under the SROs, including CAMI.

6.339 Therefore, the CVA amounts do not affect the conditions of competition between domestic and imported products, because the CVA does not require the purchase or use of domestic products. The CVA requirements, particularly those under the MVTO and the CAMI order, do not and cannot affect competitive opportunities for imported parts or other products, because companies can purchase all inputs and equipment from any country they choose, and still meet their respective CVA requirements.

6.340 The GATT and WTO cases support Canada's position that the use of domestic products must be required in order for a content or value-added requirement to be inconsistent with Article III:4. The content requirement in *Indonesia - Autos* could not be met without the use of Indonesian parts. In *FIRA*[447], the undertakings to purchase local products, while voluntarily made, were not voluntarily complied with. In *Italian Discrimination Against Imported Agricultural Machinery*[448] and in *Parts and Components*[449], the *only* means to acquire a government-offered benefit was by purchasing domestic products.

6.341 Canada's position respecting the application of Article III:4 to content requirements is confirmed by the Illustrative List in the TRIMs Agreement. Both the chapeau to paragraph 1 and sub-paragraph 1(a) make it clear that a measure must require the purchase or use of domestic products to be inconsistent with GATT Article III:4.

6.342 Inflation and growth in the industry have made the fixed CVA requirements for those companies importing vehicles under the MVTO so insignificant that they cannot be seen as a requirement to do anything, much less purchase, or even favour, domestic products. They are based on historical levels of production that were so low they cannot be expected to be seen again. Canada's *Figure 2* and Exhibit CDA-2 demonstrate that, for automobile manufacturers, reported CVA on labour alone in 1996-97 was more than three times the total required amount.[450] Total CVA reported that year was more than 11 times that required.[451]

6.343 In conclusion, the complainants have misinterpreted the findings on which they rely. Both complaining parties have argued that they have to demonstrate only that the CVA might, in some potential future circumstances, affect the conditions of competition between domestic and imported original equipment parts. None of the cases cited by the complainants has endorsed this proposition. Canada therefore submits that the CVA requirements cannot violate Article III:4.

[446] The four companies are Capital Disposal Equipment, Les Entreprises Michel Corbeil, Navistar and NovaBUS.

[447] Panel Report on *Canada - FIRA*, *supra* note 126, para. 5.4.

[448] Panel Report on *Italian Agricultural Machinery, supra* note 390.

[449] Panel Report on *EEC - Parts and Components*, *supra* note 127, para. 5.21.

[450] Labour CVA was $1.9 billion, while the total required was $611 million.

[451] Total reported CVA was almost $6.8 billion.

(iii) The Letters are not "laws, regulations or requirements"

6.344 The complainants have argued that the letters also violate Article III:4. That Article states that it applies to all "laws, regulations and requirements". Japan and the European Communities have not attempted to argue that the letters are laws or regulations because clearly they are not. They are not found in any legal instrument. The only question is whether the letters are requirements.[452]

6.345 The European Communities and Japan bear the burden of proving that the additional letters are requirements, a burden they cannot meet. The test for whether the CVA amounts in the letters are "requirements" is found in the Panel Reports in *FIRA* and *EEC - Regulation on Imports of Parts and Components*.[453] The *FIRA* panel found that voluntarily submitted undertakings could be "requirements" within the meaning of Article III:4. However, the panel explicitly noted that the undertakings at issue in *FIRA* were not complied with voluntarily. Once they were submitted, the undertakings formed part of the legally enforceable regime applying to the investment. There was, in short, a sanction for failing to comply with the requirements. This fact was central to the panel's reasoning.[454]

6.346 The Panel on *EEC - Parts and Components* distinguished between "requirements" that a company is legally bound to carry out (the *FIRA* situation) and "requirements" that a company voluntarily accepts in order to obtain an advantage. It nevertheless found that both were "requirements" within the meaning of Article III:4, but only to the extent that the requirements were conditions precedent to obtaining a benefit.[455]

6.347 The letters are not requirements under these tests. They are not part of the legally enforceable regime applying to the MVTO. Should a beneficiary fail to meet the CVA amounts in its letter, it would still qualify for its duty-free privileges. Japan's own evidence has made it clear that this is the case.[456] Indeed, should a beneficiary refuse to provide the information that would be necessary to determine whether it had met the amounts, it would still qualify. Moreover, just as there is no sanction for failing to meet the amounts in the letters, there is no reward for doing so. No additional benefits accrue to companies that honour the letters. Companies are not bound to carry out their terms, nor do they do so voluntarily in order to obtain a benefit. The letters are thus not requirements. They are completely unrelated to a company's ability to import duty free under the MVTO.

---

[452] Canada, in its response to Question 4 from the Panel, has already set out its views on the interpretation of the terms "measures" and "laws, regulations and requirements". In Canada's view, the terms do not have the same meaning, with measure being the broader term. It is thus only necessary to determine whether the letters are "requirements". If so, they are necessarily measures. Conversely, a finding that the letters are "measures" would not be determinative. It would still be necessary to determine whether the letters are "requirements", or to find that the two terms have identical meanings.

[453] Panel Report on *EEC - Parts and Components*, *supra* note 127.

[454] Panel Report on *Canada - FIRA* , *supra* note 126, para. 5.4.

[455] Panel Report on *EEC - Parts and Components*, *supra* note 127, para. 5.21.

[456] Exhibit JPN-27, p. 63.

6.348 Canada has made public its position that the letters are not requirements. Indeed, Japan has filed as evidence a public statement from Industry Canada that explicitly describes the letters as non-binding.[457] Canada has made the same statement repeatedly in the proceedings before this Panel; it should be noted that Canada makes all of its WTO submissions public upon request. These very submissions are thus also public statements that the letters are not binding and cannot be enforced.

6.349 The European Communities has made much of the wording of the letters, which it claims is mandatory. In fact, the wording varies and is at most ambiguous - the word "undertake" can mean to commit oneself formally, but it can also mean to take on a task.[458] Where there is no sanction and no reward, even the most strongly worded private undertaking cannot be considered a requirement under Article III:4.

6.350 To date, the complainants' other evidence has focused on the questions of whether the Canadian government was involved in the preparation of the letters, whether the manufacturers were required to submit letters as a *sine qua non* of Canada's signing the Auto Pact, and whether the beneficiaries believed themselves bound by the letters. The evidence provided is at best ambiguous, and does not demonstrate that the letters were ever requirements.[459]

6.351 The European Communities has also claimed that the letters are enforceable on the theory that nothing in Canadian law prevents Canada from repealing or amending the MVTO. This argument is a fundamental misstatement of WTO law. The WTO agreements do not apply to actions that Members *could* take. They apply to actions that Members have *taken*. The letters are not requirements because they are not enforceable and offer no rewards; whether the Canadian government has the constitutional authority to convert them into requirements is irrelevant.

6.352 That the letters are not requirements is clear from what would happen in the event that Canada had to implement a finding that they violate Article III:4. The Canadian government would not have to take any action in order to comply with the finding. It would not have to repeal the letters because it never passed them in the first place - there is nothing to repeal. It would not have to repudiate them, because it has already been made clear that neither the government nor the companies affected

---

[457] Exhibit JPN-38, p. 38-1.

[458] See, e.g., The New Shorter Oxford English Dictionary on Historical Principles, definition 4(a) (vol. 2 [Oxford: Clarendon Press, 1993], p. 3476, Exhibit CDA-13), and Merriam-Webster's Collegiate Dictionary, definition 1 (10th ed. [Markham: Thomas Allen, 1993], p. 1289 (Exhibit CDA-14).

[459] For example, Exhibit EC-22, p. 11 contains the following statement from an official of General Motors Corp. of the United States: I can speak for General Motors and I can say that *there have been no secret agreements, there have been no negotiations*. The Canadian Government asked us to write them a letter stating our understanding of the provisions of the agreement as it was finally determined and to ask for our endorsement of the principles to the extent that we did understand them and assigned to us an *objective* whereby, over the 4 years that are involved in this agreement, we would undertake to increase our Canadian production or our Canadian value. (emphasis added) United States-Canada Automotive Products Agreement: Hearings before the House Comm. on Ways and Means on H.R. 6960 "The Automotive Products Trade Act of 1965", 89th Cong., 1st Sess. (1965), p. 148 (testimony of James M. Roche, Executive Vice President, General Motors Corp.). This statement agrees exactly with Canada's explanation of the facts provided in response to Question 17 from the Panel.

regard themselves as bound by them. It would not have to stop enforcing them, because it does not do so.

6.353 Virtually all of the evidence the complaining parties have supplied relates to the time when the letters were written, thirty-five years ago. All of this evidence is irrelevant. Regardless of the past status of the letters, they are not requirements today, and will not become requirements in the future. Even prior to the complaining parties bringing this case, Canada had publicly stated that the letters were not binding.[460] The complainants themselves have cited the statement, and have never rebutted it. Canada has also stopped making any effort to verify whether companies achieved the amounts contained in the letters. Canada has now repeatedly made it clear that it does not regard the letters as binding. If the executives of the beneficiary companies were ever in any doubt on this point, they no longer are.

6.354 Regardless of whether the letters have ever been thought binding, they have never been enforceable. Japan has now joined the European Communities in claiming that the letters could be enforced by repealing or amending the MVTO, and even withdrawing from the Auto Pact if necessary. This argument is a fundamental misstatement of WTO law. The WTO agreements do not apply to measures that Members could take. They apply to measures that Members have taken.

6.355 In any event, Canada would never - indeed, could never - have withdrawn from the Auto Pact. First, it would punish every MVTO and SRO company, not just the non-compliant one. Second, from 1965 until 1998, when NAFTA duty phase-outs for the United States reached zero, duty-free access to the American market depended on the Auto Pact. There was never any possibility that Canada would withdraw from it under those circumstances.

6.356 For these reasons, Canada submits that the letters of undertaking do not create requirements within the meaning of GATT Article III:4. They therefore cannot give rise to a violation of that Article.

(b) The Ratio Requirements

(i) The ratio requirements do not provide less favourable treatment to domestic vehicles

6.357 The European Communities says Canada argued that less favourable treatment for some products can be balanced with more favourable treatment for others. Canada has made no such argument.

6.358 The European Communities, in its responses to questions, made it clear that its claim in this area is only with respect to vehicles imported under the MVTO and SROs - in other words, the very same vehicles it claims have an advantage under Article I. Such vehicles, the European Communities argues, are at a competitive disadvantage because the ratio requirements impose a quantitative limit on their sale, based on the value of domestic production.

6.359 According to the European Communities, MVTO and SRO beneficiaries will import vehicles in order to obtain duty-free benefits, and will then decline to sell the vehicles in order to preserve those benefits. This argument seems to have been made

[460] Exhibit JPN-38 and Exhibit EC-20.

without any regard to the measures in question. The ratios do not limit sales; they provide that imports beyond a certain value of sales will be subject to Canada's MFN duty. Manufacturers are free to sell vehicles outside their ratios - the only consequence is that they will pay duty on the value of those vehicles.

6.360 Because the ratios have no effect on total sales, whether domestic or imported, the European Communities appears to be arguing that a limit on duty-free benefits is itself a violation of Article III. Canada disagrees. The EC's argument would convert a measure setting out the terms under which importation takes place - which is manifestly a border measure - into a limitation on internal sales under Article III:4. Such a claim has no basis in the GATT. It would make every tariff rate quota or limitation on tariff preferences a violation of Article III.

(ii) The ratio requirements do not affect the internal sale of vehicles

6.361 Japan's complaint rests entirely on the hypothesis that if Canadian production were structured so that some models were produced for export, and others were directed primarily at the Canadian market, this might lead to an increase in production which could somehow disadvantage imported vehicles.

6.362 Japan's argument divides production in two: production for export and production for the domestic market. Japan theorises that if some models are directed primarily at the domestic market, an increase in the production of those models could lead to a reduction in competitive opportunities for imported vehicles. Japan has not produced any evidence to demonstrate that Canadian production is structured in this way. Nor can it, because such an inefficient structure could not be maintained in a rationalized market. Thus, it cannot substantiate its claim that domestic production "could" negatively affect the conditions of competition for imported vehicles, and Japan cannot establish a prima facie case.

6.363 In any event, the argument is difficult to reconcile with the effect of the programme, which is to remove duties from imports. It is also difficult to reconcile with market reality: beneficiaries have an incentive to *reduce* production and *increase* importation, given that their production levels far exceed what is required under the ratios.

6.364 Japan claimed that the ratio requirements could create a violation of Article III that is in some way related to an alleged production increase. However, Japan has provided no evidence and scarcely any explanation of its claim, and chose not to address it at all in its responses to the Panel's questions, in its arguments. Japan has failed to make a prima facie case, and its claim must be dismissed.

6.365 The argument of the European Communities has apparently changed through these proceedings. In presenting its claims, the European Communities seemed to argue that the ratio requirements impose a quantitative limit on all import sales of the beneficiary companies, a claim without foundation. The European Communities now seems to be limiting its argument to vehicles imported duty free under the MVTO and SROs. It concedes that sales of imported vehicles on which duty is paid receive the same treatment as sales of domestic vehicles. However, it suggests that sales of duty-free vehicles receive less favourable treatment than like domestic or duty-paid vehicles. The EC theory seems to be that a beneficiary company might reduce its production to such an extent that it would have to reduce its volume of duty-free imports for Canadian sale.

6.366 Canada rebutted the first version of the EC argument by demonstrating that it was based on a misunderstanding of how the ratios and Article III operate. The second version, however, also seems to misunderstand the operation of both Article III and the ratio requirements. It is therefore appropriate to briefly explain again exactly how the ratios work.

6.367 The MVTO and the SROs provide that each company importing vehicles under those measures must maintain a set ratio of the value of its Canadian production to the value of its Canadian sales. The sales figure includes only domestic vehicles and vehicles imported duty free. In the case of companies operating under the MVTO, the required ratio is the ratio actually achieved in the base year of 1963-64. In the case of companies operating under an SRO, each SRO specifies the workings of the required ratio. There are no other ratio amounts specified anywhere, whether in the additional letters or in the annual declarations required under the MVTO.

6.368 An example will provide the easiest means of understanding the ratio requirements. Let us assume that a company operating under the MVTO has a ratio of 95 to 100. If that company sells $100 worth of automobiles in Canada, whether imported duty free or domestic, it must also produce at least $95 worth of automobiles in Canada in that same model year. There are no requirements regarding where or how to sell that production. There are no requirements as to how much to import duty free or how much to import duty-paid. There are no requirements of any kind as to origin. The company is free to structure its imports, and its sales, as it chooses.

6.369 Furthermore, the company can always ensure that it will meet its ratio requirement, because only vehicles imported duty free are counted in the sales side, or denominator, of the ratio. In the unlikely event that the company were operating at or near its ratio, it could start paying the otherwise applicable duty on its imports. This is the same duty that would otherwise have been payable on all of its imports. In this situation, vehicles already imported into Canada would remain duty free; only vehicles to be imported could be affected, and the only effect is that they would become subject to duty. It is only in this situation that the ratio serves to cap the total value of vehicles that a company may import duty free. This cap does not limit or otherwise affect the value or volume that can be imported under the MFN duty. Manufacturers can thus import and sell as many vehicles as they choose.

6.370 As regards internal sale, all vehicles are subject to the same rules. Vehicles imported duty free under the MVTO and SROs are in precisely the same competitive position regarding their internal sale as vehicles imported duty-paid - and the European Communities has conceded that duty-paid vehicles are not discriminated against under Article III. Indeed, all vehicles, whether imported duty free or duty-paid, or whether produced domestically, are subject to precisely the same rules in respect of their internal sale.

6.371 All companies importing vehicles under either the MVTO or the SROs are currently exceeding their respective ratios by wide margins. The ratios have thus ceased to have any effect other than to qualify beneficiaries as manufacturers. There is no regulatory incentive for exceeding the required ratio. Production levels in Canada are therefore entirely the result of commercial factors such as cost and product demand.

6.372 It is possible that Canada has misunderstood the EC argument. The European Communities could be arguing that the very existence of a potential cap on the value of products that can be imported duty free itself disadvantages the internal sale of duty-free products. If this is indeed the EC argument, it fails to make the distinction between measures affecting importation of products, and measures affecting imported products. Article III:4 applies to measures affecting the competition between like domestic and imported products, after the imported products have cleared the border and any applicable duty has been paid. Article III therefore offers no basis for claiming that otherwise like imported products receive less-favourable treatment under Article III because they were subject to different tariffs. Otherwise, tariff-rate quotas and any other variable tariff rates would be a violation of Article III:4.

7. *The European Communities' Follow-Up to Canada's Response*

6.373 As a follow-up to Canada's response, the **European Communities** argues as follows:

(a) Clarification

6.374 The European Communities would like to make a clarification regarding the scope of its claims with respect to the CVA requirements. Canada attributes to the European Communities the claim that "the CVA requirements favour the use of domestic equipment manufacturing (OEM) parts in the production of vehicles in Canada".

6.375 That is not correct. The EC's claim is not limited to OEM parts. It extends to all goods used or consumed in the manufacture of motor vehicles which are counted as CVA when produced or manufactured in Canada, but not when imported. As stated in the EC's initial argumentation, in accordance with the rules contained in the MVTO 1998, that includes not only parts, but also materials, as well as certain equipment of non-permanent nature.

(b) The Letters Contain Requirements

6.376 Canada appears to have recognised that the position that the Letters of Undertaking are not "measures" is untenable. Thus, in its response to the complainant's rebuttals, Canada limits itself to argue that the Letters of Undertaking are not "laws, regulations and requirements". By way of justification, Canada explains in a footnote that since the term "measure" is "broader" than the term "requirement", it is only necessary for the Panel to determine whether the Letters are requirements.

6.377 The European Communities disagrees. Even assuming that the term "measure" was indeed "broader", the European Communities has submitted claims with respect to the CVA requirements not only under GATT Article III:4 and Article 2.1 of the TRIMs Agreement, but also under GATS Article XVII and Article 3.1 (b) of the SCM Agreement. Neither of those two provisions refers to "requirements". Therefore, a finding that the Letters are not "requirements", would not dispense the Panel from ascertaining whether they are "measures".

6.378 Canada's defence relies on an extremely narrow interpretation of the term "requirement". In essence, Canada argues that the Letters are not "requirements" because they are not "legally enforceable", either through sanctions or through rewards explicitly attached to them.

6.379 That interpretation, however, is not compelled by the ordinary meaning of the term "requirement". "Required" and "legally enforceable" are not synonyms. The existence of a explicit legal sanction furnishes the proof that something is a "requirement", but is not an inherent element.

6.380 The Letters of Undertaking contain "requirements" because they are drafted in mandatory terms and are regarded as binding by the Canadian Government and by the beneficiaries, as evidenced by the fact that compliance is regularly verified and that in practice the beneficiaries do comply with the terms of the Letters.

6.381 The statement found in Industry Canada's website to the effect that the Letters "while non-binding, typically have been met"[461] cannot be taken as evidence that the Canadian Government does not regard the Letters as "binding". That statement is not addressed to the beneficiaries, but to the general public. The Canadian Government does not need to post statements in the internet in order to convey to the beneficiaries its views on the nature of the Letters. In any event, Canada Industry uses the term "binding" in the narrow sense of "legally enforceable". In the same paragraph, Canada Industry also refers to the terms of the Letters as something the beneficiaries "undertook" and as "conditions".

6.382 For similar reasons, the statements made by the Canadian Government in these proceedings cannot be taken as evidence that it does not regard the Letters as binding or that it has repudiated them. The Big Three understand perfectly well that Canada is forced to make those arguments in order to preserve the Tariff Exemption for their benefit.

6.383 Canada claims that its interpretation of the term "requirement" is derived *from Canada - FIRA*[462] and *EC - Parts and Components*[463] Those reports, however, in no way suggest that the panels purported to formulate, or that they were applying a set of generally applicable criteria.

6.384 In any event, the Letters of Undertaking fit within the same pattern as the measures at issue in *EC - Parts and Components*. As explained by Canada, in that case the Panel found that the undertakings to increase local content given by the subsidiaries of certain Japanese companies were "requirements" because they were a "condition precedent to obtaining a benefit". The same is true of the Letters of Undertaking. The Canadian Government would not have concluded the Auto Pact if the Big Three had not submitted the Letters of Undertaking.

6.385 The only difference between the two cases is that the EC antidumping regulations envisaged that, if the undertakings were breached or withdrawn, the EC Commission could (but was not obliged to) re-institute proceedings and eventually impose anti-circumvention duties.[464] The MVTO does not envisage expressly the possibility to impose sanctions. That does not mean, however, that the Letters are unenforceable. Given the linkage between the conclusion of the Auto Pact and the submission of the Letters established by the Canadian Government, there has always been a tacit understanding between the parties that if the beneficiaries failed to comply with the Letters, the Canadian Government would withdraw the tariff benefits.

6.386 In one of the supplemental questions put by the Panel, the Panel has asked Canada whether any of the manufacturers operating under the MVTO have indicated

---

[461] Exhibit EC - 20.

[462] Panel Report on *Canada - FIRA* , *supra* note 126.

[463] Panel Report on *EEC - Parts and Components*, *supra* note 127.

[464] Ibid., para. 5.20.

in their annual reports that they have gone above the CVA requirements of the MVTO.[465]

6.387 The answer is that there is no need for the beneficiaries to do so. The samples of reporting forms included in Exhibit EC-14 show that the MVTO beneficiaries are required to report, among other things, the total CVA amount in the relevant period, as well as the net sales value of the vehicles sold in Canada during the same period. Those two amounts allow the Canadian Government to verify, by making a very simple calculation, whether the Big Three comply with the CVA requirements in the Letters. The Big Three know that. And the Canadian Government knows that the Big Three know.

C. *The TRIMs Agreement*

1. *Arguments of Japan*

6.388 **Japan** argues as follows:

6.389 By virtue of its CVA requirement, the Duty Waiver is inconsistent with Canada's obligations under Article 2.1 of the TRIMs Agreement.

6.390 Article 2 of the TRIMs Agreement reads as follows:

> "*Article 2 National Treatment and Quantitative Restrictions*
>
> 1. Without prejudice to other rights and obligations under GATT 1994, no Member shall apply any TRIM that is inconsistent with the provisions of Article III or Article XI of GATT 1994.
>
> 2. An illustrative list of TRIMs that are inconsistent with the obligation of national treatment provided for in paragraph 4 of Article III of GATT 1994 and the obligation of general elimination of quantitative restrictions provided for in paragraph 1 of Article XI of GATT 1994 is contained in the Annex to this Agreement."

6.391 To demonstrate an inconsistency with Article 2.1 of the TRIMs Agreement, it must be demonstrated that the measure in question is a TRIM and that it is inconsistent with Article III or Article XI of the GATT 1994. Both requirements are met in this case.

(a) The CVA Requirement is a TRIM within the Meaning of Article 2.1 of the TRIMs Agreement

6.392 The CVA requirement is an "investment measure". The requirement is a condition that is incorporated in the MVTO 1998, the SROs and in the letters of undertaking which are pertinent to the Canada-US Auto Pact specifically aiming at investment.[466] The publicly available letters of undertaking (Exhibit JPN-5) specifically

---

[465] Question 40 from the Panel.

[466] The preamble to the Canada-US Auto Pact includes the following statement: "Recognizing the important place that the automotive industry occupies in the industrial economy of the two countries and the interests of industry, labour and consumers in sustaining high levels of efficient production and continued growth in the automotive industry."

Article I of the Canada-US Auto Pact includes the following statement: "The Governments of the United States and Canada, pursuant to the above principles, shall seek the early achievement of

refer to investment objectives.[467] The measures today are directed at maintaining investment in Canada by the existing Auto Pact Manufacturers.

6.393 The CVA requirement is "trade-related". Such a domestic content requirement is necessarily trade-related because it favours the use of domestic products over imported products and, therefore, affects trade.[468]

6.394 Accordingly, the CVA requirement is a TRIM within the meaning of Article 2.1 of the TRIMs Agreement.

(b) The CVA Requirement is Inconsistent with Article III:4 of the GATT 1994

6.395 As discussed with respect to GATT Article III (Section VI.B), the CVA requirement is inconsistent with Article III:4 of the GATT 1994.

6.396 In the context of the TRIMs Agreement, this inconsistency is confirmed in the Agreement's Illustrative List. The relevant part of Paragraph 1 of the Illustrative List reads as follows:

> "1. TRIMs that are inconsistent with the obligation of national treatment provided for in paragraph 4 of Article III of GATT 1994 include those which are mandatory or enforceable under domestic law or under administrative rulings, or compliance with which is necessary to obtain an advantage, and which require:
>
> > (a) the purchase or use by an enterprise of products of domestic origin or from any domestic source, whether specified in terms of particular products, in terms of volume or value of products, or in terms of a proportion of volume or value of its local production;"

6.397 The Duty Waiver grants an advantage (i.e. exemption of customs duty) conditional on, *inter alia*, meeting the CVA requirement. Accordingly, the Duty Waiver is a measure for which "compliance ... is necessary to obtain an advantage" within the meaning of the chapeau of paragraph 1 of the Illustrative List.

6.398 The CVA requirement falls squarely within the example in paragraph 1(a) of the Illustrative List which states "the purchase or use by an enterprise of products of domestic origin or from any domestic source". Accordingly, the CVA requirement is a TRIM that is inconsistent with the provisions of Article III of the GATT 1994 within the meaning of Article 2.1 of the TRIMs Agreement.

2. *Arguments of the European Communities*

6.399 The European Communities argues as follows:

6.400 Article 2.1 of the TRIMs Agreement provides that:

---

the following objectives... (c) the development of conditions in which market forces may operate effectively to attain the most economic pattern of investment, production and trade."

[467] The letters signed by General Motors, Ford, Chrysler and AMC include the following understanding: "It is our understanding that the important objectives of the intergovernmental agreement are... the development of conditions in which market forces may operate effectively to attain the most economic pattern of *investment, production* and trade." (emphasis added)

[468] Panel Report on *Indonesia - Autos, supra* note 270, para. 14.82.

> "Without prejudice to other rights and obligations under GATT 1994, no Member shall apply any TRIM that is inconsistent with the provisions of Articles III or XI of GATT."

6.401 The TRIMs Agreement does not define the notion of TRIMs. Nevertheless, the Annex to that Agreement contains what Article 2.2 describes as:

> "An illustrative list of TRIMs that are inconsistent with the obligation of national treatment provided for in paragraph 4 of Article III of GATT..."

6.402 The CVA requirements and the ratio requirements are both "investment measures" and "related to trade in goods" and, consequently, constitute TRIMs within the meaning of Article 1 of the TRIMs Agreement. Since those requirements are inconsistent with GATT Article III:4 (see Section VI.B for argumentation), it follows that they infringe as well Article 2.1 of the TRIMs Agreement.

6.403 Moreover, the CVA requirements and the ratio requirements fall within Item 1 of the Illustrative List of prohibited TRIMs.

(a) The CVA Requirement and the Ratio Requirement are "Investment Measures"

6.404 The term "investment measure" is not defined in the TRIMs Agreement but has been interpreted authoritatively in *Indonesia - Autos*. In that case, the Panel found that the granting by the Indonesian Government of tariff and tax incentives conditional upon compliance by the beneficiaries with certain local content requirements was an "investment measure".

6.405 The Panel reasoned as follows:

> "[T]hose measures are aimed at encouraging the development of a local manufacturing capability for finished motor vehicles and parts and components in Indonesia. Inherent to this objective is that these measures necessarily have a significant impact on investment in these sectors. For this reason, we consider that these measures fall within any reasonable interpretation of the term 'investment measures'"[469]

6.406 The structure of the measures in dispute is similar to that of the measures applied by Indonesia. Further, the two sets of measures pursue the same objective, with the only difference that Canada's measures, having already succeeded in "developing a local manufacturing capability", now operate mainly as an encouragement for the US Big Three to maintain their investments in Canada. As such, Canada's measures, like Indonesia's measures, have a "significant impact on investment" and, therefore, must be deemed to constitute "investment measures" for purposes of the TRIMs Agreement.

(b) The CVA Requirement and the Ratio Requirement are "Related to Trade in Goods"

6.407 The CVA requirements are "related to trade in goods" because they favour the use of domestic parts and materials for the assembly of motor vehicles over imported

---

[469] Ibid., para. 14.80.

parts and materials[470] and/or the export of motor vehicles (and/or parts therefor). (See discussion below in Section VI.D, SCM Agreement).

6.408 In turn, the ratio requirements are "related to trade in goods" because they provide an incentive for limiting the sales of imported motor vehicles (discussed above in Section VI.B, Article III:4 of the GATT), as well as for exporting domestically produced motor vehicles (discussed below in Section VI.D, the SCM Agreement).

(c) The CVA Requirements and the Ratio Requirements Fall Within the Illustrative List of Prohibited TRIMs

6.409 Item 1 of the Illustrative List of prohibited TRIMs states the following in relevant part:

> "1. TRIMs that are inconsistent with the obligation of national treatment provided for in paragraph 4 of Article III of GATT include those ... compliance with which is necessary to obtain an advantage, and which require:
>
> (a) the ... use by an enterprise of products of domestic origin or from any domestic source ... specified in terms of a proportion of ... value of its local production;
>
> (b) that an enterprise's purchase or use of imported products be limited to an amount related to the ... value of local products that it exports."

6.410 The CVA requirements provide an incentive to use domestic goods instead of imported goods in the manufacture of motor vehicles. Further, as discussed below, some of the CVA requirements have been set at a level such that they cannot be met unless that the beneficiaries use a significant proportion of domestic goods in the manufacture of motor vehicles (and/or parts therefor) or, as the sole alternative, that they export part of its production of motor vehicles (and/or parts therefor). Therefore, the CVA requirements fall within Items 1(a) and/or 1(b).

6.411 In turn, as described below in arguments relating to the SCM Agreement (Section VI.D), under the ratio requirements the amount of imported motor vehicles that a beneficiary may sell in Canada (and, therefore, that it may be interested in "purchasing") varies according to the value of the motor vehicles which it exports. Therefore, the ratio requirements fall within Item 1(b) of the Illustrative List.

3. Canada's Response

6.412 **Canada** responds as follows:

[470] According to the Panel Report on *Indonesia - Autos, supra* note 270, para. 14.82, "[local content requirements are] necessarily 'trade-related, because such requirements, by definition, always favour the use of domestic products over imported products, and therefore, affect trade".

(a) The MVTO and SROs Are Not "Trade-Related Investment Measures"

6.413 Just as Japan and the European Communities cannot show a violation of Article III, they cannot show that the TRIMs Agreement has any relevance. The TRIMs Agreement, by the terms of Article 1, applies to trade-related investment measures. The term "investment measures" is not defined in the text. The only interpretation of the term was provided by the Panel in *Indonesia - Autos* which found the Indonesian measures to be TRIMs. The Panel wrote:

> "On the basis of our reading of these measures applied by Indonesia under the 1993 and the 1996 car programmes, which have investment objectives and investment features and which refer to investment programmes, we find that these measures are aimed at encouraging the development of a local manufacturing capability for finished motor vehicles and parts and components in Indonesia. Inherent to this objective is that these measures necessarily have a significant impact on investment in these sectors. For this reason, we consider that these measures fall within any reasonable interpretation of the term "investment measures"."[471]

6.414 The Panel conceded that it was not providing a complete definition of the term, and stated that other measures may relate to investment in a different manner. Nevertheless, it seems clear that an investment measure must affect investment. This is consistent with the ordinary meaning of the words.[472] The complainants have not demonstrated that Canada's measures have any current investment effects, and have therefore not shown that they are TRIMs. Changes in investment levels can have no effect on benefits under the measures. Furthermore, current production levels are far beyond those required, and are therefore based purely on commercial considerations such as labour costs, proximity to markets and the quality of the labour force.

6.415 The complaining parties have also failed to demonstrate that the CVA and ratio requirements are trade-related. Japan claims the CVA requirements of the MVTO and SROs and the CVA commitments of the additional letters are trade-related because they are a domestic content requirement. This is not true of the MVTO and SRO amounts, since Canada has already demonstrated that they do not require the use of domestic parts; indeed, they have no effect whatsoever on parts-sourcing decisions. The amounts in the additional letters are irrelevant, since they are not requirements at all.

6.416 The European Communities makes the same claims with respect to the CVA, and is wrong for the same reasons. It also claims the ratio requirements are trade-related because they create an incentive for limiting the sales of imported vehicles and for exporting domestic vehicles. Given that manufacturers are operating well above the required levels, the ratio requirements are incapable of affecting trade in goods. Manufacturers can and do increase or decrease production, imports or exports without affecting their MVTO or SRO eligibility.

---

[471] Panel Report on *Indonesia - Autos, supra* note 270, para. 14.80.

[472] See the interpretive provisions of the Vienna Convention on the Law of Treaties (May 23, 1969, CTS 1980/37, 1155 UNTS 331, (1969) 8 ILM 679), especially Article 31.

(b) The MVTO and SROs Do Not Violate the TRIMs Agreement

(i) The measures do not violate Article III or XI of GATT 1994

6.417 Assuming the TRIMs Agreement applies at all, which Canada denies, Canada's measures still do not violate Article 2. That article provides that no Member shall apply any TRIM that is inconsistent with Articles III or XI of the GATT 1994. The complainants have not raised Article XI, and they cannot demonstrate the existence of any violation of Article III. Canada has already demonstrated that the measures at issue do not violate Article III. They thus could not violate the TRIMs Agreement, even if it did apply to the case.

(ii) The CVA is not covered by the Illustrative List

6.418 It is clear from the terms of the Illustrative List that Canada is not in violation of the TRIMs Agreement. The text is explicit in stating that a prohibited TRIM must "require" the purchase or use of domestic products. The CVA requirements in the MVTO and SROs do not require the purchase or use of domestic products, notwithstanding the complainants' claims to the contrary.

6.419 The CVA is a value-added calculation that ensures a minimal level of manufacturing activity. MVTO and SRO manufacturers are free to achieve their CVA levels in the manner of their choosing. They are not *required* by law to use Canadian products: they can and do meet their CVA levels on the basis of their labour costs, which are costs necessarily incurred domestically. They could choose to import all of their parts and components, and they would still qualify for benefits under the MVTO and the SROs. The CVA is therefore not covered by the Illustrative List.

(iii) The ratio requirements are not covered by the Illustrative List

6.420 The European Communities argues that under the ratio requirement the number of imported vehicles that a manufacturer may sell varies according to the value of the vehicles it exports. It therefore claims that the ratio requirements are covered by Item 1(b) of the Illustrative List.[473]

6.421 The Illustrative List covers mandatory measures that require "that an enterprise's purchases or use of imported products be *limited* to an amount related to the ... value of local products that it exports". The ratio requirements do not in any way limit the purchase or use of imported products, let alone do so on the basis of the value of local products exported. Manufacturers can purchase, import, and use an unlimited quantity of imported vehicles. It could happen in some cases that a manufacturer may have to pay duty on some of those vehicles. This, however, is not a *limit* on the purchase or use of imported products. It simply returns the products to the situation they would have faced in the absence of the measures. The ratio require-

[473] This argument, too, appears to be premised on the EC's incorrect assumption that a ratio failure results in a complete loss of duty remission.

ment simply sets the maximum amount of duty-free importation available for any given level of production. The ratio requirements are therefore not covered by the Illustrative List, and are not TRIMs.

4. Rebuttal Arguments by Japan

6.422 **Japan** rebuts as follows:

6.423 The Government of Canada argues that the measures at issue have no current investment effect and, as such, they are not investment measures within the meaning of the TRIMs Agreement. Canada also claims that, even if they were such measures, they would not be inconsistent with Article 2.1 of the TRIMs Agreement because, according to Canada, they do not violate Article III:4 of the GATT 1994.

6.424 Canada's arguments are not supported by the facts and misinterpret the relevant provisions of the TRIMs Agreement.

(a) Investment Measures

6.425 Canada incorrectly interprets the Panel's reasoning in *Indonesia - Autos*[474] to support its contention that an investment measure must have actual investment effects. Indeed, a proper reading of the Panel's ruling in that instance can only lead to the rejection of Canada's narrow interpretation of the meaning of the term "investment measure".

6.426 In *Indonesia - Autos*, the panel made it clear that numerous measures may relate to investment in a different manner and that more than one factor can be taken into account in interpreting the term "investment measure". Far from limiting its analysis to the current investment effects of a given measure, the Panel specifically considered the objective of the Indonesian measures at issue in that case and found that such measures were aimed at encouraging the development of a local manufacturing capability for finished motor vehicles and parts and components. Then, it examined whether the measures had an impact on investment on the sectors (e.g., whether the stated objectives have been met).

6.427 In this present dispute, the measures are clearly aimed at sustaining investment in the automotive sector.

6.428 First, as discussed, the MVTO 1998, the SROs and the letters of undertaking implement the Auto Pact, a trade agreement that was explicitly aimed at investment.

6.429 Second, the fact that the only eligible recipients for the Duty Waiver are manufacturers is prima facie evidence that the Duty Waiver is an investment measure.

6.430 Third, the view that the Duty Waiver is an investment measure is supported by statements of Canadian and industry officials.

6.431 On 23 February 1999, Minister John Manley (the Minister of Industry Canada) made the following statement:

> "In the context of our consultations for this review, the industry told us that the most important decision that the government could make *to assist production in Canada* was to maintain the Auto Pact and vehi-

---

[474] Panel Report on *Indonesia - Autos, supra* note 270.

cle tariff at its current level. We did just that. We are defending the interests of GM, Ford and Daimler-Chrysler before the WTO."[475] (*emphasis added*)

6.432 This is clear evidence that the Duty Waiver "assists production" in Canada. Whether production is "maintained" or "increased", it is clearly linked to investment.

6.433 This linkage to investment is supported by the 17 November 1997 statement by the then Chairman, President and CEO of Chrysler Canada (Exhibit JPN-46) wherein he acknowledged that the CVA "has resulted in significant purchases of vehicle parts produced in Canada" and has "resulted in the dramatic rise of the Canadian vehicle parts industry" between 1964 and 1996.

6.434 With regard to the position of the Government of Canada that the CVA is not an investment measure, Japan would like to bring the Panel's attention to the 1997 statements by the then Chairman, President and CEO of Chrysler Canada, contained in our Exhibit JPN-46.

> "In the last decade alone, over $20 billion out of the $23 billion invested in total from the whole industry, came from the Auto Pact players (the domestic industry) as a result of the 1965 Auto Pact" (Exhibit JPN-46, at p.2).
>
> "Automobiles manufactured in North America by the Auto Pact members, the "Big Three", contain on average over $1,500 worth of Canadian-made parts. Automobiles manufactured by non-auto pact members, such as Honda and Toyota, contain only $360 worth of Canadian-made parts. So, you can see by these figures the potential economic ramifications of any initiatives which undermine our domestic Industry." (Ibid.)

6.435 It is also supported by 16 October 1997 statements made by the then President and CEO of Ford Canada:

> So what is so special about the Auto Pact that makes it worth fighting for?
>
> It has been acclaimed as Canada's most successful trade policy in the last 30 years because it spawned the development of a world class automotive parts and manufacturing industry in Canada.

(b) Trade-Related

6.436 The Government of Canada argues that the Duty Waiver is not trade-related. On this issue, the above discussion with respect to the inconsistency of the CVA requirement with Article III:4 of the GATT 1994 demonstrates that the Duty Waiver is trade-related and is thus governed by the TRIMs Agreement.

(c) Relevant Test

6.437 The Government of Canada argues that the CVA does not fall within the Illustrative List. This argument has no merit. First, the Illustrative List is not exhaustive. Second, the relevant legal issues are: (i) is the measure an "investment meas-

[475] Visit to Boisbriand on 23 February 1999 by Minister Manley (Exhibit JPN-49).

ure"; (ii) is the measure "trade related"; and (iii) in the context of this dispute, is the measure inconsistent with the Article III:4 of the GATT 1994. As set out above, all three questions can be answered in the affirmative. The fact that the measure is not included on the Illustrative List is not determinative.

6.438 In its response to Question 16 of the Panel, the Government of Canada takes the position that the use of the word "require" is a mandatory criterion for a TRIM that is inconsistent with Article III:4 of the GATT 1994.

6.439 Clearly, this is not the case. The qualifying word "include" applies to the remainder of paragraph 1 of the Illustrative List, including the word "require". Thus, "require" is not a mandatory criterion. It is merely illustrative.

6.440 It is necessary only to demonstrate that the TRIM in question violates Article III:4 of the GATT 1994. Thus, it is necessary only to show that the measure has the potential to change the conditions of competition between imported and like domestic products.

5. *Rebuttal Arguments by the European Communities*

6.441 The **European Communities** rebuts as follows:

6.442 Canada's main argument under the TRIMs Agreement is that the measures in dispute are not "investment measures", because they have not been shown by the complainants to have "any *current* investment effects[476]. "

6.443 The existence of an "investment measure" does not depend on its current effects on investment. The examples of prohibited TRIMs contained in the Illustrative List do not incorporate any such "current effects" test.

6.444 The Panel Report on *Indonesia - Autos*, which on this point is quoted with approval by Canada, did not look at the actual effects of the measure, but rather at the structure and the aim of the measures[477].

6.445 If the characterisation of a measure as an "investment measure" was made dependant on its actual effects on investments at a given moment, one and the same type of measure could be a prohibited TRIM when applied by a Member, but not when applied by another Member.

6.446 Indeed, that would be precisely the perverse outcome of Canada's position in this case. In *Indonesia - Autos*, the granting of a tariff exemption contingent upon compliance with a local content requirement was found to be a prohibited TRIM when applied by a developing country[478]. Yet Canada's position is, in essence, that the very same measure should be condoned by this Panel, simply because Canada is a developed country which has already succeeded in building its own local automotive industry, so that the measure has no "current" effects.

---

[476] Canada also asserts that: "Automotive production levels in Canada are based on purely commercial considerations such as labour costs, proximity to markets and the quality of the labour force". Aside from the fact that the actual effects of the measure are not relevant, Canada provides no supporting evidence for that statement. Volvo's decision to close its assembly plant in Canada casts doubts on Canada's self-confident assertions and suggests that investment incentives may still play a role even in Canada.

[477] Panel Report on *Indonesia - Autos, supra* note 270, para. 14.80.

[478] Ibid., para. 14.91.

6.447 Canada introduces the additional argument that "changes in investment levels can have no effects on benefits under the measures." That assertion is manifestly wrong. If the Big Three decided to close their production facilities in Canada and import all the motor vehicles which they sell in Canada from the United States and Mexico, they would cease to qualify for the Tariff Exemption. On the other hand, if the Big Three made new investments, so as to increase their local production, they would be entitled to sell even more vehicles imported under the Tariff Exemption than now[479].

6.448 Canada also argues that the measures are not "trade-related"; and that they do not fall within the Illustrative List. The arguments raised by Canada are essentially the same as those raised by Canada in its unsuccessful attempt to refute that the measures are inconsistent with GATT Article III:4 and with Article 3.1(a) of the SCM Agreement. Those arguments are disposed of elsewhere in the EC's argumentation.

6. *Response by Canada to the Complainants' Rebuttals*

6.449 **Canada** responds as follows:

6.450 Canada maintains its argument that the measures are not TRIMs because they have no investment effects. Manufacturers are operating well above the production levels required by the MVTO and SROs. There is no incentive to increase investment, and no need even to maintain existing levels. The measures are thus incapable of affecting investment.

6.451 The European Communities has argued that the measures are TRIMs because of their "structure and aim". Canada notes that the panel in *Indonesia - Autos* stated explicitly that the measures at issue would "necessarily" have a "significant" effect on investment.[480] It is thus incorrect to state that the previous panel "did not look at the actual effects of the measure", as the European Communities has suggested.

7. *The European Communities' Follow-Up to Canada's Response*

6.452 As a follow-up to Canada's response, the **European Communities** argues as follows:

6.453 As mentioned with respect to Article III claims, the European Communities would like to make a clarification regarding the scope of its claims with respect to the CVA requirements. Canada attributes to the European Communities the claim that "the CVA requirements favour the use of domestic equipment manufacturing (OEM) parts in the production of vehicles in Canada".

6.454 That is not correct. The EC's claim is not limited to OEM parts. It extends to all goods used or consumed in the manufacture of motor vehicles which are counted as CVA when produced or manufactured in Canada, but not when imported. In ac-

---

479 Significantly, Annex 300.A of NAFTA, which authorises Canada to continue to apply the Tariff Exemption, is entitled "Trade and Investment in the Automotive Sector" (Exhibit EC -13).

480 Panel Report on *Indonesia - Autos*, *supra* note 270, para. 14.80.

cordance with the rules contained in the MVTO 1998, that includes not only parts, but also materials, as well as certain equipment of non permanent nature.

8. Canada's Follow-Up Response

6.455 **Canada** responds as follows:

6.456 (See Canada's response to the complainants' rebuttals in Section 0.)

D. The SCM Agreement

1. Arguments of Japan

6.457 **Japan** argues as follows:

6.458 The Duty Waiver is inconsistent with the SCM Agreement. It is a subsidy that is contingent upon export performance and upon the use of domestic over imported goods. Accordingly, it is prohibited under Article 3 of the SCM Agreement.

(a) The Duty Waiver is a Subsidy under Article 1 of the SCM Agreement

6.459 Article 1 of the SCM Agreement defines a subsidy as follows:

> "1.1 For the purposes of this Agreement, a subsidy shall be deemed to exist if:
>
> (a)(1) there is a financial contribution by a government or any public body within the territory of a Member (referred to in this Agreement as "government"), i.e. where:
>
> ...
>
> (ii) government revenue that is otherwise due is foregone or not collected (*e.g.*, fiscal incentives such as tax credits);
>
> and
>
> (b) a benefit is thereby conferred."

6.460 Thus, in order to determine if a subsidy exists, two elements must be demonstrated. The alleged subsidy must be (i) a financial contribution by a government (ii) that confers a benefit.

6.461 With respect to the first element, a financial contribution under paragraph 1.1(a)(1)(ii) of the SCM Agreement exists when government revenue that is otherwise due is foregone or not collected. In the ordinary sense, "government revenue" is raised through internal taxes and other charges including customs duties. Since government revenue is foregone when a customs duty is waived, the Duty Waiver amounts to a financial contribution.

6.462 With respect to the second element, the exemption of customs duty on motor vehicles is clearly a benefit under Article 1.1(b) of the SCM Agreement.

6.463 Accordingly, the Duty Waiver is a subsidy within the meaning of Article 1 of the SCM Agreement. This is consistent with the finding of the Panel in *Indonesia -*

Autos that preferential duty treatment analogous to the Duty Waiver was a subsidy within the meaning of Article 1 of the SCM Agreement.[481]

(b) The Subsidy is Prohibited under Article 3 of the SCM Agreement

6.464 Article 3 of the SCM Agreement prohibits certain subsidies. It reads as follows:

> "3.1 Except as provided in the Agreement on Agriculture, the following subsidies, within the meaning of Article 1, shall be prohibited:
>
> (a) subsidies contingent, in law or in fact, whether solely or as one of several other conditions, upon export performance, including those illustrated in Annex I.
>
> (b) subsidies contingent, whether solely or as one of several other conditions, upon the use of domestic over imported goods.
>
> 3.2 A Member shall neither grant nor maintain subsidies referred to in paragraph 1."

6.465 The Duty Waiver is a prohibited subsidy for two independent reasons: (i) it is contingent on the use of domestic over imported goods and (ii) it is contingent on export performance.

(i) The Duty Waiver is contingent on the use of domestic over imported goods

6.466 Article 3.1(b) of the SCM Agreement prohibits subsidies that are contingent, whether solely or as one of several other conditions, upon the use of domestic over imported goods.

6.467 The Duty Waiver is conditional on compliance with the CVA requirement which requires the use of domestic over imported goods. Accordingly, the Duty Waiver is a prohibited subsidy under Article 3.1(b) of the SCM Agreement and is inconsistent with Article 3.2 of the SCM Agreement.

(ii) The Duty Waiver is contingent upon export performance

6.468 Article 3.1(a) of the SCM Agreement prohibits subsidies that are contingent, in law or in fact, whether solely or as one of several other conditions, upon export performance.

6.469 The Duty Waiver is, in fact, contingent on export performance. Eligibility for the Duty Waiver is conditional on compliance with the manufacturing requirement (i.e. the production-to-sales ratio). As discussed in argumentation relating to Article III, the application of the manufacturing requirement means that a certain value of motor vehicles is to be exported by the Auto Pact Manufacturers.

6.470 In this case, by virtue of the manufacturing requirement, the Duty Waiver is conditional on an Auto Pact Manufacturer exporting a certain amount of its produc-

---

[481] Panel Report on *Indonesia - Autos, supra* note 270, para. 14.155. The measures included a variety of tariff reductions and tariff exemptions on motor vehicles and parts.

tion. The benefit of the Duty Waiver, therefore, is contingent upon export performance.

6.471 Thus, the Duty Waiver is a prohibited export subsidy under Article 3.1(a) of the SCM Agreement and is inconsistent with Article 3.2 of the SCM Agreement.

2. *Arguments of the European Communities*

6.472 The **European Communities** argues as follows:

6.473 The Tariff Exemption is a "specific subsidy" within the meaning of Articles 1 and 2 of the SCM Agreement. Furthermore, the granting of the Tariff Exemption is contingent upon export performance, as well as upon the use of domestic over imported goods. As such, it is prohibited by both Article 3.1(a) and Article 3.1(b) *juncto* Article 3.2 of the SCM Agreement.

(a) The Tariff Exemption Constitutes a Specific Subsidy

(i) The Tariff Exemption is a "subsidy"

6.474 The notion of "subsidy" for the purposes of the SCM Agreement is defined in its Article 1.1. That provision reads in relevant part as follows:

> "1.1 For the purpose of this Agreement, a subsidy shall be deemed to exist if:
>
> (a)(1) there is a financial contribution by a government ..., i.e. where:
>
> ...
>
> (ii) government revenue that is otherwise due is foregone or not collected (e.g., fiscal incentives such as tax credits);
>
> ...
>
> and
>
> (b) a benefit is thereby conferred."

6.475 Customs duties are imposed, collected and appropriated by the Canadian Government. Accordingly, they constitute "Government revenue".

6.476 Pursuant to Canada's Customs Tariff, the importation of motor vehicles is, in principle, subject to the payment of customs duties. Thus, by exempting from customs duties the importation of motor vehicles by the beneficiaries, the Canadian Government is "foregoing" revenue that would otherwise be "due".

6.477 Finally, the Tariff Exemption provides a "benefit" to the beneficiaries because it lowers their import costs, compared to the costs that they would incur if, like any other importer of motor vehicles, they were required to pay the full amount of customs duties stipulated in Canada's Customs Tariff.

(ii) The subsidy is "specific"

6.478 Article 1.2 of the SCM Agreement provides that:

> "A subsidy as defined in paragraph 1 shall be subject to the provisions of Part II ... only if such a subsidy is specific in accordance with the provisions of Article 2."

6.479 According to Article 2.3 of the SCM Agreement:

"Any subsidy falling under the provisions of Article 3 shall be deemed to be specific."

6.480 As shown below, the Tariff Exemption falls within the provisions of both Articles 3.1(a) and 3.1(b) of the SCM Agreement. Therefore, it constitutes a "specific" subsidy for purposes of Article 1.2.

(b) The Tariff Exemption is a Prohibited Subsidy

6.481 Article 3 of the SCM Agreement reads as follows in pertinent part:

"3.1 [T]he following subsidies, within the meaning of Article 1, shall be prohibited:

a) subsides contingent, in law or in fact, whether solely or as one of several conditions, upon export performance ....

b) subsides contingent, whether solely or as one of several conditions, upon the use of domestic over imported goods.

3.2 A Member shall neither grant nor maintain subsidies referred to in paragraph 1." (footnotes omitted)

6.482 As will be demonstrated below, the ratio requirements constitute an export performance condition of the type prohibited by Article 3.1 (a).

6.483 In turn, the CVA requirements make the Tariff Exemption contingent upon: (1) the use of domestic over imported goods, contrary to Article 3.1(b); and/or (2) the exportation of motor vehicles and/or original equipment parts therefor, contrary to Article 3.1(a).

(i) The Ratio Requirements

6.484 As explained in the factual part, the production-to-sales ratio applicable to the MVTO 1998 beneficiaries is, as a general rule, at least 95 to 100 in the case of automobiles and at least 75 to 100 in the case of specified commercial vehicles and buses. In turn, the production-to-sales ratio applicable to the SRO beneficiaries is, also as a general rule, 100 to 100, irrespective of the class of motor vehicles.

6.485 In those instances where the required ratio is 100 to 100 or more, a beneficiary cannot sell in Canada any amount of motor vehicles imported under the Tariff Exemption unless it exports an equivalent amount of domestically manufactured motor vehicles.

6.486 This is illustrated by the example set out in the EC's Table 3 below. Beneficiary A sells all its production in Canada, with the consequence that it cannot sell any motor vehicles imported under the Tariff Exemption. Indeed, if Beneficiary A sold any such motor vehicles, in addition to those which it manufactures in Canada, the resulting ratio of production-to-sales would be less than 100 to 100. In contrast, Beneficiary B, which produces and sells in Canada the same amount of motor vehicles as Beneficiary A, is nevertheless entitled to sell motor vehicles imported under the Tariff Exemption up to an amount of 50$ because it exports motor vehicles for the same amount.

EC's Table 3

Ratio domestic production/domestic sales: 100 to 100

	Local production	*Exports*	*Imports*	*Total sales in Canada*
Beneficiary A	100$	0$	0$	100$
Beneficiary B	100$	50$	50$	100$

6.487 Thus, in those cases where the ratio is 100 to 100 or more, the possibility to sell motor vehicles imported under the Tariff Exemption, and consequently to benefit from the subsidy, is legally "contingent" upon export performance within the meaning of Article 3.1 a) of the SCM Agreement

6.488 In those instances where the prescribed ratio is less than 100 to 100, the beneficiaries are entitled to sell in Canada some motor vehicles imported under the Tariff Exemption, whether or not they export any domestically produced motor vehicles. For instance, if the required ratio is 95 to 100, the beneficiaries may sell imported motor vehicles for an amount equal to 5 per cent of their total sales in Canada, even if they do not export any motor vehicles.

6.489 Nonetheless, as shown by the example in the EC's Table 4, if a beneficiary exports some motor vehicles instead of selling them in Canada, the value of imported motor vehicles which it may sell in Canada increases by an amount equal to the value of the exported vehicles.

EC's Table 4

Ratio local production/local sales: 95 to 100

	Local production	*Exports*	*Imports*	*Total sales in Canada*
Beneficiary A	95$	0$	5$	100$
Beneficiary B	95$	50$	55$	100$

6.490 In the above example Beneficiary A does not export any motor vehicles. As a consequence, it may sell in Canada only a small amount of motor vehicles imported under the Tariff Exemption (5$). Beneficiary B produces the same amount as Beneficiary A but, unlike Beneficiary A, exports a substantial part thereof. As a result, Beneficiary B is entitled to sell in Canada the same amount imported under the Tariff Exemption as Beneficiary A (5$) plus an additional amount equal to the value of its exports (50$).

6.491 Thus, by exporting part of their domestic production, the beneficiaries qualify for a larger subsidy than if they sold all their domestic production in Canada. That additional subsidy is therefore "contingent" in law upon export performance within the meaning of Article 3.1 (a).

(ii) The CVA requirements

6.492 The CVA requirements do not impose explicitly the obligation to "use domestic over imported goods", but rather the obligation to reach a certain amount of Canadian Value Added. Nevertheless, parts and materials used in the manufacture of motor vehicles are one of the items, indeed the main one, included in the calculation of the CVA[482].

6.493 The Tariff Exemption is "contingent upon the use of domestic over imported goods" within the meaning of Article 3.1 (b) because using domestic parts and materials may be sufficient, or at least contribute, to meet the CVA requirements, whereas using imported parts and materials may not. As a result, the granting of the subsidy will depend, at least in some cases, on whether the beneficiaries use domestic or imported goods.

6.494 During the consultations, Canada appeared to take the position that the Tariff Exemption is not "contingent upon the use of domestic over imported goods" because in practice the beneficiaries can meet the CVA requirements without using any domestic parts and materials at all.

6.495 In order to establish a violation of Article 3.1(b), however, it is not necessary to show that the subsidy has any actual effects. The mere possibility that in some cases a beneficiary may be required to use domestic goods instead of imported goods in order to qualify for the subsidy is sufficient to trigger the application of Article 3.1(b).

6.496 At any rate, assuming *arguendo* that the actual use of domestic goods had to be a necessary condition for granting the subsidy, in the case at hand some of the CVA requirements have been set at a level such that the beneficiaries cannot possibly meet them without using some domestic parts and materials.

6.497 As set out in the factual part, the CVA requirements contained in the Letters of Undertaking have the consequence that the total CVA of the motor vehicles of a given class, and of the original equipment parts therefor, *produced* in Canada must approach 60 per cent (in the case of automobiles) or 50 per cent (in the case of specified commercial vehicles and buses) of the cost to the beneficiary of the vehicles of that class *sold* in Canada.

6.498 In turn, the SROs issued from 1984 onwards[483] provide, as a general rule, that the CVA of the motor vehicles *produced* in Canada by the beneficiaries (and in some cases, of the original equipment parts) shall be no less than 40 per cent[484] of the cost of sales of the vehicles *sold* in Canada.

6.499 In practice, however, parts and materials may account on average for as much as 80 per cent of the cost of sales of the motor vehicles assembled in Canada[485]. Consequently, the CVA contained in the motor vehicles sold in Canada by a beneficiary cannot be sufficient on its own to meet the above mentioned CVA requirements, unless those motor vehicles incorporate a substantial proportion of domestic parts and materials.

---

482 See Section VI.B on GATT Article III.

483 See *supra* para. 5.35.

484 60 per cent in the case of CAMI.

485 Based on the data shown in tables 2.10 ("Value of Shipments in Canadian Automotive Industries") and 2.16 ("Cost of Materials in the Canadian Automotive Industry) contained in the Statistical Review of the Canadian Automotive Industry: 1997 Edition, published by Industry Canada (hereinafter, "Statistical Review 1997") (Exhibit EC-18). For example, in 1995, the last year for which data are available, the total cost of materials of Canada's motor vehicles industry was C$40,680 million, whereas the value of the shipments of motor vehicles by the Canadian industry totalled C$50,473 million. Thus, the cost of materials represented, on average, 80.5 per cent of the shipment value.

6.500 It must be recalled, nevertheless, that the relevant CVA amount includes not only the CVA contained in the motor vehicles sold domestically but also the CVA of any exported motor vehicles (and in some cases of exported original equipment parts).Therefore, in theory it is conceivable that a beneficiary might be able to satisfy the CVA requirements without using any domestic parts and materials at all, by exporting such a large part of its production that the "non-parts CVA" of those exports, added to the "non-parts CVA" at of the motor vehicles sold domestically, reaches on its own the required percentage of CVA to the cost of sales of the vehicles sold domestically[486]. But in that case the CVA requirements would be operating as an export performance condition.

6.501 Thus, in definitive the CVA requirements make the Tariff Exemption "contingent" either upon the use of domestic over imported goods, contrary to the prohibition of Article 3.1 (b); and/or, as the sole alternative, upon export performance, in violation of the prohibition contained in Article 3.1(a).

3. *Canada's Response*

6.502 Canada responds as follows:

6.503 Japan and the European Communities contend that duty-free treatment pursuant to the MVTO and the SROs is a subsidy that is contingent upon export performance, contrary to Article 3.1(a) of the SCM Agreement and contingent upon the use of domestic over imported goods, contrary to Article 3.1(b) of the SCM Agreement. Both of these allegations rest on fundamental misunderstandings of the nature and effect of the measures at issue.

(a) The Duty-Free Treatment Is Not an Export Subsidy within the Meaning of Article 3.1(a) of the SCM Agreement

(i) The duty-free treatment facilitates imports: it does not distort export trade

6.504 Article 3.2 of the DSU requires that the SCM Agreement must be interpreted in good faith in accordance with the principles of treaty interpretation in customary international law as set out, in part, in Article 31 of the Vienna Convention on the Law of Treaties.[487] The starting point for interpreting the SCM Agreement is therefore the ordinary meaning of its terms, in their context and in the light of the object and purpose of the SCM Agreement.

6.505 The overriding purpose of the SCM Agreement is to discipline subsidies that distort trade. The hierarchy of disciplines the SCM Agreement imposes on its three categories of subsidies reflects this purpose: non-actionable subsidies;[488] actionable

---

[486] In practice, the "non-parts CVA" accounts for barely one third of the total CVA achieved by the beneficiaries. See Statistical Review 1997, Table 4.8 (Exhibit EC-18).

[487] Appellate Body Report on *United States - Standards for Reformulated and Conventional Gasoline*, adopted on 20 May 1996, WT/DS2/AB/R & WT/DS4/AB/R (hereinafter Appellate Body Report on *US - Gasoline*), *supra*, footnote 306, 16.

[488] See Articles 1.2 and 8.

subsidies[489]; and prohibited subsidies. Only two types of subsidies are prohibited: those that are contingent upon export performance and those that are contingent upon the use of domestic over imported goods. Such subsidies are taken to be, or are seen as intended to be, by definition trade distorting. Thus, in *Brazil - Export Financing Programme for Aircraft*, the Panel stated:

> "In our view, the object and purpose of the SCM Agreement is to impose multilateral disciplines on subsidies which distort international trade. It is for this reason that the SCM Agreement prohibits two categories of subsidies - subsidies contingent upon exportation and upon the use of domestic over imported goods - *that are specifically designed to affect trade*."[490] (*emphasis added*)

6.506 Japan and the European Communities assert that the duty-free treatment of *imported* vehicles constitutes a prohibited *export* subsidy under the SCM Agreement. The Canadian measures at issue implement Canada's obligations under the Auto Pact that was designed to facilitate the rationalization of automotive production by removing barriers to automotive trade between Canada and the United States. Canada's contribution to this rationalization was to remove the tariff on motor vehicle imports into Canada. It did this through the measures at issue.[491]

6.507 Canada's import duty waiver therefore encouraged imports into Canada. Because NAFTA-origin vehicles are not subject to duty,[492] the principal beneficiaries of the duty waiver are vehicles from Japan and the European Communities, as illustrated by Canada's *Figure 4* and Japan's Table 6.

6.508 Export subsidies are prohibited because they are trade distorting: they divert production from domestic markets to export markets. Canada's duty-free treatment for imports does not do this. If manufacturers were really exporting to receive duty-free treatment for imports, they would be exporting only up to their levels of imports and they would be exporting everywhere they could. Instead, the value of Canadian motor vehicle production is more than double that required by the production-to-sales ratios and Canadian production is directed almost exclusively to the United States.

6.509 This is exactly what one expects to see in a rationalized industry where the US market is much larger - ten times larger - than the Canadian market, and where Canadian exports to the United States have attracted no duty since the Auto Pact came in to force, first under the US GATT waiver, now under the NAFTA. In fact, this production and export pattern is followed by all Canadian motor vehicle manufacturers, and not just those qualifying for duty-free treatment for imports.

---

489 See Article 5.

490 Panel Report on *Brazil - Export Financing Programme for Aircraft*, adopted as modified by the Appellate Body on 20 August 1999, WT/DS46/R (hereinafter Panel Report on *Brazil - Aircraft*), para. 7.26.

491 Pursuant to Article II(a) and Annex A of the Auto Pact.

492 All motor vehicles from the United States and light trucks from Mexico enter Canada duty-free under the NAFTA. Other motor vehicles from Mexico are subject to a 1.3 or 2.4 per cent tariff, that will be eliminated by 2003.

6.510 The United States contribution under the Auto Pact to the rationalization of the Canada/United States automotive industry was the elimination of its duty on imports from Canada of qualifying vehicles and other automotive goods.[493]

6.511 It is the US waiver of duty on vehicles imported from Canada that has affected the export of vehicles from Canada. This is borne out by the fact that the overwhelming preponderance of exports of Canadian vehicles is to the United States.[494]

6.512 The only real *effect* on trade of the Canadian duty-free treatment is to increase the volume of duty-free imports into Canada of vehicles that would not qualify for such treatment under the NAFTA, such as those from Japan or the European Communities. This is the antithesis of the effect that underlies the prohibition of subsidies contingent upon export performance: the unfair distortion of trade in favour of exports from the subsidizing Member.

6.513 What Canada's duty-free treatment really does is to facilitate the importation of vehicles from Japan, Europe and elsewhere by permitting vehicles of any origin to enter Canada duty free. Provided that this treatment is granted on an MFN basis - and it is - this is exactly the sort of treatment that the GATT permits, and indeed encourages.

6.514 It would be contrary to the objective of trade liberalization - the very foundation of the GATT - to characterize a measure that facilitates *imports* as an improper trade distortion. It is therefore hardly surprising that nowhere does the *1965 GATT Working Party Report* suggest that any members considered Canada's duty-free treatment an export subsidy, even though export subsidies were prohibited by Article XVI:4 of the GATT at the time of the Working Party. The Working Party, by necessary implication, found no export subsidy in Canada's measures.

(ii) The duty-free treatment is unlike any of the practices on the Illustrative List of Export Subsidies

6.515 The Illustrative List of Export Subsidies in Annex I to the SCM Agreement, (the "Illustrative List"), while not exhaustive, is an important guide to identifying the practices that constitute prohibited export subsidies. It is particularly significant that in each of the practices identified on the Illustrative List there is a clear and direct nexus between the subsidy and the exported product, and the amount of the subsidy increases with the volume of exports.

6.516 Neither Japan nor the European Communities has identified any subsidy on the Illustrative List that is remotely analogous to the duty-free treatment for imports under the MVTO and SROs. The duty-free treatment is, in fact, unlike any of the measures listed as prohibited export subsidies on the Illustrative List.

---

[493] Pursuant to Article II(b) and Annex B of the Auto Pact. This elimination of duty by the United States, on Canadian vehicles only, was originally found by the Working Party to be inconsistent with Article I of the GATT. The United States therefore obtained a waiver from its GATT obligations. The US measure was subsequently subsumed into the CUSFTA and the NAFTA.

[494] See Tables 23-32 in Automotive Trade 1997, pp. 30-39 (Exhibit EC-15). The same report notes that in 1997, 97 per cent of Canada's automotive exports were to the United States, p.4.

6.517 It is contextually significant that duty or tax exemption or remission programs, such as those described in paragraphs (g) , (h) and (i) of the Illustrative List, are deemed not to constitute export subsidies when they are not excessive. By operation of footnote 5 to Article 3.1(a), these non-excessive tax or duty exemption or remission programs are explicitly not prohibited subsidies under the SCM Agreement. Footnote 5 to Article 3.1(a) provides that:

> "Measures referred to in Annex I as not constituting export subsidies shall not be prohibited under this or any other provision of this Agreement."

6.518 Moreover, under the SCM Agreement, certain exemption or remission programs are not only considered not to be prohibited export subsidies, they are considered not even to be subsidies. Footnote 1 to Article 1.1(a)(1)(ii) of the SCM Agreement provides:

> "In accordance with the provisions of Article XVI of GATT 1994 (Note to Article XVI) and the provisions of Annexes I through III of this Agreement, the exemption of an exported product from duties or taxes borne by the like product when destined for domestic consumption, or the remission of such duties or taxes in amounts not in excess of those which have accrued, shall not be deemed to be a subsidy."

6.519 Footnotes 1 and 5, together with paragraphs (g), (h) and (i) of the Illustrative List make clear that in the case of non-excessive duty or tax exemption or remission programs, there is no prohibited export subsidy - nor even a subsidy - even though government revenue that is otherwise due is foregone and a benefit is thereby conferred directly to exports.

6.520 Under the MVTO and the SROs, duty-free treatment can never result in excess remissions. Moreover, the benefit is conferred on imports. The direct correlation with exports found even in the permitted programs is entirely absent. If non-excessive exemption or remission programs do not constitute prohibited export subsidies, it would be inconsistent with the principles underlying those exemptions for MVTO and SRO duty-free treatment to be found to constitute prohibited export subsidies. To find the duty-free treatment to be an export subsidy within the meaning of Article 3.1(a) of the SCM Agreement would require an interpretation of Article 3.1(a) that is contrary to the ordinary meaning of its terms in their context and in the light of the object and purpose of the SCM Agreement.

(b) The Ratio Requirements do not Make the Duty-Free Treatment Contingent Upon Export Performance

6.521 Article 3.1(a) reaches only subsidies that are contingent upon export performance, "in law or in fact, whether solely or as one of several other conditions ...". According to the European Communities, the production-to-sales ratio requirements make the duty-free treatment contingent *in law* on export performance. By contrast, Japan appears to concede that the measures do not make the duty-free treatment *legally* contingent upon export performance, but it does contend that the "subsidy" is *de facto* contingent upon export performance.

6.522 The arguments of both complainants demonstrate the absence of *de jure* contingency. They rely on hypothetical scenarios because there is nothing on the face of the measures themselves that suggests contingency. In other words, there is no contingency in law.

6.523 Indeed, the approach of both complainants underscores that there is no *de facto* contingency either: they are forced to imagine scenarios rather than present facts. In the SCM Agreement, footnote 4 to Article 3.1(a) provides that the standard of "contingency in fact upon export performance" is met only when the facts demonstrate that the granting of a subsidy is in fact tied to actual or anticipated export earnings. The plain language of Footnote 4 demands that contingency upon exportation be demonstrated by the facts.

(i) The ratio requirement does not make the import duty relief a subsidy contingent in law upon export performance

6.524 A subsidy is contingent in law upon export performance where the underlying legal instruments of that subsidy expressly provide that the subsidy is available to enterprises only on condition of export performance. Even if the duty-free treatment could be considered a "subsidy" within the meaning of Article 1 of the SCM Agreement, nothing in either the MVTO or any of the SROs indicates that it is available only on the condition that the subject manufacturers achieve any particular export performance. The relevant legal condition expressed in the MVTO and each SRO is achievement of a production-to-sales ratio. Neither production nor sales, nor a ratio of the one to the other, is synonymous with exportation.

6.525 Despite the EC's claim, the entirety of its supporting argument consists of two examples that purport to show, by way of certain arithmetical hypotheses, that the ratio requirements force manufacturers to export even though neither the MVTO nor any of the SROs states that they must. The EC's argument fails even to establish a prima facie case that such an express condition exists. Indeed, no such condition does exist.

(ii) The ratio requirements do not make the duty-free treatment a subsidy contingent in fact upon export performance

6.526 Whether *de jure* or *de facto*, the legal standard in Article 3 is that of "contingent upon export performance". "Contingent upon" means conditioned on or dependent on.[495] "Contingent upon export performance" therefore means "conditioned or dependent upon export performance". The ordinary meaning of this phrase, interpreted in the context of Footnote 4 to Article 3.1(a) and the Illustrative List, requires more than just a linkage between the subsidy and exportation. Footnote 4 provides that the standard of "contingent in fact upon export performance":

---

[495] In the Panel Report on *Canada - Measures Affecting the Export of Civilian Aircraft*, adopted with Appellate Body Report on 20 August 1999, WT/DS70/R (hereinafter Panel Report on *Canada - Aircraft*), the Panel found that the relevant ordinary meaning of "contingent upon" is "dependent for its existence on something else", "conditional; dependent on, upon." (para. 9.331). The Panel relied on The New Shorter Oxford English Dictionary on Historical Principles, Vol. 1 (Oxford: Clarendon Press, 1993).

> "... is met when the facts demonstrate that the granting of a subsidy, without having been made legally contingent upon export performance, is in fact tied to actual or anticipated exportation or export earnings. The mere fact that a subsidy is granted to enterprises which export shall not for that reason alone be considered to be an export subsidy within the meaning of this provision. "

6.527 The fact that a subsidy is granted to enterprises that export is not sufficient to create an export subsidy. The subsidy must in fact be "tied to" exportation or export earnings. This interpretation is borne out by all of the examples on the Illustrative List, which involve a demonstrable link between an increase in exports and an increase in the size of the subsidy. In the case of the duty-free treatment at issue here, this tie is absent.

6.528 In *Canada - Aircraft*, the European Communities agreed with Canada that the following factors are useful in determining whether a subsidy is *in fact* contingent upon export performance:

- evidence that the subsidy would not have been paid but for the exports flowing from it;
- whether there are penalties - in the sense of reductions or withdrawals of payments - if exports do not take place; or
- whether there are bonuses or additional payments if exports do take place.[496]

6.529 Neither Japan nor the European Communities has produced evidence that any of these factors is present in this case. Instead, they rely on two hypothetical examples in their attempts to demonstrate export contingency. However, neither complainant has produced any evidence to substantiate their claims that the production-to-sales requirement influences qualified manufacturers to conduct their businesses in the manner suggested in these hypothetical examples.

6.530 Under the complainants' hypotheses, Canadian manufacturers export so as to receive the benefit of the duty-free treatment of imports. However, the European Communities has also characterized the ratio requirements as "restrict[ing] exclusively the sales of imported motor vehicles". Japan has argued, also with respect to Article III of the GATT, that the ratio requirements lead to increased domestic production. Japan claims that this results in increased competition for sales in Canada's domestic market - at the expense of imports. In other words, Japan and the European Communities are asking this Panel to accept, for the purposes of their SCM allegations, that the ratio requirements encourage - or even force - manufacturers to export so that they can import vehicles duty free. But they also ask the Panel to accept, for the purposes of their GATT arguments, that the same ratio requirements simultaneously restrict the sales of imported vehicles. By the complainants' reasoning, manufacturers export vehicles in order to receive duty-free treatment on imported vehicles that they then cannot sell. This illogical proposition runs counter to reality: the duty-free treatment facilitates imports; it has no nexus with exports.

6.531 The fact of the matter is that manufacturers export because of market considerations. The only "measure" in the entire context of the Auto Pact that provides an

496 Panel Report on *Canada - Aircraft, supra* note 495, para. 7.5.

incentive for Canadian manufacturers to export is the US waiver of duty on Canadian vehicles, for which the United States received a GATT waiver and which is now subsumed into the NAFTA. Manufacturers import vehicles into Canada not to obtain duty-free treatment but because there is a market for them in Canada.

6.532 There is a simple reason why neither the European Communities nor Japan relies on the factors that the European Communities proposed in *Canada - Aircraft* as indicative of *de facto* export contingency: these factors are entirely absent. The first of these factors is that the "subsidy" would not have been paid but for the exports flowing from it. As Canada has shown, exports do not flow from the Canadian duty-free treatment at all; they flow from the US duty waiver on imports of Canadian vehicles. As far as the second factor is concerned, there are no penalties if exports do not take place. With regard to the third factor, it is clear that no bonuses are paid or additional payments made if exports do take place. This is because the benefits received by a qualifying manufacturer depend wholly on its imports and not on exports.

6.533 Moreover, the fact that many of the production-to-sales ratios are set at less than 1:1[497] proves that receipt of duty-free treatment does not require exports at all. Japan's own example illustrates this.

6.534 In that example, a motor vehicle manufacturer with a ratio of 80 to 100 (*i.e.* 0.8 to 1) produces $1,000,000 worth of vehicles. Without exporting any of its production, and without exceeding its production-to-sales ratio, the manufacturer may import $250,000 worth of additional vehicles duty free. The "subsidy" is therefore available to manufacturers whether they export or not.

6.535 Moreover, the duty-free treatment available under Canada's waivers is entirely independent of export volume. The following example demonstrates this:

> A manufacturer is required to maintain a production-to-sales ratio of 1 to 1 but operates at a production-to-sales ratio of 2 to 1. It produces automobiles with a net value of $600,000 while selling $300,000 worth of domestic and imported automobiles in Canada. (In fact, as the EC's Exhibit-18 shows, qualifying manufacturers cumulatively achieve ratios of at least 2 to 1 on a regular basis.[498]) Of the $600,000 worth of automobiles produced in Canada, the manufacturer exports $500,000 and sells $100,000 domestically. The other $200,000 in domestic sales comes from imports that receive duty-free treatment.
>
> If it so chose, the same manufacturer could achieve its production-to-sales ratio by producing just $300,000 worth of automobiles and exporting them, all while importing and selling an equivalent $300,000 worth of automobiles under the duty waiver. In so doing, the manufacturer would *increase* the value of its imports, and therefore the *ad valorem* value of the duty waiver to it, by 50 per cent, while *reducing* its exports by 40 per cent and halving its Canadian production.

6.536 As this example shows, there is no direct nexus between receipt of duty-free treatment and the exportation of vehicles. Not only are there no penalties if exports

497 See Exhibit EC-18, p. 54.

498 Exhibit EC-18, p. 54.

do not take place or bonuses if additional exports do take place, but the benefit of the duty-free treatment can be increased while exports are decreased. The only way to increase the "benefit" of duty-free treatment is to increase imports, which can be done even while decreasing production and exports. If the opportunity to import vehicles duty free encouraged or rewarded exportation, manufacturers would export only to the levels necessary to maximise their imports under their production-to-sales ratios. Any other behaviour would dilute the value of the duty-free treatment per imported vehicle. However, manufacturers do not do this. They produce vehicles at values greatly in excess of their ratios and import vehicles duty free at values far below what their production would allow. This demonstrates that the duty-free treatment is not in fact "tied to" exportation. It is therefore not a subsidy contingent upon export performance.

(c) The Duty-Free Treatment is not a Subsidy Contingent Upon the Use of Domestic Over Imported Goods

6.537 Both Japan and the European Communities claim that because the duty-free treatment is conditional upon compliance with the CVA requirement, it is "contingent... upon the use of domestic over imported goods", contrary to Article 3.1(b) of the SCM Agreement.

6.538 The complainants are silent as to whether they are alleging that this "contingency" can be found *de jure* or *de facto*. Japan, in devoting a mere five lines in its argument to its Article 3.1(b) claim, has done no more than assert, incorrectly, that "the CVA requirement ... requires the use of domestic over imported goods". The European Communities, by acknowledging at the outset that "[t]he CVA requirements do not impose explicitly the obligation to 'use domestic over imported goods'", appears to be advancing a claim of *de facto* contingency.

(i) Article 3.1(b) of the SCM Agreement extends to *de jure* contingency only

6.539 In contrast with Article 3.1(a) of the SCM Agreement, which states explicitly that it applies to subsidies contingent "in law or in fact", Article 3.1(b), which immediately follows Article 3.1(a) and otherwise tracks the language of Article 3.1(a), contains no reference to *de facto* contingency. Whereas a footnote to Article 3.1(a) expands in some detail on the standard that must be met for *de facto* contingency to exist, Article 3.1(b) is again silent.

6.540 The Appellate Body has held in *Japan - Taxes on Alcoholic Beverages* that "the words actually used" in an article "provide the basis for an interpretation that must give meaning and effect to all its terms".[499] The Appellate Body made it clear in that case that textual differences in sentences within an article must be respected, and that an "omission must have some meaning".[500]

6.541 The only reasonable meaning that can be given to explicit references to *de facto* contingency in Article 3.1(a) and the omission of any such references in the

[499] Appellate Body Report on *Japan - Alcoholic Beverages, supra* note 271, at 111.
[500] Ibid.

very next sub-paragraph in Article 3.1(b) is that the prohibition in Article 3.1(b) extends to *de jure* contingency only.

6.542 The receipt of duty-free treatment is not contingent in law on the use of domestic over imported goods. The EC's own argument appears to recognize this. The complainants have not made out even a prima facie case of *de jure* contingency. Their claims in respect of Article 3.1(b) of the SCM Agreement must therefore fail.

(ii) Receipt of duty-free treatment is not de facto contingent on the use of domestic goods either

6.543 Even supposing that Article 3.1(b) of the SCM Agreement did extend to *de facto* contingency - which it does not - the facts demonstrate that no such contingency exists in the present case.

6.544 If Article 3.1(b) did extend to *de facto* contingency, then, for the reasons set out in respect of Article 3.1(a), in accordance with the customary rules of international law on the interpretation of treaties, the words "contingent upon" in Article 3.1(b) should be interpreted to apply to subsidies that are *conditional on* or *tied to* the use of domestic over imported goods. The receipt of duty-free treatment is not, as a matter of fact, conditional on or tied to the use of domestic goods over imported goods. Duty-free treatment is available to manufacturers whether they use domestic goods *or not*, provided that they meet their CVA requirements.

6.545 Japan's own argument states that, "a broad range of expenses ... are included in the calculation of CVA". These expenses include goods, services and other expenses, any of which, individually or in combination, may be sufficient to satisfy a manufacturer's CVA requirement. The EC's argument also acknowledges that a manufacturer may include in the calculation of CVA not only goods, but direct labour costs, overhead, general and administrative expenses, depreciation and capital cost allowance for land and buildings.

6.546 As a result, CVA requirements can be, and are, satisfied without the use of any domestic goods. In the case of the Big Three, CAMI and Volvo (Canada) Ltd., for example, labour costs alone (which are necessarily Canadian) are more than sufficient to achieve their CVA requirements.[501] Domestic goods are not - contrary to the assertion of the European Communities - the "main" item included by these manufacturers in their CVA calculations

6.547 The facts therefore demonstrate that the duty-free treatment is available even when domestic goods are not included in the fulfilment of a CVA requirement. The use of domestic goods plays no necessary role in determining whether a manufacturer meets its CVA requirement. While the inclusion of domestic goods in a manufacturer's CVA calculation is permitted, it is not required, *de jure* or *de facto*. Duty-free treatment cannot therefore be "contingent upon" the use of domestic over imported goods.

6.548 Manufacturers can, and do, source parts purely on the basis of commercial considerations. Duty-free treatment is not contingent upon the use of domestic over imported goods by any reasonable standard of "contingency".

---

[501] See *Figure 2*.

6.549 Faced with the facts, the European Communities states that duty-free treatment is "contingent upon" the use of domestic over imported goods not because eligibility for a duty-free treatment is conditional upon the use of domestic goods, but because using them "may be sufficient, or at least contribute, to meet the CVA requirements". As a result, according to the European Communities, the receipt of duty relief "will depend, at least in some cases" on the use of domestic goods. The European Communities then contends that "[t]he mere possibility" that a manufacturer may be required to use domestic over imported goods to qualify for the duty waiver is sufficient to trigger Article 3.1(b).[502] The European Communities offers no authority for this contention.

6.550 The contention is, in fact, diametrically opposed to the position that the European Communities itself took in *Canada - Aircraft*, where, in the context of Article 3.1(a) it argued that the term "contingent" requires conditionality; that is, that the subsidy can be obtained only if the condition is fulfilled.[503]

6.551 If *de facto* contingency is prohibited under Article 3.1(b), "contingent upon" must impose the same standard of conditionality under Article 3.1(b) that it does under Article 3.1(a). It can hardly be that the same term can require that certain circumstances *must* exist when applied to one category of prohibited subsidies, but that "mere possibility" will suffice when applied to the other category.

6.552 If even a "mere possibility" that fulfilling the CVA requirements *might* require the use of domestic goods is sufficient to transform them into a prohibited subsidy, it would establish a standard that is vastly over-broad. The EC's standard would prohibit any content requirement that even mentioned domestic goods in connection with the receipt of any government benefit such as reduced tariffs. By that measure, rules of origin requirements would also constitute prohibited subsidies. This is a result that Canada suspects most Members, including those in the European Communities, would find unacceptable.

4. *Rebuttal Arguments by Japan*

6.553 **Japan** rebuts as follows:

6.554 What constitutes a subsidy under SCM Article 1(a) does not depend on whether the measure has any effect to encourage imports, nor on whether it distorts trade. Here, a customs duty that is otherwise due is foregone and a benefit is conferred to Auto Pact Manufacturers, thus the Duty Waiver constitutes a subsidy under the definition of subsidy, expressly set forth in Article 1.1 of the SCM Agreement.

6.555 Canada has ignored this definition to contend that this Duty Waiver is a tax remission for exports. Moreover, this Duty Waiver falls within paragraph (a) of the Illustrative List of Export Subsidies in Annex I to the SCM Agreement, that is "the provision by governments of direct subsidies to a firm ... contingent upon export performance."

---

[502] The European Communities also argues that the manufacturers' letters impose additional CVA requirements. However, as Canada has shown, the letters are not requirements. Those manufacturers that have given letters can and do qualify for duty relief without fulfilling additional CVA requirements. The letters are, furthermore, unenforceable.

[503] Panel Report on *Canada - Aircraft*, *supra* note 495, para. 7.3.

6.556 Canada is mistaken in stating that "Japan appears to concede that the measures do not make the duty-free treatment legally contingent upon export performance, but it does contend that the "subsidy" is *de facto* contingent upon export performance". Actually, the MVTO and SROs by virtue of the ratio requirement provide the legal mechanism where the subsidy is contingent upon export performance. The fact that this mechanism is best understood if explained in the context of a mathematical formula does not diminish its legal effect.

(a) Article 3.1(a) of the SCM Agreement

(i) Violation of SCM Agreement in law

6.557 As clarified in its responses to Question 21 from the Panel, it is the position of the Government of Japan that, by virtue of the production-to-sales ratio, the Duty Waiver is *in law* export contingent.

(ii) Production-to-sales ratio for the MVTO 1998 manufacturers

6.558 In its response to Question 12 from the Panel, the Government of Canada acknowledges that the average of the actual production-to-sales ratio requirements for the four MVTO 1998 manufacturers is 95:100. In his above-noted 17 November 1997 remarks, the then Chairman, President and CEO of Chrysler Canada stated that the production-to-sales ratio for each Auto Pact manufacturer was 1:1. Presumably, Mr. Landry was referring to Chrysler, Ford and GM when making this statement. In her above-noted 16 October 1997 remarks, the then President and CEO of Ford Canada stated that "Ford, Chrysler and GM signed commitments that we would produce at least one vehicle in Canada for each vehicle sold here".

6.559 Taken together, these acknowledgements and statements are prima facie evidence that the production-to-sales ratio for Ford Canada, Chrysler Canada and GM Canada are 1:1. For Volvo Canada they are less than 1:1.

(iii) Canada's arguments

6.560 The Government of Canada has raised several arguments in response to the Government of Japan's challenge.

6.561 First, the Government of Canada takes the position that duty-free treatment facilitates trade and it would be contrary to the objective of the trade liberalization to prohibit such a measure.[504] The Government of Japan is challenging a duty exemption that is legally made conditional on export performance.

6.562 Second, the Government of Canada argues that there must be a clear and direct nexus between the subsidy and the exported product, and the amount of the subsidy actually increases with export volumes. In this particular case, Canada itself has offered evidence that such a clear nexus does exist. The more exports of motor vehicles that are made by the Auto Pact Manufacturers, the more motor vehicles that such eligible manufacturers can import duty free. This conclusion can be drawn from the

---

[504] Of course, duty-free treatment only facilitates or liberalizes trade for those products that receive such treatment. For products that are excluded, trade is actually hampered or restricted.

example provided by the Government of Canada. In this example, the Government of Canada assumes as a required production-to-sales ratio of 1 to 1 (but the attained production-to-sales ratio of 2 to 1) and the following circumstances:

Net Sales Value of the Vehicles Produced	Net Sales Value Sold for Consumption in Canada	Domestic Sales of Domestic Production	Duty-free Import Value	Export Value of Domestic Production
$600,000	$300,000	$100,000	$200,000	$500,000

Under this situation, assuming (1) the amount of the domestic production, the total domestic sales and the attained production-to-sales ratio are stable and (2) that export values decreased to $400,000 and $300,000 respectively, the duty-free import value will be decreased as follows:

Net Sales Value of the Vehicles Produced	Net Sales Value Sold for Consumption in Canada	Domestic Sales of Domestic Production	Duty-free Import Value	Export Value of Domestic Production
$600,000	$300,000	$200,000	$100,000	$400,000
$600,000	$300,000	$300,000	$0	$300,000

6.563 This clearly shows that the more export value increases, the more the duty-free import amount increases. In other words, this establishes that there is a clear and direct nexus between the subsidy and the exported products, and the amount of the subsidy increases with the volume of exports. Exporting is an integral component of benefiting from the Duty Waiver.

6.564 Further, the Government of Canada argues that Autopact Manufacturers may import certain motor vehicles duty free without exports. However, this does not deny the direct nexus between export performance and subsidies incorporated in the Duty Waiver regime.

6.565 Fourth, the Government of Canada argues that the Duty Waiver is not an export subsidy because it does not provide for an "excessive" duty remission. As authority for this proposition, Canada relies upon items (g), (h) and (i) of the Illustrative List and footnote 5 to the SCM Agreement. This argument has no basis in the text of the SCM Agreement. A review of the cited items in the Illustrative List and their related annexes (Annex II and III) makes it clear that the types of programmes to which their provisions apply are entirely different from the Duty Waiver. Item (g) applies to the remission of *indirect taxes* on *exported* products. Item (h) applies to the remission of *indirect* taxes on *goods used in the production of exported products.* Item (i) applies to the remission or drawback of customs duties on imported *inputs that are consumed in the production of the exported product.* All of these programmes differ fundamentally from the Duty Waiver which is a conditional waiver of customs duties on imports of a finished good.

(b) Article 3.1(b) of the SCM Agreement

6.566 While Article 3.1(b) of the SCM Agreement prohibits subsidies contingent upon the use of domestic over imported goods, the subsidy of the Duty Waiver is contingent in law upon the use of domestic over imported goods. Canada seemingly tries to argue that the term "in law" requires the costs for domestic parts be always included in the CVA but Canada shows no basis for the term to have such meaning. Rather, ordinary meaning of "in law" is "inferred by law, existing in law or by force of law" (Black's Law Dictionary) and does not support Canada's interpretation. The CVA is a legal requirement and only domestic and not imported parts, components and material costs can be counted. Thus, the Duty Waiver, by virtue of the CVA requirement, constitutes a subsidy contingent in law upon the use of domestic over imported goods.

6.567 With respect to the Government of Canada's argument that Article 3.1(b) of the SCM Agreement requires that the Government of Japan prove that the Duty Waiver requires the use of domestic over imported goods, it is the position of the Government of Japan that this argument ignores the express wording of Article 3.1(b). Article 3.1(b) prohibits "subsidies contingent ... upon the use of domestic over imported goods". This includes subsidies that are contingent on a condition that *requires* the use of domestic over imported goods as well as subsidies contingent on a condition that *favours* the use of domestic over imported goods. In this dispute, the Duty Waiver is contingent upon a requirement that favours the use of domestic parts, components and materials over imported like products.

6.568 In the event that this Panel were to find that the actual use of domestic goods is an indispensable factor of the SCM, it is still the Government of Japan's position that the Duty Waiver would be contingent upon the use of domestic over imported goods in the case of the SROs to automobile manufacturers and the letters of undertaking which impose 60 per cent CVA requirements (as evidenced in the above-noted 1997 statements by the then highest officials in Ford Canada and Chrysler Canada). The Government of Canada's response to Question 32 of the Panel which refers to CVA requirements based on a base-year and on 40-50 per cent do not apply to CAMI which is expressly bound by a 60 per cent CVA according to the terms of its SRO. Also, contrary to the Canadian assertion with no exhibits, CAMI may not achieve 60 per cent CVA requirement solely by labour cost. Furthermore, even under the MVTO 1998, labour costs might be reduced by rationalization of production facilities so that the CVA could not be satisfied by labour costs alone in the future.

6.569 The Government of Canada's argument that Article 3.1(b) does not include *de facto* contingency is unsustainable. Absence the language "in law or in fact" means that Article 3.1(b) applied to both in law and in fact contingency. Such a result would be absurd and should be avoided.

5. *Rebuttal Arguments by the European Communities*

6.570 The **European Communities** rebuts as follows:

(a) The Ratio Requirements

6.571 Canada advances several arguments in order to contest that the ratio requirements make the subsidy contingent upon export performance. They are all mistaken or irrelevant.

(i) The alleged "import facilitating" effects of the Tariff Exemption are irrelevant in determining whether it is an export subsidy

6.572 Canada alleges that it would be improper to characterise a measure that "facilitates" imports as an export subsidy.

6.573 To begin with, however, it is questionable that the Tariff Exemption "facilitates" imports at all. No doubt, it facilitates imports of motor vehicles by certain manufacturers. But this does not mean that imports are overall "facilitated".

6.574 Moreover, the measure at issue here is not the Tariff Exemption as such. The Tariff Exemption is a prohibited export subsidy only because of the ratio requirements attached thereto. Clearly, those requirements are not inherent to the Tariff Exemption and do not, of themselves, "facilitate" imports in any conceivable manner. Their only purpose is to promote local production and exports of motor vehicles.

6.575 In any event, whether or not the Tariff Exemption "facilitates " imports is irrelevant. The SCM Agreement does not provide any exception for export subsidies with "import facilitating" effects. Article 3.1(b) of the SCM Agreement prohibits all export subsidies, irrespective of their effects on imports into the subsiding country.

(ii) The contextual arguments drawn by Canada from the Illustrative List are mistaken and, in any event, irrelevant

6.576 Canada notes that the measures in dispute are unlike any of the practices in the Illustrative List of Export Subsidies in Annex I to the SCM Agreement.

6.577 This is true but irrelevant. As Canada itself concedes, the Illustrative List in Annex I is simply that, an "illustrative " list, and not an "exhaustive" one. Therefore, it is not possible to draw any *a contrario* inferences from the List, except in the well defined circumstances specified in Footnote 5. In any event, Canada's "contextual" arguments are clearly wrong.

6.578 According to Canada, it would be "particularly significant that in each of the practices identified in the Illustrative List there is a clear and direct nexus between the subsidy and the exported product".

6.579 That is not correct. The List includes practices which do not require that nexus. For example, Item (a), which reads as follows:

> "The provision by governments of direct subsidies to a firm or industry contingent upon export performance".

6.580 At any rate, the ordinary meaning of the terms of Article 3.1(a) is clear and unambiguous and leaves no scope for the "contextual" re-writing suggested by Canada. All that is required by Article 3.1(a) is the existence of a subsidy and of an export performance condition attached to that subsidy. There is no additional requirement to the effect that the goods that benefit from the subsidy must be the same as the exported goods.

6.581 In similar vein, Canada argues that the examples in the Illustrative List show that the amount of the subsidy must increase with the volume of export.

6.582 Once again, that is not correct. Assume, for instance, that the Canadian Government decided to make a $100,000 grant to any company whose exports exceed $1,000,000. That grant would fall squarely within Item (a) of the List. Yet, the amount of the subsidy would not increase with the volume of exports.

6.583 According to Canada, it is also "contextually significant" that the duty or tax exemption or remission programmes described in items (g), (h) and (i) of the Illustrative List are deemed export subsidies only to the extent that they are "excessive".

6.584 The relevance of this argument is difficult to understand other than as an attempt by Canada to obfuscate the discussion. The Items mentioned by Canada are not the expression of some sort of unwritten general principle of WTO law permitting tax or duty remissions or exemptions, provided that they are not "excessive". Instead, those Items reflect the rule set out in Footnote 1 to the SCM Agreement (which in turn reproduces the terms of Interpretative Note *ad* GATT Article XVI). That rule constitutes an exception to the definition of "subsidy" in Article 1 of the SCM Agreement and, as such, must be construed strictly.

6.585 The measures in dispute fall clearly outside the scope of Footnote 1, which reads in relevant part as follows:

> "In accordance with the provisions of Article XV I of GATT (Note to Article XVI) and the provisions of Annexes I through III of this agreement, the exemption of an exported product from duties ... borne by the like product when destined for domestic consumption, or the remission of such duties ... in amounts not in excess of those which have accrued, shall not be deemed a subsidy."

6.586 At issue in this case is an exemption of duties on imported motor vehicles, and not an exemption of duties on exported motor vehicles.

6.587 Furthermore, the Tariff Exemption cannot be assimilated to a "remission" of the duties "borne" by the products exported by the beneficiaries. The exception provided in Footnote 1 with respect to duty remissions is limited to the two situations described in Item (i) of Annex I, as further interpreted in Annexes II and III, i.e.: (i) when imported inputs are used in the manufacture of the exported products; and (ii) when domestic inputs having the same quality and characteristics are substituted for imported inputs in the production of exported products. In both cases, the inputs must be "consumed" in the manufacture of the exported goods.

6.588 The Tariff Exemption does not fall within either of those two situations. The products covered by the Tariff Exemption are not "inputs" used (let alone "consumed") in the manufacture of the motor vehicles exported by the beneficiaries, but complete motor vehicles intended for sale in Canada. For that reason, assuming that Canada levied duties on the motor vehicles now imported under the Tariff Exemption, those duties could not be deemed "borne" by the motor vehicles exported by the beneficiaries.

(iii) Canada confuses contingency "in law" with "express" contingency

6.589 The prohibition on export subsidies contained in Article 3.1(a) of the SCM Agreement applies to subsidies that are contingent upon export performance, either "in law" or "in fact". The European Communities claims and has demonstrated that the ratio requirements make the subsidy export contingent "in law".

6.590 Canada alleges that the subsidy is not export contingent "in law" because neither the MVTO 1998 nor the SROs make any express reference to the requirement to export.

6.591 The European Communities disagrees with that interpretation. Article 3.1 (a) draws a distinction between contingency "in law" and contingency "in fact", and not between "express" and "implicit" contingency. A subsidy is export contingent "in law" where the requirement to export results from the terms of the law itself, whether such requirement is stated expressly in the law or is implicit in other requirements that are so stated in the law. On the other hand, a subsidy is export contingent "in fact" where the requirement to export does not result from the terms of the law, or at least from those terms alone, but from factual elements outside the law (including the exercise of discretion by the granting authority).
6.592 In the case at hand, the requirement to export is not expressly stated in the MVTO 1998 or in the SROs. Nevertheless, that requirement is a necessary consequence of the ratio requirements, which are themselves stated expressly in the law. That makes the Tariff Exemption contingent "in law" upon export performance, and not simply "in fact".

(iv) The ratio requirements make the subsidy contingent upon export performance

6.593 Canada argues that the beneficiaries export because of market considerations and not because of the subsidy. More specifically, according to Canada, "exports do not flow from [the Tariff Exemption]; they flow from the US duty waiver on imports of Canadian vehicles".
6.594 Even if true, this would be irrelevant. Article 3.1(a) prohibits all export subsidies, whether or not they have any actual effect on the level of exports. A superfluous export subsidy would still be a prohibited subsidy. Indeed, Canada's argument puts Article 3.1(a) on its head. The relevant issue under that provision is not whether exports are contingent upon subsidisation, but whether subsidies are contingent upon export.
6.595 The European Communities has demonstrated beyond doubt that the ratio requirements make the Tariff Exemption contingent upon export performance.
6.596 In those cases where the production-to-sales ratio is 1 to 1 or more, the beneficiaries cannot sell in Canada any amount of vehicles imported under the Tariff Exemption unless they export an equivalent amount. This is not a mere "arithmetical hypothesis". It is a self-evident truth[505].
6.597 In those instances where the ratio is less than 1 to 1, the beneficiaries may sell some imported vehicles even if they do not make any exports. Nevertheless, if they export some vehicles, the value of imported motor vehicles which they may sell in Canada increases by an amount equal to the value of those exports. Thus, it is indisputable that in this situation there is an export subsidy because, to use Canada's own words, "there are bonuses or additional payments if exports do take place".

---

[505] Canada itself, perhaps inadvertently, concedes as much when it states that: "Moreover, the fact that many of the production-to-sales requirements are set at less than 1:1 proves that receipt of duty free treatment does not require exports at all." This statement involves an open admission that, at least in those cases where the ratio is 1 to 1 or more, the beneficiaries are "required" to export in order to qualify for the Tariff Exemption and, therefore, that the subsidy is contingent upon export performance.

6.598 Canada's two examples fail to demonstrate that the subsidies are not contingent upon export performance[506]. They show only that the amount of the subsidy may depend not just on the volume of exports but also on other factors, namely the volume of production, the actual ratio production-to-sales and the extent to which each beneficiary decides to make use of the Tariff Exemption.

6.599 However, the fact that other factors may also affect the size of the subsidies does not mean that that they are not contingent upon export performance. Article 3.1(a) does not require that the subsidies be contingent only and exclusively upon export performance. It prohibits subsidies contingent "...whether solely or as one of several conditions, upon export performance". The Tariff Exemption is contingent upon export performance because, all other conditions being equal, the size of the subsidy is larger if motor vehicles are exported than if they are sold in Canada.

(b) The CVA Requirements

(i) The CVA requirements make the Tariff Exemption contingent in law upon the use of domestic over imported goods

6.600 Contrary to the assumptions drawn by Canada in its argument, the European Communities claims that the CVA requirements make the Tariff Exemption contingent upon the use of local over imported goods "in law", and not simply "in fact".

6.601 Canada contends that the Tariff Exemption is not prohibited by Article 3.1(b) because the CVA requirements do not "require" the use of a certain amount of domestic goods, but rather the use of a certain amount of CVA. That argument, however, is based on a mistaken reading of Article 3.1(b).

6.602 Article 3.1(b) of the SCM Agreement does not prohibit only those conditions that require the actual use of domestic goods by the beneficiary. It prohibits any condition that gives preference to the use of domestic over imported goods, whether or not that condition results in all cases in the actual use of domestic goods by the beneficiaries.

6.603 In other words, Article 3.1(b) prohibits any subsidies that are "contingent" upon a condition that favours the use of domestic over imported goods, and not merely those subsidies that are "contingent" upon the actual use of domestic goods. In the case at hand, the subsidy is "contingent" in law upon a value added requirement that gives preference to the use of domestic over imported goods. Accordingly, the subsidy is "contingent upon the use of domestic over imported goods" in the meaning of Article 3.1(b).

6.604 That interpretation is consistent with the ordinary meaning of the wording of Article 3.1(b). That provision does not prohibit subsidies that are contingent "upon the use of domestic goods". Rather, it prohibits subsidies that are contingent "upon the use of domestic over imported goods". The terms "over imported goods" (in French, "de preference à des produits importés"; in Spanish, "con preferencia a los importados") would be totally redundant if the prohibition applied only where the

[506] The two examples assume a ratio production-to-sales 1 to 1. They provide further confirmation, if need be, that a beneficiary subject to that ratio cannot sell any imported vehicles unless it exports an equivalent amount.

subsidy is contingent upon the actual use of domestic goods. Those terms only acquire meaning if Article 3.1(b) is interpreted as prohibiting any condition that gives preference to the "use of domestic over imported goods", irrespective of whether in practice domestic goods are actually used by the beneficiary.

6.605 Further, that interpretation is consistent with the object and purpose of Article 3.1(b), which is to avoid that subsidies are used to discriminate between domestic and imported goods. Canada's interpretation would frustrate that objective. For example, assume that a Member grants a subsidy upon the condition that local valued added must represent 99 per cent of the beneficiary's sales value. If Canada's interpretation was correct, that subsidy would not be prohibited by Article 3.1(b), even though it is unquestionable that such a subsidy has both the purpose and the effect of discriminating against imported goods.

6.606 The context and the drafting history of Article 3.1(b) also supports the EC's view. Like Article 2.1 of the TRIMs, Article 3.1(b) of the SCM Agreement purported to clarify and strengthen the existing GATT disciplines with respect to local content requirements[507]. In view of that, it would be anomalous if Article 3.1 b) was interpreted so as to be less encompassing than GATT Article III:4.

6.607 In any event, assuming *arguendo* that "contingent upon the use of domestic over imported goods" meant contingent upon the actual use of domestic goods, Article 3.1(b) does not require that that condition be a necessary one. In fact, Article 3.1(b) prohibits the granting of subsidies that are contingent upon the use of domestic over imported goods, "whether solely or as one of several conditions".

6.608 This may cover the situation where a subsidy is simultaneously subject to two or more cumulative conditions. But it may as well apply to the situation where a subsidy is subject two or more alternative conditions, so that compliance with any of them gives a right to the subsidy. If one of those conditions is "the use of domestic over imported goods" the subsidy must be deemed prohibited by Article 3.1(b), even if it is also possible to qualify for the subsidy by complying with an alternative non-prohibited condition, such as using a certain amount of domestic labour or of domestic services.

6.609 Indeed, if using domestic goods had to be always a necessary condition, it would be very easy to circumvent the prohibition contained in Article 3.1(b) simply

[507] Ironically, Canada was one of the participants that proposed to insertion in the SCM Agreement of a prohibition on local content subsidies (MTN.GNG/NG10/W25). Canada explained the rationale for its proposal in the following terms (Section 1(b)): "Subsidies that are contingent, whether solely or as one of several other conditions, upon the use of domestic over imported goods or upon export performance clearly constitute distorting subsidies. Experience with existing obligations and precedents suggests that these practices should be made subject to an *explicit* GATT prohibition" (emphasis added). A Note by the Secretariat of 16 October 1989 summarised as follows the participants' views with respect to the prohibition of local content subsidies (MTN.GNG/NG10/13, p.8): "Some Participants expressed their reservation on the category of other trade related subsidies. They considered that subsidies proposed for this category were already covered by Article III of the General Agreement (subsidies that were contingent upon the use of domestic over imported goods) or by Article XVI:4 (subsidies contingent upon export performance). Some other participants explained that although these subsidies were already prohibited by other provisions of the General Agreement, their inclusion into the category of prohibited subsidies would serve the purpose of better clarity and certainty."

by providing that the beneficiaries may also qualify for the subsidy by fulfilling some irrelevant but dissuasive alternative condition. Further, that interpretation would have the absurd result that a subsidy that was conditional upon compliance with either a local content rule or an export performance requirement would be prohibited neither by Article 3.1(a) nor by Article 3.1(b).

6.610 Canada contends that the EC's interpretation of Article 3.1(b) is "vastly overbroad" and would have the consequence that "rules of origin requirements would also constitute prohibited subsidies".

6.611 This argument reflects a serious misunderstanding of the nature of origin rules. To begin with, it is obvious that origin rules may not constitute as such a subsidy, let alone a prohibited subsidy, because they involve no financial contribution.

6.612 Therefore, it may be assumed that Canada's argument is that, by the EC's standard, applying a preferential duty rate only to imports which meet a certain origin requirement would constitute a prohibited subsidy. That argument overlooks a fundamental difference between origin rules and the CVA requirements. Origin rules are used to establish the country of origin of import[508], and not whether products are "domestic" or "imported", and are generally applied in connection with border measures, such as tariffs. Thus, by definition, origin rules cannot favour the use of "domestic" over "imported" goods. If anything, origin rules would favour the use of goods originating in one exporting country over goods originating in another exporting country.

(ii) Article 3.1(b) applies to de facto contingency

6.613 Although for the reasons mentioned above, the European Communities considers that the CVA requirements are contingent "in law" upon the use of domestic over imported goods, the European Communities also submits in the alternative that the CVA requirements make the subsidy contingent "in fact" upon the use of domestic over imported goods.

6.614 Canada has argued that Article 3.1(b) does not extend to *de facto* contingency based upon the textual differences between that provision and Article 3.1(a). This argument is not compelling.

6.615 The issue of whether Article 3.1(b) should apply also to *de facto* violations was never discussed during the negotiations of the SCM Agreement. For that reason, it is not possible to draw any conclusions from the fact that Article 3.1(b) does not distinguish expressly between *de jure* and *de facto* contingency.

6.616 The ordinary meaning of Article 3.1(b) does not exclude *de facto* contingency. Previous panel and Appellate Body reports confirm that a prohibition may be applicable to *de facto* violations, even if the relevant provision does not state so expressly[509]. Moreover, if Article 3.1(b) did not apply to *de facto* contingency, it would be extremely easy to devise measures to circumvent that prohibition.

---

[508] C.f. Article 1.2 of the Agreement on Rules of Origin. Note that that provision refers to Most Favoured Nation treatment, including with respect to matters covered by GATT Article III, but not to National Treatment as matters in respect of which origin rules are used.

[509] See, e.g., Appellate Body Report on *EC - Bananas III*, *supra* note 49, para. 233.

(iii) In the alternative, the CVA Requirements make the subsidy contingent de facto upon the use of domestic over imported goods or upon export performance

6.617 Canada pretends that even if Article 3.1(b) applied to *de facto* contingency, the facts demonstrate that no such contingency exists in the present case, because the CVA requirements can be, and are satisfied on the basis of labour costs alone.

6.618 However, as shown above, Canada has not substantiated that claim. The evidence furnished by Canada only shows that, currently, the labour CVA of the Big Three and Volvo meet the CVA requirements contained in the MVTO 1998. It does not show that the Big Three meet the more onerous CVA requirements contained in the Letters of Undertaking also on the basis of labour CVA. Furthermore, Canada has conceded that some of the SRO beneficiaries do not meet their CVA requirements on the basis of CVA labour alone.

6.619 In presenting its claims, the European Communities has demonstrated that parts and materials account on average for as much as 80 per cent of the cost of sales of the motor vehicles assembled in Canada. Canada has not challenged that percentage. Indeed, it could hardly do so since it is based on official statistics of Canada's Ministry of Industry. In response to a question from the Panel, Canada merely argues that "the cost of parts and materials as a percentage of cost of sales can vary widely"[510]. Even if true, however, it would still remain that, at least in the case of some manufacturers, the percentage must be necessarily 80 per cent or higher.

6.620 The above means that, in practice, the only conceivable way in which the beneficiaries could meet the CVA requirements contained in the Letters of Undertaking and in the SROs without using any domestic goods at all is by exporting a large volume of motor vehicles and parts therefor, so that the non-parts CVA of those exports can be added to the non-parts CVA of the vehicles sold in Canada[511].

6.621 Thus, in definitive, the CVA requirements make the Tariff Exemption contingent *de facto* either upon the use of domestic over imported goods, contrary to Article 3.1(b) or upon export performance, in violation of Article 3.1(a).

6. *Response by Canada to the Complainants' Rebuttals*

6.622 **Canada** responds as follows:

[510] Canada's response to Question 24 from the Panel. In support of that proposition Canada invokes the percentages of cost of materials to "gross sales value" shown in Exhibit JPN-43-3 for Toyota and Honda. The relevance of those percentages, however, seems questionable. In the first place, they appear to correspond to the production of Honda and Toyota in Japan, where presumably more parts are made in-house, and not in Canada. Second, it is unclear whether the notion of "gross sales value" is comparable to that of "cost of sales/value of shipments", as used in Canada's regulations, which does not include selling expenses. In any event, the percentages shown in Exhibit JPN-43-3, although somewhat lower than 80 per cent (from 54 per cent to 69 per cent) confirm that a manufacturer of motor vehicles cannot meet the CVA requirements in the Letters of Undertaking and the SROs except by using a significant amount of local parts and materials or, as the sole alternative, by exporting motor vehicles or parts therefor.

[511] Note that Canada's response to Question 25 from the Panel does not deny this.

(a) The Measures at Issue do not Create a Subsidy

6.623 In their various arguments, the complainants have sometimes asserted, and at other times simply assumed, that the duty-free treatment accorded by the measures at issue constitutes a subsidy within the meaning of Article 1.1 of the SCM Agreement. When they have asserted this, they have claimed that there is a subsidy because the duty-free treatment falls under Article 1.1(a)(1)(ii) as a financial contribution in the form of government revenue that is otherwise due but is foregone or not collected. However, the complainants have offered little or no justification for their claims, beyond a mechanical recitation that an import duty waiver should be considered "revenue foregone" in the sense of Article 1.

6.624 Japan cited the *Indonesia - Autos* case in support of its proposition that duty relief is a subsidy. However, the Panel Report in *Indonesia - Autos* offers no useful analysis of the issue because the respondent Indonesia not only agreed, but also insisted, that its measures were export subsidies.[512] This was because Indonesia's defence of its illegal regime depended on persuading the panel that its duty waiver was an export subsidy and that the eight-year grace period for export subsidies of LDCs should be considered an eight year exception from other WTO obligations as well.

6.625 The European Communities alleged that Canada "admits" that the duty-free treatment is a subsidy. Canada has done no such thing. On the contrary, Canada has maintained that duty-free treatment for goods does not necessarily constitute revenue foregone under Article 1.1(a)(1)(ii) of the SCM Agreement. If it did, then a subsidy would exist whenever a Member unilaterally applied a rate of duty lower than its bound rate, as Canada does in applying a zero duty on OEM automotive parts, as many developing country Members with high bound rates do on a wide scale, and as many Members do in granting generalized preferences or duty drawbacks. Developing countries themselves do it on a wide scale: many of them have very high bound rates, but apply much lower rates. In all of these cases a benefit is conferred in accordance with Article 1.1(b) of the SCM Agreement. Specificity will also exist in many cases, for example, where the low-duty import is a component for a domestic assembly industry. To define such programmes as "subsidies" would be contrary to the object and purpose of the WTO Agreement, which explicitly identifies tariff reductions as contributing to the objectives of the parties.[513]

6.626 As Canada has also noted, Footnote 1 to Article 1.1(a)(1)(ii) excludes certain non-excessive exemptions or remissions such as duty drawbacks from the definition of a "subsidy" notwithstanding that they confer a benefit directly on exports.[514] It is

---

[512] Panel Report on *Indonesia - Autos, supra* note 270, para. 14.155.

[513] See Marrakesh Agreement Establishing the World Trade Organization in Results of the Uruguay Round of Multilateral Trade Negotiations: The Legal Texts (Geneva: GATT Secretariat, 1994), p. 6. The third preambular para. refers to contributing to the objectives of the WTO by "entering into reciprocal and mutually advantageous arrangements directed to the substantial reduction of tariffs and other barriers to trade and to the elimination of discriminatory treatment in international trade relations."

[514] Canada states that: "In accordance with the provisions of Article XVI of GATT 1994 (Note to Article XVI) and the provisions of Annexes I through III of this Agreement, the exemption of an exported product from duties or taxes borne by the like product when destined for domestic consumption, or the remission of such duties or taxes in amounts not in excess of those which have accrued, shall not be deemed to be a subsidy."

therefore difficult to justify extending the definition of "subsidy" to capture non-excessive duty exemptions or remissions on imports, particularly when tariff reductions are a *raison d'être* of the WTO.

6.627 If, however, the Panel considers that the duty-free treatment is a subsidy, it would be an import subsidy. Contrary to the complainants' assertions, duty-free treatment is available only by importing. The measures impose no requirement, either in fact or in law, to export in order to receive duty-free treatment. The duty-free treatment is available without exporting at all. The only way to receive additional benefits is by increasing the value of vehicles imported.

6.628 In the further alternative, the duty-free treatment would be a subsidy for domestic production because it is contingent upon achieving a production-to-sales ratio. The SCM Agreement does not prohibit domestic subsidies unless they cause adverse effects, none of which have been alleged by the complainants.

(b) The Duty-Free Treatment is not Inconsistent with Article 3.1(b)

6.629 Even if it were a subsidy, duty-free treatment is not a subsidy contingent upon the use of domestic over imported goods, within the meaning of Article 3.1(b) of the SCM Agreement. The claims of both Japan and the European Communities rest on interpretations of "contingent upon" that would make the concept of contingency meaningless.

6.630 The European Communities explains the "mere possibility test" it proposed, by arguing that Article 3.1(b), "prohibits any condition that gives preference to the use of domestic over imported goods, whether or not that condition results in all cases in the actual use of domestic goods".[515] Such an interpretation would replace the test of "contingency" with that of "affecting".

6.631 The European Communities further elaborates that Article 3.1(b) prohibits any subsidy that is contingent upon a "condition that favours the use of domestic over imported goods, and not merely those subsidies that are 'contingent' upon the actual use of domestic goods".[516] This would introduce an entirely new element into Article 3 that finds no support in the wording of the provision or in any authority.

6.632 The EC's test is at odds with the legal standard of Article 3, which is one of conditionality.[517] The plain meaning of a "condition" is "a thing demanded or required as a prerequisite to the granting or performance of something else; a stipulation".[518] In order to constitute a condition in Article 3.1(b), the prerequisite to the granting of a subsidy must be the requirement that domestic goods be used over imported goods. Absent such a stipulation, there is no conditionality.

6.633 In the present case, there is no such stipulation. The receipt of duty-free treatment, even if it were a subsidy, does not depend on the use of domestic over

515 EC's response to Question 19 from the Panel.

516 Ibid.

517 See Panel Report on *Canada - Aircraft, supra* note 495, para. 9.376.

518 The New Shorter Oxford English Dictionary on Historical Principles, vol. 1 (Oxford: Clarendon Press, 1993), p. 472 (Exhibit CDA-15).

imported goods, but rather, on the achievement of a CVA requirement, which may be met without the use of domestic goods at all.

6.634 The European Communities argues in the alternative that, even if Article 3.1(b) required the actual use of domestic goods, it "does not require that that condition be a necessary one".[519] By definition, an unnecessary "condition" is not a condition.

6.635 The European Communities seeks to explain its argument on the basis that under Article 3.1(b), a subsidy is prohibited if it is contingent upon the use of domestic over imported goods "whether solely or as one of several conditions".[520] The same clause appears in Article 3.1(a). The clause means that the use of domestic goods or export performance does not have to be the only condition for the receipt of the subsidy. There may be additional conditions to fulfil as well, but each condition must be mandatory. The clause does not mean, as the European Communities contends, that a subsidy can be considered contingent if the use of domestic goods or export performance is not required but is among the ways to qualify for the subsidy.[521] It does not mean, for example, that a subsidy is contingent upon export performance if receipt of the subsidy depends on either exporting or selling domestically.

6.636 Japan does not address Article 3.1(b) in its responses to the Panel's Questions. It argues only that duty-free treatment, "by virtue of the CVA requirement" is a subsidy contingent in law upon the use of domestic over imported goods because the CVA is a legal requirement and "only domestic and not imported parts, components and material costs can be counted".

6.637 Japan uses the term contingent correctly, when it states that "[t]he second condition upon which the Duty Waiver is contingent is the CVA requirement". Receipt of the duty waiver is conditional upon the fulfilment of a CVA requirement. However, the fact that duty-free treatment is legally "contingent upon" fulfilment of a CVA requirement does not make it "contingent upon" the use of domestic over imported goods, in law or in fact.

6.638 The European Communities argues in the alternative that the CVA requirements make duty-free treatment a subsidy contingent "in fact" on the use of domestic over imported goods, even though Article 3.1(b) does not mention *de facto* contingency. The European Communities contends that because it "was never discussed during the negotiations of the SCM Agreement ... it is not possible to infer any conclusions from the fact that Article 3.1 (b) does not distinguish expressly between *de jure* and *de facto* contingency".

6.639 The suggestion that a treaty cannot be given meaning in the absence of a negotiating history has no basis in treaty interpretation. It would run contrary not only to the Appellate Body's observations that an omission "must have some meaning",[522] but to the *Vienna Convention on the Law of Treaties*, which relegates a treaty's negotiating history to supplementary status behind the general rule that a treaty shall be

[519] EC's response to Question 19 from the Panel.
[520] Ibid.
[521] Ibid.
[522] Appellate Body Report on *Japan - Alcoholic Beverages, supra* note 271, at 111.

interpreted in good faith in accordance with the ordinary meaning to be given to its terms in their context and in the light of its object and purpose.[523]

6.640 The context in which sub-paragraph 3.1(b) must be interpreted is the absence of any explicit reference to contingency in fact in Article 3.1(b), in contrast to sub-paragraph 3.1(a) in the same paragraph of the same Article. The European Communities is unable to explain this difference in wording within the same paragraph. The fact that the Appellate Body has interpreted other provisions, such as Article II of the GATS, to extend to *de facto* discrimination is of little relevance; it did not involve an overt contrast in the expression of obligations in two consecutive provisions within the same Article.[524] The Appellate Body has held that textual differences between two sentences in the same Article must be respected.[525] It has held as well that a treaty interpreter is not entitled to assume that the use of different words in different places in an agreement was merely inadvertent.[526] The only way to apply these principles to Article 3.1(b) of the SCM Agreement is to find that the obligation it creates extends only to *de jure* contingency.

6.641 In any event, even if a *de facto* test could be inferred in Article 3.1(b), there is no *de facto* contingency in this case. The use of domestic over imported goods is not a condition of achieving CVA. CAMI, under its SRO, and the Big Three automobile manufacturers would meet their CVA requirements even if every part they used were imported.

(c) The Duty-Free Treatment is not Inconsistent with Article 3.1(a)

6.642 The complainants similarly fail to provide any basis for their respective claims that the duty-free treatment is inconsistent with Article 3.1(a) of the SCM Agreement. Article 3.1(a) prohibits subsidies that are contingent in law or in fact on export performance. Canada understands that Japan and the European Communities do not argue that there is any export contingency in fact. Rather, they take the view that in some theoretical circumstances there could be an incentive to export as a result of the production-to-sales ratio.

6.643 In fact, viewed as a means of encouraging exports in law, the production-to-sales ratio in conjunction with duty-free treatment, is singularly ineffective. Motor vehicle exports to Japan and the European Communities by qualifying manufacturers are practically nil. Instead, the majority of their production is exported to the United States. This is due not to the Canadian measures but to the US duty waiver,[527] as con-

[523] Vienna Convention on the Law of Treaties, May 23, 1969, Can. T.S. 1980 No. 37, 1155 U.N.T.S. 331, (1969) 8 ILM 679, Articles 32 and 31.

[524] Appellate Body Report on *EC - Bananas III, supra* note 49, paras. 233-234.

[525] Appellate Body Report on *Japan - Alcoholic Beverages, supra* note 271, at 111.

[526] Appellate Body Report on *European Communities - Measures Affecting Meat and Meat Products (Hormones)*, adopted on 13 February 1998, WT/DS26/AB/R & WT/DS48/AB/R, para. 164; Appellate Body Report on *United States - Restrictions on Imports of Cotton and Man-Made Fibre Underwear*, adopted on 25 February 1997, WT/DS24/AB/R, DSR 1997:I, 11, at 24.

[527] Initially granted under the Auto Pact and now under the NAFTA.

firmed by the fact that production by non-MVTO or SRO manufacturers in Canada follows exactly the same pattern.[528]

6.644 Japan nevertheless contends that the duty-free treatment is contingent in law upon export performance because "[t]he formula expressing such terms of the [production-to-sales] ratio as stipulated in applicable Canadian law (i.e. the MVTO and the SROs) demonstrates clearly that it makes the Duty Waiver contingent on export performance".[529] Japan has confused the legal contingency of receipt of duty-free treatment on fulfilment of the ratio with contingency upon export performance. A legal requirement to meet a production-to-sales ratio is manifestly not the same thing as a legal requirement to export or to undertake to develop exports. By simply contending that it is, unsubstantiated by any evidence, Japan has failed to establish even a prima facie case of contingency.

6.645 The European Communities suggests that the fact that the duty-free treatment facilitates imports is irrelevant because the "SCM Agreement does not provide any exception for export subsidies with 'import facilitating' effects" and that "[e]xport subsidies are always prohibited, irrespective of its [sic] effects on imports into the subsidising country". As Canada explained in its response to the Panel's Question 23, Canada has not claimed that there is an exception for export subsidies with import facilitating effects. Rather, Canada has pointed out that the duty-free treatment, if it is a subsidy at all, is a subsidy first of imports and second of production. Production subsidies are not prohibited under the SCM Agreement, and the mere fact that a subsidy is granted to an enterprise that exports, explicitly does not make the subsidy an export subsidy.[530]

6.646 The only way to receive the duty-free treatment is by importing. The European Communities cannot reconcile the standard of "contingent upon" export performance with the fact that qualifying manufacturers may receive the duty-free treatment even if they do not export at all. As Canada has already noted in the context of Article 3.1(b), contingency requires "conditionality". Exportation is not a stipulation upon which the receipt of duty-free treatment depends. That which need not be achieved is, by definition, not a condition.

6.647 According to the *New Shorter Oxford English Dictionary*, the ordinary meaning of "condition" is "a thing demanded or required as a prerequisite to the granting or performance of something else; a stipulation." In order to meet the standard of conditionality under Article 3.1(a), the prerequisite to the granting of a subsidy must be export performance. If export performance is not a prerequisite, or stipulation, for the granting of the subsidy, there is no conditionality.

6.648 Nor are there "bonuses or additional payments" if exports take place, a test of export contingency cited and endorsed by the European Communities. The only way to receive additional benefits is by increasing the value of vehicles imported. Moreover, the benefits are not payments at all.[531]

6.649 The European Communities further errs by dismissing as "'contextual' re-writing" Canada's argument that Article 3.1(a) must be interpreted in its context. The

[528] Japan's response to Question 1 from Canada.

[529] Japan's response to Question 21 from the Panel.

[530] See Footnote 4 to Article 3.1(a).

[531] Panel Report on *US - Malt Beverages*, *supra* note 427, para. 5.8.

European Communities claims that "the ordinary meaning of the terms of Article 3.1 (a) is clear and unambiguous and leaves no scope" for consideration of such context. However, the Appellate Body has consistently held that it is the context of a treaty's provisions, as well as its object and purpose, that establishes the ordinary meaning to be given to the terms of a treaty.[532] As Article 31.1 of the *Vienna Convention* provides, "A treaty shall be interpreted in good faith in accordance with the ordinary meaning to be given to the terms of the treaty in their context and in the light of its object and purpose." Contrary to the EC's contentions, context is an essential element of treaty interpretation and not merely a secondary tool to resolve ambiguity.

6.650 In the present case, context is crucial to determining what is - and is not - a subsidy contingent upon export performance. A key aspect of this context is the Illustrative List in Annex I to the SCM Agreement. As Canada noted in its answer to the Panel's Question 23, by dismissing as "irrelevant" the complete dissimilarity between the measures at issue and those on the Illustrative List, the European Communities has disregarded the guidance of the Appellate Body.[533]

6.651 In the context of the Illustrative List, it is an unjustifiable interpretative leap to contend, as the complainants do, that a non-excessive remission of import charges is not only a subsidy, but an "export subsidy". The European Communities claims that the limitation of Items (g) through (i) of the Illustrative List to excessive tax or duty exemptions or remissions are not the expression of a general principle that such remissions are permitted when non-excessive. However, the only non-excessive tax exemption or remission programs identified on the Illustrative List as an export subsidy do not involve import charges but rather, direct taxes or social welfare charges (Item (e)). Even these remissions are only deemed export subsidies when they are "specifically related to exports". The only remissions of import charges identified on the Illustrative List are those that are both excessive and linked directly to an exported product.[534] When interpreted in its context, it is clear that Article 3.1(a) does not extend to the measures at issue.

7. *Japan's Follow-Up to Canada's Response*

6.652 As a follow-up to Canada's response, Japan argues as follows:

6.653 The measures certainly constitute a subsidy in the meaning of Article 1.1(a)(1)(ii) of SCM Agreement if, for example, Canada applies 6.1 per cent customs duty on a product from certain countries while applying zero-duty on the same product from other countries. Whether or not the duty applied is lower than the bound rate does not matter in the determination of a subsidy. And such disparity in the rates of duty applied is not usually called "tariff reduction". Whether this subsidy is prohibited or not depends on the conditions attached to the subsidy. Duty-drawbacks and even GSP would be a prohibited subsidy if these schemes have conditions falling in Article 3.1 of SCM Agreement.

532 See, e.g., Appellate Body Report on *US - Gasoline*, *supra* note 487, p. 17.

533 Appellate Body Report on *Canada - Periodicals*, *supra* note 280, pp. 476-479.

534 Item (i).

8. *The European Communities' Follow-Up to Canada's Response*

6.654 As a follow-up to Canada's response, the **European Communities** argues as follows:

(a) The Tariff Exemption is a Subsidy

6.655 Canada argued in its initial response that the Tariff Exemption was not a subsidy contingent upon export performance or upon the use of domestic over imported goods. Canada has since gone one step further and claims that the Tariff Exemption is not a subsidy at all.

6.656 Canada alleges that if the Tariff Exemption were a subsidy, "then a subsidy would exist whenever a Member unilaterally applied a rate of duty lower than its bound rate".

6.657 That argument misses an essential point. The definition of subsidy in Article 1.1 of the SCM Agreement requires that the revenue that is "foregone" or not "collected" by the Government must be "otherwise due". In other words, there must be a legal obligation to pay the duty or tax which is exempted or remitted by the Government.

6.658 Bound duty rates are not "due" by importers. When a Member gives a tariff binding it assumes simply the obligation not to apply tariffs above the level of the bound rate. Since tariff bindings do not require Governments to apply the bound rates, it follows that the mere existence of a tariff binding may not, as such, impose upon the importers the obligation to pay those rates.

6.659 In its response to the complainants' rebuttals, Canada reiterates the argument that it is possible to derive from Footnote 1 and Items (g) through (i) of the Illustrative List the general principle that a duty exemption is not a subsidy unless it is "excessive".

6.660 By definition, however, an import exemption may never be "excessive". Indeed, "excessive" compared to what? The necessary consequence of Canada's argument is, purely and simply, that a duty exemption could never be a subsidy.

6.661 But, if so, there would be no reason to limit the circumstances in which the remission of import duties is not deemed a subsidy. For example, if the exemption of import duties on the machinery used for the assembly of motor vehicles is not a subsidy, why should the payment and subsequent remission of those duties constitute an export subsidy?

6.662 Yet Footnote 1 stipulates that duty remissions shall not be deemed to be a subsidy only where the import duties are "borne" by the exported goods, which in accordance with Annexes I through III means that the duties must have been levied on inputs "consumed" in the production of the exported goods.

6.663 Far from finding support in Footnote 1 and the Illustrative List, the principle asserted by Canada would render redundant Item (i) of that List as well as large portions of Annexes II and III.

(b) The Tariff Exemption is Prohibited by Article 3.1 (a)

6.664 Canada claims that, even if the Tariff Exemption were a subsidy, it would be an "import subsidy" and not an "export subsidy" because "duty-free treatment is available only by importing".

6.665 Canada's argument is based on the wrong assumption that simply because a subsidy is "contingent" upon importation, it cannot be "contingent" also upon export performance.

6.666 While it is true that "duty-free treatment is available only by importing", merely importing motor vehicles is not a sufficient condition to benefit from the subsidy. A beneficiary may not import and sell in Canada as many motor vehicles as it wishes. It may import and sell in Canada only a limited amount of motor vehicles. As demonstrated, that amount depends upon the amount of motor vehicles exported by each beneficiary. That makes the subsidy contingent upon export performance in the meaning of Article 3.1(a).

6.667 Canada also argues that, in the alternative, the duty-free treatment would not be an export subsidy but rather "... a subsidy for domestic production because it is contingent upon a production-to sales ratio".

6.668 Canada makes again the same mistake. "Production" subsidies and "export subsidies" are not mutually exclusive categories. Canada appears to overlook that "exported" goods must be "produced" first. For that reason, any "export" subsidy will normally operate also as "production" subsidy.

6.669 In the case at hand, the subsidy is contingent upon production, in the sense that the beneficiaries cannot qualify for the Tariff Exemption unless they produce some motor vehicles in Canada. But, in addition, the subsidy is also contingent upon export performance because, all other conditions being equal, the amount of the benefit is larger if motor vehicles are exported than if they are sold in Canada.

6.670 Canada also argues that the Tariff Exemption is "singularly ineffective", because the beneficiaries export "the majority of their production" to the United States, rather than to the European Communities or Japan.

6.671 As already explained by the European Communities, whether or not the Tariff Exemption has any actual effects is totally irrelevant, because the SCM Agreement prohibits all export subsidies, irrespective of their effects. In any event, the fact that there are few exports to the European Community or Japan does not mean necessarily that the subsidy causes no prejudice to those Members. The European Communities would recall that, for example, the displacement of exports from a third country market is considered as an actionable "adverse effect" under Part III of the SCM Agreement.

(c) The Tariff Exemption is Prohibited by Article 3.1 (b)

(i) Article 3.1 (b) prohibits all the subsidies that are contingent upon any condition that gives preference to the use of domestic over imported goods

6.672 The EC's position has been that Article 3.1(b) prohibits all the subsidies that are contingent upon any condition that gives preference to the use of domestic over imported goods, and not only those subsidies that require the actual use of domestic goods.

6.673 The European Communities has argued that its interpretation is consistent with the ordinary meaning of the wording of Article 3.1(b), and is supported by the context of that provision, as well as by its object and purpose and by the drafting history of the SCM Agreement.

6.674 Canada has not addressed any of those arguments. Instead, in response to the complainants' rebuttals, Canada keeps on arguing that the EC's position is inconsistent with the notion of "contingency". That argument, however, misses the point. The issue in dispute is not the meaning of the term "contingent". The European Communities has no quarrel with Canada's tautological proposition that "contingency" means "conditionality". The issue in dispute is the meaning of the terms "use of domestic over imported goods". In other words, the issues is not whether the subsidy must be "conditional", but rather what is the relevant "condition".

(ii) Article 3.1(b) does not require that the use of domestic over imported goods be a necessary condition

6.675 The European Communities has also argued that, even if "contingent upon the use of domestic over imported goods" meant "contingent upon the actual use of domestic goods", Article 3.1(b) does not require that that condition be a necessary one.

6.676 In fact, Article 3.1(b) prohibits the granting of subsidies that are contingent upon the use of domestic over imported goods "whether solely or as one of several conditions". That may cover the situation where a subsidy is subject to two or more alternative conditions, so that compliance with any of them gives a right to the subsidy.

6.677 Canada responds that, by definition, an alternative condition would not be a condition. The European Communities disagree. Assume, for example, that a Member grants a subsidy to those companies which export € 1,000,000 worth or create 1,000 jobs. Clearly, that subsidy would be "contingent" even though neither exporting nor creating jobs is a "necessary" condition to obtain the subsidy.

6.678 A subsidy subject to two or more "alternative" only ceases to be "contingent" if the admitted alternatives exhaust all possible options. For example, a subsidy granted upon exporting goods or upon selling them domestically would not be truly "contingent" upon either because the beneficiary has no other option left.

(iii) Article 3.1(b) applies also to de facto contingency

6.679 As mentioned, the European Communities considers that the CVA requirements make the Tariff Exemption contingent "in law" upon the use of domestic over imported goods. Nevertheless, the European Communities has also submitted in the alternative that the CVA requirements make the Tariff Exemption contingent "in fact" upon the use of domestic over imported goods.

6.680 Canada asserts that Article 3.1(b) does not extend to *de facto* contingency. Yet the only argument submitted by Canada is that, unlike Article 3.1(a), Article 3.1(b) does not refer expressly to contingency "in fact".

6.681 Article 3.1(a) is part of the context of Article 3.1(b) and, as such, may be a relevant element of interpretation. But it is not the only one.

6.682 As recalled by the Appellate Body in *US - Shrimps*, the interpretative analysis "must begin with, and focus upon, the text of the particular provision to be interpreted".[535] The ordinary meaning of the text of Article 3.1(a) does not exclude *de facto* contingency. A contextual interpretation based exclusively on Article 3.1(a) should not be allowed to prevail over the ordinary meaning of Article 3.1(b).

6.683 The differences in wording between Article 3.1(a) and Article 3.1(b) may be explained by their different drafting history. The explicit reference to *de facto* contingency found in Article 3.1(a) was proposed by the European Communities.[536] The EC proposal started from the premise that "the present discipline also applies to subsidies *de facto* contingent upon export".[537] Thus, the purpose of the EC proposal was not to extend the prohibition on export subsidies to *de facto* export subsidies, but rather to "provide for clearer guidance in identifying *de facto* subsidies, in order to avoid undue extensions of the category of export subsidies".[538]

6.684 The other participants agreed with the premise that *de facto* export contingency was already prohibited by existing disciplines and the negotiations focused on the text of the footnote to Article 3.1(a), which specifies the standard for the interpretation of *de facto* export contingency, rather than on the inclusion of an express reference to *de facto* export contingency in Article 3.1(a).

6.685 The mere fact that Article 3.1(b) does not refer expressly to *de facto* contingency should not be taken to mean that the drafters aimed to restrict the scope of that provision to *de jure* contingent subsidies. Rather, it reflects the fact that the drafters did not consider it necessary to define a standard for identifying *de facto* local content subsidies, simply because that notion is more easily apprehensible. By the same token, the drafters did not consider it necessary either to supplement Article 3.1(b) with an Illustrative List of prohibited local content subsidies.

6.686 In any event, Article 3.1(b) is not the only relevant contextual element. As already explained by the European Communities, Article 3.1(b) was inserted in the SCM Agreement with the purpose to clarify and reinforce the existing GATT disciplines with respect to local content requirements. In view of that, it would be anomalous if Article 3.1(b) was interpreted so as to have a narrower scope than GATT Article III:4.

6.687 Furthermore, the provisions of a treaty must be interpreted not only "in their context" but also "in light of their object and purpose". The object and purpose of Article 3.1 is to avoid that subsidies be used to discriminate between domestic and imported goods used in the manufacture of other goods. If Canada's views were upheld, it would be extremely easy for Members to devise measures to circumvent Article 3.1(b). As already explained by the European Communities, Canada's position would have the absurd result that, for example, a subsidy contingent upon a 99 per cent domestic added value requirement would not be prohibited by Article 3.1(b), even though it is unquestionable that such a subsidy would discriminate against imported goods.

(iv) In the alternative, the CVA requirements make the subsidy contingent de facto upon

[535] Appellate Body Report on *United States - Shrimp, supra* note 301, para. 114.

[536] Doc. MTN.GNG/NG10/W/31, 27 November 1989, Section 1a.

[537] Ibid.

[538] Ibid.

the use of domestic over imported goods or upon export performance

6.688 In its response to the complainants' rebuttals, Canada reiterates its position that, even if Article 3.1(b) applied to *de facto* contingency, there is no *de facto* contingency in this case because the Big Three and CAMI meet their CVA requirements on the basis of labour CVA alone.

6.689 Canada has not substantiated those assertions. The evidence provided by Canada only shows that, currently, the Big Three meet the CVA requirements in the MVTO 1998 on the basis of labour CVA alone. But it does not show that they can meet also the CVA requirements in the Letters of Undertaking without using domestic parts and materials.

6.690 Canada has provided no evidence whatsoever concerning CAMI. The European Communities has shown that, on average, the cost of materials accounts for 80 per cent of the total cost of sales of the motor vehicles assembled in Canada. Canada has not disputed that figure. Even allowing for the "wide" variations in costs among manufacturers alleged by Canada[539], it is simply impossible that labour costs alone may account for as much as 60 per cent of the cost of sales of any passenger car assembled by CAMI. The only possible way in which CAMI could meet the 60 per cent CVA requirement in its SRO without using any domestic parts and materials at all is by exporting a substantial amount of vehicles and parts, which would make the subsidy contingent upon export performance.

9. *Canada's Follow-Up Response*

6.691 **Canada** responds as follows:

(a) The Measures Are Consistent with Article 3.1(a)

6.692 Japan has asserted, on the basis of a new hypothetical example in its rebuttal, that contingency exists because duty-free treatment necessarily increases with export volumes. There is a technical error in Japan's argument in that production-to-sales ratios are based on value, not volume as Japan asserts. More significantly, the Japanese argument has two major substantive failings.

6.693 First, Japan's example shows only that an increase in the value of exportation could permit a company to import more vehicles duty-free, but not that it necessarily will. As Canada demonstrated in its initial response, the value of duty-free imports may also increase substantially while export value is decreased substantially. Nor does a manufacturer receive the alleged subsidy except by actually importing. Paradoxically, the duty-free treatment is an incentive to increase imports and reduce exports if a company wants to maximize the *ad valorem* benefit of the duty saving.

6.694 Second, even if the value of the alleged subsidy did increase with the value of exportation, that would not be sufficient to establish contingency. The same increase would also be true of any per-unit production subsidy. Such a subsidy would still not be an export subsidy because, as in the present case, exportation is not a condition

[539] Canada's response to Question 24 from the Panel.

for receipt of the benefit. In the absence of this conditionality a subsidy is not contingent upon export performance.

6.695 Japan also argues that the ratios of the MVTO automobile manufacturers are at 1 to 1 or higher, based on two statements by some company officials. Canada assumes that the officials in question were rounding off these ratios for the sake of simplicity. As Canada stated in its response to the Panel's Question 36, the ratios for these companies vary from the low 80s to 100 to the high 90s to 100. None of them are at or over 1 to 1.

6.696 The European Communities, which has elaborated its claim more than Japan, argues that even at ratios below 1 to 1, the production-to-sales ratio should be considered an export subsidy because at some point it will only be possible to increase duty-free imports by exporting more. This is as true of a ratio of 0.5 to 1 as it is of a ratio of .99 to 1. Of course, by the same theory of the European Communities, any subsidy paid in direct proportion to production is an illegal export subsidy because, at some point, domestic markets will be saturated, leaving export markets as the only alternative.

6.697 The SCM Agreement does not prohibit subsidies contingent upon production, even though a subsidy per unit of production is much more of an incentive to export than the duty-free treatment in this case. This is because a subsidy per unit of production increases with every unit of export. By contrast, as Canada has shown, the value of the duty-free treatment does not increase with increased exports but only with imports.

6.698 The complainants have also done little to challenge Canada's position that a finding that the measures are inconsistent with Article 3.1(a) would require the panel to ignore the context of the SCM Agreement. The context of the SCM Agreement, including the Illustrative List, offers no support for the complainants' contention that a non-excessive remission of import charges is not only a subsidy but an export subsidy.

6.699 In its rebuttal, the European Communities merely reiterates its arguments that the context of the SCM Agreement should be ignored, despite the Appellate Body's consistent findings that context is an essential element of treaty interpretation. As Canada noted in its response to the rebuttals, the only non-excessive tax exemption programs listed on the Illustrative List as export subsidies do not involve import duties and even these programs are only export subsidies to the extent that they are "specifically related to exports". Remissions of import duties are listed on the Illustrative List as an export subsidy only to the extent that they are both excessive and linked directly to an exported product. There is nothing on the Illustrative List that would justify extending Article 3.1(a) to the present measures, which are non-excessive and have no linkage, direct or otherwise, to an exported product.

(b The Measures Are Consistent with Article 3.1(b)

6.700 Both complainants also claim that the CVA requirement makes the duty-free treatment a subsidy contingent in law upon the use of domestic over imported goods under Article 3.1(b) of the SCM Agreement. Canada has already explained in its various arguments to this Panel why the EC's interpretation of "contingent upon" as "mere possibility" is completely unsubstantiated by the plain wording of Article 3.1(b) and is contrary to the legal standard of Article 3, which is that of conditionality.

6.701 For its part, Japan accuses Canada of ignoring the "express wording" of Article 3.1(b). It appears from Japan's arguments that Japan endorses the EC's interpretation of Article 3.1(b). Japan states that "contingent upon ... the use of domestic over imported goods" includes contingency on a condition that requires or favours the use of domestic over imported goods. This suggests strongly that Japan misunderstands the meaning of "express wording".

6.702 The express wording of Article 3.1(b) is "contingent upon the use of ...". "Contingent upon" does not mean favouring. The prerequisite to the granting of a subsidy must be the use of domestic over imported goods. In the present case, even if duty-free treatment were a subsidy, the relevant prerequisite for the receipt of duty-free treatment is the achievement of a certain CVA. Because a manufacturer may achieve its CVA with or without the use of domestic goods, the use of domestic over imported goods is not a prerequisite for receipt of duty-free treatment. The measures therefore lack the conditionality required for a prohibited subsidy.

6.703 The complainants' arguments would turn Article 3.1(b) into a prohibition of any measure that granted lower duty treatment to imported products on the basis that the imported products contained or used domestic products of the importing country. By the complainants' theory, if such measures were not subsidies contrary to Article 3.1(b), they would have to be considered to violate Article 3.1(a).

6.704 Both complainants insist in the alternative, that despite the wording of Article 3.1(b), the subsidy allegedly accorded by the measures is contingent in fact upon the use of domestic over imported goods. Neither complainant has offered any explanation for why the scope of Article 3.1(b) should be interpreted to extend to *de facto* contingency, absent the express language "in law or in fact" found in sub-paragraph (a) of the same Article. The European Communities made no new assertions on this point in its rebuttal. In today's argument it referred to its own position during the negotiation of Article 3.1(a) that: "the present discipline also applies to subsidies *de facto* contingent upon export". This hardly explains Article 3.1(b).

6.705 Japan simply asserts that in the absence of this language, sub-paragraph 3.1(b) should be taken to apply to both contingency in law and in fact. This contention fails to explain both the significance of the specific reference to "in law or in fact" in sub-paragraph 3.1(a) and the relevant findings of the Appellate Body on this issue, which Canada has discussed in its arguments.

6.706 Moreover, even if the scope of sub-paragraph 3.1(b) did extend to contingency in fact, the complainants still fail to show that the measures satisfy the legal standard of conditionality upon the use of domestic over imported goods. Nor can they, given that duty-free treatment is available even when domestic goods are not included in the fulfilment of a CVA requirement, for example, in the case of the qualifying manufacturers that fulfil their CVA requirements on labour costs alone.

E. Applicability of the GATS to the Measures

1. Arguments of Japan

6.707 **Japan** argues as follows:

6.708 The Duty Waiver and its associated conditions fall within the scope of the GATS which applies to "measures by Members affecting trade in services".[540]

6.709 The Duty Waiver and its associated conditions constitute a measure taken by a central government (i.e. the Government of Canada) in the form of a law, regulation or administrative action (i.e. the MVTO 1998, the SROs, the letters of undertaking and administrative action), within the meaning of Articles I:3 and XXVIII of the GATS.[541] Accordingly, the Duty Waiver is a "measure by a Member" under Article I:1 of the GATS.

6.710 Also, the Duty Waiver is a measure "affecting trade in services", within the meaning of Articles I and XXVIII(c) of the GATS, because it affects: (i) conditions of competition in the supply of services between wholesale trade service suppliers; and (ii) conditions of competition in the supply of services between service suppliers relating to the production of motor vehicles.[542] The panel in *EC - Bananas III* found that no measures are excluded a priori from the scope of the GATS. Rather, that panel confirmed that "sub-paragraphs (i)-(iii) [of Article XXVIII(c) of the GATS] do not contain a definition of 'measures by Members affecting trade in services' as such, but rather are an illustrative list of matters in respect of which such measures could be taken".[543] The *EC - Bananas III* panel also determined that the expression "affecting" in Article I:1 of the GATS had to be given a broad interpretation. It noted that Article I:1 of the GATS refers to measures in terms of their effect, which means "they could be of any type or relate to any domain of regulation".[544] On this issue, the Panel concluded that:

> "... the drafters consciously adopted the terms 'affecting' and 'supply of a service' to ensure that the disciplines of the GATS would cover any measure bearing upon conditions of competition in supply of a service, regardless of whether the measure directly governs or indirectly affects the supply of the service."[545]

6.711 The Duty Waiver and its associated conditions have two effects on the conditions of competition in the supply of services. First, the discriminatory provision of

---

540 Article I:1 of the GATS states "[t]his Agreement applies to measures by Members affecting trade in services".

541 Article I:3 of the GATS defines "measures by Members" to include measures taken by ... central, regional or local governments and authorities. GATS Article XXVIII defines the term "measures" to mean any measure by a Member, whether in the form of a law, regulation, rule, procedure, decision, administrative action, or any other form.

542 Article XXVIII(c) of the GATS provides:

(c) "measures by Members affecting trade in services" include measures in respect of

- (i) the purchase, payment or use of a service;
- (ii) the access to and use of, in connection with the supply of a service, services which are required by those Members to be offered to the public generally;
- (iii) the presence, including commercial presence, of persons of a Member for the supply of a service in the territory of another Member.

543 Panel Reports on *EC - Bananas III*, *supra* note 269, para. 7.280. The substance of the Panel's statement was supported by the Appellate Body in its Report on *EC - Bananas III*, *supra* note 49, para. 220.

544 Ibid.

545 Ibid., para. 7.281. At para. 220 of its Report, *supra*, note 49, the conclusions of the Appellate Body support the Panel's reasoning on this point.

duty-exempt status that is limited to the Auto Pact Manufacturers (who are also wholesale trade service suppliers of motor vehicles) necessarily affects the conditions of competition in the supply of services between wholesale trade service suppliers. The Duty Waiver necessarily reduces the cost for the supply of wholesale trade services for the Auto Pact Manufacturers and places them at a competitive advantage in offering their wholesale trade services in the Canadian market. The effect of the Duty Waiver on the conditions of competition in this instance is indirect in that it directly affects the cost of the good being distributed and indirectly affects the cost and/or profitability of the related wholesale trade services.[546] However, the panel in *EC - Bananas III* explicitly addressed this situation and found irrelevant "whether the measure directly governs or indirectly affects the supply of the service".[547] The supply of wholesale trade services by Non-Auto Pact Manufacturers is quite clearly less profitable than would be the case if the prices charged for those automobiles did not have to recoup the cost of the discriminatory MFN duty. Accordingly, the Duty Waiver has "a bearing upon conditions of competition in supply of services" and is a measure affecting trade in services within the meaning of Articles I and XXVIII(c) of the GATS.

6.712 Second, following the reasoning of the Panel of *EC - Bananas III*, by virtue of the domestic content requirement (i.e. the CVA), the Duty Waiver has an effect on the purchase, payment or use of services related to the production of motor vehicles. Items listed in the definition of the CVA include payments made by the Auto Pact Manufacturers in respect of the use of services in the following service sectors:

(i) repair and maintenance services;

(ii) engineering services; and

(iii) administrative and general services (e.g., accounting, management and consulting services).

6.713 The domestic content requirement in practice requires the Auto Pact Manufacturers to purchase and use certain specified services supplied by service suppliers in Canada to the detriment of like services supplied by service suppliers outside Canada. In this way, it has an effect on the conditions of competition in the supply of services. It is, therefore, a measure affecting trade in services within the meaning of Articles I and XXVIII(c) of the GATS.

2. *Arguments of the EC*

6.714 The **European Communities** argues as follows:

6.715 GATS Article I:1 provides that: "[t]his Agreement applies only to measures by Members affecting trade in services". Thus, a "measure covered by the GATS" is a measure "affecting trade in services[548].

6.716 The Tariff Exemption is a "measure covered by GATS" because:

- it is a "measure by a Member";

---

[546] As discussed below, the Government of Canada has scheduled its relevant GATS commitments.

[547] Panel Reports on *EC - Bananas III, supra* note 269, para. 7.281.

[548] See, e.g., Panel Report on *EC - Bananas III (USA), supra* note 269, para. 7.298.

- the beneficiaries are suppliers of "services" covered by the GATS, namely of wholesale trade services for automobiles;
- the Tariff Exemption "affects" the "supply" of those services; and
- in so doing, the Tariff Exemption "affects" the "trade" in wholesale trade services for automobiles.

(a) The Tariff Exemption is a "Measure by a Member"

6.717 The Tariff Exemption is contained in "Orders-at-Council" issued by the Governor General of Canada. Therefore, it is clearly a " measure by a Member" in the meaning of GATS Articles I:3 (a) and XXVIII (a).

(b) The Beneficiaries Are Suppliers of Wholesale Trade Services Covered by the GATS

6.718 In addition to manufacturing automobiles in Canada, the beneficiaries also are engaged in the wholesale distribution in Canada of automobiles imported by them from other Members. Typically, the beneficiaries purchase the automobiles to foreign manufacturers, import them into Canada and sell them to local dealers which, as a general rule, re-sell them to the final users.

6.719 In connection with that activity, the beneficiaries also perform a series of related activities such as maintaining a stock, delivering the automobiles to the dealers, commissioning and/or funding promotional activities, providing after-sales maintenance and repair services, etc.

6.720 GATS Article I.3(b) stipulates that the term "services" includes "any service in any sector except services supplied in the exercise of governmental authority". Thus, the sectoral coverage of GATS is, in principle, universal[549].

6.721 The distribution of goods, both at wholesale and at retail level, is a "service" within the meaning of the GATS. That activity is listed in the Services Sectoral Classification List[550]. Moreover, many Members (including Canada[551]) have given market access and/or national treatment commitments with respect to wholesale distribution services. Further confirmation is provided by *EC - Bananas III*, where the provision of wholesale trade services with respect to bananas was found to be an activity covered by the GATS[552].

6.722 The CPC describes "wholesale trade services" as a sub-set of "distributive services", which is defined in a headnote to Section 6 of the CPC as consisting of:

> *"selling merchandise to retailers, to industrial, commercial, institutional, or other professional business users, or to other wholesalers,*

---

549 Ibid., para. 7.288.

550 In the Uruguay Round negotiations, participants agreed to follow a set of guidelines for the scheduling of specific commitments under the GATS. Those guidelines encouraged participants to use the so-called Services Sectoral Classification List (Document MTN.GNS/W/120, dated 10 July 1991), which is largely based on the United Nations' Central Product Classification (the "CPC"). Although the use of the Services Sectoral Classification List is not mandatory, most Members, including Canada, have adopted it as a basis for scheduling their commitments.

551 Exhibit EC-19.

552 Ibid.

or acting as agent or broker (wholesaling services) or selling merchandise for personal or household consumption including services incidental to the sale of goods (retailing services). *The principal services rendered by wholesalers and retailers may be characterised as reselling merchandise, accompanied by a variety of related, subordinated services such as: maintaining inventories of goods*; physically assembling, sorting and grading goods in large lots, breaking bulk and redistribution in smaller lots; *delivery services*; refrigeration services; *sales promotion services rendered by wholesalers*; and services associated with retailer' business, e.g., processing subordinated to selling, warehousing and garage services." (*emphasis added*)

6.723 Under Section 6, the CPC contains a sub-division entitled "Wholesale trade services of motor vehicles" (CPC 61111), which includes, *inter alia*, the "wholesaling of passenger motor cars".

6.724 Thus, the activities performed by the beneficiaries with respect to the automobiles that they import from other Members fall squarely within the definition of the CPC category of "wholesale trade services".

(c) The Tariff Exemption "Affects" the "Supply" of Wholesale Trade Services

6.725 The considerations made below with respect to the meaning of the term "affecting the supply of services" in the context of GATS Article XVII are equally applicable with respect to GATS Article II.

6.726 The granting of a tariff exemption for importing automobiles modifies the conditions of competition between the beneficiaries and other wholesale distributors of imported automobiles which do not benefit from a similar exemption for importing the automobiles that they re-sell in Canada. Hence, the tariff exemption "affects" the "supply" of wholesale distribution services.

6.727 This analysis is confirmed by *EC - Bananas III*. In that case, the Panel found that, by favouring certain categories of wholesalers of bananas with respect to the allocation of a tariff quota for bananas, the measures "affected" the supply of wholesale trade services for bananas within the European Communities.

6.728 On appeal, that conclusion was affirmed by the Appellate Body. In response to an argument to the effect that "when buying or importing [bananas], a wholesale trade services supplier is a buyer or importer and not covered by the GATS", the Appellate Body noted that:

"It is difficult to conceive how a wholesaler could engage in the 'principal service' of reselling a product if it could not also purchase or, in some cases, import the product. Obviously, a wholesaler must obtain the goods by some means in order to resell them ....[553]

[553] Appellate Body Report on *EC - Bananas III*, *supra* note 49, para. 226.

(d) The Tariff Exemption "Affects" the "Trade" in Wholesale Distribution Services

6.729 Article I:2 of GATS defines "trade in services" as the "supply of a service" through any of the four modes listed therein, i.e. cross-border supply, consumption abroad, commercial presence and presence of natural persons. Thus, a measure "affects trade in services" if it affects the "supply of services" through any of those four modes.

6.730 In the present case, the Tariff Exemption affects the "trade in services" because it affects the "supply" of wholesale distribution services through commercial presence (Mode 3) by persons of other Members.

3. Canada's Response

6.731 **Canada** responds as follows:

(a) The Measures at Issue are not Covered by the GATS

6.732 Measures covered by the GATS are set out in Article I. Article I:1 provides that: "This Agreement applies to measures by Members affecting trade in services".

6.733 Article I:2 defines "trade in services" as the supply of a service according to any of four so-called "modes".[554] Thus, measures covered by the GATS are measures affecting the supply of a service according to these modes.

6.734 According to the arguments of both complainants, the services allegedly affected by the measures at issue are wholesale distribution services for automobiles. Japan's argument does not specify the mode of wholesale distribution service supply that is allegedly affected by the measures at issue. The EC's argument contends that the affected mode is the supply of wholesale distribution services through the commercial presence of persons of other Members (mode 3).

6.735 Japan and the European Communities rely on *EC - Bananas III* for the proposition that the scope of the GATS is broad enough to extend to the measures at issue. However, the fact that the scope of the GATS is broad does not mean that it is unlimited. Virtually all goods must be distributed in order to be marketed and the distribution of goods is a service. If the term "affecting" is interpreted too broadly, all measures affecting trade in goods would be found to affect, at a minimum, the distribution services for those goods. Thus, all measures affecting trade in goods would also affect trade in services. To avoid this result, the Appellate Body has held that a measure must affect a service supplier in its supply of a service to fall within the GATS. It is not enough for the measure to affect the service supplier in a capacity unrelated to the supply of a service.

6.736 The Appellate Body has made this critical distinction in two separate findings in *EC - Bananas III*. In considering the extent to which the GATS applies to vertically-integrated companies, the Appellate Body stated that:

[554] The modes are, respectively, the supply of a service: from the territory of one Member into the territory of any other Member; in the territory of one Member to the service consumer of any other Member; by a service supplier of one Member, through commercial presence in the territory of any other Member; and by a service supplier of one Member, through presence of natural persons of a Member in the territory of any other Member.

> "...to the extent that it is also engaged in providing "wholesale trade services" and is therefore *affected in that capacity* by a particular measure of a Member *in its supply of those "wholesale trade services"*, that company is a service supplier within the scope of the GATS."[555] (*emphasis added*)

6.737 Implicit in this finding is the requirement that "affecting" means affecting *in the capacity of a service provider* and *in its supply of services*.

6.738 The Appellate Body's distinction is borne out by the definitions in Article XXVIII(b) and (c) of the GATS. "Supply of a service", as the phrase is used in Article I, is defined in Article XXVIII(b) to include the "production, distribution, marketing, sale and delivery of a service". Without exception, these examples relate to the activity of carrying on a service business.

6.739 Similarly, Article XXVIII(c) defines "measures by Members affecting trade in services" to include measures respecting such things as the purchase of a service, the payment for a service, the use of a service, access to services and the presence of persons to supply a service. Again, without exception, these examples relate to the activity of carrying on a service business. None of the examples in either of the foregoing definitions relates to access to or taxation of goods provided by a service supplier.

6.740 The Appellate Body's distinction upholds the unambiguous statement in the Addendum to the Explanatory Note on the Scheduling of Initial Commitments in Trade in Services issued by the Group of Negotiations on Services.[556] The Addendum takes the form of questions and answers. In response to Question 6, "Is it necessary to reserve the right to impose customs duties and regulations on the movement of goods in relation to the supply of a service?", the Addendum answers:

> "There is no requirement in the GATS to schedule a limitation to the effect that the cross-border movement of goods associated with the provision of a service may be subject to customs duties or other administrative charges. *Such measures are subject to the disciplines of the GATT.*"[557] (*emphasis added*)

6.741 In considering the relationship between the GATT 1994 and the GATS, the Appellate Body also found that there are three categories of measures: those affecting the supply of services as services; those involving a service related to or supplied in conjunction with a good; and those affecting only trade in goods as goods.[558]

6.742 At the core of the Japanese and EC argument is the proposition that every measure that affects the cost of or access to goods also affects the trade in the services supplied by the distributors of such goods. This proposition runs contrary to the finding of the Appellate Body in *EC - Bananas III*; it would read out of existence the category of measures that affect only trade in goods as goods.

---

[555] Appellate Body Report on *EC - Bananas III*, *supra* note 49, para. 227.

[556] Addendum to the Explanatory Note on the Scheduling of Initial Commitments in Trade in Services, MTN.GNS/W/164/Add.1, 30 November 1993 (Exhibit CDA-8).

[557] Ibid., p. 2.

[558] Appellate Body Report on *EC - Bananas III*, *supra* note 49, para. 221.

6.743 As noted, the *activity* of distributing goods is undoubtedly a service. A measure affecting the activity of supplying the service of distributing goods is a measure *affecting the supply of a service* within the scope of the GATS. However, a measure affecting goods themselves but not the supply of distribution services related to those goods is not a measure affecting trade in services because it does not affect supply of a service. It therefore does not fall within the scope of the GATS.

6.744 Duties or tariffs are measures affecting trade in goods as goods. So too are measures providing for relief from duties or tariffs. The MVTO and SROs are pure tariff measures. Tariff measures fall within the disciplines of the GATT, as its very title indicates. Such measures affect trade in goods as goods. The extension or non-extension of MVTO and SRO duty-free treatment may affect the cost of automobiles, but it does not, either directly or indirectly, affect in any way trade in wholesale distribution services for those automobiles. It does not affect the suppliers of wholesale distribution services *in their capacity a*s providers of wholesale distribution services.

6.745 The complainants' claim in respect of Article II of the GATS relates to the duty-free treatment afforded to certain goods. These measures fall into the first category of measures identified by the Appellate Body: measures affecting only trade in goods as goods. The extension of duty-free treatment to automobiles may affect the cost of the automobiles but it does not affect wholesale distribution services in those automobiles.

6.746 Accepting the arguments of the European Communities and Japan would have absurd and far-reaching consequences. If the mere fact that a measure affects goods means that it also affects the suppliers of distribution trade services for such goods in their capacity as service suppliers, the GATS could be used to impugn and override measures that are permitted under the GATT and other WTO Agreements. Thus for example, Article XXIV of the GATT permits Members to form customs unions and free-trade areas that by definition entail discrimination in the rates of duty imposed on the goods of parties and the like goods of non-parties.

6.747 If the complainants' arguments on this issue were accepted, any differential treatment of goods authorized by Article XXIV of the GATT could be used to found a claim of inconsistency with the GATS, on the basis that such measures "affect" the suppliers of distribution services in those goods. This very concern was raised by the European Communities itself in *EC - Bananas III* when it argued that even the *prohibitive* tariffs under its banana import licensing regime were outside the scope of the GATS.[559] Similarly, the legitimate imposition of an anti-dumping or countervailing duty on imported goods, while consistent with Article VI of the GATT, would almost certainly affect the foreign suppliers of distribution services for those goods, and could therefore, according to the complainants' reasoning, be inconsistent with the GATS.

6.748 Japan and the European Communities seek to escape the implications of their argument by claiming that the measures at issue do in fact affect service suppliers as service suppliers. Japan, for example, insists that "[t]he Duty Waiver [sic] necessarily reduces the cost for the supply of wholesale trade services for the Auto Pact manufacturers", and that "[t]he supply of wholesale trade services by Non-Auto Pact

559 Ibid., para. 43.

manufacturers is quite clearly less profitable than would be the case if the prices charged for those automobiles did not have to recoup the cost of the discriminatory MFN duty".

6.749 However, Japan offers no substantiation whatsoever for these claims. It offers no explanation why wholesale trade service providers are "affected" by the measures at issue any more than the providers of distribution services for any goods are affected by the duties imposed on those goods. The EC's claim is equally deficient. Neither complainant has made out even a prima facie case that the measures at issue "affect" the supply of wholesale distribution services. They have failed to show that the MVTO and SROs are measures covered by the GATS.

6.750 The absence of any substantiated effect of the measures on the supply of wholesale motor vehicle distribution services stands in stark contrast to the facts *of EC - Bananas III*, where the European Communities maintained an import licensing regime. Under the EC's tariff quota system, over-quota imports of bananas faced a prohibitive tariff, while the right to import bananas at preferential rates within the EC's quota was allocated by a system of import licenses. Effectively, those wholesalers that received in-quota import licences could purchase or import bananas. Those that did not receive licences effectively could not. Thus, the allocation of import licences necessarily affected the ability of distribution service providers to provide their services: it affected their ability to purchase or import goods. As the Appellate Body noted:

> "It is difficult to conceive how a wholesaler could engage in the 'principal service' of reselling a product if it could not also purchase or, in some cases, import the product. Obviously, a wholesaler must obtain the goods by some means in order to resell them ..."[560]

6.751 The MVTO and SROs have no effect whatsoever on the ability of the identified entities to obtain automobiles, to import automobiles, or to otherwise engage in the provision of automobile distribution services. Thus, in 1997, according to Japan's own figures, over 181,000 motor vehicles were imported into Canada without benefit of a MVTO or SRO duty waiver or the NAFTA. Over 82 per cent of these imports came from Japan.[561]

6.752 Moreover, because in *EC - Bananas III*, licences to import bananas from certain countries or were far more valuable than licences to import bananas from other countries, the allocation of the more valuable licenses necessarily affected both the service suppliers that received them and those that did not. The benefits of receiving the more valuable licences affected the service suppliers in their capacity as service suppliers.

6.753 There are no comparable circumstances in the present case. There is no licencing mechanism for any wholesale service supplier engaged in the distribution of motor vehicles in Canada, nor any instrument akin to a licence which permits - or the absence of which limits - the supply of such distribution services. The only possible point of comparison is that the EC's bananas regime applied differential duties to the

[560] Appellate Body Report on *EC - Bananas III*, *supra* note 49, para. 226.

[561] Japan's Table 6.

products handled by different wholesale operators. Significantly, this was not even raised as a GATS issue in *EC - Bananas III*.

6.754 In sum, the import quota and licencing system in *EC - Bananas III* was critical to the scope and profitability of the provision of services by the independent banana distributors and to the ability of even the integrated distributors to import at all. The mere existence of differential duties was not. The "effect" of the EC's banana importer licencing regime was therefore fundamentally different from the measures at issue.

6.755 In the absence of even a prima facie case that the MVTO and SROs affect the supply of services, the claims by Japan and the European Communities under Articles II of the GATS must fail.

4. *Rebuttal Arguments by Japan*

6.756 **Japan** rebuts as follows:

6.757 The Government of Canada argues that the MVTO 1998 and SROs are "pure tariff measures" that do not affect the supply of wholesale trade services and thus are not covered by the GATS. It then argues that duties and tariff measures affect only trade in goods as goods and, as such, are disciplined only by the GATT 1994. The Government of Canada cited as authority for this position the Appellate Body Report for *EC - Bananas III*, claiming that "affecting" within the meaning of Article I means "affecting in the capacity of a service provider and its supply of services". The Government of Canada also referred, in order to support its position, to the 1993 GATS Addendum that states there is no requirement in the GATS to schedule a limitation to the effect that the cross-border movement of goods associated with the provision of a service may be subject to "customs duties or other charges". The argument simply fails to defend that the Duty Waiver is outside of the scope of the GATS.

6.758 First, the Government of Canada's above citation of the relevant part in the Appellate Body for *EC - Bananas III* does not address the definition of "affecting" within the meaning of GATS Article I. Rather, it only recognizes that, even if it is vertically integrated, a company is a wholesale service supplier, to the extent that it is engaged in providing wholesale trade services and is therefore affected in that capacity by a particular measure of a Member. It does in no way determine the interpretation of "affecting" within the meaning of Article I of the GATS.

6.759 The Government of Canada's argument on the Addendum is also unconvincing. The Addendum simply states that Members are not required to schedule general customs duties or other charges as limitation in the Schedule of Specific Commitments on trade in services. It neither permits Canada to take tariff measures that are in violation of GATS Article II, nor exempts Canada from the requirement to list such discriminatory custom duties or other charges as an MFN exemption. Canada's emphasis on the phrase in the Addendum that "such measures are subject to the disciplines of the GATT" does little help its position: the Appellate Body for *EC - Bananas III* confirms the fact that measures that are covered by the GATT are not *a priori* excluded from the coverage by the GATS.

6.760 The Government of Canada's narrow interpretation of the word "affecting" in Article I:1 of the GATS is contrary to its ordinary meaning in the light of the object and purpose of the GATS. In *EC - Bananas III*, the Panel stated that the word "affecting" was chosen by the drafters of the GATS to ensure that any measures bearing upon the conditions of competition in the supply of a service be covered by the GATS. It determined that the word "affecting" had to be given a broad interpretation and that a measure affecting trade in services "could be of any type and relate to any domain of regulation".[562] It follows from this interpretation that contrary to what Canada is suggesting, no measures are *per se* excluded from a review under the GATS.

6.761 As the Government of Canada admits itself, the Appellate Body Report in *EC - Bananas III* divides measures into three categories and recognizes that "measures that involve a service relating to a particular good or a service supplied in conjunction with a particular good" fall within the scope of both the GATT 1994 and the GATS. The Appellate Body then supports the Panel's finding that the EC-banana import licensing procedures are subject to both the GATT 1994 and GATS.

6.762 As the Appellate Body Report in *EC - Bananas III* confirms, and as the Government of Canada also admits, measures affecting trade in goods can have an effect on the supply of services and be also governed by the GATS. The Government of Japan submits that such an effect can also be indirect and still give rise to a violation of the GATS, as was the case of the measures at issue in *EC - Bananas III*, tariff quotas, which were restrictions of trade in goods. In fact, tariff quotas are simply two-tier "customs duties". The fact that they had an indirect effect on trade in services was sufficient for them to fall within the scope of the GATS. In *EC - Bananas III*, it was determined that, by favouring certain categories of wholesalers of bananas with respect to the allocation of tariff quotas for bananas, the measures affected the supply of wholesale services.

6.763 As the Government of Canada admits in its initial response, the Duty Waiver affects the cost of automobiles procured and then distributed by wholesale trade service suppliers, as the EC tariff quota system affected the cost of bananas procured and then distributed by operators. Thus, in a manner almost identical to the measures at issue in *EC - Bananas III*, the Duty Waiver, which involves a service relating to or supplied in conjunction with automobiles and by creating two-tier "custom duties," affects trade in wholesale trade services of motor vehicles. The only difference between the Duty Waiver in this case and the tariff quota system in *EC - Bananas III* is the magnitude of the duty.

6.764 The Government of Canada also attempted to stand out differences between this case and *EC - Bananas III* by claiming that "the import quota and licensing system in *EC - Bananas III* was critical to the scope and profitability of the provision of services by the independent banana distributors and to the ability of even the integrated distributors to import at all" because those who did not receive licenses faced a prohibitive tariff. However, as the Government of Canada admits itself, "critical" is not a test to determine whether a measure affects trade in services, and it is irrelevant whether the higher tariff is "prohibitive" or not, as long as measures affect the ability of wholesale trade service suppliers and do not accord no less favourable treatment to service and service suppliers of all WTO Members. The Duty Waiver also affects

[562] Panel Reports on *EC - Bananas III, supra* note 269, para. 7.280. The Appellate Body supported the substance of this statement, Appellate Body Report on *EC - Bananas III, supra* note 49, para. 220.

the ability of Auto Pact Manufacturers (who are also wholesale service suppliers) to import and distribute motor vehicles by reducing their procurement cost. Again, the difference is just a magnitude of the discrimination of the customs duty in question, not its nature.

6.765 The effects of the Duty Waiver on wholesale trade services have already been discussed extensively in the Government of Japan's response to Question 35 of the Panel.

6.766 Also unconvincing in this context is the Government of Canada's argument that the acceptance of Japan's interpretation on the scope of GATS would have far-reaching and absurd consequences.[563] The Government of Canada argues that such interpretation would make differential treatment of goods authorized by the GATT 1994 such as an anti-dumping and countervailing duty inconsistent with the GATS. However, the Duty Waiver is not an anti-dumping or countervailing duty. It is a discriminatory tariff measure entirely different in nature from differential treatment of goods categorically authorized by the GATT and other WTO Agreements. Therefore, Japan views that the Panel is not required to decide on the consistency between these GATT-consistent measures and the GATS, which is irrelevant to this isolated case of discriminatory tariff measures not at all authorized by the GATT 1994.

5. *Rebuttal Arguments by the European Communities*

6.767 The **European Communities** rebuts as follows:

6.768 Canada argues that the EC's claim implies that "every measure which affects the cost of or access to goods also affects the trade in the services supplied by the distributors of such goods" Before addressing more specifically the different aspects of Canada's argument, it should be recalled that the fact that a measure affects trade in services in itself is not sufficient to establish a violation of GATS Article II, for it is still necessary to show, as the European Communities has done, that like services or service suppliers of some WTO Members are accorded less favourable treatment. Thus, the EC's interpretation of the term "affect" would not have the "absurd and far-reaching" consequences claimed by Canada[564].

6.769 Canada submits that "duties and tariffs are measures affecting trade in goods as goods". This is certainly true, but does not rule out that they may *also* affect trade in services. The Appellate Body in *EC - Bananas III* has recognised that one and the same measure, because of its specific content, may affect both the provision of goods

[563] Ibid., paras. 153-154.

[564] For example, although anti-dumping measures or countervailing duties, or a preferential duty rate applied under a free-trade area agreement, may conceivably affect the supply of distribution services, it does not follow necessarily that those measures are contrary *per se* to GATS Article II. A complainant would still have to show that in their application those measures provide an advantage to the service suppliers of one Member over the suppliers of other Members. In this connection, it is also worth recalling that, contrary to what is implied by Canada at several points (see e.g., Canada's response to Question 33 from the Panel), the EC does not claim that the free-trade area for goods established by NAFTA leads to a de facto violation of GATS Article II. The EC's claim is that the violation of Article II results from the privileges accorded under the Tariff Exemption to the US Big Three, in derogation of NAFTA 's generally applicable rules.

and the provision of services and therefore may be reviewed under both GATT and GATS[565].

6.770 The measures reviewed in *EC - Bananas III* were quite similar to the ones at issue in this dispute, and indeed measures like tariff quotas are measures *par excellence* affecting trade in goods. However, this did not prevent the Appellate Body to conclude that EC measures were subject to both the GATT and the GATS[566].

6.771 The similarity is clear if one has regard to the *EC - Bananas III* Panel Report. First, the Panel recognised that operators (the banana importers) providing wholesale services in respect of the products that they have imported are wholesale service suppliers[567]. Likewise, the Tariff Exemption beneficiaries providing wholesale services in respect of the automobiles which they have imported are wholesale service suppliers.

6.772 Second, wholesale services as defined in the headnote to Section 6 of the CPC classification consist in "resale to retailers". There can be no question that this equally applies to this case.

6.773 Third, certain operators (the initial licence holders) were found to be able to retain the "tariff quota rent" (i.e. the advantage of importing in-quota goods at preferential rates)[568]. Likewise, the beneficiaries of the Tariff Exemption are able to retain the benefit of importing duty free.

6.774 In a nutshell, in *EC - Bananas III* the Panel recognised that a tariff advantage allowing to import under more favourable conditions allows to resell under more favourable conditions too. Its finding was affirmed by the Appellate Body. Therefore, the same principle should be recognised as applying in this case.

6.775 Canada's attempts to distinguish the Tariff Exemption from the measures reviewed in *EC - Bananas III* are unsuccessful.

6.776 Canada suggests that the standard upheld in EC - Bananas III is that a measure would only fall under GATS provisions if "prohibitive", that is, if it prevented importation.

6.777 The Panel *EC - Bananas III* in did not rule on the assumption that importation outside the tariff quotas were prohibitive. In fact the Panel took into account the fact that licences were freely tradeable. Thus, contrary to what Canada says, those distributors who had not been allocated licences by the European Communities could still import bananas provided that they bought licences. Indeed, large numbers of licenses were actually traded on the market[569].

6.778 Nevertheless, the Panel considered that in that case the buyers of the licences would not reap the tariff quota rent which would still remain with the seller. Thus, the Panel found that the effect of the measures was to confer on certain operators (initial licence holders) an economic advantage (the tariff quota rent) which enabled them to compete on the market under better conditions[570].

---

565 Appellate Body Report on *EC - Bananas III, supra* note 49, para. 221.

566 Ibid., para. 222.

567 Panel Reports on *EC - Bananas III, supra* note 269, para.7.320.

568 Ibid., para. 7.336.

569 Panel Reports on *EC - Bananas III, supra* note 269, para. 7.336.

570 Ibid.

6.779 This means, on the one hand, that the tariff quota system was taken into account by the Panel to review whether certain operators were afforded more "favourable conditions" within the meaning of GATS, and thus to establish a violation thereof. On the other hand, it shows that the Panel did not base its finding on the condition that the measures totally prevented importation by other operators. This point was not modified by the Appellate Body. Thus, any attempt to distinguish measures on the basis of the intensity of their restrictive effect on importation has no basis in *EC - Bananas III*.

6. *Canada's Response to the Complainants' Rebuttals*

6.780 **Canada** responds as follows:

6.781 Japan, in its response to the Panel's Question 27,[571] simply repeats its position that the duty-free treatment "necessarily affects the profitability in supplying wholesale trade services". It offers no evidence or explanation for its conclusion. The burden is on Japan to show that the duty reduces the profitability of wholesale distribution. Having failed to do this, it has failed to make out a prima facie case.

6.782 Japan goes so far as to contend that differences in retail prices caused by the duty-free treatment will "necessarily" affect sales volumes and by extension profitability in the supply of wholesale trade services. The implication of this argument is that any difference in retail prices between domestic and imported goods due to a measure will necessarily affect the relative profitability of wholesale service suppliers in those goods. By Japan's reasoning, every tariff becomes a potential violation of national treatment for distribution services in any product sector where manufacturers tend to do their own distribution. According to Japan, the tariff will "affect the profitability" of the foreign manufacturers/distributors of imported products while domestic distributors of domestic products face no tariff. For example, where a Member has made commitments for distribution services, it would violate Article XVII of the GATS that those who manufacture and distribute automobiles in the Member can sell them without paying duty, while imported cars are subject to a tariff.

6.783 The European Communities seeks to justify its assertion that the present measures fall within the scope of the GATS on the basis that they are similar to the measures found to affect services in *EC - Bananas III*. However, none of the EC's points of comparison is valid.

6.784 In the first place, the EC's contention that the measures in *EC - Bananas III* are "quite similar" to those at issue in this case is absurd. The measures at issue in both cases affect trade in goods, as the European Communities states. However, that is where the similarity ends. From a GATS perspective, the effect of the EC's scheme on trade in services was readily evident. The scheme involved (i) the creation of a tariff quota system with an over-quota tariff rate that made over-quota imports prohibitive; and (ii) the creation of a licensing system to allocate in-quota licences. Thus, the lack of a licence meant that an importer effectively could not import. Access to the quota was essential to the ability of distributors to carry on their business, particularly when the only source of the product being distributed was from imports.

571 Japan's response to Question 27 from the Panel.

By taking quotas away from operators in category A and allocating them to Category B operators, the EC's system fundamentally limited or disrupted the distribution businesses of Category A operators. The allocations put the Category A operators in the competitively disadvantageous position of having to pay quota rents to their Category B competitors in order to acquire licences to enable them to remain in business or maintain their market share.

6.785 The duty-free treatment in the present case is not even remotely equivalent to the quota scheme in *EC - Bananas III*. Indeed, it should be noted that in the *EC - Bananas III* case there was also a tariff preference for certain bananas that was not even alleged as a GATS measure, notwithstanding that it reduced the cost of only certain bananas.

6.786 The European Communities also contends that the ability of the operators receiving the initial licences in *EC - Bananas III* to extract tariff quota rent from the Category A operators is analogous to the receipt of duty-free benefits by qualifying manufacturers in the present case. This ignores both that the EC banana licences were tradeable and that they were essential for the ability of banana distributors to sell in the EC market. The receipt of a licence to import bananas in-quota affected both the distribution service suppliers that received them and those that did not and had to purchase them. The licence allocations effectively determined which suppliers could engage in the business of distributing bananas in the EC market and which ones would have to pay large rents for the ability to do so. Licence allocations in these circumstances, and the necessity to pay quota rents, are central to the equality of competitive opportunities that GATS Article II is intended to preserve.

6.787 The EC's assertion that the *EC - Bananas III* panel "did not rule on the assumption that importation outside the tariff quotas were prohibitive" because licences were tradeable is a misrepresentation. In the face of prohibitive over-quota tariffs, tradability of licences gave a further competitive advantage to the licence recipients by enabling them to extract quota rents from those distributors who needed licences. No such elements are present in this case. All distributors can import and sell as many automobiles as the market will bear.

6.788 The European Communities further argues that, because most of the operators not receiving bananas licences were foreign operators, the panel found that they were subject to less favourable conditions of competition than their EC counterparts. Because the qualifying manufacturers of automobiles are mostly of US origin, the European Communities argues that other wholesale service suppliers are subject to less favourable conditions of competition.

6.789 Even if it were true that most of the automobile manufacturers are service suppliers of the United States, the EC's reasoning is conclusory. It has skipped the critical step of demonstrating an effect of the measures on wholesale service suppliers in their capacity as such. The EC measures were found to violate Article II of the GATS because, for the reasons just described, they fundamentally altered competition in distribution services by introducing a system where licences were essential to conduct a distribution business, and by allocating those licences in a new and discriminatory way. No similar effect arises from the duty-free treatment at issue in this case.

6.790 Nor, contrary to the EC's assertion, did either the panel or the Appellate Body in *EC - Bananas III* recognize "that a (tariff) advantage allowing to import [sic] under more favourable conditions allows to resell under more favourable conditions too". The "advantage" recognized in *EC - Bananas III* was not the difference in tariff rates but the allocation, to certain operators, of licences the absence of which rendered importation effectively impossible or forced the payment of quota rents. As previously noted, the mere difference in tariff rates in *EC - Bananas III* was not even argued as an issue of discrimination against competing service suppliers under the GATS.

7. *Japan's Follow-Up to Canada's Response*

6.791 Following up on Canada's response to the complainants' rebuttals, **Japan** argues as follows:

6.792 With respect to the Government of Japan's claim that the Duty Waiver by virtue of the eligibility restriction is inconsistent with Article II of the GATS, contrary to the assertions of the Government of Canada, the Government of Japan has presented a prima facie case with respect to the fact that the Duty Waiver "affects" wholesale trade services.

6.793 As discussed in Japan's rebuttal, the difference between the Duty Waiver and the measure at issue in *EC - Bananas III* is the magnitude of the customs duties. In both instances, the regimes are analogous to a tariff quota whereby higher and lower tier duties are applied. In the case of the Duty Waiver, although the higher tier duty may not be prohibitive, it is still significant (6.1 per cent). While its effect may not be as great as that encountered in *EC - Bananas III*, there is still an effect. Whether or not it is "prohibitive" is irrelevant to determine whether a measure "affects" the supply of services. The payment of the 6.1 per cent MFN duty by a wholesale trade service supplier *per se* increases its procurement costs and, therefore, *per se,* decreases the profitability of that service supplier in comparison with service suppliers who are exempted from payment of the duty by the Duty Waiver, thus affecting the conditions of competition in favour of the latter to attract dealers (see response of the Government of Japan to Panel Question 35 and Japan's rebuttal. The Government of Japan has also demonstrated in these documents that competition exists between wholesale trade service suppliers in attracting the retail service suppliers, regardless of their integration with manufacturers in their resale to retail service suppliers. In this way, the supply of wholesale trade services is "affected" by the Duty Waiver.

6.794 The Government of Canada's concern that this argument could bring every tariff into the potential violation of the GATS is unfounded. Canada distorted Japan's argument by stating that it implies "any difference in retail prices between domestic and imported goods due to a measure will necessarily affect the relative profitability", and thus "every tariff becomes a potential violation of national treatment for distribution services". The Government of Japan simply argues that certain measures affecting trade in goods also affects trade in services and thus can also be governed by the GATS. Just because a measure is covered by the GATS does not mean at all that it is in violation of the GATS. Violation occurs when such a measure is inconsistent with one or more of the GATS obligations, which is clearly the case with the Duty Waiver. To the extent that tariffs are also covered by the GATS, it simply means that those tariffs must be imposed in a manner consistent not only with the GATT 1994 but also with the GATS. In this instance, as the Government of Japan has already demonstrated, discriminatory imposition of the duty-free treatment through the Duty Waiver is inconsistent with GATS as well.

8. *The European Communities' Follow-Up to Canada's Response*

6.795 Following up on Canada's response to the complainants' rebuttals, the **European Communities** argues as follows:

6.796 In its response to the rebuttals, Canada restates its GATS Article II test, based on which in order for a violation to be established Canada's Tariff Exemption should affect wholesale trade services in some specific way "that would not make every import duty, and most other goods measures, into measures covered by the GATS".

6.797 That requirement, however, is nowhere stated in the GATS. In accordance with Article I:1 of the GATS, all that is required in order to establish that a measure is "covered" by the GATS is to show that the measure in question "affects the supply of services". This does not, however, mean that *every* import duty is covered by Article II of the GATS.

6.798 Rather, the scope of Article II is limited by another requirement in addition to the one that a measure affect the provision of services. In fact, to establish a violation of Article II it is further necessary to show that the measure at issue modifies the conditions of competition in favour of providers of a certain WTO Member compared to providers of other Members. The European Communities had already refuted this argument of Canada's and set out the proper Article II test. Yet even if one wanted to follow Canada's test, it is clear that the Tariff Exemption does affect trade in wholesale services in a way different from other import duties, in the sense that while not all tariff measures discriminate in favour of some importers only, Canada's measure does.

6.799 This conclusion can be illustrated by referring to Canada's example of the supposedly absurd consequences of the Complainants' position. Canada argues that if the Complainants' reasoning is followed, then "where a member has made commitments for distribution services, it would violate Article XVII of the GATS that those who manufacture and distribute automobiles in the member can sell them without paying duty, while imported cars are subject to a tariff".

6.800 That example, however, is clearly different from the measures in dispute. The application of the same import duty on all imports of cars by all importers would not modify the conditions of competition in favour of domestic distributors: all distributors would have the opportunity to import automobiles under the same conditions and/or to manufacture them domestically.

6.801 Canada's reconstruction of the *EC - Bananas III* Appellate Body Report in its response to the rebuttals is striking. Canada appears to argue that the regime reviewed *EC - Bananas III* was different from Canada's Tariff Exemption because (a) its effect on trade in services was readily evident, and (b) the decisive element to find the EC's bananas regime in breach of Article II was that "the lack of a licence [for in-quota imports] meant that an importer effectively could not import".

6.802 Indeed, considering that "the lack of licence meant that an importer effectively could not import" simply begs the question, as this is an inherent feature in any licensing system. It sounds somehow like saying that the lack of fuel in a car prevents one from driving. However, the real issue is obviously whether fuel can be procured, and under which conditions.

6.803 In this connection, the European Communities has already recalled that the decisive element in the *EC - Bananas III* case was not merely the imposition of a licensing system, as the licences were freely tradable and were actually traded. It was rather that the original licence holders could retain their "tariff quota rent" (that is, the benefit of a preferential tariff scheme) even if they sold their licences.[572]

6.804 Canada also makes much of the fact that in *EC - Bananas III* the measures at issue were not differences in tariff rates, but rules for the allocation of import licenses under a tariff quota. That difference, however, is superficial.

6.805 The import licenses at issue in *EC - Bananas III* conferred to certain distributors the right to import a certain amount of bananas at a preferential duty rate. The amount was based on certain performance criteria, including in particular the amount of EC and ACP bananas previously marketed by those distributors.

6.806 Likewise, the MVTO 1998 and the SROs confer to certain designated importers (the beneficiaries) the right to import a certain amount of motor vehicles at a preferential duty rate. That amount is based on certain performance criteria, namely their local production-to-sales ratio.

6.807 In any event, if anything, the measures at issue are *more* discriminatory than the measures in dispute in *EC - Bananas III*. In the first place, in *EC - Bananas III* any distributor was entitled to apply by licenses. Chiquita and the other US distributors did get licenses from the EC authorities. By contrast, the list of beneficiaries of the Tariff Exemption has been closed since 1989.

6.808 Second, as already recalled, in *EC - Bananas III*, licenses were freely transferable. Again, in contrast, the only possible way in which a non-beneficiary could qualify for the Tariff Exemption is by taking over one of the beneficiaries. Compared with the price of buying GM, the quota rents paid by Chiquita are negligible.

6.809 In conclusion, in its structure and effects the EC's bananas import scheme is much more similar to the preferential tariff scheme constituted by the Tariff Exemption than Canada pretends. The difference comes down to one of degree, i.e. to a difference between the alleged "large rents" paid to buy banana import licences and the preference margin afforded by Canada's Tariff Exemption. As the European Communities has said elsewhere, there is no place for a *de minimis* threshold under Article II of the GATS.

6.810 In its response to the rebuttals, Canada again submits that in order to establish an Article II violation "an effect of the measures on wholesale trade services suppliers in their capacity as such" must be demonstrated. Contrary to what Canada argues, this was not "critical" to the Appellate Body's ruling in *EC - Bananas III*. It was not considered as a separate element to show to establish a violation. There is no support for this additional requirement in the *EC - Bananas III* Appellate Body Report. In fact on the one hand, when evaluating whether GATT and GATS may overlap, the Appellate Body found that the "Under GATS, the focus is on how the measure affects the supply of a service or the services suppliers involved".[573]

6.811 On the other hand, when specifically dealing with integrated companies, the Appellate Body found that "to the extent that [an integrated company] is also engaged in providing 'wholesale trade services' *and is therefore* affected in that capacity by a particular measure of a Member in its supply of those 'wholesale trade services',

---

[572] Panel Report on *EC - Bananas III (USA)*, *supra* note 269, para. 7.336.

[573] Appellate Body Report on *EC - Bananas III*, *supra* note 49, para. 221.

that company is a service supplier within the scope of the GATS".[574] It clearly results from this passage that the effect on service providers "in their capacity as such" is not a separate element from the fact that a company must provide services.

9. *Canada's Follow-Up Response*

6.812 **Canada** responds as follows:

6.813 Both Japan and the European Communities insist that the duty-free treatment under the measures affects trade in services, but their explanations for how this is so remain vague. In particular, the complainants are unable to explain how the duty-free treatment affects trade in wholesale services in any way that would not make every import duty, and most other goods measures, measures subject to the GATS. The difficulty the complainants face is that the duty-free treatment affects trade in goods, and may affect the price of goods, but it does not affect trade in distribution services in any way independent of its effect on the price of goods.

6.814 Japan and the European Communities seek to evade this fundamental flaw in their argument. They assert baldly that the present case is just like *EC - Bananas III* and that if the measures in that case were found to affect trade in services, then the same must be true of the duty-free treatment. Japan goes so far as to suggest that the only difference between the measures in *EC-Bananas III* and those in the present case is the magnitude of a tariff.

6.815 There are two basic flaws with these contentions. The first is that because the complainants are claiming effects that arise in fact, not in law, all of the facts, including the magnitude of the tariff, are relevant. The other flaw is that the measures at issue in the present case are fundamentally different from those in *EC - Bananas III*.

6.816 Despite the complainants' repeated attempts to suggest otherwise, the offending GATS measure in *EC - Bananas III* was not the tariff quota itself but the import license allocation system. That system took licenses away from Category A operators. It fundamentally limited or disrupted their distribution businesses and put them in the competitively disadvantageous position of having to pay quota rents to their Category B competitors in order to reacquire their licenses to enable them to remain in business or maintain market share.

6.817 The situation was particularly egregious in *EC - Bananas III* because for the most part, the product could be sourced only by importing. It was impossible to carry on a banana distribution business without an import licence. The measures in question went to the very heart of the ability of distribution service suppliers to deliver distribution services and properly fell within the scope of the GATS.

6.818 A fact that Canada has previously noted, and the complainants have studiously ignored, is that in *EC - Bananas III*, in addition to the ordinary tariff quota and the licence distribution system, there was a tariff preference for certain (ACP) bananas over Latin American bananas. That tariff differential was not even argued to be a GATS measure by any of the many parties to that dispute, nor by the panel or the Appellate Body. It may be surmised that it was simply inconceivable to the parties that such a measure would be considered to affect trade in services.

---

574 Ibid., para. 227.

6.819 It was also inconceivable to the drafters of the GATS, as evidenced by the Addendum to the Explanatory Note cited by Canada. Despite Japan's attempts to explain it away, and the EC's decision to ignore it, the Addendum assured Members that there was no requirement to schedule a GATS limitation for the effect that customs duties might have on the cross-border movement of goods associated with the provision of a service.

6.820 Neither Japan nor the European Communities have claimed any effect of the measures except the potential effect on the price of goods. This, they contend, is sufficient to constitute an effect on the distributors of those goods. The implications of accepting this contention, which Canada has considered in more detail, include that it could make otherwise legal differential treatment of goods, such as anti-dumping and countervailing duties and end-use requirements, inconsistent with the GATS.

6.821 The European Communities responds that while this is conceivable, it does not necessarily follow that such measures are contrary *per se* to GATS Article II because a complainant would still have to show that the measures accord an advantage to the service suppliers of one or more Members over those of other Members. This offers little comfort. Measures such as anti-dumping duties specifically disadvantage the goods of certain Members. Due to vertical integration in manufacturing and distribution, these disadvantages would, by the complainants' reasoning, affect the service suppliers of those goods and those Members, in some cases under Article II, in others under Article XVII.

6.822 Japan responds that the Panel should ignore this problem because these other measures are "categorically authorized by the GATT and other WTO Agreements". However, a measure is not immune from one WTO obligation merely because it may be consistent with another.[575] It is precisely because an overly broad interpretation of "measures affecting trade in services" would have the bizarre and unwarranted consequence of making illegal all kinds of legal tariff measures that the Panel must exercise caution.

6.823 The complainants might want to do the same. As Canada just noted, there are cases throughout the world where, due to the vertically-integrated distribution of goods, foreign distribution service suppliers pay tariffs on the goods they import while domestic distribution service suppliers distribute goods that are not subject to duty. The mechanical application of the complainants' erroneous interpretation would render all such import duties a violation of a GATS commitment on distribution services. A tariff measure affects the cost of the goods purchased. The likely foreign-owned distributor of the import would pay a duty while the domestic distributor of a domestic good would not. Therefore, by the complainants' reasoning, a host of legal import duties would become violations of the GATS.

6.824 Moreover, if the duty-free treatment is offensive because it favours the distribution service suppliers of certain countries, then free-trade areas must be offensive too. Under the NAFTA for example, distribution service suppliers of North American-manufactured vehicles are able to import vehicles into Canada, the United States and Mexico duty-free. Honda and Toyota are significant beneficiaries of this treatment but Korean manufacturers and distributors are not. There is no provision of the

[575] Appellate Body Report on *EC - Bananas III*, *supra* note 49, para. 221.

GATS that exempts free-trade areas that create differentials in duty treatment, doubtless because the drafters of the GATS never imagined that it would be necessary to have one for a tariff measure of the kind at issue here.

6.825 In fact, in their rebuttals, the complainants make much of Article V of the GATS. As Canada noted in its response to Question 33 from the Panel, if the Panel finds that measures at issue do fall within the scope of the GATS in respect of the duty-free treatment of goods, the measures at issue would be subject to the MFN exception conferred by Article V:1 of the GATS. Neither complainant has made a persuasive case to the contrary.

6.826 However, as Canada also noted in its response to Question 33, the principal relevance of Article V is that it demonstrates that the scope of the GATS was never intended to extend to measures according duty-free treatment to goods. If it was, the exemption in Article V:1 would have been extended to agreements liberalizing trade in goods and not just agreements liberalizing trade in services.

6.827 In presenting its claims, Japan attempted to incorporate into Article II the "affecting conditions of competition test" from Article XVII of the GATS. Part of Canada's response was to note that there is no competition among wholesale distribution trade service suppliers to affect due to the close relationships between manufacturers and their distribution service providers.

6.828 The complainants have since offered two responses. The first, by the European Communities, is that such competition does exist, as demonstrated by the Big Three's distribution arrangements, such as with Chrysler and Mitsubishi. The European Communities describes Mitsubishi as unrelated to Chrysler. Despite the EC's statement that it was Canada's position that these imports always required an ownership link, what Canada actually said in its response to the complainants' rebuttals was that Mitsubishi and Chrysler had an equity relationship or a manufacturing relationship, or both throughout the duration of their distribution arrangement. The Mitsubishi example merely demonstrates the absence of independent competition in wholesale distribution services.

6.829 In its latest argument, the European Communities offers two more examples, Ford's distribution of Kias and GM's distribution of Isuzus, but these suffer from the same flaw. In neither case were the distributors independent of the manufacturers whose vehicles they distributed. In both cases the distribution was a function of other relationships, including substantial equity interests in the manufacturer. The GM/Isuzu relationship is ongoing, but Ford's distribution of Kias ended in 1994.

6.830 The complainants' second response was that manufacturers compete to sell automobiles to retail dealers. Even if this is true, and the EC's own regulations, submitted as Exhibit CDA-16, seem to say the contrary, it is merely another way of arguing that the measures affect distribution service suppliers by affecting the price of the goods distributed by them. This is evident for example, in Japan's contention that by reducing the procurement cost of automobiles, the duty-free treatment confers an advantage on qualifying manufacturers to supply their services to dealers. The European Communities makes similar claims.

6.831 Canada has already addressed the far-reaching implications of these assertions. Canada has also noted that these assertions would nullify the three distinct categories of measures the Appellate Body identified in *EC - Bananas III*. Neither complainant has suggested otherwise, or has offered a theory of what falls into the Appellate Body's category of measures affecting goods only.

6.832 Even if retailers were not bound by exclusive agreements with manufacturers, what they are choosing to purchase, in the complainants' own scenario, is not distribution services as such, but automobiles. Even if the dealers had a choice among the suppliers of the automobiles they wish to purchase - which they do not - the duty-free treatment would not affect their choice of supplier. It would merely affect their choice of automobile. In other words, to use the language of the Appellate Body, the duty-free treatment does not affect wholesale trade service suppliers in the supply of their wholesale trade services.

F. Article II of the GATS

1. Arguments of Japan

6.833 **Japan** argues as follows:

(a) Article II of the GATS Requires Immediate and Unconditional MFN Treatment for Wholesale Trade Services and Service Suppliers of Motor Vehicles

6.834 Restricting eligibility to the Duty Waiver to the Auto Pact Manufacturers under the MVTO 1998 and the SROs who are wholesale trade service suppliers is inconsistent with Article II of the GATS, which requires the "immediate and unconditional" extension of general most-favoured-nation treatment to like services and service suppliers of any other WTO Member.

6.835 In accordance with the definition stipulated in Article XXVIII of the GATS, particularly subparagraphs (m) and (n) of the Article, the Government of Japan found in Japan's Tables 1 and 2 that the Auto Pact Manufacturers include US and Swedish service suppliers (e.g., Ford Canada, GM Canada and Volvo Canada) and do not include Japanese service suppliers (e.g., Honda Canada and Toyota Canada).[576]

6.836 The first paragraph of Article II of the GATS provides:

> "With respect to any measure covered by this Agreement, each Member shall accord immediately and unconditionally to services and service suppliers of any other Member treatment no less favourable than that it accords to like services and service suppliers of any other country."

6.837 The second paragraph of the same Article provides:

> "A Member may maintain a measure inconsistent with paragraph 1 provided that such a measure is listed in, and meets the conditions of, the Annex on Article II Exemptions."

---

[576] CAMI, which is 50 per cent owned by General Motors Corp. (a US corporation) and 50 per cent owned by Suzuki Motor Corporation (a Japanese corporation) is not a Japanese service supplier since it is neither owned nor controlled by natural persons or judicial persons of Japan within the meaning of subpara. (m) of Article XXVIII of the GATS. This is because i) more than 50 per cent of the equity interest in CAMI is *not* beneficially owned by Japanese persons within the meaning of subpara. (n)(i) of the Article; and ii) Japanese persons *do not* have the power to name a majority of its directors or otherwise to legally direct its actions within the meaning of subpara. (n)(ii) of the same Article.

Canada, however, has not listed any measures relating to "wholesale trade services" in the Annex. Therefore, Canada is fully bound by its obligations under Article II:1 of the GATS in relation to "wholesale trade services".

6.838 In *EC - Bananas III*, the WTO panel articulated the following two-part test to determine whether the contested measure violates Article II of the GATS:

> "We note that two elements need to be demonstrated in order to establish a violation of the GATS MFN clause: (i) the EC has adopted or applied a measure covered by GATS; (ii) the EC's measure accords to services or service suppliers of Complainants' origin treatment less favourable than that it accords to the like services suppliers of any other country."[577]

6.839 The first element of the two-part test set out by the panel in *EC - Bananas III* is met in this case. The Government of Japan has shown that the Duty Waiver constitutes a measure affecting trade in services. As the Panel in *EC - Bananas III* clarified, "any measure bearing upon conditions of competition in supply of a service" constitutes a measure "affecting the supply of services". By exempting the imports of the Auto Pact Manufacturers from otherwise applicable MFN customs duty, the Duty Waiver reduces the cost that must be borne by the Auto Pact Manufacturers in supplying wholesale trade services. Therefore, the Duty Waiver constitutes a measure bearing upon condition of competition and thus is covered by the GATS.

6.840 As to the second element, according to the panel in *EC - Bananas III*, if the answers to both of the following questions are "yes", then the Duty Waiver is inconsistent with Article II of the GATS:

(i) Does the Duty Waiver confer an advantage?

(ii) If it does, is such an advantage conferred on services or service suppliers from certain members but not on like services or service suppliers from other WTO Members including Japan?

Further, the Appellate Body in *EC - Bananas III* concluded that, in determining whether a measure meets the MFN obligation of Article II:1 of the GATS, "treatment no less favourable" should be interpreted to include both *de facto* and *de jure* discrimination.[578] Finally, Article II of the GATS requires that MFN Treatment be accorded "immediately and unconditionally".

(b) The Duty Waiver Accords More Favourable Treatment to Wholesale Trade Service and Service Suppliers of the United States and Sweden in Violation of Article II of the GATS

(i) The services and service suppliers at issue are like

6.841 As discussed above, importers who are eligible for the Duty Waiver (i.e. the Auto Pact Manufacturers) offer wholesale trade services to distribute domestically

---

[577] Panel Reports on *EC - Bananas III, supra* note 269, para. 7.344.

[578] Appellate Body Report on *EC - Bananas III, supra* note 49, para. 234.

produced and imported motor vehicles. Similarly, importers who are not eligible for the Duty Waiver (i.e. Non-Auto Pact Manufacturers) offer like wholesale trade services to distribute domestically produced and/or imported motor vehicles.

6.842 In *EC - Bananas III*, the panel found:

> "In our view, the nature and the characteristics of wholesale transactions as such, as well as of each of the different subordinated services mentioned in the headnote to Section 6 of the CPC, are "like" when supplied in connection with wholesale services, irrespective of whether these services are supplied with respect to bananas of EC and traditional ACP origin, on the one hand, or with respect to bananas of third-country or non-traditional ACP origin, on the other. Indeed, it seems that each of the different service activities taken individually is virtually the same and can only be distinguished by referring to the origin of the bananas in respect of which the service activity is being performed. Similarly, in our view, to the extent that entities provide these like services, they are like service suppliers."[579]

6.843 This finding applies with equal force to the instant case. As discussed above, the Auto Pact Manufacturers (e.g., Chrysler Canada, Ford Canada, General Motors Canada and Volvo Canada) and Non-Auto Pact Manufacturers (e.g. Honda Canada, Mazda Canada, Nissan Canada and Toyota Canada) are rendering "like" services "in connection with wholesale trade services", "irrespective of whether these services are supplied with respect to automobiles imported by the Auto Pact Manufacturers or their related companies on the one hand or with respect to automobiles imported by the Non-Auto Pact Manufacturers on the other hand". Further, to the extent that the Auto Pact Manufacturers and the Non-Auto Pact Manufacturers "provide these like services, they are like service suppliers"[580], regardless of whether or not they have production facilities in Canada.

(ii) The Duty Waiver confers an advantage on wholesale trade services and service suppliers who are eligible for the Duty Waiver (i.e. the Auto Pact Manufacturers)

6.844 The Appellate Body concluded in *EC-Bananas III*:

> "treatment no less favourable" in Article II:1 of the GATS should be interpreted to include *de facto*, as well as *de jure*, discrimination. We should make it clear that we do not limit our conclusion to this case.[581]

6.845 As discussed above, the Auto Pact Manufacturers are limited to United States or Canadian automobile manufacturers (i.e. service suppliers) with one exception. This is a reflection of the fact that the Canada-US Auto Pact was originally intended to address trade in automobiles and original equipment parts on a duty-free basis between Canada and the United States. Since the NAFTA entered into force, with respect to automobile manufacturers, only Canadian subsidiaries of three major

579 See Panel Reports on *EC - Bananas III, supra* note 269, para. 7.322 (see also para. 7.346).
580 Ibid., para. 7.346.
581 Appellate Body Report on *EC - Bananas III, supra* note 49, para. 234.

United States automobile manufacturers and a Swedish manufacturer and two manufacturers that are allowed remission of duties under SROs (i.e. CAMI and Intermeccanica), all of which are also wholesale trade service suppliers, have been allowed to import motor vehicles duty-free for wholesale trade in Canada.

6.846 No Japanese wholesale trade service suppliers may enjoy the advantages of importing automobiles duty-free, since they are prevented from doing so by the eligibility restriction. Moreover, the restriction freezes the status quo, i.e. the situation where only importers that are United States or Swedish wholesale trade service suppliers may import automobiles duty-free from third countries. This constitutes *de facto* discrimination against Japanese wholesale trade services and service suppliers, and is therefore inconsistent with Canada's obligations under Article II of the GATS.

6.847 As noted by the Appellate Body, any other interpretation would allow a Member to "devise discriminatory measures aimed at circumventing the basic purpose of" Article II:1 of the GATS.[582]

6.848 As also clarified by the panel in *EC - Bananas III* (para. 7.349), "the obligations contained in Article II:1 of the GATS to extend 'treatment no less favourable' should be interpreted to require providing 'no less favourable conditions of competitions'". Although the Panel in *EC - Bananas III* based its holding on prior interpretations of Article III of the GATT 1994, the Appellate Body affirmed the substance of its holding. Also, a number of panels have found that the MFN obligation of Article I of the GATT 1994 extends to *de facto* discrimination of the type the Government of Canada has engaged in here.[583]

6.849 The Duty Waiver necessarily affects the conditions of competition because the Auto Pact Manufacturers need not pass on import duties in the sales price of automobiles nor incur any financial carrying costs associated with the import duties, while Non-Auto Pact Manufacturers are required to do so. Thus, wholesale trade service suppliers who pay the MFN duty (or that distribute motor vehicles for which the MFN duty is paid) are put at a competitive disadvantage (i.e. accorded less favourable treatment) in offering their services as compared to like service suppliers who do not pay the duty (or that distribute motor vehicles for which the MFN duty is waived).

6.850 Thus, Japanese service suppliers are subject to less favourable treatment than United States or Swedish service suppliers.[584] This discrimination is the result of the provision of duty-free status to a very limited number of importers in conjunction with the eligibility restriction.

---

[582] Ibid., para. 233.

[583] See, e.g., Panel Report on *Japan - SPF Lumber, supra* note 282, paras. 6.9, 5.10, 5.13 and 5.14: Panel Report on *EEC - Beef from Canada, supra* note 282, paras. 4.2(a) and (b), and 4.3. See also Panel Report on *Spain - Unroasted Coffee, supra* note 282.

[584] As discussed in footnote 591, CAMI is not of Japanese-origin pursuant to Article XXVIII of the GATS.

(iii) The favourable treatment is not accorded "immediately and unconditionally" to like services and service suppliers

6.851 Article II:1 of the GATS obliges the Government of Canada to accord no less favourable treatment "immediately and unconditionally" to like services and service suppliers of WTO Members.

6.852 Although no case in the context of the GATS has referred to lack of conditionality, as discussed above in the context of Article I:1 of the GATT 1994, the Panel on *Indonesia - Autos* discussed this requirement in detail. The findings of the *Indonesia - Autos* Panel regarding the "immediate and unconditional" provision of benefits apply equally to the equivalent MFN obligation in the GATS.

6.853 Under the Duty Waiver, in order for an importer/wholesale trade service supplier to benefit from the duty-exempt treatment, it must meet certain pre-requisites, including eligibility, domestic content and manufacturing requirements. Accordingly, the Duty Waiver creates "conditional most-favoured- nation" treatment and, therefore, violates Article II:1 of the GATS.

2. *Arguments of the European Communities*

6.854 The **European Communities** argues as follows:

6.855 The Tariff Exemption is inconsistent with Canada's obligations under GATS Article II in that *de facto* it provides more favourable treatment to US suppliers of wholesale distribution services for automobiles than to like service suppliers of other Members.

6.856 Article II of GATS states as follows in relevant part:

> "1. With respect to any measure covered by this agreement, each Member shall accord immediately and unconditionally to services and service suppliers of any other Member treatment no less favourable than that it accords to like services and service suppliers of any other country.
>
> 2. A Member may maintain a measure inconsistent with paragraph 1 provided that such a measure is listed in, and meets the conditions of, the Annex on Article II exemptions."

6.857 Therefore, the Panel is required to address the following issues in order to decide on the EC's claim under GATS Article II:

- whether the Tariff Exemption is a "measure covered by the GATS";
- whether the Tariff Exemption is covered by the Annex on Article II exemptions;
- whether the beneficiaries are "like" the service suppliers of other Members; and
- whether the Tariff Exemption affords more "favourable treatment" to US service suppliers than to like service suppliers of other Members.

(a) The Tariff Exemption is a "Measure Covered by the GATS"

6.858 (*See* Section VI.E, Applicability of the GATS to the Measures.)

(b) The Tariff Exemption is not Covered by the Annex on Article II Exemptions

6.859 Canada has not listed in the Annex on Article II exemptions any measures relating to the supply of "wholesale trade services". Therefore, Canada is fully bound by its obligations under Article II:1 in relation to those services.

(c) The Beneficiaries are "Like" Other Suppliers of Wholesale Distribution Services

6.860 The beneficiaries supply the same type of distribution services as the other firms established in Canada which are engaged in the purchase, importation and resale of automobiles to local dealers.

6.861 In fact, the distinction between the beneficiaries and the other wholesale distributors is based exclusively on the fact that the beneficiaries: (1) were engaged in the manufacture of automobiles prior to 1989; and (2) have undertaken to comply with certain CVA and ratio requirements. Clearly, however, neither of those two factors may have, as such, any bearing on the nature and the characteristics of the distribution services supplied by the beneficiaries with respect to imported automobiles.

6.862 To the extent that they provide "like" services, the beneficiaries and the other wholesale distributors are "like" service suppliers[585].

(d) The Tariff Exemption Affords "More Favourable Treatment" to US Service Suppliers than to the Service Suppliers of Other Members

6.863 In *EC - Bananas III*, the Appellate Body clarified that Article II of GATS applies not only to formal, or *de jure* discrimination, but also to *de facto* discrimination between services or service suppliers. According to the Appellate Body:

> "The obligation imposed by Article II is unqualified. The ordinary meaning of this provision does not exclude *de facto* discrimination. Moreover, if Article II was not applicable to *de facto* discrimination, it would not be difficult - and, indeed, it would be a good deal easier in the case of trade in services, than in the case of trade of goods - to devise discriminatory measures aimed at circumventing the basic purpose of that Article.[586]

6.864 On that premise, the Appellate Body affirmed the Panel's finding that, although the so-called "operator category rules" for the allocation of a tariff quota did not distinguish formally among service suppliers on the basis of their country of origin, they were nonetheless inconsistent with GATS Article II because *de facto* "most" of the service suppliers of Complainants' origin were classified within the less fa-

---

585 See, e.g., Panel Reports on *EC - Bananas III*, *supra* note 269, paras. 7.322, 7.346, 7.359.

586 Appellate Body Report on *EC - Bananas III*, *supra* note 49, para. 233.

voured category of operators, whereas "most" of the suppliers of ACP fell within the more favoured category[587].

6.865 The present dispute concerns a similar situation. The Tariff Exemption does not distinguish formally among suppliers of wholesale distribution services for automobiles according to their country of origin. Nonetheless, *de facto* it affords more favourable treatment to US suppliers than to the suppliers of other Members.

6.866 As explained in the factual part, the category of firms authorised to import automobiles under the Auto Pact duty-free is a closed one, consisting of just five beneficiaries[588].

6.867 As set out in the EC's Table 5 below, three of those beneficiaries (namely, the subsidiaries of the US Big Three) are wholly owned by juridical persons constituted under the law of the United States and with substantial business operations in the territory of the United States. Therefore, those beneficiaries can be considered as service suppliers of the United States in application of the rules contained in GATS Article XXVIII (m)[589] and (n)[590].

6.868 Another beneficiary, CAMI Automotive Inc., is a joint venture between General Motors Corp., a US company, and Suzuki Motor Corp., a Japanese company, of which General Motors Corp. is the largest shareholder[591]. CAMI is devoted exclusively to manufacturing and does not distribute in Canada the automobiles that it is entitled to import duty-free under the Auto Pact. Instead, those automobiles, like the automobiles manufactured in Canada by CAMI, are distributed by the two parent companies under their respective nameplates[592].

6.869 Thus, there is currently only one beneficiary without any ownership links with US firms: Volvo (Canada) Ltd., which is a wholly owned subsidiary of Volvo AB, a Swedish company. This situation, nevertheless, will change soon, following the an-

---

587 Ibid., paras. 242-244. The Appellate Body followed the same reasoning with respect to the allocation of the so-called "hurricane licenses" (para. 248).

588 Intermeccanica, an artisanal producer of replicas of racing cars, may be disregarded for the purposes of this analysis.

589 GATS Article XXVIII (m) reads as follows:

"(m) 'juridical person of another Member' means a juridical person which is either:

(i) constituted or otherwise organised under the law of that other Member, and is engaged in substantive business operations in the territory of that Member or any other Member; or

(ii) in the case of the supply of a service through commercial presence, owned or controlled by:

natural persons of that Member; or

juridical persons of that other Member identified under subpara. (i)."

590 GATS Article XXVIII (n) provides that:

"(n) a juridical person is:

(i) 'owned' by persons of a Member if more than 50 per cent of the equity interest in it is beneficially owned by persons of that Member;

(ii) 'controlled' by persons of a Member if such persons have the power to name a majority of its directors or otherwise to legally direct its actions;

(iii) 'affiliated' with another person when it controls, or is controlled by, that other person; or when it and the other person are both controlled by the same person."

591 In September 1998, General Motors Corp increased its shareholding in Suzuki Motors Corp. from 3.3 per cent to 10 per cent.

592 In practice, most of CAMI's production is for General Motors.

nouncement made on 29 January 1999 of the sale of Volvo AB's passenger car business to Ford Motor Co.[593]

6.870 As shown in the EC's Table 6, in contrast with the subsidiaries of the US Big Three, both Suzuki Canada Inc. and Volvo (Canada) Ltd. are minor players in the Canadian market for automobiles and account for a very small share of imports under the Auto Pact.

6.871 Moreover, as mentioned above, Volvo (Canada) Ltd. ceased the production of automobiles as of December 1998, with the consequence that it will lose the right to import automobiles duty-free under the Auto Pact at the end of the current model year.

6.872 The fact that the Tariff Exemption benefits mainly US service suppliers is by no means fortuitous. As already explained in the factual part, until 1989 Canada was committed to extend the Tariff Exemption to any manufacturer which met CVA and ratio requirements equivalent to those imposed upon the original Auto Pact beneficiaries in 1965. Canada was forced to repudiate that commitment as a result of the conclusion of the CUFSTA, which contains a express provision prohibiting Canada from granting the Tariff Exemption to any other manufacturers. That prohibition was inserted in the CUFSTA at the demand of the United States and has the clear purpose of reserving the Tariff Exemption for the subsidiaries of the US Big Three.

EC's Table 5

Country of origin of the beneficiaries

Service supplier	**Parent**	**% of shares owned by parent**	**Country of incorporation of the parent**
Ford Motor Co. of Canada Ltd.	Ford Motor Co.	100	USA
General Motors of Canada Ltd.	General Motors Corp.	100	USA
Chrysler Canada Ltd	Daimler Chrysler Corp.[594]	100	USA
CAMI Automotive Inc.	General Motors Corp	50	USA
	Suzuki Motor Corp.	50	Japan
Volvo (Canada) Ltd.	Volvo AB	100	EC (Sweden)

Source: Based on the documents attached (Exhibit EC-21).

[593] The sale has been approved by the shareholders of Volvo AB at an extraordinary General Meeting held on 8 March 1999 and cleared by the EC anti-trust authorities on 26 March 1999.

[594] In May 1998, Daimler-Benz and Chrysler agreed to merge their businesses. Daimler Chrysler Corp. (formerly Chrysler Corp.) is a wholly owned subsidiary of Daimler Chrysler AG, a holding company incorporated in Germany which also controls Daimler-Benz AG. It is believed that Chrysler Canada Ltd. now imports motor vehicles of the marque Mercedes under the Auto Pact.

EC's Table 6

Sales of automobiles by distributor in 1997

Distributor	Produced in Canada (units) (A)	Imported (units) (B)	Market share (A + B)
Ford Motor Co. of Canada Ltd.[595]	107,676*	1,992**	14.84%
General Motors of Canada Ltd.[596]	242,014	3,873**	33.27%
Chrysler Canada Ltd.	87,292*	---**	11.81%
Volvo (Canada) Ltd.	9,224	1,796	1.49%
Volkswagen Canada Inc.	---	26,541	3.59%
BMW Canada Inc.	---	7,117	0.96%
Mercedes-Benz Canada Inc.	---	5,703	0.77%
Porsche Canada Ltd.	---	1,796	0.24%
Toyota Motor Mfg. Canada Inc.	34,119	46,009	10.84%
Honda Canada Inc.	43,151	47,152	12.20%
Nissan Canada Inc.	---	20,570	2.78%
Subaru Canada Inc.	---	7,944	1.08%
Mazda Canada Inc.	---	22,195	3.00%
Suzuki Canada Inc.	2,572	2,311	0.66%
Lada Canada Inc.	---	646	0.09%
Hyundai Canada Inc.	---	19,285	2.61%

*Including sales of automobiles produced in the United States and Mexico.

**Excluding sales of automobiles imported from the United States and Mexico.

Source: Quarterly Automotive Circular, January-December 1997, Industry Canada, Table 1.7 (Exhibit EC-16).

3. *Canada's Response*

6.873 **Canada** responds as follows:

6.874 Article II of the GATS imposes an MFN obligation. Article II:1 provides:

> "With respect to any measure covered by this Agreement, each Member shall accord immediately and unconditionally to services and service suppliers of any other Member treatment no less favourable than that it accords to like services and service suppliers of any other country."

6.875 Article II:2 of the GATS allows Members to exempt certain measures from the scope of Article II by listing them in an Annex. No such exemptions are at issue in this case.

6.876 In order to succeed in their claims, Japan and the European Communities must establish:

i) that the measures at issue are covered by the GATS;

ii) that the services and service suppliers at issue are "like"; and

---

[595] Ford Motor Co. of Canada, Ltd. also imports and distributes in Canada the marques Jaguar and Kia.

[596] General Motors of Canada Ltd. also imports and distributes the marques Saab and Isuzu.

(iii) that the measures at issue accord more favourable treatment to the service suppliers of certain countries than it does to the service suppliers of other Members.

6.877 The claims of Japan and the European Communities cannot satisfy this test. The measures at issue are neither measures covered by the GATS, nor do they accord more favourable treatment to the service suppliers of some countries than to those of other Members.

(a) The Measures at Issue are not Covered by the GATS

6.878 (*See* Section VI.E, Applicability of the GATS to the Measures.)

(b) The MVTO and SROs do not Accord More Favourable Treatment to the Service Suppliers of Certain Countries

(i) The Complainants' evidence does not demonstrate de facto discrimination

6.879 The complainants' arguments on the third element of the test under Article II of the GATS - in particular that of the European Communities - come down to a numbers game. Japan and the European Communities acknowledge that the measures do not distinguish *de jure* among the suppliers of wholesale distribution services for automobiles, but claim that they do so on a *de facto* basis.

6.880 The complainants attempt to identify the number of manufacturers that are eligible to import automobiles pursuant to the MVTO or the SROs. The totals they arrive at, six in the case of Japan, five in the case of the European Communities, differ in that Japan includes Intermeccanica, a Canadian speciality automobile manufacturer, while the European Communities does not. The totality of their argument is that, on the basis of the "nationality" of certain of these five or six manufacturers, the measures *de facto* accord more favourable treatment to certain Members than to others. Japan argues that manufacturers of the United States and Sweden (a member of the European Communities) receive more favourable treatment. The European Communities claims that manufacturers of the United States alone do. It is a testament to their insufficient evidence that the complainants cannot agree on this fundamental point.

6.881 In fact, when the nationality of service suppliers is ascertained in accordance with the GATS rules, no particular Member is favoured or disadvantaged. Changes in ownership of MVTO beneficiaries over the period that the measures have been in effect demonstrate that the measures are indifferent to the nationality of the beneficiaries' ownership.

6.882 According to the rules in GATS Article XXVIII(m) and (n) for determining which company is a juridical person of which Member, Chrysler Canada is a juridical person of the European Communities, in that it is wholly owned by DaimlerChrysler of the United States which is in turn 100 per cent owned by DaimlerChrysler AG of the Federal Republic of Germany. Volvo (Canada) Ltd. is, as the European Communities notes, a wholly owned subsidiary of Volvo AB of Sweden. However, its passenger car business is now or will soon become American by virtue of its sale to the

Ford Motor Company. On the other hand, the European Communities notes that Volvo (Canada) Ltd. is about to lose its qualifying status under the MVTO because it is ceasing production in Canada. In addition, CAMI, a 50/50 joint venture of General Motors of Canada Limited and Suzuki Motor Company is probably, under the GATS, a juridical person of both the United States and Japan.

6.883 Thus, of the automobile manufacturers alleged to be foreign service suppliers benefiting from the MVTO and SROs among the possible conclusions are that two-and-a-half are US companies, two are EC companies and half is a Japanese company; or three-and-a-half are US companies, one is an EC company and half is a Japanese company; or two-and-a-half are US companies, one is an EC company and half is a Japanese company.

6.884 Other permutations are also possible. What is clear is that the nationality of the wholesales service suppliers at issue reveals that the MVTO and SROs do not *de facto* afford more favourable treatment to the service suppliers of certain countries than to those of other Members.

(ii) The MVTO and the SROs do not modify conditions of competition

6.885 According to the Panel Report in *EC - Bananas III*, the obligation in Article II of the GATS to accord "treatment no less favourable" requires Members to provide "no less favourable conditions of competition" to the service suppliers of another Member than they accord to the like service suppliers of any other country.[597]

6.886 Only Japan relies on this interpretation of Article II, which was subsequently cast into some doubt by the Appellate Body Report.[598] Even if Japan's interpretation of Article II is correct, its application of that interpretation to the facts of this case is not.

6.887 Japan asserts that duty-free treatment under the MVTO and SROs "necessarily" affects the conditions of competition "because the Auto Pact Manufacturers need not pass on import duties in the sales price of automobiles nor incur any financial carrying costs associated with the import duties, while Non-Auto Pact Manufacturers are required to do so." However, the cost of duties is borne by the sales price of the goods on which the duties are imposed. Duties affect the cost of the goods as goods and not the conditions of competition in the supply of distribution services.

6.888 If it were otherwise so, as Canada has noted above, any duty measure would also be a measure affecting the supply of distribution services for the dutiable good. Duty-free treatment reduces the cost of goods, not services. The fact that automobiles imported by Honda Canada are subject to duty while automobiles imported by Chrysler Canada are not does not mean that conditions of competition between Chrysler Canada and Honda Canada in the provision of wholesale distribution services are affected.

6.889 Moreover, the commercial presences engaged in the supply of wholesale distribution services for automobiles are integrally related to the manufacturers of the motor vehicles they distribute. Unlike the distributors in *EC - Bananas III*, they do

---

597 Panel Reports on *EC - Bananas III*, *supra* note 269, para. 7.349.

598 Appellate Body Report on *EC - Bananas III*, *supra* note 49, para. 231.

not engage in genuine competition in buying and reselling. They are mere conduits for the vehicles produced by the manufacturers to which they are related. The MVTO and SROs do not therefore affect the conditions of competition among the suppliers of wholesale distribution trade services.

6.890 In the supply of wholesale distribution services for automobiles, there is no competition to affect. The structure of the motor vehicle industry allows for considerable competition among manufacturers in the sale of automobiles (*i.e.* goods as goods). However, because wholesale service suppliers are subordinated to those manufacturers, competition among them in the supply of wholesale distribution services is precluded.

6.891 All of the commercial presences identified by the complainants as providing wholesale distribution services are closely related to the manufacturers of the automobiles they distribute. They do not compete independently of these relationships to provide distribution trade services for the automobiles produced by other manufacturers. Thus, for example, the Ford Motor Company of Canada does not and cannot compete with Honda Canada to provide wholesale distribution services for Honda automobiles manufactured by the Honda Motor Company of Japan. Those services, such as they are, are the exclusive domain of Honda Canada by virtue of its relationship with its parent manufacturer. Nor does Honda Canada compete with the Ford of Canada for the distribution of Fords. That non-NAFTA vehicles imported by Honda are subject to a duty whereas those imported by Ford of Canada are not has absolutely no bearing on these distribution relationships. It does not affect the conditions of competition between the providers of wholesale distribution services because no such competition exists.

6.892 Once again, the situation in the automobile industry is starkly different from that in *EC - Bananas III*, where not all of the relevant services were supplied by vertically-integrated companies and even those that were had "the capability and opportunity to enter the wholesale service market" rather than transferring bananas within their integrated company.[599] Such opportunities in practice simply are not available to any of the suppliers of wholesale distribution services for automobiles.

6.893 Lastly, Japan has offered no evidence that the effect of the measures on conditions of competition is attributable to the nationality of the service suppliers. As Canada has shown, service suppliers from Japan and the European Communities as well as the United States benefit from duty-free treatment under the measures.

(iii) The treatment of wholesale service suppliers is not made "conditional" by the MVTO and SROs

6.894 Japan transplants to Article II of the GATS its argument under Article I of the GATT that because manufacturers must meet certain conditions to qualify for duty-free importation under the MVTO or the SROs, the treatment accorded to wholesale trade service suppliers is "conditional". As Japan admits, "no case in the context of the GATS has referred to lack of conditionality". To the extent that any requirement of unconditionality can be transplanted from the GATT to the GATS, Canada's ar-

[599] Panel Reports on *EC - Bananas III*, *supra* note 269, para. 7.320.

guments in respect of Article I of the GATT that Japan has misconstrued this requirement apply equally to Article II of the GATS.

4. *Rebuttal Arguments by Japan*

6.895 **Japan** rebuts as follows:

6.896 As discussed in the Government of Japan's presentation of its clams, the Duty Waiver is inconsistent with Canada's obligations under GATS Article II. It accords more favourable treatment to wholesale trade services and service suppliers of motor vehicles of the United States and Sweden than to like services and service suppliers of other WTO Members including Japan.

(a) The Duty Waiver is Within the Scope of the GATS

6.897 (*See* Section VI.E, Applicability of the GATS to the Measures.)

(b) The Duty Waiver Discriminates Between Like Service Suppliers

6.898 The Government of Canada has also claimed that the measures are indifferent to the nationality of the beneficiaries' ownership, which is also far from convincing to us. The Government of Japan would not repeat its effective response to the claim which has already been provided. It simply suffice to refer that at the core of Japan's argument for the discriminatory nature of the Duty Waiver is that Japanese service suppliers are excluded from ever qualifying for the Duty Waiver while US and Swedish service suppliers are not.

(c) Competition Exists Between Wholesale Trade Service Suppliers

6.899 Also unconvincing is Canada's reasoning that wholesale trade service suppliers of motor vehicles are "integrally related to the manufacturers of the motor vehicles they distribute" and thus "they do not engage in genuine competition." When wholesale trade service suppliers are subordinated to those manufacturers, as Canada emphasizes, those vertically integrated companies are wholesale trade service suppliers, to the extent that they are engaged in providing wholesale trade services, as confirmed in paragraph 227 of the Appellate Body Report for *EC - Bananas III*. And those wholesale service suppliers compete against each other in their resale to retail service suppliers, even when they are integrated with respective manufacturers. More detail on this has been provided in the Government of Japan's response to Question 35 from the Panel.

6.900 From the Government of Japan's point of view, the Government of Canada's response to Question 35 of the Panel ignores transactions between the wholesale service suppliers and their dealers (i.e. the transactions between the wholesale service suppliers and the consumers of those services) in determining whether there is competition between integrated wholesale trade service suppliers of a automobiles. There is no question that the wholesale trade service suppliers must attract dealers who consume their services and further distribute automobiles at the retail level, and therefore there is competition amongst wholesale trade service suppliers to attract dealers. To the extent that the Duty Waiver reduces the procurement cost of automobiles for the Auto Pact Manufacturers (who are also wholesale trade service suppliers) and, thereby, confers an advantage to supply their services to dealers, competition between them exists and its conditions are modified within the meaning of the GATS.

(d) Article V of the GATS

6.901 In its argumentation as a third party (see Section VIII), the United States Government raises Article V as a provision that, in its view, may be of relevance to the facts of this case. Further, the Government of Canada supports this argument in its reply to the Question of the Panel.

6.902 However, Article V has no application to the facts of this dispute. By its express wording, Article V of the GATS applies to parties "entering into an agreement liberalizing trade in services between or among the parties to such an agreement". There is no such agreement relevant to this instance. The Auto Pact is no longer in force as it is not being implemented by the United States, and even if it were (which is not), it would not qualify as an agreement of the type mentioned in Article V:1 of GATS, as the US admits in its response to Question 1(a) of European Communities.

6.903 Moreover, the Duty Waiver is in no way part of the NAFTA. Rather, it is inconsistent with the NAFTA as evidenced by the express exceptions in NAFTA Annex 300-A.1 (which excludes the Duty Waiver from the prohibition on Duty Waivers in NAFTA Article 304) and NAFTA Annex I-Canada (which excludes the Duty Waiver from the prohibition against performance requirements in NAFTA Article 1106). Without these exceptions, the Duty Waiver could not have been permitted to continue under the NAFTA.

6.904 Therefore, as the Government of Japan has demonstrated, the Duty Waiver is solely a domestic measure implemented under Canadian domestic laws.

5. Rebuttal Arguments by the European Communities

6.905 The **European Communities** rebuts as follows:

(a) The Tariff Exemption Affects the Provision of Services Within the Meaning of Article I:1 of the GATS

6.906 (*See* Section VI.E, Applicability of the GATS to the Measures.)

(b) Vertical Integration does not Exclude Competition Among Providers of Wholesale Distribution Services for Automobiles

6.907 Canada has argued that "because service suppliers are subordinated to ... manufacturers, competition among them in the supply of wholesale services is precluded".

6.908 A similar argument was rejected in *EC - Bananas III*. According to that Panel Report, the mere fact that the wholesale distributors of bananas were vertically integrated did not exclude *per se* a violation of GATS Article II, because those wholesalers had the "capability and opportunity to enter the wholesale service market"[600].

6.909 The Appellate Body affirmed the Panel's view and further added:

> "... even if a company is vertically-integrated, and even if it performs other functions related to the production, importation, distribution and processing of a product, to the extent that it is also engaged in providing 'wholesale trade services' and is therefore affected in that capacity by a particular measure of a Member in its supply of those 'wholesale trade services', that company is a service supplier within the scope of the GATS."[601]

6.910 Although the major wholesale distributors of automobiles present in the Canadian market are vertically integrated with manufacturers[602], they have the "capability and opportunity" to compete amongst them with respect to the purchase of motor vehicles from manufacturers for wholesale resale.

6.911 While it may be true that Honda Canada and Ford Canada would not compete for the distribution in Canada of vehicles manufactured by Ford in the United States, they may compete, not only with other integrated distributors but also with independent distributors, for the distribution of vehicles produced by a foreign manufacturer without a distribution network in Canada.

6.912 By way of example, in the past Chrysler has imported and distributed in Canada motor vehicles manufactured by Mitsubishi, an unrelated Japanese producer[603]. Similarly, Ford imports and distributes in Canada motor vehicles manufactured by Kia and Mazda, while General Motors does the same with Isuzu's motor vehicles, even though they do not have a controlling interest in those manufacturers[604].

6.913 The Tariff Exemption confers upon the beneficiaries a competitive advantage in respect of the purchase of vehicles for resale because it lowers their import costs and, therefore, gives them the possibility to offer better purchasing terms to the foreign manufacturer.

6.914 In any event, Canada's argument is built on the erroneous assumption that wholesale distribution services are provided exclusively to manufacturers. Yet the relationship between wholesalers and retailers is at least equally relevant. Wholesale distributors of automobiles act as an intermediary between manufacturers and retail distributors. Thus, they also provide a service to retail distributors. In fact, except in the rare cases where wholesale distributors of automobiles act as mere agents for the manufacturers, the "buyer" of the service, i.e. the person who actually "pays" for the distribution service, is the retailer and not the manufacturer.

6.915 Vertical integration between manufacturers and wholesale distributors of automobiles, even if it were complete, would not exclude *per se* competition among wholesale distributors with respect to sales to retailers and final consumers. Vertical integration has the only consequence that Honda Canada and Ford Canada, for ex-

600 Panel Reports on *EC - Bananas III*, *supra* note 269, para. 223.

601 Appellate Body Report on *EC - Bananas III*, *supra* note 49, para. 227.

602 The affiliation of some distributors, such as Lada Canada Inc., is nevertheless unclear, as shown in the EC's response to Question 34 from the Panel, Table 7.

603 See Exhibit EC-16, Table 1.7.

604 See Exhibit JPN-10.

ample, cannot compete to resell the *same* automobiles to retailers. But it does not prevent them from competing in order to resell to dealers automobiles manufactured by their respective parents which are directly competitive and substitutable with each other. In other words, the absence of intra-brand competition among wholesalers does not exclude inter-brand competition.

6.916 In response to a question by the Panel, Canada argues that wholesalers cannot compete for sales to retailers due to the existence of exclusive distribution arrangements between manufacturers and wholesalers. For example, according to Canada, GM Canada could not supply Honda cars to an Honda dealer because Honda Canada has the exclusive right to distribute those cars[605]. That example, however, misses the point raised by the Panel. GM Canada and Honda Canada compete for sales to retailers because, as admitted by Canada itself in the same response[606], a dealer selling Honda cars may decide to switch to GM cars, if GM Canada offers betters terms than Honda Canada. The Tariff Exemption affects competition between Honda Canada and GM Canada in respect of their sales to retailers because, by lowering the imports cost of GM Canada, it allows GM Canada to offer better terms to dealers.

6.917 In the same response, Canada raises the curious argument that the Complainants have not proven that the service suppliers " purchase" the automobiles from the manufacturers and, therefore, that they "re-sell" them in the meaning of the headnote to Section 6 of the CPC[607]. The ordinary meaning of "re-selling", however, does not exclude the sale of products previously purchased from a related seller. A sale between two related, but legally distinct juridical persons, is still a "sale".

(c) The Tariff Exemption Accords More Favourable Treatment to Service Suppliers of the United States

6.918 Canada argues that the Tariff Exemption does not afford more favourable treatment to US service suppliers because not all the beneficiaries are service suppliers of the United States. More specifically, Canada contends that Chrysler Canada Ltd., CAMI Automotive Inc., and Volvo Canada Ltd. are, at least in part, service suppliers of other Members.

6.919 In the case of Chrysler Canada Ltd., Canada alleges that it is not a service supplier of the United States but of Germany, because its parent company, DaimlerChrysler Corp., a US juridical person, is fully owned by DaimlerChrysler AG, a juridical person constituted under the law of Germany.

6.920 That argument is based on a mistaken reading of Article XXVIII(m). In accordance with the plain meaning of that provision, if a service supplier established in Member A is owned or controlled by a juridical person of Member B, then that service supplier can be considered as a service supplier of Member A, irrespective of who owns or controls the juridical person in Member B[608].

---

605 Canada's response to Question 35 from the Panel.

606 Ibid.

607 Ibid.

608 A different matter is whether in case that the juridical person of Member B was in turn controlled by a person of Member C, Member C could *also* assert rights under the GATS in respect of the service supplier in Member A.

6.921 The above is confirmed by EC - Bananas III[609], where the Panel held that the EU subsidiaries of Del Monte, a company constituted under Mexican law, were service suppliers of Mexico, even though Del Monte was controlled by a Jordanian national[610].

6.922 As regards CAMI Automotive Inc., the evidence available suggests that, although it is owned 50/50 by Suzuki Motor Co. of Japan, and General Motors Corp, of the United States, actual control is exercised by the latter[611]. Canada takes the view, nevertheless, that CAMI is "a juridical person of both the United States and Japan[612]. That position is clearly mistaken. If neither General Motors nor Suzuki "owns" or "controls" CAMI in accordance with the criteria of Article XXVIII (n), the inescapable conclusion is that CAMI is not a "service supplier of another Member", but service supplier of Canada. That would have the consequence that, in addition to being contrary to GATS Article II, the Tariff Exemption would also violate GATS Article XVII.

6.923 Volvo Canada Ltd., was controlled by Volvo AB, of Sweden, until January 1999, when Volvo AB agreed to sell its passenger car business to Ford Motor Co., of the United States. At any rate, Volvo Canada Ltd closed its Canadian assembly plant in December 1998, with the consequence that it will loose the right to import motor vehicles under the Tariff Exemption as of July 1999.

6.924 In any event, more relevant that the number of suppliers of each Member that benefit from the Tariff Exemption, is their share of imports under the Tariff Exemption[613]. The evidence made available by the European Communities shows that the US Big Three account for the vast majority of those imports.

6.925 The EC's Table 1 provides data on imports of automobiles under the Tariff Exemption. Together, imports originating in the United States and Mexico accounted in 1997 for 97.23 per cent of all imports under the Tariff Exemption. To the EC's best knowledge, neither Volvo nor Suzuki is engaging in imports of automobiles from the United States and/or Mexico. Accordingly, the 97.23 per cent import figure from US and Mexico actually means imports by the Big Three.

6.926 As regards the residual 2.77 per cent of automobile imports under the Tariff Exemption, which are those originating in "MFN countries" within the meaning of the MVTO of 1998, information provided in the EC's Table 6 shows that in 1997 the Big Three's total imports amounted to 5.865 units. In turn, imports by Volvo and Suzuki amounted to 4.107 units. Thus, the Big Three's imports from "MFN countries" under the Tariff Exemption represented 58.81 per cent of all such imports. Therefore, it may be estimated that overall the Big Three accounted in 1997 for about

---

609 Panel Reports on *EC - Bananas III, supra* note 269, footnote 493.

610 Furthermore, by Canada's own logic, before reaching the conclusion that DaimlerChrysler AG is a service supplier of Germany, it would be necessary to establish that it is "owned" or "controlled" by German persons rather than by US persons.

611 General Motors Corp., is the largest single shareholder of Suzuki Motor Co. Furthermore, Japanese nationals seem to constitute a minority within the Board of Directors of CAMI Automotive Inc. (See CAMI's page in the Corporations Directorate of Industry Canada (Exhibit EC-21).)

612 Canada's response to Question 34 from the Panel. In contrast, Canada stated that CAMI "is probably, under the GATS, a juridical person of both the United States and Japan".

613 See Panel Reports on *EC - Bananas III, supra* note 269, paras. 7.333 and 7.334.

99 per cent of total imports of automobiles made into Canada under the Tariff Exemption.

6.927 While the main beneficiaries of the Tariff Exemption are US service suppliers, all major wholesale distributors of automobiles which do not benefit from the Tariff Exemption are, with only one exception (Nissan Canada Inc.), service suppliers of Members other than the United States[614].

(d) The Violation of Article II is not Exempted by Article V

6.928 In reply to a question from the Panel, Canada has indicated that even if the Tariff Exemption was found to be inconsistent with GATS Article II, it would nevertheless be "subject to the MFN exception conferred by Article V:1 of the GATS"[615].

6.929 The European Communities recalls that Article V:1 of GATS is an affirmative defence. Therefore, in accordance with well settled case law[616], it is for Canada to prove that the Tariff Exemption is covered by GATS Article V:1, and not for the Complainants to prove the opposite. Clearly, the laconic answer given by Canada to the Panel's question cannot be considered sufficient to meet its burden of proof.

6.930 Without prejudice to the above, the European Communities submits that for the reasons set forth below the Tariff Exemption fails to meet the requirements of GATS Article V:1.

6.931 In the first place, Article V:1 provides an exception only with respect to "agreements" between Members, and not with respect to unilateral measures by Members. The wording of Article V:1 is clear and unambiguous in that respect:

> "This agreement shall not prevent any of its Members from being a party to or entering into an agreement liberalising trade in services between or among the parties to such an agreement..."

6.932 The Tariff Exemption is not an "agreement". As already explained, the Tariff Exemption is neither part of, nor required by NAFTA. NAFTA permits, but does not oblige Canada to maintain the Tariff Exemption, which constitutes a derogation from generally applicable NAFTA rules. The decision to maintain the Tariff Exemption is a unilateral decision of Canada, except to the extent that the Tariff Exemption implements the provisions of the Auto Pact[617]. The Auto Pact, however, lacks the "substantial sectoral coverage" required by letter (a) of Article V:1.

6.933 Second, GATS Article V:1 requires that the agreement must "liberalise" trade in services. The meaning of that term is further specified in letter (b) of that Article, which provides that the agreement must:

---

614 See Table 7 in EC's response to Question 33 from the Panel.

615 Canada's response to Question 33 from the Panel.

616 See the Appellate Body Report on *US - Wool Shirts*, *supra* note 283, at 337-338, and the panel reports cited therein.

617 The Auto Pact only requires Canada to grant duty free treatment to imports from the United States.

"... provide for the absence or elimination of substantially all discrimination, in the sense of Article XVII, between or among the parties, ... through:

(i) elimination of existing discriminatory measures, and/or

(ii) prohibition of new or more discriminatory measures,

... except for measures permitted under Articles XI, XII, XIV and XIV bis."

6.934 Canada cannot claim that the Tariff Exemption is necessary in order to "eliminate discrimination" between US suppliers and Canadian suppliers of distribution services for automobiles because, according to Canada, no Canadian supplier of those services benefits from the Tariff Exemption. Thus, if anything, the Tariff Exemption would give raise to "reverse discrimination" against Canadian suppliers.

6.935 In any event, assuming that there was a Canadian beneficiary of the Tariff Exemption, since the Tariff Exemption applies only to a few US suppliers, it would fail to "eliminate substantially all discrimination" against US and Mexican suppliers.

6.936 The truth is that, far from "eliminating" discrimination, the Tariff Exemption actually "creates" additional discrimination, not only between the beneficiaries and the service suppliers of third countries, but also *vis-à-vis* the remaining US suppliers (actual or potential) and the Canadian and Mexican suppliers (actual or potential). That result is clearly incompatible with the objective to "liberalise " trade in services among the parties stated in Article V:1.

6.937 The same is true of the CVA requirements attached to the Tariff Exemption, which are of themselves inconsistent with GATS Article XVII and, consequently, "discriminatory" for purposes of Article V:1(b).

6.938 Moreover, assuming that the Tariff Exemption qualified as an "agreement" in the meaning of Article V:1, as being part of NAFTA, it would be inconsistent with the additional requirement contained in Article V:4, which provides that:

"Any agreement referred to in paragraph 1 shall be designed to facilitate trade between the parties to the agreement and shall not in respect of any Members outside the agreement raise the overall level of barriers to trade in services within the respective sectors or subsectors compared to the level applicable prior to such an agreement"

6.939 CUFSTA and then NAFTA have raised the barriers to trade in services in the subsector of distribution services for motor vehicles because they prevent Canada from issuing any new SROs to service suppliers of other Members, effectively "freezing" the list of beneficiaries of the Tariff Exemption as of 1989.

6.940 Likewise, assuming that the Tariff Exemption was an agreement covered by Article V:1, it would also infringe Article V:6, which stipulates that:

"A service supplier of any other member that is a juridical person constituted under the laws of a party to an agreement referred to in paragraph 1 shall be entitled to treatment granted under such agreement, provided that it engages in substantive business operations in the territory of the parties to such agreement"

6.941 Article V:6 would thus require Canada to extend the treatment granted to the Big Three to any juridical person constituted under the law of the United States or of Mexico and with substantial business operations in those countries that are controlled or owned by EC nationals or juridical persons.

6. Response by Canada to the Complainants' Rebuttals

6.942 **Canada** responds as follows:

(a) The Duty-Free Treatment does not Affect Trade in Wholesale Services

6.943 (*See* Section VI, page 185, Applicability of the GATS to the Measures.)

(b) The Measures do not Accord More Favourable Treatment to Service Suppliers of Certain Countries

6.944 Even if they could demonstrate some effect of the duty-free treatment on wholesale service suppliers in the supply of such services, the complainants are unable to substantiate their claims that the measures *de facto* accord more favourable treatment to the service suppliers of certain countries. As Canada has argued from the outset, the nationality of the manufacturers qualifying for duty-free treatment reveals no *de facto* discrimination, and changes in the ownership of qualifying MVTO manufacturers prove that the measures are indifferent to nationality.

6.945 When services are supplied by a commercial presence, in accordance with Article XXVIII(m) of the GATS, the nationality of a service supplier is determined by where the juridical person owning or controlling it is constituted or otherwise organized.

6.946 The European Communities argues that one cannot proceed in such an enquiry beyond one level of ownership or control.[618] According to the European Communities, DaimlerChrysler Canada Inc. remains a service supplier of the United States, despite the purchase of Chrysler Corp. by DaimlerChrysler AG. Similarly, Nissan Canada is a US service supplier because it is majority owned by a US company, although that company is in turn wholly-owned by Nissan Motor Co. Ltd. of Japan. Japan rejects this characterization of Nissan Canada, and therefore appears to reject the EC's argument, although for reasons left unspecified, it considers Chrysler Canada (now DaimlerChrysler Canada Inc.) to be a US service supplier.[619]

6.947 The European Communities claims support for its test in a footnote to the Panel Report in *EC - Bananas III*.[620] However, that footnote consists of *obiter dicta* remarks regarding the application of Article XXVIII when not all of the juridical persons in a chain of ownership or control are juridical persons of a WTO Member. In the present case, when all of the juridical persons at issue are juridical persons of a Member, the nationality of a service supplier should be determined by the nationality of the juridical persons with ultimate ownership or control, as such persons have the actual power to legally direct the actions of the service supplier. By this test, DaimlerChrysler Canada Inc. is a service supplier of the European Community, while Nissan Canada is a service supplier of Japan.

6.948 However, even if the test proposed by the European Communities were correct, the mere fact that three of the four current qualifying automobile manufactur-

[618] EC's response to Question 34 from the Panel.

[619] Japan's response to Question 34 from the Panel.

[620] EC's response to Question 34 from the Panel, citing footnote 493 of Panel Reports on *EC - Bananas III*, *supra* note 269.

ers[621] would be US-owned is a function of geography and the historical commercial role of the Big Three in North America rather than governmentally-imposed discrimination. It is more significant that if for example, DaimlerChrysler reorganized such that DaimlerChrysler Canada Inc. became directly rather than indirectly owned by DaimlerChrysler AG, it would have no effect whatsoever on its qualifying status, because the measures do not discriminate on the basis of the nationality of the service supplier. It should also be noted that although the European Communities lists Mercedes-Benz Canada Inc. as a non-beneficiary of duty-free treatment,[622] imports of Mercedes-Benz vehicles qualify for duty-free treatment as MVTO imports of DaimlerChrysler Canada Inc.

6.949 Both complainants have disputed Canada's position that the distribution structure of the motor vehicle industry precludes competition among wholesale service suppliers in their capacity as service suppliers. Japan, for example, has cited the Report of the Appellate Body in *EC - Bananas III* for the proposition that there is competition among wholesale service suppliers even when they are vertically-integrated. However, the relevant paragraph of the Appellate Body Report merely noted that vertically-integrated companies may provide wholesale trade services, and may be service suppliers within the scope of the GATS to the extent that they are affected in their capacity as a wholesale trade service suppliers by a measure in their supply of those wholesale trade services.[623] The Appellate Body Report offers no support for the proposition that there is competition among distribution service suppliers to import and distribute automobiles.

6.950 The European Communities has also asserted that such competition exists. It has twice cited Chrysler Canada's importation and distribution of vehicles manufactured by Mitsubishi of Japan as a "concrete example" of such competition, on the basis that Chrysler and Mitsubishi were "unrelated" to each other.[624] The facts are otherwise. Throughout the period that Chrysler Canada imported Japanese vehicles from Mitsubishi, Chrysler Canada and/or its parent, Chrysler Corp. had an equity interest in Mitsubishi or jointly manufactured vehicles with Mitsubishi, or both. When these relationships ended, Chrysler ceased to import or distribute vehicles from Mitsubishi of Japan. The facts of the Chrysler/Mitsubishi relationship confirm the absence of competition in the provision of distribution services.

6.951 Both complainants have also argued that even if relationships with manufacturers preclude competition among distribution service suppliers to import automobiles, the measures affect competition among distributors in the sale of automobiles to retail dealers.[625] Canada rebutted these arguments in its Response to the Panel's Question 35.[626] Canada noted that because the distribution service suppliers have

[621] The fourth, CAMI, is jointly-owned by judicial persons of the United States and Japan, while Volvo Canada, which was a judicial person of the EC, is no longer manufacturing automobiles in Canada.

[622] EC's response to Question 34 from the Panel, Table 7.

[623] Appellate Body Report on *EC - Bananas III*, *supra* note 49, para. 227.

[624] EC's response to Question 35 from the Panel.

[625] Japan's responses to Questions 27 and 35 from the Panel; EC's response to Question 35 from the Panel.

[626] Canada's response to Question 35 from the Panel.

exclusive relationships with manufacturers of particular vehicles, retailers cannot select among distributors for the supply of those vehicles.

6.952 Moreover, the absence of competition in the distribution of automobiles is acknowledged in the EC's own laws. Commission Regulation (EC) No. 1475/95 of 28 June 1995 exempts certain motor vehicle distribution and servicing arrangements from the EC's competition laws. Paragraph 4 of the preamble to the Regulation justifies this exemption on the grounds that: "... exclusive and selective distribution clauses can be regarded as indispensable measures of rationalization in the motor vehicle industry ...".[627]

6.953 Finally, Japan has asserted that differences in the retail prices of automobiles caused by the duty-free treatment "means that the conditions of competition between manufacturers/wholesale trade service suppliers for sales to retailers will be negatively affected".[628] It is telling that Japan is unable to decide whether those allegedly affected are manufacturers or wholesale service suppliers. More fundamentally, as Canada has already explained, Japan's legal theory would produce the absurd result that every tariff, by affecting the price of a product, violates national treatment for distribution services for any product, such as automobiles or photographic film, in which there is a tendency to single-brand distribution. Indeed, by Japan's reasoning, every import duty, and most other goods measures, would potentially violate the GATS.

7. *The European Communities' Follow-Up to Canada's Response*

6.954 As a follow-up to Canada's response, the **European Communities** argues as follows:

(a) The Tariff Exemption Affects Trade in Wholesale Distribution Services

6.955 (*See* Section VI.E, Applicability of the GATS to the Measures.)

(b) The Measure Accords More Favourable Treatment to US Suppliers

6.956 To refute the EC's *de facto* violation claim under GATS Article II, notably to object to the EC's characterizing DaimlerChrysler Canada as a US supplier, Canada refers again to the "chain of ownership" and "ultimate ownership" notions. These notions, however, are simply not relevant under Article XXVIII. This is so irrespec-

---

[627] Commission Regulation (EC) No 1475/95 of 28 June 1995 on the application of Article 85(3) of the Treaty to certain categories of motor vehicle distribution and servicing agreements, cited to Official Journal L 145, 29/06/95 p. 0025-0034, from *http://europa.eu.int/eur-lex/en/lif/dat/1995/en_395R1475.html* (Exhibit CDA-16). See also Article 81(3) (ex Article 85) of the Treaty in Exhibit CDA-17: Consolidated Version of the Treaty Establishing the European Community, cited to Official Journal C 340, 10.11.1997, pp. 173-308, from *http://europa.eu.int/eur-lex/en/treaties/ index.html.*

[628] Japan's response to Question 35 from the Panel.

tive of whether a company's "ownership chain" includes WTO Members' "juridical persons" only, or also "persons" of non-WTO Members.

6.957 In fact, Article XXVIII(m)(ii) simply refers to "ownership" or "control" to determine what is a "juridical person of another Member". The application of that rule to the present case is rather straightforward. This case is concerned with the nationality of DaimlerChrysler Canada. As DaimlerChrysler US owns 100 per cent of DaimlerChrysler Canada shares, then it "owns" DaimlerChrysler Canada.

6.958 On the other hand, Article XXVIII(m)(ii) adds no further requirement to determine the "nationality" of a juridical person. In particular, it makes no reference to any further ownership or control relationship. Therefore, whether DaimlerChrysler US is in turn owned by some other company is not relevant to review a claim in respect of DaimlerChrysler Canada. It would only be relevant if a claim were to be assessed in respect of DaimlerChrysler US.

6.959 The fact that in *EC - Bananas III* the Panel considered Jordanian ownership to be irrelevant does not constitute a special derogation from the general Article XXVIII(m) rule for cases where the ultimate control/ ownership is exercised by a juridical person of a third country. In the Panel's words, the dispute concerned "the commercial presence of service suppliers which are "persons" or owned or controlled by such persons of a complainant and *subsidiary companies owned or controlled by parent companies that are constituted or otherwise organized under the law of a complainant and are engaged in substantive business operations in the territory of any other Member*".[629] Based on this premise, the Panel then continued:

> "*As a result*, suppliers which are commercially present within the EC territory and owned or controlled by, *for example*, Del Monte Mexico would be entitled to benefit from GATS rights because it *would not matter under Article XXVIII(m)* whether Del Monte Mexico was owned or controlled by natural or juridical persons of Jordan, i.e. a WTO non-Member, as long as Del Monte Mexico was *incorporated in Mexico and engaged in substantive business operations in the territory of Mexico or any other Member*".[630]

6.960 It clearly results from the emphasized words that in the *EC - Bananas III* dispute the first owner was considered to be the relevant one. The same must apply to the present case, as the owner of DaimlerChrysler Canada is incorporated in the United States and engages in substantive business operations in the territory of the United States. Article XXVIII includes no exception or special rule for cases where ultimate ownership or control is exercised by a non-Member company. It has a single rule where the relevant factor is whether the supplier, whose nationality is at issue, is owned or controlled by a company incorporated in a WTO Member and conducts substantial business operations in a Member.

6.961 Canada's response to the rebuttals calls for one last remark in respect of the "nationality" issue. The fact that most Tariff Exemption beneficiaries are US-owned, including pursuant to Article XXVIII(m) ownership test, is not a function of geography or other accident, contrary to what Canada argues. It is a consequence of a delib-

---

[629] Panel Report on *EC - Bananas III (USA), supra* note 269, para. 7.318.

[630] Ibid., footnote 493.

erate choice to close the Tariff Exemption beneficiaries list in 1989. That choice was the function of a bilateral agreement between two WTO Members' governments - the Government of Canada and the Government of the United States.

(c) Vertical Integration does not Exclude Competition Among Providers of Services

6.962 Canada's reading of the Appellate Body *EC - Bananas III* Report must also be corrected.

6.963 In paragraph 227 of its Report, the Appellate Body did not consider that integrated companies "may be services suppliers within the scope of the GATS to the extent that they are affected in their capacity as a wholesale trade services suppliers by a measure in their supply of those wholesale trade services". The Appellate Body rather said that the fact of providing services would make integrated companies services suppliers and would *therefore* make them affected as service suppliers. In other words, there is no separate requirement that service suppliers be affected "in their capacity as wholesale trade services providers".

6.964 Canada eventually takes a position on the imports of Mitsubishi cars by Chrysler to the effect that these imports would have always taken place while the two companies had an ownership link. Canada does not supply any evidence in support of this allegation. The European Communities notes that according to the information on the Panel's record Chrysler has had no ownership interests in Mitsubishi at least since 1993. Yet, imports of Mitsubishi vehicles by Chrysler continued until 1996.[631]

6.965 Canada even goes as far as to state that EC law "acknowledge[s] the absence of competition" in the car sector. The European Communities has difficulty to see how a piece of legislation operating in a different territory and market may have any relevance to assess the situation in the Canadian market for the purposes of establishing a violation of GATS by Canada.

6.966 At any rate, the European Communities wishes to clarify that Commission Regulation (EC) No 1475/95 of 28 June 1995 does not do what Canada says it does. It rather exempts certain restrictions on competition under strict conditions and limits. It does so, however, on the assumption and to the extent that this is necessary to enhance and promote *more* competition on the car market. That pro-competition rationale is so deeply rooted in the regulation that pursuant to Article 3.3 of the Regulation contract clauses whereby distributors would be completely prohibited from multi-brand distribution cannot be exempted.

6.967 Furthermore, under Article 8.1 of Regulation 1475/9[5] the exemption from competition rules may be withdrawn if a contract, which would otherwise meet the Regulation requirements, concerns goods which are *not subject to competition*. The rationale of this provision is explained in paragraph 30 of the Preamble in the following terms:

> "(30) Distribution and servicing agreements can be exempted, subject to the conditions laid down in Articles 5 and 6, so long as the application of obligations covered by Articles 1 to 4 brings about an im-

[631] Exhibit EC-16.

provement in distribution and servicing to the benefit of the consumer and *effective competition exists*, not *only between manufacturers' distribution systems* but also to a certain extent *within each system* within the common market. *As regards the categories of products set out in Article 1, the conditions necessary for effective competition,* including competition in trade between Member States, *may be taken to exist at present*, so that European consumers may be considered in general to take an equitable share in the benefit from the operation of such competition."

6.968 It is apparent from the last emphasized language that Commission Regulation 1475/95 does exactly the opposite of what Canada argues. It does not "acknowledge the absence of competition". It rather acknowledges the existence of competition and sets adequate rules to preserve and further promote it.

8. *Canada's Follow-Up Response*

6.969 **Canada** responds as follows:

(a) The Measures do not Affect Trade in Services

6.970 (*See* Section VI.E, Applicability of the GATS to the Measures.)

(b) Duty-Free Treatment does not Accord More Favourable Treatment

6.971 In order to succeed under Article II, the complainants would have to demonstrate as well that the measures accord more favourable treatment to the service suppliers of certain countries.

6.972 Both the complainants claim that the measures do this on a *de facto* basis but they cannot agree on the facts. In particular, Japan complains that one of the long-time beneficiaries of the duty-free treatment was Volvo, a Swedish company, a fact that the European Communities ignores.

6.973 Japan's sole contention on the question of more favourable treatment is that it need not offer substantial evidence because its service suppliers are clearly excluded from ever qualifying for the duty-free treatment. However, even this is belied by the cases of DaimlerChrysler Canada Inc. and CAMI.

6.974 The European Communities takes the more mechanistic, but equally unenlightening approach of comparing the ownership of qualifying companies. As Canada has shown, this approach can produce a variety of results and ignores benign geographic and historical explanations for why, by some measures, there are more qualifying US manufacturers than others.

6.975 The European Communities argues that by operation of Article XXVIII of the GATS, DaimlerChrysler Canada Inc. is not a service supplier of the European Communities, because it is not directly owned by DaimlerChrysler AG. However, it misses the larger point: the nationality of DaimlerChrysler Canada Inc's ownership is entirely irrelevant to its qualifying status because the measures do not discriminate on the basis of the nationality of the service supplier. If DaimlerChrysler AG were to directly own DaimlerChrysler Canada Inc., it would not affect its qualifying status for duty-free treatment.

6.976 In any event, the EC's interpretation of Article XXVIII is not correct. For the most part, Canada has addressed this issue in its response to the rebuttals. However, Canada cannot leave unchallenged the EC's suggestion that the "plain meaning" of Article XXVIII(m) leads to a particular result. According to the European Communities, Article XXVIII(m) means that a service supplier established in a Member is a service supplier of that Member, even if it is owned or controlled by a juridical person of another Member and irrespective of who owns or controls that juridical person.

6.977 First, Canada suspects that the European Communities intended to argue that the service supplier in the foregoing case must be considered a service supplier of the Member where the juridical person that owns or controls it is established, irrespective of who owns or controls that juridical person.

6.978 Second, even assuming the European Communities misstated its position, the absolutist position it may have intended to argue is also wrong. Article XXVIII(m) of the GATS defines who or what is a "juridical person of another Member". Neither Article XXVIII(m) nor any other paragraph of Article XXVIII directly defines who or what is a "service supplier of another Member", which is the pertinent question in Articles II and XVII of the GATS. In order to determine who or what is a service supplier of another Member, Article XXVIII(m) must be read in conjunction with Articles XXVIII(g), (j) and (n), which respectively define "service supplier", "person" and ownership and control of a juridical person.

6.979 Article XXVIII(g) provides that a service supplier is any person that supplies a service. Article XXVIII(j) provides that a person is a natural or a juridical person. Thus, a service supplier of another Member is a natural or juridical person of another Member that supplies a service. The relevant definition for the present case is a juridical person of another Member that supplies a service.

6.980 Article XXVIII(m)(ii) provides that in the case of the supply of a service through a commercial presence, a juridical person of another Member is a juridical person *owned or controlled* by juridical persons of that Member identified in Article XXVIII(m)(i); that is, a juridical person of another Member is a juridical person owned or controlled by a juridical person constituted or otherwise organized under the law of that other Member and engaged in substantive business operations in that other Member or any other Member.

6.981 Article XXVIII(n) defines ownership or control. A juridical person is owned by persons of a Member if those persons own more than 50 per cent of the equity interest in it. A juridical person is controlled by persons of a Member if those persons have the power to name the majority of its directors or otherwise to legally direct its actions.

6.982 All of the foregoing comes down to a simple principle: the nationality of a commercial presence can be determined either by who owns it, or by who controls it. If "ownership" is used as the defining criterion, Article XXVIII could conceivably be read to mean that one looks only to the direct ownership, although as Canada has noted, the source cited by the European Communities in support of this approach is *obiter dicta* and relates to persons of non-Members. The better approach is to determine nationality by who has ultimate ownership because those persons have the real power to direct the actions of the commercial presence.

6.983 If "control" is used as the defining criterion, the answer to who has the power to legally direct the actions of a commercial presence will always be the person with the ultimate ownership. In the case of DaimlerChrysler Canada Inc., that person is DaimlerChrysler AG. DaimlerChrysler AG, which is organized under the laws of Germany, is the successor corporation to Daimler-Benz AG of Germany, and is majority owned by the former stockholders of Daimler-Benz AG.[632] It is, by all measures, a juridical person of Germany.

6.984 In the case of CAMI, the European Communities appears to be suggesting that if two juridical persons of Members other than Canada own a juridical person in Canada in its entirety, that juridical person is Canadian because neither of the non-Canadian persons individually exercises majority ownership or control, even though they jointly exercise absolute ownership and control. This makes little sense. It is the nationals of other Members that both own and legally direct the actions of the juridical person in Canada. By this measure, CAMI is a service supplier of both the United States and Japan.

6.985 The mechanistic and arbitrary nature of the enterprise of determining the nationality of service suppliers demonstrates just how unhelpful it is for identifying *de facto* discrimination. By the EC's logic, if Suzuki owned one more share of CAMI, or if DaimlerChrysler AG owned DaimlerChrysler Canada Inc. directly, the entire nationality equation would change. Yet neither change would make the slightest difference to the qualifying status of the companies at issue. The measures governing qualification, the MVTO and the SROs are completely neutral as to national origin.

6.986 The European Communities appears to recognize this when it argues that other data are more relevant. However, it is wrong when it insists that the relevant data are the share of imports receiving duty-free treatment. That data relates to goods, not to the supply of distribution services. It cannot be passed off as relevant for the purposes of Article II of the GATS.

6.987 If market share data is relevant at all, the data to consider is the share of wholesale distribution trade services in automobiles held by each commercial presence. Due to vertical integration, that data will correspond almost exactly with their shares of automobile sales in Canada. By this measure, even assuming that DaimlerChrysler Canada Inc. is a service supplier of the United States, Japanese distribution service suppliers have approximately 33 per cent of automobile distribution in Canada, EC distribution service suppliers have approximately 9 per cent and US distribution service suppliers have approximately 55 per cent. If DaimlerChrysler AG is treated as a service supplier of Germany, the EC share rises to approximately 20 per cent, while the US share falls to approximately 43 per cent. These figures offer no basis for a finding that the duty-free treatment discriminates against distribution service suppliers of particular Members.

9. *Further Follow-Up by the European Communities*

6.988 As further follow-up to Canada's response, the **European Communities** argues as follows:

6.989 The European Communities has noted that, by Canada's own logic, before reaching the conclusion that Chrysler Canada Ltd. is a service supplier of Germany,

[632] "Summary of Proxy Statement/Prospectus for Chrysler Corporation Stockholders," 6 August 1998. (Exhibit CDA-24).

it would be necessary to establish that DaimlerChrysler AG is "owned" or "controlled" by German persons, rather than by US persons.

6.990 In response, Canada contends that Daimler Chrysler AG "is majority owned by the former stockholders of Daimler Benz AG" and, therefore, that "it is by all measures a juridical person of Germany". As evidence, Canada cites the document included in Exhibit CDA-24.

6.991 It is well known that, as stated in that document, upon the merger of Chrysler Corporation and Daimler Benz AG, the stockholders of Chrysler Corporation received approximately 42 per cent of the shares of DaimlerChrysler AG, whereas the former stockholders of Daimler Benz AG received the remaining 58 per cent.

6.992 However, contrary to what is implied by Canada, the above does not mean that German persons "own" or "control" DaimlerChrysler AG in the sense of Article XXVIII of GATS. Canada makes the erroneous assumption that all the former stockholders of Daimler Benz AG were German persons. The truth, however, is that a considerable number of shares of Daimler Benz AG' shares was owned by US persons.

6.993 As shown by the table below, it may be estimated that the shares of DaimlerChrysler AG issued to the holders of shares of Chrysler Corporation traded in the United States, together with the shares of DaimlerChrysler AG issued to US persons holding shares of Daimler Benz AG, accounted upon the conclusion of the merger for 50.88 per cent of the share capital of DaimlerChrysler AG. Thus, even assuming that, as claimed by Canada, only the "ultimate ownership" was relevant, Chrysler Canada Ltd. would still be a US service supplier.

	Number of shares	*% of total outstanding shares DaimlerChrysler AG*
• Total outstanding ordinary shares of DaimlerChrysler AG[633]	960.1 million	100 %
• Shares of DaimlerChrysler AG issued to former stockholders of Chrysler Corporation[634]	430. 4 million	44.82 %
• Shares of DaimlerChrysler AG issued to US persons holding shares of Daimler Benz AG[635]	58.2 million	6.06 %

633 Combined Consolidated Statement of Income of DaimlerChrysler AG, included in the Proxy Statement/Prospectus of DaimlerChrysler AG distributed to the shareholders of Chrysler Corporation prior to the merger, p. 108 (Exhibit EC-23).

634 Registration Statement under the Securities Act of 1933, Form F-4, filed by DaimlerChrysler AG with the Securities and Exchange Commission of the United States (Exhibit EC-24).

635 Ibid.

G. Article XVII of the GATS

1. Arguments of Japan

6.994 **Japan** argues as follows:

6.995 Canada is required to accord, pursuant to Article XVII of the GATS and its Schedule of Specific Commitments, national treatment for wholesale trade services and service suppliers as well as for certain services and service suppliers related to the production of motor vehicles.

6.996 With respect to wholesale trade services, the provision of duty-free import status to certain domestic manufacturers (which are or can be wholesale trade service suppliers) is inconsistent with Article XVII of the GATS, because: (i) Canada has undertaken a commitment in a relevant sector and mode of supply; (ii) Canada has adopted or applied a measure affecting the supply of services in that sector and mode of supply; and (iii) the measure accords to service suppliers of other Members treatment less favourable than it accords to like Canadian service suppliers.[636] Canada grants a Canadian Auto Pact Manufacturer, that is also a wholesale trade service supplier, the Duty Waiver but does not extend no less favourable treatment to like service suppliers of other Members, including Japan. This is inconsistent with Canada's obligations under Article XVII of the GATS.

6.997 With respect to certain services related to the production of motor vehicles, the CVA requirement in practice requires the Auto Pact Manufacturers to purchase and use services supplied by service suppliers in Canada instead of services supplied by those located outside Canada. This requirement results in a situation whereby the services supplied under Mode 1 (cross-border supply) and Mode 2 (consumption abroad) by service suppliers of other Members are accorded treatment less favourable than the treatment accorded to like services supplied by Canadian service suppliers located in Canada. This requirement is also inconsistent with the Government of Canada's obligations under Article XVII of the GATS.

6.998 Article XVII of the GATS provides:

> "1. In the sectors inscribed in its Schedule, and subject to any conditions and qualifications set out therein, each Member shall accord to services and service suppliers of any other Member, in respect of all measures affecting the supply of services, treatment no less favourable than that it accords to its own like services and service suppliers (footnote omitted).
>
> 2. A Member may meet the requirement of paragraph 1 by according to services and service suppliers of any other Member, either formally identical treatment or formally different treatment to that it accords to its own like services and service suppliers.
>
> 3. Formally identical or formally different treatment shall be considered to be less favourable if it modifies the conditions of competition in favour of services or service suppliers of the Member compared to like services or service suppliers of any other Member."

---

[636] See Panel Reports on *EC - Bananas III*, *supra* note 269, para. 7.314.

6.999 These provisions indicate that a three-step analysis is required to determine whether the Duty Waiver is inconsistent with Article XVII of the GATS:

(i) Are wholesale trade services and other services related to the production of motor vehicles covered in the Government of Canada's Schedule of Specific Commitments, and what conditions and qualifications, if any, apply?

(ii) Are those services and service suppliers at issue are "like"?

(iii) Does the Duty Waiver modify the conditions of competition in favour of services or service suppliers of Canada?

6.1000 The answer to each inquiry is yes. Accordingly, the Duty Waiver is inconsistent with Article XVII of the GATS.

(a) The Duty Waiver Accords More Favourable Treatment to Canadian Wholesale Trade Services and Service Suppliers in Violation of Article XVII of the GATS

6.1001 Japan has found that more than one hundred manufacturers regarded as Canadian service suppliers within the meaning of Article XXVIII of the GATS are allowed to import automobiles - including passenger cars, buses and specified commercial vehicles - duty-free from other Members. Among them, one passenger car manufacturer, Intermeccanica, is a Canadian service supplier within the meaning of Article XVII of the GATS.[637] Other Auto Pact Manufacturers of Canadian origin manufacture buses and commercial motor vehicles, which Japanese automobile industries may export to meet demand if latent demand exists. The Japanese motor vehicle industry may also offer wholesale trade services for such buses and commercial vehicles if such demand exists.[638] This demonstrates that there are Canadian motor vehicle wholesale trade service suppliers in Canada.

(i) Canada's specific commitment covers wholesale trade services of motor vehicles through commercial presence

6.1002 As discussed by the panel in *EC - Bananas III*, during the Uruguay Round negotiations, the participants agreed to follow a set of guidelines for the scheduling of specific commitments under the GATS.[639] Among other things, the guidelines suggested that the participants employ the *United Nations Central Product Classification System* (CPC). Canada adopted the CPC as the basis for scheduling its GATS commitments. Applying the panel's reasoning, any legal definition of the scope of Canada's GATS commitments should be based on the CPC description of the sector and the activities that it covers.

---

[637] In the past there were a few other domestic automobiles manufacturers that were eligible for the Duty Waiver—Bombardier Inc. and Aurora. See Bombardier Inc., Logistic Equipment, Division Remission Order (Exhibit JPN-6, p. 73), and Aurora Cars Limited Remission Order (Exhibit JPN-6, p. 102).

[638] See Appellate Body Report on *Korea - Alcoholic Beverages*, *supra* note 280, pp. 32-37

[639] See Panel Reports on *EC - Bananas III*, *supra* note 269, para. 7.289.

6.1003 CPC describes "wholesale trade services" as a sub-set of the broader sector of distributive trade services which is described in the headnote to Section 6 as follows:

> Distributive trade services consisting of selling merchandise to retailers, to industrial, commercial, institutional or other professional business users, or to other wholesalers, or acting as agent or broker (wholesaling services) or selling merchandise for personal or household consumption including services incidental to the sale of goods (retailing services). The principal services rendered by wholesalers and retailers may be characterized as reselling merchandise, accompanied by a variety of related, subordinated services, such as: maintaining inventories of goods; physical assembling; sorting and grading goods in large lots; breaking bulk and redistribution in smaller lots; delivery services; refrigeration services; sales promotion services rendered by wholesalers; and services associated with retailers business, e.g., processing subordinated to selling, warehousing and garage services.

6.1004 CPC division 61 applies to the sale, maintenance and repair services of motor vehicles and motorcycles.

6.1005 CPC subclass 61111 applies to wholesale trade services for motor vehicles. It reads as follows:

> "Wholesaling and commission agents' services of passenger motor cars, motor buses and motor coaches, motor lorries and trucks, over-the-road truck tractors, semi-trailers and trailers."

6.1006 As discussed by the panel in *EC - Bananas III*, wholesale trade services such as those covered by CPC subclass 61111 are fully covered by the GATS.[640] Companies such as General Motors Canada, Ford Canada, Chrysler Canada, Toyota Canada, Honda Canada and Intermeccanica are wholesale trade service suppliers of motor vehicles within the meaning of the GATS.

6.1007 Canada's specific commitment covers wholesale trade services under CPC class 6111 (sale of motor vehicles including automobiles and other road vehicles) through commercial presence without conditions and qualifications within the meaning of Article XVII:1 of the GATS.[641] CPC 61111 is a subclass of CPC 6111 and is, therefore, covered by the commitment.

6.1008 Canada has not limited, conditioned or qualified its commitment to these services. Thus, it is obliged to accord to services and service suppliers of any other Member in this sector including those of Japan treatment no less favourable than the treatment that it accords to its own like services and service suppliers.

(ii) The services and service suppliers at issue are "like "

6.1009 As discussed in the section regarding Article II of the GATS services supplied by Japanese wholesale trade service suppliers and services supplied by Canadian

[640] Ibid., para. 7.288.

[641] Canada-Schedule of Specific Commitments, GATS/SC/16, 15 April 1994 pp. 47-49 (hereinafter *Canada's GATS Schedule*).

service suppliers are "like", regardless of whether the suppliers perform other functions related to the manufacturing of motor vehicles, as discussed by the Panel in *EC - Bananas III* and confirmed by the Appellate Body.[642] And to the extent that Canadian service suppliers supply these "like" services, they and Japanese wholesale trade service suppliers are "like" service suppliers.

(iii) The Duty Waiver modifies the conditions of competition in favour of Canadian services and service suppliers

6.1010 As discussed, "any measure bearing upon conditions of competition in supply of a service" constitutes a measure "affecting the supply of services". By exempting the imports of a Canadian Auto Pact Manufacturer from customs duties, the Duty Waiver reduces the cost that must be borne by such a manufacturer in supplying wholesale trade services. In this manner, less favourable treatment that the Government of Canada accords to motor vehicles imported by Japanese wholesale trade service suppliers modifies the conditions of competition in favour of Canadian services or service suppliers compared to like services or service suppliers of other Members, including Japan.

6.1011 Therefore, Canada, by virtue of the Duty Waiver, accords to Japanese wholesale trade services and service suppliers of motor vehicles treatment less favourable than it accords to its own like services and service suppliers. This is inconsistent with Canada's national treatment obligation under Article XVII of the GATS.

(b) The Duty Waiver Accords More Favourable Treatment to Canadian Services and Service Suppliers Related to the Production of Motor Vehicles

6.1012 In order to comply with the CVA requirement, the Duty Waiver in practice requires the Auto Pact Manufacturers to procure certain services supplied in Canada. This favours certain Canadian services, and thereby, service suppliers and accords less favourable treatment to like services and service suppliers of other WTO Members. In this way, the Duty Waiver is inconsistent with Canada's obligations under Article XVII of the GATS.

(i) The services at issue

6.1013 Subsection 1(1) of the Schedule to the MVTO 1998 establishes which services qualify as Canadian value added for the purposes of determining whether the CVA requirement is met. The relevant part of the CVA definition reads as follows:

"Canadian value added" means

(a) ...

(iv) the part of the following costs that is reasonably attributable to the production of the vehicles, namely ...

---

642 Panel Reports on *EC - Bananas III, supra* note 269, para. 7.320 and Appellate Body Report on *EC - Bananas III, supra* note 49, para. 255 (q).

(I) the cost of maintenance and repair work *executed in Canada* on buildings, machinery and equipment used for production purposes.

(K) the cost of engineering services, experimental work and product development work *executed in Canada*,

...

(v) administrative and general expenses *incurred in Canada* that are reasonably attributable to the production of the vehicles ... (*emphasis added*)

6.1014 Item (a)(iv)(I) refers to the cost of "maintenance and repair work on ... machinery and equipment used for production purposes". Item (a)(iv)(K) refers to the cost of "engineering services used for production purposes". Finally, item (a)(v) refers to "administrative and general services".

6.1015 Since information on the services claimed under these elements of the CVA is not publicly available, it is not possible to explicitly identify such services. However, the CVA permits the Auto Pact Manufacturers to claim the cost of such services with only one qualification - i.e. that the cost of such services be "reasonably attributable to the production of motor vehicles".

6.1016 Accordingly, the specific types of services covered or potentially covered by these elements of the CVA are very broad. In the case of repair and maintenance services related to machinery and equipment, such services include the repair and maintenance of potentially all of the equipment and components of equipment related to the manufacturing process. In the case of engineering services, such services include process and production engineering services as well as engineering design services. In the case of administrative and general services, the list of potential services is immense, and includes accounting services, data processing services, software services, and management consulting services.

(ii) Canada's Schedule of Specific Commitments

6.1017 Maintenance and repair work on machinery and equipment used for the production process (item (a)(iv)(I) of the CVA), engineering services (item (a)(iv)(K) of the CVA) and administrative and general expenses (item (a)(v) of the CVA) are included in service sectors inscribed in Canada's Schedule of Specific Commitments. As discussed below, with only minor exceptions, Canada has committed to providing national treatment for the various relevant services (maintenance and repair, engineering, etc.), which are procured by the Auto Pact Manufacturers.

6.1018 With respect to *maintenance and repair work* on machinery and equipment, Canada has inscribed the following in its Schedule of Specific Commitments:

- repair services incidental to metal products, machinery and equipment including computers and communication equipment on a fee or contract basis (CPC 8861 to 8866).

6.1019 The CPC defines these services broadly as "repair services incidental to metal products, machinery and equipment".

6.1020 Canada has not inscribed any limitations on its national treatment obligation with respect to the first three modes of supply (cross-border supply, consumption abroad, and commercial presence) of these services.

6.1021 With respect to *engineering services*, Canada has inscribed the following in its Schedule of Specific Commitments:

- advisory and consultative engineering services (CPC 8672);
- engineering design for industrial processes and production (CPC 86725);
- engineering design services n.e.c. (CPC 86729); and
- other engineering services (CPC 86729).

6.1022 According to the CPC, "advisory and consultative engineering services" include recommendation services concerning engineering matters and study of the efficiency gains in production as a result of alternative process, technology or plant layout. "Engineering design for industrial processes and production" include engineering design services for production processes, procedures and facilities; material flows, equipment layout, material handling systems, processes and process control (which may integrate computer technology) for manufacturing plants; special machinery, equipment and instrumentation systems; and any other design services for production procedures and facilities. Design services include preliminary plans, specifications and cost estimates, including working drawings, specifications regarding materials to be used, methods of construction and/or installation. "Engineering design services n.e.c." refer to other specialty engineering design services, including prototype development and detailed designs for new products. Other engineering services include all engineering services not elsewhere classified.

6.1023 Canada has inscribed one narrow limitation on its national treatment commitment regarding these services. This limitation pertains to cross-border supply of engineering services in the province of Saskatchewan where a residency requirement applies for obtaining accreditation as an engineer. In all other provinces, including those where Canada's motor vehicle production plants are located, Canada's national treatment obligation regarding the supply of these engineering services via modes 1, 2 and 3 is not limited.

6.1024 With respect to *administrative and general expenses*, the following types of services are inscribed in Canada's Schedule of Specific Commitments:

- accounting, auditing and book-keeping services (CPC 862);
- taxation services (CPC 863);
- consultancy services related to the installation of computer hardware (CPC 841);
- software implementation services (CPC 842);
- data processing services (CPC 843);
- database services (CPC 844);
- maintenance and repair services of office machinery and equipment including computers (CPC 845);
- computer services (CPC 849);
- market research and public opinion polling (CPC 864);
- management consulting services (CPC 865):
    - financial management (CPC 86502);
    - marketing management (CPC 86503);
    - human resources management (CPC 86504); and

- production management (CPC 86505);
- services related to management consulting (CPC 866);
- public relations services (CPC 86506);
- placement and supply of personnel (CPC 866);
- packaging services (CPC 876);
- duplicating services (CPC 87904);
- translation and interpretation services (CPC 87905);
- commercial courier services (CPC 75121);
- electronic data interchange (CPC 7523); and
- on-line information and/or data processing including transaction processing (CPC 843).

6.1025 The only relevant limitations to the national treatment commitments undertaken by Canada in the service sectors and sub-sectors listed above relate to accounting, auditing and book-keeping services and to translation and interpretation services. With respect to auditing, Canada inscribed in its Schedule a residency requirement for accreditation as an auditor in the provinces of Alberta, Newfoundland, Nova Scotia, Prince Edward Island, Manitoba and Saskatchewan. This requirement limits the scope of Canada's national treatment commitment with respect to cross-border supply of such services as well as the supply through commercial presence of service suppliers of other Members. As for translation and interpretation services, Canada inscribed a citizenship requirement for using the title "Certified translator" in the province of Québec. This qualification limits Canada's commitment with respect to cross-border supply of translation services.

6.1026 Consequently, Canada's national treatment obligation is not limited with respect to all of the other services listed above (through modes 1, 2 and 3), which form part of the administrative and general expenses incurred by motor vehicle manufacturers.

(iii) The CVA requirement accords less favourable treatment to "like" services and service suppliers

The services and service suppliers at issue are "like"

6.1027 As discussed in paragraph 6.842, the Panel in *EC - Bananas III* discussed the issue of "like" services and service suppliers. In that case, the Panel had to determine whether wholesale trade services provided by companies originating from the EC and ACP countries and those provided by companies originating from other countries were like. The Panel concluded as follows:

> "... the nature and characteristics of wholesale transactions as such, as well as of each the different subordinated services ... are 'like' when supplied in connection with wholesale services, irrespective of whether these services are supplied with respect to bananas of EC and traditional ACP origin, on the one hand, or with respect to bananas of third country origin or non traditional ACP origin on the other. Indeed, it seems that the different service activities taken individually is virtually the same and can only be distinguished by referring to the origin of bananas in respect of which the service activity is be-

ing performed. Similarly, in our view, to the extent that entities provide these like services, they are like service suppliers."[643]

6.1028 It can be deducted from the reasoning of the Panel that the nature and characteristics of services are "like" irrespective of where they are supplied. The CVA requirement and the equivalent requirements in the SROs cover the above-noted services generally and distinguish between services solely on the basis of whether the services are "executed in Canada" (in the case of CVA Items (a)(iv)(I) and (a)(iv)(K)) or whether the expenses related to the services are "incurred in Canada" (in the case of CVA Item (a)(v)). Accordingly, the services of Canada and other Members are *per se* "like".[644] And to the extent that Canadian service suppliers provide these "like"" services, they and Japanese service suppliers are "like" service suppliers.

Services and service suppliers outside Canada are accorded less favourable treatment

(a) Modes of supply

6.1029 Article I:2(a) of the GATS defines Mode 1 (cross-border supply) as the supply of a service "from the territory of one Member into the territory of any other Member", and Mode 2 (consumption abroad) as the supply of a service "in the territory of one Member to the service consumer of any other Member". Also, Article XXVIII(f)(i) of the GATS defines a service of another Member as a service which is supplied "from or in the territory of that other Member", in the case of Mode 1 (cross-border supply) or Mode 2 (consumption abroad).

6.1030 The discrimination that is created by the domestic content requirement arises from the use in the definition of the CVA of the phrases "executed in Canada" and "incurred in Canada".

6.1031 In the case of CVA Items (a)(iv)(I) and (a)(iv)(K), where the services in question are "executed in Canada", their costs can be included in the definition of Canadian value added. Conversely, where the services are not executed in Canada, their costs cannot be included in the CVA calculation.

6.1032 In the case of CVA Item (a)(v), where the costs associated with the services in question are "incurred in Canada", they can be included in the definition of Canadian value added. Conversely, where the costs in question are not incurred in Canada, they cannot be included in the CVA calculation.

6.1033 These phrases prevent the inclusion of costs in the CVA requirement where the services in question are supplied under Mode 1 (cross-border supply) or under Mode 2 (consumption abroad), whereas costs of "like" services supplied in Canada are included in the CVA requirement.

---

643 Panel Reports on *EC - Bananas III*, *supra* note 269, para. 7.322.

644 In the context of trade in goods, this "principled" or "*per se*" approach to establishing like products has been applied by the Panel in *Indonesia - Autos*, *supra* note 270, para. 14.141 and by the Panel in *US - Non-Rubber Footwear*, *supra* note 269, para. 6.12. The same reasoning can be applied in the case of services where the measure in question applies to services or a class of services generally.

(b) Nature of the Less Favourable Treatment

6.1034 In the sectors inscribed in its Schedule of Specific Commitments which, as established above, include the relevant elements of the CVA requirement, Canada has bound itself to accord no less favourable treatment to services and service suppliers of any other WTO Member than that it accords to its own like services and service suppliers. Article XVII:3 of the GATS provides that the treatment accorded to services and service suppliers of other WTO Members, whether formally identical or formally different, "shall be considered to be less favourable if it modifies the conditions of competition in favour of services and service suppliers of the Member maintaining the measure compared to like services and service suppliers of any other Member".

6.1035 Since costs associated with services supplied under Mode 1 (cross-border supply) and Mode 2 (consumption abroad) are not eligible for the CVA calculation, the domestic content requirement modifies the conditions of competition in favour of services supplied in Canada compared to like services supplied under either Mode 1 or Mode 2 from or in the territory of other Members. Accordingly, services and thereby service suppliers of the former benefit from the economic inducement created by the domestic content requirement while like services and service suppliers of the latter do not.

6.1036 In the case of item (a)(iv)(I) of the CVA, only the cost of maintenance and repair work on machinery and equipment executed in Canada is included in the calculation of the CVA. *A contrario*, this means that the cost of like maintenance and repair work executed outside Canada will not be included in the calculation of the CVA. Clearly, this requirement modifies the conditions of competition in favour of maintenance and repair services on machinery and equipment supplied in Canada, over like services supplied under Mode 1 or Mode 2 from or in the territory of other Members. Hence, item (a)(iv)(I) of the CVA accords less favourable treatment to like repair and maintenance services of other Members, and thereby their service suppliers. This is inconsistent with Canada's national treatment commitment in respect of the supply of repair and maintenance services and service suppliers.

6.1037 Similarly, item (a)(iv)(K) of the CVA provides that only the cost of engineering services, experimental work and product development work executed in Canada is included in the calculation of the CVA. *A contrario*, this implies that the cost of like engineering services executed outside Canada will not be included in the calculation of the CVA. Again, this requirement modifies the conditions of competition in favour of engineering services offered in Canada over like services supplied under Mode 1 or Mode 2 from or in the territory of other WTO Members. Thus, item (a)(iv)(K) of the CVA accords less favourable treatment to like engineering services of other Members, and thereby their service suppliers. This is inconsistent with Canada's national treatment commitment in respect of the supply of engineering services.

6.1038 Item (a)(v) of the CVA definition provides that costs associated with services classified as "general and administrative expenses" are included in the CVA only if they are incurred in Canada. *A contrario*, this implies that the cost of like services that are incurred outside Canada will not be included in the CVA calculation. This requirement modifies the conditions of competition in favour of such services supplied in Canada over like services supplied under Mode 1 or Mode 2 from or in the territory of other Members. Thus, item (a)(v) of the CVA accords less favourable treatment to like services of other Members, and thereby their service suppliers. This is inconsistent with Canada's national treatment commitment in respect of the supply of such services.

6.1039 Accordingly, by virtue of the domestic content requirement, the Duty Waiver is inconsistent with Article XVII of the GATS.

2. *Arguments of the European Communities*

6.1040 The **European Communities** argues as follows:

6.1041 The cost of certain services used by the beneficiaries as inputs for the manufacture of motor vehicles is counted as CVA only when those services are supplied within the territory of Canada. As a consequence, the CVA requirements provide an incentive for the beneficiaries to use Canadian services over like services supplied from the territory of other Members into Canada through Mode 1 ("cross-border delivery") or in the territory of other Members through Mode 2 ("consumption abroad"), thereby infringing Canada's obligations under GATS Article XVII.

6.1042 Specifically, the CVA calculation rules stipulate that the following items are to be counted as CVA:

> "(iv) the part of the following costs that is reasonably attributable to the production of the vehicles, namely:
>
> ...
>
> (G) fire and other insurance premiums, in respect of production inventories and the production plant and equipment, paid to a company authorised by federal or provincial law to *carry on business in Canada or a province*.
>
> ...
>
> (I) the cost of ... repair work *executed in Canada* on ... machinery and equipment used for production purposes.
>
> ...
>
> (K) the cost of engineering services ... *executed in Canada*.
>
> ...
>
> (v) administrative and general expenses *incurred in Canada* that are reasonably attributable to the production of the vehicles ..." (*emphasis added*).

6.1043 The meaning of the terms "carried on in Canada", "executed in Canada" and "incurred in Canada" is not defined in the CVA calculation rules. During the consultations, the European Communities asked Canada to confirm whether those terms mean that services supplied into Canada from the territory of another Member or in the territory of another Member cannot be counted as CVA. In view of the responses given by Canada, the European Communities understands that the services of other Members supplied through modes 1 and 2 are not counted as CVA.

6.1044 Article XVII:1 of GATS reads as follows:

> "1. In the sectors inscribed in its Schedule, and subject to any conditions and qualifications set out therein, each Member shall accord to services and service suppliers of any other Member, in respect of all measures affecting the supply of services, treatment no less favourable than that it accords to its own like services and service suppliers." (footnote omitted).

6.1045 Accordingly, in order to rule on the EC's claim under GATS Article XVII the Panel is required to make the following determinations:

- whether Canada has undertaken in its Schedule national treatment commitments for modes 1 and 2 with respect to the relevant sectors;
- whether the services of other Members supplied through modes 1 and 2 are "like" the Canadian services;
- whether the CVA requirements "affect the supply" of the services concerned; and
- whether the CVA requirements afford "less favourable treatment" to the services of other Members than to Canadian services.

(a) The Relevant Sectors and Modes of Supply are Covered by Canada's Commitments on National Treatment

6.1046 Canada has inscribed in its Schedule[645] national treatment commitments for modes 1 and 2 with respect to the following relevant sub-sectors:

- non-life insurance services (CPC 8129). This commitment covers *inter alia* the insurance services referred to in item (iv) G of the CVA calculation rules;
- repair services incidental to machinery and equipment, including computers and communications equipment on a fee or a contract basis (CPC 8861 to 8866). This commitment covers *inter alia* the services described as "repair work executed on machinery and equipment used for production purposes" in item (iv) I of the CVA calculation rules; and
- engineering services (CPC 8672). This commitment covers the services described as "engineering services" in item (iv) K.

6.1047 Canada has also undertaken national treatment commitments for modes 1 and 2 with respect to a wide range of other services that are likely to figure among the beneficiaries' "general and administrative expenses" mentioned in item (v) of the CVA calculation rules. For example, that category of expenses may include:

(1) (1) professional services (e.g., the services falling within CPC* 861, CPC 862 and CPC* 863);

(2) (2) computer related services (e.g., CPC 841, CPC 842*, CPC 843*, CPC 844*, CPC 845, CPC 849);

(3) (3) other business services (e.g., CPC 86501, 86502, 86504, 86505, 86506, 86509, CPC 8676 and CPC 872);

(4) (4) banking services (e.g., CPC 81115 to 81119, CPC 8113, CPC 8112, CPC 81339* and CPC 81199*);

(5) (5) telecommunication services (e.g., subsectors (a), (b), (c), (d), (e), (f) and (g)); or

(6) (6) travel services (e.g., CPC 641, CPC 642/3 and CPC 7471).

645 A copy of Canada's GATS Schedule of Specific Commitments is attached (Exhibit EC -19).

6.1048 While Canada's relevant national treatment commitments are subject to certain horizontal limitations, as well as to some sector and/or mode specific limitations, none of those limitations allows the application of the CVA requirements.

(b) The CVA Requirement is a "Measure Affecting the Supply of Services"

6.1049 As shown above, the CVA requirements, including those contained in the Letters of Undertaking, are "laws, regulations or requirements" for purposes of Article III of GATT. For the same reasons, the CVA requirements also are "measures" for purposes of GATS Article XVII[646].

6.1050 The term "supply of a service" has a broad coverage[647]. According to GATS Article XXVIII(b) it includes "... the production, distribution, marketing, sale and delivery of a service".

6.1051 The term "affecting" is not defined in the GATS. In *EC -Bananas III*, the Panel interpreted that term as covering:

> "[A]ny measure bearing upon conditions of competition in supply of a service, regardless of whether the measure directly governs or indirectly affects the supply of the service."[648]

6.1052 The Panel's interpretation was upheld by the Appellate Body, which noted that:

> "[T]he use of the term 'affecting' reflects the intent of the drafters to give a broad reach to the GATS. The ordinary meaning of the word 'affecting' implies a measure that has 'an effect on', which indicates a broad scope of application. This interpretation is further reinforced by the conclusions of previous panels that the term 'affecting' in the context of Article III of the GATT is wider in scope than such terms as 'regulating ' or 'governing''"[649] (footnotes omitted).

6.1053 In the present case, the CVA requirements "affect the supply of a service" because, as shown below, they provide an incentive for the beneficiaries to use services supplied within the Canadian territory over like services supplied in or from the territory of other Members, thereby modifying the conditions of competition between them.

(c) Canadian Services Are "Like" the Services of Other Members Provided Through Modes 1 and 2

6.1054 The distinctions drawn by the CVA requirements are based exclusively on the territory where the service is supplied, and not on the nature and characteristics of the services themselves. Clearly, however, the mere fact that a service is supplied within

---

646 The term "measure" is defined in GATS Article XXVIII (a) as comprising: "any measure by a Member, whether in the form of a law, regulation, rule, procedure, decision, administrative action, or any other form." In turn, GATS Article I:3 (a) provides in relevant part that: "(a) 'measures by Members' means measures taken by: (i) central, regional or local governments; [...]".

647 See, e.g., Panel Reports on *EC - Bananas III*, *supra* note 269, para. 7.281.

648 Ibid.

649 Appellate Body Report on *EC - Bananas III*, *supra* note 49, para. 220.

the territory of Canada does not, of itself, confer to that service any attribute which makes it, by definition, "unlike" any service of another Member supplied through modes 1 or 2.

6.1055 For example, if one of the beneficiaries commissioned a legal opinion on the WTO compatibility of the Auto Pact, the services provided by a trade lawyer based in Brussels would not be, by definition, "unlike" those provided by a trade lawyer of Ottawa.

(d) Services of Other Members Supplied Through Modes 1 and 2 Are Afforded "Less Favourable Treatment" Than Canadian Services

6.1056 The "no less favourable treatment" requirement set forth in paragraph 1 of GATS Article XVII has been specified in paragraphs 2 and 3 of that Article, which state that:

> "2. A Member may meet the requirement of paragraph 1 by according to services and service suppliers of any other Member, either formally identical treatment or formally different treatment to that it accords to its own like service and service suppliers.
>
> 3. Formally identical or formally different treatment shall be considered to be less favourable if it modifies the conditions of competition in favour of services or service suppliers of the Member compared to like services or service suppliers of any other Members."

6.1057 In the present case, the services of other Members receive "formally different treatment": while Canadian services are always counted as CVA, the services of other Members are not counted as CVA when supplied through modes 1 and 2.

6.1058 That difference in treatment confers a competitive advantage to Canadian services. Using Canadian services makes it easier for the beneficiaries to reach the required level of CVA, and hence to qualify for the Tariff Exemption, than using like services of other Members supplied through modes 1 or 2. Consequently, all other conditions being equal, the beneficiaries will give preference to Canadian services over like services of other Members supplied through modes 1 or 2. Thus, services of other Members are afforded "less favourable treatment" than like Canadian services.

3. Canada's Response

6.1059 **Canada** responds as follows:

6.1060 Japan, but not the European Communities, claims that the MVTO and the SROs, by granting duty-free treatment to qualifying manufacturers, contravene Canada's national treatment obligations under Article XVII of the GATS.

6.1061 Article XVII:1 of the GATS provides:

> "In the sectors inscribed in its Schedule, and subject to any conditions and qualifications set out therein, each Member shall accord to services and service suppliers of any other Member, in respect of all measures affecting the supply of services, treatment no less favourable than that it accords to its own like services and service suppliers."

6.1062 According to the analytical framework established by the Panel in *EC - Bananas III*, in order to establish a breach of Article XVII, all three of the following elements need to be demonstrated:

(i) the Member has undertaken a commitment in a relevant sector and mode of supply;

(ii) the Member has adopted or applied a measure affecting the supply of services in that sector and/or mode of supply; and

(iii) the Member's measure accords to service suppliers of another Member treatment less favourable than that it accords to the Member's own like service suppliers.

6.1063 Japan has failed to establish the existence of any of these elements. It has failed to show the existence of a specific commitment by Canada for wholesale trade services of motor vehicles, because Canada has not made one; it has failed to show that the measures, insofar as they accord duty-free treatment to certain imported vehicles, affect service suppliers in their capacity as service suppliers; and it has failed to show either that the measures modify the conditions of competition as between Canadian services and service suppliers and like services and service suppliers of other Members, or even that such like services and service suppliers exist.

(a) Canada Has Not Undertaken a Commitment in a Relevant Sector

6.1064 Canada's specific commitments are those listed and bound in its GATS Schedule[650] on the basis of the UN *Provisional Central Product Classification* (CPC).[651] According to Japan's argument, the services at issue are wholesale trade services of motor vehicles. However, Canada has not made a specific commitment in respect of wholesale trade services of motor vehicles.

6.1065 Wholesale trade services of motor vehicles is listed in the Provisional CPC as classification 61111:

> Wholesaling and commission agents' services of passenger motor cars, motor buses and motor coaches, motor lorries and trucks, over-the-road truck tractors, semi-trailers and trailers. (Goods classified in CPC 491, 492.)[652]

6.1066 Classification 61111 is one of several breakouts from classification 6111 "Sales of motor vehicles", which in turn forms part of Division 61 of the Provisional CPC, "Sale, Maintenance and Repair Services of Motor Vehicles and Motorcycles".[653] A separate division, Division 62, covers "Commission Agents' and Wholesale Trade Services, *Except of Motor Vehicles and Motorcycles*" (*emphasis added*).

---

[650] *Canada's GATS Schedule*, *supra* note 641.

[651] United Nations Statistical Office, *Provisional Central Product Classification*, UN Doc.ST/ESA/STAT/SER.M/77 (New York: United Nations, 1991) (hereinafter "*CPC*"). See relevant sections in Exhibit CDA-9. See e.g., *EC - Bananas - Recourse to Arbitration by the European Communities under Article 22.6 of the DSU*, Decision by the Arbitrators, WT/DS27/ARB, 9 April 1999, para. 6.24.

[652] Ibid., p. 189.

[653] Ibid., p. 130.

Division 62 includes a classification for "Wholesale trade services", classification 622.[654]

6.1067 Canada's Schedule distinguishes between commitments in respect of "Wholesale trade services", and those in respect of "Retailing services".[655] Under "Wholesale trade services", Canada has made commitments only in respect of certain services in classification 622; that is, for certain wholesale trade services other than of motor vehicles.[656]

6.1068 The commitment to which Japan refers, under CPC 6111, is listed in Canada's Schedule of Specific Commitments only under "Retailing Services". It is not listed under "Wholesale trade services". Canada's specific commitments therefore do not extend, and were not intended to extend, to wholesale trade services for motor vehicles. In the absence of such a commitment, there can be no breach of Article XVII of the GATS.

(b) Duty-Free Treatment Under the MVTO and the SROs does not Affect the Supply of Wholesale Trade Services

6.1069 As Canada has argued above, in respect of Article II of the GATS, Japan has failed to show that the MVTO and the SROs, by providing duty-free importation of automobiles for qualifying manufacturers, affects wholesale distribution trade service suppliers in their capacity as service suppliers. Japan has therefore failed to show that the measures affect trade in services and are thereby covered by the GATS. Japan has thus also failed to demonstrate the second element of a breach of Article XVII of the GATS.

(c) The MVTO and the SROs do not Accord Less Favourable Treatment to Like Services and Service Suppliers

(i) Japan has failed to identify like service suppliers

6.1070 Even if Japan could satisfy the first two elements to demonstrate a breach of Article XVII of the GATS, it would still have to show that the measures accord less favourable treatment to Japanese wholesale distribution service suppliers than to like Canadian service suppliers.

6.1071 In the case of automobiles, there are no like Canadian wholesale distribution service suppliers. As Japan itself has acknowledged, all of the wholesale distribution service suppliers for mass-produced automobiles are juridical persons of other Members.

6.1072 The only Canadian supplier of wholesale trade services for passenger cars that Japan has identified is Intermeccanica. Even the European Communities has acknowledged that Intermeccanica is not "like", describing it as an "artisanal pro-

---

654 Ibid., p. 131-134.

655 Canada's GATS Schedule, *supra* note 641, pp. 47-49.

656 Ibid., II.4.B, p. 47.

ducer of replicas of racing cars". To the extent that it is a wholesale distribution service supplier at all, it is not like Honda Canada or Toyota Canada or any other of the commercial presences identified by Japan as wholesale distribution service suppliers. Japan has therefore failed to satisfy the third element of the test in respect of wholesale distribution services for passenger cars.

6.1073 Japan has offered no evidence whatsoever to substantiate its claim that there are Canadian suppliers of wholesale distribution services for buses or specialized commercial vehicles that are advantaged by the duty-free treatment under the MVTO or the SROs. Nor has it identified any like Japanese service suppliers. The services provided by distributors of automobiles are no more like the services provided by the distributors of buses or specialized commercial vehicles than the goods that they distribute are like. Even if there were like service suppliers, the measures would not modify the conditions of competition among them, because, as Canada has argued in respect of Article II, there is no such competition, due to the integrated structure of the motor vehicle industry. Japan has failed to make even a prima facie case regarding the third element of the test in respect of wholesale distribution services for specialized commercial vehicles and buses.

(ii) Duty-free treatment does not modify conditions of competition because there is no competition

6.1074 Article XVII:2 of the GATS provides that:

> "A Member may meet the requirement of paragraph 1 by according to services and service suppliers of any other Member, either formally identical treatment or formally different treatment to that it accords to its own like services and service suppliers."

6.1075 Article XVII:3 of the GATS elaborates that:

> "Formally identical or formally different treatment shall be considered to be less favourable if it modifies the conditions of competition in favour of services or service suppliers of the Member compared to like services or service suppliers of any other Member."

6.1076 Thus, unlike Article II of the GATS, Article XVII explicitly provides that the test of the standard of treatment accorded by Members is whether it modifies the conditions of competition as between the services and service suppliers of that Member and the like services and service suppliers of any other Member.

6.1077 For the same reasons that the measures, insofar as they accord duty-free treatment to certain imported vehicles, do not affect the conditions of competition in respect of Article II of the GATS, they do not do so in respect of Article XVII of the GATS either. All of the Japanese subsidiaries that Japan has claimed are wholesale trade service suppliers are part of integrated entities that compete with one another for product sales at the retail level but not at the wholesale level. Due to the structure of the motor vehicle industry, there is simply no competition among wholesale distribution trade service suppliers.

6.1078 Japan has therefore failed to demonstrate any of the three elements necessary to show a violation of Article XVII of the GATS.

(d) Article XVII of the GATS - CVA Requirements

6.1079 Japan and the European Communities also claim that the CVA requirement under the measures is inconsistent with Article XVII of the GATS. In order to establish a breach of Article XVII in respect of the CVA requirement, the complainants must establish the same three elements that Japan failed to establish in respect of duty-free treatment.[657] They cannot do so.

(i) Canada has limited commitments in relevant sectors and modes of supply

6.1080 The complainants have identified certain CVA eligible services in respect of which Canada has scheduled a specific national treatment commitment under Article XVII of the GATS. They are:

- CVA item (a)(iv)(I): maintenance and repair work on buildings, machinery and equipment; (CPC 8861 to 8866);[658]
- CVA item (a)(iv)(K): engineering services, experimental work and product development work (CPC 8672); and
- CVA item (a)(iv)(G): fire and insurance premiums (CPC 8129) (identified only by the EC).

Both complainants have also alleged Canadian commitments in respect of a wide range of services allegedly constituting "general and administrative expenses" under CVA item (a)(v).

6.1081 Canada's national treatment commitments in respect of many of these services are subject to limitations inscribed in its Schedule of Specific Commitments.[659]

- In respect of "Engineering services" (CPC 8672), Canada has limited its commitments by scheduling limitations on market access. The limitation is that most provinces, including those where automobiles are produced - Ontario and Quebec - require either permanent residency or citizenship for accreditation. These limitations apply in respect of modes of supply (1), (2), and (4).
- According to Article XX:2 of the GATS and the *Explanatory Note for the Scheduling of Initial Commitments in Trade in Services*,[660] a measure that is scheduled in respect of Article XVI (market access) and that is also inconsistent with Article XVII (national treatment) is to be regarded as a scheduled limitation or qualification in respect of Article XVII as well. Thus, the provincial residency and citizenship requirements for engineering services, although scheduled as market

[657] (i) the Member has undertaken a commitment in a relevant sector and mode of supply; (ii) the Member has adopted or applied a measure affecting the supply of services in that sector and/or mode of supply; and (iii) the Member's measure accords to service suppliers of another Member treatment less favourable than that it accords to the Member's own like service suppliers.

[658] For CVA items, see MVTO 1998. For CPC references, see *supra* note 651.

[659] See Canada's GATS Schedule, *supra* note 641.

[660] Scheduling of Initial Commitments in Trade in Services: Explanatory Note, MTN.GNS/W/164., 3 September 1993 (Exhibit CDA-10).

access limitations, limit Canada's national treatment commitments as well.

- In respect of "Insurance and insurance-related services" which includes the "Non-life insurance services" (CPC 8129) identified by the EC, Canada has scheduled several mode 1 market access limitations to the effect that services must be provided through a commercial presence.[661] As noted above, these limitations apply to national treatment as well as market access.
- Canada has also scheduled as a national treatment limitation in respect of the mode 2 supply of insurance services (consumption abroad), its 10 per cent excise tax on net premiums paid to foreign direct insurance providers on a contract against risk ordinarily within Canada.[662]

6.1082 Three of the services identified by the European Communities and/or Japan as falling within "general and administrative expenses" are also subject to relevant limitations:

- In respect of "Accounting, auditing and bookkeeping services (CPC 862), Canada has scheduled as modes 1 and 2 market access limitations, provincial requirements, (including in Ontario) that auditing services be supplied by a commercial presence, and citizenship or residence requirements for accreditation (including Quebec and Ontario respectively). As noted above, such limitations apply equally to Canada's national treatment commitments.
- In respect of "Placement and supply services of personnel" (CPC 872), Canada has scheduled as a mode 2 market access limitation a requirement that services must be supplied through a commercial presence. As noted above, this limitation also limits Canada's national treatment commitments.
- In respect of "Travel agency and tour operator services" (CPC 7471), Canada has scheduled as mode 1 limitations on market access the requirements that in Ontario, travel agency and wholesalers services must be supplied through a commercial presence and that in Quebec travel agencies services must be supplied through a commercial presence. As noted above, these limitations also limit Canada's national treatment commitments.
- In respect of "Travel agency and tour operator services" (CPC 7471), Canada has also scheduled as mode 1 limitations on national treatment, residency requirements in Ontario for travel agents and wholesalers and residency requirements in Quebec for travel counsellors.

---

661 Canada: Schedule of Specific Commitments, Supplement 4, GATS/SC.16/Suppl.4, 26 February 1998, p. 4 (Exhibit CDA-11).

662 Canada's GATS Schedule, *supra* note 641, Sec. II.7.A, p. 54. See also CPC, *supra* note 651, pp. 141-142.

(ii) The only modes of supply that may be "affected" are modes 1 and 2

6.1083 The second element that the complainants must show is that the measures affect the supply of services in a sector and/or mode of supply. Two of the four different modes by which a service may be supplied under the GATS are entirely unaffected by the CVA rules.

6.1084 Pursuant to the measures, the calculation of CVA may include the costs of certain services if those services are "executed in Canada" in the case of maintenance and repair work or engineering services; "incurred in Canada" in the case of administrative and general expenses"; and, in respect of insurance premiums, paid to a company authorized to carry on business in Canada. All of these services may therefore be included in CVA calculations if they are provided by a commercial presence of another Member in Canada (mode 3); or provided by the presence of foreign nationals in Canada (mode 4).

6.1085 Accordingly, any "effect" that the measures may have on the supply of services can only be on the supply of certain services according to modes 1 or 2. The complainants' claims must therefore be limited to the alleged effect of the measures on the provision of the identified services, in respect of which Canada has made an unlimited commitment for those modes.

(iii) The measures do not accord less favourable treatment to foreign services or service suppliers

6.1086 As previously noted, pursuant to Article XVII.3, the test for less favourable treatment under Article XVII of the GATS is whether the measure at issue modifies the conditions of competition as between the domestic services and service suppliers and those of another Member. The measures at issue do not do so.

6.1087 Although the only applicable modes of supply are modes 1 and 2, one of the relevant categories of CVA eligible services - maintenance and repair work on buildings, machinery and equipment - in most cases must be provided in Canada; that is, other than by those modes. The maintenance of buildings and, generally, the repair work on production machinery and equipment in those buildings can neither be done across a border nor consumed abroad. General Motors cannot reasonably be expected to ship its Canadian factories or heavy equipment to Japan to be maintained or repaired.

6.1088 Similarly, although Japan and the European Communities have identified hotel and other lodging services (CPC 641) and food and beverage services (CPC 642/3) as being disadvantaged by the CVA requirement, in general, the sole criterion that a manufacturer will use in determining whether to consume those services abroad will be whether it is geographically advantageous to do so. A General Motors employee visiting Canada will not stay in a hotel in Japan. Nor will that employee go to Europe to eat or arrange to have meals catered from Brussels. These choices have everything to do with geography. They have nothing to do with CVA requirements.

6.1089 Any competitive disadvantages in the foreign provision of these services are inherent in their foreign character. They do not arise from CVA requirements. Canada is under no obligation to compensate for such disadvantages, as Note 10 to Article XVII:1 of the GATS makes clear:

> "Specific commitments assumed under this Article shall not be construed to require any Member to compensate for any inherent competitive disadvantages which result from the foreign character of the relevant services or service suppliers."

6.1090 Given the foregoing, the complainants' claims must be limited to those services that (a) may be provided from another Member into Canada or consumed abroad; (b) are not the subject of relevant limitations; and (c) are not inherently disadvantaged by their foreign character. The complainants' claims are effectively limited to certain of the services that may constitute "general and administrative expenses".

6.1091 Any assertion that the conditions of competition between the foreign suppliers of these remaining services and like services supplied in Canada are modified by the CVA requirement is demonstrably incorrect. The general and administrative expenses related to those services are trivial compared to other CVA eligible costs such as labour, heating, lighting and power, taxes, pension contributions and depreciation, all of which are necessarily incurred in Canada.

6.1092 Canada's *Figure 2* demonstrates that MVTO manufacturers exceed their CVA requirements on the basis of labour costs alone. So does the only relevant SRO manufacturer, CAMI. Qualifying manufacturers readily satisfy their CVA requirements without including the cost of any services relating to these general and administrative expenses. It simply cannot be that qualifying manufacturers would choose where to source those services on the basis of CVA eligibility. The inclusion of those services in the list of CVA-eligible expenses therefore does not affect the conditions of competition as between Canadian and foreign service suppliers. As the evidence makes clear, most of the qualifying manufacturers exceed their CVA requirements on the basis of labour costs alone.

6.1093 It is therefore inconsistent with the facts for the complainants to suggest that the CVA requirements in the MVTO and SROs would cause qualifying manufacturers to prefer to obtain these remaining services in Canada rather than abroad when they can readily satisfy their CVA requirements without including the costs of those services. Accordingly, the inclusion of those services in the list of CVA-eligible expenses does not in any way affect the conditions of competition as between Canadian and foreign service suppliers.

4. *Rebuttal Arguments by Japan*

6.1094 **Japan** rebuts as follows:

(a) Wholesale Trade Services

6.1095 Contrary to its allegations, Canada has made a specific commitment in respect of wholesale trade services of motor vehicles. Canada has made a commitment in respect of services in classification 6111 of the CPC. The Government of Canada acknowledged that it made this commitment in its initial response. Had the Government of Canada wanted to limit its commitment to retail sale services, as it now argues, it would have had to inscribe CPC subclass 61112, a subclass that narrows the broad scope of coverage of classification 6111 to retail services. However, the Government of Canada did not. Therefore, Canada's commitment covers wholesale trade services for motor vehicles.

6.1096 Moreover, Canada inscribed on its schedule an express limitation to its commitments in respect of *wholesale trade services* for motor vehicles. This limitation, which relates to the sales of motor vehicles in the province of Saskatchewan, is not relevant in the present dispute but confirms that the Government of Canada's admission that Canada's commitments extend to wholesale trade services of motor vehicles. It is simply due to the fact that accepting the Government of Canada's argument would result in the contradictory situation where Canada limits a commitment that it has not even made. Rather, the only logical proposition is that the Government of Canada deemed it necessary to inscribe the above-noted limitation simply because it wanted to restrict the commitment that it undertook with respect to wholesale trade services of motor vehicles.

6.1097 The Government of Canada in this context argued in its arguments and its response to Question 30 of the Panel that there are no like Canadian wholesale service suppliers since (a) Intermeccanica is not a wholesale trade service supplier, and (b) even if it were, it would not be like service suppliers since its size and sales volume are vastly different from Japanese wholesale trade service suppliers that the Government of Japan has identified, both of which fall short of proving the Government of Canada's argument. The Government of Canada argues that Intermeccanica does not import automobiles for resale or distribute them at all. But the fact is that it is qualified for the Duty Waiver, and it has the capability and opportunity to import automobiles duty free at any time, whereas Japanese service suppliers are excluded from qualifying for the Duty Waiver.

6.1098 The difference in the scale of companies and in the nature of their products do not affect the likeness of the service suppliers insofar as those service suppliers supply services listed in the same CPC category: wholesale trade services of motor vehicles. The Panel on *EC - Bananas III* made this clear by stating when determining the likeness of green and ripened bananas that "the CPC descriptions do not make any distinction between green and ripened bananas." Those wholesale trade service suppliers the Government of Japan identified and Intermeccanica should be therefore all regarded as like wholesale trade service suppliers of motor vehicles, unless otherwise specified in Canada's schedule.

6.1099 The Government of Canada also emphasized in this context that the Government of Japan has offered no evidence to substantiate the claim that there are Canadian wholesale trade service suppliers for buses or specialized vehicles. The defense, however, is no longer valid in the presence of the factual information that Canada provided: in response to Question 2(4) from Japan, Canada listed eight companies who have imported and distributed vehicles other than automobiles under the MVTO and seven companies under an SRO, which are wholesale trade services suppliers of Canada and certain other WTO Members (but not including Japanese like service suppliers) as shown in Exhibit JPN-50. And since Japanese wholesale trade service suppliers have the capability to produce and distribute buses or specified commercial vehicles as argued by Japan, as in its response to the Question 34 of the Panel, and at least one Japanese service supplier (Hino Diesel Trucks (Canada), Ltd. imports and distributes trucks in Canada without enjoying the benefit under the Duty Waiver, Japan would like to simply repeat the claim made already. In addition, the argument that no Japanese service suppliers are treated unfavourably because there existed no Japanese service suppliers does not affect the determination of the violation of the GATS[663], as confirmed in *Canada - Periodicals.*[664]

(b) CVA

6.1100 Canada emphasizes in relation to Article XVII that it has not undertaken a commitment in respect of wholesale trade services of motor vehicles, by claiming that because Canada has made commitments only in respect of certain wholesale trade services other than those of motor vehicles. This claim is directly in contradiction with the definition given in CPC Classification List, where category 6111 "Sale of motor vehicles" includes explicitly category 61111 "Wholesale trade services of motor vehicles" and category 61112 "Retail sales of motor vehicles." Canada's commitment lists CPC 6111 without further specification.

6.1101 Moreover, Canada itself appears to think that it has committed wholesale trade services of motor vehicles, since on page 47 of Canada's Schedules of commitments, under the heading Wholesale trade services, Canada lists as one of the limitations on market access "Sale of Motor Vehicles (Saskatchewan): Services must be supplied through a commercial presence" (GATS/SC/16, at page 47). If Canada claims Wholesale trade services do not include sales of motor vehicles, why was there the need to put the limitation on market access?

6.1102 The Government of Japan also alleges that the CVA requirement for the Duty Waiver explicitly excludes from the CVA calculation the cost of certain services related to motor vehicles that are not executed in or incurred in Canada. Thus, as in the case of parts, components and materials (discussed above), the CVA requirement de jure favours those services supplied in Canada and accords less favourable treatment to like services supplied under Mode 1 or Mode 2 from or in the territory of other WTO Members. Thus the Duty Waiver is, by virtue of this domestic content requirement, inconsistent with Canada's obligations under Article XVII of the GATS.

6.1103 In response, Canada points out that its commitments in certain relevant service sectors are subject to limitations. However, there are still other commitments in a number of relevant service sectors which are not subject to limitations, including maintenance and repair work on buildings, machinery and equipment, and thus Canada is not entirely exempted from its obligations under Article XVII in those sectors.

6.1104 Second, Canada also fails to prove that the CVA requirement accords no less favourable treatment to like foreign services or service suppliers. It argues that "any competitive disadvantages in the foreign provision of these services are inherent in their foreign character," not arising from the CVA requirement. However, apart from any disadvantage which may result from the foreign character of relevant services and service suppliers, the CVA requirement itself gives a competitive disadvantage, which is not inherent to services supplied under Mode 1 or Mode 2 from or in the

[663] The existence of the domestic service suppliers which may enjoy favourable treatment needs to be proven with respect to the buses and specified commercial vehicles, but under the MVTO 1998 domestic and foreign companies may acquire the Autopact Manufacturers as discussed, subject to certain conditions. Such a possibility is sufficient for the establishment of the violation of Article XVII of the GATS.

[664] Panel and Appellate Body Reports on *Canada - Periodicals*, *supra* note 280.

territory of other WTO Members, including engineering design services, over like services supplied in Canada. Therefore, the CVA requirement can not be justified by Canada's incorrect assertion that any disadvantages in these sectors are inherent in their foreign character.

6.1105 Canada also asserts that the conditions of competition are not modified since "most of qualifying manufacturers exceed their CVA requirement on the basis of labour cost alone" and thus they are not induced by the requirements to purchase services supplied in Canada. However, as long as there is discrimination in favour of services supplied in Canada against like services supplied outside of Canada, how the requirement is actually met does not matter, the CVA requirement constitutes a violation of Article XVII of the GATS.

5. *Rebuttal Arguments by the European Communities*

6.1106 The **European Communities** rebuts as follows:

6.1107 The European Communities has argued that since only services supplied in Canada may be computed as CVA, the CVA requirements provide an incentive to use services supplied within the Canadian territory, instead of like services of other Members supplied "cross-border" (mode 1) or through "consumption abroad" (mode 2). Therefore, they amount to formally different, and less favourable, treatment of certain services, which are " CVA eligible" to the detriment of foreign services and suppliers.

(a) The Limitations on Canada's National Treatment Commitments do not Cover CVA Requirements

6.1108 Canada admits that it has undertaken national treatment commitments in respect of certain CVA-eligible services mentioned by the European Communities (maintenance and repair, engineering, insurance, and services which Canada admits fall within "general and administrative expenses" class). However, Canada points out that its schedules also include limitations to the above commitments and relies on such limitations to attempt refuting EC's arguments. Yet Canada has not succeeded in its demonstration.

6.1109 Although Canada may have to some extent limited some of its relevant national treatment commitments, that limitation does not authorise the application of CVA requirements or of other additional requirements: in other words, it does not mean that Canada's commitments keep no residual value at all.

6.1110 This is made clear by the example of *residency (and nationality) requirements*, limiting national treatment on *engineering services* and on two services falling within "*general and administrative expenses*". Residency and nationality requirements or commercial presence requirements may in practice exclude the possibility to provide services through modes 1 and 2. However, this does not mean that those limitations may cover any kind of restrictions on national treatment. If a Member has scheduled a limitation requiring commercial presence or residence, but nevertheless decided not to enforce it, it cannot impose "other limitations" instead. The CVA requirements, however, will apply regardless of whether Canada enforces a commercial presence or residence requirement in respect of relevant services.

6.1111 The EC's position is confirmed by *Addendum 1* to the Explanatory Note circulated during the Uruguay Round by the Group of Negotiations on Services. *Ad-*

dendum 1 makes clear that a residence requirement does not amount to an across-the-board exemption in respect of modes 1 and 2. It spells out that only the expression "unbound" ensures that there is absolutely no commitment in respect of a given mode:

> "It is correct to use the term "unbound" for a mode of supply in a given sector where a Member wishes to remain free to introduce or maintain measures inconsistent with market access or national treatment".[665]

6.1112 The use of the term "unbound" is contrasted in *Addendum 1* with the possibility to use more specific limitations, including residency requirements, which are considered to provide "the certainty that there are no other limitations with respect to the cross-border mode" additional to those which the terms "residence" or "nationality" express.[666]

6.1113 It is clear from *Addendum 1* that any limitations and requirements in respect of a given service that are not listed, including CVA requirements, could only be covered if that service were "unbound" as regards mode 1 and 2. Irrespective of whether residence requirements may, as a matter of fact, render provision of these services through mode 1 or 2 impossible, they do not cover different legal requirements.

6.1114 Another illustration of this principle is provided by limitations attached to *insurance and insurance-related services*. For example, if one has regard to mode 2 limitations, Canada's national treatment column includes a reference to an insurance subsector, that is "Direct insurance other than life",[667] which is the CVA-relevant one. As Canada admits, on that specific subsector there is simply no commercial presence requirement, but only a tax (10 per cent) on non-resident insurers' services. Moreover, the very fact that a limited restriction on mode 2 exists in Canada's national treatment limitations column also means that *no other* limitation is authorised, hence not either the one resulting from the application of the CVA requirements. Otherwise, there would have been no reason to inscribe this narrower limitation in the national treatment column.

6.1115 In the light of the above Canada cannot pretend that its schedule of National Treatment commitments includes " relevant limitations" for the CVA requirements in respect of modes 1 and 2. If this inference were correct, it would be sufficient for a Member to have attached even the slightest limitation to its commitments to be effectively exempted from respecting them at all.

---

[665] See Scheduling of Initial Commitments in Trade in Services: Explanatory Note, Addendum, MTN.GNS/W/164/Add.1, 30 November 1993, point 7 (Exhibit CDA-8).

[666] Ibid.

[667] See Canada: Schedule of Specific Commitments, Supplement 4, GATS/SC.16/Suppl.4, 26 February 1998.

(b) The AVA Requirements Accord "Less Favourable Treatment" to Foreign Services and Service Providers

6.1116 Canada has also tried to refute that CVA requirements favour services supplied within the Canadian territory by alleging that resort to domestic services depends on some inherent difficulty to use/supply services through modes 1 and 2.

6.1117 It cannot go unnoticed that by doing so Canada is actually questioning the very rationale of the condition that CVA-eligible services must be carried on in Canada in order to be actually counted as CVA: why is Canada defending and enforcing those requirements if Canadian services and service providers are favoured anyway by objective characteristics of the services at issue or of the market?

6.1118 Apart from that basic contradiction, Canada's defence is affected by some fatal flaws.

6.1119 First, Canada has again drawn too general a conclusion from certain isolated elements of its regime. In fact, based exclusively on its analysis of the *maintenance and repair services* and *of hotel services* (which follow within the CVA class of "general and administrative expenses") Canada argues that *no* CVA requirements accord "less favourable treatment" within the meaning of Article XVII of the GATS.

6.1120 Moreover, even for those two categories Canada is arriving at its conclusion on the basis of largely incorrect assumptions. As to maintenance and repair of equipment, it may be true that shipment abroad of heavy machinery may prove less eased than repair on the spot, just as it is true that modes 1 and 2 may be ruled out for building maintenance. But what about e.g., electronic equipment, whether employed in actual manufacturing processes, or in monitoring, or perhaps in the administrative units of a factory? How about software sent abroad for update or virus removal? And, as regards hotels, let us suppose that a new import arrangement is to be negotiated by GM Canada with a foreign supplier. CVA rules on general and administrative expenses mean that if negotiations take place in the supplier's country, hotel expenses incurred by the relevant Canadian sales manager will not be computed as CVA, while if the foreign supplier is invited to Canada his hotel expenses will.

6.1121 Examples like those just quoted simply disprove that there is some "inherently domestic" character even in the two only services to which Canada has referred. The truth of the matter is rather that normally all services referred to in the EC's arguments can be provided through mode 1 and /or mode 2. The European Communities has also provided several additional examples in its reply to Panel's Question 28[668]. They further confirm that resort to domestically provided services is not a geographical necessity.

6.1122 Last, in its arguments Canada rightly recalls that it is under no GATS obligation to make up for "any inherent competitive disadvantages which result from the

[668] Indeed, the possibility for these services to be provided by telecommunications makes them suitable for provision through mode 1. According to para. 19 of Scheduling of Initial Commitments in Trade in Services: Explanatory Note (MTN.GNS/W/164, 3 September 1993 (Exhibit CDA-10): "(a) Cross border supply - International transport, the supply of a service through telecommunications or mail, and services embodied in exported goods (e.g., a computer diskette, or drawings) are all examples of cross-border supply, since the service provider is not present within the territory of the Member where the service is delivered."

foreign character of the relevant services". This is true, but it certainly does not authorise Canada to interfere in the competitive situation so as to adversely affect the competitive conditions of foreign services and providers. The European Communities is not requesting of Canada that it take any compensatory step. It is simply requesting that Canada abstain from changing the conditions of competition to the detriment of foreign services and suppliers.

6.1123 As regards Canada's contention that CVA requirements may already be met on the basis of labour costs only, it has already been refuted in respect of Article III:4 (see Section VI.B).

6. *Response by Canada to the Complainants' Rebuttals*

6.1124 **Canada** responds as follows:

(a) Article XVII - CVA

6.1125 The European Communities acknowledges that residency, nationality and commercial presence requirements "may in practice exclude the possibility to provide services through modes 1 and 2". The European Communities nevertheless contends that even if such requirements "render the provision of services through modes 1 or 2 impossible, they do not cover different legal requirements". While this may be true, it is beside the point. The CVA cannot possibly have any effect on the supply by modes 1 or 2 of engineering services, insurance services, accounting, auditing and bookkeeping services, placement and supply services, travel agency and tour operator services or any other services identified by the complainants if the provision of services by those modes is already impossible.

6.1126 In their responses to the Panel's Question 34, Japan and the European Communities also argue whether some of the services are physically capable of being provided by modes 1 or 2 and the extent to which some foreign service suppliers may be inherently disadvantaged by their foreign character within the meaning of Footnote 10 to Article XVII. However, they have not identified the services or suppliers that remain unaffected by the factors Canada has raised. Japan, for example, argues that engineering services are not inherently disadvantaged by their foreign character within the meaning of Footnote 10, while ignoring that such services are subject to residency and citizenship requirements that render impossible their provision by modes 1 or 2. Moreover, neither of the complainants addresses the fundamental point that manufacturers can meet their CVA requirements without including the cost even of those services that do remain in issue, after all the limiting factors have been taken into account.

6.1127 Japan seeks to reverse the burden of proof when it argues that Canada "fails to prove that the CVA requirement accords no less favourable treatment to like foreign services or service suppliers". However, the burden does not lie with Canada. It lies with the complainants to show that the CVA requirements do accord less favourable treatment to their services or service suppliers. As Canada has demonstrated, the CVA requirements do not do so.

(b) Canada Has not Undertaken a Commitment

6.1128 Japan's assertion that Canada has made a relevant commitment because "Canada's commitment lists CPC 6111 without further specification" ignores entirely that

Canada's commitment is scheduled only in respect of the retailing services sector.[669] By scheduling its commitment only under retailing services, Canada plainly indicated that it did not apply to other types of services. In any event, Article XVII of the GATS imposes obligations in respect of specific - that is, positive - commitments. It is binding on Members only in respect of sectors and sub-sectors in which they have made commitments.

6.1129 Japan refers to Canada's scheduled market access limitation requiring a commercial presence for the sale of motor vehicles in Saskatchewan as evidence that Canada's wholesale trade services commitments extend to motor vehicles. That commitment should have been listed under retailing services but was incorrectly listed under wholesale trade services. The fact that it was placed under wholesale trade services in error is confirmed by the scope of Canada's wholesale trade services commitments which are explicitly limited to CPC 622, which expressly excludes wholesale trade services of motor vehicles.[670] Japan has offered no rebuttal for this explicit limitation. Canada notes that Japan has not referred to the market access limitation for "Automobile Dealers and Salvage Dealers" in Newfoundland, which immediately follows the Saskatchewan limitation. The Newfoundland limitation is also listed in the wholesale trade services sector, although it very clearly relates to retail services. The fact that Canada inadvertently listed two limitations incorrectly cannot be the basis for construing a Canadian commitment in the face of Canada's express limitation of its wholesale services commitments to CPC 622, its scheduling of a CPC 6111 commitment only in respect of the retail services sector. To construe a commitment where Canada has not explicitly made one would contravene Article XVII:1 of the GATS, which limits Members' obligations to specific commitments only.

(c) The Measures do not Accord Less Favourable Treatment

6.1130 It is unclear if Japan has abandoned its Article XVII claim that duty-free treatment under the measures adversely affects conditions of competition for suppliers of wholesale services for specified commercial vehicles and buses. Japan appears in its rebuttal to limit its Article XVII argument to automobile importers only. It states that "[t]he measure, which allows importation of automobiles by service suppliers of certain Members including Canada duty-free, whereas importation of automobiles by like service suppliers of other Members at MFN duty, constitutes a violation of Article ... XVII".

6.1131 As Canada has explained, there are no "like" Canadian automobile wholesale service suppliers. Apart from its assertions with respect to Intermeccanica, which are unsubstantiated and wrong, as explained in Canada's Response to the Panel's Question 30,[671] Japan has failed to list any such service suppliers let alone make out a prima facie case.

---

669 See Canada's response to Question 31 from the Panel.

670 See Canada's response to Question 31 from the Panel.

671 Canada's response to Question 30 from the Panel.

6.1132 In its response to the Panel's Question 34,[672] Japan makes an oblique reference to service suppliers that distribute buses and specified commercial vehicles. Without indicating the claim in respect of which these service suppliers are relevant, Japan states that it has "insufficient information" relating to them. Japan indicates that there may be one Japanese truck service supplier but does not specify what sort of services it supplies. It then contends that information as to the nationality of *Japanese* service suppliers is "uniquely in the hands of the Government of Canada" and should be provided by Canada. In effect, Japan seeks to reverse the burden of proof, arguing that there may be Japanese service suppliers and there may be discrimination against them. Canada knows of no such discrimination and has no responsibility to respond to such vague, unsubstantiated speculation.

6.1133 When Japan alleges that its service suppliers have been disadvantaged, the onus rests on Japan to make out a prima facie case that this is so.[673] This includes identifying those of its service suppliers that it alleges to be affected. It cannot demand that Canada make its case for it. Having failed to identify any alleged Japanese wholesale service suppliers of buses or specified commercial vehicles, Japan has failed to make out a prima facie case that the duty-free treatment under the measures is inconsistent with Article XVII of the GATS.

7. *Japan's Follow-Up to Canada's Response*

6.1134 As a follow-up to Canada's response, **Japan** argues as follows:

6.1135 With respect to the Government of Japan's claim that the Duty Waiver by virtue of the eligibility restriction is inconsistent with Article XVII of the GATS, the Government of Japan has demonstrated at paragraphs 127-130 of its second written submission that Canada's specific commitments cover wholesale trade services for motor vehicles, and that a Canadian wholesale trade service supplier (i.e. Intermeccanica) is a "like" service supplier which is qualified for the Duty Waiver and has the capability and opportunity to import automobiles duty-free. Thus, the Government of Japan maintains that Canada, by virtue of the Duty Waiver, accords to Japanese wholesale trade services and service suppliers of motor vehicles, less favourable treatment than it accords to its own like services and service suppliers.

6.1136 The Government of Japan has also demonstrated in Exhibit JPN-50 and paragraph 131 of its second written submission that there exist several like domestic service suppliers which compete with at least one wholesale trade service supplier of Japanese origin (i.e. Hino Diesel Trucks (Canada), Ltd.) in the case of specified commercial vehicles covered by the Duty Waiver.

6.1137 With respect to the Government of Japan's claim that the CVA is inconsistent with Article XVII of the GATS, the Government of Japan has demonstrated in its response to Question #28 of the Panel and its second written submission that services covered by the CVA and Canada's specific commitments could be supplied through mode 1, that these foreign services supplied from outside Canada, either through mode 1 or mode 2, are excluded from ever being included in the CVA calculation, and that the disadvantages caused by the CVA requirement are not inherent from

[672] Japan's response to Question 34 from the Panel.

[673] See Appellate Body Report on *US - Wool Shirts*, *supra* note 283, p. 333 et seq.

their foreign character. Accordingly, as in the case of parts, components and materials, the CVA, which itself is a mandatory requirement, expressly discriminates against the supply of like foreign, including Japanese, services in favour of like domestic services. Accordingly, it violates Canada's obligations under Article XVII of the GATS.

8. *The European Communities' Follow-Up to Canada's Response*

6.1138 As a follow-up to Canada's response, the **European Communities** argues as follows:

6.1139 In its response to the complainants' rebuttals, Canada argues that the costs of CVA-eligible services are counted irrespective of whether the service supplier is Canadian or foreign. This statement is misleading and irrelevant at the same time. It is misleading, because it is only true in respect of supply trough commercial presence or movement of natural persons modes. It is irrelevant, because as both the European Communities and Canada agree, EC's claim under Article XVII concerns modes 1 and 2 only.

6.1140 Canada seems to concede that residence requirements do not cover other limitations on national treatment commitments. Contrary to Canada's view this is not beside the point, but rather the basic point of the EC's claim for the whole range of the services that the European Communities has mentioned in its presentation of its claims

6.1141 The truth is that the premise of Canada's conclusion is false. The provision by modes 1 or 2 of the services listed by the European Communities is not "already impossible". Canada has mentioned certain limitations in respect of a limited range of the services at issue and has tried to draw a general conclusion from them. The European Communities has replied to Canada's specific objections.[674] The other services are clearly unaffected by the factors that Canada has mentioned.

6.1142 In any event, it must be recalled that the European Communities is not required to show that the CVA requirements have any actual effects. Article XVII is concerned with "conditions of competition", not with the actual effects of a measure, and a measure is inconsistent with it if it creates less favourable conditions for like service suppliers of foreign origin.[675] The CVA requirements would apply even if Canada decided not to enforce its commercial presence and residency requirements and therefore modify the conditions of competition.

9. *Canada's Follow-Up Response*

6.1143 **Canada** responds as follows:

---

[674] EC's argumentation and response to Question 28 from the Panel.

[675] Appellate Body Report on *EC - Bananas III*, *supra* note 49, para 244; Panel Report on *EC - Bananas III (USA)*, *supra* note 269, paras. 7.320 and 7.337.

(a) The Measures do not Deny National Treatment to Wholesale Distribution Trade Service Suppliers

6.1144 At this late stage in the proceedings, Japan remains unable to demonstrate any of the three elements required to make out a violation of Article XVII of the GATS concerning the suppliers of wholesale distribution trade services. Those elements are: (i) a commitment in a relevant sector and mode of supply; (ii) a measure affecting the supply of services in that sector and mode of supply; and (iii) less favourable treatment accorded to services or service suppliers of another Member by the measure.

6.1145 With respect to the first of these elements, Japan continues to attempt to hold Canada to a commitment that Canada has not made. Japan claims that in order for Canada to have limited its motor vehicles services commitment to retail services, Canada would have had to limit its commitment to subclass 61112 of the CPCs. Japan's claim completely ignores that Canada's commitment is expressly limited to retail services by its location in the "Retailing services" sector/subsector. Japan's claim seeks in effect to rewrite Canada's schedule of specific commitments. It runs directly contrary to the principle, confirmed by the Panel in *EC - Bananas III*, that commitments are binding on Members only in the sectors and sub-sectors in which they have made commitments.[676] By scheduling its specific commitment in the "Retailing services" sector only, Canada limited its commitment to that sector. It is not for Japan to ignore the sectoral limitations on Canada's commitments in order to hold Canada to an obligation to which it has not specifically agreed to be held.

6.1146 As to the second element, whether the duty-free treatment affects the supply of services, it does not. All of Canada's arguments on this issue in Article II of the GATS are equally relevant here and Canada relies on those arguments. There is nothing new to say that Canada has not already said under Article II.

6.1147 In respect of the third element, Japan has still failed to demonstrate the existence of "like" service suppliers. Japan claims that the difference in the scale of companies and the nature of their products does not affect their likeness as service suppliers. Japan continues to insist against all reason that Intermeccanica, an artisanal manufacturer that neither imports nor distributes vehicles at all, is somehow like Toyota Canada or Honda Canada when it comes to the supply of wholesale distribution trade services.

6.1148 The passage Japan cites from the *EC - Bananas III* Panel Report[677] in support of its contention addresses only whether banana ripening should be considered a part of wholesaling.[678] It has nothing to do with the likeness of service suppliers. Even if Intermeccanica did import vehicles, its complete production run consists of less than 20 hand-built cars each year. Its entire duty-free import entitlement would be approximately what Honda Canada distributes in half-an-hour. Intermeccanica cannot by any measure be considered a like service supplier to the Japanese automotive giants.

6.1149 Japan also relies on its Exhibit JPN-50, for the proposition that the measures discriminate against Japanese suppliers of wholesale trade services in trucks or

[676] Panel Reports on *EC - Bananas III*, *supra* note 269, para. 7.305.

[677] Ibid., *supra* note 269, para. 7.292.

[678] Ibid., paras. 7.287 and 7.293.

buses. Keeping in mind that Article XVII of the GATS concerns national treatment, JPN-50 actually demonstrates that nine of the twelve beneficiaries identified are non-Canadian, and that five of them are European. JPN-50 offers no evidence that Canada accords less favourable treatment to the service suppliers of other Members than it does to its own like service suppliers. On the contrary, JPN-50 helps to explain not only why the European Communities did not make an Article XVII claim but also why it limited its Article II claim to automobiles only. JPN-50 demonstrates that in fact as well as law, non-Canadian and non-US manufacturers do qualify for duty-free treatment under the measures.

VII. QUESTIONS[679] AND REPLIES

A. *Factual Arguments of the Parties*

1. *Questions and Replies Relating to Factual Arguments on the Measures at Issue*

(a) Question 12 (the Ratio Requirement)

The Auto Pact and the MVTO 1998 set the ratio requirement at 75:100 for automobile manufacturers benefiting from the duty waiver. In light of this, could Canada please clarify why an explanation of the "Auto Pact Background", found on an Industry Canada website, says this ratio is 95:100? (See, Exhibit EC-20.)

(i) Reply from Canada

7.1 The minimum allowable ratio requirement is 75:100. The average of the actual ratio requirements for the four MVTO automobile manufacturers is approximately 95:100.

(b) Question 36 (the "Actual" Ratio Requirements for MVTO Automobile Manufacturers)

In its reply to question 12 from the Panel following the first substantive meeting, Canada writes: "The minimum allowable ratio requirement is 75:100. The average of the actual ratio requirements for the four MVTO automobile manufacturing companies is approximately 95:100." Could Canada please clarify what it means by "actual ratio requirements" and indicate in what instrument(s) this average actual ratio requirement for the four MVTO automobile manufacturers can be found.

(i) Reply from Canada

7.2 The "actual ratio requirement" for each MVTO automobile manufacturer was determined on a company-by-company basis for each class of vehicle, and represents the production to sales ratio for that company during the base year (August 1, 1963 through July 31, 1964), as confirmed by audit. Each company was informed of the

679 Unless otherwise indicated, Questions are those put forward by the Panel.

amount it had achieved in the base year. This is the ratio that each company must maintain in order to qualify each year as an MVTO beneficiary.

7.3 The actual amounts for the four automobile manufacturers are confidential information, and cannot be released without the express permission of the companies. The amounts range from a ratio in the low-80s to 100, to a ratio in the high-90s to 100. The average of the four amounts is approximately 95 to 100. There is no statutory instrument setting out the ratio requirement for each company.

(c) Question 37 (SROs - Documents and Beneficiaries)

Memorandum D-10-16-2 (para. 3) indicates that the Appendix listing manufacturers qualifying for the duty waiver by SROs will be updated as required.

- *Does this mean that the list may be expanded, and if so, how? If not, would updates be geared toward eliminating SRO companies?*

(i) Reply from Canada

7.4 The statement does not mean the list may be expanded. It means that the list would be updated if any changes to the list of qualified manufacturers were required. For example, updates would be required to reflect a change in a company's name, or to remove companies that have ceased manufacturing.

- *Does Exhibit EC-6, on the SROs (along with Summary Table of SROs in Exhibit EC-7) contain in their current form all SROs in force? If not, please supply copies of missing ones.*

(ii) Reply from Canada

7.5 The European Communities stated that it has provided evidence concerning all the SROs. However, Exhibit EC-6 does not contain the current form of all the SROs still in force. Exhibit EC-6 was apparently based on Memorandum D-10-16-2. That memorandum lists the SROs for every company still manufacturing, but it does not include companies that are still in existence but no longer manufacturing. The orders for those companies remain in force, and are publicly available, but they are not in use. An order would only be repealed if the company concerned has ceased to exist, for example as a result of bankruptcy.

7.6 Canada notes that the European Communities appears to be taking the position that the orders themselves are the only evidence it needs to file in order to make a prima facie case that the SROs are inconsistent with Canada's WTO obligations. Obviously, Canada disagrees, but given the European position, and the fact that all the orders are publicly available, it was for the European Communities to file copies of every SRO it wanted the Panel to consider. It is now past the deadline set by the Panel for the submission of new evidence, and the European Communities has failed to provide even the most basic elements of proof in respect of the SROs that it has not provided. Nevertheless, given the Panel's request, Canada is collecting all the missing orders, and will provide them no later than the Second Substantive Meeting. Canada submits, however, that these orders should not be considered as part of the record before the Panel.

- *Could Canada please indicate which of the SRO beneficiaries are Canadian owned or controlled.*

(iii) Reply from Canada

7.7 Canada does not have this information readily available. This is because the Government of Canada does not collect this information for the purposes of administering the SROs: the ownership and control of SRO companies are irrelevant to their status under the Auto Pact. However, some of this information may be obtained by conducting searches of the companies' reports filed with provincial securities regulation bodies. Provincial laws require publicly-traded companies to file reports annually regarding ownership and other information. Canada explained to Japan during the consultations that this was the only way this information could be obtained.

7.8 In contrast, privately-owned companies are under no obligation to report any information concerning the ownership of their shares. This information can only be obtained directly from the companies, assuming they are willing to provide it. Private companies that are subsidiaries of publicly-traded companies are an exception to this general rule. Information concerning their ownership can be obtained through the public filings of their parent corporations.

(d) Question 38 (Letters - Comprehensiveness of Exhibits)

Does Exhibit EC-2, which includes letters to the Minister of Industry from General Motors of Canada, Ltd., Ford Motor Co. of Canada, Ltd., Chrysler Canada, Ltd. and American Motors (Canada), Ltd., contain all the letters written in 1965 by vehicle manufacturers to the then Canadian Minister of Industry (which Japan and the EC refer to as "Letters of Undertaking")?

(i) Reply from Canada

7.9 No. For example, Volvo (Canada) Ltd. also supplied a letter.[680]

- *Have these same companies written subsequent letters updating the 1965 ones? If so, please* prov*ide copies.*

(ii) Reply from Canada

7.10 All four companies provided subsequent letters in 1968. These letters do not update the original letters, contain no undertakings of any sort, and are irrelevant. They express the companies' opinions as to how well the system had worked in the first three years, and in some cases make suggestions for future improvements. In view of the Panel's question, Canada has requested permission from the companies to provide them to the Panel.

---

680 Attached as Exhibit CDA-18.

(iii) EC Comments on Exhibits submitted with Canada's Reply

7.11 With reference to Exhibit CDA-22, the European Communities argues that, as already explained by the European Communities, the Letters of Undertaking submitted by the Big Four in 1965 envisaged that the Canadian Government and the beneficiaries would enter into new "discussion" before the end of model year 1968. The Big Four testified to the US Congress that in the course of those "discussions" the Canadian Government requested them to sign further letters of undertaking providing for an additional increase in CVA.

7.12 The Big Four did not accede to those requests. The letters contained in Exhibit CDA - 22 were submitted by the Big Four in place of the letters of undertaking requested by the Canadian Government. The Big Four's reluctance to submit any further undertakings confirms that they did regard the Letters of Undertaking submitted in 1965 as imposing binding requirements upon them, rather than as a mere statement of the "results" they "hoped to achieve"[681]. That distinction is clearly made in the following passage of the letter submitted by Ford Motor Company of Canada, Ltd.:

7.13 "While we are opposed to any further letters of undertaking with respect to production commitments, we do believe that additional increases in our future Canadian production will take place, subject, of course to the normal uncertainties ..."

- *Have other vehicle manufacturers signed letters of this nature as well? If so, please provide copies.*

(iv) Reply from Canada

7.14 No other manufacturers provided updating letters. Other manufacturers did provide original letters. Canada submits these letters are irrelevant, because they are not requirements within the meaning of Article III:4. Nevertheless, Canada will attempt to provide all the letters, because the Panel has asked for them. They are confidential information and cannot be released without the permission of the originating company. Canada has requested such permission. Letters provided will be submitted as confidential information within the meaning of section 3 of the Working Procedures of the *Dispute Settlement Understanding*.

(v) EC Comments on Exhibits submitted with Canada's Reply

7.15 With reference to Exhibit CDA-20, the European Communities argues that with only one exception[682], all the Letters of Undertaking included in this Exhibit are drafted in identical terms. This confirms that, far from being unilateral acts of the beneficiaries, the Letters are little else than an official form filled in by the beneficiaries at the request of the Government.

---

[681] See Canada's response to Question 17 from the Panel.

[682] The remaining Letter (submitted by Kaiser Jeep Canada Ltd) is very similar to the Letters submitted by Canada Chrysler Ltd. and American Motors(Canada) Ltd. (Exhibit EC-2).

7.16 With the same exception, all the Letters were submitted after the conclusion of the Auto Pact in 1965, some of them as a late as in 1984. Nevertheless, all of them continue to refer to the "objectives" of the Auto Pact as the reason for giving the additional CVA commitments. Despite the carefully chosen language, that reference confirms the linkage between the submission of the Letters and the tariff benefits provided for in the Auto Pact.

7.17 It is worth noting that the Letters place the obligation to comply with the additional CVA requirement on the same level as the obligation to comply with the legally binding terms of the MVTO or of the relevant SRO. Thus, by way of example the Letter of Undertaking submitted by Collins Manufacturing Company Ltd. reads as follows in relevant part:

> "... we are pleased to advise that our company *undertakes* to meet the conditions stipulated by Motor Vehicles Tariff Order 1965.
>
> "... our company *also undertakes*: ...
>
> 1. To achieve an increase in Canadian Value Added... " (*italics supplied*)

7.18 It is also worth nothing that, like some of the Letters submitted by the Big Four, all the Letters in this Exhibit include the additional undertaking to:

> "... report to the Minister of Industry, Trade and Commerce such information as the Minister requires pertaining to progress achieved by our company, as well as to report the plans we make to fulfil *our obligations under this letter*." (*emphasis added*)

7.19 Furthermore, the Letters state that the beneficiary:

> "understands that the Government will conduct an audit each year with respect to the matters described in this letter".

(e) Questions 39 (Annual Declarations by Beneficiaries)

Under the MVTO 1998, each model year the beneficiaries must submit, before they make their first importations, a signed declaration to the Minister of National Revenue, in which they undertake for the model year to comply with the CVA and ratio requirements (stipulated in MVTO 1998). Could Canada please indicate whether any of these undertakings in the signed declarations have gone above the production-to-sales ratio and CVA requirements of the MVTO?

(i) Reply from Canada

7.20 Signed declarations do not contain any undertakings. There are no figures contained in the statement, which is in a form of declaration that is prescribed by the MVTO and is identical for all companies. The companies just fill in the blank spaces to identify the company, signing officer, year of importation, etc. The declaration contains only the following statements regarding the production-to-sales ratio and CVA requirements:

> (c) the ratio of the net sales value of the vehicles of that class that are to be produced in Canada by the company to the total net sales value of all vehicles of that class to be sold for consumption in Canada by the company during the period August 1, 19... to July 31, 19.... will be

equal to or higher than the ratio achieved by the company in the base year; and

(d) the vehicles of that class that are to be produced in Canada during the period August 1, 19.... to July 31, 19.... will have a Canadian value added that is equal to or greater than the Canadian value added in respect of all vehicles of that class that were produced by the company in Canada during the base year.

A sample copy of the declaration is attached as Exhibit CDA-19. It can also be found in Exhibit JPN-7 (at page 7-6); an older version is available in Exhibit EC-9, as page 10 of Memorandum D-10-16-3. Other early versions can be found in the earlier versions of this memorandum, which form part of Exhibit CDA-7.

- *Have vehicle manufacturers operating under SROs submitted declarations in which they undertake to go above their respective production-to-sales ratio and CVA requirements?*

(ii) Reply from Canada

7.21 No. There is no requirement in the SROs for manufacturers to submit any declarations, annually or otherwise, and nor do they do so.

7.22 Canada would draw the Panel's attention to paragraph 6 of Memorandum D-10-16-2, which states that companies must file a bond or renewal notice annually, in accordance with the terms of their respective orders. Neither the bond nor the "renewal notice" is a declaration. The bond is a security deposit for duties waived that might have to be collected at the end of the importation period in the event of a failure to meet the legal requirements in the order. Some companies have provided bonds with expiry dates; in those cases, when the bond expires, the company must provide a new bond or send a notice renewing the old one.

(f) Question 40 (Annual Reports by Beneficiaries)

The arguments indicate that departmental memoranda spell out conditions for duty remission and require manufacturer-beneficiaries to submit reports demonstrating compliance with MTVO conditions (and Letters of Undertaking, according to the EC) or their individual SROs, with these reports detailing production costs, output and sales.

Are there relevant departmental memoranda other than D-10-16-3 (concerning the MVTO 1998) and D-10-16-2 (concerning SROs)? If so, please provide copies.

(i) Reply from Canada

7.23 All the relevant memoranda have been filed as exhibits for the Panel. Japan and the European Communities between them have provided the current versions of memoranda D-10-16-2 and D-10-16-3. Canada has provided all previous versions of these memoranda (see Exhibits CAD-7-1, 7-3, 7-4, 7-5). The only other memoranda that deal even indirectly with the MVTO and SROs are D-10-16-1 and D-17-3-1 (Exhibits CDA-7-7 and 7-8).

- *Is it accurate to say that Revenue Canada audits the manufacturers' reports after the close of each model year, and if so, for what purpose?*

(ii) Reply from Canada

7.24 Revenue Canada receives copies of the reports at the conclusion of each model year. It then conducts an audit for the purpose of ensuring that the legal requirements of the MVTO 1998 or the applicable SRO have been satisfied.

7.25 Neither Revenue Canada, nor any other department, conducts an audit or other verification of any figures that may be submitted in respect of the additional letters. Industry Canada has in the past reviewed the figures submitted in respect of the additional letters, but it no longer does so. If a company provides the information, it is simply filed as reported. No other action is taken, regardless of whether the numbers provided indicate that the company has met the letter amounts.

- *Have any of the manufacturers operating under the MVTO indicated in their annual reports that they have gone above the production-to-sales ratio and CVA requirements of the MVTO? If so, do these indications correspond to what had been undertaken in the signed declarations for the relevant time-periods?*

(iii) Reply from Canada

7.26 Respecting the first part of the question, companies in their annual reports state their actually achieved ratio and CVA, without reference to whether the required amounts have been exceeded. (See the sample reporting forms at Exhibit EC-14.) However, as a matter of fact, the MVTO companies generally report figures far in excess of their requirements.

7.27 Respecting the second part of the question, Canada refers the Panel back to Paragraph 1 of Canada's answer to Question 39, and, in particular, to clauses (c) and (d) of the prescribed form of declaration. As is clear from these clauses, the ratio and CVA requirements referred to in the declaration are always the ratio and CVA achieved by the company in the base year. Nothing is undertaken in the declaration; the company only declares its intention to meet its base-year requirements. Contrary to what is implied in the second part of the question, there can never be a difference between the ratio and CVA referred to in a declaration and the ratio and CVA requirements of the MVTO.

- *Have any of the manufacturers operating under the SROs indicated in their annual reports that they have gone above the production-to-sales ratio and CVA requirements of their SROs? If so, do these indications correspond to what had been undertaken in the signed declarations for the relevant time-periods?*

(iv) Reply from Canada

7.28 The answer to the first part of this question is the same as above: companies report just the amounts they have achieved, without reference to the amounts required.

7.29 Respecting the second part of the question, Canada refers the Panel to paragraph 3 of Canada's answer to Question 39, and reiterates that manufacturers covered by SROs are not required to file declarations, annually or on any other basis. The legal ratio and CVA requirements are always specified in the applicable SRO.

(g) Question 41 (Claims - the Measures and Products Concerned)

Could the EC and Japan please clarify the scope of the measures and products concerned thereby of their claims under GATT Article I and GATS Article II.

(i) Reply from Japan

7.30 Throughout its argument, including its claims under GATT Article I and GATS Article II, the Government of Japan has consistently referred to the measures at issue as the "Duty Waiver". Canada implements and applies the Duty Waiver through domestic legislation, regulations, statutory instruments, departmental memoranda and administrative practices. More specifically, Canada implements the Duty Waiver pursuant to: (i) section 115 of the *Customs Tariff* and section 23 of the *Financial Administration Act*; (ii) the *Motor Vehicles Tariff Order, 1998* (MVTO 1998); (iii) letters of undertaking signed by individual manufacturers upon the demand of the Government of Canada; (iv) Special Remission Orders (SROs) providing for the remission of customs duties on motor vehicles imported by specified manufacturers; (v) departmental memoranda relating to the MVTO 1998 and the SROs; and (vi) implementing measures taken thereunder. The Government of Canada also exercises administrative discretion regarding certain aspects of the Duty Waiver. The scope of the products concerned is all products covered by the Duty Waiver.

(ii) Reply from the EC

7.31 The claims submitted by the European Communities under GATT Article I and GATS Article II concern the category of "automobiles", as defined in the MVTO 1998.

7.32 The measures concerned are the Auto Pact, the MVTO 1998 and the SRO issued to CAMI.

7.33 All the other claims submitted by the European Communities concern the three categories of motor vehicles defined in the MVTO 1998 (i.e. "automobiles", "specified commercial vehicles" and "buses").

(h) Question 1 from the EC (SRO Beneficiaries)

Canada has referred to CAMI (twice) as being the only "relevant" SRO beneficiary in connection with claims regarding the CVA requirements raised by the EC under GATT Article III:4 and GATS Article XVII. The EC's Panel request, however, covers all SROs. What is the basis for Canada's assertion that CAMI is the only "relevant" SRO beneficiary in this dispute.

(i) Reply from Canada

7.34 Both Japan and the European Communities raised specific allegations only with respect to the Canadian Big Three and Volvo (Canada) as MVTO beneficiaries, and to the two SRO automobile manufacturers, namely CAMI Automotive Inc. and Intermeccanica. That company was described by the European Communities as, "an artisanal manufacturer of hand-built replicas of famous racing cars." Canada, as the defending party, is not required to rebut the contents of the EC's panel request, but only the evidence presented to the Panel. Accordingly, Canada's rebuttal focuses on the Big Three, Volvo (Canada) and CAMI.

(i) Question 2 from the EC (Auto Pact and Measures at Issue)

Canada has asserted that the Auto Pact is not a "measure". Does that mean that, in Canada's view, the Auto Pact is not a "measure" within the scope of this dispute? If so, why?

(i) Reply from Canada

7.35 Yes, that is exactly what it means. In Canada, treaties are not self-executing. The provisions of a treaty must be implemented in new or existing domestic law in order to be enforceable. Accordingly, the Auto Pact itself is not a Canadian measure. Rather, the measures are the domestic laws, regulations and requirements implementing the Auto Pact; that is, the MVTO 1998 and the various SROs.

(j) Question 3 from the EC (SROs' Relation to the Auto Pact)

Canada has indicated that the only measures in dispute are those that "implement" Canada's obligation under the Auto Pact, i.e. the MVTO 1998 and the SROs. However, the EC understands that the Auto Pact does not require the adoption of SROs, which therefore are purely unilateral measures. Nor does the Auto Pact require the granting of a tariff exemption for imports from third countries. Is the EC's understanding correct?

(i) Reply from Canada

7.36 Paragraph 3 of Annex A to the Auto Pact provides for the issuance of SROs. It states: "The Government of Canada may designate a manufacturer not falling within the categories set out above as being entitled to the benefit of duty-free treatment in respect of the goods described in this Annex.[683]

(k) Question 5 from the EC (CVA and Cost of Sales for U.S. Big Three and Volvo)

Canada's Figure 2 shows that [sic] the total CVA reported by the US Big Three and Volvo as well as the labour CVA of those manufacturers. Could Canada complete that information with the aggregate total cost of sales in Canada of those producers?

---

683 See Exhibit EC-1, JPN-1.

(i) Reply from Canada

7.37 The information is complete as presented. Cost of sales is not relevant to those companies' CVA requirements, which were calculated on the basis of their performance in the 1963-64 base year.

(l) Question 1 from Japan (Canada's Response to Factual Assertions)

In its initial responses, the Government of Canada did not respond in full to the factual assertions made by the Government of Japan and the European Communities. In this connection, the Government of Canada stated as follows:

The fact that Canada does not dispute a particular contention or allegation of Japan or the EC is not to be taken as an admission that any such contention or allegation is accepted as true. Many of the contentions are either irrelevant to this dispute or are bald assertions made without any proof, and are therefore not to be taken into account by the Panel in making its decision. Canada will focus on the main arguments and the matters the Panel needs to have before it in order to arrive at a correct decision.

To the extent that Canada is of the view that a factual assertion is irrelevant to the dispute or is unsupported, it should indicate its views expressly to the Panel. Therefore, the Government of Japan requests the Government of Canada:

- *to identify the factual statements in the initial arguments of Japan and the European Communities that Canada views as being irrelevant to this dispute and explain the nature of the irrelevancy.*
- *to identify the factual statements in such arguments that Canada views as being unsupported, and provide reasons for such views.*
- *to identify the factual statements in such arguments that Canada disagrees with and explain such disagreement and, if necessary, provide rebuttal evidence.*

(i) Reply from Canada

7.38 Japan's question demonstrates a fundamental misunderstanding of the nature of dispute settlement under the DSU. It is well settled in WTO jurisprudence that as complaining parties, Japan and the European Communities must put forward the factual and legal arguments to establish their claims. Only once the complaining parties have presented sufficient evidence to establish a presumption of a WTO violation does the burden shift to Canada as the defending party to rebut the presumptions[684]

7.39 As Canada has made clear, neither Japan nor the European Communities has established a prima facie case of violation of any WTO obligation by Canada. There-

[684] Appellate Body Report on *US - Wool Shirts*, *supra* note 283, pp. 333-338.

fore, the burden has not shifted to Canada to rebut their contentions and Canada is not under any legal burden to provide rebuttal evidence.

7.40 Nevertheless, throughout its argumentation, Canada demonstrated the factual and legal errors of the cases put forward by Japan and the European Communities. It noted where the complainants' allegations were irrelevant or unsupported and provided ample evidence to rebut those claims. Japan need only look at the Canadian arguments for the response to its question.

(m) Question 2(1) from Japan (Purpose of CVA and Ratio Requirements)

The Government of Canada argues that the CVA requirement does not play a substantial role and all the automobile manufacturers operate far in excess of the required production-to-sales ratios. Nevertheless, the Government of Canada still maintains these two requirements. Thus, there must be reasons for maintaining them. What are the reasons and background for setting and maintaining the CVA and manufacturing requirements?

(i) Reply from Canada

7.41 The purpose of setting the CVA requirement and the production-to-sales ratio was to ensure that only qualified manufacturers receive the benefits of duty-free importation.

7.42 The CVA for each manufacturer was calculated for each class of vehicles (automobiles, specified commercial vehicles and buses) in the 1963-1964 base year. CVA levels in subsequent years had to attain this threshold for the manufacturer to continue to qualify for duty-free importation. The amount was expressed as a fixed dollar amount, and has remained constant throughout the operation of the Auto Pact.

7.43 Similarly the production-to-sales ratio was ascertained for the 1963-1964 base year from the net sales value of all vehicles of each class produced in the base year compared to the net sales value of all vehicles of that class sold for consumption. The ratio had to exceed 75 to 100; it had to attain at least that level in subsequent years to permit duty-free importation. The ratios have remained constant for each manufacturer for each class of vehicles.

7.44 Today, these requirements ensure that importers claiming a duty exemption are qualified manufacturers. Such manufacturers receive duty free treatment of im ports from all non-NAFTA countries, including Japan, Korea and EC member states.

(n) Question 2(2) from Japan (Similarity of Letters)

Please explain why (i) the required percentages of the CVA set forth in the respective Letters of Undertaking from the Auto Pact Manufacturers (Exhibit JPN-5) are identical to each other and (ii) the form and substance of such respective Letters of Undertaking are very similar even though the Government of Canada states that the CVA requirements set forth in such letters were set voluntarily by the Auto Pact Manufacturers? Please explain in detail the role of the Government of Canada in drafting or otherwise participating in the preparation of these letters.

(i) Reply from Canada

7.45 Please refer to the answer provided for the Panel's Question 17.

(o) Question 2(3) from Japan (DaimlerChrysler Merger and MVTO Satus)

Please confirm whether the Government of Canada has extended to DaimlerChrysler the privilege to import motor vehicles duty-free in Canada. If so, what are the criteria and requirement for such an extension?

(i) Reply from Canada

7.46 There is no question of extending to DaimlerChrysler the privilege to import vehicles duty-free. The question is whether DaimlerChrysler Canada Inc. will retain its MVTO status after the merger. The Government of Canada has not yet made this decision, which will be effective to the date of the merger.

7.47 The criteria that establish the conditions under which the waiver of customs duties would cease to be granted can be found in the footnote to Annex 1002.1 of the Canada-US FTA.

(p) Question 2(4) from Japan (Beneficiaries Importing Vehicles other than Automobiles)

Please provide the names of the six vehicle manufacturers that currently utilize the MVTO to import vehicles other than automobiles referred to and the names of seven vehicle manufacturers that currently utilise the SROs to import vehicles other than automobiles, respectively.

(i) Reply from Canada

7.48 The following companies have given permission to the Canadian government to state that they have imported vehicles other than automobiles under the MVTO or an SRO at least once in the last 10 years (note that the resulting total exceeds the number previously referred to):

- MVTO: General Motors of Canada Ltd., Ford of Canada Ltd., Chrysler Canada Ltd., Canadian Blue Bird Coach, Ltd., Freightliner Corporation, Thomas Built Buses of Canada Ltd., Prevost Highway Coach Manufacturer, New Flyer.
- SRO: Capital Disposal Equipment Inc., MCI Motorcoach Industries, A. Girardin Inc., Navistar International Corporation, Nova BUS, Western Star Trucks Inc., Les entreprises Michel Corbeil Inc.

(q) Question 2(5) from Japan (Imports under the NAFTA and the MVTO/SROs)

Canada stated that "Eligible manufacturers may import vehicles from outside the NAFTA area duty free." Does this statement mean that eligible manufacturers may import vehicles from the NAFTA area duty free under the Duty Waiver as well? If not, are eligible manufacturers prohibited from importing vehicles from the NAFTA area duty free under the Duty Waiver? If so, what is the legal basis for this prohibition?

(i) Reply from Canada

7.49 Yes, eligible manufacturers may also import vehicles from the NAFTA area duty free. As stated, "Vehicles are entitled to the remission on condition that the goods are imported into Canada on or after January 18, 1965 from any country entitled to the Most-Favoured-Nation Tariff".

(r) Question 8 from the EC (Letters - Verification of Compliance)

Canada has admitted that it reviewed compliance with the Letters of Undertaking until 1996.

- *Could Canada please provide any evidence that compliance is no longer verified?*

(i) Reply from Canada

7.50 Canada cannot provide evidence of what it is not doing. For decades, Canada accepted the numbers provided by the companies, and performed the calculation for growth CVA on that basis, without making any attempt to determine whether the amounts provided were correct. Since model year 1996, Canada has not even made the calculation. If the companies provided information relating to growth CVA, it was simply filed, and no other action was taken.

- *How did Canada collect the necessary information to verify compliance? Did Canada request the Big Three to provide that information? If so, on what legal basis? Has that legal basis been amended or repealed? Could Canada please provide a copy of the requests for information addressed to the Big Three? If no requests for information were addressed, why did the Big Three provide that information?*

(ii) Reply from Canada

7.51 Canada requested the information on an annual basis. There is no legal authority for collecting the information. In contrast, the MVTO - in the Schedule, s. 2(b) - and the SROs provide explicit legal authority for the collection of information relevant to their administration.

- *Have the Canadian authorities informed officially the Big Three that they are no longer monitoring compliance with the Letters of Undertaking? If so, please provide a copy of the relevant document. If not, how do the Big Three know that they are no longer required to provide the necessary information to enforce compliance?*

(iii) Reply from Canada

7.52 Canada has not informed the Big Three in writing that it is no longer calculating whether the letter amounts have been met. The companies have been informed verbally, through the regular formal and informal contacts that occur between government officials and company executives.

- *Did the Big Three report the information required to verify compliance with the Letters of Undertaking at the end of model years 1997 and 1998?*

(iv) Reply from Canada

7.53 Only two of them provided the information.

B. Legal Arguments of the Parties

1. Questions and Replies Relating to Claims ander Article I of the GATT

(a) Question 1 (Test for *De Facto* Discrimination)

Canada states that:

> *GATT and WTO cases demonstrate that to prove a de facto violation of Article I, claimants must prove that a criterion that is neutral on its face is in fact able to be met only by products of a particular origin or origins, such that national origin determines the tariff treatment the product receives. The simple fact is that MVTO and SRO duty remissions have been and are still applied to products from a number of sources, including notably the complaining parties. There is no incentive to source from any particular country.*

Could Japan and the EC please comment on this test of de facto discrimination proposed by Canada.

(i) Reply from Japan

7.54 The Government of Japan has never seen an instance in which a recognition was given to such a test as is described by Canada using the language "GATT and WTO cases demonstrate that to prove a *de facto* violation of Article I, claimants must prove that a criterion that is neutral on its face is in fact able to be met only by products of a particular origin or origins, such that national origin determines the tariff treatment the product receives". Japan is of the view that such a test has never been established in any panel or Appellate Body report, despite the Canadian assertion. If Canada claims that it has been so established, we would like to see such concrete examples.

7.55 To be precise, as Canada mentioned, the Panel Report on *EC - Import of Beef from Canada* case, as referred to in para. 232 of the Appellate Body Report for *EC - Banana III* case, established the following criteria for *de facto* discrimination under Article I of GATT 1994. The Panel found that the EC's measure "had the effect of preventing access of 'like products' from other origin than the United States, thus being inconsistent with most-favoured-nation principle in Article I."

7.56 When judged against this criteria, the Duty Waiver's discriminatory effect is evident as follows.

7.57 The MVTO and SROs are on their face origin neutral as to motor vehicles imported duty-free by Auto Pact Manufacturers. However, as demonstrated in argumentation and confirmed by Exhibit CDA-6, the Duty Waiver has been "in effect" granted largely to products originating in Sweden and Belgium and not so granted to "like" products originating in the territory of Japan. As Canada admitted, Auto Pact Manufacturers have strong tendency to import automobiles from certain specific sources in certain countries. In fact, the evidence on record demonstrates that capital or other business relationships between Auto Pact Manufacturers in Canada and other entities in those countries are decisive in the determination of the countries of origin of duty-free imports, as shown in Exhibits JPN-10 and JPN-11.

7.58 Thus, MVTO and SROs have the effect of preventing duty-free access of like products from other origins than the particular countries and thus they constitute a violation of Article I of GATT 1994.

(ii) Reply from the EC

7.59 The test advanced by Canada is unduly restrictive and would make it virtually impossible to prove the existence of *de facto* discrimination. In order to establish a *de facto* violation of GATT Article I:1 it is not necessary to show that "*only*" imports of a certain origin may benefit from the advantage concerned. Instead, it may be sufficient to show that imports of a certain origin benefit *disproportionately* from that advantage. The relevant test is thus whether the disputed measure results in an allocation of imports among supplying Members which is different from that that would have prevailed in the absence of that measure.

7.60 Contrary to Canada's assertion, previous GATT and WTO cases do not support Canada's very narrow interpretation of the notion of *de facto* discrimination.

7.61 For example, in *Spain - Unroasted Coffee*[685], the Panel ruled that Spain had acted inconsistently with GATT Article I:1 by applying higher import duties on imports of certain varieties of coffee ("unwashed arabica" and "robusta") that on a "like" variety ("mild" coffee). Under the test put forward by Canada, the complainant (Brazil) would have been required to show that no "mild" coffee could be grown in Brazil, so that *de facto* "*only*" imports from other countries could benefit from the lower duty rate. The Panel, however, deemed it sufficient that Brazil exported to Spain "*mainly*" the varieties subject to the higher duty rate:

7.62 "The Panel further noted that Brazil exported to Spain mainly 'unwashed Arabica' and also 'Robusta' coffee which were both presently charged with higher duties than that applied to 'mild' coffee. Since these were considered to be 'like products' the Panel concluded that the tariff regime as presently applied by Spain was discriminatory *vis-à-vis* coffee originating in Brazil".[686]

7.63 Further confirmation is provided by *EC - Bananas III*. In that case, the Panel ruled that the so-called "operator rules" used for allocating a tariff quota among different categories of distributors of bananas violated *de facto* Article II of GATS be-

[685] Panel Report on *Spain - Unroasted Coffee, supra* note 282.

[686] Ibid., para. 4.10.

cause while "*most*" service suppliers of Complainants' origin fell in the less favoured category, "*most*" service suppliers of ACP origin fell within the more favoured category.[687]

7.64 Yet, under the test proposed by Canada, the Panel could not have concluded that there was a *de facto* violation unless it had ascertained previously that "only" service suppliers of ACP origin, to the exclusion of any actual or potential service supplier of any other Member, could ever qualify for the more favoured category.

7.65 More specifically, in *EC - Bananas III* the Panel based its finding that the "operator rules" discriminated *de facto* in favour of ACP suppliers on the fact that foreign suppliers of non-ACP origin accounted for only 10 per cent of the relevant imports.[688] In comparison, imports under the MVTO 1998 and the SROs from countries other than the United States and Mexico account for less than 3 per cent.[689] Thus, if anything, *de facto* discrimination is even more blatant in this case than in *EC - Bananas III*.

7.66 The above mentioned findings of *EC - Bananas III* concerned Article II of GATS and not Article I of GATT. Nevertheless, it is submitted that the test of *de facto* discrimination cannot be different under those two provisions. Indeed, it must be recalled that in *EC - Bananas III* the Appellate Body based its conclusion that Article II of GATS may apply to *de facto* violations precisely on its similarity with GATT Article I:1.[690]

7.67 Further guidance is provided by the Panel Report on *Japan - Film,* where the Panel held that the relevant test in order to determine whether a measure violates *de facto* Article III:4 is whether it has "a disparate impact on imports" compared to domestic products.[691] Once again, there is no reason why the relevant standard of *de facto* discrimination under GATT Article III should be different from that under GATT Article I:1. In fact, the Panel on *Japan - Film* cited expressly past practice under GATT Article I:1 in support of its interpretation of Article III:4.[692]

(b) Question 2 (Test for *De Facto* Discrimination)

Is the complainants' basis for a claim of de facto discrimination that beneficiaries do not include all potential importers of automobiles in Canada? Is it also the complainants' view that there would still be an MFN violation if all potential importers were eligible beneficiaries under the scheme?

---

687 Panel Reports on *EC - Bananas III, supra* note 269, paras. 7.350-7.351. The Panel followed the same reasoning in order to conclude that the "export certificates" and the "hurricane licenses" were also contrary to GATS Article II (ibid., paras. 7.393 and 7.396). These findings of the Panel were expressly upheld by the Appellate Body, Appellate Body Report on *EC - Bananas III, supra* note 49, paras. 243-244 and 248.

688 Panel Reports on *EC - Bananas III, supra* note 269, paras. 7.332-7.334.

689 See EC's Tables 1 and 2.

690 Appellate Body Report on *EC - Bananas III, supra* note 49, paras. 231-232.

691 Panel Report on *Japan - Film, supra* note 93, paras. 10.85-10.86 and 10.380-10.381.

692 Ibid., para. 10.86.

(i) Reply from Japan

7.68 There would be no *de facto* discrimination under GATT Article I if *all* potential importers of motor vehicles may import motor vehicles duty-free without meeting any conditions for the Duty Waiver—i.e. the eligibility restriction, the production-to-sales ratio and the CVA requirement.

7.69 Considering the private companies' trade tendency mentioned in the response above, even if the eligibility will become open to all manufacturers in Canada including Toyota or Honda, the motor vehicles produced by manufacturers in Japan having no manufacturing facilities in Canada such as Nissan, or Fuji Heavy (Subaru) would not enjoy the benefits under the Duty Waiver and thus the mere removal of the eligibility restrictions will not cure the violation of Article I of the GATT.

(ii) Reply from the EC

7.70 Yes. The main beneficiaries of the Tariff Exemption are the Canadian subsidiaries of the US Big Three, all of which have large manufacturing facilities in the USA and Mexico. As a result, the Tariff Exemption provides an advantage to imports from those two countries over imports from those countries where the non-beneficiaries of the Tariff Exemption have their main manufacturing facilities.

7.71 No. If the Tariff Exemption was available under the same conditions to any potential importer, there would be no *de facto* violation of Article I of GATT.

7.72 The European Communities is not arguing that the Tariff Exemption discriminates *de facto* in favour of US and Mexican imports simply because those imports account currently for the majority of imports into Canada. It is very likely that, even in the absence of the Tariff Exemption, imports from Mexico and the USA would still account for a large share of imports into Canada due to the existence of NAFTA as well as to purely commercial factors, such as the closeness of the USA and Mexico to the Canadian market.

7.73 The EC's complaint is that reserving the Tariff Exemption to the Big US Three has the consequence that the share of US and Mexican imports into Canada is even larger than it would be if the Tariff Exemption was available to all importers. As already shown, this is demonstrated by the fact that the share of US and Mexican imports under the Tariff Exemption (97 per cent in 1997) is larger than their share of total imports (80 per cent in the same year).[693]

(c) Question 3 (Foreign Trade Zones, Drawback Programs and End-Use Tariff Classifications)

Canada has stated that "conditions that do not affect the origin from which a good must come are not inconsistent with Article I. Witness the widespread use of foreign trade zones, drawback programs and end-use tariff classifications. All of these result in like products bearing different rates of duty. But the distinctions are without regard to national origin". Could Japan and the EC please comment on these statements.

---

693 EC's Table 2.

(i) Reply from Japan

7.74 As to the three measures referred to by Canada, Japan requested Canada to make clarification by lodging our question previously.

7.75 As far as Japan knows at this point, these measures are clearly distinguishable from the Duty Waiver. Unlike the three measures above, the Duty Waiver is not available to all potential recipients for importing motor vehicles from all potential source countries, because of its eligibility restriction, its other conditions, and the nature of the facts and circumstances within which it is implemented. Such distinctions can be deduced from the questions posed by the Government of Japan.

(ii) Reply from the EC

7.76 The European Communities is not arguing that any condition unrelated to the imported goods is as such contrary to the obligation to provide most favoured national treatment "unconditionally" laid down in GATT Article I:1. As explained above, the EC's claim is that restricting the availability of the Tariff Exemption to certain importers linked to US producers with large manufacturing facilities in the USA and Mexico has the consequence of providing *de facto* an advantage to goods originating in the USA and Mexico over like goods originating in the European Communities.

(d) Question 4 (Private vs. Governmental Action)

The panel in Japan - Measures affecting Consumer Photographic Film and Paper stated that "past GATT cases demonstrate that the fact that an action is taken by private parties does not rule out the possibility that it may be deemed to be governmental if there is sufficient government involvement with it" and that this "possibility will need to be examined on a case-by-case basis" (WT/DS44/R, para. 10.56). The panel also stated that the words "laws, regulations and requirements" in Article III:4 "should be interpreted as encompassing a [similarly] broad range of government action and action by private parties that may be assimilated to government action" (Ibid., para. 10.376). Could all parties please comment on this statement.

(i) Reply from Japan

7.77 In *Japan - Film*, the main issue was whether or not a governmental measure *existed*. However, the measures at issue are clearly and indisputably governmental measures (i.e. the MVTO 1998, the SROs). Although production and trade actions taken by motor vehicle manufacturers/importers are private ones, those government measures affecting those private actions bring about GATT Article I violation.

7.78 Assuming that the Panel had the letters of undertaking on its mind when posing this question, it is the position of the Government of Japan that such letters are clearly "requirement" within the meaning of Article III:4 of the GATT 1994.

(ii) Reply from the EC

7.79 As noted in the first of the passages of the Panel Report on *Japan - Film*[694] quoted by the Panel, it is now well established that formally "private" action may nevertheless be deemed Governmental action subject to dispute settlement, provided that there is sufficient involvement of the Government in it.

7.80 In the present case, for the reasons already explained by the European Communities, Canada's position that the Letters of Undertaking are purely "private acts" of the Auto Pact beneficiaries is clearly untenable. The submission of the Letters of Undertaking was requested by the Canadian Government as a condition *sine qua non* for signing the Auto Pact. Further, the content of the Letters was the subject of negotiations between each beneficiary and Canada's Ministry of Industry. Moreover, the Canadian Government collects on a regular basis the necessary statistical information to ascertain compliance with the Letters of Undertaking and there is evidence that it does so in practice.

7.81 The Panel Report on *Japan - Film*[695], as well as the previous Panel Reports on *Japan - Semiconductors*[696] and *Japan - Agricultural Products*[697], also stand for the proposition that non-binding "measures", such as Government recommendations or administrative guidance, may constitute a "measure" subject to dispute settlement.

7.82 In *Japan - Film*, the Panel discussed the issue of whether the words "laws, regulations and requirements" used in GATT Article III:4 have the same scope as the term "measure" in GATT Article XXIII: 1(b) or in GATT Article XI, but did not consider it necessary to reach a conclusion.[698]

7.83 According to the complainant in that dispute, the United States, the terms "laws, regulations and requirements" would reflect the drafters' intention to cover "all" possible forms of governmental action.[699] In turn, the defendant, Japan, maintained that for a party to be subject to a government "requirement",

> "it must either (i) be legally obligated to carry out the request, or (ii) receive some advantage from the government in exchange for compliance. In other words, there must be either a government sanction or the withholding of a government benefit that is attached, formally or substantively, to non-compliance." [700]

---

694 Panel Report on *Japan - Film, supra* note 93, para. 10.56.

695 According to the Panel Report on *Japan - Film, supra* note 93, para. 10.49: "...Moreover, we also consider it conceivable ... that even non-binding, hortatory wording in a government statement of policy could have a similar effect on private actors to a legally binding measure...".

696 See Panel Report on *Japan - Semiconductors, supra* note 112, para. 117: "The Panel considered that the complex of measures exhibited the rationale as well as the essential elements of a formal system of export control. The only distinction in this case was the absence of formal legal legally binding obligations... However, the Panel concluded that this amounted to a difference in form rather than substance because the measures were operated in a manner equivalent to mandatory requirements...".

697 Panel Report on *Japan - Restrictions on Imports of Certain Agricultural Products*, adopted on 21 August 1991, BISD 35S/163, 242.

698 Panel Report on *Japan - Film, supra* note 93, para. 10.376.

699 Ibid., para. 10.375.

700 Ibid.

7.84 The European Communities agrees with the view expressed by the United States. Japan's position was based on the textual differences between GATT Article III:4, on the one hand, and GATT Articles XI and XXIII (b), on the other hand. That argument, however, is far from compelling. The national treatment obligation contained in Article III:4 complements the prohibition on import restrictions contained in Article XI.[701] It would be absurd if non-binding border measures that restrict imports were prohibited by Article XI, but then non-binding internal measures that discriminate against imported products were permitted by Article III:4.

7.85 In any event, the Letters of Undertaking would qualify as "requirements" even if Japan's narrower interpretation of that term was adopted. As already explained, unlike the measures at issue in *Japan - Film*, which were often purely hortatory statements, the Letters of Undertaking are worded in unequivocally mandatory language and purport to impose binding obligations upon the beneficiaries. Furthermore, to use Japan's words, there is a sanction attached "substantively", if not "formally", to non-compliance: the withdrawal of the Tariff Exemption.

(iii) Reply from Canada

7.86 The Panel in *Japan -Film* examined whether certain actions were "measures" in the sense of Article XXIII:1(b), and considered whether they were also "laws, regulations and requirements" in the sense of Article III:4. That analysis offers little assistance to the Panel in this case. The analysis of "measure" was related to a very particular set of facts not present here. The discussion of "laws, regulations and requirements" was predicated on an assumption for the purposes of analysis and does not reflect a finding that the phrase should be interpreted as encompassing private action.

7.87 The Panel's analysis of the word "measure" centered on considerations particular to the country whose "measure" was under review. The Panel noted:

> In Japan, it is accepted that the government sometimes acts through what is referred to as administrative guidance. In such a case, the company receiving guidance from the Government of Japan may not be legally bound to act in accordance with it, but compliance may be expected in light of the power of the government and a system of government incentives and disincentives arising from the wide array of government activities and involvement in the Japanese economy.[702]

7.88 The Panel also noted that another Panel Report had concluded that Japanese administrative guidance was a "measure" because it emanated from the government

---

[701] As noted by the Panel Report on *Italian Agricultural Machinery, supra* note 390, para. 11: "... the intention of the drafters of the Agreement was clearly to treat the imported products in the same way as the like domestic products once they had been cleared through customs. Otherwise indirect protection could be given".

Similarly, the Panel Report on *US - Petroleum, supra* note 73, noted, para. 5.2.2: "... The general prohibition of quantitative restrictions under Article XI... and the national treatment obligation of Article III... have essentially the same rationale, namely to protect expectations of the contracting parties as to the competitive relationship between their products and those of the other contracting parties...".

[702] Panel Report on *Japan - Film, supra* note 93, para. 10.44.

and was effective in the Japanese context. The Panel therefore found that its own analysis would have to be sensitive to the context in which government actions are taken, and the effect they have on private actors.[703]

7.89 The Panel then concluded that the definition of "measure" must be a broad one, including government actions that are non-binding on their face, provided they have effects similar to binding ones, such as sufficient incentive or disincentive to cause parties to act in a particular manner. Here again, the conclusion was premised on the Japanese context of the measures at issue. The Panel referred specifically to situations in which there is a high degree of collaboration between government and industry, as exists in Japan. The Panel stated that in such instances, even hortatory wording could have effects similar to binding measures.[704]

7.90 The Canadian regulatory system is quite different from that of Japan. The concept of "administrative guidance" that was central to the Panel's definition of "measure" does not exist. Canada governs through a system of laws and regulations that impose definite obligations and provide specific consequences for failure to comply. A non-binding act will not have the same consequences as it would in Japan. These factors should be taken into account in deciding what is or is not a "measure" in this case.

7.91 The Panel then turned to the question of whether private acts could be deemed to be governmental. The Panel noted previous decisions in which private acts were found to be "measures". The Panel cited, *inter alia*, *Japan - Trade in Semiconductors*[705], in which the Panel found that apparently private acts had been taken in an administrative structure that exerted "maximum possible pressure" to influence private decisions. This system had the same "rationale as well as the essential elements of a formal system".[706] The Panel therefore concluded that private acts could be deemed to be governmental where there was sufficient government involvement.

7.92 Whether any given private act can be attributed to the government is therefore a question of fact, to be determined by the degree of government involvement in the act at issue. As the Panel in *Japan - Film* noted, this question must be answered on a case-by-case basis.[707] Canada would emphasize the differences between the Canadian and Japanese administrative systems; in Canada, there is no general administrative system exerting "maximum possible pressure" on private actions. The Canadian government does not have the sort of pervasive influence on private decisions that was present in the cases where private acts were attributed to governments - the government must take direct action through a law or regulation. Canada therefore submits that the additional letters, as private actions, cannot be "measures" in the Canadian context. They are not statutes or regulations, are non-binding, and cannot be enforced.

7.93 Even if the Panel were to decide that the letters are measures, there remains the question of whether they are "laws, regulations and requirements" within the meaning of Article III:4. The Panel in *Japan - Film* made no findings on the inter-

[703] Ibid., para. 10.46.

[704] Ibid., para. 10.49.

[705] Panel Report on *Japan - Semiconductors, supra* note 112.

[706] Panel Report on *Japan - Film, supra* note 93, para. 10.54.

[707] Ibid., para. 10.56.

pretation of this phrase. It concluded that none of the alleged measures violated GATT Article III:4. It could thus assume that all the actions at issue were "laws, regulations and requirements", without actually deciding the point. The Panel said explicitly that for the purposes of argument, it would treat *every* action at issue as a requirement, including those it had already found were not even "measures".[708] To conclude that the Panel was deciding that any of these "measures" were in fact requirements would be a serious misinterpretation of the Panel's decision.

(e) Question 5 (Criteria for Advantage)

Japan has stated, inter alia, that "it is clear from Article I that the granting of any advantage cannot be made conditional on any criteria not related to the imported product itself. This is embodied in the words 'immediately and unconditionally' and has been verified in the Indonesia - Autos Panel Report (paras.14.144-14.147)". ... "Applying the foregoing legal interpretation to the facts of this case, the advantage of the Duty Waiver has been made conditional on an eligibility restriction and on the fulfilment of Canadian content and manufacturing requirements. None of these criteria are related to the imported motor vehicles themselves. Accordingly, Canada is not granting unconditional MFN treatment to motor vehicles originating in the territories of all WTO Members in its application of the Duty Waiver" (emphasis added). Could Canada please comment on these statements.

(i) Reply from Canada

7.94 Japan has misinterpreted the meaning of "unconditionally" in Article I. Canada addressed this point in its argumentation. There is no prohibition in Article I of origin-neutral terms and conditions on importation that apply to the *importers* as opposed to the *products* being imported. Article I prohibits only conditions related to the national origin of the imported product.

7.95 Japan's argument is based on a single passage in a single, unappealed, WTO case: *Indonesia -Autos.*[709] The Panel was examining Indonesian measures under which "Pioneer companies" could import parts and components duty free. Only one company qualified as an importer. It could import duty free under three conditions. First, parts and components had to be used in the assembly of a "National Car" (of which there was only one). Second, they had to be imported by Pioneer companies (of which there was only one) producing National Cars. Third, the company had to meet a local content requirement.[710]

7.96 Japan has argued from this that the limitation on the identity of importers, and the CVA and ratio requirements are "conditions" within the meaning of Article I. Thus Japan argues that the tariff treatment of vehicles in Canada is "conditional" upon the manufacturer being on a list of companies operating under the MVTO or an SRO, and upon that importer meeting its CVA and ratio requirements.

7.97 This cannot be what the Panel meant, since it has no basis in GATT jurisprudence. Not the least of its problems is the fact that it would read Article II out of the

708 Ibid., paras. 10.376 and 10.377.

709 Panel Report on *Indonesia - Autos, supra* note 270.

710 Ibid., para. 14.146.

GATT. That Article specifically contemplates tariff bindings being subject to "terms, *conditions* or qualifications". In any event, Article I prohibits only treatment that discriminates on the basis of nationality. Thus, as Canada made clear in its initial response:

> "[T]he proper test of whether the imposition of a condition or criterion infringes Article I is whether that condition or criterion is both a) insufficient to afford a basis to distinguish the products as not "like", *and* b) of a nature that results in discriminatory import treatment on the basis of the national origin of the product."

7.98 Article I simply does not apply to origin-neutral conditions on importation, including tariff rate quotas, end-use tariff distinctions or foreign trade zone programmes.

7.99 In Canada's view the Panel in *Indonesia - Autos* did not intend its analysis to be given the broad reading offered by Japan. It quite properly found that Indonesia's measures were *de facto* violations of Article I, because only Korean products were in fact capable of meeting the conditions imposed by Indonesia. The Panel therefore found that the Indonesian measures, in their application, amounted to differential treatment on the basis of national origin.

7.100 In summary, all three Indonesian conditions, in spite of their apparent neutrality, were inconsistent with the requirement of Article I:1 that an "advantage, favour or privilege" be accorded "unconditionally". In practice they determined the national origin of the products that could be imported duty free, and as such violated Article I. There is no such condition in any of Canada's impugned automotive measures, and hence no violation of Article I.

(f) Question 6 (Eligibility Restriction and *De Facto* Discrimination)

Japan has stated that "the fact that the eligibility restriction de facto excludes certain motor vehicles from certain countries from benefiting from the Duty Waiver amounts to a violation of the MFN obligation in GATT Article I". Could Canada please comment on this statement.

(i) Reply from Canada

7.101 Japan's statement is false: the MVTO and the SROs do not exclude motor vehicles of any national origin, whether *de facto* or *de jure*. Manufacturers are free to import vehicles of any national origin; the evidence led by Japan itself in Japan's Table 6 proves that MVTO and SRO beneficiaries import vehicles of many national origins, including Japan and member states of the EC.

(g) Question 7 (Criteria for SRO Status)

Japan has stated that: "The criteria for determining initial eligibility for SRO status were uncertain and arbitrary as the Government of Canada reserved the right under the Canada - US Auto Pact to designate manufacturers as entitled to the Duty waiver and there is no mentioning of the criteria that might be applied for such designations." Could Canada please comment on this statement, and also explain the criteria that were used for granting SROs.

(i) Reply from Canada

7.102 The criteria for determining initial eligibility for SRO status were neither uncertain nor arbitrary. Vehicle manufacturers not in operation during the base year (August 1, 1963 to July 31, 1964) only had to request the issuance of an SRO. The request could be made verbally or in writing to the responsible officials in the Department of Industry.

7.103 The Canadian government would determine whether the company in question was capable of matching the CVA and ratio performance of the MVTO companies. If so, the order was granted. It would then be duly passed, following the same procedures as would be used for any other Canadian regulation.

(h) Question 8 (Measures at Issue and Applicability of GATT Article XXIV)

The EC has stated that "the measures in dispute are neither part of, nor required by NAFTA, but rather a derogation from that agreement. Accordingly, they cannot be 'exempted' from Article I by virtue of Article XXIV". Could Canada please comment on these statements.

(i) Reply from Canada

7.104 The EC's statement is incorrect. The measures are not, and cannot be, a derogation from the NAFTA. Annex 300-A of the NAFTA specifically provides both for the continuation of the Auto Pact and for the maintenance by Canada of its duty-free treatment pursuant to the Auto Pact.

7.105 Even if the NAFTA did not so provide, Article XXIV of the GATT exempts from Article I the provision of duty-free treatment to products of members of a free-trade area. Nothing in Article I states that preferential duty-free treatment is only exempt from Article I to the extent that it is "part of" or "required by" the principal agreement establishing a free-trade area. For example, parties to an interim free-trade agreement (or customs union) often accelerate the elimination of duties among themselves. Nothing in Article XXIV would preclude the parties from accelerating duty-free treatment through a separate agreement or even unilaterally, even though they are not "required" to do so by the principal agreement.

(i) Question 9 (Measures at Issue and Applicability of GATT Article XXIV)

The EC has stated that "Article XXIV:5 does not provide a legal basis for adopting all sorts of measures otherwise incompatible with Article I. That provision merely authorises the 'formation of a free-trade *area'. Consequently, only those measures that are inherent in that objective can be exempted by Article XXIV". Could Canada please comment on these statements.*

(i) Reply from Canada

7.106 Canada has not claimed an Article XXIV exemption for "all sorts of measures". Canada has raised Article XXIV in response to the EC's complaint that Canada has accorded its duty-free treatment on a basis inconsistent with Article I of the GATT because most of the vehicles that receive duty-free treatment originate in the

United States or Mexico. Canada has noted that a party to a free-trade agreement, or an interim agreement for the formation of a free-trade area, is exempt from Article I by reason of Article XXIV when it grants duty-free treatment to the products of other parties to the free-trade agreement. This is what Canada has done with respect to products from the United States and Mexico.

7.107 The Panel does not need to define the legal limits of the Article XXIV exception, nor to devise tests such as what measures are "inherent" in the objective of a free-trade area. Whatever else may be exempted by Article XXIV, and whatever else may be "inherent" in the objective of a free-trade area, duty-free treatment clearly is.

(j) Question 10 (U.S. Big Three vs. Foreign Producers and Other Manufacturers in the United States)

Could Canada please comment on the EC's statement that the "only and exclusive purpose [of the measures in dispute] is to provide an advantage to the US Big Three, not only vis-à-vis the foreign producers of motor vehicles but also vis-à-vis other manufacturers established in the United States". (emphasis added)

(i) Reply from Canada

7.108 The European Communities seeks to substantiate its claim that the measures do not fall within the NAFTA. In fact they do, as Canada explained in its response to question 9.

7.109 The EC's particular complaint identified by the Panel in paragraph 18 is rather obscure. One of the original beneficiaries of the measures was the Canadian subsidiary of an EC manufacturer, Volvo. Moreover, the status of manufacturers in the United States is irrelevant to this dispute. The measures accord duty-free treatment to qualifying manufacturers in Canada. They have no bearing on the ability of manufacturers established in the United States to import vehicles from Canada, and vehicles produced in the United States by all manufacturers may enter Canada duty free, whether under the Auto Pact or the NAFTA.

(k) Question 11 (CVA and Ratio Requirements and Article XXIV:8(b))

In view of Canada's contention that any preferential treatment of products of the United States and Mexico is justifiable under GATT Article XXIV, could Canada please clarify how it regards the CVA and ratio requirements found in the Auto Pact, given that Article XXIV:8(b) provides: "A free-trade area shall be understood to mean a group of two or more customs territories in which the duties and other restrictive regulations of commerce ... are eliminated on substantially all the trade between the constituent territories in products originating in such territories". (emphasis added)

(i) Reply from Canada

7.110 The CVA and ratio requirements are not restrictive regulations of commerce within the meaning of Article XXIV:8. They are the eligibility requirements contained in the MVTO and SRO definition of "manufacturer", existing to ensure that beneficiaries actually manufacture in Canada. They do not in any way restrict commerce between Canada, the United States or Mexico, and thus do not disqualify the North American free-trade area from the definition in Article XXIV:8(b).

7.111 In any event, the question as to whether the CVA and ratio requirements are restrictive regulations of commerce is moot. Anybody meeting the NAFTA certification of origin can import any vehicle from the United States and Mexico under the NAFTA, without regard to the CVA and ratio requirements. These requirements apply only to imports made under the MVTO or an SRO. This can be clearly seen in the case of the American manufacturing arms of Toyota and Honda. Vehicles built by these companies enter Canada duty-free under the NAFTA without regard to the CVA and ratio requirements. The same is true of vehicles imported by MVTO or SRO companies. If the vehicles are certified as NAFTA-originating, they can enter Canada from the United States duty-free, irrespective of the CVA and ratio requirements.

(l) Question 42 (Canada's *Figure 4* - Imports under the MVTO and SROs)

Could Canada please supplement the import data shown in Canada's original Figure 4 with data for imports receiving duty-free treatment under (i) the MVTO or SROs from the United States and Mexico, and (ii) imports coming in under NAFTA by meeting NAFTA rules of origin. (Please distinguish the data by these two groups.)

(i) Reply from Canada

7.112 The information provided in *Figure 4* was intended to respond to Japan's claims regarding discrimination in favour of Belgian and Swedish manufacturers as depicted in Japan's Table 5. The data used to produce *Figure 4*, which shows that Japanese-origin vehicles represent a significant percentage of import sales, were purchased from the same source that Japan used to create its Table 5. Both Table 5 and *Figure 4* show sales of imported vehicles by *units*. The company that provided the data does not separate sales of North American origin. Canadian, American and Mexican sales are provided as a single number representing domestic sales, and Canada cannot separate the data. Canada has not been able to obtain sales data for US and Mexican vehicles from any other source. Therefore, as an alternative, Canada is providing the information based on *value* of imports. *Figure 5* (below) shows the percentage of MVTO imports originating in North America, Japan, Europe, and the rest of the world. The actual values of these imports are provided in Exhibit CDA-25.

Canada's Figure 5

Figure 5 - Imports Under MVTO and SROs
(Percentage of Vehicles Imported by Origin, Based on Value)

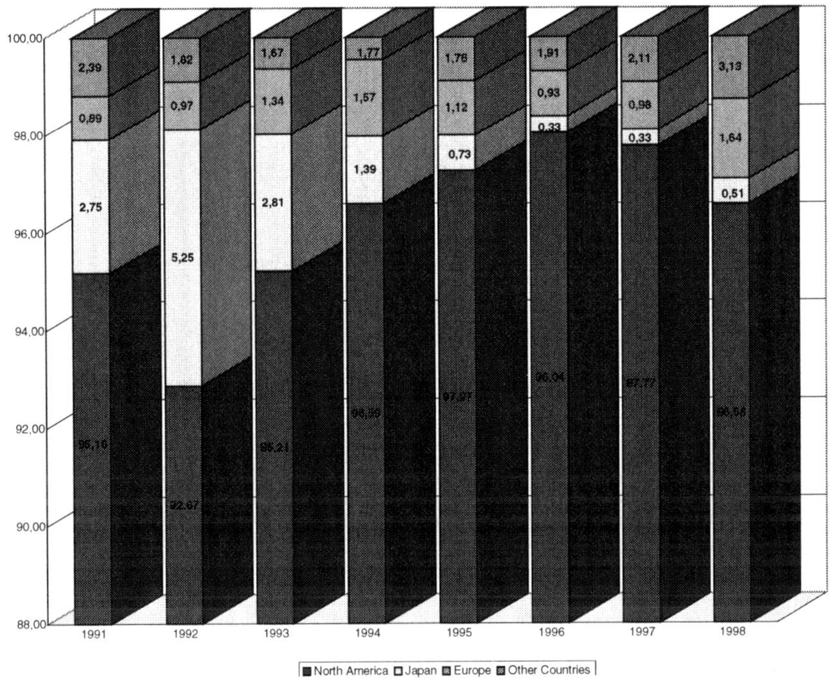

7.113 NAFTA came into effect on 1 January 1994. Canada does not have records of sales of NAFTA imports - again, sales statistics available to the Canadian government treat all North American vehicles as domestic. As an alternative, Canada is providing the information based on *value* of NAFTA imports for each year since 1994. The following numbers represent the total value of all vehicles imported under the NAFTA, without regard to the identity of the importer:

1994: $431,736,609
1995: $557,865,152
1996: $697,478,247
1997: $845,203,530
1998: $1,655,496,286

7.114 The European Communities requested that Canada provide NAFTA certificates for the vehicles imported from the United States in 1998. The 1998 certificates for Chrysler Corporation are attached. Also attached are the 1998 and 1999 certificates for the Ford Motor Company. Canada does not have 1998 certificates for General Motors Corp., but it does have them for 1999. It should be noted, however, that General Motors of Canada Ltd. did not import any models in 1998 that it did not also import in 1999. Those models were produced in the same factories in both years. The Certificates are attached as Exhibit CDA-26.

7.115 The companies obtained certificates because they are necessary for vehicles entering the United States and Mexico. They were provided to Canada for information purposes to confirm their ability to meet NAFTA rules of origin requirements. Canada understands that the companies also provide certificates to major customers buying large numbers of vehicles, some of whom want confirmation that they are purchasing North American vehicles.

7.116 The companies continued to import North American vehicles under the MVTO because that is the practice they have been following since 1965. As 1998 was the first year that duty-free importation from the United States under the NAFTA was possible, some had not completely adjusted their administrative practices to the new regime.

(m) Question 43 (Data on Cost of Sales)

Could Canada please supplement the data shown in Exhibit CDA-2 by indicating the aggregate cost of sales each year for each of the producers listed.

(i) Reply from Canada

7.117 Exhibit CDA-27 shows the aggregate cost of sales data for each model year since 1963-64 for General Motors of Canada Ltd., Ford of Canada Ltd., Chrysler Canada Ltd., (as it then was) and Volvo (Canada) Ltd. *Figures 6* and *7* contrast the differing CVAs applicable to the MVTO, SROs, and letters. *Figure 7* demonstrates how the cost of sales number would be used to calculate the growth amounts specified in the letters. The cost of sales from the base year would be subtracted from the cost of sales in each subsequent model year. The resulting amount would then be multiplied by 60 per cent (in the case of the Big Three) or 40 per cent (in the case of Volvo (Canada) Ltd.). The result of this calculation would then be added to the base year requirement, producing the growth amount for the particular company.

Canada's Figure 6

Figure 6 - How Does the Canadian-Value-Added (CVA) Requirement Work for Automobile Manufacturers

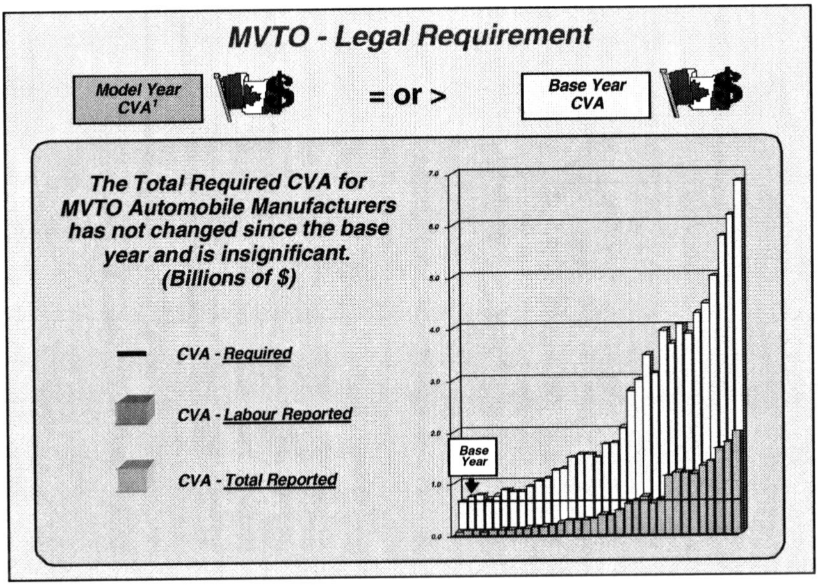

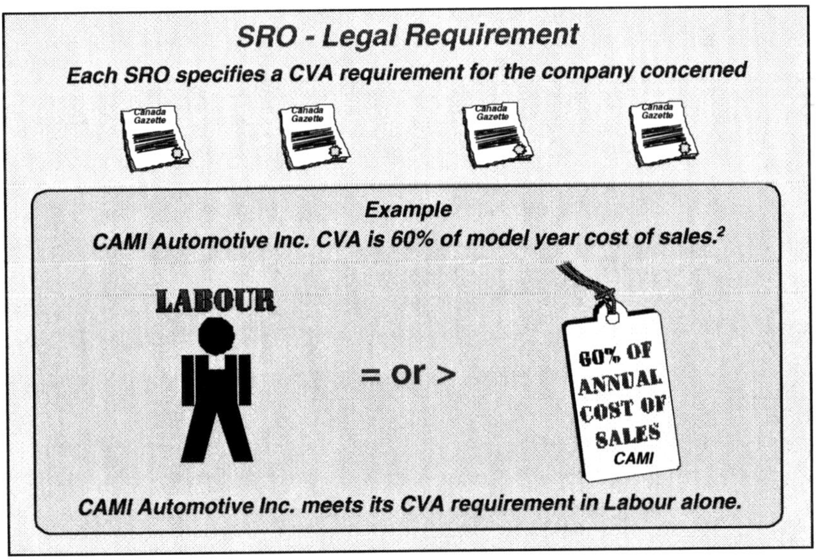

1 *Model Year = August 1 - July 31*

2 *Cost of Sales = Cost of Production for Automobiles Produced in Canada and Sold for Consumption in Canada + Cost of Automobiles Imported for Consumption in Canada (based on Value for Duty)*

Canada's Figure 7

Figure 7 - The Canadian-Value-Added (CVA) Amount in the Letters

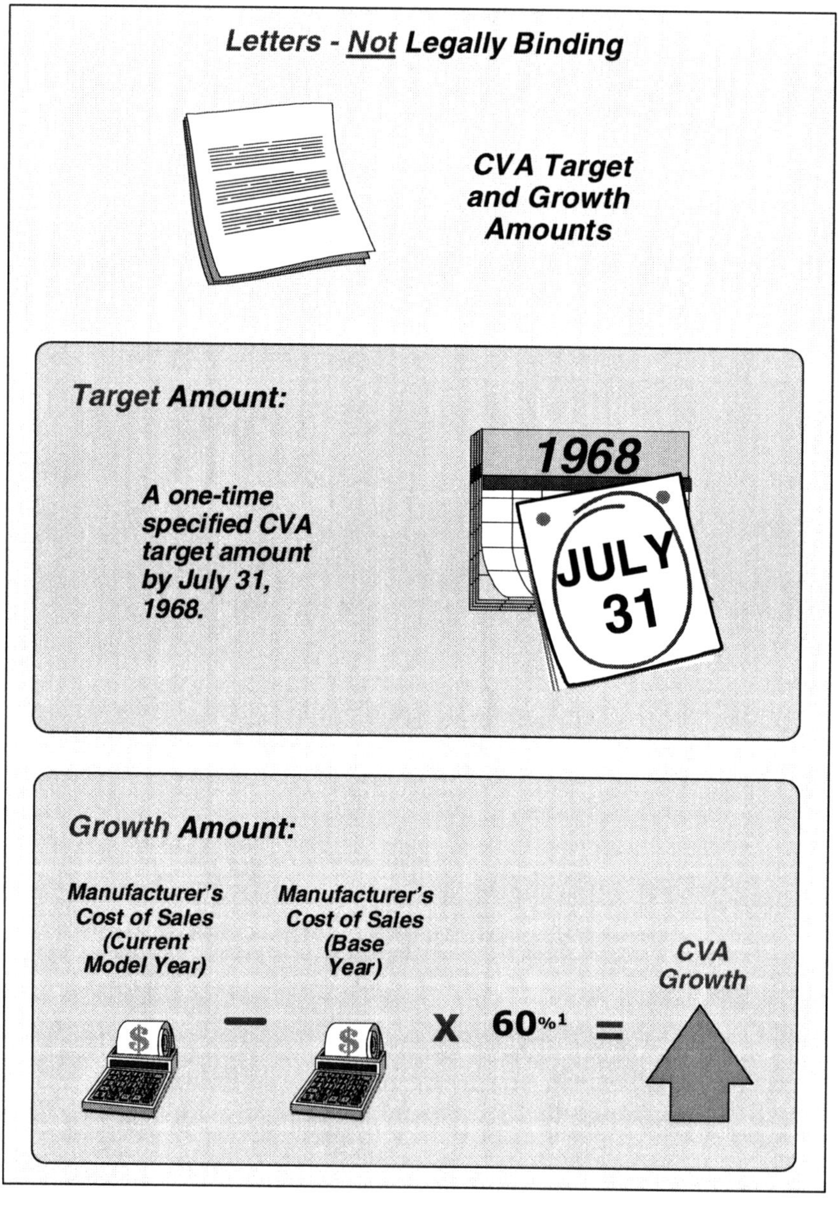

1 The amount for the Big Three is 60%. The amount for Volvo (Canada) Ltd. is 40%.

7.118 Note that the calculation in some letters refers to subtracting the cost of sales of the previous year, rather than the base year. In practice, however, when calculations were performed, they were done always using the base year.

(n) Question 44 (Imports and Companies' Capital Relationships)

Could Canada please comment on Japan's statement that "[e]ach qualified manufacturer in fact imports vehicles only from countries where its parent company, or a company with which it has a capital relationship, has production facilities."

(i) Reply from Canada

7.119 In practice, Canada understands that it is characteristic of the globalized automotive industry that there be some sort of capital, manufacturing or similar relationship between the automobile manufacturers and companies from whom they import. This appears to be true not only of the qualified manufacturers but also of Japanese and EC manufacturers. Certainly, neither of the complainants has offered any evidence to the contrary.

7.120 Canada notes that, at least in Canada, this practice is the choice of the companies, and is in no sense required by Canadian measures. Nothing in the Canadian measures requires or induces such relationships as a condition of importation, nor do Canadian measures limit the choice of relationships on the part of the companies. Under the Canadian measures, the qualified manufacturers are entitled to source vehicles from wherever they choose regardless of any relationships. When companies do choose to enter into relationships, they are free to establish such relationships without limitation as to company or country.

7.121 The breadth of these private choices demonstrates the globalization of the automotive industry. The affiliations of manufacturers extend to virtually all significant producing countries. For example, according to information provided by the Big Three, those companies alone currently have vehicle manufacturing affiliations involving at least 24 separate countries, including Japan, France, Germany, Portugal, Sweden and the United Kingdom. Canada refers the Panel to its response to the complainants' rebuttals, where, in responding to Japan's Article I allegation, Canada lists all of these 24 countries. Canada also refers the Panel to its Exhibit CDA-12, in which Canada has provided a complete list of global automotive affiliations for 1999.

7.122 Again, these are private decisions. Canadian measures do not require such a wide geographic spread of company relationships, nor do Canadian measures in any way limit manufacturers from expanding their relationships to other companies or countries. Canada points out that, independent of any requirements of Article I, it is evident that the companies' choices have resulted in a wide geographic sweep of relationships and of imports.

(o) Questions 45 (MFN Import Duty Rates on Motor Vehicles since 1965)

Could Canada please provide figures showing the applicable Canadian MFN import duty rates on motor vehicles since 1965, including any evolution in these rates.

(i) Reply from Canada

Canada's MFN Tariff on Motor Vehicles Since 1963

EFFECTIVE DATE	BOUND RATE
April 1, 1963	17.5%
June 1, 1969	15.0%
January 1, 1980	14.3% (Tokyo Round Reductions Commence)
January 1, 1981	13.6%
January 1, 1982	12.8%
January 1, 1983	12.1%
January 1, 1984	11.4%
January 1, 1985	10.7%
January 1, 1986	9.9%
January 1, 1987	9.2%
January 1, 1995	8.6% (Uruguay Round Reductions Commence)
January 1, 1996	8.0%
January 1, 1997	7.3%
January 1, 1998	6.7%
January 1, 1999	6.1%

(p) Question 2(6) from Japan (Foreign Trade Zones, Drawback Programs and End-Use Tariff Classification)

Canada has referred to foreign trade zones, drawback programs and end-use tariff classification. Japan does not understand the relevance of these measures to this present case.

- *Under Canada's own analogy between the Auto Pact and foreign trade zones, must the Auto Pact Manufacturers pay the customs duty exempted at the border under the Duty Waiver on the imported vehicles when they sell those vehicles to any person within Canada? Can Canada provide the definition of the foreign trade zone and an example in which the Auto Pact is administered in such a manner?*
- *Under Canada's own analogy between the Auto Pact and drawback programs, must the Auto Pact manufacturers re-export the vehicles imported duty free under the Duty Waiver to any other country in order to enjoy the benefit of the duty drawback? Can Canada provide the definition and an example in which the Auto Pact is administered in such a manner?*
- *Under Canada's own analogy between the Auto Pact and end-use tariff classification, must the vehicles imported duty free under the Duty Waiver be used in any product other than the imported vehicle itself? Can Canada provide the definition of the end-use tariff classification and an example in which the Auto Pact is administered in such a manner?*

- *Under each of the respective schemes described above, is it supposed that importers must be qualified to enjoy the duty exemption? If so, what are the conditions for the qualification or eligibility?*

(i) Reply from Canada

7.123 Japan has misunderstood Canada's argument. Canada did not at any time claim the MVTO and SROs are themselves foreign-trade-zone programmes, duty drawback programmes, or end-use tariff classifications. Canada was responding to Japan's argument that *any* condition on importation that is not related to the product itself must be a violation of Article I. This argument is wrong, as demonstrated by the existence of numerous programmes that create conditions on importation that are not related to the product itself.

7.124 Foreign-trade-zone programmes require products to be imported by particular importers, for a particular use. Duty drawback programmes require products to be incorporated into finished products and re-exported. End-use classifications require products to be put to a particular use. Each of these is plainly a *condition* on importation, unrelated to the products themselves. Each is permitted.

7.125 The mere fact that the MVTO and SROs set conditions for importation does not in and of itself determine whether those measures violate Article I. That Article does not prevent the imposition of terms and conditions on importation. It does not prevent Members from limiting the number of eligible importers, or from setting eligibility criteria for those importers. If it did, all import licensing schemes would be prohibited. Article I only prevents the granting of an advantage to the products of one country without immediately and unconditionally extending that advantage to the products of all Members.

(q) Question 4 from the EC (Canada's *Figure 4* - Imports under the MVTO and SROs)

Canada's Figure 4 appears not to show the imports under the MVTO 1998 and SROs originating in the USA and Mexico. Also, the percentages shown in that figure do not appear to take into account those imports. Could Canada explain that apparent omission? Does it mean that since 1991 all imports from the US and Mexico were made under the CUSFTA/NAFTA? Could Canada indicate what would be the relevant percentages if US and Mexican imports made under the MVTO 1998 and the SROs are taken into account?

(i) Reply from Canada

7.126 There was no omission. Canada prepared Figure 4 on the basis of the list of countries in Japan's Table 6. The supporting data for the figure is found in Exhibit CDA-6. This does not mean that since 1991 all imports from the United States and Mexico were made under CUSFTA/NAFTA. The percentages are irrelevant to the Japanese argument that Canada was rebutting.

(r) Question 6 from the EC (Data on Cost of Parts and Materials and Cost of Sales)

Could Canada please provide the following data, on average for all the MVTO and SRO beneficiaries of each class of vehicles, for the most recent model year for which the information is available:

- *the percentage of the cost of parts and materials to the cost of sales.*
- *the percentage of CVA to the cost of sales of the vehicles produced in Canada.*
- *the percentage of CVA to the cost of sales of the vehicles sold in Canada.*

(i) Reply from Canada - preliminary note

7.127 The figures provided are all for model year 1996-97.

(ii) Reply from Canada - the percentage of the cost of parts and materials to the cost of sales.

7.128 Note: Cost of sales is a term that includes only the cost to the manufacturer of vehicles sold for consumption in Canada. In other words, cost of sales is the sum of (i) the cost of producing domestic vehicles sold for consumption in Canada, and (ii) the cost of vehicles imported for sale in Canada (based on their value for duty). Cost of sales excludes vehicles sold for export. Canada does not collect, and does not have, a "cost of sales" for all vehicles produced in Canada. Thus, when the European Communities asks for the percentage of parts and materials to cost of sales, the result is meaningless. It takes the value of all parts and materials used in Canadian production, and compares it to the cost of only those vehicles sold for consumption in Canada (whether imported or domestic). This obviously inflates the percentages.

7.129 The percentages of parts and materials to cost of sales (of vehicles sold for consumption in Canada) are as follows:

Automobiles: 167%;

SCVs: 211%;

Buses: 192%.

(iii) Reply from Canada - the percentage of CVA to the cost of sales of the vehicles produced in Canada.

7.130 Note: This question asks for a comparison of CVA to the cost of sales of only those vehicles produced in Canada. As Canada explained above, Canada does not have the cost of sales figure requested, because it would include the cost of vehicles exported. Canada is providing the percentage of CVA to the cost of sales of vehicles produced in Canada and sold for consumption in Canada. This inflates the percentages, because it compares *total* CVA to only a portion of the cost of sales (that is, it leaves out the cost of sales of imported vehicles).

7.131 The percentages of CVA to the cost of vehicles produced in Canada and sold for consumption in Canada are:

Automobiles: 204%;

SCVs: 203%;

Buses: 188%.

(iv) Reply from Canada - the percentage of CVA to the cost of sales of the vehicles sold in Canada.

7.132 Note: Canada does not have the cost of sales of all vehicles sold in Canada, which would include vehicles sold for export. As stated above, Canada can only provide the percentage of CVA to the cost of sales of vehicles sold for consumption in Canada. This is the calculation used in determining whether companies like CAMI Automotive Inc. have met the CVA requirements in their respective SROs.

7.133 The available percentages are:

Automobiles: 47%;

SCVs: 57%;

Buses: 116%.

(s) Question 7 from the EC (1998 Automobile Imports from the US and Mexico under the MVTO)

Could Canada please indicate how many automobiles (units and/or value) were imported during 1998 from the USA and Mexico by the MVTO beneficiaries:

- *under the Tariff Exemption*
- *under NAFTA*
- *under the MFN duty rate*

(i) Reply from Canada

- *under the Tariff Exemption*

7.134 The total value of automobiles imported from the United States under the MVTO in 1998 was $9,541,000,000. The total value of automobiles imported from Mexico under the MVTO in 1998 was $419,000,000. These numbers added together amount to $9,960,000,000.

7.135 Note: This number is not the same as that provided for "North America" for 1998 in Exhibit CDA-25, provided in response to the Panel's Question 42. That question asked for the total for all *vehicles* imported under both the MVTO and the SROs, not just the MVTO.

- *under NAFTA*

7.136 The total for all vehicles is provided in response to the Panel's Question 42. Because the European Communities has asked for information relating only to the MVTO beneficiaries, and not the SROs, it would be necessary to determine the import values for each company individually, and then aggregate them. Canada does not have individual company data, and therefore cannot provide the information requested.

- *under the MFN duty rate*

7.137 Canada does not have this information for the same reason discussed above.

(t) Question 52 (Private vs. Governmental Action)

Could the EC and Japan respond to the arguments by Canada in its response to Panel Question 4 that the Panel Report in Japan - Measures Affecting Consumer Photographic Film and Paper offers little assistance to the Panel in this case, especially because "[t]he Panel's analysis of the word 'measure' centred on considerations particular to the country whose 'measure' was under review"?

(i) Reply from Japan

7.138 As the Government of Japan stated in its response to Panel Question 4, it shares ultimate conclusion with Canada that the Film case is not relevant to the present case. Every measure subject to a WTO panel procedure has its own unique characteristics reflecting the economic, social and political situations in the country under review. In Canada's response to the Panel Question 4, Canada seemingly attempts to dismiss Japan's claim on the Letters of Undertaking being in violation of Article III:4 by way of discussing the "measure" in the sense of Article XXIII:1(b) of GATT at length, instead of discussing the "requirements" in the sense of Article III:4. It is the latter provision of GATT that Japan is claiming the violation of in the present case, as stated in its response to Panel's Question 51 and other documents.

(ii) Reply from the EC

7.139 The Panel on *Japan - Film* is relevant for this case in two different respects.

7.140 First, the panel held that "the fact that action is taken by private parties does not rule out the possibility that it may be deemed governmental if there is sufficient government involvement in it".[711]

7.141 That finding was presented by the Panel as a restatement of a well-established and generally applicable principle, and not as an exceptional finding justified by the unique features of the Japanese political system. If anything, the degree of Government involvement in the Letters of Undertaking is greater than in some of the actions that were considered as Government "measures" in *Japan - Film.*[712]

7.142 Second, the panel ruled that "even non-binding, hortatory wording in a government statement of policy could have a similar effect on private actors to legally binding measure".[713]

7.143 Again, the Panel formulated that conclusion in generally applicable terms and did not confine it to the specific circumstances of the case under consideration. In any event, as already explained by the European Communities, this issue does not even arise in this case. Unlike the Japanese measures, the Letters of Undertaking are not mere statements of Government policy. They are drafted in mandatory language and have been regarded as binding by both parties. Moreover, the submission of the Letters of Undertaking was a necessary condition for the granting of the Tariff Ex-

[711] Panel Report on *Japan - Film, supra* note 93, para. 10.56.

[712] See, e.g., ibid., paras. 10.298-10.299.

[713] Ibid., para. 10.49.

emption. By contrast, in *Japan - Film* there was no direct link between the measures and the granting of any specific government benefit.

2. *Questions and Replies Relating to Claims under Article III:4 of the GATT*

(a) Question 13, in Part (the Ratio Requirements)

The EC argues that the ratio requirement is inconsistent with GATT Article III:4 because the maximum limit on the total sales value in practice operates "so as to restrict exclusively the sales of imported motor vehicles". In this connection, the EC further states that "the ratio requirements have the consequence that the beneficiaries cannot, without losing the entitlement to the Tariff Exemption, sell in Canada any imported motor vehicles in excess of a certain amount that is directly related to the sales value of their domestic production of motor vehicles".

The EC also that the ratio requirement is inconsistent with Article 2.1 of the TRIMs Agreement because it falls within the scope of Item 1(b) of the Illustrative List. The EC explains this view by stating that "under the ratio requirements the amount of imported motor vehicles that a beneficiary may sell in Canada (and, therefore, that it may be interested in 'purchasing') varies according to the value of the motor vehicles which it exports".

- *Is the EC's argument regarding the inconsistency of the ratio requirement with Article III:4 of the GATT identical to its argument on the inconsistency of that requirement with Item 1(b) of the Illustrative List annexed to the TRIMs Agreement?*

(i) Reply from the EC

7.144 No. They are similar but not identical. The European Communities claims that the ratio requirements violate Article III:4 because they place a quantitative limit on the sales of motor vehicles imported under the Tariff Exemption. Whether or not that limit is linked to the volume of exports is irrelevant in order to establish a violation of Article III:4. For that, it is sufficient to show that sales of imported goods are limited, while sales of like domestic goods are not.

7.145 On the other hand, the EC's claim under Item 1 (b) of the Illustrative List is that the ratio requirements place a limit on the sale of imported vehicles which is "related" to the amount of vehicles exported by each beneficiary. Thus, this claim involves an additional element, which is not required in order to establish a violation of Article III:4, namely that the limitation on internal sales be related to the value of exports.

(b) Question 14 (the Ratio Requirements)

In support of the view that the production-to-sales ratio requirement is inconsistent with Article III:4 of the GATT, Japan describes a situation in which an Auto Pact Manufacturer decides to sell additional motor vehicles produced in Canada, which "would increase the competition for sales of like imported motor vehicles".

- *Is it the view of Japan that any measure which leads to increased domestic production of a product and hence increases the competitive pressure faced by like imported products as a result of an increase in domestic sales of that product is per se inconsistent with Article III:4?*
- *How does Japan respond to the argument of Canada that the production-to-sales ratio is comparable to "a production-based subsidy, which requires a certain level of production to receive a certain level of benefits", and that such a production-based subsidy is not a violation of Article III?*
- *Related to this, what is the view of Japan on the argument advanced by Canada that "[N]either the GATT not any other WTO Agreement prohibits measures that increase production levels; there is no authority anywhere for the proposition that a mere increase in domestic production negatively affects the conditions of competition for like imported products"?*

(i) Reply from Japan

Japan will address these points in its rebuttal.

(c) Question 15 (the Ratio Requirements)

With reference Canada's previous arguments, could Canada please explain its views on whether or not the production-to-sales ratio affects the internal sale in Canada of imported motor vehicles other than those imported by MVTO and SRO beneficiaries?

(i) Reply from Canada

7.146 The production-to-sales ratios do not affect the internal sale of any vehicles in Canada, imported or domestic. Canada's previous arguments address the EC argument that the ratios operate to cause beneficiary companies to limit their sales of imports, without limiting their sales of domestic vehicles. The paragraphs thus explain why the ratios do not affect the internal sale of MVTO and SRO imports. The ratios merely determine whether the company's imports will be dutiable or duty-free. MVTO and SRO companies are free to import and sell as many vehicles as they choose. As long as sales are within the relevant ratio, imports remain duty-free. Once sales exceed that ratio, the manufacturer must pay the normal MFN duty on subsequent imports. In either case, there is no effect on the conditions of sale on the internal market in Canada.

7.147 The ratios determine whether or not products are subject to duty. In other words, the only possible effect relates to the importation of the products.

7.148 The production-to-sales ratios also do not affect the internal sale of vehicles imported by non-MVTO or SRO companies. These companies are not required to keep any ratio whatsoever and can import and sell vehicles, subject only to Canada's MFN duty on motor vehicles. The EC's argument cannot apply to them.

7.149 Canada would also note that the ratios have no actual or intended effects on market conditions in Canada. As Canada stated, Canadian production levels are well above the minimal levels required by the ratios. The ratios thus have not increased the number of domestic vehicles available for sale in the Canadian market. Manufacturers are producing vehicles for commercial reasons, and not in order to increase their ability to import.

(d) Question 16 (Meaning of "Require" in Chapeau of TRIMs Illustrative List)

Canada states that the text of the TRIMs Agreement "is explicit in stating that a prohibited TRIM must 'require' the purchase or use of domestic products." Could Canada further elaborate on its views on the meaning of the word "require" in the Chapeau of the Illustrative List of the TRIMs Agreement especially in light of the statement that "TRIMs which are inconsistent with Article III:4 of GATT 1994 include those ...compliance with which is necessary to obtain an advantage, and which require..."

(i) Reply from Canada

7.150 The Chapeau to paragraph 1 of the Illustrative List refers to "TRIMs that are inconsistent with the obligation of national treatment provided for in paragraph 4 of Article III of GATT 1994." It therefore deals only with measures that have already been found to be TRIMs, and sets out a two-step test to determine whether they are covered by the List.

7.151 First, the measure must be *either* mandatory or enforceable under domestic law or under administrative rulings, *or* such that compliance with it is necessary to obtain an advantage. Second, the alleged measure must *require* one of the actions set out in sub-paragraphs (a) and (b).

7.152 The first part of the test in the Chapeau goes to whether the alleged prohibited TRIM is a binding measure. If the answer to this question is "no", then the TRIM is not covered by the Illustrative List. If the answer is "yes", then it must be determined whether the binding is of the type listed in sub-paragraphs (a) or (b).

7.153 The CVA requirements contained in the MVTO and SROs are binding measures within the meaning of the Chapeau. They are mandatory and enforceable. However, these requirements are not covered by the second part of the test in the Chapeau because they do not "require" the actions listed in sub-paragraphs (a) and (b). They do not (a) "require" the purchase or use of domestic products, and they do not (b) "require" that purchase or use of imported products be limited to an amount related to the volume or value of domestic products exported. They are not included in the examples of prohibited TRIMs.

7.154 The additional CVA amounts found in the letters do not fall within the scope of Article III:4, and are not covered by the first part of the test in the Chapeau, because they are neither mandatory nor enforceable, and they need not be complied with in order to obtain an advantage.

(e) Question 17 (the Letters)

Canada submits that the arguments of the EC that certain Letters of Undertaking were required of the manufacturers as a condition of Canada's signing the Auto Pact, and that the beneficiaries have assumed that a failure to meet them would result in Canada withdrawing the Tariff Exemption, are without basis in fact. Canada states that a failure to meet the voluntary undertakings would not lead to denial of duty-free treatment and that revenue Canada does not review whether MVTO companies have met their commitments under the letters.

In light of the statements of the EC and of Japan, and without prejudice to the Panel's view on whether the Letters of Undertaking are properly described as "requirements" within the meaning of GATT Article III:4, could Canada provide a detailed explanation of:

- *the circumstances surrounding the submission of the Letters of Undertaking, in particular as regards the nature of the role, if any, of Canadian authorities and the relationship of the Letters to the Auto Pact;*
- *the nature of the commitments contained in the Letters;*
- *the current practical significance, if any, of these commitments;*
- *the relationship of the commitments contained in the Letters to the requirements of the MVTO 1998 and the SROs; and*
- *arrangements, if any, for gathering information on the application of the commitments contained in the Letters.*

(i) Reply from Canada

7.155 At the conclusion of the Auto Pact, the Canadian government sought assurance from the affected companies that they understood the new system. It provided them with a draft letter outlining what the requirements would be under the Pact, and what it hoped would be achieved as a result. The companies were free to modify the letter in any way they chose - for example, the letter from General Motors of Canada Ltd. is different in both form and substance from the others, and in no way affected that company's MVTO status.

7.156 The commitments in the letters are statements of what was hoped to be achieved under Canada's implementation of the Auto Pact system. They have no legal status or existence in Canada, because they are not contracts, statutes, or regulations. They cannot create any form of obligation or duty. As Canada stated, the Canadian government lacks the legal authority to deny MVTO and SRO benefits for a failure to meet the commitments. No other form of punishment can be imposed either.

7.157 The letters have no current practical significance. No benefits depend on meeting the CVA levels contained in the letters and no sanctions exist for failing to do so. Neither the government, nor the affected companies, consider the letters to be binding in any way.

7.158 The CVA amounts in the letters are unrelated to the requirements of the MVTO and the SROs. Those requirements determine whether companies are entitled to duty-free benefits in any given year. They stand on their own, and are complete in themselves. The letters are an expression of what was hoped would be achieved through the Auto Pact system. Success or failure in meeting those expectations has no bearing on meeting MVTO or SRO requirements.

7.159 There are no arrangements for collecting the information relating to the application of the letters. Some of it is contained in the information collected to verify whether companies are meeting their legal requirements under the MVTO and SROs. Much of it is not, and the Canadian government makes no effort to collect it. While some companies provide it anyway, the government does not audit or otherwise verify the amounts those companies report.

(f) Question 18 (the Letters and Private vs. Governmental Action)

Canada argues that certain Letters of Undertaking are not "requirements" within the meaning of GATT Article III:4 on the grounds that they have no legal status and no legal effect, and that the Canadian Government lacks the legal authority to deny duty-free eligibility in case of a failure to meet the voluntary undertakings in such Letters. What is Canada's view on the argument of the EC and Korea that GATT/WTO case law, as stated most recently in the Panel Report on Japan - Measures affecting Consumer Photographic Film and Paper (WT/DS44/R), supports the characterization of the Letters of Undertaking as measures which are attributable to the Government of Canada?

(i) Reply from Canada

7.160 The arguments of the European Communities and Korea are wrong. The letters are not measures within the meaning of Article III:4 because they are not binding on the companies that submitted them.

7.161 The panel in *Japan - Film* was clear in stating that whether an act is a "measure" must be determined on a case-by-case basis, having regard to the context in which the act was taken. Private acts can only be measures where there is sufficient government involvement, for example where the administrative structure exerts "maximum possible pressure" on private actions, and has the "rationale as well as the essential elements of a formal system".[714] In the Canadian context, there is no system of administration beyond the formal regulatory system. The government cannot direct private action without a specific law or regulation. No law or regulation required the submission of the letters, and no law or regulation requires the companies to meet the commitments they gave. The letters therefore cannot be measures.

7.162 Even if the Panel were to find that the letters are "measures", there would remain the question of whether they are "laws, regulations and requirements" within the meaning of Article III:4. Canada recalls here its answer to the Panel's question 4. The panel in *Japan - Film* did not address the interpretation of this phrase; instead, it twice noted that "requirement" appears to be narrower in meaning than "measure". It subsequently assumed for the purposes of its analysis that "laws, regulations and

---

[714] Panel Report on *Japan - Film, supra* note 93, para. 10.54, citing Panel Report on *Japan - Semiconductors, supra* note 112.

requirements" encompassed a broad range of government actions and private actions that may be assimilated to government action.

7.163 Japan and the European Communities, as the complaining parties, bear the burden of demonstrating that the letters are attributable to the Canadian government and are "laws, regulations or requirements" within the meaning of Article III:4. Since the circumstances present in previous cases are not present here, the complaining parties cannot discharge this burden.

(g) Question 46 (the Ratio Requirements)

The EC states that "the ratio requirements have the consequences that the beneficiaries cannot, without losing the entitlement to the Tariff Exemption, sell in Canada any imported motor vehicles in excess of a certain amount that is directly related to the sales value of their domestic production of motor vehicles."

In its response to Panel Question 13, the EC observes that "the ratio requirements violate Article III:4 because they place a quantitative limit on the sales of motor vehicles imported under the Tariff Exemption."

The EC also has argued that "the ratio requirements are internal measures subject to Article III, and not to Article XI, because they do not affect the right to import motor vehicles, but the right to sell them in Canada."

Could the EC further explain whether its argument is that the ratio requirements restrict the internal sale in Canada of any imported motor vehicles or that they restrict the internal sale in Canada of those motor vehicles that are imported duty-free?

(i) Reply from the European Communities

7.164 The European Communities claims that the ratio requirements limit the sale in Canada of motor vehicles imported under the Tariff Exemption.

(h) Question 47 (the Ratio Requirements)

What is the EC's response to the argument of Canada that the only possible effect of the ratio requirement relates to the importation of products in question (Canada's response to Panel Question 15) and to the observation of Canada that "the EC's argument would convert a measure setting out the terms under which importation takes place - which is manifestly a border measure - into a limitation on internal sales under Article III:4"?

(i) Reply from the EC

7.165 The ratio requirements do not restrict the right to import motor vehicles under the Tariff Exemption. They limit the right to sell in Canada vehicles already imported in Canada under the Tariff Exemption. Therefore, the ratio requirements are internal measures in the sense of Article III of GATT and not border measures. As already explained by the European Communities, the distinction between import measures subject to GATT Article XI and internal measures subject to GATT Article III is a formal one, and not one based on the effects of the measures on the volume of imports.

(i) Question 48 (the Ratio Requirements)

With reference to Canada's argument that the ratio requirements do not affect the internal sale of imported motor vehicles, could Canada respond to the argument of the EC that "any increase in the sales value of motor vehicles produced in Canada by the beneficiary will give rise automatically to an identical increase in the value of permitted domestic sales," whereas "an increase in imports of motor vehicles does not entail any increase in the value of permitted domestic sales"?

(i) Reply from Canada

7.166 The EC's argument is based on a mistaken premise. There is no limit on domestic sales under any circumstances for any manufacturer or any other person. Therefore, the EC's reference to "permitted domestic sales" is inapt. Canada refers the Panel to its previous arguments, which explain the workings of the ratios. Production does not affect in any way the value of vehicles that can be sold in Canada. It has the potential to affect only the value of vehicles that can be imported duty-free.

7.167 The production-to-sales ratio does not set any type of quantitative restriction on either the value or volume of domestic sales, either of domestic or imported vehicles. In the event that a company were operating at or near its ratio, the company would simply begin paying duty on its vehicle imports. Of course, as Canada made clear in its initial response, manufacturers are in fact operating well above the required ratios. But there is no limit in either case on how many imported vehicles may be sold in Canada.

7.168 As Canada now understands the EC argument, it relates exclusively to vehicles imported duty-free under the MVTO or SROs. It argues that because there is a limit on the value that can be imported duty-free, the vehicles so imported are disadvantaged in respect of their internal sale. The European Communities concedes that other imported vehicles receive treatment no less favourable than that accorded to domestic vehicles, as required by Article III.

7.169 There is no basis in Article III for distinguishing between otherwise like products on the basis of whether the products were subject to an import duty. The question is whether imported vehicles - regardless of whether some or all of them were subject to import duty at the border - are treated less favourably than like domestic vehicles for purposes of internal laws, regulations or requirements affecting their sale. The answer in the case of the Canadian measures is clearly no. There is no limit on how many like imported vehicles can be sold. There is a potential limit on how many of those like vehicles will have been imported duty free, but that is not an Article III question. Article III applies to measures affecting internal competition between imported and domestic products, after imported products have cleared the border, and any customs duties have been paid.

(j) Question 49 (the Ratio Requirements)

Could Canada further explain whether its position that the ratio requirements do not affect the internal sale of imported motor vehicles is based on the fact that current production levels exceed the ratio requirements?

(i) Reply from Canada

7.170 While it is true that the level of Canadian production is such that the companies could be importing substantially more vehicles duty free than they currently choose to do, that is *not* the reason that Canada has said that the ratio requirements do not affect the internal sale of imported motor vehicles. Rather, the reason is as explained above in the response to Question 48. There is no restriction on the internal sale of vehicles, whether a manufacturer is below, at or above its ratio. All vehicles, whether imported or domestic or, if imported, whether imported duty-free or subject to duty, or imported by a qualifying manufacturer or a non-qualifying manufacturer, are subject to exactly the same rules respecting internal sale, and all other matters subject to Article III. There are no limits of any kind on internal sale; any manufacturer can always sell as many vehicles as the market demands.

(k) Question 50 (the Letters)

With respect whether or not the Letters of Undertaking are "requirements" within the meaning of GATT Article III:4, could Canada comment on:

- *the argument of the EC that "the Letters of Undertaking had been negotiated with the Canadian Ministry of Industry and that their submission was regarded by Canada as a condition sine qua non for signing the Auto Pact"*

(i) Reply from Canada

7.171 The European Communities has failed to support these allegations with any evidence. Moreover, the historical record does not support the EC's allegations. Canada's files do not indicate either that the texts were "negotiated" or that submission of the letters was a *sine qua non* for signing the Auto Pact. Canada's response to the Panel's Question 17 was based on such information as it has. Government records show that Canada provided a draft of the letters, but it is inaccurate to say that the letters were "negotiated". Neither do the records support the EC position that the letters were a condition *sine qua non* for signing the Auto Pact. There is nothing in the records to indicate what Canada would have done if the companies had not delivered the letters. However, it is illogical to believe that Canada would have annulled the agreement without the letters, given that it was a carefully negotiated bilateral treaty.

7.172 What the European Communities claims as support for its argument on this point is at best ambiguous. The reference provided is to a statement in Exhibit EC-22 made by a Chrysler Corporation executive, who said that prior to the signing of the Auto Pact, Canada sought assurances that its industry would remain viable. He did not state that Canada made the provision of letters a condition *sine qua non*.

- *the argument of the EC that the Canadian Government requested affected companies to make specific commitments with respect to increases in Canadian value added*

(ii) Reply from Canada

7.173 The record shows that Canada did request undertakings respecting Canadian-value-added.

- *the arguments of the EC regarding the alleged monitoring by Canadian authorities of compliance with the Letters of Undertaking*

(iii) Reply from Canada

7.174 These EC arguments are speculative and without support on the record. The European Communities invokes a thirty-five year old letter containing prospective expectations of an industry executive. However, whether or not there ever were such "audits" on a quarterly or annual basis in the early years of the Auto Pact, there are no such audits now. Indeed, the Canadian Government does not now review any information pertaining to the letters. As the letters were never enforceable, there is no clear record as to when Canada ceased informal reviews of information provided in respect of the letters. At this point it is clear that there is no practice of review at all. It is Canada's understanding that the companies are fully aware that no reviews are carried out.

7.175 The European Communities descends into speculation and innuendo in claiming that the Government monitors CVA under the MVTO only to obtain information pertinent to the letters. The CVA in the MVTO is a binding obligation, and is monitored and enforced for that reason.

7.176 The European Communities tries to find support for its speculations by citing the Canadian Government's own public avowal that the letters are not binding. The European Communities claims that because the Government website also observes that the letters "typically" have been met, this demonstrates that the government must be monitoring to make such a statement. Leaving aside that the word "typically" connotes something less than full compliance with what the European Communities alleges to be binding letters, it should be noted that the Big Three at least have long publicly and proudly boasted of the extent of their activities in Canada, much as companies and corporations do throughout the world to get credit for the good things they do for the countries in which they operate. That does not mean that those good things are required.

7.177 It follows that the EC's conclusions are as bereft of merit as the speculations on which they are built. As Canada explained, whatever may have been in the minds or aspirations or expectations of government and industry in years past, there is no truth to the EC claim that these letters have any current effect, nor does Canada ascertain, audit or otherwise review "compliance" with the letters.

- *the argument of Japan that statements of the Chief Executive Officers of two of the Auto pact beneficiaries demonstrate that the letters of Undertaking are "binding and operative"*

(iv) Reply from Canada

7.178 While the Canadian Government was not involved in or consulted regarding the apparently informal remarks that were quoted, it may be doubted whether, even as an expression of company perception, there was any intended legal significance in the choice of words on the part of these executives. There perhaps should be some allowance for hyperbole in an informal setting in any event, and this was a time of some tension between auto companies as to their relative contributions to the Canadian economy. Regardless, Canada doubts very much that executives of these companies or of any other qualifying manufacturer would make these statements using the same words today, because Canada has made it clear that the letters are not binding.

(l) Question 51 (the Letters and FIRA and EEC-Regulation on Imports of Parts and Components)

Could the EC and Japan state their views on the argument that under the tests articulated in FIRA and EEC-Regulation on Imports of Parts and Components the letters of Undertaking are not "requirements" within the meaning of GATT Article III:4.

(i) Reply from Japan

7.179 The Government of Japan has refuted the Canadian argument that the letters of undertaking are not "requirements" within the meaning of Article III of the GATT. Canada tries to focus only on the surface of the letters and other legal instruments and hide substantial role and significance of the letters. It is quite implausible that private companies voluntarily submit to the government the commitments of local contents in their production when such commitments only restrict those companies' activities. It is of no merit for Canada to argue that the letters have not been expressly implemented by a Canadian law or regulation and that the MVTO 1998 and SROs do not, on their face, provide for sanctions in the event that the commitments in the letters are not complied with. The signatories of the letters viewed them as binding, the letters contain audit and reporting requirements, and there is no expiry date on the letters. The MVTO 1998 and the SROs are "Orders in Council" which are statutory instruments that can be revoked or amended by the Government of Canada. The letters of undertaking are enforceable as the Government of Canada is capable of revoking or amending the relevant instruments if the commitments in the letters are not implemented.

7.180 In any event, the Government of Japan is of the view that the Canadian characterisation of the tests articulated in the FIRA and Parts and Components cases is inaccurate at best. Both of these cases found the "voluntary" undertakings to be "requirements" within the meaning of Article III:4.

7.181 In *Canada - FIRA*, the voluntary undertakings were "requirements" primarily because they became conditions for which compliance could be enforced (para. 5.4). As noted, the letters of undertaking were conditions for the original duty-free treatment and were and continue to be enforceable through withdrawal of the advantage via revocation or amendment of the MVTO 1998 and the SROs. In *EEC - Parts and Components*, the Panel found that Article III:4 refers not only to requirements which an enterprise is legally bound to carry out (as in the *FIRA* case) but also those which an enterprise voluntarily accepts in order to obtain an advantage from the government. The letters of undertaking were entered into by the signatories in order to obtain the advantage of the Duty Waiver from the Government of Canada.

7.182 Thus, the letters of undertaking in this dispute are clearly "requirements" within the meanings in both Panel Reports. Had Canada been able to point to a case where a panel found similar undertakings falling outside the scope of "requirements" under Article III:4, the Canadian argument would have been more persuasive.

(ii) Reply from the European Communities

7.183 The European Communities has already addressed this argument. For ease of reference, the relevant passages are reproduced here below:

> "Canada claims that its interpretation of the term "requirement" is derived from *Canada - FIRA*[715] and *EC - Parts and Components.*[716] Those reports, however, in no way suggest that the panels purported to formulate, or that they were applying, a set of generally applicable criteria.
>
> "In any event, the Letters of Undertaking fit within the same pattern as the measures at issue in *EC - Parts and Components*. As explained by Canada, in that case the Panel found that the undertakings to increase local content given by the subsidiaries of certain Japanese companies were "requirements" because they were a "condition precedent to obtaining a benefit". The same is true of the Letters of Undertaking. The Canadian Government would not have concluded the Auto Pact if the Big Three had not submitted the Letters of Undertaking.
>
> "The only difference between the two cases is that the EC antidumping regulations envisaged that, if the undertakings were breached or withdrawn, the EC Commission *could* (but was not obliged to) reinstitute proceedings and eventually impose anti-circumvention duties.[717] The MVTO does not envisage expressly the possibility to impose sanctions. That does not mean, however, that the Letters are unenforceable. Given the linkage between the conclusion of the Auto Pact and the submission of the Letters established by the Canadian Government, there has always been a tacit understanding between the parties that if the beneficiaries failed to comply with the Letters, the Canadian Government would withdraw the tariff benefits."

(m) Question 53 (the Letters)

The EC argues that, because of the link between the submission of the Letters of Undertaking and the conclusion of the Auto Pact, "the beneficiaries have assumed that, were they to disregard the commitments contained in the Letters, the Canadian Government would withdraw the Tariff Exemption. The Canadian Government could do so simply by repealing or amending the MVTO 1998. There is nothing, either in the MVTO 1998, or in any other provision of Canadian law, that could prevent the Canadian Government from taking that action."

---

[715] Panel Report on *Canada - FIRA*, *supra* note 126.

[716] Panel Report on *EEC - Parts and Components*, *supra* note 127.

[717] Panel Report on *EEC - Parts and Components*, *supra* note 127, para. 5.20.

- *Could the EC further explain the factual basis for its contention that the beneficiaries have assumed that non-compliance with the commitments in the Letters of Undertaking would result in withdrawal of the tariff exemption?*

(i) Reply from the European Communities

7.184 As shown by the European Communities, the Letters of Undertaking were negotiated by the beneficiaries and Canada's Ministry of Industry in parallel with the negotiation of the Auto Pact, and submitted only a few days before the conclusion of the Auto Pact.

7.185 Furthermore, chief executives of the US Big Three, as well as the US officials who negotiated the Auto Pact, testified before the US Congress that the Canadian Government made of the submission of the Letters of Undertaking a necessary condition for the conclusion of the Auto Pact and, indeed, regarded the Letters as being an "important part" of the Auto Pact..

7.186 The European Communities has also shown that, for their part, the Big Three gave the undertakings contained in the Letters subject to the condition that the Canadian Government would sign the Auto Pact and adopt the necessary implementing regulations.

7.187 Thus, although the Letters are formally unilateral acts of the beneficiaries, they embody an agreement between the beneficiaries and the Canadian Government involving mutual obligations for both parties. Even in the absence of any express provision to that effect, it is implicit in any agreement involving mutual obligations that if one of the parties fails to fulfil its obligations, the other party is released from complying with its own obligations.[718] In view of that, the beneficiaries could but assume that, if they did not comply with their part of the agreement, the Canadian Government could legitimately reciprocate by withdrawing the tariff benefits.

- *What are the views of the EC on the argument that to argue that the Letters are enforceable because nothing in Canadian law prevents Canada from repealing or amending the MVTO is a fundamental misstatement of WTO law because WTO agreements apply to actions that Members have taken and not to actions that Members could take?*

(ii) Reply from the EC

7.188 Canada's argument mischaracterize the EC position. The European Communities has not argued that the Letters are "enforceable" simply because "nothing in Canadian law prevents Canada from repealing or amending the MVTO". The EC's position is that the Letters of Undertaking are "enforceable" because the granting of the Tariff Exemption was conditional upon the submission of the Letters and the Canadian Government has the necessary authority to withdraw the Tariff Exemption, should the beneficiaries fail to comply with the terms of the Letters. The European Communities made the argument mentioned by the Panel in response to a previous

[718] In the law of contracts, this basic notion is reflected in the so-called *exceptio non adimpleti contractus*, an exception to the effect that the plaintiff is not entitled to sue unless it has performed its own part of a contract. The same principle finds expression in Article 60 of the Vienna Convention on the Law of Treaties, of 23 May 1969.

argument raised by Canada to the effect that the European Communities "has provided no legal basis under which Canada could withdraw benefits for a failure to meet the commitments under the Letters".

7.189 In any event, the measures in dispute in this case are not the sanctions that Canada could impose in case of violation of the Letters of Undertaking, but rather the Letters themselves, which are an action "taken" by the Canadian Government already in 1965. The possibility to withdraw the Tariff Exemption has been cited by the European Communities only as a further indication that the Letters are "requirements".

7.190 Finally, it must be recalled that, as confirmed by *Japan - Film*, the WTO Agreements may apply where the Government has not even the possibility to impose a sanction in the event of lack of compliance, such as for example in the case of a simple statement of government policy. *A fortiori*, the WTO Agreement may apply also in cases where the Government can impose a sanction, even if is not mandatorily required to do so. Indeed, as mentioned above in response to question 51, *EC - Parts and Components* concerned precisely that type of situation.

3. *Questions and Replies Relating to Claims under the TRIMS Agreement*

(a) Question 13 (the Ratio Requirements)

The EC argues that the ratio requirement is inconsistent with GATT Article III:4 because the maximum limit on the total sales value in practice operates "so as to restrict exclusively the sales of imported motor vehicles". In this connection, the EC further states that "the ratio requirements have the consequence that the beneficiaries cannot, without losing the entitlement to the Tariff Exemption, sell in Canada any imported motor vehicles in excess of a certain amount that is directly related to the sales value of their domestic production of motor vehicles".

The EC also argues that the ratio requirement is inconsistent with Article 2.1 of the TRIMs Agreement because it falls within the scope of Item 1(b) of the Illustrative List. The EC explains this view by stating that "under the ratio requirements the amount of imported motor vehicles that a beneficiary may sell in Canada (and, therefore, that it may be interested in 'purchasing') varies according to the value of the motor vehicles which it exports".

- *Is the EC's argument regarding the inconsistency of the ratio requirement with Article III:4 of the GATT identical to its argument on the inconsistency of that requirement with Item 1(b) of the Illustrative List annexed to the TRIMs Agreement?*

(i) Reply from the European Communities

7.191 No. They are similar but not identical. The European Communities claims that the ratio requirements violate Article III:4 because they place a quantitative limit on the sales of motor vehicles imported under the Tariff Exemption. Whether or not that limit is linked to the volume of exports is irrelevant in order to establish a violation of Article III:4. For that, it is sufficient to show that sales of imported goods are limited, while sales of like domestic goods are not.

7.192 On the other hand, the EC's claim under Item 1 (b) of the Illustrative List is that the ratio requirements place a limit on the sale of imported vehicles which is "related" to the amount of vehicles exported by each beneficiary. Thus, this claim involves an additional element, which is not required in order to establish a violation of Article III:4, namely that the limitation on internal sales be related to the value of exports.

- *With regard to the EC's argument concerning Item 1(b) of the TRIMs Illustrative List, could the EC further explain its view that the ratio requirement limits "an enterprise's purchases or use of imported products to an amount related to the volume or value of local products that it exports"?*

(ii) Reply from the European Communities

7.193 The ratio requirements do not limit expressly the "purchase" or "use" of imported goods but their internal "sale". Nevertheless, it seems obvious that by limiting the "sales" of imported goods, the ratio requirements limit necessarily their "purchase". In any event, it must be recalled that the Illustrative List of prohibited TRIMs is not an exhaustive one. Even if Item 1 (b) did not cover measures that restrict the "sale" of imported goods, it would be necessary to conclude by analogy that a measure that limits the sale of imported goods to an amount related to the value of exports of the company concerned is also a TRIM inconsistent with GATT Article III:4 and, therefore, prohibited by Article 2.1 of the TRIMs Agreement.

- *In light of the reference made by the EC in its arguments on Item 1(b) of the TRIMs Illustrative List to its analysis of the inconsistency of the ratio requirement with Article 3.1(a) of the SCM Agreement, does the EC consider that the ratio requirement is inconsistent with Item 1(b) of the TRIMs Agreement and with Article 3.1(a) of the SCM Agreement for the same reason, i.e. because it makes the duty-free treatment legally contingent upon export performance ? Could the EC in this regard further explain its view of the relationship between Item 1(b) of the Illustrative List of the TRIMs Agreement, on the one hand, and Article 3.1(a) of the SCM Agreement, on the other?*

(iii) Reply from the European Communities

7.194 No. The same facts give raise to two violations, but the "reason" for each violation is different. The European Communities claims that the ratio requirements fall within Item 1(b) because they limit the internal sale of vehicles imported under the Tariff Exemption to an amount "related" to the value of exports. Whether or not the Tariff Exemption is a "subsidy" in the meaning of Article 1 of the SCM Agreement, and whether it is "contingent upon export performance" in the sense of Article 3.1(a) of the SCM Agreement are not pertinent considerations in deciding that claim.

7.195 In turn, the European Communities considers that the Tariff Exemption constitute a "subsidy" prohibited by Article 3.1(a) of the SCM Agreement, because the ratio requirements attached thereto make it "contingent upon export performance". The success of that claim does not depend on whether the ratio requirements limit the sale of imported vehicles in violation of Article III:4 and Item 1(b) of the Illustrative List.

7.196 The relationship between the TRIMs Agreement and the SCM Agreement has been discussed in detail in the Panel Report on Indonesia - Automobiles.[719] That report concluded, amongst other things, that:

> "... the SCM and TRIMs Agreement cannot be in conflict, as they cover different subject matters and do not impose mutually exclusive obligations. The TRIMs Agreement and the SCM Agreement may have overlapping coverage in that they may both apply to a single legislative measure, but they have different foci, and they impose different types of obligations."[720]

7.197 The European Communities agrees with that analysis.

(b) Question 16 (Meaning of "Require" in Chapeau of TRIMs Illustrative List)

Canada states that the text of the TRIMs Agreement "is explicit in stating that a prohibited TRIM must 'require' the purchase or use of domestic products." Could Canada further elaborate on its views on the meaning of the word "require" in the Chapeau of the Illustrative List of the TRIMs Agreement especially in light of the statement that "TRIMs which are inconsistent with Article III:4 of GATT 1994 include those ...compliance with which is necessary to obtain an advantage, and which require..."

(i) Reply from Canada

7.198 The Chapeau to paragraph 1 of the Illustrative List refers to "TRIMs that are inconsistent with the obligation of national treatment provided for in paragraph 4 of Article III of GATT 1994." It therefore deals only with measures that have already been found to be TRIMs, and sets out a two-step test to determine whether they are covered by the List.

7.199 First, the measure must be *either* mandatory or enforceable under domestic law or under administrative rulings, *or* such that compliance with it is necessary to obtain an advantage. Second, the alleged measure must *require* one of the actions set out in sub-paragraphs (a) and (b).

7.200 The first part of the test in the Chapeau goes to whether the alleged prohibited TRIM is a binding measure. If the answer to this question is "no", then the TRIM is not covered by the Illustrative List. If the answer is "yes", then it must be determined whether the binding is of the type listed in sub-paragraphs (a) or (b).

7.201 The CVA requirements contained in the MVTO and SROs are binding measures within the meaning of the Chapeau. They are mandatory and enforceable. However, these requirements are not covered by the second part of the test in the Chapeau because they do not "require" the actions listed in sub-paragraphs (a) and (b). They do not (a) "require" the purchase or use of domestic products, and they do not (b) "require" that purchase or use of imported products be limited to an amount related

719 Panel Report on *Indonesia - Autos, supra* note 270, paras. 14.47-14.55.

720 Ibid., para. 14.52.

to the volume or value of domestic products exported. They are not included in the examples of prohibited TRIMs.

7.202 The additional CVA amounts found in the letters do not fall within the scope of Article III:4, and are not covered by the first part of the test in the Chapeau, because they are neither mandatory nor enforceable, and they need not be complied with in order to obtain an advantage.

(c) Question 46 (the Ratio Requirements)

The EC states that "the ratio requirements have the consequences that the beneficiaries cannot, without losing the entitlement to the Tariff Exemption, sell in Canada any imported motor vehicles in excess of a certain amount that is directly related to the sales value of their domestic production of motor vehicles."

In its response to Panel Question 13, the EC observes that "the ratio requirements violate Article III:4 because they place a quantitative limit on the sales of motor vehicles imported under the Tariff Exemption."

The EC argues that "the ratio requirements are internal measures subject to Article III, and not to Article XI, because they do not affect the right to import motor vehicles, but the right to sell them in Canada."

Could the EC further explain whether its argument is that the ratio requirements restrict the internal sale in Canada of any imported motor vehicles or that they restrict the internal sale in Canada of those motor vehicles that are imported duty-free?

(i) Reply from the EC

7.203 The European Communities claims that the ratio requirements limit the sale in Canada of motor vehicles imported under the Tariff Exemption.

4. *Questions and Replies Relating to Claims under the SCM Agreement*

(a) Question 13, in Part (the Ratio Requirements)

In light of the reference made by the EC in its arguments on Item 1(b) of the TRIMs Illustrative List to its analysis of the inconsistency of the ratio requirement with Article 3.1(a) of the SCM Agreement, does the EC consider that the ratio requirement is inconsistent with Item 1(b) of the TRIMs Agreement and with Article 3.1(a) of the SCM Agreement for the same reason, i.e. because it makes the duty-free treatment legally contingent upon export performance ? Could the EC in this regard further explain its view of the relationship between Item 1(b) of the Illustrative List of the TRIMs Agreement, on the one hand, and Article 3.1(a) of the SCM Agreement, on the other?

(i) Reply from the European Communities

7.204 No. The same facts give raise to two violations, but the "reason" for each violation is different. The European Communities claims that the ratio requirements fall within Item 1(b) because they limit the internal sale of vehicles imported under the Tariff Exemption to an amount "related" to the value of exports. Whether or not the Tariff Exemption is a "subsidy" in the meaning of Article 1 of the SCM Agreement, and whether it is "contingent upon export performance" in the sense of Article 3.1(a) of the SCM Agreement are not pertinent considerations in deciding that claim.

7.205 In turn, the European Communities considers that the Tariff Exemption constitute a "subsidy" prohibited by Article 3.1(a) of the SCM Agreement, because the ratio requirements attached thereto make it "contingent upon export performance". The success of that claim does not depend on whether the ratio requirements limit the sale of imported vehicles in violation of Article III:4 and Item 1(b) of the Illustrative List.

7.206 The relationship between the TRIMs Agreement and the SCM Agreement has been discussed in detail in the Panel Report on *Indonesia - Autos.*[721] That report concluded, amongst other things, that:

> "... the SCM and TRIMs Agreement cannot be in conflict, as they cover different subject matters and do not impose mutually exclusive obligations. The TRIMs Agreement and the SCM Agreement may have overlapping coverage in that they may both apply to a single legislative measure, but they have different foci, and they impose different types of obligations."[722]

7.207 The European Communities agrees with that analysis.

(b) Question 19 ("Mere Possibility" and Contingency)

The EC states: "The mere possibility that in some cases a beneficiary may be required to use domestic goods instead of imported goods in order to qualify for the subsidy is sufficient to trigger the application of Article 3.1(b)". Could the EC please elaborate on this statement in light of the drafters' use of the term "contingent" in Article 3.1(b). Further, could the EC also elaborate on the relevance of GATT Article III:8(b), which reads: "The provisions of this Article shall not prevent the payment of subsidies exclusively to domestic producers ... ", in particular, with regard to whether a value-added test as a criterion for determining who falls within the class of "domestic producers" would be in violation of SCM Article 3.1(b).

(i) Reply from the European Communities

7.208 For the reasons already explained, the European Communities is of the view that Article 3.1(b) of the SCM Agreement does not prohibit only those conditions that require the actual use of domestic goods by the beneficiary. It prohibits any condition that gives preference to the use of domestic over imported goods, whether or not that condition results in all cases in the actual use of domestic goods by the beneficiaries.

7.209 In other words, Article 3.1(b) prohibits any subsidy that is "contingent" upon a condition that favours the use of domestic over imported goods, and not merely those subsidies that are "contingent" upon the actual use of domestic goods. In the case at hand, the subsidy is "contingent" in law upon a value added requirement that

---

[721] Panel Report on *Indonesia - Autos, supra* note 270, paras. 14.47-14.55.

[722] Ibid., para. 14.52.

gives preference to the use of domestic over imported goods. Consequently, the subsidy is "contingent upon the use of domestic over imported goods" in the meaning of Article 3.1(b).

7.210 In any event, assuming *arguendo* that "contingent upon the use of domestic over imported goods" meant contingent upon the actual use of domestic goods, Article 3.1(b) does not require that that condition be a necessary one. In fact, Article 3.1(b) prohibits the granting of subsidies that are contingent upon the use of domestic over imported goods, "whether solely or as one of several conditions".

7.211 This may cover the situation where a subsidy is simultaneously subject to two or more cumulative conditions. But it may as well apply to the situation where a subsidy is subject two or more alternative conditions, so that compliance with any of them gives a right to the subsidy. If one of those conditions is "the use of domestic over imported goods" the subsidy must be deemed prohibited by Article 3.1(b), even if it is also possible to qualify for the subsidy by complying with other alternative non-prohibited conditions, such as using domestic labour or domestic services.

7.212 Finally, although for the reasons above mentioned, the European Communities considers that the CVA requirements are contingent "in law" upon the use of domestic over imported goods, it has also submitted in the alternative that the CVA requirements make the subsidy contingent "in fact" upon the use of domestic over imported goods.

7.213 Regarding the relevance of GATT Article III:8(b), and, in particular, with regard to whether a value-added test as a criterion for determining who falls within the class of "domestic producers" would be in violation of SCM Article 3.1(b): The Tariff Exemption is not a subsidy "paid" to domestic producers in the meaning of GATT Article III:8(b). As confirmed by the Appellate Body in *Canada - Periodicals*, Article III:8 (b) exempts from the obligations of Article III only the payment of subsidies involving the expenditure of revenue by the government.[723] Thus, for example, tax exemptions[724] or reductions in transportation or postal rates[725] have been found not to be covered by Article III:8(b). For the same reason, a subsidy in the form of a tariff exemption is not exempted by that provision either.[726]

7.214 Furthermore, assuming *arguendo* that Article III:8(b) applied to subsidies in the form of tariff exemptions, the terms of Article III:8(b) only exempt the "payment" of the subsidy. The exemption does not extend to any conditions attached to the subsidy, such as local content or value added requirements[727], which have discriminatory effects additional to those of the subsidy itself.

---

723 Appellate Body Report on *Canada - Periodicals, supra* note 280, p.34.

724 See the Panel Reports on *US - Malt Beverages, supra* note 427, para. 5.10; and Panel Report on *Indonesia - Autos, supra* note 270, paras. 14.41-14.46.

725 Appellate Body Report on *Canada - Periodicals, supra* note 280, pp. 32-35.

726 In the Panel Report on *Indonesia - Autos, supra* note 270, paras. 14.83-14.92, the granting of tariff benefits contingent upon compliance with certain local content requirements was found to be inconsistent with GATT Article III:4 and prohibited by Article 2.1 of the TRIMs Agreement.

727 According to the Panel Report on *Indonesia - Autos, supra* note 270, "... the purpose of Article III:8 (b) is to confirm that subsidies to producers do not violate Article III, so long as they do not have any component that introduces discrimination between imported and domestic products..." (para. 14.43) "... Article III:8 (b) of GATT does not constitute a defence to any measure providing

7.215 The application of a value added requirement is not necessary for determining who is a "domestic producer". Moreover, if that justification was accepted, Panels would have to ascertain in each case what level of domestic value added is sufficient to confer the status of "domestic producer". In fact, if that determination was left to each Member's discretion, the prohibition on local content requirements would become dead letter. Members could easily circumvent that prohibition simply by setting the level of domestic value added at a level such that it requires necessarily the use of domestic goods. Yet, the incompatibility with GATT Article III:4 of local content requirements, including those compliance with which is necessary to obtain an advantage, is now well established by precedent and has been confirmed beyond any possible doubt in Item 1(a) of the Illustrative List of prohibited TRIMs. Canada itself has conceded that the granting of subsidies contingent upon a local content requirement is inconsistent with GATT Article III:4.
7.216 Finally, since the Panel has raised this question under the heading of "The SCM Agreement", the European Communities would like to recall that, by its own terms, Article III:8(b) of GATT only provides an exemption from the obligations contained in the other paragraphs of GATT Article III. It does not provide an exception with respect to the prohibition of subsidies contingent upon the use of domestic over imported goods contained in Article 3.1(b) of the SCM Agreement. To the extent that there was a conflict between GATT Article III:8(b) and Article 3.1(b) of the SCM Agreement, the latter would prevail in accordance with the General Interpretative Note to Annex 1 A.

(c) Question 20 ("Duties Borne" and Inputs)

The EC remarks: "Duties 'borne' by an exported product means duties on inputs that are consumed in the production of that product". Please explain the legal basis for your view.

(i) Reply from the European Communities

7.217 The remark by the European Communities quoted in the Panel's question refers to Footnote 1 of the SCM Agreement. That Footnote is introduced by the clause: "In accordance with the ... provisions of Annexes I through III of this Agreement". That clause limits the scope of the exception to the definition of "subsidy" in Article 1 provided for in Footnote 1 with respect to the remission of import duties to the two situations described in Item (i) of Annex I, as further interpreted in Annexes II and III, i.e.: (i) when imported inputs are used in the manufacture of the exported products; and (ii) when domestic inputs having the same quality and characteristics are substituted for imported inputs in the production of exported products. Item (i) makes it clear that in both cases the inputs must be "consumed" in the production of the exported products.

---

discrimination between domestic and imported products, including local content requirements" (footnote 686).

(d) Question 21 (the Ratio Requirements)

Japan states: "Actually, the MVTO and SROs by virtue of the ratio requirement provide the legal mechanism where the subsidy is contingent upon export performance. The fact that this mechanism is best understood if explained in the context of a mathematical formula does not diminish its legal effect". Is Japan arguing that the duty waiver is export-contingent in law? Please elaborate.

(i) Reply from Japan

7.218 It is the position of the Government of Japan that the production-to-sales ratio is in law export contingent. The formula expressing such terms of the ratio as stipulated in applicable Canadian law (i.e. the MVTO 1998 and the SROs) demonstrates clearly that it makes the Duty Waiver contingent on export performance.

(e) Question 22 (the Measures at Issue and Production-Based Subsidies)

Canada states: "Yet production-based subsidies are not violations of GATT Article III". Could Canada further elaborate on this point and on the possible relevance of GATT Article III:8(b).

(i) Reply from Canada

7.219 Canada's statement that production-based subsidies are not violations of GATT Article III was a reference to the fact that such subsidies are actionable, not prohibited, under the SCM Agreement.

7.220 Canada's statement was made to refute what appears to be Japan's contention that the production-to-sales ratios are inconsistent with Article III:4 of the GATT because they serve to increase domestic production and therefore competition against imported vehicles. In its argument, Canada noted that Japan's underlying assumption was incorrect - the ratios do not increase domestic production beyond what would otherwise be achieved, as demonstrated by the fact that all of the automobile manufacturers produce vehicles far in excess of what the ratios require.

7.221 However, even if Japan's assumption were correct, it would be wrong at law to conclude that an increase in domestic production as a result of the ratios was inconsistent with Article III:4 of the GATT. This is because this argument would read Section III of the SCM Agreement out of existence. Furthermore, Article III:8(b) of the GATT explicitly recognizes that production-based subsidies to domestic producers, which inherently increase domestic production, are not subject to Article III of the GATT.[728] By Japan's argument, any subsidy that increases domestic production would be a violation of Article III of the GATT. This would read out of existence both Article III:8 of the GATT and Part III of the SCM Agreement which makes production-based subsidies actionable rather than prohibited.

7.222 The receipt of duty-free treatment contingent on achieving certain production-to-sales ratios may not be a subsidy at all, by analogy with the exemptions in the

[728] See Panel Report on *United States - Measures Affecting the Importation, Internal Sale and Use of Tobacco*, adopted 4 October 1994, BISD 41S/131, paras. 109, 111.

SCM Agreement and in particular, footnote 1 to the SCM Agreement. In the alternative, if the Panel finds that it is a subsidy, it is a subsidy maintained on imports: it is imported vehicles that are exempted from Canada's 6.1 percent MFN duty.

7.223 In the further alternative, it is a production-based subsidy, by virtue of the requirement to achieve production-to-sales ratios in order to qualify for duty-free treatment (although benefits are not linked to production in the sense that production beyond the ratio does not increase benefits). It is not a subsidy contingent upon either export performance or the use of domestic over imported goods because of the absence of either sort of contingency.

(f) Question 23 (Subsidies and Import Facilitation)

Canada states: "... that the duty-free treatment under the MVTO and the SROs amounts to a subsidy contingent upon exportation ... is an odd allegation, because duty-free treatment is granted to imports". The EC responds: "In any event, whether or not the tariff exemption "facilitates" imports is irrelevant. The SCM Agreement does not provide any exception for export subsidies with 'import facilitating' effects." How would Canada rebut the EC's response?

(i) Reply from Canada

7.224 Canada is not suggesting that the SCM Agreement provides an exception for export subsidies with "import facilitating effects". Canada maintains that the duty-free treatment is not an export subsidy at all.

7.225 The Appellate Body has stated that a proper interpretation of a provision of an agreement must be made on the basis of a careful examination of the text, context and object and purpose of that provision.[729] This is what Canada has proposed for Article 3.1(a) of the SCM Agreement.

7.226 The Appellate Body has also found that illustrative lists, although not exhaustive, "exemplify the kinds of programmes" covered by a provision.[730] This is precisely why Canada has relied on the Illustrative List of Export Subsidies in Annex I to the SCM Agreement. Canada's measures are not even remotely like those on the Illustrative List. The European Communities concedes this, but describes it as "irrelevant", because the Illustrative List is not exhaustive. On the contrary, as the Appellate Body has found, it is highly relevant.

(g) Question 24 (the Letters and CVA Figures)

Without prejudice to whether the Letters of Undertaking constitute "requirements" under GATT Article III:4, could Canada please respond to the EC arguments in this regard, including the figures relating to CVA levels.

---

729 Appellate Body Report on *US - Gasoline, supra* note 487, at 16.

730 Appellate Body Report on *Canada - Periodicals, supra* note 280, at 478.

(i) Reply from Canada

7.227 The letters do not constitute "requirements". Even if they did, it is incorrect to assume that some beneficiaries "cannot possibly" meet their CVA requirements without using some domestic parts and materials. The EC's suggestion that "parts and materials may account on average for as much as 80 per cent of the cost of sales of motor vehicles assembled in Canada" is belied by Japan's Exhibit JPN-43-3 (which Canada understands was not withdrawn, unlike the Japanese language exhibits JPN-43 and JPN-43-2). JPN-43-3 demonstrates that the cost of parts and materials as a percentage of cost of sales can vary widely. For Honda, it was 54 per cent in both 1996 and 1997. For Toyota, it was 69 per cent in 1996 and 63 per cent in 1997. It is unclear from the exhibit whether these statistics include Honda and Toyota's manufacturing facilities in Canada.

(h) Question 25 (the CVA Requirements and Export Performance)

Could Canada please respond to the EC argument that "... the CVA requirements would be operating as an export performance condition".

(i) Reply from Canada

7.228 The EC's argument again depends on the incorrect premise that the letters are requirements. Moreover, the argument, like the EC's "mere possibility" argument, stretches the definition of "contingent upon" well past what it can reasonably bear. The argument appears to be that in some cases, manufacturers would export vehicles, in order to meet their CVA requirements, in order to qualify for the right not to pay duty on other vehicles that they would then import from Europe or Japan (and that according to the EC's GATT Article III arguments, they could then not sell). Even if such treatment constitutes a subsidy, receipt of such treatment is not, *de jure* or *de facto*, conditional upon, dependent upon or tied to the export of vehicles. Manufacturers may achieve their CVA requirements by any means they choose.

(i) Question 26 (Contingency - "in Law" and "in Fact" vs. "Express" and "Implicit")

The EC states: "Article 3.1(a) draws a distinction between contingency 'in law' and contingency 'in fact', and not between 'express' and 'implicit' contingency". Could Canada please respond to this comment.

(i) Reply from Canada

7.229 The European Communities has cited no authority for its assertion and has offered no explanation of what it considers to be the difference between implicit contingency and contingency in fact. It is a generally accepted principle that laws must be explicit, not implicit. Accordingly, under Article 3.1(a), a subsidy is contingent in law upon export performance where the underlying legal instruments of that subsidy expressly provide that the subsidy is available to enterprises only on the condition that they export or undertake to develop exports. A subsidy is contingent in fact upon export performance where there is no express requirement to export, but the facts and circumstances are such that there is an implicit requirement to export (or to undertake export development) for it to benefit from a subsidy.

(j) Question 54 (the CVA Requirements and Exportation)

The EC states: "Thus, in definitive, the CVA requirements make the tariff exemption 'contingent' either upon the use of domestic over imported goods, contrary to the prohibition of Article 3.1(b); and/or, as the sole alternative, upon export performance, in violation of the prohibition contained in Article 3.1(a)". If, as the EC observes, " ... the relevant CVA amount includes not only the CVA contained in the motor vehicles sold domestically but also the CVA of any exported motor vehicles (and in some cases of exported original equipment parts)" (Emphasis added), could the EC explain why a manufacturer not using any domestic goods would need to export in order to meet the CVA requirements.

(i) Reply from the European Communities

7.230 The CVA requirements contained in the Letters of Undertaking and in the SROs stipulate that the total CVA contained in the motor vehicles *sold in Canada or exported* (and in some cases also in the OEM parts) must represent a certain percentage of the cost of sales of the motor vehicles *sold in Canada*, i.e. not including the cost of sales of the vehicles produced in Canada and exported, but including the cost of sales of any imported vehicles sold in Canada.

7.231 Thus, if a beneficiary exports some motor vehicles (or OEM parts) the denominator of the fraction (i.e. the cost of sales in Canada) is less than if those vehicles are sold in Canada. On the other hand, the numerator (i.e. the CVA amount) remains the same, irrespective of whether the vehicles are exported or sold in Canada.

7.232 As shown by the European Communities, the cost of parts and materials a accounts, on average, for 80 per cent of the cost of sales of the motor vehicles produced in Canada, while labour and other manufacturing overheads account for the remaining 20 per cent. This means that a beneficiary which does not export any motor vehicles or parts will not be able to meet the CVA requirements in the Letters or in the SROs (from 40 per cent to 60 per cent of the cost of sales in Canada), unless it uses a substantial amount of domestic parts and materials (at least 20 per cent to 40 per cent of the cost of sales).

7.233 The only conceivable way in which a beneficiary could meet the CVA requirements in the Letters and the SROs without using any domestic parts or materials at all is by exporting, so that the non-parts CVA contained in the exported cars can be added to the non-parts CVA of the vehicles sold in Canada.

7.234 The above may be illustrated by means of the following example. Assume that a beneficiary subject to a 40 per cent CVA requirement produces in Canada 1,000 vehicles with a cost of sales of 10,000 \$ each. Assume further that: 1) parts and materials account for 80 per cent of their cost of sales, i.e. 8,000 \$ per unit; 2) the vehicles contain no domestic parts and materials at all; and 3) labour and all the other costs included in the cost of sales, with a total value of 2,000 \$ per unit, are exclusively of Canadian origin. If the beneficiary sold all the vehicles in Canada, the ratio CVA to cost of sales in Canada would be 20 per cent (1,000 units X 2,000 $ / 1,000 units X 10,000 $). On the other hand, if the beneficiary exported 500 units, the ratio CVA to cost of sales in Canada would be 40 per cent (1,000 units X 2,000 $ / 500 units X 10,000 $).

7.235 For the sake of simplicity, the above example does not take into account the cost of sales in Canada of imported vehicles. Nevertheless, as explained above, the cost of those sales increases the denominator, which means that in the above example the beneficiary would have to export even a larger share of its domestic production in order to meet the CVA requirements without using any Canadian parts or materials.

(k) Question 55 (Paragraphs (g), (h), and (i) of the SCM Illustrative List and the Measures at Issue)

Canada states: "It is contextually significant that duty or tax exemption or remission programmes, such as those described in paragraphs (g), (h), and (i) of the Illustrative List, are deemed not to constitute export subsidies when they are not excessive." Could Canada please elaborate on how, in Canada's view, paragraphs (g), (h), and (i) of the Illustrative List should inform the Panel's determination of whether the Canadian duty-free treatment is an export subsidy. Is Canada arguing that, even if the import duty exemption were in excess of 6.1%, it would only be an export subsidy if it was linked directly to exported goods?

(i) Reply from Canada

7.236 Canada is not claiming that the duty exemption in this case is identical to those listed in items (g), (h) and (i) of the Illustrative List. Rather, Canada's point is that those three items consider a tax or duty rebate to be actionable *only* if it is excessive. An excessive duty rebate would be, in practical terms, no different from a legal duty exemption coupled with a cash subsidy. Whether such a subsidy was an export subsidy would depend on whether it was contingent upon export performance. However, in item (i) of the Illustrative List, a non-excessive duty exemption was specifically considered not to be an export subsidy even in the case of blatant export contingency. That context supports Canada's position that the duty waiver in this case is neither a subsidy nor an export subsidy.

(l) Question 61 (Implementation Time-Period)

Article 4.7 of the Agreement on Subsidies and Countervailing Measures states:

> *If the measure in question is found to be a prohibited subsidy, the panel shall recommend that the subsidizing Member withdraw the subsidy without delay. In this regard, the panel shall specify in its recommendation the time-period within which the measure must be withdrawn.*

In the event that the Panel were to find the existence of a prohibited subsidy, what would Canada consider to be an appropriate time-period for implementation, given the use of the phrase "without delay" in Article 4.7?

(i) Canada's reply

7.237 It is difficult to respond to this hypothetical question, given that Canada does not agree that the duty-free treatment in this case is a subsidy. Nevertheless, assuming for the purposes of this question that the Panel would find the existence of a prohibited subsidy, Canada submits that "without delay" should be interpreted in a manner that would allow Canada a reasonable opportunity to implement the Panel's findings.

7.238 The rationale for creating an expedited dispute settlement process in Article 4 of the SCM Agreement is that prohibited subsidies are assumed to have trade-distorting effects harmful to the interests of other Members. Thus, while the existence of such effects is not relevant to determining whether a "subsidy" is prohibited, their presence or absence should be taken into account in determining the appropriate time period to be accorded under Article 4.7 in any particular case.

7.239 The measures in this case have no prejudicial or trade-distorting effects. Moreover, there is no demonstrable urgency in dealing with measures that have been in place for thirty-five years, the only effect of which is to increase imports from countries other than the United States and Mexico - principally the European Communities and Japan.

7.240 The Canadian measures clearly have no trade distorting effects in any export market, and their structure makes it unlikely that this will ever change. The alleged subsidy is a grant of duty-free treatment in direct proportion to imports, and the formulas for the CVA and the production-to-sales ratios are such that both exports and domestic purchases could be *reduced* without any loss in duty-remission benefit.

7.241 Empirical evidence confirms this. Canadian exports of vehicles to the European Communities and Japan are negligible; the alleged subsidy therefore cannot be causing any distortions in those markets. Canadian exports to the United States are attributable to the US duty waiver, and to proximity, not to any alleged subsidy, as explained in paragraphs 97-98 of Canada's first written submission.

7.242 Canada also draws the Panel's attention to the arguments it made in paragraphs 21 and 22 of its first written submission. This case is not about a single discrete measure - what Japan has called the "Duty Waiver" and the European Communities "the Tariff Exemption". Canada's implementation of the Auto Pact involves complex measures; indeed, the complaining parties have purported to challenge a wide variety of matters, not all of which can even be characterized as "measures". Japan, for example, has cited the MVTO 1998, the SROs, the *Customs Tariff*, the *Financial Administration Act*, the letters of undertaking, departmental memoranda, and unidentified "implementing measures". (Japan's first written submission, para. 16.) Irrespective of the status of these so-called measures, the duty-free treatment cannot be withdrawn without affecting every aspect of Canada's regime.

7.243 For Canada, implementing changes to measures of such long duration will involve consultations with provinces and stakeholders, the requisite changes to legislation, and the design of replacement measures. For the manufacturers, it will involve a change in years of business practice, which cannot be accomplished quickly.

7.244 Finally, Canada notes that the measures have been in existence for decades, and that the complaining parties themselves have not made any suggestion during these proceedings that there is an urgent need for action. Should such a claim be made at this late stage of the proceedings, it should be rejected.

7.245 Having regard to the foregoing, "without delay" should not require Canada to make any adjustments until 12 months after the adoption of the Panel's recommendations and rulings.

(ii) Comment from Japan on Canada's Reply

7.246 With respect to the determination of an appropriate time-period for implementation, there is a significant difference between the relevant rules and procedures of the DSU and the special and additional rules and procedures set forth in Article 4.7 of the SCM Agreement. Japan recognizes that paragraph 3 of Article 21 of the DSU allows an implementing Member "a reasonable period of time" to implement the recommendations or rulings of the DSB, where it is impracticable to comply immediately. In contrast, Article 4.7 of the SCM Agreement requires a panel to recommend that a subsidy be withdrawn "without delay".

7.247 Canada claims that the measures at issue are "complex," citing even the *Financial Administration Act*, apparently in support of its contention that changes to the WTO-inconsistent programs "would effect every aspect of Canada's regime." However, not a single Canadian statute would need to be altered in any way to abolish the illegal aspects of the regime. Instead, Canada would only need to repeal the offending portions of the statutory and administrative orders that actually implement the regime, to withdraw the prohibited subsidies. Canadian authorities should be able to accomplish within a few months the process of consulting with the provinces and "stakeholders" - all of which are or should be aware of the challenges to the regime and the likelihood that it would be adjudged to be WTO-inconsistent.

7.248 In *Brazil - Export Financing Programme for Aircraft*, the Appellate Body confirmed the Panel's interpretation that "without delay" meant 90 days in the circumstances of that case. In Japan's view, we find nothing in the current case which warrants a period longer than the one granted in the *Brazil case*. Thus, the period of twelve months requested by Canada is far too long.

7.249 Canada's argument that the presence or absence of trade distorting effects should be taken into account in determining the appropriate time-period for implementation under Article 4.7 is neither justified by the text of the SCM Agreement nor supported by any authority. As a matter of fact, however, as argued in Japan's prior submissions to the Panel, the measures do have trade-distorting effect, which should not be permitted to continue.

7.250 In paragraph 6 of Canada's response, Canada merely repeats its previous assertions that are not relevant to the Question, and this should simply be dismissed as irrelevant.

7.251 With regard to paragraph 8 of Canada's response, it must also be noted that it is irrelevant to the interpretation of "without delay", whether or not any suggestion for "an urgent need for action" was made by the complaining parties during the proceedings of the current panel.

7.252 In conclusion, in the circumstances of this case, the words "without delay" in Article 4.7 should be interpreted to mean just that. There is no reason to delay unduly the withdrawal of the prohibited subsidies. To permit a long and drawn-out process of implementation would signal to other WTO Members who may appear before other panels that the orders of the panel are less than mandatory and that compliance need not occur promptly. Accordingly, Japan suggests that all recommendations be implemented within no longer than 90 days.

(iii) Comment from the European Communities on Canada's Reply

7.253 In response to Question 61, Canada advances the extraordinary claim that, in the event that the Panel were to find the existence of a prohibited subsidy, Canada should be accorded no less than twelve months in order to adopt the necessary implementing measures[731].

7.254 Canada's main justification for that request is that the subsidy has "no prejudicial or trade distorting effect[732]" and that there is no need for "urgent action[733]".

7.255 The European Communities disagrees with those unsupported assertions. Canada's argument begs the question: if the ratio and the CVA requirements have no effects at all, why are they enforced? Contrary to Canada's claims, there is no "empirical evidence[734]" whatsoever that the subsidy has no effect on the level of exports. No doubt, both NAFTA and geographical proximity facilitate Canadian exports to the Unites States. That does not exclude, however, that the subsidy may result in an even higher level of exports to the United States[735].

7.256 The best proof that the subsidy does have harmful effects is that the European Communities and Japan, which together with the United States (the beneficiary of the measures in dispute) are the world's largest manufacturers of motor vehicles and parts and components thereof, have brought this case. Furthermore, they have been supported by Korea, another major manufacturer.

7.257 In any event, whether or not the subsidy has any prejudicial effects is not a relevant consideration in determining the duration of the time period for implementation under Article 4.7 of the SCM Agreement.

7.258 Article 4.7 constitutes a departure from the general rule contained in Article 21.3 of the Dispute Settlement Understanding (the "DSU")[736]. The chief purpose of Article 4.7 is to provide faster remedies than those available under the DSU. Thus, whereas Article 21.3 of the DSU allows a "reasonable period of time" to implement whenever it is impracticable to comply immediately, Article 4.7 requires that prohibited subsidies be withdrawn "without delay" in all cases.

7.259 Logic demands that implementation "without delay" should not take longer than implementation within "a reasonable period of time". Yet Canada's argument would have precisely that absurd result.

7.260 The effects of a measure found to be inconsistent with the WTO Agreement have not been deemed relevant in determining the duration of the "reasonable period of time". As made clear by a long line of cases, "the reasonable period of time should be the shortest period possible within the legal system of the Member to implement

---

731 Canada's response to Question 61 from the Panel.

732 Ibid.

733 Ibid.

734 Ibid.

735 In any event, this argument does not address the claim that the subsidy violates Article 3.1 b) of the SCM Agreement.

736 The provisions of Article 4.2 though 4.12 are listed as "special or additional rules and procedures" in Appendix 2 to the DSU.

the recommendations and rulings of the DSB" [737]. Consequently, the effects of a measure may not *a fortiori* be a relevant factor in assessing what constitutes implementation "without delay" for the purposes of Article 4.7.

7.261 The following argument recently put forward by Canada in *Brazil - Aircraft* is also pertinent:

> "... Article 7.9 of the SCM Agreement provides that countermeasures may be imposed if actionable subsidies are not withdrawn within six months of the adoption of the Panel or Appellate Body reports. It is logical that where a subsidy is required to be withdrawn *without delay*, the timeframe for withdrawal must be shorter than the six month period provided under Article 7.9 and in no circumstances should be longer than six months[738]".

7.262 Previous cases under Article 4.7 confirm that the effects of a subsidy are not a relevant consideration. To this date, Article 4.7 of the SCM Agreement has been applied in three occasions[739]. In all the three cases, the Panel recommended that the subsidy be withdrawn within 90 days. The Panels seem to have reached that conclusion in light of the nature of the measures and of the internal procedures required in order to implement the Panel's ruling. On the other hand, there is no indication in the reports that the Panels took into account the effects of the subsidy.

7.263 Even assuming that the effects of the subsidy were a relevant factor, Canada's request for twelve months would still be unwarranted. Panels enjoy some discretion to specify in each particular case the time period within which the subsidy must be withdrawn. But they cannot depart from the benchmark of "without delay".

7.264 Implementation twelve months after the adoption of the Panel Report can under no circumstances be regarded as implementation "without delay". The ordinary meaning of the terms "without delay" (*sans retard* in French; *sin demora* in Spanish) is "at once"[740], "le plus vite possible[741]". Canada's request is incompatible with the ordinary meaning of "without delay" and would effectively read out of Article 4.7 that requirement.

7.265 In this regard, it is worth recalling that in *Australia - Automotive Leather* the panel took the view that the implementation period of seven months and one-half

---

[737] Arbitration award in *EC - Measures concerning Meat and Meat Products (Hormones)*, WT/DS26/15, WT/DS48/13, 29 May 1998, para. 26. See also the Arbitration awards in *Indonesia - Certain Measures affecting the Automobile Industry*, WT/DS54/15, WT/DS55/14, WT/DS59/13, WT/DS64/12, 7 December 1998 (hereinafter Arbitration Report on *Indonesia - Autos*), para. 22; *Australia - Measures affecting the Importation of Salmon*, WT/DS18/9, 23 February 1999, para. 38; and Appellate Body Report on *Korea - Alcoholic Beverages*, *supra* note 280, para. 37.

[738] Appellate Body Report on *Brazil - Export Financing Programme for Aircraft*, adopted on 20 August 1999, WT/DS46/AB/R, (hereinafter Appellate Body Report on *Brazil - Aircraft*), para. 52.

[739] Panel Report on *Australia - Subsidies Provided to Producers and Exporters of Automotive Leather*, WT/DS126/R (hereinafter, Panel Report on *Australia - Automotive Leather*) paras. 10.6 and 10.7; Panel Report on *Canada - Aircraft*, *supra* note 495, para. 10.4; and Panel Report on *Brazil - Aircraft*, *supra* note 490, para. 8.5.

[740] The Shorter Oxford English Dictionary on Historical Principles, Third Edition, p. 511.

[741] Dictionnaire alphabetique et analogique de la Langue Francaise Paul Robert, 1964, VI, p.164

months requested by Australia could not "reasonably be described as corresponding to the requirement that the measure must be withdrawn without delay[742]".

7.266 Canada also claims that "implementing changes ... will involve consultations with provinces and stakeholders, the requisite changes to legislation and the design of replacement measures"[743]. While it is arguable, in the light of the precedents above mentioned, that the duration of the internal procedures required for implementation may be a relevant factor, Canada has provided no evidence of the existence in Canadian law of any mandatory procedural requirements which may delay the withdrawal of the subsidy for as much as twelve months.

7.267 The truth is that the MVTO 1998 and the SROS are both Orders-in-Council, i.e. acts of the executive branch, which can be amended or repealed within a relatively short period of time. The Letters of Undertaking, being informal acts of the Government, could be dealt with even more expeditiously. The Customs Tariff and the Financial Administration Act[744] confer to the Canadian executive the necessary authority for the adoption of the MVTO 1998 and the SROs but are not themselves measures in dispute. Therefore, there is no need to repeal or amend them in order to withdraw the subsidy. Finally, the Auto Pact is, according to Canada, a non self-executing agreement which would fall outside the scope of this dispute[745]. In any event, the Auto Pact merely requires Canada to grant duty-free treatment to imports by the Auto Pact manufacturers from the United States. On the other hand, the Auto Pact does not require Canada to grant duty-free treatment to imports by the Auto Pact beneficiaries from third countries, nor to imports by the SRO beneficiaries, irrespective of the source. Thus, there is no need to amend the Auto Pact in order to withdraw those subsidies.

7.268 Canada also raises the argument that "for the manufacturers, it will involve a change in years of business practice, which cannot be accomplished quickly[746]". The pertinence of this type of considerations has been rejected in arbitrations under Article 21.3 DSU. As noted by the Arbitrator in *Indonesia - Autos*:

> "In virtually every case in which a measure has been found to be inconsistent with a member's obligations under the GATT 1994 or any other covered agreement, and therefore, must be brought into conformity with that agreement, some degree of adjustment by the domestic industry of the Member concerned will be necessary [...] Structural adjustment to the withdrawal or the modification of an inconsistent measure, therefore, is not a 'particular circumstance' that can be taken into account in determining the reasonable period of time under Article 21.3 c)."[747]

7.269 The same considerations are valid *a fortiori* in assessing what constitutes implementation "without delay" in the sense of Article 4.7 of the SCM Agreement.

---

742 Panel Report on *Australia - Automotive Leather, supra* note 739, para. 10.6.
743 Canada's response to Question 61 from the Panel.
744 See Canada's response to Question 61 from the Panel.
745 Canada's response to Question 2 from the EC.
746 Canada's response to Question 61 from the Panel.
747 Arbitration Report on *Indonesia - Autos, supra* note 737, para. 23.

7.270 For the above reasons, the European Communities submits that the Panel should recommend that the subsidy be withdrawn within 90 days from the adoption of the report.

5. *Questions and Replies Relating to Claims Regarding Applicability of the GATS*

(a) Question 27 (the Duty Waiver and Article XXVIII)

Canada argues that none of the examples listed in Article XXVIII relates to access to or to taxation of goods provided by a service supplier. Could the EC and Japan please elaborate on how the duty waiver relates to the measures listed in Article XXVIII.

(i) Reply from Japan

7.271 Judging from the wording of the definitions of "the supply of a service" and "measures by Members affecting trade in services" in GATS Article XXVIII, it is appropriate to interpret that the listed definitions are not exhaustive.

7.272 The procurement of automobiles is an integral part of the "supply" of wholesale trade services of motor vehicles within the meaning of Article XXVIII (b), since the supply of wholesale trade services mainly consists of procuring products from manufacturers and reselling them to retailers.

7.273 The Duty Waiver, by reducing the procurement cost of automobiles that is borne by the Auto Pact Manufacturers (who are also wholesale trade service suppliers), necessarily affects the profitability in supplying wholesale trade services - procuring and reselling automobiles. In turn, it affects the conditions of competition between wholesale trade service suppliers in selling automobiles to retail service suppliers (dealers) and the maintenance and expansion of their dealer networks. Thus, the Duty Waiver constitutes measures by Members affecting trade in wholesale trade services within the meaning of Article XXVIII.

(ii) Reply from the European Communities

7.274 Contrary to what is implied by the question, GATS Article XXVIII (c) does not contain a list of "measures" affecting trade in services, but rather a list of matters in respect of which such measures could be taken.[748]

7.275 The use of the term "include" in GATS Article XXVIII (c) makes it clear that the list contained in that provision does not purport to be exhaustive, but merely illustrative.

7.276 A Note prepared by the GATT Secretariat in 1991[749] in order to clarify the definitions of the terms contained in the then draft GATS described as follows the limited purpose of Article XXVIII (c) [Article XXXIV (c) in the draft]:

7.277 "The definition supplements that of supply of a service. It specifies that measures dealing with the consumer side of the transaction (purchase, payment and

[748] Panel Reports on *EC - Bananas III, supra* note 269, para. 7.280.
[749] MTN.GNS/W/139, 15 October 1991, para. 6.

use), transportation and communication, as well as constraints on physical or juridical presence, are within the scope of the agreement..."

7.278 Thus, the purpose of Article XXVIII (c) is merely to confirm that measures adopted in respect of certain matters are *also* within the scope of GATS, rather than attempting to define the scope of application of GATS, something which is already done in GATS Article I:1.[750]

7.279 The illustrative nature of Article XXVIII (c) is evidenced by the fact that, for example, it does not include measures in respect of the "production" of services. Yet, there can be no question that a measure limiting the output of a service provider is a measure "affecting the supply of services". Indeed, that type of measure is expressly mentioned in GATS Article XVI:2 (c) as a limitation on market access.

7.280 The illustrative nature of Article XXVIII (c) has been confirmed by the Panel Report on *EC - Bananas III*.[751] According to that Report, the controlling criterion in order to determine whether a measure is covered by GATS is not whether it regulates a matter listed in Article XXVIII (c), but whether it "affects" trade in services:

7.281 "... In principle no measures are excluded a priori from the scope of the GATS as defined by its provisions. The scope of the GATS encompasses any measure of a Member to the extent it affects the supply of a service...".[752]

7.282 That finding was affirmed by the Appellate Body.[753] Further, the Appellate Body confirmed that that the term "affect" must be interpreted broadly[754] and upheld the Panel's finding that the rules for the allocation of a tariff quota for bananas "affected" the provision of distribution services for those goods.

7.283 In view of the above, there is no scope left for arguing that the measure in dispute in this case, which is also a tariff measure, like the one at issue in *EC - Bananas III*, is excluded *a priori* from the GATS' coverage simply because it is not explicitly listed in Article XXVIII (c).

(b) Question 29 ("Critical to the Scope and Profitability" and "Measure Affecting Trade in Services")

Canada argues against the analogy between the measures at issue in this case and the EC import licensing regime on bananas, on the grounds that the latter was "critical" to the scope and profitability of the provision of distribution services. Could Canada please clarify the meaning of the term "critical" in this context and how it is used to determine whether a certain measure would be considered a "measure affecting trade in services".

---

[750] The Note by the Secretariat of 15 October 1991, observes the following with respect to Article I:1 of GATS, para. 4: "This important provision determines the scope of the GATS. Its full meaning is clarified through the definition of each of its elements: measures, by Parties, affecting, trade in services."

[751] Panel Reports on *EC - Bananas III*, *supra* note 269, para. 7.280.

[752] Ibid., para. 7.285.

[753] Appellate Body Report on *EC - Bananas III*, *supra* note 49, para.220.

[754] Ibid.

(i) Reply from Canada

7.284 Canada was not proposing "critical" as a test. The test, as established by the Appellate Body in *EC - Bananas III*[755] is whether a measure does or does not affect a service supplier in its capacity as a service provider and in its supply of services. Canada used the term "critical" to contrast the very significant effect that access to import licences had on importers in *EC - Bananas III* in their capacity as importers, i.e. their ability to compete for the provision of the service of importing bananas, with the absence of any effect whatsoever of the 6.1 per cent duty on the ability of vehicle distributors to compete for the service of distributing vehicles.

7.285 As Canada noted, under the EC's bananas regime, the right to import bananas within the tariff-rate quota was allocated by a system of licences. It was critical to the outcome of *EC - Bananas III* that the EC measures deliberately and drastically took distribution business away from certain suppliers and gave it to others. Those distributors that did not receive licences faced a prohibitive tariff, which meant that they were effectively prevented from distributing bananas in the EC, unless they were prepared to pay an exorbitant quota rent to the licence holder. That is, they were affected by the import licensing regime in their capacity as distributors.

7.286 The EC's measures in *EC - Bananas III* also imposed differential levels of duty, but it is significant that these were not even mentioned in relation to trade in services but, properly, only in relation to trade in goods. Differential duties may affect goods as goods, but they do not and cannot affect service suppliers in their capacity as service suppliers. To hold that they do would render null the three categories of measures identified by the Appellate Body in *EC - Bananas III*[756] would ignore the definitions of "supply of a service" and "measures by Members affecting trade in services" in Article XXVIII of the GATS, would contradict the *Addendum* to the *Explanatory Note on the Scheduling of Initial Commitments in Trade in Services*, and would create conflicts between the GATS and differential treatment of goods authorized under the GATT. The GATS complements the rights and obligations of the GATT, but was not intended to subsume or contradict them.

(c) Question 58 (Interface of GATT and GATS)

Canada has raised the point that differential tariffs arise for a number of reasons. Such differential tariff treatment may have adverse commercial consequences for certain service suppliers in the importing country compared with other service suppliers, particularly where the industry is characterised by a high degree of vertical integration.

Assuming such differential tariffs are fully consistent with GATT 1994, it may be held that they "affect trade in services", which is not to imply that such measures necessarily breach GATS obligations. In the case of differential tariffs arising from regional economic integration agreements, it would seem logical for any examination of that matter to proceed directly to GATS Article V that deals with the matter.

[755] Appellate Body Report on *EC - Bananas III*, *supra* note 49.
[756] Ibid., para. 221.

However, in other cases unrelated to regional economic integration agreements and thus where GATS Article V is irrelevant - anti-dumping and CVD orders which are themselves fully consistent with the provisions of GATT 94 and the Anti-dumping or SCM Agreements, for example - such differential tariffs may also be considered to have the incidental consequence of "affecting trade in services" and, moreover, raise the question as to whether less favourable treatment is being accorded to certain services providers either in terms of GATS Article II or Article XVII.

Could the delegations of Japan and the EC comment on this?

(i) Reply from Japan

7.287 As this question is answered in the rebuttal of Japan, the Duty Waiver is not an anti-dumping or countervailing duty, and therefore the Panel is not required to decide on the consistency between these GATT-consistent measures and the GATS. The Panel in *the EC - Bananas III* also wisely rejected the argument on the consistency between GATT-consistent measures and the GATS, saying that the Panel "need not decide in this case how to resolve a conflict that may never arise "between GATT and GATS provisions.

7.288 It is the position of the Government of Japan that to the extent that this Panel is considering this issue in the context of this dispute, the only difference between the Duty Waiver and the measure at issue in *the EC - Bananas III* is the magnitude of the discrimination of the customs duty in question, not its nature. It is therefore the position of the Government of Japan that to the extent that such argument was irrelevant to *the EC - Bananas III* case, it is equally irrelevant to this dispute.

(ii) Reply from the European Communities

7.289 Differential tariff treatment may "affect the supply of services" in the sense of GATS Article I:1. Nevertheless, as rightly noted in the Panel's question, that does not mean that tariff differentials are *per se* contrary to GATS Article XVII or Article II. For that, it would still be necessary to show that *in casu* the tariff differential provides more favourable treatment to domestic service suppliers than to foreign service providers, or to service suppliers of one or more Members than to service suppliers of other Members, respectively.

7.290 The tariff differential at issue in this case is fundamentally different from those resulting from the existence of a free trade area ("FTA") established in conformity with Article XXIV GATT. Canada grants the Tariff Exemption only to a limited number of importers/distributors. By contrast, in a FTA any importer/distributor is entitled to import duty free any goods from the other constituent territories of the FTA. For that reason, the mere existence of a FTA is unlikely to give a competitive advantage to service suppliers of a particular Member at the expense of service suppliers of other Members. In fact, in the present case neither the European Communities nor Japan claim that the FTA between Canada and the United States established by NAFTA gives raise to a violation of Article II. Rather the complainants' claim is that Article II of GATS is breached by the additional privileges granted to certain US importers/distributors under the Tariff Exemption.

7.291 Contrary to what is implied in the question, whether or not a FTA gives raise to a violation of GATS Article II is not a question to be examined directly within the framework of Article V GATS. As a first step, it is necessary to establish that there is a prima facie violation of GATS Article II. Indeed it must be recalled that the existence of a FTA formed in accordance with GATT Article XXIV does not necessarily presuppose the existence of an Economic Integration Agreement meeting the requirements of Article V GATS and vice-versa.

7.292 The Tariff Exemption also is easily distinguishable from anti-dumping ("AD") and countervailing ("CV") duties. In the first place, unlike the Tariff Exemption, AD and CV duties do not discriminate formally among importers/distributors. AD and CV duties apply to all imports from a given exporting country, or at least to all imports manufactured by a certain undertaking, irrespective of the identity of the importer/distributor. By contrast, the Tariff Exemption applies only and exclusively to imports by a limited number of designated importers/distributors.

7.293 Second, even those importers/distributors which are related to an exporter/manufacturer subject to AD/CV measures have several options to import the goods that they distribute without being required to pay AD or CV duties: (a) to purchase the goods from an unrelated supplier in the same exporting country; (b) to purchase the goods from a supplier (related or unrelated) in another country not covered by the AD/CV measure; or (c) to stop selling at dumped prices or to renounce the subsidy. In contrast, there is nothing that a non-beneficiary can do in order to obtain the Tariff Exemption, short of taking over one of the existing beneficiaries.

7.294 Finally, it must be recalled that AD and CV duties are remedies against practices that distort competition among goods, and consequently also among the distributors of those goods. Furthermore, both AD[757] and CVD duties[758] must be applied on non-discriminatory basis on imports from all sources. Therefore, AD and CV duties do not "modify the conditions of competition" in favour of those service suppliers who distribute goods not subject to those measures. Rather, AD and CV duties serve to re-establish a level playing field between those suppliers who distribute dumped/subsidised goods and those suppliers who distribute non dumped/non subsidised goods.

6. *Questions and Replies Relating to Claims under Article II of the GATS*

(a) Question 33 (the Measures at Issue and GATS Article V)

Without prejudice to Canada's stated position that the duty waiver is not inconsistent with Article II of the GATS and in the light of the third-party argument from the United States, could Canada clarify whether it sees any relevance of Article V of the GATS to the arguments put forward by the complainants?

(i) Reply from Canada

7.295 Article V of the GATS is relevant to demonstrate that the scope of the GATS was not intended to extend to measures according duty-free treatment to goods. Had

---

757 C.f. Article 9.2 of the Agreement on Implementation of Article VI of GATT 1994.

758 C.f. Article 19.3 of the SCM Agreement.

those drafting the GATS ever imagined that trade-in-goods provisions such as duty remission programs might constitute measures "affecting trade in services", the exemption in Article V:1 of the GATS would have been extended to agreements liberalizing trade in goods, and not just agreements liberalizing trade in services. To hypothesize the relevance of Article V of the GATS in the event that the GATS was found to apply to the duty-free treatment of goods would require contorting the scope of the GATS beyond the intentions of its drafters.

7.296 If the Panel nevertheless finds that the measures according duty-free treatment to goods fall within the scope of the GATS, then Canada agrees with the United States that with respect to any more favourable treatment allegedly accorded to US service suppliers, the measures would be subject to the MFN exception conferred by Article V:I of the GATS.

(b) Question 34 (Ownership and Control)

Canada argues that when the nationality of service suppliers (distributors) is ascertained in accordance with the GATS provisions, no service suppliers of a particular Member are favoured or disadvantaged. Please clarify whether service suppliers, as individual economic operators (which in some cases might be distinct from manufacturers), are service suppliers of other Members according to Article XXVIII. And, to the extent possible, provide factual information on the ownership and control situation of these operators.

(i) Reply from Japan

7.297 With respect to wholesale trade services related to automobiles, the relevant service suppliers and their ownership are set out in Japan's Tables 1 and 2.

7.298 To summarise the evidence, in Japan's Table 1 the wholesale trade service suppliers of the Auto Pact Manufacturers are identified—Chrysler Canada, Ford Canada, GM Canada, Volvo Canada and CAMI and their ownership is specified. Applying the ownership test in paragraphs (m) and (n) of GATS Article XXVIII, the first three companies are US service suppliers and the fourth is a Swedish service supplier.[759] With respect to the fifth company, it is not a Japanese service supplier within the meaning of paragraph (n) of GATS Article XXVIII.[760]

7.299 Japan's Tables 1 and 2 list the following wholesale trade service suppliers of the non-Auto Pact Manufacturers: Toyota Canada Inc., Nissan Canada Inc., Mazda Canada Inc., Suzuki Canada, Honda Canada Inc., Subaru Canada Inc., BMW Canada Inc. and Volkswagen Canada Inc. Others not listed on these tables include subsidiaries of South Korean manufacturers (e.g., Hyundai, etc). As evident from those ta-

[759] This could change to a US service supplier as a result of Ford Motor Co's 1 March 1999 agreement with AB Volvo to purchase Volvo's world-wide passenger car business. On 8 March 1999, AB Volvo's shareholders approved the transaction. The transaction will close following the receipt of regulatory approvals. Source: Ford Motor Co., Form 10-K Annual Report (US Securities and Exchange Commission), fiscal year ended December 31, 1998.

[760] According to the information given to the Ministry of International Trade and Industry of the Government of Japan by Suzuki Motor Corporation, only General Motors Group owns 40,237,358 preferred shares of CAMI in addition to ordinary shares equally owned by and between General Motors Corporation and Suzuki Motor Corporation.

bles, all of these companies are non-Canadian and non-US, according to paragraphs (m) and (n) of Article XXVIII.

7.300 It can be concluded from the foregoing evidence that US subsidiaries that supply wholesale trade services benefit from the Duty Waiver and *none* of the Japanese subsidiaries that supply like services benefit from the Duty Waiver.

7.301 For the sake of avoidance of misunderstanding, the Government of Japan would like to emphasize that even if one or more Japanese service suppliers were granted duty-free treatment under the Duty Waiver (which is not the case), Canada could not justify according less favorable treatment to other Japanese service suppliers.

7.302 The Government of Japan has only insufficient information relating to service suppliers which distribute buses and specified commercial vehicles imported from abroad into Canada, although, to the extent of the knowledge of the Government of Japan, there is at least one Japanese service supplier named *Hino Diesel Trucks (Canada), Ltd.* Since the information as to the nationality of the service suppliers is uniquely in the hands of the Government of Canada, the information on this aspect should be provided by the Government of Canada. Accordingly, the Government of Japan has submitted a question to Canada on this issue. It is, nevertheless, the understanding of the Government of Japan that no Japanese service suppliers are eligible for the duty exemption in connection with buses and specified commercial vehicles.

(ii) Reply from the European Communities

7.303 The European Communities has already provided the requested factual information on ownership and control with respect to the five wholesale distributors that are entitled to import automobiles under the Tariff Exemption in the EC's Table 5.

7.304 As shown in that Table, three of those five wholesale distributors (Ford Motor Co. of Canada Ltd., General Motors Co. of Canada Ltd and Chrysler Canada Ltd.) can be considered as service suppliers of the United States in accordance with the criteria set forth in GATS Article XXVIII m) and n), while another distributor (CAMI Automotive Inc.) is a joint venture between a Japanese company (Suzuki Motors Corp.) and a US company (General Motors Corp.).

7.305 The fifth wholesale distributor (Volvo Canada Ltd.) was controlled by Volvo AB, of Sweden, until January 1999, when Volvo AB agreed to sell its passenger car business to Ford Motor Co., of the United States. At any rate, Volvo Canada Ltd closed its Canadian assembly plant in December 1998, with the consequence that it will loose the right to import motor vehicles under the Tariff Exemption as of July1999.

7.306 Ford Motor Co. of Canada Ltd, General Motors Co. of Canada Ltd and Chrysler Canada Ltd. account for the vast majority of sales of automobiles imported under the Tariff Exemption.

7.307 As clarified by the Panel Report in *EC - Bananas III*[761], the fact that a juridical person of Member A that controls a service supplier established in Member B is in turn controlled by another person of Country C does not prevent from considering

[761] Panel Reports on *EC - Bananas III, supra* note 269, footnote 493.

that service supplier as a service supplier of Member A for GATS purposes. Thus, contrary to Canada's assertions, Chrysler Canada Ltd., can still be regarded as a service supplier of the United States, despite the fact that its US parent company, DaimlerCrhysler Corp, is controlled by DaimlerChrysler AG of Germany following the merger of Chrysler with Daimler-Benz.

7.308 The EC's Table 7 (below) provides the requested ownership information with respect to the major wholesale distributors which are *not* entitled to import automobiles under the Tariff Exemption. The Table reflects the information available to the EC's and does not purport to be exhaustive.

7.309 The EC's Table 7 shows that, with only one exception (Nissan Canada Inc.) all the major wholesale distributors of automobiles which do not benefit from the Tariff Exemption are service suppliers of Members other than the United States. Thus, for example, Volkswagen Canada Inc. is a service supplier of Germany because it is owned by a juridical person constituted under German law, Volkswagen AG, which is engaged in substantial business operations within the German territory.

EC's Table 7

Country of origin of the major suppliers of wholesale trade services for automobiles which do not befit from the Tariff Exemption

Service supplier	Parent company	% of shares owned by parent company	Country of incorporation of parent company
Volkswagen Canada Inc.	Volkswagen AG	100	Germany
BMW Canada Inc.	BMW AG	100	Germany
Mercedes-Benz Canada Inc.	DaimlerChrysler AG	100	Germany
Honda Canada Inc.	Honda Motor Co.	50.14	Japan
	American Honda Motor Co.*	49.86	USA
Toyota Canada Inc.	Toyota Motor Corp.	50	Japan
	Mitsui & Co.	50	Japan
Nissan Canada Inc.	Nissan Motor Co. Ltd.	38.3	Japan
	Nissan North America Inc.**	61.7	USA
Subaru Canada Inc.	Fuji Heavy Industries Ltd.	100	Japan
Mazda Canada Inc.	Mazda Motor Corp.	60	Japan
	Itochu Corp.	40	Japan
Hyundai Canada Inc.	Hyundai Motor Co.	100	Korea
Porsche Canada Ltd.	Porsche AG	100	Germany
Lada Canada Inc.	???	???	???

* A fully owned subsidiary of Honda Motor Co., of Japan.

** A fully owned subsidiary of Nissan Motor Co. Ltd., of Japan.

(iii) Reply from Canada

7.310 Article XXVIII(m) of the GATS provides that a "juridical person of another Member" is a juridical person which is either: (i) constituted or otherwise organized under the law of that other Member ... or (ii) in the case of the supply of a service through commercial presence, owned or controlled by ... juridical persons of that other Member identified under subparagraph (i).

7.311 Article XXVIII(n)(i) of the GATS provides that a juridical person is "owned" by persons of a Member if more than 50 per cent of the equity interest in it is beneficially owned by persons of that Member.

7.312 Chrysler Canada Ltd. is now DaimlerChrysler Canada Inc.. It is a wholly-owned subsidiary of the DaimlerChrysler Corporation (a United States company), which in turn is 100 per cent owned by DaimlerChrysler AG of Germany.

7.313 According to Article XXVIII(m)(i), DaimlerChrysler AG is a juridical person constituted under the law of Germany. DaimlerChrysler Canada Inc. is owned by DaimlerChrysler AG through DaimlerChrysler Corporation. DaimlerChrysler Canada Inc. is therefore a juridical person of Germany, according to Article XXVIII(m)(ii) and XXVIII(n)(i).

7.314 Similarly, Nissan Canada Inc. is a juridical person of Japan, although according to Japan's Table 2, it is majority-owned by Nissan North America Inc. of the United States. This is because Nissan North America Inc. is itself 100 per cent owned by Nissan Motor Co. Ltd. of Japan.

7.315 While Volvo Canada Limited was operating as a manufacturer in Canada, it was wholly-owned by Volvo AB of Sweden. It was therefore a juridical person of Sweden by operation of Articles XXVIII(m) and (n). Volvo Canada Limited is now indirectly wholly-owned by the Ford Motor Company.

7.316 CAMI Automotive Inc. is 50 percent owned by General Motors of Canada Limited and 50 per cent owned by the Suzuki Motor Company of Japan. General Motors of Canada is wholly-owned by the General Motors Corporation of the United States, making it a juridical person of the United States for the purposes of Article XXVIII. CAMI is therefore owned 50/50 by juridical persons of the United States and Japan. Under Article XXVIII(n)(i), ownership by persons of a Member requires an equity interest greater than 50 per cent. Persons of neither the United States or Japan own CAMI individually because neither General Motors nor Suzuki individually owns greater than 50 per cent. Together however, they own 100 per cent of CAMI. CAMI can therefore be said to be a juridical person of both the United States and Japan.

(c) Question 35 (Vertical Integration)

Canada argues that in the supply of wholesale trade services for automobiles there is no competition between wholesale trade service suppliers since wholesale suppliers are subordinated to manufacturers and therefore the question of an effect on conditions of competition does not arise. Does vertical integration between manufacturers and suppliers of wholesale trade services exclude any actual or potential competition at the wholesale trade level? To what extent does vertical integration between manufacturers and suppliers of wholesale trade services also exclude competition with respect to sales to retailers?

(i) Reply from Japan

7.317 As the Appellate Body Report for *EC - Bananas III* confirmed, even if wholesale trade service suppliers are integrated with manufacturers, to the extent they are engaged in providing wholesale trade services, they are wholesale trade service suppliers.

7.318 And vertical integration between manufacturers and suppliers of wholesale trade services does not exclude any actual and potential competition at the wholesale trade level, since an integrated manufacturer, in its capacity as a wholesale trade service supplier, competes with other wholesale trade service suppliers as to the sales of automobiles to retail service suppliers (dealers) and the maintenance and expansion of their dealers networks. This type of competition is relevant to this dispute because dealers are consumers of the wholesale trade services provided by the service suppliers in question. To the extent that manufacturers/wholesale trade service suppliers are to sell automobiles to retail service suppliers (i.e. dealers), there is competition between those manufacturers/wholesale trade service suppliers with respect to sales to retailers, notwithstanding their vertical integration.

7.319 Further, differences in the retail prices of automobiles caused by the Duty Waiver will necessarily affect sales volumes and will lead to differences in profitability in supplying wholesale trade services between manufacturers/wholesale service suppliers. This means that the conditions of competition between manufacturers/wholesale trade service suppliers for sales to retailers will be negatively affected.

(ii) Reply from the European Communities

7.320 No. Although the major wholesale distributors of automobiles present in the Canadian market are vertically integrated with manufacturers[762], that does not exclude any actual or potential competition amongst them with respect to the purchase of motor vehicles from manufacturers for wholesale resale.

7.321 In the first place, some foreign manufacturers of automobiles have little or no presence at all in the Canadian market (e.g., Renault, Peugeot-Citroen, Fiat, Mitsubishi, Proton or Tata).

7.322 Those potential new entrants have basically three options in order to penetrate into the Canadian market: to set up their own distributors; to designate an independent distributor; or to appoint as a distributor an existing integrated distributor. The last option is not unusual, in particular when the model ranges of the two manufacturers concerned are complementary. By way of example, in the past Chrysler has imported and distributed in Canada motor vehicles manufactured by Mitsubishi, an unrelated Japanese producer (see Exhibit EC-16, Table 1.7).

7.323 Thus, while it may be true that, as argued by Canada, Honda Canada and Ford Canada would not compete for the distribution in Canada of vehicles manufactured by Ford in the United States, they may compete, not only with other integrated distributors but also with independent distributors, for the distribution of vehicles produced by a foreign manufacturer without a distribution network in Canada. The Tariff Exemption confers upon the beneficiaries a competitive advantage in that market because it lowers their import costs and, therefore, gives them the possibility to offer better purchasing terms to the foreign manufacturer.

7.324 Secondly, even with respect to motor vehicles of the parent company's brand, vertically integrated distributors may face competition from parallel importers.

[762] The affiliation of some distributors, such as Lada Canada Inc., is nevertheless unclear, as shown in Table 7.

Regarding the question, "To what extent does vertical integration between manufacturers and suppliers of wholesale trade services also exclude competition with respect to sales to retailers?":

7.325 Canada's argument is built on the wrong assumption that wholesale distribution services are provided by the wholesalers exclusively to the manufacturers. The truth, however, is that wholesaler distributors of automobiles act as intermediaries between the manufacturers and the retailers (and in some cases final consumers, e.g., in the case of so-called "fleet sales" to big purchasers). They provide a service to retailers as much as to the manufacturers. In fact, except in the rare cases where wholesale distributors of automobiles act as mere agents for the manufacturers, the "buyer" of the service, i.e. the person who actually "pays" for the distribution service, is the retailer and not the manufacturer.

7.326 Quite clearly, vertical integration between manufacturers and wholesale distributors of automobiles, even if it were complete, would not exclude *per se* competition among wholesale distributors with respect to sales to retailers and final consumers. Vertical integration has the only consequence that Honda Canada and Ford Canada cannot compete to resell the *same* automobiles to retailers. But it does not prevent them from competing in order to resell to dealers automobiles manufactured by their respective parents which are directly competitive and substitutable with each other. In other words, the absence of intra-brand competition among wholesalers does not exclude inter-brand competition.

(iii) Reply from Canada

7.327 Canada notes that the arguments in question are found in its initial response.

7.328 It is not clear if the question refers to vertical integration in the motor vehicle industry only, or to vertical integration generally. In the motor vehicle industry, a combination of vertical integration and exclusive distribution arrangements does exclude any actual or potential competition at the wholesale trade level. The same is not necessarily true of other industries. For example, it is not the case in the bananas business, where even those companies that were vertically integrated had the "capability and opportunity to enter the wholesale service market".[763]

7.329 Contrary to what was implied by the European Communities in its argument, the Appellate Body's findings in *EC - Bananas III* in respect of integrated wholesalers were specific to the facts of the case. The Appellate Body stated that: "even if a company is vertically-integrated, ... to the extent that it is also engaged in providing "wholesale trade services" *and is therefore affected in that capacity by a particular measure of a Member in its supply of those 'wholesale trade services',* that company is a service supplier within the scope of the GATS".[764] (*emphasis added*)

7.330 The fact that a wholesale service supplier is integrated does not mean that it is necessarily outside the scope of the GATS, but nor does it mean that it necessarily falls within the scope of the GATS either. The determining factor is whether that service supplier is affected in its capacity as a service supplier and in its supply of those services. The nature of the motor vehicle industry is such that there is no com-

[763] Panel Reports on *EC - Bananas III, supra* note 269, para. 7.320.

[764] Appellate Body Report on *EC - Bananas III, supra* note 49, para. 227.

petition among wholesale service suppliers in the supply of wholesale trade services. Japan confirmed this in its arguments.

[Regarding the question "to what extent does vertical integration between manufacturers and suppliers of wholesale trade services also exclude competition with respect to sales to retailers?":]

7.331 If the EC's reference to retailers was meant to suggest that retailers could choose among wholesale service suppliers, the suggestion is wrong. Wholesaling by definition entails sales to retailers. Wholesalers purchase goods from manufacturers and resell them to retailers. A headnote to Division 6 of the CPC states that: "*The principal services rendered by wholesalers and retailers may be characterized as reselling merchandise*, accompanied by a variety of related, subordinated services ...". (*emphasis added*)

7.332 "Reselling" necessarily implies that the reseller has purchased the good in the first place. It is uncertain to what extent the commercial presences of the motor vehicle manufacturers identified by the complainants as "wholesalers" have purchased the vehicles from the manufacturers. If they have not, they cannot be said to be wholesalers at all. The complainants have offered no evidence on this point.

7.333 Even assuming that these commercial presences are wholesalers, they do not compete for sales to retailers for the same reason that they do not compete to distribute the vehicles of particular manufacturers. The so-called wholesalers have exclusive distribution arrangements with the manufacturers. Accordingly, retailers of specific brands of vehicles cannot select among wholesale service suppliers for the supply of those vehicles. Retail dealers of Honda automobiles cannot for example, approach General Motors of Canada and ask General Motors to supply them with Hondas from the Honda Motor Company of Japan. Those retailers must rely on Honda Canada Inc. to provide those vehicles.

7.334 It is possible that the European Communities was suggesting that duty-free treatment may influence which brands of vehicles retailers choose to sell and that this consequentially influences their choice of service supplier. However, this simply underscores that what benefits from the duty-free treatment is particular goods (the vehicles) and that there is no competition in the provision of distribution services for those goods. To contend that the measure affects wholesale service suppliers through retailers implies that every measure affecting goods not only affects wholesale service suppliers of those goods but also the retailers of the goods as well. No measures affecting goods would not also "affect" services. The EC's argument would obliterate the distinction among the three categories of measures by the Appellate Body in *EC - Bananas III*.[765]

(d) Question 56 (the Measures at Issue and GATS Article V)

In its reply to question 33 from the Panel, Canada said that if the Panel found that the duty waiver fell within the scope of the GATS it agreed with the United States that with respect to any more favourable treatment allegedly accorded to US service

[765] Appellate Body Report on *EC - Bananas III*, *supra* note 49, para. 221.

suppliers, the measures would be subject to the MFN exception conferred by Article V:1 of the GATS. Could Canada elaborate further on how the mesures at issue could be considered consistent with the paragraph 6 of Article V, concerning the treatment of service suppliers of Members not parties to the economic integration agreement?

(i) Reply from Canada

7.335 Canada did not invoke the Article V:1 exception, because the tariff measures in question do not affect trade in services and hence are not subject to the GATS. Article V:1 of the GATS covers agreements liberalizing trade in services but it does not cover tariff measures taken pursuant to agreements liberalizing trade in goods, such as those creating free-trade areas or customs unions. Canada submits that such measures are not exempted under Article V:1 because, until the EC and Japanese claims in this case, no one, including the drafters of the GATS and those involved in *EC - Bananas III,* had ever thought that tariff measures were within the scope of the GATS.

7.336 Canada stated that if the Panel nevertheless found that the measures according duty-free treatment fell within the scope of the GATS, Canada would endorse the suggestion of its NAFTA partner, the United States, that by extension, Article V:1 of the GATS would apply to any alleged MFN violation arising from a provision of the NAFTA. This would be because the NAFTA is, among other things, an agreement liberalizing trade in services and therefore falls within Article V:1 of the GATS.

7.337 It is not entirely clear to Canada why the Panel is raising Article V:6 in the context of Article V:1. Article V:6 of the GATS creates an obligation on Members to grant service suppliers that are juridical persons of another Member constituted under the laws of a party to an agreement liberalizing trade in services the treatment granted under the services liberalizing agreement, provided that the juridical person engages in substantive business operation in the territories of the parties to the services liberalization agreement. Because neither of the complainants claimed a violation of Article V:6 in its request for a panel, alleged violations of Article V:6 of the GATS are not properly within the Panel's terms of reference.

7.338 If the Panel's question is intended to suggest that an inconsistency with Article V:6 would negate the exception afforded by Article V:1, Canada cannot agree. In contrast with paragraphs (a) and (b) of Article V:1, there is nothing in Article V:6 itself or elsewhere in Article V to suggest that Article V:6 constitutes a condition limiting the application of the Article V:1 exception. If it had been intended as such a condition, it would have been included in Article V:1 rather than drafted as an independent obligation.

7.339 In any event, the NAFTA fully satisfies Article V:6. The treatment granted by the NAFTA chapters that specifically address trade in services (Chapters 11, 12 and 14) is granted to service suppliers that are juridical persons of other Members constituted under the laws of the NAFTA parties and engaging in substantial business activities there. To the extent that the tariff treatment granted by the trade in goods provisions of the NAFTA affects trade in services - and in Canada's view it does not - that tariff treatment is also granted to service suppliers that are juridical persons of other Members constituted under the laws of the NAFTA parties and engaging in substantial business activities there. This includes Canada's duty-free treatment for qualifying manufacturers, as permitted under the NAFTA.

- *Also, hypothetically, what would be Canada's justification for more favourable treatment accorded to non-NAFTA service suppliers?*

7.340 Canada does not understand the question but would be pleased to receive a clarification of it and an opportunity to respond. [The Panel decided not to pursue this matter.]

(e) Question 57 (the Measures at Issue and *De Facto* Discrimination)

The EC and Japan claim that Auto-Pact manufacturers, as suppliers of wholesale trade services, are accorded more favourable treatment in a manner which constitutes de facto discrimination against other like service suppliers. Does this imply that Auto-Pact manufacturers and other service suppliers receive formally identical treatment? How could this relate to the Auto-Pact manufacturers being a closed list?

(i) Reply from Japan

7.341 The claim of the Government of Japan with regard to the eligibility restriction is that Japanese service suppliers are *de facto* excluded from ever qualifying for the Duty Waiver due to various conditions set forth under the MVTO 1998 and the SROs as outlined in Japan's arguments as well as the fact that Auto Pact Manufacturers are limited to those on "a closed-list". Since GATS Article II applies to *de facto* discrimination as well as *de jure* discrimination, it is not necessary to address the significance of "formally identical treatment" in the context of this dispute.

(ii) Reply from the European Communities

7.342 No. The treatment received by the Big Three and CAMI is formally, and not simply *de facto*, more favourable than that accorded to the other suppliers of wholesale distribution services for automobiles. The European Communities claims that the Tariff Exemption results in *de facto* discrimination in the sense that, although those differences in treatment are not formally based on the origin of the service suppliers, *de facto* US suppliers receive more favourable treatment than the suppliers of other Members.

7.343 The fact that the list of beneficiaries was frozen as of 1989 reinforces the discriminatory effects of the Tariff Exemption, because it means that other suppliers of distribution services for automobiles cannot obtain the Tariff Exemption, even if they are also established as manufacturers in Canada and meet CVA and ratio requirements equivalent to those imposed upon the beneficiaries.

7.344 Finally, the fact that the list was frozen at the request of the United States evidences that the effects of the Tariff Exemption are by no means the result of geography or accident, as claimed by Canada, but the intended consequence of a deliberate policy to provide an advantage to the US suppliers over the suppliers of other Members.

(f) Question 59 (Origin of Wholesale Trade Service Suppliers)

Could Japan please clarify on what basis it has classified three suppliers of wholesale trade services for buses and specified commercial vehicles as Canadian in Exhibit JPN-50.

Could Japan please provide necessary material to support the Canadian origin of these suppliers.

7.345 As for the nationality of the "juridical person", Article XXVIII (m)(i) and (ii) and (n)(i) of the GATS prescribe as follows:

> (m) "juridical person of another Member" means a juridical person which is either:
>
> (i) constituted or otherwise organized under the law of that other Member, and is engaged in substantive business operations in the territory of that Member or any other Member; or
>
> (ii) in the case of the supply of a service through commercial presence, owned or controlled by:
>
> 1. natural persons of that Member; or
> 2. juridical persons of that other Member identified under subparagraph (i);
>
> (n) a juridical person is:
>
> (i) "owned" by persons of a Member if more than 50 per cent of the equity interest in it is beneficially owned by persons of that Member;
>
> ...

7.346 Based on the information provided by the Government of Canada in its response to Question (4) of the Government of Japan, the three suppliers of wholesale trade services classified as Canadian in Exhibit JPN-50, which are A. Girardin Inc., Les Enterprises Michel Corbeil Inc. and Western Star Trucks Inc., have imported vehicles from other countries into Canada. Those companies provide services through a commercial presence in Canada. If those companies are not owned or controlled by natural persons of a country other than Canada or juridical persons of countries other than Canada identified under subparagraph (m)(i), those companies are not "juridical persons of another Member", and it follows that those companies are juridical persons of the Member (Canada).

7.347 On the homepage of the Canadian Department of Industry (Industry Canada) (http://strategis.ic.gc.ca/), Industry Canada stated that "Both Thomas Built and Canadian Bluebird are American-owned. A. Girardin and Michel Corbeil Enterprises Inc. are wholly-owned Canadian companies." (See page 3 of attachment 1 to this response [assigned name: Exhibit JPN-51].) Therefore, Japan concluded that A. Girardin and Michel Corbeil Enterprises Inc. are service suppliers of Canadian origin.

7.348 On the homepage of Industry Canada (*http://strategis.ic.gc.ca/*), it is also indicated that ownership of Les Enterprises Michel Corbeil Inc. (see attachment 2 [assigned name: Exhibit JPN-51]) and Michel Corbeil Enterprises Inc. (see attachment 3 [assigned name: Exhibit JPN-51]) is Canadian. This homepage also indicates that the ownership of Western Star Trucks Inc. is Canadian (see attachment 1 [assigned name: Exhibit JPN-51]). Based on the information from Industry Canada on the ownership of those three companies, it is reasonable to presume that more than 50 per cent of their equity interests is owned by Canadians.

7.349 Please see attachments 1-3 [assigned name: Exhibit JPN-51], which substantiates Japan's above conclusion.

(g) Question 60 (Origin of Wholesale Trade Service Suppliers)

Could Canada please confirm that the three suppliers of wholesale trade services for buses and specified commercial vehicles, listed as Canadian in Exhibit JPN-50, are of Canadian origin.

7.350 The three companies listed as Canadian in Exhibit JPN-50 are A.Girardin Inc., Les Entreprises Michel Corbeil Inc., and Western Star Trucks Inc. Canada has the following information about their "origin": A.Girardin Inc. and Les Entreprises Michel Corbeil Inc. are both privately-owned companies incorporated in Canada. To Canada's knowledge, both companies are Canadian-owned. Western Star Trucks Inc. is a company incorporated in Canada. It is wholly-owned by a Canadian-incorporated company, Western Star Trucks Holdings Ltd., which in turn is controlled by a Singapore-incorporated company, Western Star International, which owns 42 per cent of Western Star Holdings.

7.351 Canada notes that Japan has not adduced any evidence in the record to support its assertion that the three companies at issue are "suppliers of wholesale trade services". As Canada noted in its Response of 25 June 1999 to the Panel's Question 35, wholesalers purchase goods and resell them to retailers. A headnote to Division 6 of the CPC states that: "the principal services rendered by wholesalers and retailers may be characterized as reselling merchandise..." Manufacturers that import vehicles but do not resell them to retailers are not "suppliers of wholesale trade services".

7.352 Eligible manufacturers that do import buses or SCVs are not necessarily "wholesale trade service suppliers". For example, they may import bus or SCV chassis (which are considered to be vehicles under the MVTO and the SROs) as inputs for finished vehicles of their own manufacture; they may re-import vehicles of their own manufacture that have been exported for modification in other countries; or they may import vehicles as retailers (i.e. for direct sale to end-users). None of these activities would constitute the supply of wholesale trade services.

7.353 In its Response of 25 June 1999 to Japan's Question 2(4), Canada stated only that the three companies in question, among others, "have imported vehicles other than automobiles under the MVTO or an SRO at least once in the last 10 years". At paragraph 131 of its Second Written Submission of 2 July 1999, Japan subsequently declared all of these companies to be "wholesale trade service suppliers". It has offered no evidence to substantiate this assertion.

7. *Questions and Replies Relating to Claims under Article XVII of the GATS*

(a) Question 28 (Services Supplied Through Mode 1)

The EC quotes some examples of services potentially affected by the CVA, which can be supplied through mode 1 and which cannot be considered to be inherently disadvantaged due to their foreign character. Could the EC and Japan please identify all services sectors affected by the C VA which can be supplied through mode 1.

(i) Reply from Japan

7.354 Since the CVA applies to services in general and only the Government of Canada has full information on the types of services that are or could be included in the CVA, it is not possible for the Government of Japan to identify all service sectors affected by the CVA which can be supplied through mode 1. However, only one example of discrimination is sufficient to establish a violation of GATS Article XVII.

7.355 Japan's initial argumentation lists three general categories of services that, on their face, would qualify for inclusion in the CVA calculation. These services could be supplied through mode 1. For example:

- *Repair and maintenance services* - These services could be supplied through mode 1 in situations where machinery and/or equipment would be repaired with the technical advice rendered through telecommunications means. Examples of such machinery and/or equipment include computer hardware, control boards, and moveable mechanical equipment and devices. Other examples include repair and maintenance services of high-tech machines supplied through telecommunications means from outside of Canada.
- *Engineering Services* - These services could be supplied through mode 1 in situations where experimental work and/or product development work in relation with motor vehicle manufacturing is conducted in the form of technical advice rendered through telecommunications means. Examples of such services include engineering services related to the design of a motor vehicle assembly line supplied through telecommunications means from outside of Canada. Engineering services related to the operation of such line of production could also be supplied through telecommunications means from outside of Canada. As a result, engineering services are not inherently domestic as incorrectly suggested by the Government of Canada. For example, it is possible for engineers outside of Canada to monitor the production process of facilities located in Canada.
- *General Services* - Accounting, data processing, software implementation, and management consulting are a few examples of general services that could be supplied through mode 1. Examples of such services include production data processing services rendered through telecommunications means from outside of Canada, software that can be upgraded through telecommunications means, book keeping that could be performed through telecommunications means, management, corporate governance and human resources studies that could be performed through telephone conference by foreign firms upon receipt of relevant information from the manufacturer.

(ii) Reply from the European Communities

7.356 As a preliminary remark, it should be noted that the examples quoted by the European Communities included not only examples of supply through mode 1 ("cross-border" supply), but also examples of supply through mode 2 ("consumption abroad").

7.357 The European Communities considers that in principle *all* the service sectors listed in its initial argumentation (i.e. "non-life insurance services", "repair services incidental to machinery and equipment", "engineering services", "professional services", "computer related services", "banking services", "telecommunication services", "travel services" and other "business services") can be supplied through mode 1 and/or mode 2. Further, most of them, if not all, can be supplied through mode 1.

7.358 As regards, "non-life insurance services" (CPC 8129) and "engineering services" (CPC 8672), Canada applies some limitations to the supply through mode 1. While for the reasons explained elsewhere, those limitations do not exclude a violation of Article XVII, their very existence demonstrates that provision through mode 1 is not impossible.

7.359 The same is true of many sub-sectors falling within the category of "general and administrative expenses" such as "accounting, auditing and book-keeping services" (CPC 862[766]); "management consulting services" (CPC 865[767]); "placement and supply services of personnel" (CPC 872[768]); "travel agencies and tour operator services" (CPC 7471[769]); "telecommunication services" (sub-sectors a), b), c), d) e) and f)[770]); and "banking services"[771].

7.360 As regards the remaining services mentioned in the EC argument, it is not difficult to conceive examples of supply though mode 1:

7.361 *Foreign legal consultants (CPC 861*)*: the Canadian Association of Auto Pact beneficiaries requests from a Brussels law firm with no commercial presence in Canada, to give a legal opinion on the WTO compatibility of the Auto Pact. In response, that law firm sends by fax a memorandum setting out the reasons why the Auto Pact violates the WTO Agreement.

7.362 *Taxation services (CPC 863*)*: Intermeccanica is considering to set up a subsidiary in the EU. It requests a tax consultant based in Brussels to advise on what member State would constitute the best location from a tax point of view. Both the request and the answer are delivered through e-mail.

7.363 *Computer related services*: GM Canada asks Siemens Germany to design the computer hardware and software for its new factory in Quebec (CPC 841 and 842*); GM Canada outsources the processing of bills to a company in Bangalore (India) (CPC 843*); GM Canada subscribes to the electronic version of the EC Official Journal published in Luxembourg (CPC 844*).

7.364 *Technical testing and analysis services (CPC 8676)*: the R & D department of GM Canada sends a sample of a new ecological fuel made from maple syrup to the

[766] GATS/SC/16, p. 18 (Exhibit EC-19).
[767] Ibid., p. 30.
[768] Ibid., p. 33.
[769] Ibid., p. 70.
[770] GATS/SC/16/Suppl.3, p.2 (Exhibit EC-19).
[771] GATS/SC/16/Suppl.4, p. 1 (Exhibit EC-19).

Max Planck Institute in Hamburg for further testing. The results are delivered by e-mail.

7.365 Arguably, a few of the sub-sectors identified by the European Communities (e.g., "repair services incidental to machinery and equipment" (CPC 8861 to 8866) and "hotel and lodging" (CPC 641) and "food and beverage serving" (CPC 642/3) cannot be supplied through mode 1. Nevertheless, as evidenced by the examples provided by the European Communities, all of them can be provided though mode 2.

(b) Question 30 ("Like" Service Suppliers)

Canada argues that there are no Canadian wholesale distribution service suppliers which are "like" Japanese suppliers. Could Canada please clarify on what grounds Intermeccanica should not be considered "like" other suppliers of wholesale trade services for automobiles. Could it also clarify on what grounds Canadian suppliers of wholesale trade services for buses and specialised commercial vehicles should not be considered "like" suppliers of wholesale trade services for automobiles.

(i) Reply from Canada

7.366 Canada notes that it is Japan that has the burden of proof in making its claim that Intermeccanica is a "like" service supplier. Japan has provided no evidence or explanation for this claim. Japan has simply asserted that "Intermeccanica is a Canadian service supplier within the meaning of Article XVII of the GATS". It neither substantiated that assertion nor addressed whether the services Intermeccanica allegedly supplies are wholesale distribution trade services. In keeping with the well-established principle, confirmed by the Appellate Body in *United States - Measure Affecting Imports of Woven Wool Shirts and Blouses from India*[772], that the initial burden of proof lies on the complaining party to establish a prima facie case, the onus is on Japan to explain why Intermeccanica should be considered "like" other suppliers of wholesale trade services for automobiles. Japan has failed to meet its burden. The onus has not shifted to Canada because Japan has not made out a prima facie case.

7.367 In any event, there are two fundamental reasons why Intermeccanica is not "like" other suppliers of wholesale trade services for automobiles. In the first place, it is not a supplier of wholesale trade services at all. As the European Communities acknowledged, it is a *producer* of automobiles. It is not a wholesaler and is irrelevant for the purposes of a GATS analysis. It does not import automobiles for resale or distribute them at all.

7.368 Secondly, even if it were a wholesale distribution supplier, which it clearly is not, its size and sales volumes, and the vehicles it "distributes", are vastly different from those of any of the commercial presences identified by Japan as wholesale distribution service suppliers. Intermeccanica has 8 employees.[773] It has never produced more than 22 vehicles in a year. The vehicles it does produce are hand-built replicas of famous automobiles. It is simply preposterous to contend that it is a potential

---

[772] Appellate Body Report on *US - Wool Shirts*, *supra* note 283, at 333 *et seq.*

[773] See Exhibit JPN-12.

competitor[774] for the wholesale distribution business of companies like Toyota or Honda, which import tens of thousands of cars each year. Even if Intermeccanica were a wholesale distribution service supplier, it would be utterly "unlike" the foreign service suppliers listed by Japan.

(ii) Reply from Canada

7.369 Regarding "on what grounds Canadian suppliers of wholesale trade services for buses and specialised commercial vehicles should not be considered 'like' suppliers of wholesale trade services for automobiles", again, the burden of proof lies with Japan to substantiate its allegations. Again, it has failed to do so. In its initial arguments, Japan stated that:

> ... Auto Pact Manufacturers of Canadian origin manufacture buses and commercial motor vehicles, which Japanese automobile industries may export to meet demand if latent demand exists. The Japanese motor vehicle industry may also offer wholesale trade services for such buses and commercial vehicles if such demand exists. This demonstrates that there are Canadian motor vehicle wholesale trade service suppliers in Canada.

7.370 Of course, Japan has demonstrated nothing of the sort. It has simply asserted that there are Canadian *manufacturers* of buses and (specified) commercial vehicles. However, it has failed to adduce any evidence whatsoever that there are Canadian suppliers of wholesale trade services for buses and specified commercial vehicles. The manufacture of a good and the wholesale distribution of that good are two distinct activities. The GATS arguments of both complainants with respect to the effect of duty-free treatment seek to erase this distinction. The Panel must not permit this.

7.371 Whether Canadian suppliers of wholesale trade services for buses and specified commercial vehicles are "like" Japanese suppliers of wholesale trade services for automobiles should be determined on a case-by-case basis, just as it must with like goods.[775] This determination is rendered impossible (and moot) by Japan's failure to identify any Canadian suppliers of wholesale trade services for buses and specified commercial vehicles. Moreover, such "likeness" cannot be assumed. In the passage quoted above from Japan's arguments, Japan did not even claim that its automobile manufacturers produce, or have the ability to produce, buses or specified commercial vehicles, let alone that they or their related commercial presences in Canada are capable of providing wholesale distribution services for either class of vehicle.

---

[774] Even if such competition were feasible, which it is not due to the relationships between the parent manufacturers and their Canadian subsidiaries.

[775] See the Report of the *Working Party on Border Tax Adjustments*, adopted 2 December 1970, BISD 18S/97, para. 18 and the Appellate Body Report on *Japan - Alcoholic Beverages, supra* note 271, at 113.

(c) Question 31 (Commitments in Canada's GATS Schedule)

The entry B. "wholesale trade services" in Canada's schedule does not explicitly exclude wholesale trade services for motor vehicles. On what grounds is Canada claiming that it is excluded?

(i) Reply from Canada

7.372 The entry B. "Wholesale trade services" at page 47 of Canada's Schedule of Specific Commitment[776] does explicitly exclude wholesale trade services for motor vehicles. It does this in the first column, which indicates the sector or sub-sector to which Canada's commitments apply, by noting at the bottom of that column that the commitments apply to the services in CPC 622 only. CPC 622 covers certain wholesale trade services excluding those for motor vehicles. CPC 622 falls under Division 62 of the CPC which is entitled "Commission Agents' and Wholesale Trade Services, *Except of Motor Vehicles*". (*emphasis added*)

Canada argues that the commitment under CPC 6111, listed under retailing services, does not extend to wholesale trade services. Why did Canada not indicate in this entry the exclusion of wholesale trade of motor vehicles?

(ii) Reply from Canada

7.373 Canada did indicate the exclusion of wholesale trade services for motor vehicles in this entry by scheduling its commitment under "Retailing Services". Article XVII of the GATS extends only to specific commitments. That is, it is binding on Members only in sectors and sub-sectors in respect of which they have made commitments.[777] By scheduling its CPC 6111 commitments in the "Retailing Services" sector only, Canada did not bind itself in respect of other sectors such as "Wholesale trade services".

(d) Question 32 (the CVA requirements and mode 4)

Canada argues that most of the qualifying manufacturers exceed their CVA requirements on the basis of labour costs alone. Could Canada please provide factual information on those manufacturers who do not meet the CVA requirements on the basis of labour costs alone. To what extent do labour costs include the purchase of services which could be supplied by natural persons under mode 4?

(i) Reply from Canada

7.374 All of the MVTO manufacturers meet their CVA requirements on the basis of labour costs alone, as do all SRO manufacturers operating under a base-year CVA requirement. Four SRO manufacturers operating under 40 or 50 per cent CVA re-

---

776 *Canada's GATS Schedule*, *supra* note 641.

777 Panel Reports on *EC - Bananas III*, *supra* note 269, para. 7.305.

quirements have, in some recent years, not met those requirements on the basis of labour costs alone.

7.375 The cost of any service supplied by mode 4 is fully CVA-eligible. Services supplied by mode 4 are not included in the heading for labour costs, but may be included under other CVA headings.

(e) Question 34 (Ownership and Control)

7.376 (See p. 3417)

(f) Question 35 (Vertical Integration)

Canada argues that in the supply of wholesale trade services for automobiles there is no competition between wholesale trade service suppliers since wholesale suppliers are subordinated to manufacturers and therefore the question of an effect on conditions of competition does not arise. Does vertical integration between manufacturers and suppliers of wholesale trade services exclude any actual or potential competition at the wholesale trade level? To what extent does vertical integration between manufacturers and suppliers of wholesale trade services also exclude competition with respect to sales to retailers?

(i) Reply from Japan

7.377 As the Appellate Body Report for *EC - Bananas III* confirmed, even if wholesale trade service suppliers are integrated with manufacturers, to the extent they are engaged in providing wholesale trade services, they are wholesale trade service suppliers.

7.378 And vertical integration between manufacturers and suppliers of wholesale trade services does not exclude any actual and potential competition at the wholesale trade level, since an integrated manufacturer, in its capacity as a wholesale trade service supplier, competes with other wholesale trade service suppliers as to the sales of automobiles to retail service suppliers (dealers) and the maintenance and expansion of their dealers networks. This type of competition is relevant to this dispute because dealers are consumers of the wholesale trade services provided by the service suppliers in question. To the extent that manufacturers/wholesale trade service suppliers are to sell automobiles to retail service suppliers (i.e. dealers), there is competition between those manufacturers/wholesale trade service suppliers with respect to sales to retailers, notwithstanding their vertical integration.

7.379 Further, differences in the retail prices of automobiles caused by the Duty Waiver will necessarily affect sales volumes and will lead to differences in profitability in supplying wholesale trade services between manufacturers/wholesale service suppliers. This means that the conditions of competition between manufacturers/wholesale trade service suppliers for sales to retailers will be negatively affected.

(ii) Reply from the European Communities

7.380 No. Although the major wholesale distributors of automobiles present in the Canadian market are vertically integrated with manufacturers[778], that does not exclude any actual or potential competition amongst them with respect to the purchase of motor vehicles from manufacturers for wholesale resale.

7.381 In the first place, some foreign manufacturers of automobiles have little or no presence at all in the Canadian market (e.g., Renault, Peugeot-Citroen, Fiat, Mitsubishi, Proton or Tata).

7.382 Those potential new entrants have basically three options in order to penetrate into the Canadian market: to set up their own distributors; to designate an independent distributor; or to appoint as a distributor an existing integrated distributor. The last option is not unusual, in particular when the model ranges of the two manufacturers concerned are complementary. By way of example, in the past Chrysler has imported and distributed in Canada motor vehicles manufactured by Mitsubishi, an unrelated Japanese producer (see Exhibit EC-16, Table 1.7).

7.383 Thus, while it may be true that, as argued by Canada, Honda Canada and Ford Canada would not compete for the distribution in Canada of vehicles manufactured by Ford in the United States, they may compete, not only with other integrated distributors but also with independent distributors, for the distribution of vehicles produced by a foreign manufacturer without a distribution network in Canada. The Tariff Exemption confers upon the beneficiaries a competitive advantage in that market because it lowers their import costs and, therefore, gives them the possibility to offer better purchasing terms to the foreign manufacturer.

7.384 Secondly, even with respect to motor vehicles of the parent company's brand, vertically integrated distributors may face competition from parallel importers.

Regarding the question, "To what extent does vertical integration between manufacturers and suppliers of wholesale trade services also exclude competition with respect to sales to retailers?":

7.385 Canada's argument is built on the wrong assumption that wholesale distribution services are provided by the wholesalers exclusively to the manufacturers. The truth, however, is that wholesaler distributors of automobiles act as intermediaries between the manufacturers and the retailers (and in some cases final consumers, e.g., in the case of so-called "fleet sales" to big purchasers). They provide a service to retailers as much as to the manufacturers. In fact, except in the rare cases where wholesale distributors of automobiles act as mere agents for the manufacturers, the "buyer" of the service, i.e. the person who actually "pays" for the distribution service, is the retailer and not the manufacturer.

7.386 Quite clearly, vertical integration between manufacturers and wholesale distributors of automobiles, even if it were complete, would not exclude *per se* competition among wholesale distributors with respect to sales to retailers and final consumers. Vertical integration has the only consequence that Honda Canada and Ford Canada cannot compete to resell the *same* automobiles to retailers. But it does not

[778] The affiliation of some distributors, such as Lada Canada Inc., is nevertheless unclear, as shown in Table 7.

prevent them from competing in order to resell to dealers automobiles manufactured by their respective parents which are directly competitive and substitutable with each other. In other words, the absence of intra-brand competition among wholesalers does not exclude inter-brand competition.

(iii) Reply from Canada

7.387 Canada notes that the arguments in question are found in its initial response on these points.

7.388 It is not clear if the question refers to vertical integration in the motor vehicle industry only, or to vertical integration generally. In the motor vehicle industry, a combination of vertical integration and exclusive distribution arrangements does exclude any actual or potential competition at the wholesale trade level. The same is not necessarily true of other industries. For example, it is not the case in the bananas business, where even those companies that were vertically integrated had the "capability and opportunity to enter the wholesale service market".[779]

7.389 Contrary to what was implied by the European Communities, the Appellate Body's findings in *EC - Bananas III* in respect of integrated wholesalers were specific to the facts of the case. The Appellate Body stated that: "even if a company is vertically-integrated, ... to the extent that it is also engaged in providing "wholesale trade services" *and is therefore affected in that capacity by a particular measure of a Member in its supply of those 'wholesale trade services',* that company is a service supplier within the scope of the GATS".[780] (*emphasis added*)

7.390 The fact that a wholesale service supplier is integrated does not mean that it is necessarily outside the scope of the GATS, but nor does it mean that it necessarily falls within the scope of the GATS either. The determining factor is whether that service supplier is affected in its capacity as a service supplier and in its supply of those services. The nature of the motor vehicle industry is such that there is no competition among wholesale service suppliers in the supply of wholesale trade services. Japan confirmed this in its arguments.

[Regarding the question "*to what extent does vertical integration between manufacturers and suppliers of wholesale trade services also exclude competition with respect to sales to retailers?*":]

7.391 If the EC's reference to retailers was meant to suggest that retailers could choose among wholesale service suppliers, the suggestion is wrong. Wholesaling by definition entails sales to retailers. Wholesalers purchase goods from manufacturers and resell them to retailers. A headnote to Division 6 of the CPC states that: "*The principal services rendered by wholesalers and retailers may be characterized as reselling merchandise*, accompanied by a variety of related, subordinated services ...". (*emphasis added*)

7.392 "Reselling" necessarily implies that the reseller has purchased the good in the first place. It is uncertain to what extent the commercial presences of the motor vehi-

---

[779] Panel Reports on *EC - Bananas III, supra* note 269, para. 7.320.

[780] Appellate Body Report on *EC - Bananas III, supra* note 49, para. 227.

cle manufacturers identified by the complainants as "wholesalers" have purchased the vehicles from the manufacturers. If they have not, they cannot be said to be wholesalers at all. The complainants have offered no evidence on this point.

7.393 Even assuming that these commercial presences are wholesalers, they do not compete for sales to retailers for the same reason that they do not compete to distribute the vehicles of particular manufacturers. The so-called wholesalers have exclusive distribution arrangements with the manufacturers. Accordingly, retailers of specific brands of vehicles cannot select among wholesale service suppliers for the supply of those vehicles. Retail dealers of Honda automobiles cannot for example, approach General Motors of Canada and ask General Motors to supply them with Hondas from the Honda Motor Company of Japan. Those retailers must rely on Honda Canada Inc. to provide those vehicles.

7.394 It is possible that the European Communities was suggesting that duty-free treatment may influence which brands of vehicles retailers choose to sell and that this consequentially influences their choice of service supplier. However, this simply underscores that what benefits from the duty-free treatment is particular goods (the vehicles) and that there is no competition in the provision of distribution services for those goods. To contend that the measure affects wholesale service suppliers through retailers implies that every measure affecting goods not only affects wholesale service suppliers of those goods but also the retailers of the goods as well. No measures affecting goods would not also "affect" services. The EC's argument would obliterate the distinction among the three categories of measures by the Appellate Body in *EC - Bananas III*.[781]

(g) Question 59 (Origin of Wholesale Trade Service Suppliers)

Could Japan please clarify on what basis it has classified three suppliers of wholesale trade services for buses and specified commercial vehicles as Canadian in Exhibit JPN-50.

Could Japan please provide necessary material to support the Canadian origin of these suppliers.

7.395 As for the nationality of the "juridical person", Article XXVIII (m)(i) and (ii) and (n)(i) of the GATS prescribe as follows:

> (m) "juridical person of another Member" means a juridical person which is either:
>
> (i) constituted or otherwise organized under the law of that other Member, and is engaged in substantive business operations in the territory of that Member or any other Member; or
>
> (ii) in the case of the supply of a service through commercial presence, owned or controlled by:
>
> natural persons of that Member; or

[781] Ibid., para. 221.

juridical persons of that other Member identified under subparagraph (i);

(n) a juridical person is:

(i) "owned" by persons of a Member if more than 50 per cent of the equity interest in it is beneficially owned by persons of that Member;

...

7.396 Based on the information provided by the Government of Canada in its response to Question (4) of the Government of Japan, the three suppliers of wholesale trade services classified as Canadian in Exhibit JPN-50, which are A. Girardin Inc., Les Enterprises Michel Corbeil Inc. and Western Star Trucks Inc., have imported vehicles from other countries into Canada. Those companies provide services through a commercial presence in Canada. If those companies are not owned or controlled by natural persons of a country other than Canada or juridical persons of countries other than Canada identified under subparagraph (m)(i), those companies are not "juridical persons of another Member", and it follows that those companies are juridical persons of the Member (Canada).

7.397 On the homepage of the Canadian Department of Industry (Industry Canada) (http://strategis.ic.gc.ca/), Industry Canada stated that "Both Thomas Built and Canadian Bluebird are American-owned. A. Girardin and Michel Corbeil Enterprises Inc. are wholly-owned Canadian companies." (See page 3 of attachment 1 to this response [assigned name: Exhibit JPN-51].) Therefore, Japan concluded that A. Girardin and Michel Corbeil Enterprises Inc. are service suppliers of Canadian origin.

7.398 On the homepage of Industry Canada (*http://strategis.ic.gc.ca/*), it is also indicated that ownership of Les Enterprises Michel Corbeil Inc. (see attachment 2 [assigned name: Exhibit JPN-51]) and Michel Corbeil Enterprises Inc. (see attachment 3 [assigned name: Exhibit JPN-51]) is Canadian. This homepage also indicates that the ownership of Western Star Trucks Inc. is Canadian (see attachment 1 [assigned name: Exhibit JPN-51]). Based on the information from Industry Canada on the ownership of those three companies, it is reasonable to presume that more than 50 per cent of their equity interests is owned by Canadians.

7.399 Please see attachments 1-3 [assigned name: Exhibit JPN-51], which substantiates Japan's above conclusion.

(h) Question 60 (Origin of Wholesale Trade Service Suppliers)

Could Canada please confirm that the three suppliers of wholesale trade services for buses and specified commercial vehicles, listed as Canadian in Exhibit JPN-50, are of Canadian origin.

7.400 The three companies listed as Canadian in Exhibit JPN-50 are A.Girardin Inc., Les Entreprises Michel Corbeil Inc., and Western Star Trucks Inc. Canada has the following information about their "origin": A.Girardin Inc. and Les Entreprises Michel Corbeil Inc. are both privately-owned companies incorporated in Canada. To Canada's knowledge, both companies are Canadian-owned. Western Star Trucks Inc. is a company incorporated in Canada. It is wholly-owned by a Canadian-incorporated company, Western Star Trucks Holdings Ltd., which in turn is controlled by a Singapore-incorporated company, Western Star International, which owns 42 per cent of Western Star Holdings.

7.401 Canada notes that Japan has not adduced any evidence in the record to support its assertion that the three companies at issue are "suppliers of wholesale trade services". As Canada noted in its Response of 25 June 1999 to the Panel's Question 35, wholesalers purchase goods and resell them to retailers. A headnote to Division 6 of the CPC states that: "the principal services rendered by wholesalers and retailers may be characterized as reselling merchandise..." Manufacturers that import vehicles but do not resell them to retailers are not "suppliers of wholesale trade services".

7.402 Eligible manufacturers that do import buses or SCVs are not necessarily "wholesale trade service suppliers". For example, they may import bus or SCV chassis (which are considered to be vehicles under the MVTO and the SROs) as inputs for finished vehicles of their own manufacture; they may re-import vehicles of their own manufacture that have been exported for modification in other countries; or they may import vehicles as retailers (i.e. for direct sale to end-users). None of these activities would constitute the supply of wholesale trade services.

7.403 In its Response of 25 June 1999 to Japan's Question 2(4), Canada stated only that the three companies in question, among others, "have imported vehicles other than automobiles under the MVTO or an SRO at least once in the last 10 years". At paragraph 131 of its Second Written Submission of 2 July 1999, Japan subsequently declared all of these companies to be "wholesale trade service suppliers". It has offered no evidence to substantiate this assertion.

8. *Questions and Replies Relating to Third-Party Arguments*

(a) Question 1 from the European Communities to the United States (the Measures at Issue and GATS Article V)

The United States have suggested that even if the measure in dispute were found to be inconsistent with GATS Article II, they would nevertheless be covered by the exception conferred by GATS Article V:1.

That position appears to be based on a misunderstanding of the nature of the measures in dispute. Those measures are not part of, nor required by NAFTA. Some of the measures implement the provisions of the 1965 Auto Pact between the USA and Canada (namely, the tariff exemption for importing vehicles from the United States granted to a number of manufacturers already established in Canada in 1956 under the MVTO 1998). The remaining measures are purely unilateral ones, not required either by NAFTA or by the Auto Pact (namely, the tariff exemption granted to the same manufacturers under the MVTO 1998 for importing vehicles from third countries, including Mexico, as well as the so-called Special Remission Orders issued to manufacturers not established in Canada in 1965).

(a) Is it the view of the United States that the Auto Pact qualifies as an agreement of the type mentioned in Article V:1 of GATS?

(b) Does the United States take the view that Article V:1 of GATS provides an exception also with respect to the adoption of purely unilateral measures

that are not part of, nor required by an agreement of the type mentioned in that provision?

(i) Reply from the United States

7.404 (a) No.

(b) Article V:1 may apply to such measures in some cases depending, *inter alia*, on their nature.

(b) Question 2 from the European Communities to the United States (the Measures at Issue and GATS Article V)

It is generally admitted that Panels cannot take into account affirmative defenses unless invoked by one of the main parties to a dispute.

(a) Does the United States take the view that the panel could reject a claim on the basis of Article V:1 GATS, even if that provision was not invoked by Canada?

(b) Who bears the burden of proving that an agreement fulfils the conditions of Article V:1?

(i) Reply from the United States

7.405 The United States agrees with the European Communities that a panel cannot take into account affirmative defenses unless such defenses are invoked by one of the parties to the dispute. The panel in *United States - Customs User Fee* arrived at a similar conclusion, noting "GATT practice has been for panels to make findings only on those issues raised by the parties to the dispute."[782] This practice is reflected in Article 7.2 of the WTO Understanding on Rules and Procedures Governing the Settlement of Disputes.

(c) Question 3 from the European Communities to the United States (the Measures at Issue and GATT Article XXIV)

The United States has indicated that even if the measures in dispute were found to be inconsistent with GATT Article I in that de facto they provide more favourable treatment to goods originating in Mexico and the USA, such violation would nevertheless be covered by GATT Article XXIV.

Yet in 1996 the United States requested a renewal of the 1965 waiver for the Auto Pact, notwithstanding the fact that in the meantime the United States had concluded the CUSFTA and the NAFTA with Canada, both of which purport to establish a free-trade *area. Why did the United States consider it necessary to make such a request?*

---

[782] Panel Report on *United States - Customs User Fee*, adopted on 2 February 1998, BISD 35S/290, para. 124.

(i) Reply from the United States

7.406 In view of the fact the European Communities has noted that "[t]he Auto Pact is an asymmetrical agreement that imposes different obligations on each of the two signatories, the US waiver does not appear to be relevant in a case involving Canadian measures.

(d) Question 4 from the European Communities to the United States (the Measures at Issue and GATT Article XXIV and GATS Article V)

Do Article XXIV GATT and Article V:1 GATS provide an exception only with respect to the claims submitted by the EC under GATT Article I and GATS Article II respectively, or also with respect to all the other claims submitted by the EC under the GATT, the TRIMs Agreement, the SCM Agreement and the GATS?

(i) Reply from the United States

7.407 As a third party in these proceedings the United States limited its presentation to a few points that may be of relevance to the Panel in examining this dispute. The questions raised by the European Communities in question 4 range beyond the scope of the US presentation, and the United States is not prepared to provide views on these matters at this time.

(e) Question 5 from the European Communities to the United States (freezing of SRO List of Beneficiaries)

The EC has alleged, and Canada has not disputed, that Article 1200.1 of the CUSFTA, which "froze" the list of beneficiaries of the Auto Pact and of the Special Remission Orders as of 1989, was inserted at the request of the United States.

(a) Why did the United States demand the inclusion of that provision?

(b) How did Article 1200.1 of the CUSFTA contribute to the liberalisation of trade in motor vehicles and distribution services for automobiles between the United States and Canada, as compared to the pre-existing situation?

(i) Reply from the United States

7.408 For purposes of clarification, the United States notes that the European Communities appears to have erroneously cited to Article 1200.1 of the US-Canada Free-Trade Agreement; the United States believes the relevant provision is Annex 1002.1 of that agreement. As a third party in these proceedings the United States limited its presentation to a few points that may be of relevance to the panel in examining this dispute. The questions raised by the European Communities in question 5 range beyond the scope of the US presentation, and the United States is not prepared to provide views on these matters at this time.

VIII. THIRD-PARTY ARGUMENTS

A. *India's Arguments as a Third Party*

8.1 As a third party, **India** argues as follows:

8.2 The complaining parties, i.e. Japan and the European Communities, have argued that the Tariff exemption and CVA requirements granted, pursuant to the signing of the 1965 Agreement between USA and Canada on the import of automotive products (hereinafter referred to as the 'Auto Pact') are inconsistent with various provisions of the WTO Agreement, including the MFN obligation set out in Article I of GATT; the national treatment obligation set out in Article III of GATT; the provisions of the TRIMs Agreement and the provisions of the Subsidies and Countervailing Measures Agreement.

8.3 These are important issues and their legal status and consistency with WTO provisions has to be examined very carefully. However, as a third party, India will not be addressing all of the factual and legal issues raised in this proceeding. Instead, India will be presenting its views on two issues - namely, Article I and III of GATT, which in India's view are the cornerstone of the multilateral trading system, the primacy of which India strongly believes in. If India does not make comments on a particular factual or legal claim, it does not mean that India either agrees or disagrees with the position taken by any of the parties on these issues.

8.4 It is India's view that the Panel will need to determine whether the measures under dispute afford "less favourable treatment" to imported products than to domestic products, that is whether the measure is consistent with the provisions of Article III of GATT, or not. It is our view that a mere contending that certain provisions of the Auto Pact give preference, all other conditions being equal, to Canadian goods over like imported goods, is not sufficient. It must be established that the provisions specifically grant certain privileges to the domestic industry, which are otherwise not available to foreign industry, irrespective of the conditions that the latter may satisfy. Canada is not a developing country. Otherwise, India would have also suggested for the Panel to go beyond the legal framework and also examine the basic objectives of the domestic law, since developing countries have to at times provide certain incentives to encourage domestic industry. Such measures are usually not inconsistent with the provisions of Article III of GATT, even though they may at times appear to be so.

8.5 Similarly, the Panel would also need to determine whether the 'Auto Pact' is consistent with the provisions of Article I - that is, whether or not it fulfils the MFN obligation. The important issue in India's view is to see whether the Auto Pact provides any advantage to imports of automobiles originating in the US and Mexico, *vis-à-vis* imports of like products originating from other Member countries. Even though on its face value the tariff exemption provided by the Auto Pact appears to be non-discriminatory, the Panel will need to examine whether the beneficiaries of this exemption have largely been companies based in the US and Mexico, or whether companies based outside the NAFTA parties have also been able to benefit, from what Canada terms as an instrument which has helped transformed Canada "from a highly protective automotive market into one of the most open markets in the world for automotive products and investment, both as a matter of law and in practice". While regional trading arrangements are important building blocks of the multilateral trading system, the benefit that they give to Members which are parties to the arrangement cannot under any circumstance be at the cost of the rights and benefits of Members which are not parties to the RTA.

B. Korea's Arguments as a Third Party

8.6 As a third party, **Korea** argues as follows:

1. Introduction

8.7 The Government of the Republic of Korea wishes to note that, as a manufacturer and exporter of motor vehicles and components, as well as a provider of services related thereto, it has a substantial trade interest in the matters raised in the present dispute. In this regard, the Korean Government emphasizes that it shares the view advanced by the complainants in this proceeding that the measures under dispute[783] with respect to the selective and discriminatory removal of customs duties on the importation of certain motor vehicles involve numerous inconsistencies with Canada's obligations under the GATT 1994, the TRIMS Agreement, the SCM Agreement and the GATS, respectively. In this respect, Korea wishes to clarify its position with respect to some of the main legal issues relevant to this dispute.

2. GATT 1994

(a) Article I:1 GATT 1994

8.8 With regard to Article I:1 of the GATT 1994, Korea considers that the Tariff Exemption applied by Canada is clearly inconsistent with this provision in that Canada has failed to accord "immediately and unconditionally" the removal of customs duties with respect to like products originating in or destined for the territories of all other WTO Members. Article I:1 embodies a very broadly worded and unconditional obligation to accord Most-Favored-Nation Treatment with respect to trade in goods. Indeed, while MFN-type treaty clauses have existed in treaties for centuries prior to the entry into force of the GATT 1994 and the WTO Agreement, the precise obligations under such clauses have not always been as broadly formulated as under Article I:1 of the GATT 1994.[784] Against this background, the original drafters of Article I:1 of the GATT clearly intended to emphasize the wide application and unconditional nature of the obligations specified therein with respect to MFN treatment for the purposes of trade in goods. Specifically, in the present case, if Canada affords, with respect to "customs duties," any "advantage" in connection with the importation of motor vehicles originating in any other country, its obligation under Article I:1 of the GATT 1994 is to "immediately and unconditionally" accord the same treatment with respect to like products originating in the territories of all other WTO Members.

---

[783] The tariff exemption selectively applicable to certain imports of motor vehicles, including the "ratio" requirements as well as the CVA requirements contained in the Auto Pact, as supplemented by the letters of undertaking, and in the MVTO 1998; and the tariff exemptions applicable to the importation of motor vehicles, including the "ratio" and CVA requirements attached thereto, provided for in the SROs.

[784] For an overview of the historical meaning applied to MFN-type clauses, please refer to The World Trading System: Law and Policy of International Economic Relations, John H. Jackson.

(b) The Tariff Exemption Relates to a Customs Duty within the terms of Article I:1 of the GATT 1994

8.9 The Tariff Exemption clearly relates to a customs duty within the meaning of Article I:1, as it waives the otherwise applicable normal MFN duty applied by Canada.

(c) The Tariff Exemption is an Advantage within the Meaning of Article I:1 of the GATT 1994

8.10 Although these issues have been dealt with at some length in the complainants' arguments, Korea notes that the Tariff Exemption clearly constitutes an "advantage" within the meaning of Article I:1 of the GATT 1994 relating to customs duties because certain imported motor vehicles are exempt from otherwise applicable customs duties. The exemption from the outset was limited to the imports of the original qualifying Auto Pact manufacturers and imports made pursuant to company-specific SROs, thereby conferring an advantage over non-beneficiaries.

(d) The Products Are "Like" Products

8.11 As the Tariff Exemption is designed to cover all motor vehicles (with some minor exceptions), and does not involve criteria based on the characteristics of those products, it is clear that the motor vehicles for which the duty waiver applies and other imported motor vehicles which cannot benefit from the duty waiver are 'like products'.

(e) The Advantage is not Accorded Immediately and Unconditionally to Like Products Originating in all WTO Members

8.12 In the view of Korea, the clear and unqualified obligation under Article I:1 of the GATT 1994 is to accord "immediately and unconditionally" any advantage to like products originating in the territories of all WTO Members. Under the Tariff Exemption, however, the advantages with respect to the waiver of customs duties are limited to the beneficiaries under the Auto Pact. In addition, the advantage provided under the Tariff Exemption is subject to several conditions relating, inter alia, to the CVA and ratio requirements. These conditions imposed do not relate to the imported products themselves. In this respect, in *Indonesia - Autos*, the panel clearly stated that under Article I:1 of the GATT 1994, any advantage "cannot be made conditional on any criteria not related to the imported product itself."

(f) The Advantages Accorded to Products Originating in Particular WTO Members Has Not Been Accorded to Like Products Originating in the Territories of All WTO Members

8.13 Under the terms of the Auto Pact and subsequent instruments, the beneficiaries under the Auto Pact are restricted to a closed group. The Auto Pact beneficiaries are, in principle, allowed to import motor vehicles from any national origin. However, as was detailed in Japan's argument, in reality these manufacturers have tended to choose imports from a limited number of countries, based on previous commercial links and other factors. The majority of vehicles entitled to the Tariff Exemption are of particular national origin. Furthermore, due to the fact that the list of eligible importers has been frozen since 1 January 1989, it is clear that in practice, the duty waiver advantage has not been accorded to like products originating in all WTO Members and importers with capital or commercial links with producers in other WTO Member countries, such as Korea, have not been accorded the same advantage.

8.14 The advantage of the Duty Waiver is clearly linked in law and fact to production of Canadian origin motor vehicles by the importer in accordance with the Requirements of MVTO 1998. Therefore, contrary to Canada's allegations, the advantage discriminates based on the origin of the products because a producer/importer of Korean origin motor vehicles cannot obtain the benefit of the Duty Waiver which is only granted to producers/importers of Canadian origin cars. Thus, Canada's allegation that "Which Member's products benefit at any given time depends entirely on commercial decisions made by the manufacturers" as stated in its argument is groundless.

8.15 Canada argues that the preponderance of vehicles imported from the United States and Mexico is irrelevant because any advantage they may receive is due to Canada's free-trade agreement with these countries. Finally, Korea wishes to emphasize that, contrary to Canada's implicit assertion, there is no decision or finding in any WTO bodies that NAFTA is consistent with Article XXIV of the GATT 1994. Moreover, contrary to Canada's unsupported allegation, GATT 1994 does not explicitly state that the formation of a free-trade agreement consistent with Article XXIV (assuming, *arguendo*, that this were to be the case) of the GATT 1994 provides "[...] an exception to Article I:1, *de jure* and *de facto*."

G. Article III:4 of the GATT 1994

8.16 With respect to Article III:4 of the GATT 1994, Korea considers that the Canadian requirements relating to minimum CVA targets, one of the conditions upon which the Tariff Exemption is based, affords "less favorable treatment" within the meaning of Article III:4 with respect to "laws, regulations and requirements affecting" the internal sale, offering for sale, purchase, transportation or use of imported parts and materials which are used in the manufacture of motor vehicles, or parts of motor vehicles, than the treatment afforded to like domestic goods.

8.17 Korea notes that, with respect to the CVA requirements expressly contained in the MVTO 1998 and the SROs, such instruments are considered statutory instruments under the Canadian *Statutory Instruments Act.*[785] As such, they clearly constitute "laws, regulations or requirements" within the meaning of Article III:4. With regard to the CVA requirements set forth in the letters of undertaking signed by the Auto Pact manufacturers, Korea considers that the substantive undertakings contained in these letters and the circumstances under which these commitments were undertaken mean that they fall within the definition of "requirements" under Article III:4 and that, therefore, Article III:4 is equally applicable with respect to the CVA commitments contained therein. In this respect, the inclusion of the word "requirements" in addition to "laws [and] regulations" in Article III:4 suggests that acts in-

[785] Statutory Instruments Act, R.S.C. 1985, c.S-22, s.2.

volving private parties which might not have immediate or apparent legal consequences in the formalistic sense were nonetheless intended to fall within the scope of this provision if the surrounding circumstances reveal that the parties in fact considered themselves bound to the relevant rule or requirement. This view was confirmed in *Japan - Film*[786] in which it was stated that an action taken by private parties may be deemed governmental if there is "sufficient government involvement with it."

8.18 In this respect, the letters of undertaking were signed by the Auto Pact beneficiaries as a condition by the Canadian government for its agreeing to conclude the Auto Pact. As has been noted by the European Communities, the fact that non-compliance has remained exceptional despite the lack of articulated sanctions for failing to meet the CVA requirements, in addition to the establishment of certain procedures to monitor compliance of the beneficiaries, indicates that the letters of undertaking are not considered voluntary by either party and as such properly fall within the definition of "requirements" under Article III:4.

8.19 In the view of Korea, the CVA requirements as described above "affect" the internal sale, offering for sale etc. with respect to the relevant parts, materials and equipment. In this regard, Korea notes that the term "affect" as used in Article III:4 is intended to have a broad meaning, which was confirmed in *Italian Agricultural Machinery*[787] in which the Panel concluded that the term encompassed "laws or regulations which might adversely modify the conditions of competition between the domestic and imported products on the internal market." In this regard, the CVA requirements clearly adversely affect conditions of competition on the market as a constant incentive exists to use domestic over imported goods in order to reach the required CVA levels and thus benefit from the Tariff Exemption. Finally, Korea considers that the CVA requirements entail a less favorable treatment for imported goods within the meaning of Article III:4 in that, as the Tariff Exemption is directly linked to the attainment of certain CVA targets, imported goods are placed at a competitive disadvantage. Canada's allegations that Canadian-produced products play no role in determining whether an automobile manufacturer meets its CVA levels is clearly contradicted by the MTVO 1998 itself which lists the cost of parts produced in Canada (and the cost of materials to the extent that they are of Canadian origin) as one of the elements included in the definition of CVA.

3. *TRIMS Agreement*

(a) The Applicability of the TRIMs Agreement to the Present Dispute

8.20 With respect to the TRIMs Agreement, Korea notes that Article 2.1 of this Agreement provides, in relevant part, that:

> "[N]o Member shall apply any TRIM that is inconsistent with the provisions of Article III [...] of the GATT."

8.21 With respect to Article 2.1, it was stated in *Indonesia - Autos*[788] that:

786 Panel Report on *Japan - Film, supra* note 93, para. 10.56.

787 Panel Report on *Italian Agricultural Machinery, supra* note 390, 64, para. 12.

788 Panel Report on *Indonesia - Autos, supra* note 270, para. 14.64.

> "By its terms, Article 2.1 requires two elements to be shown to establish a violation thereof: first, the existence of a TRIM; second, that TRIM is inconsistent with Article III [...] of GATT."

8.22 In this regard, Korea believes that the CVA requirements as well as the ratio requirements which are conditions that must be met for the application of the Tariff Exemption, clearly fall within the ordinary meaning of "investment measures" and are "trade-related." In addition, the requirements as applied are inconsistent with Article III:4 of the GATT 1994. In particular, the requirements fall clearly within paragraph 1(a) of the illustrative list of TRIMs which are inconsistent with Article III:4 of the GATT 1994 contained in the Annex to the TRIMs Agreement.

(b) The CVA Requirements and Ratio Requirements Are "Investment Measures"

8.23 The Tariff Exemption is conditioned upon, *inter alia*, meeting the relevant CVA and ratio requirements.[789] In this respect, the requirements expressly seek to influence the behaviour of the beneficiaries with regard to, among others, their maintenance of certain levels of production in Canada as well as choices with respect to sources of supply as between Canadian and non-Canadian sources. Thus, the requirements are directly linked to encouraging patterns of investment in the Canadian automotive industry which are in line with the Canadian Governments policy objectives in this sector. The CVA and ratio requirements therefore naturally fall within the scope of any reasonable interpretation of the term "investment measures."

8.24 In *Indonesia - Autos*, the Panel found that certain Indonesian measures with respect to the automobile industry conditioned various customs and tax benefits upon the compliance with particular local content requirements. The Panel found that the Indonesian measures were:

> "[...] aimed at encouraging the development of local manufacturing capability for finished motor vehicles and parts and components in Indonesia. Inherent to this objective is that these measures necessarily have a significant impact on investment in these sectors. For this reason we consider that these measures fall within any reasonable interpretation of the term "investment measures".

8.25 In this respect, by conditioning the granting of the Tariff Exemption on the maintenance of specified levels of domestic content as well as defined ratios of Canadian production to sales in Canada, these requirements certainly involve a "significant impact on investments." The requirements therefore fall plainly within the definition of investment measures for the purposes of the TRIMs Agreement.

(c) The CVA and Ratio Requirements Are "Trade-Related"

8.26 In *Indonesia - Autos* the Panel noted that local content requirements are necessarily trade-related "[...] because such requirements, by definition, always favor the use of domestic products over imported products, and therefore affect trade." The

---

[789] As applicable under the Auto Pact, Letters of Undertaking, the MVTO 1998 and the SROs.

CVA requirements, insofar as they are obligatory in order to obtain the Tariff Exemption, constitute local content requirements and hence will "always" affect trade.

8.27 The ratio requirements are also clearly trade-related or "related to trade in goods" as is specified in Article 1 of the TRIMs Agreement. The ratio requirement obliges a beneficiary to maintain a specified proportion between the sales value of each category of vehicle sold in Canada and the sales value of the motor vehicles of that category manufactured in Canada and therefore is directly related to and affects the conditions of trade with respect to those goods. Canada appears to take the position that because the ratio requirements are mostly complied with, this fact alone somehow means that the measures cannot be trade-related. This assertion is clearly baseless. The fact that particular manufacturers are, at a given time, complying with the ratio requirements clearly does not operate to alter the determination as to whether the measures which include the ratio requirements are themselves trade-related.

(d) The CVA and Ratio Requirements Fall under the Illustrative List of prohibited TRIMs

8.28 Paragraph 1 of the Illustrative List of prohibited TRIMs provides, in relevant part, that:

> "TRIMs that are inconsistent with the obligation of national treatment provided for in paragraph 4 of Article III of GATT include those [with which compliance is necessary] to obtain an advantage, and which require:
>
> (a) the purchase or use by an enterprise of products of domestic origin or from any domestic source, whether specified in terms of particular products, in terms of volume or value of products, or in terms of a proportion of volume or value of its local production; or
>
> (b) that an enterprise purchases or use of imported products be limited to an amount related to the volume or value of local products that it exports."

8.29 As noted above, the CVA requirements are TRIMs which must be complied with in order to obtain an "advantage" within the meaning of paragraph 1, which, in this context, consists of the Tariff Exemption. In addition, the CVA requirements clearly require the "purchase or use [...] of products of domestic origin or from any domestic source, [...] in terms of a proportion of volume or value of its local production." Under the MVTO 1998, for example, the calculation of CVA, which is required in order to obtain the Tariff Exemption, includes, *inter alia,* "the cost of parts *produced* in Canada, and the cost of materials *to the extent that they are of Canadian origin.*" (*emphasis added*).

8.30 Given that, in many, if not most, circumstances, the required level of CVA cannot be attained without resorting to the purchase of parts produced in Canada or materials of Canadian origin, the CVA requirements therefore effectively impose an obligation to purchase or use products of domestic origin or from a domestic source in order to qualify for the Tariff Exemption and therefore fall within the scope of paragraph 1(a) of the Annex.

8.31 In addition, the ratio requirements fall within the scope of paragraph 1(b). For example, as has been noted by the European Communities, in those cases where the ratio requirement is 100 to 100, if a beneficiary sells all its production in Canada, the consequence of this would be that such beneficiary could not sell any motor vehicles imported under the Tariff Exemption because this would result in a production-to-sales ratio of less than 100 to 100. Therefore, for the purposes of obtaining the Tariff Exemption, the beneficiaries' purchase of imported products is limited to an amount which is "related" to the value of local products which it exports within the meaning of paragraph 1(b). Canada itself notes that if the ratio requirements are not complied with "[...] a manufacturer may have to pay duty on some of those vehicles." Canada asserts, however, that this does not constitute a limit on the purchase or use of imported products. This reasoning completely ignores the fact that it is sufficient for the purposes of item 1 of the illustrative list that compliance with the ratio requirements is necessary to obtain an advantage, which in this case consists of the Tariff Exemption. It is not necessary to demonstrate that the ratio requirements must be complied with in order to import vehicles at all.

8.32 In addition, Korea notes that the use of the words "related to" in paragraph 1(b) suggests that investment measures falling within this provision do not have to expressly stipulate that imports are limited in relation to the value of local products exported by the beneficiary. Rather, it is sufficient that the circumstances of the operation of the measure reveal that there are actual or potential limitations on the purchase or use of imported products, and that there is some logical relation or connection between this limitation and the level of local products exported.

4. *SCM Agreement*

(a) Applicability of the SCM Agreement to the Present Dispute

8.33 With respect to the SCM Agreement, Korea considers that the Tariff Exemption constitutes a countervailable subsidy within the meaning of Articles 1 and 2 of the SCM Agreement. Moreover, Korea believes that this subsidy falls within the scope of prohibited subsidies within the meaning of Article 3.1(a) and 3.1(b).

(b) The Tariff Exemption Constitutes a Countervailable Subsidy Within the Meaning of Articles 1 and 2 of the SCM Agreement

8.34 Article 1.1 of the SCM Agreement provides, in relevant part, that:

> "[A] subsidy shall be deemed to exist if:
>
> (a)(1) there is a financial contribution by a government [...] i.e. where:
>
> ...
>
> (ii) government revenue that is otherwise due is foregone or not collected (e.g., fiscal incentives such as tax credits);
>
> ...
>
> and
>
> (b) a benefit is thereby conferred."

8.35 In this regard, Korea notes that customs duties clearly constitute a source of "government revenue." Moreover, the requirement to pay customs duties upon imports of motor vehicles is generally applicable and the waiver of such customs duties operates by way of exception. Thus the ordinarily applicable customs duties constitute government revenue "that is otherwise due," and, where the Exemption operates, this revenue is "foregone or not collected" within the meaning of Article 1.1(a)(1)(ii). Finally, the Tariff Exemption clearly provides a "benefit" within the meaning of Article 1.1(b). As was noted in *Canada - Aircraft*[790] "[...] the ordinary meaning of 'benefit' clearly encompasses some form of advantage." The Tariff Exemption clearly provides an advantage in that only a limited number of beneficiaries are exempted from payment of the customs duties on imports while the generally applicable customs duties continue to apply with respect to other importers.

C. *The Tariff Exemption Constitutes a Prohibited Subsidy Within the Meaning of Article 3.1(a) and 3.1(b) of the SCM Agreement*

8.36 Article 3 of the SCM Agreement provides, in relevant part, that:

> "[T]he following subsidies, within the meaning of Article 1, shall be prohibited:
>
> (a) subsidies contingent in law or in fact, whether solely or as one of several conditions, upon export performance [...]
>
> (b) subsidies contingent, whether solely or as one of several conditions, upon the use of domestic over imported goods.

8.37 In the view of Korea, the CVA requirements, which form part of the conditions for the application of the Tariff Exemption, fall within the scope of Article 3.1(b). For the purposes of calculating CVA, the MVTO 1998 provides that the relevant costs shall include "the cost of parts produced in Canada, and the cost of materials to the extent that they are of Canadian origin." Therefore, a component in reaching the required levels of CVA depends upon the use of the use of domestic over imported goods. The attainment of the required amounts of CVA is an express condition for the availability of the Tariff Exemption and the cost of Canadian parts and materials constitute a *de jure* component in reaching these amounts.

8.38 In addition, Korea considers that the ratio requirements, the fulfilment of which are conditions for the availability of the Tariff Exemption, fall within the scope of Article 3.1(a) in that they are "contingent" upon "export performance." As noted in the EC's argument, where the ratio requirement imposed on the beneficiary is 100 to 100, the possibility of making any imports under the Tariff Exemption, and thus the ability to obtain any subsidy, will directly depend on, and therefore be "contingent" upon whether the beneficiary exports any of its motor vehicles manufactured in Canada. If the beneficiary exports no such vehicles it cannot make any imports under the Tariff Exemption without falling below the required Ratio. In addition, in other cases where the relevant Ratio is lower than 100 to 100, the value of the imports which can be made under the Duty Exemption is still directly related (and

[790] Panel Report on *Canada - Aircraft*, *supra* note 495.

therefore contingent) upon the value of vehicles manufactured in Canada which are exported by the beneficiary.

8.39 Thus, Canada's allegation that "[I]t is abundantly clear that under the Canadian measures, the benefit of the duty-free treatment is contingent upon import performance, not export performance." as stated in its argument is not true.

5. *GATS*

(a) Article II GATS

8.40 With regard to Article II of the GATS, Korea considers that the Tariff Exemption is inconsistent with the MFN obligation provided therein. Article II:1 provides that:

> "With respect to any measure covered by this Agreement, each Member shall accord immediately and unconditionally to services and service suppliers of any other member treatment no less favorable than it accords to like services and service suppliers of any other country."

8.41 Article II:2 provides for exceptions to this obligation, provided that any measures inconsistent with the MFN obligation are listed in the Annex on Article II exemptions. As has been noted by the complainants, however, Canada has not listed any exemption which would cover "wholesale trade services."

8.42 Consequently, a violation of Article II of the GATS will be established where it is shown that a measure is covered by GATS, and, with respect to services and service suppliers of any other Member, Canada accords treatment less favorable than it accords to like services and service suppliers of any other country.

(b) The Tariff Exemption is a Measure Covered by GATS

8.43 The Tariff Exemption clearly falls within the meaning of Article I:1, which states that this Agreement applies to measures "affecting trade in services." In *EC - Bananas III,* it was noted that the term "affecting" in Article I:1 was to be given a broad interpretation. In particular, it was noted that "the use of the term 'affecting' reflects the intent of the drafters to give a broad reach to the GATS. The ordinary meaning of the word 'affecting' implies a measure that has 'an effect on', which indicates a broad scope of application."

8.44 This interpretation contrasts sharply with Canada's very restrictive interpretation." In particular, Canada seeks to distinguish the present measures from the measures in dispute in *EC - Bananas III* on the grounds that in the latter case the application of the measures were "[...] *critical* to the scope and profitability of the provision of services [...] and to the ability of [distributors] to import *at all.*" Conversely, Canada appears to suggest that the present measures can only be deemed to be "affecting" trade in services if they are similarly "critical" to the ability to import or provide the relevant services "at all." Clearly, such a test bears no resemblance to the ordinary meaning of the term "affecting" nor to the clear indications as to the broad meaning attributed to this term in *EC - Bananas III* noted above. In this respect, the Tariff Exemption clearly affects trade in services, *inter alia,* because it reduces the cost for the limited number of beneficiaries in supplying wholesale trade services and therefore modifies competition by placing such beneficiaries at a competitive advantage for the supply of such services. The measures thus produce an effect on trade in services and, consequently, are covered by GATS.

(c) The Tariff Exemption Accords an Advantage to Wholesale Trade Service and Service Suppliers of the United States and Sweden, and, Consequently, Less Favorable Treatment to Like Services and Service Suppliers in Other Countries

The services and service providers at issue are like

8.45 Importers who are beneficiaries under the Tariff Exemption offer trade services to distribute domestically produced and imported motor vehicles. Similarly, Non-Auto Pact manufacturers offer like wholesale trade services. In *EC - Bananas III* it was stated that:

> "[T]he nature and characteristics of wholesale transactions as such, as well as of each of the different subordinated services [...] are 'like' when supplied in connection with wholesale services, irrespective of whether these services are supplied with respect to bananas of EC and traditional ACP origin, on the one hand, or with respect to bananas of third country origin or non traditional ACP origin on the other. Indeed, it seems that the different service activities taken individually is virtually the same and can only be distinguished by referring to the origin of bananas in respect of which the service activity is being performed. Similarly, in our view, to the extent that entities provide these like services, they are like service suppliers."[791]

8.46 By analogy, both Auto Pact manufacturers and non-Auto Pact manufacturers are rendering "like" services "in connection with wholesale trade services." In addition, "to the extent that Auto Pact manufacturers and non-Auto Pact manufacturers provide like services, they are like suppliers."

8.47 The Tariff Exemption clearly fails to accord treatment no less favourable with respect to services and service suppliers of any other country. The advantages accorded under the Tariff Exemption are only available to a closed category of manufacturers which are also service suppliers. This closed category is comprised almost exclusively of Service suppliers of the United states and Canada. This fact, coupled with the prohibitive eligibility criteria ensures that the advantage conferred under the Tariff Exemption is not accorded immediately and unconditionally to service suppliers in any other country. In this respect, the Tariff Exemption operates to discriminate against services and service suppliers of certain WTO Members in favour of others and is therefore inconsistent with the MFN requirement under Article II of GATS.

The Tariff Exemption confers an advantage on wholesale trade services and service suppliers that are eligible for the exemption

[791] Panel Reports on *EC - Bananas III, supra* note 269, para. 7.322.

8.48 In *EC - Bananas III* it was noted that the obligations contained in Article II:1 of the GATS to extend "treatment no less favorable" should be interpreted to require proving "no less favorable conditions of competitions." In this respect, the Tariff Exemption affects the conditions of competition because Auto Pact manufacturers do not need to pass on import duties in the sales price of automobiles while non-Auto Pact manufacturers are required to do so. Therefore, wholesale trade service suppliers who pay the MFN duty are placed at a competitive disadvantage and are therefore accorded less favorable treatment.

(d) Article XVII GATS

8.49 With regard to the national treatment obligation in Article XVII of the GATS, Korea considers that the Tariff Exemption is inconsistent with this provision. Canada is obliged under Article XVII of the GATS and its schedule of specific commitments to grant national treatment with respect to wholesale trade services and service suppliers including such services and service suppliers relating to the production of motor vehicles.

8.50 Article XVII of GATS, paragraphs 1, 2 and 3, respectively, provide that:

> "In the sectors inscribed in its schedule, and subject to any conditions and qualifications set out therein, each Member shall accord to services and service suppliers of any other Member, in respect of all measures affecting the supply of services, treatment no less favorable than it accords to its own like service suppliers.

8.51 A Member may meet the requirement of paragraph 1 by according to services and service suppliers of any other member, either formally identical treatment or formally different treatment to that it accords to its own like services and service suppliers.

8.52 Formally identical or formally different treatment shall be considered to be less favorable if it modifies the conditions of competition in favor of services or service suppliers of the member compared to like services or service suppliers of any other Member."

(e) Wholesale Trade Services of Motor Vehicles Through Commercial Presence Are Covered in Canada's Schedule of Specific Commitments

8.53 Canada's specific commitment covers wholesale trade services under CPC[792] class 6111 (sale of motor vehicles including automobiles and other road vehicles) through commercial presence without conditions or qualifications under Article XVII:1 of the GATS. As Canada has not limited, conditioned or qualified its commitment in these services it is required to accord to services and service suppliers of any other member in this sector treatment no less favorable than the treatment it accords its own like services and service suppliers.

[792] United Nations Central Product Classification System.

(f) The Services and Service Suppliers Are "Like"

8.54 Korea endorses the argument by Japan, with respect to the interpretation of *EC - Bananas III*, that Auto Pact manufacturers and Non-Auto Pact manufacturers are rendering "like" services "in connection with wholesale trade services," "irrespective of whether these services are supplied with respect to automobiles imported by the Auto Pact manufacturers or their related companies on the one hand or with respect to automobiles imported by the Non-Auto Pact manufacturers on the other hand." And that, to the extent that the Auto Pact manufacturers and Non-Auto Pact manufacturers "provide these like services, they are like service suppliers," whether or not they have production facilities in Canada.

(g) The Tariff Exemption Modifies the Conditions of Competition in Favor of Canadian Services and Service Suppliers

8.55 The Tariff Exemption modifies conditions of competition in favor of only certain service suppliers in that it applies the Tariff Exemption only to Auto Pact manufacturers who are also wholesale trade service suppliers. The savings in import duty costs due to the Duty Waiver provides the Auto Pact Manufacturers a competitive advantage in wholesale services because of the lower import duty costs and corresponding financing costs savings. Therefore, the less favorable treatment accorded by Canada to imports by Non-Auto Pact Manufacturers' wholesale trade service suppliers modifies the conditions of competition between certain Canadian services and service suppliers and like services or service suppliers of other Members who are granted less favorable treatment. Consequently, the application of the Tariff Exemption by Canada is inconsistent with its obligation of national treatment under Article XVII of the GATS.

(h) The Tariff Exemption Accords More Favorable Treatment to Canadian Services and Service Suppliers Related to the Production of Motor Vehicles

8.56 Korea notes that, in order to achieve stipulated CVA requirements, Auto Pact manufacturers are in effect obliged to obtain certain services supplied in Canada. In this respect, Canadian services and service suppliers are accorded more favorable treatment as compared with like services and service suppliers of other WTO Members. In this regard, therefore, the Tariff Exemption is inconsistent with Canada's obligations under Article XVII of the GATS. The types of services which may be counted towards the achievement of CVA are defined in the MVTO 1998.[793] The definition of CVA in the MVTO 1998 with respect to services includes:

> (a)(iv) "the part of costs that is reasonably attributable to the production of vehicles, namely,
>
> (I) the cost of maintenance and repair work executed in Canada on buildings, machinery and equipment used for production purposes.

[793] Subsection 1(1) of the Schedule to the MVTO 1998.

(K) the cost of engineering services, experimental work and product development executed in Canada.

[...]

(v) administrative and general expenses incurred in Canada that are reasonably attributable to the production of the vehicles."

8.57 The types of services which might be covered in these CVA categories is potentially very broad. In this regard, as noted by Japan, Canada's schedule of specific commitments contains very few limitations on its commitment to provide national treatment with respect to these various services (with regard to modes 1, 2 and 3), which are procured by the Auto Pact manufacturers.

(i) The CVA Requirements Accord Less Favorable Treatment to "Like" Services and Service Suppliers

Like services and service suppliers

8.58 In *EC - Bananas III*, the Panel considered the issue of "like" services and suppliers. With respect to whether wholesale trade services provided by companies originating in the European Communities and ACP countries on the one hand, and companies originating from other countries on the other hand, were like, it was stated that:

> "[T]he nature and characteristics of wholesale transactions as such, as well as of each of the different subordinated services [...] are 'like' when supplied in connection with wholesale services, irrespective of whether these services are supplied with respect to bananas of EC and traditional ACP origin, on the one hand, or with respect to bananas of third country origin or non traditional ACP origin on the other. Indeed, it seems that the different service activities taken individually is virtually the same and can only be distinguished by referring to the origin of bananas in respect of which the service activity is being performed. Similarly, in our view, to the extent that entities provide these like services, they are like service suppliers."[794]

8.59 By analogy, the nature and characteristics of the services at issue are "like" irrespective of where they are supplied. Therefore, to the extent that Canadian service suppliers and other service suppliers provide these "like" services, they are "like" suppliers.

I.2 Services and service suppliers outside Canada are accorded less favorable treatment

I.3 Modes of supply

8.60 The CVA requirements, insofar as they require that the services in question be "executed in Canada," as applicable under items (a)(iv)(I) and (a)(iv)(K), or that the cost for services be "incurred in Canada" in the case of item (a)(v), accord less

[794] Panel Reports on *EC - Bananas III*, *supra* note 269, para. 7.322.

favorable treatment to service suppliers outside Canada in that they prevent the inclusion of costs in calculating CVA where the services are supplied under Mode 1 (cross-border supply) or under Mode 2 (consumption abroad). Conversely, the cost of "like" services which are supplied in Canada are included for the purposes of calculating CVA.

J. Scope of the less favorable treatment

8.61 Under Article XVII:3 of the GATS, treatment accorded to services and service suppliers of other WTO Members shall be considered to be "less favorable if it modifies the conditions of competition in favor of services and service suppliers of the member maintaining the measure compared to like services and service suppliers of any other Member."

8.62 Under the CVA requirements, costs associated with services supplied under Mode 1 (cross-border supply) and Mode 2 (consumption abroad) are excluded from the calculation of CVA. Consequently, the exclusion of these costs for the purpose of CVA in these cases modifies the conditions of competition in favor of services supplied in Canada compared to like services under Mode 1 or Mode 2 from or in the territory of other Members.

6. Conclusion

8.63 On the basis of the factual and legal considerations above, Korea considers that the inconsistency of the Canadian Tariff Exemption with its obligations under Articles I:1 and III:4 of the GATT 1994, Article 2.1 of the TRIMs Agreement, Articles 3.1(a), 3.1(b) and 3.2 of the SCM Agreement and Articles II and XVII of the GATS has been conclusively demonstrated.

C. The United States' Arguments as a Third Party

8.64 As a third party, the **United States** argues as follows:

8.65 As a third party, the United States does not attempt to respond to *all* of the factual and legal issues raised in this proceeding. Instead, the United States reserves its comments for one issue that it believes bears emphasis; that is, the relevance of Article XXIV of the *General Agreement on Tariffs and Trade 1994* ("GATT 1994") to these proceedings. Further, the United States would raise one issue that has not yet been addressed, but which the panel may wish to keep in mind; namely, the possible relevance of Article V of the *General Agreement on Trade in Services* ("GATS") to this case. The fact that no comment is made on a particular factual or legal claim does not mean that the United States agrees or disagrees with the position of any of the parties in this case.

1. Legal Arguments

(a) GATS Article V

8.66 It is appropriate to mention one issue that thus far has not been mentioned by any party: namely, the possible relevance of GATS Article V. That Article, which is analogous to GATT Article XXIV, recognizes that GATS members may enter into agreements liberalizing trade in services.

8.67 Specifically, Article V provides that:

> 1. This Agreement shall not prevent any of its Members from being a party to or entering into an agreement liberalizing trade in services between or among the parties to such an agreement, provided that such an agreement:
>
> (a) has substantial sectoral coverage (*footnote omitted*), and
>
> (b) provides for the absence or elimination of substantially all discrimination, in the sense of Article XVII, between or among the parties, in the sectors covered under subparagraph (a), through:
>
> (i) elimination of existing discriminatory measures, and/or
>
> (ii) prohibition of new or more discriminatory measures,
>
> either at the entry into force of that agreement or on the basis of a reasonable time-frame, except for measures permitted under Articles XI, XII, XIV and XIV *bis*.
>
> 2. In evaluating whether the conditions under paragraph 1(b) are met, consideration may be given to the relationship of the agreement to a wider process of economic integration or trade liberalization among the countries concerned.

8.68 In 1994, the United States, Canada, and Mexico implemented the North American Free Trade Agreement ("NAFTA"), a comprehensive free-trade agreement governing trade in goods and services, trade-related intellectual property rights, and other matters. NAFTA Chapters 11 (Investment), 12 (Trade in Services), 13 (Telecommunications), 14 (Financial Services), and 16 (Temporary Entry), together with other services-related provisions of the NAFTA, create a North American free-trade zone for services.

8.69 The services provisions of the NAFTA fall squarely within the terms of GATS Article V:1. The NAFTA provides the elimination or absence of substantially all discrimination among the three Parties across the range of services sectors. The agreement is substantial both in terms of the number of sectors it covers and the volume of trade affected. Moreover, it applies across all modes of supply.

8.70 The European Communities and Japan argue that duty-free treatment offered under the Auto Pact confers, *de facto*, certain benefits on US-owned automobile companies that, in the complainants' view, are wholesale services suppliers for purposes of the GATS. The European Communities and Japan argue that those benefits contravene GATS Article II. Canada has rejected the complainants' claim.

8.71 The United States takes no position here on the merits of the EC's GATS Article II arguments, or Canada's rebuttal. However, should it ultimately sustain the EC's position on this issue, the Panel should consider the application of GATS Article V to the measures at issue.

8.72 To the extent that they provide more favorable treatment to US services suppliers than to like services suppliers of other Members, as the European Communities asserts, Canada's measures would be subject to the implied exception to GATS Article II conferred by GATS Article V:1. Specifically, the more favourable treatment that the European Communities is seeking to condemn is being accorded by a member of an economic integration agreement of the type specified by Article V:1 to the services suppliers of another member of that agreement.

(b) GATT Article XXIV

8.73 In a parallel argument with respect to trade in goods, the European Communities alleges that "the Tariff Exemption is inconsistent with GATT Article I:1 in that *de facto* it provides an advantage to imports of automobiles originating in the United States and Mexico *vis-à-vis* imports of like products originating in other Members."

8.74 The arguments offered above with respect to GATS Article V are also relevant in response to this assertion. As Canada has noted, to the extent the United States and Mexico attain benefits that other countries do not, GATT Article XXIV sanctions such treatment. As partners in a free-trade area, Canada, the United States, and Mexico are permitted to offer to each other advantages that are not extended to other countries.

IX. INTERIM REVIEW

9.1 On 27 October 1999, Canada and Japan requested the Panel to review certain aspects of the interim report that had been transmitted to the parties on 13 October 1999, in accordance with Article 15.2 of the DSU.[795] The European Communities indicated that it had no comments. As for a possible review meeting with the Panel, Canada and Japan expressed a preference to respond in writing to each other's comments. The Panel thus invited the parties to submit written responses to each other's comments by 11 November 1999; Canada and Japan did so. No further comments were accepted after that date.

9.2 We have reviewed the arguments and suggestions presented by Canada and Japan and have finalized our report, taking into account those comments by the parties which we considered justified.

9.3 For the descriptive part (i.e. Sections I-VIII), where requested, we inserted language found in the original submissions of the parties, unless that language already appeared in the descriptive part. These insertions may be found in paragraphs 5.132-5.138, 5.142-5.143, 5.217-5.220, 6.15, 6.42-6.45, 6.66, 0-6.94, 6.121-6.123, 6.162, 6.190-6.194, 6.274, 6.361-6.363, 6.436, 6.450, 6.792, and 6.1134-6.1137, as well as in footnotes 34 and 308; Canada's *Figures 1-7* were also inserted. Although appearing in the Legal Arguments section (Section VI), paragraphs 5.90-5.116 and 5.271 were duplicated in Section V for completeness, as requested. Paragraph 4.6 and footnotes 44, 46 and 275 were added for clarification, as requested. Paragraphs 2.3-2.6, 2.8, 2.10, 2.14, 2.29, 2.35 and 6.417, as well as footnote 33, were revised in the light of Canada's comments. In addition, other typographical and technical re-

[795] The descriptive part of the report (i.e. Sections I-VIII) was issued to the parties on 5 August 1999 for comment. On 20 August 1999 Canada and Japan submitted comments and the European Communities indicated that it did not wish to do so.

finements were made. Paragraph 4.3 was left intact despite a request that it be deleted.

9.4 For both the Findings and the Conclusions and Recommendations sections (i.e. Sections X and XI), we made minor linguistic, typographical and technical corrections and also added clarifications. Specifically, footnotes 800 and 811 were added for clarification, as requested; paragraph 10.4 was revised, with paragraphs 10.3-10.6 reordered; and terminology as to the measures at issue was corrected in paragraphs 10.264, 10.290, 10.308, 11.1(g) and 11.1(i).

9.5 A number of more substantive modifications were also made in response to comments from the parties. In particular, paragraph 10.39 was revised as requested to reflect Canada's position better. In that paragraph, the key issue is Canada's view of what constitute "origin-neutral" conditions on importers, referred to in the second sentence, to which no objection was posed. A sentence summarizing Canada's argument as to the relevant test of Article I:1 consistency was deleted from the end of the paragraph because these ideas are already presented in paragraph 10.35. Paragraph 10.44 was revised as requested to provide a more accurate reflection of Canada's position on the issue of intra-firm trade in the automotive sector; the basic point of the paragraph - i.e. that the importers will import only from related parties - is not altered. Paragraphs 10.52-10.54 were revised to provide a more detailed reflection of Canada's arguments, thus adding balance. Paragraph 10.81 has been revised to make it clear that the idea expressed in this paragraph is not that use of imported products prevents a manufacturer from benefitting from the import duty exemption, but rather that the use of imported products does not contribute to meeting the conditions for benefitting from the exemption. Paragraphs 10.83 and 10.84 were revised to reflect better Canada's position that measures only affect the internal sale or use of products if they have a potential effect under current circumstances and not, as previously stated in paragraph 10.83, if they have an actual effect under current circumstances. Paragraphs 10.225, 10.230, 10.292 and 10.293 were revised to reflect Canada's comment that their argument that the import duty exemption is not a measure affecting trade in services does not also extend to the CVA requirements.

9.6 In addition, and taking into consideration Japan's view that remedies may be a relevant consideration when determining whether to apply judicial economy, we have elaborated on Section X.C.2 (Claims under the SCM Agreement: CVA requirements) by undertaking an examination of the consistency of the CVA requirements with Article 3.1(b).[796]

---

[796] Initially we chose not to examine claims under Article 3 of the SCM Agreement regarding the CVA requirements. Japan took issue with this decision with respect to claims under Article 3.1(b) of the SCM Agreement but not claims under Article 3.1(a) of that Agreement. Hence, we only elaborated findings on those claims under 3.1(b).

X. FINDINGS

A. *Introduction*

1. *Measures at issue*

10.1 The parties to this dispute disagree as to the consistency with various provisions of the GATT 1994 (GATT), the TRIMs Agreement, the SCM Agreement and the GATS, of an exemption from customs duties accorded by Canada on the importation of motor vehicles subject to certain conditions ("import duty exemption"). This import duty exemption arises out of Canada's implementation of the Auto Pact, which was concluded between Canada and the United States in January 1965. It is currently applied by Canada pursuant to the Motor Vehicles Tariff Order 1998 (MVTO 1998) and a number of Special Remission Orders (SROs).[797]

10.2 The MVTO 1998 provides that the importation of certain categories of motor vehicles[798] is free from payment of the otherwise applicable MFN tariff if imported by a manufacturer of a category of motor vehicles in accordance with the conditions set out in the schedule to the MVTO 1998. The schedule to the MVTO 1998 provides that the term "manufacturer" means:

> "...a manufacturer of a class of vehicles who
>
> (a) produced vehicles of that class in Canada in each of the four consecutive quarters of the base year; and
>
> (b) produced vehicles of a class in Canada in the 12-month period ending on July 31 in which the importation is made where
>
> > (i) the ratio of the net sales value of the vehicles produced to the net sales value of all vehicles of that class sold for consumption in Canada by the manufacturer in that period is equal to or higher than the ratio of the net sales value of all vehicles of that class produced in Canada by the manufacturer in the base year to the net sales value of all vehicles of that class sold for consumption in Canada by the manufacturer in the base year, and is not in any case lower than 75 to 100, and
> >
> > (ii) the Canadian value added is equal to or greater than the Canadian value added in respect of all vehicles of that class produced in Canada by the manufacturer in the base year."

The term "base year" means the 12-month period beginning on 1 August 1963 and ending on 31 July 1964.

10.3 A number of motor vehicle manufacturers who had no production operations in Canada during the 1963-64 base year have been accorded the right to import motor vehicles duty free into Canada pursuant to company-specific SROs which provide that the manufacturers must meet criteria with respect to the ratio between the net

---

[797] The MVTO 1998 and the SROs also provide for an import duty exemption with respect to certain parts and components for use as original equipment in the manufacture of motor vehicles. That exemption has not been contested in this dispute.

[798] We note that the MVTO 1998 defines "motor vehicles" as comprising (i) automobiles, (ii) specified commercial vehicles, and (iii) buses. The SROs follow this definition.

sales value of vehicles produced in Canada and the net sales value of all vehicles sold for consumption in Canada and with respect to the Canadian value added in the production of motor vehicles.

10.4 In sum, to qualify for the import duty exemption, an eligible manufacturer of a class of vehicles must meet the following conditions: (1) a manufacturing presence in Canada which, with respect to the MVTO 1998, is expressed in terms of a base year, along with local production of vehicles of the class being imported in the current year ("manufacturing presence"); (2) a production-to-sales ratio requirement, as reflected in the MVTO 1998 and the SROs ("ratio requirement"); and (3) a Canadian value added requirement, as reflected in the MVTO 1998 and the SROs ("CVA requirement"). We also note that, according to complainants, additional CVA requirements are contained in various Letters of Undertaking.[799]

10.5 In 1989, the category of motor vehicle manufacturers eligible for the import duty exemption under the then applicable MVTO or pursuant to company-specific SROs was closed in accordance with an obligation assumed by Canada under the Canada-United States Free Trade Agreement.[800]

10.6 While the eligibility for the import duty exemption provided for under the MVTO 1998 and the SROs is thus confined to certain motor vehicle manufacturers, the right of those manufacturers to import motor vehicles duty free is not subject to a limitation with respect to the origin of such vehicles.

10.7 We note the difference in product coverage of the various claims of Japan, on the one hand, and the European Communities on the other. The product coverage of Japan's claims - those under the GATT, the TRIMS Agreement, the SCM Agreement and the GATS - includes the three categories of "motor vehicles" as defined in the MVTO 1998 (with certain exceptions not relevant to this proceeding), including "automobiles", "buses" and "specified commercial vehicles".[801] Similarly, the product coverage of the European Communities' claims under GATT Article III, the TRIMS Agreement, the SCM Agreement and Article XVII of the GATS also include all three categories of motor vehicles.[802] However, the European Communities' claims under GATT Article I and GATS Article II are limited in their product coverage to "automobiles" as defined in the MVTO 1998.[803]

10.8 For the purposes of our analysis of all the parties' claims, unless otherwise specified, in referring to "product(s)" we mean to include all three categories of "motor vehicles" as defined in the MVTO 1998.

2. *Order of Consideration of Claims*

10.9 In our analysis of the legal issues in this case, we shall follow the order in which the complainants presented their claims. Accordingly, we shall first address

---

[799] Although we note the statement by the European Communities in Section V.A.1(b), *supra*, that it is also challenging the Canada-US Auto Pact as such, no claims are made as to the Auto Pact as distinct from those made against the MVTO 1998, the SROs and the Letters of Undertaking.

[800] We note that the Canada-United States Free Trade Agreement as such is not at issue in this dispute.

[801] See *supra* para. 2.19.

[802] See *supra* para. 5.20.

[803] See *supra* para. 5.19.

claims under GATT Article I:1, followed by those under GATT Article III:4, and those under the TRIMs Agreement. We shall then turn to claims under the SCM Agreement. Finally, we shall address claims under the GATS.

3. Rules of Treaty Interpretation

10.10 Article 3.2 of the DSU directs panels to clarify WTO provisions "in accordance with customary rules of interpretation of public international law". It is generally considered that the fundamental rules of treaty interpretation set out in Articles 31 and 32 of the Vienna Convention have attained the status of rules of customary international law. These Vienna Convention articles provide as follows:

> Article 31
>
> *General rule of interpretation*
>
> 1. A treaty shall be interpreted in good faith in accordance with the ordinary meaning to be given to the terms of the treaty in their context and in the light of its object and purpose.
>
> 2. The context for the purpose of the interpretation of a treaty shall comprise, in addition to the text, including its preamble and annexes:
>
> (a) any agreement relating to the treaty which was made between all the parties in connexion with the conclusion of the treaty;
>
> (b) any instrument which was made by one or more parties in connexion with the conclusion of the treaty and accepted by the other parties as an instrument related to the treaty.
>
> 3. There shall be taken into account together with the context:
>
> (a) any subsequent agreement between the parties regarding the interpretation of the treaty or the application of its provisions;
>
> (b) any subsequent practice in the application of the treaty which establishes the agreement of the parties regarding its interpretation;
>
> (c) any relevant rules of international law applicable in the relations between the parties.
>
> 4. A special meaning shall be given to a term if it is established that the parties so intended.
>
> Article 32
>
> *Supplementary means of interpretation*
>
> Recourse may be had to supplementary means of interpretation, including the preparatory work of the treaty and the circumstances of its conclusion, in order to confirm the meaning resulting from the application of article 31, or to determine the meaning when the interpretation according to article 31:
>
> (a) leaves the meaning ambiguous or obscure; or

(b) leads to a result which is manifestly absurd or unreasonable.

10.11 As noted by the Appellate Body in its report on *Japan - Alcoholic Beverages*, "Article 31 of the Vienna Convention provides that the words of the treaty form the foundation for the interpretive process: 'interpretation must be based above all upon the text of the treaty'. The provisions of the treaty are to be given their ordinary meaning in their context. The object and purpose of the treaty are also to be taken into account in determining the meaning of its provisions".[804]

10.12 Our understanding of these rules of interpretation is that, even though the text of a term is the starting-point for any interpretation, the meaning of a term cannot be found exclusively in that text; in seeking the meaning of a term, we also have to take account of its context and to consider the text of the term in light of the object and purpose of the treaty. Article 31 of the Vienna Convention explicitly refers to the "ordinary meaning to be given to the terms of the treaty in their [the terms'] context and in the light of its [the treaty's] object and purpose".[805] The three elements referred to in Article 31 - text, context and object and purpose - are to be viewed as one integrated rule of interpretation rather than a sequence of separate tests to be applied in a hierarchical order.[806] Of course, context and object and purpose may simply confirm the textual meaning of a term. In many cases, however, it is impossible to give meaning, even "ordinary meaning", without looking also at the context and/or object and purpose.[807]

10.13 It is in accordance with these rules of treaty interpretation that we will examine the WTO provisions at issue in this case.

B. Claims Under the GATT and the TRIMs Agreement

1. Claims under Article I:1 of the GATT

(a) Introduction

10.14 As described above in the introductory section of the findings, Canada accords an import duty exemption on motor vehicles if imported by importers who

---

804 Appellate Body Report on *Japan - Alcoholic Beverages, supra* note 271, pp. 105-106.

805 See Appellate Body Report on *Brazil - Measures Affecting Dessicated Coconut*, adopted on 20 March 1997, WT/DS22/AB/R, DSR 1997:I, 167, pp. 180 *et seq.*

806 "The Commission by heading the article 'General rule of interpretation' in the singular and by underlining the connection between para.s 1 and 2 and again between para. 3 and the two previous para.s, intended to indicate that the application of the means of interpretation in the article would be a single combined operation. All the various elements, as they were present in any given case, would be thrown into the crucible and their interaction would give the legally relevant interpretation". Yearbook of the International Law Commission (1966) Vol. II, A/CN.4/SER.A/1966/Add.1, 219 and 220.

807 To find "ordinary meaning", reference is often made to an authoritative language dictionary. However, very few - if any - words have only one dictionary meaning. Thus, even the step of choosing the relevant dictionary meaning(s) in pursuit of "ordinary meaning" - often the very first step in treaty interpretation - necessarily involves a reference to the context in which the word is used. Referring to the object and purpose of an agreement may also be indispensable to arriving at the meaning of a word.

meet certain conditions. This import duty exemption is provided for in the MVTO 1998 and certain SROs.

10.15 The European Communities and Japan claim that this import duty exemption is inconsistent with Article I:1 of the GATT, which provides in relevant part:

> "With respect to customs duties and charges of any kind imposed on or in connection with importation ..., any advantage, favour, privilege or immunity granted by any contracting party to any product originating in ... any other country shall be accorded immediately and unconditionally to the like product originating in ... the territories of all other contracting parties."

10.16 The parties do not dispute that the import duty exemption is an "advantage" within the meaning of Article I:1 with respect to "customs duties and charges of any kind on or in connection with importation". It is also not in dispute that there are imported products which do not benefit from this exemption which are like imported products which benefit from the exemption.

10.17 Two main arguments have been advanced with respect to the alleged inconsistency of this import duty exemption with Article I:1. Firstly, Japan argues that the import duty exemption is inconsistent with Article I:1 because, by conditioning the exemption on criteria which are unrelated to the imported product itself, Canada fails to accord the exemption immediately and unconditionally to like products originating in the territories of all WTO Members. Secondly, both the European Communities and Japan argue that the limitation of the eligibility for the import duty exemption to certain motor vehicle manufacturers is inconsistent with Article I:1 on the grounds that it entails *de facto* discrimination in favour of products of certain countries.

(b) Whether the Import Duty Exemption is Awarded "Immediately and Unconditionally"

10.18 We first consider the argument of Japan that, by making the import duty exemption conditional upon criteria which are unrelated to the imported product itself, Canada fails to accord the import duty exemption immediately and unconditionally to like products originating in all WTO Members. By "criteria unrelated to the imported products themselves," Japan means the various conditions which confine the eligibility for the exemption to certain motor vehicle manufacturers in Canada.

10.19 We note that in developing this argument, Japan refers to the Concise Oxford Dictionary definition of the word "unconditional" as meaning "not subject to conditions", and cites *Indonesia Autos*[808] and *Belgian Family Allowances*[809], as well as the *Working Party Report on the Accession of Hungary*[810], as authority for the proposition that the subjecting of an advantage to *any* condition *unrelated to the product* is inconsistent with Article I:1.

10.20 We also recall Canada's response that Japan misinterprets the "immediately and unconditionally" clause in Article I:1 and that Article I:1 contains no prohibition of origin-neutral terms and conditions on importation that apply to the *importers* as

[808] Panel Report on *Indonesia - Autos, supra* note 270.

[809] Panel Report on *Belgian Family Allowances, supra* note 276.

[810] Report of the *Working Party on the Accession of Hungary, supra* note 276.

opposed to the *products* being imported. According to Canada, Article I:1 prohibits only conditions related to the national origin of the imported product. Canada thus argues that it is entitled to treat like products differently so long as the distinction in treatment is based on criteria other than national origin. Canada argues that in the instant case the conditions under which the import duty exemption is accorded are consistent with Article I:1 in that they are based on the activities of importing manufacturers and not on the origin of the products. Canada further argues that to hold otherwise would be to "read Article II out of the GATT", given that Article II specifically contemplates tariff bindings being subject to "terms, *conditions* or qualifications"[811].

10.21 We note that the argument of Japan that the import duty exemption is inconsistent with Article I:1 because it is conditioned upon criteria that are unrelated to the imported products is distinct from Japan's argument that the import duty exemption violates Article I:1 because it discriminates in practice in favour of products of certain countries. Thus, Japan advances an interpretation of Article I:1 which distinguishes between, on the one hand, the issue of whether the advantage arising out of the import duty exemption is accorded "unconditionally" as required by Article I:1, and, on the other, the issue of whether that advantage is accorded without discrimination as to the origin of products.

10.22 As explained below, we believe that this interpretation of Japan does not accord with the ordinary meaning of the term "unconditionally" in Article I:1 in its context and in light of the object and purpose of Article I:1. In our view, whether an advantage within the meaning of Article I:1 is accorded "unconditionally" cannot be determined independently of an examination of whether it involves discrimination between like products of different countries.

10.23 Article I:1 requires that, if a Member grants any advantage to any product originating in the territory of any other country, such advantage must be accorded "immediately and unconditionally" to the like product originating in the territories of all other Members. We agree with Japan that the ordinary meaning of "unconditionally" is "not subject to conditions". However, in our view Japan misinterprets the meaning of the word "unconditionally" in the context in which it appears in Article I:1. The word "unconditionally" in Article I:1 does not pertain to the granting of an advantage *per se*, but to the obligation to accord to the like products of all Members an advantage which has been granted to any product originating in any country. The purpose of Article I:1 is to ensure unconditional MFN treatment. In this context, we consider that the obligation to accord "unconditionally" to third countries which are WTO Members an advantage which has been granted to any other country means that the extension of that advantage may not be made subject to conditions with respect to the situation or conduct of those countries. This means that an advantage granted to the product of any country must be accorded to the like product of all WTO Members without discrimination as to origin.

10.24 In this respect, it appears to us that there is an important distinction to be made between, on the one hand, the issue of whether an advantage within the meaning of Article I:1 is subject to conditions, and, on the other, whether an advantage,

---

[811] *Supra* para. 7.97.

once it has been granted to the product of any country, is accorded "unconditionally" to the like product of all other Members. An advantage can be granted subject to conditions without necessarily implying that it is not accorded "unconditionally" to the like product of other Members. More specifically, the fact that conditions attached to such an advantage are not related to the imported product itself does not necessarily imply that such conditions are discriminatory with respect to the origin of imported products. We therefore do not believe that, as argued by Japan, the word "unconditionally" in Article I:1 must be interpreted to mean that making an advantage conditional on criteria not related to the imported product itself is *per se* inconsistent with Article I:1, irrespective of whether and how such criteria relate to the origin of the imported products.

10.25 We thus find that Japan's argument is unsupported by the text of Article I:1. We also consider that there is no support for this argument in the GATT and WTO reports cited by Japan. A review of these reports shows that they were concerned with measures that were found to be inconsistent with Article I:1 not because they involved the application of conditions that were not related to the imported product but because they involved conditions that entailed different treatment of imported products depending upon their origin.

10.26 Thus, the measure at issue in *Belgian Family Allowances* was "the application of the Belgian law on the levy of a charge on foreign goods purchased by public bodies when these goods originated in a country whose system of family allowances did not meet specific requirements."[812] The panel determined that this levy was an internal charge within the meaning of Article III:2 of the GATT and found that it was inconsistent with Article I:1:

> "According to the provisions of paragraph 1 of Article I of the General Agreement, any advantage, favour, privilege or immunity granted by Belgium to any product originating in the territory of any country with respect all matters referred to in paragraph 2 of Article III shall be granted immediately and unconditionally to the like product originating in the territories of all contracting parties. Belgium has granted exemption from the levy under consideration to products purchased by public bodies when they originate in Luxemburg and the Netherlands, as well as in France, Italy, Sweden and the United Kingdom. If the General Agreement were definitively in force in accordance with Article XXVI, it is clear that the exemption would have to be granted unconditionally to all other contracting parties (including Denmark and Norway). *The consistency or otherwise of the system of family allowances in force in the territory of a given contracting party with the requirements of the Belgian law would be irrelevant in this respect, and the Belgian legislation would have to be amended insofar as it introduced a discrimination between countries having a given system of family allowances and those which had a different system or no sys-*

[812] Panel Report on *Belgian Family Allowances*, *supra* note 276, para. 1.

> *tem at all, and made the granting of the exemption dependant on certain conditions.*"[813] (*emphasis added*)

10.27 Similarly, the reference made by Japan to the *Working Party Report on the Accession of Hungary* concerns tariff exemptions and reductions granted in the framework of co-operation contracts. The GATT Secretariat, in response to a request for a legal opinion, commented that "the prerequisite of having a co-operation contract in order to benefit from certain tariff treatment appeared to imply conditional most-favoured-nation treatment and would, therefore, not appear to be compatible with the General Agreement".[814]

10.28 With respect to the Panel Report on *Indonesia - Autos,* we note that the panel determined that certain customs duty and tax benefits provided by Indonesia to imports of "National Cars" and parts and components thereof from Korea were advantages within the meaning of Article I, and that these "National Cars" and their parts and components imported from Korea were like other similar motor vehicles and parts and components from other Members. The panel then proceeded to

> "...examine whether the advantages accorded to national cars and parts and components thereof from Korea are unconditionally accorded to the products of other Members, as required by Article I. The GATT case law is clear to the effect that any such advantage (here tax and customs duty benefits) cannot be made conditional on any criteria that is not related to the imported product itself."[815]

Significantly, in support of the statement that "the GATT case law is clear to the effect that any such advantage (...) cannot be made conditional on any criteria that is not related to the imported product itself", the panel referred to the Panel Report on *Belgian Family Allowances.*[816] As discussed above, that Panel Report dealt with a measure which distinguished between countries of origin depending upon the system of family allowances in force in their territories. We further note that, following this statement, the panel on *Indonesia - Autos* identified certain conditions which entailed discrimination between imports of the subject products from Korea and like products from other Members, and found that these measures were thus inconsistent with Article I of the GATT.[817] The statement in the Panel Report that an advantage within the meaning of Article I "cannot be made conditional on any criteria that is not related to the imported product itself" must therefore in our view be seen in relation to conditions which entailed different treatment of like products depending upon their origin.

10.29 In sum, we believe that the panel decisions and other sources referred to by Japan do not support the interpretation of Article I:1 advocated by Japan in the present case according to which the word "unconditionally" in Article I:1 must be interpreted to mean that subjecting an advantage granted in connection with the importation of a product to conditions not related to the imported product itself is *per se*

---

[813] Ibid., para. 3.

[814] Report of the *Working Party on the Accession of Hungary, supra* note 276, para. 12.

[815] Panel Report on *Indonesia - Autos, supra* note 270, para. 14.143.

[816] Ibid., para. 14.144.

[817] Ibid., paras. 14.145-148.

inconsistent with Article I:1, regardless of whether such conditions are discriminatory with respect to the origin of products. Rather, they accord with the conclusion from our analysis of the text of Article I:1 that whether conditions attached to an advantage granted in connection with the importation of a product offend Article I:1 depends upon whether or not such conditions discriminate with respect to the origin of products.

10.30 In light of the foregoing considerations, we reject Japan's argument that, by making the import duty exemption on motor vehicles conditional on criteria that are not related to the imported products themselves, Canada fails to accord the exemption immediately and unconditionally to the like product originating in the territories of all WTO Members. In our view, Canada's import duty exemption cannot be held to be inconsistent with Article I:1 simply on the grounds that it is granted on conditions that are not related to the imported products themselves. Rather, we must determine whether these conditions amount to discrimination between like products of different origins.

(c) Whether the Import Duty Exemption Discriminates in Favour of Motor Vehicles of Certain Countries

10.31 We thus turn to the issues raised by the complainants to support their view that the import duty exemption involves discrimination in favour of motor vehicles of certain countries. We begin by recapitulating the main arguments of the parties.

10.32 Japan argues that, by virtue of the eligibility restriction, the import duty exemption accorded by Canada on motor vehicles discriminates in practice by according an advantage to motor vehicles from certain countries while effectively denying the same advantage to like motor vehicles originating in the territories of other WTO Members. Japan submits that, although the beneficiaries of the import duty exemption are ostensibly permitted to import motor vehicles of any national origin, in practice they have chosen and will continue to choose to import the products of particular companies from particular countries, in consideration of their previous history of transactions, capital relationships, and the nationality of companies investing in the beneficiaries. In the view of Japan, this means that the eligibility restriction and other conditions attached to the exemption effectively limit access to the advantage to certain Members having the companies with which the beneficiaries have certain commercial relationships. Japan further argues that the discriminatory nature of the exemption was strengthened due to the fact that the list of eligible importers has been frozen since 1 January 1989. As evidence of the discriminatory character of the import duty exemption, Japan adduces statistics which show that in 1997, 96% of Sweden's imports into Canada, and 94% of Belgium's were duty-free (in both cases these were imports of Volvos and of Saabs, the latter partly owned by GM, with Volvo Canada and GM Canada both being eligible manufacturer beneficiaries). Japan compares this with just under 30% of duty-free imports for the whole of the European Communities, and of just under 5% for Korea and just under 3% for Japan.[818] Japan also points to the fact that Volvos and Saabs are imported under the import duty exemption from Belgium or Sweden while like vehicles produced by Japanese manu-

818 *Supra* Japan's Table 6.

facturers are imported subject to the MFN rate.[819] We note that at the initial stage of this proceeding Japan's argument concentrated on the discrimination in favour of imports from Belgium and Sweden as compared with imports from Japan; subsequently Japan has also contended that there is discrimination in favour of imports from the United States and Mexico.

10.33 The European Communities argues that, although the import duty exemption on its face is non-discriminatory in that it applies equally with respect to all imports of automobiles by the beneficiaries, irrespective of their country of origin, in reality the main beneficiaries are subsidiaries of US companies with large manufacturing facilities in the United States and Mexico, and the benefit of the exemption therefore accrues almost exclusively to imports from these two countries. In support of this, the European Communities states that in 1997, imports of automobiles from the United States and Mexico accounted for 97% of all duty-free imports into Canada, when in contrast imports from these two countries accounted for only 80% of all imports of automobiles into Canada.[820] According to the European Communities, this "disproportionate" share is not a result of commercial factors but is the result of the import duty exemption. Moreover, whereas in 1997 the vast majority of imports from Mexico and the United States benefited from the import duty exemption, most imports from other sources were subject to customs duties.[821]

10.34 Both Japan and the European Communities argue that their claim that the import duty exemption gives rise to *de facto* discrimination is supported by relevant GATT and WTO Panel Reports.

10.35 Canada argues that the claim of the complainants that the import duty exemption involves *de facto* discrimination in favour of products of certain countries is without foundation in law or in fact. According to Canada, GATT and WTO dispute settlement cases demonstrate that to prove a *de facto* violation of Article I:1 it must be shown that a criterion that is neutral on its face is in fact able to be met only by products of a particular origin or origins such that national origin determines the tariff treatment the product receives. In the case at hand, there are no such criteria that determine the origin of the products which may be imported under the import duty exemption. In the view of Canada, the mere limitation of the number of eligible importers is not inconsistent with Article I:1 given that there are no conditions restricting the origin of products imported by the beneficiaries. In this connection, Canada submits that there is no basis in GATT and WTO case law for the view that a *de facto* violation of Article I:1 can be established on the basis of the commercial decisions of importers with respect to their sources of supply.

10.36 Canada further submits that the complainants have failed to adduce evidence supporting their claim of discrimination. The lack of factual support for this claim is illustrated by the fact that the complainants differ on which third countries benefit from the allegedly more favourable treatment. In addition, the statistics adduced by the complainants to demonstrate that the products of some countries receive a disproportionate share of the duty-free benefit do not provide evidence of discrimina-

[819] *Supra* Japan's Tables 9 and 10.
[820] *Supra* EC's Table 1.
[821] *Supra* EC's Table 2.

tion. With respect to the data presented by Japan, Canada argues that these data are inaccurate, incomplete and irrelevant to the establishment of a violation of Article I:1. In any event, even Japan's data show that in 1996 there were 1,776 duty-free import sales of vehicles from Sweden, compared with 4,502 duty-free import sales from Japan. Canada also submits data[822] showing that during the years 1991-98 Japanese-origin vehicles have benefitted from the import duty exemption to a much greater extent than have vehicles of Belgium, Sweden and several other WTO Members. Canada rejects as irrelevant Japan's comparison between luxury models imported from Belgium and Sweden and luxury models imported from Japan. With respect to the statistics adduced by the European Communities, Canada argues that the European Communities fails to explain how these statistics constitute evidence of discrimination within the meaning of Article I:1, and that, even if it were true that an advantage is granted *de facto* to products of the United States and of Mexico, such advantage would be exempted from Article I:1 by virtue of Article XXIV.

10.37 In respect of this disagreement between the parties on whether or not the import duty exemption accorded by Canada under the MVTO 1998 and SROs involves discrimination in favour of products of certain countries, we note first that Japan and the European Communities do not contest the fact that this exemption applies to imports from any country entitled to Canada's MFN rate. We therefore consider that the fundamental legal question before us is how the MFN requirement in Article I:1 must be applied to a measure which, on the one hand, involves a limitation to certain importers of an advantage granted in connection with the importation of a product but which, on the other hand, does not impose conditions regarding the origin of the products which can benefit from such advantage. More specifically, the question arises whether such a measure can be considered to give rise to *de facto* discrimination between like products originating in the territories of different Members.

10.38 In this regard, we note that GATT/WTO jurisprudence has established that Article I:1 encompasses both *de jure* and *de facto* forms of discrimination.[823] The instant case differs from situations addressed in some of the Panel Reports referred to by the parties with respect to the issue of *de facto* discrimination under Article I:1 in that in the present case such discrimination is alleged to arise from conditions with regard to the importers eligible for the import duty exemption rather than from conditions applied with respect to the products imported by such importers: the complainants essentially argue that there is *de facto* discrimination as a result of the fact that only certain importers in Canada qualify for the import duty exemption. In their view, this effectively limits the benefit of that exemption to the products of certain Members in whose territories are located companies related to those importers.

10.39 By contrast, Canada submits that Article I:1 does not prohibit the imposition of origin-neutral terms and conditions on importation that apply to importers as opposed to the products being imported. As we understand this argument, Canada takes the view that terms and conditions that apply to importers are "origin-neutral" if they

822 *Supra* Canada's Figure 4.

823 See Appellate Body Report on *EC - Bananas III*, *supra* note 49, para. 232. See also Panel Report on *EEC - Beef from Canada*, *supra* note 282; Panel Report on *Spain - Unroasted Coffee*, *supra* note 282; and Panel Report on *Japan - SPF Lumber*, *supra* note 282.

do not provide for limitations with respect to the origin of products which may be imported by the importers.

10.40 Though we do not contest the validity of the proposition that Article I:1 does not prohibit the imposition of origin-neutral terms and conditions on importation that apply to importers, we believe that the interpretation advocated by Canada of what "origin-neutral" means in this context is unduly narrow. We see no basis in the text of Article I:1 to hold that, where a measure reserves an import duty exemption to certain importers, the consistency of that measure with Article I:1 depends solely on whether or not there are restrictions on the origin of products imported by such importers. Rather, we believe that account should also be taken of the possibility that the limitation of the exemption to certain importers may by itself have a discriminatory impact on the treatment of like products of different origins.

10.41 As described above in the introductory section of these findings, the category of importers eligible for the import duty exemption accorded by Canada under the MVTO 1998 and the SROs is confined to manufacturers who were present in Canada in a particular base year and who meet certain performance requirements. In addition, since 1989 no new motor vehicle manufacturers have been able to qualify for the exemption. We note in this regard that among the manufacturers who currently benefit from the exemption are companies which have links of ownership or control with motor vehicle producers based in certain countries. Thus, with respect to automobiles, the current beneficiaries of the MVTO 1998 are fully-owned subsidiaries of General Motors, Ford, Chrysler and Volvo.[824] On the other hand, there are automobile manufacturers in Canada which are subsidiaries of companies based in other countries and which do not enjoy the import duty exemption.

10.42 We consider that, for the purpose of determining whether the limitation of eligible importers has an impact on the origin of products imported under the import duty exemption, the foreign affiliation of automobile manufacturers in Canada which benefit from the import duty exemption, as compared with the foreign affiliation of automobile manufacturers who are not entitled to the exemption, is of particular significance when viewed in conjunction with the evidence before us regarding the predominantly, if not exclusively, "intra-firm" character of trade in automotive products.

10.43 In this regard, we note the arguments and evidence presented by the complainants that the global automotive industry is highly integrated and characterized by a high degree of intra-firm trade. In particular, evidence adduced in this proceeding shows that the import patterns of the major automotive corporations in Canada are such that they import only their own make of motor vehicles and those of related companies.[825] Thus, General Motors in Canada imports only GM motor vehicles and those of its affiliates; Ford in Canada imports only Ford motor vehicles and those of its affiliates; the same is true of Chrysler and of Volvo. These four companies all have qualified as beneficiaries of the import duty exemption. In contrast, other motor vehicle companies in Canada, such as Toyota, Nissan, Honda, Mazda, Subaru, Hyundai, Volkswagen and BMW, all of which also import motor vehicles only from

[824] We note the recent changes that have occurred in the ownership of Chrysler and Volvo, as described in the factual arguments section of this report, and, in the case of Volvo, the implications of these changes for its status as a beneficiary of the import duty exemption.

[825] See Exhibit JPN-10.

related companies, do not benefit from the import duty exemption. The evidence also shows that General Motors has imported Saabs and Suzukis duty free into Canada and that General Motors has an ownership in the foreign producers of these vehicles. Similarly, between 1971-1993 when Mitsubishi and Chrysler ran a joint venture, Chrysler imported motor vehicles from Mitsubishi into Canada duty-free, but these imports ceased after the termination of the joint-venture affiliation.

10.44 We further note the statement by Canada that it is characteristic of the globalized automotive industry that there be some sort of capital, manufacturing or similar relationship between the automobile manufacturers and companies from which they import.[826] We also note that, as part of its defence to the claims raised under Article II of the GATS, Canada stresses the vertical integration between distributors and manufacturers of motor vehicles and the fact that distributors will not import and distribute motor vehicles produced by other manufacturers unless there is that capital, manufacturing or similar relationship.

10.45 We conclude from this analysis that the limitation of the eligibility for the import duty exemption to certain importers in Canada who are affiliated with manufacturers in certain countries affects the geographic distribution of the imports of motor vehicles under the import duty exemption. While these eligible importers are not in law or in fact prevented from importing vehicles under the exemption from any third country, in view of their foreign affiliation and the predominantly, if not exclusively, "intra-firm" character of trade in this sector, imports will tend to originate from countries in which the parent companies of these manufacturers, or companies related to these parent companies, own production facilities. Whether or not a like product of a WTO Member in practice benefits from the import duty exemption depends upon whether producers in the territory of that Member are related to any of the eligible Canadian motor vehicle manufacturers. Thus, in reality the conditions on which Canada accords the import duty exemption on motor vehicles entail a distinction between exporting countries depending upon whether or not producers in such countries are related to the eligible manufacturers. We therefore consider that, in a context of intra-firm trade, the limitation of the availability of the import duty exemption to certain manufacturers, including fully-owned subsidiaries of firms based in a very limited number of third countries, discriminates as to the origin of products which will benefit from the import duty exemption.

10.46 We note Canada's argument that the origin of products imported under the import duty exemption is determined by commercial decisions of the importers and that such decisions cannot be the basis for finding a violation of Article I:1. In this regard, we wish to stress that, in finding that the conditions attached to the import duty exemption discriminate as to the origin of products imported under this exemption, we are not denying that the decisions taken by individual importers as to the sourcing of their supplies are commercial decisions in which the Government of Canada is not involved. In our view, however, the issue is not whether the Government of Canada is somehow directing importers to import from particular sources; it clearly is not. While there is no involvement of the Government of Canada in decisions by individual importers, what is attributable to the Government of Canada is

[826] *Supra* para.7.119.

that, as a result of the limitation of the number of eligible importers, the geographic distribution of imports benefitting from the import duty exemption is determined by the commercial decisions of a closed category of importers mainly consisting of subsidiaries of firms based in certain countries, rather than by the commercial decisions of a broader, open-ended group of importers.

10.47 We have carefully considered the evidence provided by the parties with respect to the origin of imports under the import duty exemption. In this respect, we note in particular the argument of Canada that the available evidence, such as the data contained in Canada's Figure 4, shows that imports under the import duty exemption originate from a number of countries, including Japan, Belgium and Sweden, and that in recent years imports from Japan have accounted for a greater percentage of imports under the import duty exemption than imports from some other countries, such as Sweden, Belgium and the United Kingdom.

10.48 We consider that the evidence presented by Canada shows that the conditions attached to the import duty exemption do not prevent imports of motor vehicles from a range of countries, including the complainants, from benefitting from the exemption. This evidence also confirms the point made by Canada that the eligible manufacturers have affiliations with companies in a range of countries. At the same time, we do not believe that these data are in contradiction with our view that the import duty exemption favours products of certain countries depending upon the affiliation of producers located in those countries to the importers in Canada who are eligible for the import duty exemption. We note in this connection that other data before us, presented by the European Communities and Japan, reveal very significant differences between the percentages of imports of automobiles from individual countries that have benefitted from the import duty exemption. The difference between the United States, Mexico, Sweden and Belgium, on the one hand, and other European countries and Japan on the other - not to mention other major motor vehicle producers such as Korea - is particularly striking.[827] We also consider significant the data presented by the European Communities and Japan regarding imports of automobiles from different sources as percentages of total imports under the import duty exemption.[828] We therefore believe that the fact that imports under the import duty exemption have originated from a number of countries, as a consequence of the capital relationship between eligible importers and producers in those countries, does not warrant a conclusion that the import duty exemption is accorded on equal terms to like products of different origin.

10.49 As explained above, our view of the discriminatory character of the import duty exemption is based on an analysis of the consequences, in the context of an industry characterized by intra-firm trade, of the limitation of the number of eligible importers to manufacturers with particular foreign affiliations. We believe that, while not of decisive importance, the historical context of the import duty exemption provides further support for this view. We recall that this measure stems from a bilateral agreement between Canada and the United States designed to resolve a long-standing trade dispute between Canada and the United States over trade in automotive prod-

[827] *Infra* EC's Table 2, Japan's Table 6.
[828] *Infra* EC's Table 1, Japan's "New" Figure 4.

ucts. This agreement was designed *inter alia* to achieve rationalization of production in the North-American market. From the perspective of Canada this involved the granting of import duty exemptions as an encouragement to US owned motor vehicle manufacturers to expand their production operations in Canada. We therefore consider that at the outset the import duty exemption was expected to benefit mainly imports from particular sources.

10.50 In light of the foregoing considerations, we **find** that, by reserving the import duty exemption provided for in the MVTO 1998 and the SROs to certain importers, Canada accords an advantage to products originating in certain countries which advantage is not accorded immediately and unconditionally to like products originating in the territories of all other WTO Members. Accordingly, we find the application of this measure to be inconsistent with Canada's obligations under Article I:1of the GATT.

(d) Applicability of Article XXIV of the GATT

10.51 Having found that the import duty exemption is inconsistent with Article I:1 of the GATT, we now turn to the arguments of the parties with respect to the applicability of Article XXIV to the exemption.

10.52 We note that Canada raises Article XXIV in response to the complaint of the European Communities that Canada has accorded duty-free treatment on a basis inconsistent with Article I of the GATT, because most of the vehicles that receive duty-free treatment originate in the United States or Mexico. Canada notes that it had formed a free-trade area with the United States and Mexico and, therefore, granting duty-free treatment to products of its free-trade partners is exempt from Article I:1 by reason of Article XXIV.

10.53 The European Communities submits that there is currently no free-trade area between Mexico and Canada; that the import duty exemption is neither part of nor required by NAFTA; that, to the extent the import duty exemption is based on an international agreement, that agreement - the Auto Pact - lacks the necessary coverage to bring it within the ambit of Article XXIV; and that the import duty exemption is not a measure necessary for the formation of a free-trade area.

10.54 Canada contests the arguments of the European Communities, indicating that there is no doubt about the existence of a free-trade area between Canada, the United States and Mexico; that Article XXIV status does not require the total elimination of all duties among the members of a free-trade area; that the European Communities is in error in arguing that the measures in dispute are not part of NAFTA because the NAFTA specifically provides for the continuation of duty-free treatment pursuant to the Auto Pact; that in any event nothing in Articles I or XXIV states that preferential duty-free treatment is exempt from Article I only to the extent that it is "part of" or "required by" the principal agreement establishing the free-trade area, and that the objective of a free-trade area is, if nothing else, duty-free treatment among its Members.

10.55 We recall that in our analysis of the impact of the conditions under which the import duty exemption is accorded, we have found that these conditions entail a distinction between countries depending upon whether there are capital relationships of producers in those countries with eligible importers in Canada. Thus, the measure not only grants duty-free treatment in respect of products imported from the United States and Mexico by manufacturer-beneficiaries; it also grants duty-free treatment in respect of products imported from third countries not parties to a customs union or free-trade area with Canada. The notion that the import duty exemption involves the granting of duty-free treatment of imports from the United States and Mexico does not capture this aspect of the measure. In our view, Article XXIV clearly cannot justify a measure which grants WTO-inconsistent duty-free treatment to products originating in third countries not parties to a customs union or free trade agreement.

10.56 We further note that the import duty exemption does not provide for duty-free importation of all like products originating in the United States or Mexico and that whether such products benefit from the exemption depends upon whether they are imported by certain motor vehicle manufacturers in Canada who are eligible for the exemption. While in view of the particular foreign affiliation of these manufacturers, the exemption will mainly benefit products of the United States and Mexico, products of certain producers in these countries who have no relationship with such manufacturers are unlikely to benefit from the exemption. Thus, in practice the import duty exemption does not apply to some products that would be entitled to duty-free treatment if such treatment were dependant solely on the fact that the products originated in the United States or Mexico. We thus do not believe that the import duty exemption is properly characterized as a measure which provides for duty-free treatment of imports of products of parties to a free-trade area.

10.57 Based on the foregoing considerations, we **find** that Article XXIV of the GATT does not provide a justification for the inconsistency with Article I of the import duty exemption made pursuant to the measures at issue. We see no need to address other issues raised by the parties regarding the application of Article XXIV to the import duty exemption.

2. *Claims Under Article III:4 of the GATT and the TRIMs Agreement*

10.58 The claims presented under Article III:4 of the GATT pertain to conditions concerning the level of Canadian value added and the maintenance of a certain ratio between the net sales value of vehicles produced in Canada and the net sales value of vehicles sold for consumption in Canada.

10.59 We note that the complainants have also raised claims under the TRIMs Agreement with respect to these aspects of the measures at issue in this dispute. Both complainants claim that the conditions regarding Canadian value added are inconsistent with Article 2.1 of the TRIMs Agreement. The European Communities claims that the conditions regarding the maintenance of a ratio between the net sales value of motor vehicles produced in Canada and the net sales value of motor vehicles sold for consumption in Canada are also inconsistent with that provision.

10.60 We note that, in two recent dispute settlement proceedings, consideration has been given to the issue of the sequence of the examination of claims raised with respect to the same measure under Article III:4 of the GATT and the TRIMs Agreement.

10.61 In *EC - Bananas III* (ECU), claims were raised under Article III:4 of the GATT and Article 2.1 of the TRIMs Agreement regarding aspects of the European

Communities' import licensing procedures for bananas. The panel in that dispute decided to treat the claims under Article 2.1 of the TRIMs Agreement together with its consideration of the claims under Article III:4 of the GATT.[829] The panel found that the allocation to certain operators of a percentage of the licences allowing the importation of third-country and non-traditional ACP bananas at in-quota tariff rates was inconsistent with the requirements of Article III:4 of the GATT.[830] In light of that finding, the panel did not consider it necessary to make a specific ruling on whether this aspect of these import licensing procedures was also inconsistent with Article 2.1 of the TRIMs Agreement.[831]

10.62 In *Indonesia - Autos*, claims under Article III:4 of the GATT and Article 2.1 of the TRIMs Agreement were raised with respect to certain local content measures applied by Indonesia regarding automobiles. The panel in that dispute decided that it should first examine the claims under the TRIMs Agreement on the grounds that "the TRIMs Agreement is more specific than Article III:4 as far as the claims under consideration are concerned".[832] After finding that the measures at issue were inconsistent with Article 2.1 of the TRIMs Agreement,[833] the panel determined that it was not necessary to make a finding on the question of whether these measures were inconsistent with Article III:4 of the GATT.[834]

10.63 In the present dispute, the parties have not explicitly addressed this question of which of the claims raised under Article III:4 of the GATT and Article 2.1 of the TRIMs Agreement should be examined first. Implicit in the order in which they have presented their claims is the view that these claims should be addressed first under Article III:4 of the GATT. While we are aware of the statement made by the Appellate Body in *EC - Bananas III*, and referred to by the panel in *Indonesia - Autos,* that a claim should be examined first under the agreement which is the most specific with respect to that claim, we are not persuaded that the TRIMs Agreement can be properly characterized as being more specific than Article III:4 in respect of the claims raised by the complainants in the present case. Thus, we note that there is disagreement between the parties not only on whether the measures at issue can be considered to be "trade-related investment measures" but also on whether the Canadian value added requirements and ratio requirements are explicitly covered by the Illustrative List annexed to the TRIMs Agreement. It would thus appear that, assuming that the measures at issue are "trade-related investment measures", their consistency with Article III:4 of the GATT may not be able to be determined simply on the basis of the text of the Illustrative List but may require an analysis based on the wording of Article III:4. Consequently, we doubt that examining the claims first under the TRIMs Agreement will enable us to resolve the dispute before us in a more efficient manner than examining these claims under Article III:4.

---

829 Panel Report on *EC - Bananas III (ECU), supra* note 269, para. 7.168.

830 Ibid., para. 7.182.

831 Ibid., paras. 7.185-7.187.

832 Panel Report on *Indonesia - Autos, supra* note 270, para. 14.63.

833 Ibid., para. 14.91.

834 Ibid., para. 14.93.

10.64 In light of the foregoing considerations, we decide that, consistent with the approach of the panel in *EC - Bananas III*, we will examine the claims in question first under Article III:4 of the GATT.

(a) CVA Requirements

10.65 The European Communities and Japan claim that Canada acts inconsistently with Article III:4 of te GATT by reason of conditions with respect to the level of CVA requirements as set forth in the MVTO 1998, SROs and certain Letters of Undertaking.

10.66 We first examine the claims raised with regard to the CVA requirements provided for in the MVTO 1998 and the SROs and next examine the claims raised with regard to the CVA requirements contained in the Letters of Undertaking.

(i) CVA requirements provided for in the MVTO 1998 and in the SROs

10.67 The MVTO 1998 provides that one of the conditions which must be met by a manufacturer in order to be eligible for duty-free importation of motor vehicles is that the Canadian value added in the production of vehicles of a class is equal to or greater than the Canadian value added in respect of all vehicles of that class produced in Canada by the manufacturer in the base year.[835] The term "base year" in this context means the 12 month period beginning on August 1, 1963 and ending on July 31, 1964. Because the Canadian value added requirement is expressed in terms of value added in the base year, it is essentially a requirement to achieve a fixed nominal amount of value added.

10.68 CVA requirements as a condition for eligibility for duty-free importation of motor vehicles are also provided for in the SROs.[836] In SROs issued before 1984, these CVA requirements are expressed in terms of a combination of a specified percentage of cost of production and a level of Canadian value added achieved during the base period applicable to each individual SRO. SROs issued after 1984 contain CVA requirements expressed in terms of a percentage of cost of sales.[837]

10.69 In this connection, the term "Canadian value added" has been defined as including (i) the costs of parts produced in Canada and of materials of Canadian origin that are incorporated in the motor vehicles; (ii) direct labour costs incurred in Canada; (iii) manufacturing overheads incurred in Canada; (iv) general and administrative expenses incurred in Canada that are attributable to the production of motor vehicles; (v) depreciation in respect of machinery and permanent plant equipment located in Canada that is attributable to the production of motor vehicles, and (vi) a capital cost allowance for land and buildings in Canada that are used in the production of motor vehicles.[838]

10.70 The complainants claim that the CVA requirements in the MVTO 1998 and the SROs are inconsistent with Article III:4 by reason of the treatment accorded to

[835] *Supra* para. 2.23.
[836] *Supra* para. 2.32.
[837] *Supra* para. 2.33.
[838] *Supra* para. 2.26.

imported parts, materials and non-permanent equipment for use in the production of motor vehicles.

10.71 Article III:4 of the GATT provides in relevant part:

> "The products of the territory of any contracting party imported into the territory of any other contracting party shall be accorded treatment no less favourable than that accorded to like products of national origin in respect of all laws, regulations and requirements affecting their internal sale, offering for sale, purchase, transportation, distribution or use."

10.72 Accordingly, in order to substantiate this claim, it must be demonstrated that (i) the CVA requirements involve a law, regulation or requirement affecting the internal sale, offering for sale, purchase, transportation, distribution or use of such imported parts, materials and non-permanent equipment, and (ii) this law, regulation or requirement accords less favourable treatment to imported parts, materials and non-permanent equipment products than that accorded to like domestic products.[839]

10.73 We note that it has not been contested in this dispute that, as stated by previous GATT and WTO panel and appellate body reports, Article III:4 applies not only to mandatory measures but also to conditions that an enterprise accepts in order to receive an advantage,[840] including in cases where the advantage is in the form of a benefit with respect to the conditions of importation of a product.[841] The fact that compliance with the CVA requirements is not mandatory but a condition which must be met in order to obtain an advantage consisting of the right to import certain products duty-free therefore does not preclude application of Article III:4.

10.74 We further note that the parties agree that the MVTO 1998 and the SROs are legal instruments that fall within the scope of the notion of "laws, regulations or requirements" within the meaning of Article III:4. In addition, it has not been contested that the distinction made between domestic products and imported products in the definition of Canadian value added is based solely on origin and that, consequently, there are imported products which must be considered to be like the domestic products the costs of which are included in the definition of Canadian value added.

10.75 However, the parties disagree on whether or not the CVA requirements affect the "internal sale,...or use" of imported products within the meaning of Article III:4 and provide less favourable treatment in this respect to imported products than to like domestic products. The arguments of the parties on these issues can be briefly summarized as follows.

10.76 Central to the claim of the European Communities and Japan is the fact that the definition of Canadian value added for purposes of the MVTO 1998 and the SROs includes the costs of domestic parts, materials and non-permanent equipment, but excludes the costs of like imported products. The complainants argue that, as a result of the exclusion of imported products from the definition of Canadian value added, the CVA requirements affect the "internal sale,..or use" of products because

---

[839] See, e.g., Panel Report on *US - Gasoline, supra* note 306, pp. 70-71, para. 6.5, and Panel Report on *Japan - Film, supra* note 93, para. 10.369.

[840] See, e.g., Panel Report on *EEC - Parts and Components, supra* note 127, para. 5.21.

[841] See, e.g., Appellate Body Report on *EC - Bananas III, supra* note 49, para. 211.

they modify the conditions of competition between domestic and imported products, and that the CVA requirements accord less favourable treatment to imported products by providing an incentive to use domestic products. They reject Canada's argument that, because the CVA requirements do not stipulate that use of domestic products is a necessary condition and can be easily met on the basis of labour costs alone, they play no role in parts sourcing decisions, and therefore do not affect the "internal sale,...or use" of products. According to the complainants, this argument disregards the discrimination against the use of imported products resulting from the exclusion of the costs of imported products from the definition of Canadian value added. In addition, the complainants consider that this argument is inconsistent with the principle articulated in GATT and WTO case law according to which Article III should be interpreted in light of its objective of protecting the effective equality of competitive opportunities and with the principle that the actual trade effects of a measure are in this respect of no legal relevance. The complainants also contest that the evidence adduced by Canada actually shows that motor vehicle manufacturers can easily meet the CVA requirements on the basis of labour costs alone.

10.77 Canada argues that the CVA requirements in the MVTO 1998 and the SROs do not in law require the use of domestic products because they can be met on the basis of other elements of value added, such as labour costs. Canada also submits that, as a factual matter, evidence shows that the required CVA amounts are at such a low level that they can be easily met through labour costs alone. Because the use of domestic products is not in law or in fact required, the CVA requirements do not affect the conditions of competition between imported and domestic products and do not play a role in parts sourcing decisions of the motor vehicle manufacturers. As a consequence, the CVA requirements do not affect the "internal sale,...or use" of imported products, nor do they provide less favourable treatment to imported products. Thus, in the view of Canada, there is an important distinction to be made between, on the one hand, a value added requirement which does not necessitate the use of domestic products and, on the other, a local content requirement which can only be met by the use of domestic products. According to Canada, the notion that the mere inclusion of domestic products in the definition of a value added requirement is *per se* inconsistent with Article III:4 is contradicted by relevant GATT and WTO panel reports and is inconsistent with established principles of burden of proof in WTO dispute settlement because it would free complainants from having to demonstrate that contested measures have any effects on the conditions of competition between imported and domestic products. Canada submits that the Illustrative List in the TRIMs Agreement confirms its view that the use of domestic products must be required in order for a local content or value added requirement to be inconsistent with Article III:4.

10.78 In our examination of the merits of these arguments, we take into account certain well established considerations regarding the interpretation of Article III:4. The "no less favourable treatment obligation" in Article III:4 has been consistently interpreted as a requirement to ensure effective equality of opportunities between imported products and domestic products. In this respect, it has been held that, since a fundamental objective of Article III is the protection of expectations on the competitive relationship between imported and domestic products, a measure can be found to be inconsistent with Article III:4 because of its potential discriminatory impact on imported products.[842] The requirement of Article III:4 is addressed to "relative competitive opportunities created by the government in the market, not to the actual choices made by enterprises in that market."[843] Both in relation to Article III:2 and Article III:4 it has been established that the actual trade effects of a disputed measure are not a decisive criterion in determining whether the requirements of these provisions are met in a given case.[844] Finally, as stated by the Appellate Body, a determination of whether there has been a violation of Article III:4 does not require a separate consideration of whether a measure affords protection to domestic production.[845]

10.79 As noted above, Canada's principal argument in response to the claim that the CVA requirements provide less favourable treatment within the meaning of Article III:4 is that these requirements do not affect the "internal sale,... or use" of imported products because they do not in law or in fact require the use of domestic products and therefore play no role in the parts sourcing decisions of manufacturers.

10.80 With respect to whether the CVA requirements affect the "internal sale,...or use" of products, we note that, as stated by the Appellate Body, the ordinary meaning of the word "affecting" implies a measure that has "an effect on" and thus indicates a broad scope of application.[846] The word "affecting" in Article III:4 of the GATT has been interpreted to cover not only laws and regulations which directly govern the conditions of sale or purchase but also any laws or regulations which might adversely modify the conditions of competition between domestic and imported products.[847]

10.81 We note that it is undisputed that the definition of Canadian value added includes the costs of domestic, i.e. Canadian, parts, materials and non-permanent equipment but excludes the costs of imported parts, materials and non-permanent equipment. Given that the CVA requirements are among the conditions that must be met to obtain the benefit of duty-free importation of motor vehicles, the exclusion of imported products from the calculation of the Canadian value added means that, whereas the use of domestic products by a manufacturer in Canada can contribute to the fulfilment of a condition necessary to obtain an advantage, the use of imported products cannot contribute to the fulfilment of this condition.

10.82 In light of our interpretation of the word "affecting" in Article III, we consider that a measure which provides that an advantage can be obtained by using domestic products but not by using imported products has an impact on the conditions of competition between domestic and imported products and thus affects the "internal sale,... or use" of imported products, even if the measure allows for other means to obtain the advantage, such as the use of domestic services rather than products. Consequently, the CVA requirements, which confer an advantage upon the use of do-

842 Panel Report on *US - Section 337, supra* note 280, paras. 5.11 and 5.13.

843 Panel Report on *US - Malt Beverages, supra* note 427, para. 5.31.

844 See, e.g., Appellate Body Report on *Japan - Alcoholic Beverages, supra* note 271, at 110; Panel Report on *EC - Bananas III (ECU), supra* note 269, para. 7.179.

845 Appellate Body Report on *EC - Bananas III, supra* note 49, para. 216.

846 Ibid., para. 220.

847 Panel Report on *Italian Agricultural Machinery, supra* note 390, para. 12.

mestic products and deny that advantage in case of the use of imported products, must be regarded as measures which "affect" the "internal sale,... or use" of imported products, notwithstanding the fact that the CVA requirements do not in law require the use of domestic products.

10.83 We also see no merit in Canada's argument that the CVA requirements do not in practice "affect" the internal sale or use of imported parts and materials because the CVA levels are so low that they can be easily met on the basis of labour costs alone. As discussed above, based on the ordinary meaning of the term "affecting", the CVA requirements must be considered to affect the internal sale or use of imported products because they have an effect on the competitive relationship between imported and domestic products by conferring an advantage upon the use of domestic products while denying that advantage if imported products are used. Thus, we consider that the fact that it is easier to meet the CVA requirements and thus to obtain the benefit of the import duty exemption if domestic products are used than if imported products are used is sufficient to find that these requirements affect the internal sale or use of products, and we do not believe that we need to examine how important the CVA requirements are under present circumstances as a factor influencing the decisions of motor vehicle manufacturers in Canada regarding the choice between domestic parts, materials and non-permanent equipment, on the one hand, and imported parts, materials and non-permanent equipment, on the other.

10.84 The idea that a measure which distinguishes between imported and domestic products can be considered to affect the internal sale or use of imported products only if such a measure is shown to have an impact under current circumstances on decisions of private firms with respect to the sourcing of products is difficult to reconcile with the concept of the "no less favourable treatment" obligation in Article III:4 as an obligation addressed to governments to ensure effective equality of competitive opportunities between domestic and imported products, and with the principle that a showing of trade effects is not necessary to establish a violation of this obligation. In this respect, it should be emphasized that, contrary to what has been argued by Canada, the present case does not involve "the possibility of a future change in circumstances creating the potential for discrimination" or "discrimination that might exist after a change in circumstances that could occur at some unspecified time in the future."[848] Rather, the present case clearly involves formally different treatment of imported and domestic products albeit that the actual trade effects of this different treatment may be minimal under current circumstances. We therefore disagree with Canada's assertion that the CVA requirements do not entail a "current potential for discrimination under present circumstances."[849] As a consequence, whether or not in practice motor vehicle manufacturers can easily meet the CVA requirements of the MVTO 1998 and the SROs on the basis of labour costs alone does not alter our finding that the CVA requirements affect the internal sale or use of products. We therefore do not consider it necessary to examine the factual issues raised by the parties in support of their different views on this matter.

---

848 *Supra* paras. 6.335and 6.336.

849 *Supra* para. 6.336.

10.85 In light of the foregoing considerations, we find that the CVA requirements affect the internal sale or use in Canada of imported parts, materials and non-permanent equipment for use in the production of motor vehicles. We further consider that the CVA requirements accord less favourable treatment within the meaning of Article III:4 to imported parts, materials and non-permanent equipment than to like domestic products because, by conferring an advantage upon the use of domestic products but not upon the use of imported products, they adversely affect the equality of competitive opportunities of imported products in relation to like domestic products.

10.86 In the latter regard, we note Canada's argument that GATT and WTO panel reports and the Illustrative List in the TRIMs Agreement support its view that a local content requirement or a value added requirement is inconsistent with Article III:4 only if the use of domestic products is required.

10.87 We find this argument not persuasive. First, the equality of competitive opportunities between domestic and like imported products is affected if a measure accords an advantage to the sale or use of domestic products but not to the sale or use of like imported products, regardless of whether or not that advantage can also be obtained by other means. The less favourable treatment of imported products which is the result of the denial of the advantage in case of sale or use of imported products is not negated by the fact that the advantage may also be obtained by other means than sale or use of domestic products. We therefore find that Canada's argument is unsupported by the plain meaning of the "no less favourable treatment" obligation in Article III:4.

10.88 Second, while it is true that GATT and WTO panel reports which have found local content requirements to be in violation of Article III:4 have dealt with conditions which could only be met through the use of domestic products,[850] nothing in the reasoning in these reports suggests that they support the general proposition that measures relating to local content or value added are inconsistent with Article III:4 only if the use of domestic products is a necessary condition.

10.89 Third, as to Canada's argument that the Illustrative List in the TRIMs Agreement supports its view that a measure linking an advantage to the use of domestic products is inconsistent with Article III:4 only if the measure "requires" the use of domestic products, we consider that by definition the illustrative nature of the List means that it does not constitute an exhaustive statement of measures incompatible with Article III:4.

10.90 In light of the foregoing considerations, we **find** that Canada acts inconsistently with Article III:4 of the GATT by according less favourable treatment to imported parts, materials and non-permanent equipment than to like domestic products with respect to their internal sale or use as a result of the application of CVA requirements as one of the conditions for eligibility for the import duty exemption of motor vehicles under the MVTO 1998 and the SROs.

10.91 In light of the finding in the preceding paragraph, we do not consider it necessary to make a specific ruling on whether the CVA requirements provided for in

[850] Panel Report on *Italian Agricultural Machinery, supra* note 390; Panel Report on *Canada - FIRA, supra* note 126; Panel Report on *Indonesia - Autos, supra* note 270.

the MVTO 1998 and the SROs are inconsistent with Article 2.1 of the TRIMs Agreement. We believe that the Panel's reasoning in *EC - Bananas III* as to why it did not make a finding under the TRIMs Agreement after it had found that certain aspects of the EC' licensing procedures were inconsistent with Article III:4 of the GATT also applies to the present case.[851] Thus, on the one hand, a finding in the present case that the CVA requirements are not trade-related investment measures for the purposes of the TRIMs Agreement would not affect our finding in respect of the inconsistency of these requirements with Article III:4 of the GATT since the scope of that provision is not limited to trade-related investment measures. On the other hand, steps taken by Canada to bring these measures into conformity with Article III:4 would also eliminate the alleged inconsistency with obligations under the TRIMs Agreement.

(ii) Commitments with regard to CVA contained in certain Letters of Undertaking

10.92 In addition to the provisions regarding Canadian value added contained in the MVTO 1998 and the SROs, the complainants contest the consistency with Article III:4 of the GATT of conditions regarding Canadian value added contained in certain Letters of Undertaking, dated 13 and 14 January 1965, which were addressed by four Canadian motor vehicle producers[852] to the Canadian Minister of Industry.

10.93 In response to a question from the Panel, Canada indicated that other manufacturers had also submitted letters containing undertakings regarding Canadian value added. Canada subsequently provided copies of eighteen such letters written over the period 1965-1984. We consider that, since the complainants in their arguments specifically mention only the four Letters of Undertaking written on 13 and 14 January 1965, these other letters are not at issue.

10.94 The Letters written in January 1965 set forth certain undertakings by the four companies that were additional to the requirement in the proposed Auto Pact to maintain Canadian value added at a level equal to or greater than the level of Canadian value added in the period 1 August 1963-31 July 1964. Specifically, the Letters state that the manufacturers will: (i) increase in each ensuing model year over the base model year Canadian value added in the production of vehicles and original equipment parts by an amount equal to 60 per cent of the growth in their market for automobiles sold for consumption in Canada and by an amount equal to 50 per cent of the growth in their market for commercial vehicles sold for consumption in Canada, and (ii) achieve a specified increase in the annual Canadian value added by the end of the model year 1968.

10.95 The information available to the Panel indicates that the undertakings made in 1965 by the four motor vehicle producers have not been revoked or terminated. A publication by Industry Canada dated 10 June 1998 containing background information on the Auto Pact states:

---

[851] Panel Report on *EC - Bananas III (ECU)*, *supra* note 269, para. 7.186.

[852] General Motors of Canada, Ltd., Ford Motors Co. of Canada, Ltd., Chrysler Canada, Ltd., and American Motors (Canada) Ltd.

> "Assemblers also undertook to achieve CVA in vehicle assembly and/or parts production by a fixed dollar amount set for each company (1964 value) plus 60 percent of the annual growth in the value of their Canadian sales of cars, by 50 percent of growth in truck sales, and by 40 percent of growth in bus sales. These conditions are outlined in a letter of undertaking by each company and, while non-binding, typically have been met."

10.96 Japan and the European Communities submit that the conditions in these Letters with respect to the achievement of Canadian value added are "requirements" within the meaning of Article III which accord less favourable treatment to imported parts and materials than to like domestic products with respect to their internal sale or use. Canada argues that the Letters are not "requirements" covered by Article III:4.

10.97 It follows that we must first address the question of whether Article III:4 is applicable to the Letters of Undertaking as "requirements."[853] There is no dispute between the parties that these Letters are not "laws" or "regulations" for purposes of Article III:4.

10.98 While there is no disagreement between the parties as to the principle that it is possible for action of private parties to constitute a "requirement" within the meaning of Article III:4, they differ on whether or not in the case at hand the involvement of the Government of Canada has been such that the conditions mentioned in the Letters can be properly treated as "requirements."

10.99 The European Communities submits, first, that the Letters are acts which are attributable to Canada because of the role played by Canadian authorities in the submission of the Letters. In the view of the European Communities, the Letters were submitted in response to a request from the Government of Canada and their text was based on a model provided by the Canadian Ministry of Industry; the commitments made in the Letters did not advance the commercial interests of the firms; and statements made by the chief executive officers of the firms in question in a debate on the Auto Pact in the United States Congress indicate that the Letters were negotiated by the firms with the Canadian Ministry of Industry and that the Letters were regarded by Canada as a *sine qua non* for signing the Auto Pact. Second, the European Communities argues that the wording of the Letters indicates that the commitments contained therein were regarded as binding obligations. Third, the European Communities considers that the Letters are enforceable by the Government of Canada, notwithstanding that there is not explicitly a sanction attached to the non-compliance with the conditions stipulated in the Letters. Because of the link between the submission of the Letters and the conclusion of the Auto Pact, the firms in question have assumed that in case of non-compliance with the commitments given in the Letters, the Government of Canada would withdraw the import duty exemption. Finally, the European Communities refers to reporting and auditing procedures provided for in

[853] We note that the parties have also expressed different views on the more general issue of whether the Letters constitute "measures" which are subject to WTO disciplines. However, in connection with the claims presented under Article III:4 we only need to consider whether these conditions constitute "requirements" within the meaning of that provision.

the Letters and to steps taken by the Government of Canada to ascertain compliance with the commitments contained in the Letters.

10.100 Japan argues that the Letters of Undertaking were submitted by Canadian motor vehicle manufacturers, at the request of the Government of Canada, in order to obtain the advantage of the import duty exemption. Japan further submits that the commitments contained in the Letters are binding, that the Letters contain audit and reporting requirements, and that there is no expiry date in the Letters. In the view of Japan, the Letters are enforceable in that the Government of Canada can revoke or amend the MVTO 1998 or the SROs in case of non-compliance with the Letters. It is therefore irrelevant that the Letters have not been implemented in Canadian law and that the MVTO 1998 and the SROs do not provide for sanctions in the event that the commitments contained in the Letters are not complied with.

10.101 Canada denies that the Letters were required of the motor vehicle producers as a condition of Canada's signing the Auto Pact, that the Letters were negotiated between the Government of Canada and the firms in question, and that the firms have assumed that a failure to meet the commitments in the Letters would result in a withdrawal of the import duty exemption. Canada explains that at the conclusion of the Auto Pact the Canadian Government sought assurances from the affected companies that they understood the new system and provided them with a draft letter outlining what the requirements would be under the Auto Pact and what it hoped would be achieved as a result. The commitments contained in the Letters are statements of what was hoped to be achieved under Canada's implementation of the Auto Pact system. Canada submits that the Letters are not legally binding under Canadian law. The Letters are not contracts or statutory instruments. Neither the Government of Canada nor the companies consider the Letters binding in any way. Canada also submits that the Letters are not enforceable because the Government of Canada lacks the legal authority to deny the benefits under the MVTO or SROs for a failure to meet the commitments in the Letters. The Panel Reports on *Canada - FIRA* and on *EEC - Parts and Components* support the view that the Letters are not "requirements" within the meaning of Article III:4 because compliance with the Letters is neither legally enforceable nor a condition necessary to obtain an advantage. Finally, Canada points out that it does not gather information pertaining to status of compliance with the commitments contained in the Letters.

10.102 We note that several GATT and WTO Panel Reports have found that actions by private parties can constitute "requirements" within the meaning of Article III:4.

10.103 The Panel Report in *Canada - FIRA* discusses the status of certain undertakings offered by foreign investors as "requirements" within the meaning of Article III:4:

> "The Panel first examined whether the purchase undertakings are to be considered 'laws, regulations or requirements' within the meaning of Article III:4. As both parties had agreed that the Foreign Investment Review Act and the Foreign Investment Review Regulations -whilst providing for the possibility of written undertakings- did not make their submission obligatory, the question remained whether the undertakings given in individual cases are to be considered "requirements" within the meaning of Article III:4. In this respect the Panel noted that Section 9(c) of the Act refers to "any written undertakings...relating to the proposed or actual investment given by any party

thereto conditional upon the allowance of the investment" and that section 21 of the Act states that 'where a person who has given a written undertaking...fails or refuses to comply with the undertaking' a court order may be made "directing that person to comply with the undertaking". The Panel further noted that written purchase undertakings -leaving aside the manner in which they may have been arrived at (voluntary submission, encouragement, negotiation, etc)- once they were accepted, became part of the conditions under which the investment proposals were approved, in which case compliance could be legally enforced. The Panel therefore found that the word "requirements" as used in Article III:4 could be considered a proper description of existing undertakings."[854]

10.104 The Panel Report on *EEC - Parts and Components* states the following: "The Panel noted that Article III:4 refers to 'all laws, regulations or requirements affecting the internal sale, offering for sale, purchase, transportation, distribution or use'. The Panel considered that the comprehensive coverage of 'all laws, regulations or requirements affecting (emphasis added) the internal sale, etc. of imported products suggests that not only requirements which an enterprise is legally bound to carry out, such as those examined by the FIRA Panel (BISD 30S/140, 158), but also those which an enterprise voluntarily accepts in order to obtain an advantage from the government constitute 'requirements' within the meaning of that provision."[855]

10.105 More recently, the question of the interpretation of the phrase "laws, regulations and requirements" in Article III:4 was considered in the Panel Report on *Japan - Film* but the Panel did not actually make findings on this question.[856]

10.106 It is evident from the reasoning of the Panel Reports in *Canada - FIRA* and in *EEC - Parts and Components* that these Reports do not attempt to state general criteria for determining whether a commitment by a private party to a particular course of action constitutes a "requirement" for purposes of Article III:4. While these cases are instructive in that they confirm that both legally enforceable undertakings and undertakings accepted by a firm to obtain an advantage granted by a government can constitute "requirements" within the meaning of Article III:4, we do not believe that they provide support for the proposition that either legal enforceability or the existence of a link between a private action and an advantage conferred by a government is a necessary condition in order for an action by a private party to constitute a "requirement." To qualify a private action as a "requirement" within the meaning of

---

854 Panel Report on *Canada - FIRA*, *supra* note 126, para. 5.4.

855 Panel Report on *EEC - Parts and Components*, *supra* note 127, para. 5.21.

856 The Panel stated: "A literal reading of the words all laws, regulations and requirements in Article III:4 could suggest that they may have a narrower scope than the word measure in Article XXIII:1(b). However, whether or not these words should be given as broad a construction as the word measure, in view of the broad interpretation assigned to them in the cases cited above, we shall assume for the purposes of our analysis that they should be interpreted as encompassing a similarly broad range of government action and action by private parties that may be assimilated to government action. " Panel Report on *Japan - Film*, *supra* note 93, para. 10.376.

Article III:4 means that in relation to that action a Member is bound by an international obligation, namely to provide no less favourable treatment to imported products than to domestic products.

10.107 A determination of whether private action amounts to a "requirement" under Article III:4 must therefore necessarily rest on a finding that there is a nexus between that action and the action of a government such that the government must be held responsible for that action. We do not believe that such a nexus can exist only if a government makes undertakings of private parties legally enforceable, as in the situation considered by the Panel on *Canada - FIRA*, or if a government conditions the grant of an advantage on undertakings made by private parties, as in the situation considered by the Panel on *EEC - Parts and Components*. We note in this respect that the word "requirement" has been defined to mean "1. The action of requiring something; a request. 2. A thing required or needed, a want, a need. Also the action or an instance of needing or wanting something. 3. Something called for or demanded; a condition which must be complied with."[857] The word "requirements" in its ordinary meaning and in light of its context in Article III:4 clearly implies government action involving a demand, request or the imposition of a condition but in our view this term does not carry a particular connotation with respect to the legal form in which such government action is taken. In this respect, we consider that, in applying the concept of "requirements" in Article III:4 to situations involving actions by private parties, it is necessary to take into account that there is a broad variety of forms of government of action that can be effective in influencing the conduct of private parties.

10.108 In light of these considerations, we proceed to analyze whether in the case at hand there is a connection between the undertakings given by the four motor vehicle manufacturers and actions of the Government of Canada such that these undertakings must be regarded as "requirements" within the meaning of Article III:4. To this end, we consider first the arguments and evidence presented by the parties with respect to the nature of the involvement of the Government of Canada in the submission of the Letters. We next examine the arguments and evidence presented by the parties with respect to the question as to whether or not the commitments contained in the Letters are binding and enforceable, and whether or not the Government of Canada monitors compliance with these commitments.

10.109 With respect to the circumstances surrounding the submission of the Letters of Undertaking, the evidence before us shows that the Letters were submitted by Canadian motor vehicle manufacturers in response to a request made by the Government of Canada in the context of the anticipated conclusion of the Auto Pact between Canada and the United States.

10.110 That the Letters were submitted in response to a request from the Canadian Government is evident from the text of the Letters. First, the opening sentence of one of these Letters reads:

> "This letter is in response to your request for a statement with respect to the proposed agreement between the Governments of Canada and

[857] The New Shorter Oxford English Dictionary (Clarendon Press, 1993) Vol. II, 2557.

the United States concerning trade and production in automotive products, as you have described it to us."

10.111 Second, there is substantial similarity in structure and content and wording of the Letters. In this regard, it has been confirmed by Canada in the proceedings before the Panel that the Government of Canada provided the motor vehicle manufacturers in question with a draft letter. Third, the text of the Letters shows that the Canadian Government had made requests for specific commitments regarding Canadian value added.[858] In the proceedings before the Panel, Canada has confirmed that the Government of Canada did request undertakings respecting Canadian value added. Finally, testimony before the United States Congress of the chief executives of the companies in question also confirms that the Letters were written in response to a request by the Government of Canada.[859]

10.112 The European Communities and Canada disagree on the question of whether the Letters were the subject of "negotiations" between the companies in question and the Government of Canada.[860] We believe that the evidence before us is not conclu-

---

[858] One of the Letters states: "You have requested that we should increase Canadian value added in our products by $121 million between 1964 and the end of the model year 1968, as outlined under condition (4). Also you have requested that the amount should be further increased to the extent required under condition (3) stated above."

[859] *Supra* para. 5.62.

[860] In support of its view that the Letters were negotiated with the Government of Canada, the European Communities refers to the following statements made before the US Congress: "The Canadian Government asked us to write them a letter stating our understanding of the provisions of the agreement as it was finally determined and to ask for our endorsement of the principles to the extent that we did understand them and assigned to us an objective whereby, over the 4 years that are involved in this agreement, we would undertake to increase out Canadian production or our Canadian value."

"The agreement was entered into by Canada only after Canada received assurances from the Canadian vehicle manufacturers which were designed to protect and stimulate Canada's much smaller and less developed manufacturing industry."

"...it ought to be a matter of record that there have been such conversations between the Canadian Government and each of the Canadian automobile manufacturers, and that the results of those conversations -that is the letters of assurance, or statements of intentions, are an important part of this agreement as a whole from the Canadian standpoint."

"...we knew during the course of the negotiations that went on for many, many months that the Minister of Industry of Canada was holding conversations with the automobile manufacturing companies in Canada in respect of their intentions as to production under the differing conditions of the prospective agreement. ...It took the Canadian government some time to formulate what was in the letters but I would say [that we became aware of the terms of the letters] in the winter certainly of 1964. ...I imagine that during the separate conversations that the companies had with the Minister of Industry, that the discussion was perhaps a common one, and perhaps the Minister of Industry drafted a proposed letter that he discussed with each of them that had identical language in it, and that these letters were taken by the Canadian companies and modified to suit their particular circumstances and returned to the ministry with a lot of common language remaining."

By contrast, Canada has referred to the following statement of a chief executive of one of the companies in question:

"I can speak for General Motors and I can say that *there have been no secret agreements, there have been no negotiations.* The Canadian Government asked us to write them a letter stating our understanding of the provisions of the agreement as it was finally determined and to ask for our endorsement of the principles to the extent that we did understand them and assigned to us an objec-

sive with respect to whether or not the Letters were the subject of negotiations between the motor vehicle manufacturers and the Government of Canada. However, this lack of clarity as to whether or not the content of the Letters was the subject of negotiations between the manufacturers and the Government of Canada does not detract from the undisputed evidence that the Letters were submitted in response to a request from the Government of Canada.

10.113 Another relevant aspect of the role of the Government of Canada with regard to the submission of the Letters of Undertaking concerns the relationship between the submission of these Letters and the conclusion of the Auto Pact. In this respect, the evidence before us shows that the Letters were requested by the Government of Canada, and submitted by the companies in question, in connection with the anticipated conclusion of the Auto Pact. The Letters were submitted several days before the signature of the Auto Pact. The opening sentence of each of the Letters refers to "the agreement between the Governments of Canada and the United States concerning trade and production in automotive products." It is evident that the companies had been informed of the objectives and provisions of the proposed agreement: the Letters mention the main objectives of the agreement, express the companies' support for these objectives, and note the conditions under which the Auto Pact provides for the duty-free importation of motor vehicles and certain automotive parts into Canada. In three of the Letters, the paragraph containing the undertakings with regard to Canadian value added starts with the following sentence:

> In addition to meeting these stipulated conditions *and in order to contribute to meeting the objectives of the agreement..." (emphasis added)*

10.114 Finally, in two Letters the implementation of the Auto Pact is mentioned as a condition for the undertakings:

> "The following comments assume that the proposed agreement for duty-free treatment has the full support of the respective Governments, and that the program may be expected to continue for a considerable period of time."
>
> and
>
> "Our undertakings are, of course, conditional upon the execution of that agreement, upon the adoption of an order in council, and regulations substantially in the form of the drafts that you have already delivered to us, and upon an acceptable response in respect of the enclosed supplementary letter."

10.115 It follows that the anticipation of the conclusion of the Auto Pact was a key factor in the decision of the companies to respond positively to the request of the Government of Canada that the companies make commitments with regard to the growth in the level of Canadian value added in their operations. The companies made their undertakings conditional upon the conclusion and implementation of the Auto Pact and viewed these undertakings as contributing to the objectives of the Auto Pact. Given that, in submitting the undertakings before the conclusion of the Auto

---

tive whereby, over the 4 years that are involved in this agreement, we would undertake to increase our Canadian production or our Canadian value." (emphasis added by Canada).

Pact, the companies in question were motivated by expectations concerning the benefits they would derive from this agreement through the import duty exemption, it is possible to view this aspect of the relationship between the action of the private parties and the role of the Government of Canada in terms of an undertaking offered by private parties as a condition for obtaining a benefit from a government. Though the information before us does not establish conclusively that, as alleged by the European Communities, the undertakings contained in the Letters were regarded by the Government of Canada as a condition *sine qua non* for the conclusion of the Auto Pact, there is sufficient evidence to conclude that the actions of the companies manifestly depended upon (anticipated) action by the Government of Canada in the form of the conclusion of an international agreement.

10.116 We now turn to the issues raised by the parties with respect to whether or not the Letters of Undertaking are binding and enforceable and whether or not the Government of Canada monitors compliance with the Letters.

10.117 The parties differ as to whether or not the commitments contained in the Letters of Undertaking are "binding". In this respect, we note first that the Letters provide that the companies "undertake" to achieve very specific, verifiable objectives with respect to the level of Canadian value added in their operations. Several Letters discuss in detail the companies' understanding of, and their concerns regarding, particular technical aspects of the implementation of the value added criteria, notably the methodology for the computation of Canadian value added, and draw attention to factors that may limit the ability of the companies to meet the stated objectives. Second, various statements in the Letters indicate that the word "undertake" was used in the sense of a formal commitment. For example, one of the Letters states:

> "Subject to the imponderables mentioned above, it is our intention and that of our affiliates to make every effort feasible to meet the objectives of the agreement to be made between the Governments of Canada and the United States, and to achieve the indicated goal as rapidly as possible.
>
> (...)
>
> In conclusion, therefore, I am prepared to say at this time that, first (name of the company) has plans underway to increase Canadian value added by about $ 30 million in each of the first 2 years of the plan; and, second, we are continuing our studies of ways to accomplish the remainder of the program and will undertake to meet the full objective of $121 milion by the end of the model year 1968.
>
> It is anticipated that these studies will take between 3 and 4 months to finish, and I will be prepared to discuss the results with you when they are completed. From time to time, as requested, we will be glad to discuss our current operations and our plans for future development with the Minister of Industry, and to receive and consider his suggestions."

In three of the four Letters of Undertaking the final paragraphs read as follows:

> "(name of the company) also agrees to report to the Minster of Industry, every 3 months beginning April 1, 1965, *such information as the Minister of Industry requires pertaining to progress achieved by our company, as well as plans to fulfill our obligations under this letter.* In addition, (name of the company) understands that the Government

> will conduct an audit each year with respect to the matters described in this letter. (*emphasis added*)
>
> We understand that before the end of model year 1968 we will need to discuss together the prospects for the Canadian automotive industry and our company's program."

In one of these Letters, these paragraphs are preceded by the following statement:

> "The undertakings given in this letter are to be adjusted to the extent necessary for conditions not under the control of the (name of the company) or of any affiliated (name of the company) company, such as acts of God, fire, earthquake, strikes at any plant owned by (name of the company) or by any of our suppliers, and war."

10.118 In view of the specificity of the undertakings; the precision as regards the modalities of their implementation; the reference to the undertakings as "obligations"; the commitment to provide information "required" by the Ministry of Industry pertaining to "progress achieved...as well as plans to fulfill" these obligations; and the explicit reference to the need to adjust the undertakings in case of *force majeure*, it is reasonable to conclude that the companies, by submitting these Letters, accepted responsibility *vis-à-vis* the Government of Canada with respect to the achievement of the conditions contained in the Letters. We therefore consider that the commitments contained in the Letters were intended to be binding as obligations of the companies in question notwithstanding that, as argued by Canada, the Letters do not have a specific legal status under Canadian law.

10.119 Japan and the European Communities argue that the Letters are enforceable because there is nothing to prevent Canada from amending or repealing the MVTO 1998 or the SROs to withdraw the import duty exemption as a response to non-compliance with the commitments contained in the Letters of Undertaking. The European Communities also submits that, because of the link between the submission of the Letters of Undertaking and the conclusion of the Auto Pact, the beneficiaries have assumed that, were they to disregard the commitments contained in the Letters, the Canadian Government would withdraw the import duty exemption. Canada points out that the Letters are not enforceable because there is no legal basis upon which Canadian authorities can deny the right of duty free importation in response to a failure to meet a commitment in the Letters. In Canada's view, whether or not the letters could be made enforceable through amendments to the MVTO and the SRO is irrelevant as the WTO Agreements only deal with measures actually applied by Members. Canada further rejects as unsupported by evidence the argument of the European Communities that there has been a tacit understanding between the companies and the Government that the import duty exemption would be revoked in case of non-compliance with the commitments provided for in the Letters.

10.120 The information before us shows that Canada has not taken steps to create specific legal authority under its domestic law that would enable the Government of Canada to take action in response to a failure by the companies to meet the commitments given in the Letters of Undertaking. Specifically, there is nothing in the legal instruments adopted by Canada in connection with its domestic implementation of the Auto Pact to indicate that the import duty exemption can be withdrawn in case of a failure to meet these commitments. In this respect, we consider that the arguments of the European Communities and Japan regarding steps that Canada could take to make the Undertakings enforceable by amending relevant regulations are somewhat speculative.

10.121 However, we do not believe that the issue of whether or not the Letters of Undertaking are enforceable through the use of sanctions in case of non-compliance through the withdrawal of the import duty exemption is of decisive importance. Rather, the procedures for the provision of information to the Minister of Industry, the commitment "to discuss together the prospects for the Canadian industry and our company's program" and the conduct of a yearly audit demonstrate that the Government of Canada would play an active role in ascertaining implementation of the commitments. The choice of an informal mechanism with regard to the implementation of the Letters rather than a formal enforcement mechanism involving the possibility of sanctions in case of non-compliance does not mean that there was no active involvement of the Government of Canada with regard to compliance with these commitments. In the latter regard, we note that in the proceedings before the Panel Canada has confirmed that at least until model year 1996 it gathered information on an annual basis with respect to the achievement of the Canadian value added levels stipulated in the Letters of Undertaking.

10.122 In sum, the evidence before the Panel shows that: (i) in making the undertakings contained in the Letters, the companies acted at the request of the Government of Canada; (ii) the anticipated conclusion of the Auto Pact was a key factor in the decision of the companies to submit these undertakings; (iii) the companies accepted responsibility *vis-à-vis* the Government of Canada with respect to the implementation of the undertakings contained in the Letters, which they described as "obligations" and in respect of which they undertook to provide information to the Government of Canada and indicated their understanding that the Government of Canada would conduct yearly audits; and (iv) at least until model year 1996, the Government of Canada gathered information on an annual basis concerning the implementation of the conditions provided for in the Letters.

10.123 In light of this evidence, we consider that the involvement of the Government of Canada in the action taken by the four companies was such that the commitments contained in the Letters of Undertaking can be regarded as "requirements" within the meaning of Article III:4. Where a government requests a firm to make commitments as specific as those contained in the Letters of Undertaking and to record them in writing in letters addressed to the government, and these commitments are described by the firms as "obligations" in respect of the fulfilment of which they undertake to provide information to, and to consult with, the government, it is evident that there is action of private parties directed by, or at the very least expected by, the government. That the Letters do not have a specific legal status under Canadian law in the sense that they are not contracts or statutory instruments does not negate the fact that government action was effective in inducing companies to make commitments *vis-à-vis* the Canadian Government with respect to the conduct of their business operations in Canada in a manner that was regarded as binding by the companies. The ordinary meaning of the term "requirement" does not support the proposition that, where a government induces a firm to make a clearly specified, verifiable commitment *vis-à-vis* that government to act in a particular manner, such a commitment only qualifies as a "requirement" if it is embodied in an instrument with a defined legal status under the law of the country in question.

10.124 We note Canada's argument that, regardless of the past status of the Letters, they are not "requirements" today. Canada submits that, even before the complaints had brought this case, Canada had publicly stated that the Letters were not binding, and that it has stopped making any effort to verify whether companies achieved the amounts contained in the Letters.

10.125 We note that, except for the conditions relating to the achievement of a specific level of Canadian value added in 1968, the commitments made in the Letters of Undertaking were not limited in time. The commitments to increase Canadian value added by a specified percentage of market growth applied to "each model year over the preceding model year." The Letters contain no expiry date. Evidence before the Panel indicates that the undertakings have not been terminated.

10.126 The information before us does not indicate that the companies in question no longer consider themselves to be bound *vis-à-vis* the Government of Canada in respect of the commitments contained in the Letters. On the contrary, statements made in October and November 1997 by chief executive officers of the Ford Motor Company of Canada and of Chrysler Canada Ltd. suggest that these companies continued to regard these commitments as binding on them ("each member must meet a 60 per cent Canadian value added commitment" and "we have exceeded those requirements by a country mile").[861] We also note that in a publication dated 10 June 1998 which provides background information on the Auto Pact, Industry Canada explicitly mentions commitments made by manufacturers with respect to Canadian value added:

> "Assemblers also undertook to achieve CVA in vehicle assembly and/or parts production by a fixed dollar amount set for each company (1964 value) plus 60 percent of the annual growth in the value of their Canadian sales of cars, by 50 percent of growth in truck sales, and by 40 percent of growth in bus sales. These conditions are outlined in a letter of undertaking by each company and, while non-binding, typically have been met."

10.127 This clearly suggests that as recently as June 1998 the Government of Canada viewed such undertakings as part of its policy respecting the implementation of the Auto Pact and that at least at that time the Government of Canada possessed the information necessary to ascertain the status of compliance with the conditions contained in the Letters of Undertaking. Finally, while Canada has indicated that it has ceased verifying compliance with the undertakings, we recall that nothing in the information before us suggests that the Government of Canada has taken steps to terminate the Undertakings.

10.128 Under these circumstances, we believe that the information provided by Canada during the Panel proceedings that it has recently ceased gathering information on the CVA amounts contained in the Letters of Undertaking is not a sufficient basis for us to conclude that the Letters should no longer be treated as "requirements" within the meaning of Article III:4 as of the date on which the terms of reference of this Panel were established.

10.129 We consider that, as requirements within the meaning of Article III:4, the commitments contained in the Letters of Undertaking with respect to Canadian value

---

[861] *Supra* paras. 5.49 and 5.50.

added affect the internal sale or use of imported products and afford less favourable treatment to imported products than to like domestic products because these commitments are easier to meet if domestic products are used than if imported products are used. In this connection, we recall that in our analysis of the claims raised with respect to the CVA requirements provided for in the MVTO 1998 and the SROs we have rejected Canada's argument that a measure relating to the use of domestic products is inconsistent with Article III:4 only if that measure in law or in fact requires the use domestic products. Similarly, we recall our view expressed in that connection that the actual trade effects of the CVA requirements are of no legal consequence in the context of Article III:4. We therefore do not believe it is necessary to examine the arguments of the parties on the question of whether or not the commitments contained in the Letters of Undertaking in practice can easily be met by the firms in question.

10.130 In light of the foregoing considerations, we **find** that Canada acts inconsistently with Article III:4 of the GATT by according less favourable treatment to imported products than to like domestic products with respect to their internal sale or use as a result of the conditions contained in Letters of Undertaking with respect to Canadian value added.

10.131 For reasons explained in paragraph 10.91, we do not consider it necessary to make a finding on whether these conditions are inconsistent with Article 2.1 of the TRIMs Agreement.

(b) Ratio Requirements

10.132 We now proceed to examine whether Canada acts inconsistently with Article III:4 of the GATT by reason of the provisions of the MVTO 1998 and of the company-specific SROs which stipulate that, as a condition for eligibility for duty-free importation of motor vehicles, manufacturers must maintain a certain ratio between the net sales value of vehicles produced in Canada and the net sales value of all vehicles of that class sold for consumption in Canada ("ratio requirements").

10.133 We note that, while the European Communities explicitly requests us to find that these ratio requirements are inconsistent with Article III:4 of the GATT, Japan's initial presentation of its arguments does not include a request for such a finding.[862] In this argumentation, Japan presents several arguments on this issue and reserves its right to elaborate on the claims presented on this matter in Japan's request for the establishment of a panel.[863] At the first meeting with the parties, we rejected a preliminary objection raised by Canada with respect to Japan's reservation of its right to elaborate on these claims.[864] At that meeting, we also posed several questions to Japan on the arguments presented by Japan in its initial argumentation regarding the inconsistency of the ratio requirements with Article III:4.[865] Though Japan responded that it would address the issues raised by the Panel in its rebuttal, Japan's subsequent

862 *Supra* para. 3.1.
863 *Supra* para. 4.2.
864 *Supra* Section VI.C.
865 Question 14 from the Panel.

argumentation is completely silent on the matter of the alleged inconsistency of the ratio requirements with Article III:4.

10.134 In light of the fact that Japan's request for findings as set out in its initial argumentation does not include the issue of the inconsistency of the ratio requirements with Article III:4, that subsequently Japan has offered no further argumentation on this matter during the course of the panel proceedings, and that it has not responded to our questions on this issue, we conclude that Japan has not presented a claim that the ratio requirements are inconsistent with Article III:4 of the GATT. Alternatively, assuming *arguendo* that the arguments presented by Japan in its initial argumentation can properly be described as amounting to a claim, we find that Japan has failed to substantiate this claim. We therefore limit ourselves to a consideration of the claim raised by the European Communities.

10.135 The European Communities claims that the ratio requirements provided for in the MVTO 1998 and the SROs are inconsistent with Article III:4 because they provide less favourable treatment to imported motor vehicles than to like domestic motor vehicles with respect to their internal sale.

10.136 As noted above, the parties agree that the MVTO and the SROs are covered by the term "laws, regulations or requirements" in Article III:4. It is also undisputed that the ratio requirements apply to imported and domestic motor vehicles that are like products within the meaning of Article III:4.

10.137 In the view of the European Communities, the ratio requirements "affect" the internal sale of motor vehicles because they provide an incentive to limit the sales of imported motor vehicles, thereby modifying the conditions of competition between those vehicles and domestic motor vehicles the internal sale of which is not subject to any similar restriction.

10.138 In support of its view that the ratio requirements afford less favourable treatment to imported motor vehicles than to like domestic vehicles with respect to their internal sale, the European Communities submits that the ratio requirements place a maximum limit on the total sales value of all motor vehicles sold for consumption in Canada which in practice operates so as to restrict exclusively the sales of imported motor vehicles. While an increase in the sales value of motor vehicles produced in Canada by the beneficiary will automatically give rise to an identical increase in the value of permitted domestic sales, an increase in imports of motor vehicles does not entail an increase in the value of permitted domestic sales. As a result, the beneficiaries cannot, without losing the entitlement to the import duty exemption, sell in Canada any imported motor vehicles in excess of a certain amount which is directly related to the sales value of their domestic production of motor vehicles. Because no similar limit is placed on the internal sale of domestic motor vehicles, the ratio requirements afford less favourable treatment to imported motor vehicles with respect to their internal sale in Canada.

10.139 In response to questions from the Panel, the European Communities has stated that it claims that the ratio requirements limit the internal sale in Canada of motor vehicles *imported under the tariff exemption*[866] and that the ratio requirements are internal measures in the sense of Article III and not border measures because

[866] *Supra* para. 7.164.

"they limit the right to sell in Canada vehicles already imported in Canada under the tariff exemption."[867] We therefore proceed on the understanding that the claim of the European Communities concerns the implications of the ratio requirements with respect to the internal sale of those motor vehicles which have been imported duty-free.

10.140 Canada submits that the ratio requirements do not fall within the scope of Article III:4 because they do not affect the internal sale of any motor vehicles in Canada, imported or domestic. In the view of Canada, the argument of the European Communities that the ratio requirements entail a restriction on the internal sale of imported motor vehicles rests on a misunderstanding of the operation of the ratio requirements. In this regard, Canada points out that, since manufacturers can always ensure that they stay within their ratios by paying duty on imported motor vehicles, the ratios cannot limit the internal sale of imported vehicles. The ratio requirements have an effect on the importation of motor vehicles in that they limit the total value of motor vehicles that a manufacturer may import duty-free. However, the ratio requirements do not affect the conditions of sale of motor vehicles after their importation. In this connection, Canada argues that the European Communities fails to make a distinction between measures affecting the importation of products and measures affecting imported products after their importation.

10.141 In light of the claim of the European Communities and the counterarguments of Canada, we must determine whether and how the ratio requirements affect the conditions of the internal sale in Canada of motor vehicles imported under the import duty exemption, i.e. motor vehicles imported duty-free by beneficiaries of the MVTO 1998 and of the company-specific SROs, as compared with the conditions of sale of like vehicles produced in Canada by the beneficiaries. Specifically, we must establish whether or not the ratio requirements entail a restriction on "the right to sell in Canada vehicles already imported under the tariff exemption", as alleged by the European Communities and as contested by Canada.

10.142 The ratio requirements mean that a certain ratio must be maintained between the net sales value of vehicles produced by a manufacturer and the net sales value of all vehicles of that class sold for consumption in Canada by the manufacturer. The net sales value of all vehicles sold for consumption in Canada includes the value of domestic vehicles and the value of vehicles which have been imported duty free but does not include the value of motor vehicles on the importation of which import duties have been paid. As a consequence of the ratio requirements, the net sales value of all vehicles of a class sold for consumption in Canada by a manufacturer cannot exceed the sales value of vehicles of that class produced in Canada by the same manufacturer by a certain amount.

10.143 Since the ratio requirements apply to "the net sales value of all vehicles of that class sold for consumption in Canada" there is no formal distinction between vehicles on the basis of their origin. Thus, on its face, the limitation on the sales value of vehicles sold for consumption in Canada operates without distinction between imported and domestic vehicles. The question before us is whether in practice this limitation has the effect of restricting the internal sale of motor vehicles which

[867] *Supra* para. 7.165.

have been imported duty-free, without imposing a similar restriction on the internal sale of like domestically produced motor vehicles.

10.144 We note that, if a vehicle imported under the import duty exemption is sold for consumption in Canada, the sales value of that vehicle will lead to an increase in the net sales value of vehicles sold for consumption in Canada but will not affect the net sales value of vehicles produced in Canada. The ratio between these values will therefore decline. On the other hand, in the case of a domestically produced vehicle, production and sale of such a vehicle lead to identical increases in the net sales value of vehicles produced in Canada and the net sales value of vehicles sold for consumption in Canada. Hence, the ratio between these values will not be affected.

10.145 It follows that, as a result of the ratio requirements, the net sales value of vehicles sold for consumption in Canada and imported duty-free is subject to a limitation. The maximum possible sales value of vehicles sold for consumption in Canada and imported duty-free is realized if a manufacturer exports its entire production of domestically produced vehicles, in which case the net sales value of vehicles sold for consumption in Canada and accounted for by vehicles which have been imported duty free is equal to the net sales value of the vehicles produced in Canada by the manufacturer.

10.146 However, the notion of a limitation of the net sales value of motor vehicles sold for consumption in Canada and imported duty free is not by itself sufficient to find in favour of the claim of the European Communities. Rather, to substantiate this claim, it must be shown that this limitation arises from a restriction on the internal sale of such imported motor vehicles. In other words, it must be demonstrated that, because of the ratio requirements, motor vehicles which have been imported duty-free are subject to a restriction as regards the internal sale of such vehicles in Canada.

10.147 In this respect, we note that, where the net sales value of duty-free imported motor vehicles sold for consumption in Canada reaches the limit allowed under the ratio requirements, the beneficiary is no longer entitled to duty-free treatment of imports. Further sales in Canada of imported motor vehicles will therefore be sales of vehicles on which import duties will have been paid. At the same time, vehicles already imported duty-free will not be affected. We note that the European Communities has not contested Canada's explanation of this aspect of the operation of the ratio requirements.[868]

10.148 We therefore consider that the effect of the ratio requirements in limiting the share of the net sales value of all vehicles sold for consumption in Canada which is accounted for by vehicles that have been imported duty-free is a direct consequence of the fact that, beyond a certain value of imports, further imports of motor vehicles become subject to payment of import duty. This limitation on the net sales value of duty-free imported motor vehicles is not effected through a restriction on the internal sale of such motor vehicles subsequent to their importation. While the European Communities claims that the ratio requirements "limit the right to sell in Canada vehicles already imported under the Tariff Exemption", it has not shown how the ratio requirements could create a situation in which a motor vehicle manufacturer who has

[868] *Supra* para. 6.369.

been allowed to import a vehicle duty-free is subsequently confronted with a limitation of his "right to sell" such a vehicle in Canada. What is referred to by the European Communities as a "limitation" on the internal sale of such vehicles in fact is a limitation on the value of vehicles that can be imported duty-free.

10.149 For purposes of Article III, the manner in which the ratio requirements affect the treatment accorded to motor vehicles with respect to the conditions of their importation is irrelevant. That there is a limitation on the net sales value of vehicles which can be imported duty-free therefore cannot constitute a grounds for finding a violation of Article III:4. The fact that internal sales of domestic vehicles are not subject to a "similar" limitation is also without relevance. By definition, a violation of Article III cannot be established on the basis of a comparison between the conditions of internal sale of domestic products with the conditions of importation of imported products.

10.150 In light of the foregoing considerations, we **find** that the European Communities has failed to demonstrate that, by applying ratio requirements under the MVTO 1998 and the SROs as one of the conditions determining the eligibility of duty-free importation of motor vehicles, Canada is according to motor vehicles imported duty free less favourable treatment with respect to their internal sale than to like domestic motor vehicles. The claim of the European Communities regarding the inconsistency of the ratio requirements with Article III:4 must therefore be rejected. Because of this finding with respect to the claim of the European Communities regarding the consistency of the ratio requirements with Article III:4 of the GATT, we must also reject the claim of the European Communities that these requirements are inconsistent with Article 2.1 of the TRIMs Agreement. We note in this regard that the European Communities claims that these ratio requirements are trade-related investment measures which are inconsistent with Article 2.1 of the TRIMs Agreement because they violate Article III:4 of the GATT.

C. Claims Under the SCM Agreement

10.151 The European Communities and Japan claim that the import duty exemption provided by the Canadian Government to certain motor vehicle manufacturers under the MVTO 1998 and the SROs constitutes a subsidy within the meaning of Article 1 of the Agreement on Subsidies and Countervailing Measures (SCM Agreement). They further claim that, because this import duty exemption is accorded upon fulfilment of certain ratio requirements and CVA requirements, it is contingent upon export performance within the meaning of Article 3.1(a) of the SCM Agreement and contingent upon the use of domestic over imported goods within the meaning of Article 3.1(b) of the SCM Agreement and is thus prohibited under those provisions.

1. Ratio Requirements

10.152 In the view of the European Communities and Japan, the import duty exemption constitutes "revenue ... foregone" which is "otherwise due", and hence a financial contribution exists within the meaning of Article 1.1(a)(1)(ii) of the SCM Agreement. This import duty exemption confers a benefit on the manufacturers in question in that the manufacturers are allowed to retain funds that they would otherwise have been obliged to pay as import duties. The complainants further consider that the import duty exemption is contingent, in law and in fact, upon export performance, because eligibility for it is based on the fulfilment of production-to-sales ratios which require a manufacturer beneficiary to export.

10.153 Canada contends that the import duty exemption does not represent a subsidy within the meaning of Article 1 of the Agreement or an export subsidy within the meaning of Article 3.1(a) of the Agreement. The overriding purpose of the SCM Agreement is to discipline subsidies that distort trade, and it would be contrary to the objective of trade liberalisation to characterise a measure that facilitates imports as an improper trade distortion. Further, the import duty exemption is unlike any of the practices identified in the Illustrative List of Export Subsidies contained in Annex I to the SCM Agreement (Illustrative List).

10.154 Canada submits that the ratio requirements do not make the import duty exemption contingent in law upon export performance, because nothing in either the MVTO 1998 or any of the SROs indicates that the import duty exemption is available only on the condition that the subject manufacturers achieve any particular export performance. Canada also argues that the ratio requirements do not make the import duty exemption contingent in fact upon export performance, because the import duty exemption is not "tied to" exportation or export earnings within the meaning of footnote 4 of the SCM Agreement. In this context, Canada explains how, in its view, the import duty exemption is entirely independent of export volume.

(a) Order in Which Issues Will Be Addressed

10.155 Article 3.1(a) of the SCM Agreement provides that subsidies "within the meaning of Article 1" which are contingent upon export performance are prohibited. Consequently, in order for a measure to be an export subsidy within the meaning of Article 3.1(a) of the SCM Agreement, it must be a subsidy within the meaning of Article 1 of that Agreement. Accordingly, we will first examine whether the import duty exemption identified by the European Communities and Japan is a subsidy within the meaning of Article 1 of the SCM Agreement, and then consider whether that subsidy is contingent upon export performance within the meaning of Article 3.1(a) of the Agreement.

(b) Whether the Import Duty Exemption is a Subsidy Within the Meaning of Article 1

10.156 Article 1.1 of the SCM Agreement provides, in relevant part, that:

> "For the purposes of this Agreement, a subsidy shall be deemed to exist if:
>
> (a)(1) there is a financial contribution by a government or any public body within the territory of a Member (referred to in this Agreement as "government"), i. e. where:
>
> ...
>
> (ii) government revenue that is otherwise due is foregone or not collected (e. g. fiscal incentives such as tax credits) (*footnote omitted*);
>
> ...
>
> and
>
> (b) a benefit is thereby conferred."

It is clear from Article 1.1 that two criteria must be met in order for a subsidy to exist within the meaning of that Article. First, there must be a financial contribution by a government. Second, a benefit must thereby be conferred. We will consider each criterion in turn.

(i) Financial contribution by a government

10.157 The European Communities argues that, because customs duties are imposed, collected and appropriated by the Canadian Government, they constitute "government revenue". Given that the importation of motor vehicles into Canada is, in principle, subject to customs duties, an exemption from such duties means that the Canadian Government is "foregoing" revenue that would otherwise be "due". A financial contribution therefore exists within the meaning of Article 1.1(a)(1)(ii) of the SCM Agreement. Japan argues that "government revenue" is raised through internal taxes and other charges, including customs duties. Since government revenue is foregone when a customs duty is waived, the import duty exemption amounts to a financial contribution

10.158 Canada argues that an import duty exemption for goods does not necessarily constitute revenue foregone under Article 1.1(a)(1)(ii). If it did, then a subsidy would exist whenever a Member unilaterally applied a rate of duty lower than its bound rate. To define such a programme as "subsidies" would be contrary to the object and purpose of the WTO Agreement, which explicitly identifies tariff reductions as contributing to the objectives of the Agreement.

10.159 It will be recalled that, under Article 1 of the SCM Agreement, there is a financial contribution and hence a possible subsidy where "government revenue that is otherwise due is foregone or not collected (e.g. fiscal incentives such as tax credits)". The term "revenue" has been defined, *inter alia*, as "[t]he annual income of a government or State, from all sources, out of which public expenses are met".[869] The word "otherwise" has been defined, *inter alia*, to mean "in other circumstances".[870] The adjective "due" has been defined, *inter alia*, to mean "[t]hat is owing or payable as an obligation or debt".[871]

10.160 Examining the Canadian import duty exemption in light of the ordinary meaning of the words above, we consider that customs duties represent "government revenue". In respect of whether the customs duties at issue in this case represent government revenue otherwise due, we recall that the import duty exemption is accorded to particular importers and not to others, and further consider that, in the absence of the import duty exemption, imports by manufacturer beneficiaries which are shielded from duties by that exemption would be subject to duties. In respect of whether those customs duties represent the foregoing of government revenue otherwise due, we recall that Canada applies an MFN duty on motor vehicles originating in non-NAFTA countries at the rate of 6.1 per cent. We further recall that certain duties continue to apply with respect to imports originating in NAFTA countries. While light trucks from Mexico and all motor vehicles from the United States enter Canada

[869] The New Shorter Oxford English Dictionary (Clarendon Press, 1993), Vol. 2, 2579.
[870] Ibid., 2032.
[871] The New Shorter Oxford English Dictionary (Clarendon Press, 1993), Vol. 1, 761.

duty-free under the NAFTA, motor vehicles from Mexico other than light trucks are subject to 1.3 or 2.4 per cent duties.[872] Finally, we recall that, in order for motor vehicles to qualify for the preferential duty treatment applicable with respect to imports originating in NAFTA countries, they must satisfy certain rules of origin and reporting requirements which are not applicable in order to receive the import duty exemption at issue in this dispute. Thus, even motor vehicles imported from Mexico and the United States in a tariff category subject to zero duty would not necessarily be eligible for duty-free treatment absent the import duty exemption. Accordingly, absent the import duty exemption accorded to certain companies under the MVTO 1998 and the SROs, those companies would be liable to pay duties of up to 6.1 per cent on the motor vehicles in question. We find, therefore, that the import duty exemption constitutes the "foregoing" of government revenue which is "otherwise due".

10.161 We now address Canada's argument that, if an import duty exemption were necessarily treated as revenue foregone, a subsidy would exist every time a WTO Member applied a rate lower than its bound rate, and this would be contrary to the object and purpose of the WTO Agreement, which explicitly identifies tariff reductions as contributing to the objectives of the Agreement. In our view, a Member's bound rate merely represents the *maximum* duty a Member may impose in respect of imports from WTO Members; the mere fact that a WTO Member applies a level of duties lower than the bound rate would not mean that it is foregoing revenue that is "otherwise due". More importantly, while the preamble to the WTO Agreement recognises that the "substantial reduction of tariffs" contributes to fulfilling certain objectives of the WTO Agreement, it does not follow that tariff reductions will always be WTO-consistent. For example, the reduction of tariffs in a discriminatory manner could give rise to a violation of Article I of GATT 1994. Similarly, we consider that the foregoing of government revenue otherwise due, in the form of customs duties, and in a manner which is specific within the meaning of Article 2, may give rise to a subsidy which is subject to the disciplines of the SCM Agreement.[873]

10.162 Canada also argues that, if an import duty exemption were necessarily treated as revenue foregone, a subsidy would exist every time generalised preferences or duty drawbacks were granted by a WTO Member. In our view, however, these examples advanced by Canada involve factual and legal considerations distinct from those in the case at hand. For instance, a generalised system of preferences accords favourable treatment to certain products from certain countries, and *all* such products from those countries receive favourable treatment. That situation is distinct from the case at hand, where *some* importers of a product - the manufacturer beneficiaries - are accorded favourable treatment as compared with other importers of *the same product from the same country*. As for duty drawbacks, item (i) of the Illustrative List indicates the circumstances in which the remission or drawback of import charges on imported inputs consumed in the production of the exported product constitutes an export subsidy. When read in conjunction with footnote 1 to the SCM Agreement, item (i) would appear to indicate - although this is not an issue we need decide in this

[872] See *supra* footnote 492.

[873] Our conclusions in this respect are consistent with those reached by the panel in *Indonesia - Autos*. In that dispute, the panel found that exemptions from import duties involved the foregoing of government revenue otherwise due. Panel Report on *Indonesia - Autos, supra* note 270, para. 14.155.

dispute - that non-excessive duty drawback is not to be considered a subsidy within the meaning of Article 1 of the Agreement.

10.163 Having concluded that the Canadian import duty exemption constitutes the "foregoing" of government revenue which is "otherwise due" within the meaning of Article 1.1(a)(1)(ii) of the SCM Agreement, we find that it gives rise to a financial contribution within the meaning of Article 1.1(a)(1) of the Agreement.

(ii) Benefit

10.164 Having found that a financial contribution exists on the part of the Canadian Government through the import duty exemption provided to certain motor vehicle manufacturers, we must now consider the second criterion set out in the definition of a subsidy in Article 1, that is, benefit.

10.165 A benefit has been defined, *inter alia*, as "(An) advantage".[874] Further, the Appellate Body has stated in *Canada - Aircraft*:

> "The dictionary meaning of 'benefit' is 'advantage', 'good', 'gift', 'profit', or, more generally, 'a favourable or helpful factor or circumstance'. (*footnote omitted*) ... These definitions also confirm that the Panel correctly stated that 'the ordinary meaning of 'benefit' clearly encompasses some form of advantage.' (*footnote omitted*)"[875]

In our view, the fact that the manufacturer beneficiaries need not pay customs duties that would otherwise be due - and that would be paid by non-qualifying manufacturers - constitutes just such an advantage. We find that the financial contribution made through the import duty exemption, therefore, confers a benefit within the meaning of Article 1.1(a)(2) of the SCM Agreement.

(iii) Illustrative List as context

10.166 Canada posits that footnotes 1 and 5, in conjunction with items (g), (h) and (i) of the Illustrative List of Export Subsidies, make it clear that non-excessive exemption or remission programmes are not subsidies. Footnote 1 to Article 1.1(a)(1)(ii) excludes certain non-excessive exemptions or remissions such as duty drawbacks from the definition of a "subsidy", notwithstanding that they confer a benefit directly on exports. It is therefore difficult, in Canada's view, to justify extending the definition of "subsidy" to capture non-excessive duty exemptions or remissions on imports.

10.167 We note that Canada does not contend that the measure at issue here falls within the scope of footnote 1. Rather, it would appear that Canada is making the contextual argument that, based on a principle derived from footnotes 1 and 5 and items (g), (h) and (i) of the Illustrative List, "non-excessive exemptions [from] or remissions" of duties are not subsidies, and that the import duty exemption in this case is just such a "non-excessive" exemption or remission. In response to a question

---

[874] The New Shorter Oxford English Dictionary (Clarendon Press, 1993), Vol. 1, 214.

[875] Appellate Body Report on *Canada - Measures Affecting the Export of Civilian Aircraft*, adopted on 20 August 1999, WT/DS70/AB/R (hereinafter Appellate Body Report on *Canada - Aircraft*), para. 153.

from the Panel, Canada explains that "[a]n excessive duty rebate would, in practical terms, be no different from a legal duty exemption coupled with a cash subsidy."[876]

10.168 We recall that footnote 1 to Article 1.1(a)(1)(ii) provides that:

> "In accordance with the provisions of Article XVI of GATT 1994 (Note to Article XVI) and the provisions of Annexes I through III of this Agreement, the exemption of an exported product from duties or taxes borne by the like product when destined for domestic consumption, or the remission of such duties or taxes in amounts not in excess of those which have accrued, shall not be deemed to be a subsidy."

Items (g), (h) and (i) of the Illustrative List (i. e., Annex I referred to in footnote 1) provide further elaboration regarding the application of this principle.

10.169 Item (i) of the Illustrative List relates to import charges, and is thus most closely related to the measures at hand. Under item (i), the remission or drawback of import charges "in excess of those levied on imported inputs that are consumed in the production of the exported product" is a prohibited export subsidy. Thus, the concept of "excessive" remission or drawback of import charges involves a comparison between the import duties levied on inputs consumed in the production of an exported product[877], on the one hand, and the amount of the remission or drawback granted on the other. In the case at hand, Canada has never contended that the import duty exemption in question represents the remission or drawback of import charges on imported inputs that are consumed in the production of exported products. On the contrary, qualifying motor vehicle manufacturers earn an import duty exemption in respect of motor vehicles that are sold in the Canadian market. Nor has Canada made any effort to demonstrate that the amount of the import duty exemption was calculated as a function of, or in fact bears any relationship to, the import charges levied on imported inputs that are consumed in the production of an exported product. Thus, we fail to understand how the concept of "excessive" exemption or remission is of relevance to this dispute, or in what sense it could be said that Canada's import duty exemption in this case is not "excessive".[878]

10.170 Having concluded that the import duty exemption represents a financial contribution by the Canadian Government and that a benefit is thereby conferred, we **find** that the import duty exemption constitutes a subsidy within the meaning of Article 1 of the SCM Agreement.

(iv) Specificity

10.171 We note that Article 1.2 of the SCM Agreement states:

> "A subsidy as defined in paragraph 1 shall be subject to the provisions of Part II ['Prohibited Subsidies'] or shall be subject to the provisions

876 *Supra* para. 7.236.

877 As defined in footnote 61 to Annex II of the SCM Agreement.

878 Our views with respect to para.s (g) and (h) of the Illustrative List, relating to indirect taxes, are similar. Put simply, an export subsidy exists under these two items if the Member exempts or remits indirect taxes "in excess" of the amount of indirect taxes that would be payable if the product were sold in the domestic market. Given that the measure in question here has no relation to the amount of indirect taxes that would be payable if the exported product had been sold in the domestic market, we fail to grasp how the concept of "excessive" remission is relevant to the case at hand.

> of Part III ['Actionable Subsidies'] or V ['Countervailing Measures'] only if such a subsidy is specific in accordance with the provisions of Article 2."

10.172 We further note that Article 2.3 of the SCM Agreement states:

> "Any subsidy falling under the provisions of Article 3 shall be deemed to be specific."

Given that the central issue of the claims under the SCM Agreement in this dispute is whether the import duty exemption falls within the provisions of Article 3, we need not, and do not, address the question of specificity separately.

(c) Whether the Import Duty Exemption is "contingent ... Upon export performance"

10.173 In the previous section, we have concluded that the import duty exemption under the MVTO 1998 and the SROs gives rise to a financial contribution that confers a benefit, and thus represents a subsidy within the meaning of Article 1 of the SCM Agreement. We now consider whether that subsidy is contingent upon export performance within the meaning of Article 3.1(a) of the Agreement.

10.174 Article 3.1 of the SCM Agreement provides, in relevant part:

> "Except as provided in the Agreement on Agriculture, the following subsidies, within the meaning of Article 1, shall be prohibited:
>
> (a) subsidies contingent, in law or in fact (*footnote omitted*), whether solely or as one of several other conditions, upon export performance, including those illustrated in Annex I (*footnote omitted*);

10.175 The European Communities and Japan argue that the import duty exemption is contingent upon export performance by reason of the ratio requirements. The European Communities explains how, where the required ratio is 100:100 or higher, a beneficiary cannot sell in Canada any value of motor vehicles imported under the import duty exemption unless it exports an equivalent value of domestically manufactured motor vehicles. Where the requirement is less than 100:100, by exporting part of its domestic production, a beneficiary would see the value of motor vehicles which it may import duty-free into Canada increase by an amount equal to the value of the exported vehicles. It would therefore qualify for a larger subsidy than if it sold all its domestic production in Canada. The ratio requirements hence function as requirements to export. Japan explains how, where the ratio requirement is 100:100, the only way for a manufacturer beneficiary importing motor vehicles and selling them in Canada to maintain compliance with this requirement is to export the vehicles it produces. Where the ratio requirement is less than 100:100, the only way for a manufacturer beneficiary importing motor vehicles and selling them in Canada to maintain compliance with this requirement is to export the vehicles it produces, but a lower requirement imposes a lesser degree of pressure in comparison with the situation in which the requirement is 100:100.

10.176 In Canada's view, even if there is a subsidy, there is no export contingency in law. A subsidy is export-contingent in law where the underlying legal instruments establishing that subsidy expressly provide for it to be available only on condition of export performance. The relevant legal condition for the import duty exemption is achievement of a production-to-sales ratio, and neither production nor sales, nor a ratio of the one to the other, is synonymous with exportation.

10.177 Canada further argues that there is no export contingency in fact, because the import duty exemption is available to manufacturer beneficiaries whether they export or not and the import duty exemption is entirely independent of export volume. Specifically, there is no direct nexus between receipt of the import duty exemption and the exportation of vehicles. Not only are there no penalties if exports do not take place or bonuses if additional exports do take place, but the benefit of the import duty exemption can be increased while exports are decreased. The only way to increase the benefit of the import duty exemption is to increase imports, which can be done even while decreasing production and exports.

10.178 As a threshold matter, we note the disagreement of the parties regarding the concepts of "in law" and "in fact" export contingency. The European Communities argues that, where the requirement to export is stated expressly in the law or is implicit in other requirements that are so stated in the law, the subsidy is contingent in law upon export performance. Where the requirement to export does not result from the terms of the law, or at least from those terms alone, but from factual elements outside the law, the subsidy is contingent in fact upon export performance. Japan does not specifically address this issue. Canada, on the other hand, argues that a subsidy is contingent in law upon export performance where the underlying legal instruments of that subsidy expressly provide that the subsidy is available to enterprises only on condition of export performance. In response to a question from the Panel, Canada argues that a subsidy is contingent in fact upon export performance where there is no express requirement to export, but the facts and circumstances are such that there is an implicit requirement to export.

10.179 The term "law" has been defined, *inter alia*, as "that which is laid down, ordained, or established."[879] Following from this definition, export contingency *in law*, in our view, must refer to the situation where one can ascertain, on the face of the law (or other relevant legal instrument), that export contingency exists. In other words, an examination of the terms of the underlying legal instruments of the subsidy in question would suffice to determine whether or not export contingency in law exists. We do not mean by this, however, that the terms of the law must - as Canada suggests - "expressly provide" that the subsidy is contingent upon export performance, but rather, that the existence of export contingency can be demonstrated on the basis of the law or other relevant legal instrument, without reference to external factual elements.

10.180 We find confirmation of our view on this issue in a recent statement of the Appellate Body in *Canada - Aircraft*:

> "In our view, the legal standard expressed by the word 'contingent' is the same for both *de jure* or *de facto* contingency. There is a difference, however, in what evidence may be employed to prove that a subsidy is export contingent. *De jure export contingency is demonstrated on the basis of the words of the relevant legislation, regulation or other legal instrument.* Proving *de facto* export contingency is a much more difficult task. There is no single legal document which will demonstrate, on its face, that a subsidy is 'contingent ... in fact ...

[879] Black's Law Dictionary (West Publishing Co.,1968, Fourth Edition), 1028.

upon export performance'. Instead, the existence of this relationship of contingency, between the subsidy and export performance, must be *inferred* from the total configuration of the facts constituting and surrounding the granting of the subsidy, none of which on its own is likely to be decisive in any given case."[880] (*first emphasis added*)

10.181 In light of our view regarding the distinction between "in law" and "in fact" export contingency, we now consider whether the Canadian import duty exemption is contingent in law upon export performance.

10.182 We note that the ratio requirements applicable to the MVTO 1998 beneficiaries are, "as a general rule", 95:100 for automobiles, at least 75:100 for SCVs and at least 75:100 for buses.[881] With respect, specifically, to the four automobile manufacturer beneficiaries under the MVTO 1998, Canada has stated, in response to a question from the Panel, that the amounts of the ratio requirements are confidential.[882] Canada adds that they range from the low-80s:100 to the high-90s:100, and the average of the four amounts is approximately 95:100. We further note that the SROs issued prior to 1997 set the minimum ratio requirement at 75:100. Regarding the SROs issued since 1997, almost all such SROs have the ratio requirement set at 100:100.[883]

10.183 The word "contingent" has been defined, *inter alia*, as "conditional, dependent".[884] Further, the Appellate Body has stated in *Canada - Aircraft*:

> "In our view, the key word in Article 3.1(a) is 'contingent'. As the Panel observed, the ordinary connotation of 'contingent' is 'conditional' or 'dependent for its existence on something else'. (*footnote omitted*) This common understanding of the word 'contingent' is borne out by the text of Article 3.1(a), which makes an explicit link between 'contingency' and 'conditionality' in stating that export contingency can be the sole or 'one of several other *conditions*'."[885]

10.184 In light of the above ordinary meaning of the word "contingent", we first examine the situation in which the ratio requirement is 100:100 or higher[886]. For instance, a company selling $100 worth of motor vehicles in Canada must produce $100 worth of motor vehicles in Canada in order to receive an import duty exemption for its imports of motor vehicles. However, for every unit value of motor vehicles

[880] Appellate Body Report on *Canada - Aircraft, supra* note 875, para. 167.

[881] *Supra* para. 2.25.

[882] *Supra* para. 7.3. We recall the Appellate Body's statement in *Canada - Aircraft*: " . . . [A] panel has broad legal authority to request information from a Member that is a party to a dispute, and . . . a party so requested has a *legal duty* to provide such information." (*emphasis added*) While we do not consider that the precise amounts of the ratio requirements for the MVTO manufacturers are necessary to our analysis, we note that the Appellate Body further stated: " . . . [A] panel should be willing expressly to remind parties - during the course of dispute settlement proceedings - that a refusal to provide information requested by the panel may lead to inferences being drawn about the inculpatory character of the information withheld." Appellate Body Report on *Canada - Aircraft, supra* note 875, paras. 197 and 204.

[883] *Supra* para. 2.34.

[884] The New Shorter Oxford English Dictionary (Clarendon Press, 1993), Vol. 1, 494.

[885] Appellate Body Report on *Canada - Aircraft, supra* note 875, para. 166 (*emphasis in original*).

[886] We note that one ratio requirement - that for Navistar International - is higher than 100:100.

that it imports duty-free, it would have to export an equivalent unit value of motor vehicles produced in Canada, in order to maintain its production-to-sales ratio. Notwithstanding the fact that the requirement is set out as a production-to-sales ratio, we fail to see how a manufacturer beneficiary could access the import duty exemption - and still maintain its production-to-sales ratio - without exporting. In cases where the production-to-sales ratio is 100:100, the only way to import any motor vehicles duty-free is to export, and the amount of import duty exemption allowed is directly dependent upon the amount of exports achieved. Given that, where the ratio requirement is 100:100, it is impossible to import duty-free without exporting, the import duty exemption is clearly "conditional" or "dependent" upon exportation.

10.185 Canada contends that a manufacturer beneficiary subject to a 100:100 ratio requirement which is in fact performing at a higher-than-required ratio could increase its duty-free imports while at the same time reducing its exports. We agree with Canada that such a situation is in fact possible. Thus, for example, a manufacturer might, in year x, produce $500 worth of motor vehicles in Canada, export $450 worth of motor vehicles from Canada, import $50 worth of motor vehicles pursuant to the import duty exemption and thus, in total, sell $100 worth of motor vehicles in Canada. In this case, the manufacturer beneficiary has achieved a production-to-sales ratio of 500:100. The following year, that manufacturer beneficiary might continue to produce $500 worth of motor vehicles in Canada, but reduce its exports to $400 while increasing its duty-free imports to $100 (leaving an actual production-to-sales ratio of 500:200, well in excess of the required ratio). Under these circumstances, the manufacturer beneficiary has decreased its exports while increasing the amount of its duty-free imports (and thus the amount of the subsidy).

10.186 Canada considers that the type of situation set out above establishes that there is no sufficient "nexus" between the exports and the subsidy and that the import duty exemption is not, therefore, "contingent ... upon export performance". We disagree. In our view, the situation posited by Canada simply demonstrates that a manufacturer beneficiary may in a given year choose not to fully exercise its entitlement to the import duty exemption, while in a subsequent year more fully availing itself of that entitlement. Looked at from another angle, it could be said that the manufacturer beneficiary exceeded the production-to-sales ratio necessary in order to obtain the amount of import duty exemption it required, and that it therefore had a certain margin of flexibility to reduce exports and/or increase duty-free imports in subsequent years. The fact remains, however, that the manufacturer beneficiary could not have imported *any* motor vehicles duty-free in either year without exporting an equivalent value of motor vehicles in that year. Thus, the subsidies are clearly contingent upon export performance, in as much as the import duty exemption obtained was conditional or dependent upon exporting an equivalent value of motor vehicles. The fact that the manufacturer beneficiary exceeded the amount of exports necessary to obtain the amount of subsidy in question in no way changes this.

10.187 We have noted that ratio requirements for some manufacturer beneficiaries are set at 100:100 or higher and for others at less.[887] We have examined the situation in which the ratio requirement is 100:100 in light of the ordinary meaning of the

[887] See *supra* para. 10.182.

word "contingent". Accordingly, we now consider the situation in which the ratio requirement is less than 100:100 in light of the ordinary meaning of the word "contingent".

10.188 Let us assume that the ratio requirement is 75:100, the "minimum allowable ratio requirement"[888]. A manufacturer beneficiary sells $100 worth of motor vehicles in Canada and must, therefore, produce $75 worth of motor vehicles in Canada in order to satisfy the ratio requirement. Having done so, it is entitled to import $25 worth of motor vehicles duty-free or, in other words, has a duty-free "allowance" or "entitlement" of up to $25. Admittedly, no exports have occurred, nor do they need to, for the manufacturer beneficiary to receive the import duty exemption up to this amount. We accept that the import duty exemption is not contingent upon export performance up to this amount.

10.189 However, if the manufacturer beneficiary wishes to import any amount *above* its duty-free "allowance" and still receive the import duty exemption, it would have to export an amount equivalent to that exceeding this "allowance", so as to ensure that the production-to-sales ratio remains unaltered. In the present case, if it wishes to import $75 rather than $25 worth of motor vehicles duty-free, which is $50 more than its "allowance", it would have to export $50 worth of motor vehicles. For every unit value of duty-free imports above the "allowance", it is required to export an equivalent unit value of its production in Canada. Indeed, other things being equal, the more the manufacturer beneficiary exports, the more it can import duty-free. For instance, if it then exports $100 worth of motor vehicles, it can import $125 worth of motor vehicles duty-free. In our view, the relationship between the import duty exemption and export performance in this situation is such that the former is "conditional" or "dependent" on the latter.

10.190 Of course, the manufacturer beneficiary could steadily increase its domestic production and its domestic sales, all the while respecting the 75:100 ratio, and the value of duty-free imports that it is allowed would increase proportionally without any exports occurring. However, this does not change the fact that, to import duty-free in excess of its "allowance", the manufacturer beneficiary is obliged to export an amount equivalent to that in excess.

10.191 We therefore find that, with the exception of the one situation where the ratio requirement is less than 100:100 and the manufacturer beneficiary wishes to access an import duty exemption only up to the amount of its duty-free "allowance", there is a clear relationship of contingency between the import duty exemption and export performance. The fact that, where the ratio requirement is less than 100:100, some amount of import duty exemption is accessible without exports occurring cannot possibly mean that the import duty exemption in its totality should be considered not to be export-contingent. In other words, the import duty exemption is contingent upon export performance even if, where the ratio requirement is less than 100:100, the manufacturer beneficiary may fulfil it to receive a certain amount of import duty exemption without exporting, because, *in order to receive a greater amount of import duty exemption, it is obliged to export.*

[888] *Supra* para. 7.1.

10.192 We note that it is the *law* (or other relevant legal instrument) - the MVTO 1998 and the SROs - that creates this construct, *i.e.*, an import duty exemption upon condition of meeting certain ratio requirements. It is the *law* that determines what a particular manufacturer beneficiary's ratio requirement will be. And, in the case of a ratio requirement lower than 100:100, although the manufacturer beneficiary has a choice as to the amount of the import duty exemption it wishes to access, it is the *law* that determines the consequences of that choice for the manufacturer beneficiary, or, otherwise put, it is the *law* that then establishes contingency upon export performance. We **find**, on the basis of our foregoing discussion, that the MVTO 1998 and the SROs demonstrate, on their face, that the import duty exemption is contingent upon export performance, and we have not needed to refer ourselves to "the total configuration of the facts constituting and surrounding the granting of the subsidy"[889]. Being demonstrable "on the basis of the words of the relevant legislation, regulation or other legal instrument"[890], export contingency in respect of the Canadian import duty exemption exists in law.

10.193 With specific reference to the four MVTO automobile manufacturer beneficiaries, Canada claims, in response to a question from the Panel, that there is no statutory instrument setting out the ratio requirement.[891] Canada submits that the actual ratio requirement for each MVTO automobile manufacturer beneficiary was determined on a company-by-company basis for each class of vehicle. Each company was informed of the production-to-sales ratio it had achieved in the base year, and that is the ratio that each company must maintain in order to qualify as an MVTO manufacturer beneficiary each year.[892] We consider, however, that, while no statutory instrument sets out the ratio requirement for each automobile manufacturer beneficiary, it is the Canadian Government which determined, *pursuant to the MVTO 1998*, the ratio requirement for each automobile manufacturer beneficiary. That is, the MVTO 1998 requires that each automobile manufacturer beneficiary be subject to a ratio requirement and establishes a formula on the basis of which the individual ratio requirement for each automobile manufacturer beneficiary is to be calculated. Thus, the existence of export contingency with respect to the four MVTO automobile manufacturer beneficiaries can be determined on the basis of the MVTO 1998 itself.

10.194 We note that the European Communities and Japan have, *in the alternative*, made an argument as to export contingency in fact. Having found that the Canadian import duty exemption is contingent in law upon export performance, we need not, and do not, address this argument.

10.195 Having examined the import duty exemption in light of the ordinary meaning of the text of Article 3.1(a), we now address what Canada considers to be the context in which Article 3.1(a) must be interpreted, *i.e.* the Illustrative List. Canada argues that the Illustrative List is an important guide to identifying the practices that constitute export subsidies, and the Canadian import duty exemption is unlike any of the measures in the Illustrative List. Canada emphasises that, in each of the practices identified in the Illustrative List, there is a clear and direct nexus between the subsidy

889 Appellate Body Report on *Canada - Aircraft, supra* note 875, para. 167.
890 Ibid.
891 *Supra* para. 7.3.
892 *Supra* para. 7.2.

and the exported product, and the amount of the subsidy increases with the volume of exports. We recall, however, that the test set out in Article 3.1(a) is contingency upon export perfomance, and not a "nexus" between the subsidy and the exported product. And we have established that the import duty exemption is contingent upon export performance by reason of the ratio requirements.

10.196 Canada posits that, because the only remissions of import charges identified in the Illustrative List are those that are both excessive and linked directly to an exported product, only such remissions of import charges may be considered subsidies contingent upon export performance. We recall that Article 3.1(a) prohibits "subsidies contingent ... upon export performance, *including those illustrated in Annex I* [the Illustrative List]". It is thus reasonable, in our view, to consider that the Illustrative List may be of some utility in informing the notion of export contingency in certain precise situations. We find it difficult to accept, however, that the practices identified in the Illustrative List represent a circumscription - in the manner suggested by Canada - of the conditions under which a subsidy is deemed to be contingent upon export performance. Indeed, the use of the words "including" and "illustrated" makes it clear that, while all practices identified in the Illustrative List are subsidies contingent upon export performance, there may be other practices not identified in the Illustrative List that are also subsidies contingent upon export performance.

10.197 Accordingly, the Illustrative List does not establish any general definition of the circumstances in which an exemption or remission is to be considered an export subsidy. Specifically, we do not find any basis in the cited provisions - or, for that matter, anywhere else in the SCM Agreement - for Canada's view that, because the only remissions of import charges identified in the Illustrative List are those that are both excessive and linked directly to an exported product, only such remissions of import charges may be considered subsidies contingent upon export performance. Item (i) is the only one in the Illustrative List that deals with the remission of import charges, but it is specific to imported inputs. It cannot be considered to establish a general rule as to *all* remissions of import charges.

10.198 Turning now to the object and purpose of the SCM Agreement, Canada submits that the purpose of the SCM Agreement is to discipline subsidies that distort trade, and that the only real effect on trade of the Canadian import duty exemption is to increase the volume of duty-free imports into Canada of vehicles that would not qualify for such treatment under the NAFTA. Canada also argues that, even assuming that the import duty exemption can be considered a subsidy, it is a subsidy of imports, not of exports. In response to a question from the Panel, Canada submits that, in the alternative, the import duty exemption is a production-based subsidy by virtue of the production-to-sales ratio requirements.

10.199 In order for a measure to fall within the scope of the SCM Agreement's prohibition of export subsidies, it need only be a subsidy within the meaning of Article 1 which is contingent upon export performance within the meaning of Article 3.1(a). In this case, while the subsidy in question is provided through the mechanism of a duty exemption for imports and thus arguably "facilitates imports", that does not change the fact that the subsidy is contingent upon export performance and thus falls within the scope of Article 3.1(a). In any event, and whether or not it also "facilitates imports", a subsidy which is contingent upon export performance can be expected to affect exporters' behaviour. Thus, even if a showing that an export subsidy did not have any "real effect" on exports were a defence to a claim under Article 3.1(a) - which of course it is not - Canada has not convinced us that the subsidy in question has not had any "real effect" in increasing Canadian exports of motor vehicles. Finally, we note that Canada's argument could, taken to its extreme, lead to the conclusion that a financial contribution in the form of the foregoing of import duties could never give rise to an export subsidy or, indeed, to any subsidy. Item (i) of the Illustrative List, however, clearly foresees that the excessive remission or drawback of certain import charges constitutes a prohibited export subsidy.

10.200 We recall Japan's argument that the Canadian import duty exemption falls within item (a) of the Illustrative List of Export Subsidies, that is, "the provision by governments of direct subsidies to a firm ... contingent upon export performance." Having established that the Canadian import duty exemption violates Article 3.1(a) of the SCM Agreement by reason of its being contingent upon export performance, we need not, and do not, address this argument.

10.201 For the reasons discussed in this section, we **find** that the Canadian import duty exemption is a subsidy within the meaning of Article 1 of the SCM Agreement which is "contingent ... in law ... upon export performance" within the meaning of Article 3.1(a) of the Agreement. We therefore **find** that Canada acts inconsistently with its obligations under Article 3.1(a) of the SCM Agreement.

2. *CVA Requirements*

10.202 In the previous section of this report, we concluded that the import duty exemption provided by the Canadian Government to certain motor vehicle manufacturers under the MVTO 1998 and the SROs constitutes a subsidy within the meaning of Article 1 of the SCM Agreement (*supra* paras. 10.156-10.170). We now consider whether, as the European Communities and Japan claim, the import duty exemption is contingent upon the use of domestic over imported goods within the meaning of Article 3.1(b) of the SCM Agreement because it is accorded upon fulfilment of certain Canadian value-added ("CVA") requirements, and is thus prohibited under that provision.

(a) Factual Considerations

10.203 We recall that three types of CVA requirements are at issue in this dispute.

10.204 *First*, there are the CVA requirements under the MVTO 1998 itself. Under the MVTO 1998, a manufacturer is entitled to benefit from the import duty exemption if, *inter alia*, that manufacturer's total Canadian value added with respect to a class of vehicles is equal to or greater than that manufacturer's total value added with respect to that same class of vehicles in the base year. The term "Canadian Value Added" is defined in the MVTO 1998 as including: (i) the cost of parts produced in Canada and of materials of Canadian origin that are incorporated in the motor vehicles; (ii) direct labour costs incurred in Canada; (iii) manufacturing overheads incurred in Canada; (iv) general and administrative expenses incurred in Canada that are attributable to the production of motor vehicles; (v) depreciation in respect of machinery and permanent plant equipment located in Canada that is attributable to the production of motor vehicles; and (vi) a capital cost allowance for land and buildings in Canada that are used in the production of motor vehicles.

10.205 *Second*, there are CVA requirements in the SROs. SROs issued after 1984 typically require that the total CVA of a manufacturer's vehicles produced in Canada in a given year must be at least 40 per cent of the cost of sales of vehicles sold in Canada in the same year. By way of exception, one manufacturer (CAMI) must meet a requirement that the total CVA of its vehicles and original equipment manufacturing parts produced in Canada in a given year must be at least 60 per cent of the cost of sales of vehicles sold in Canada in the same year.

10.206 *Third*, there are Letters of Undertaking. Letters signed by General Motors, Ford, Chrysler and American Motors provide for two additional commitments with respect to CVA, i.e., to increase in each ensuing model year over the base model year CVA in the production of vehicles by an amount equal to 60 per cent of the growth in their market for automobiles sold for consumption in Canada and by an amount equal to 50 per cent of the growth in their market for commercial vehicles sold for consumption in Canada, and to achieve a stipulated increase in the annual CVA by the end of model year 1968.

(b) Arguments of the Parties

10.207 The European Communities acknowledges that access to the import duty exemption is not explicitly conditioned upon the use of domestic over imported goods, but that it is rather conditioned upon reaching a certain level of CVA. It asserts, however, that because the use of domestic parts and materials may be sufficient, or at least contribute, to meeting the CVA requirements, the import duty exemption is contingent in law upon the use of domestic over imported goods. In short, the European Communities considers that Article 3.1(b) prohibits any condition that gives preference to domestic over imported goods, irrespective of whether in practice domestic goods are actually used by the beneficiary. The European Communities further argues in the alternative that the import duty exemption is in fact contingent upon the use of domestic over imported goods. In this respect, the European Communities asserts that parts and materials amount on average to as much as 80 per cent of the cost of sales of motor vehicles assembled in Canada.

10.208 Japan claims that the import duty exemption is contingent in law upon the use of domestic over imported goods, in that Article 3.1(b) prohibits subsidies that are contingent upon a condition that *requires* the use of domestic over imported goods, as well as subsidies contingent on a condition that *favours* the use of domestic over imported goods. Japan further argues in the alternative that the import duty exemption is contingent in fact upon the use of domestic over imported goods in the case of the SROs to automobile manufacturers and the Letters of Undertaking which impose 60 per cent CVA requirements.

10.209 Canada responds that the import duty exemption is not contingent in law on the use of domestic over imported goods. Moreover, Canada contends that Article 3.1(b) contains no reference to contingency in fact and extends only to contingency in law. Even if Article 3.1(b) did extend to contingency in fact, the import duty exemption is not contingent in fact upon the use of domestic goods, because the words "contingent upon" should be interpreted to apply to subsidies that are *conditional upon* or *tied to* the use of domestic over imported goods. The import duty exemption is available to manufacturers whether or not they use domestic goods, provided they meet their CVA requirements. Canada points to the fact that a manufacturer may include in the calculation of CVA not only goods, but direct labour costs, overhead, general and administrative expenses, depreciation and capital cost allowance for land and buildings.

(c) Contingency in Law

10.210 We first consider whether the Canadian import duty exemption is contingent in law upon the use of domestic over imported goods.

10.211 Article 3.1 provides, in relevant part:

> "Except as provided in the Agreement on Agriculture, the following subsidies, within the meaning of Article 1, shall be prohibited:
>
> ....
>
> (b) subsidies contingent, whether solely or as one of several other conditions, upon the use of domestic over imported goods."

10.212 In our examination of the complainants' claims under Article 3.1(a) of the SCM Agreement, we examined the concepts of "in law" and "in fact" export contingency (*supra* paras. 10.178-10.179) and concluded that export contingency in law refers to the situation where one can ascertain, on the face of the law (or other relevant legal instrument), that export contingency exists. Equally, contingency in law upon the use of domestic over imported goods must refer to the situation where the contingency is demonstrable "on the basis of the words of the relevant legislation, regulation or other legal instrument"[893] rather than "the total configuration of the facts constituting and surrounding the granting of the subsidy"[894]. Accordingly, we must first examine the legal instruments in question here in order to determine whether eligibility for the import duty exemptions is contingent in law upon the use of domestic over imported goods.

10.213 As we noted in the section of our report relating to claims under Article 3.1(a) of the SCM Agreement, the word "contingent" has been defined, *inter alia*, as "conditional, dependent".[895] It is in light of this ordinary meaning of the word "contingent" that we must examine whether, under the CVA requirements outlined above, access to the import duty exemption is conditional or dependent upon the use of domestic over imported goods.

10.214 We recall the view of the European Communities and Japan that Article 3.1(b) extends to subsidies contingent on a condition that favours or gives preference to the use of domestic over imported goods. The complainants argue that the words "over imported" would be redundant if this provision were interpreted to mean simply "contingent on the use of domestic goods". We note however that the text of Article 3.1(b) refers to subsidies "contingent upon the use" of domestic over imported goods. This language thus creates a direct link between the subsidy and the use of domestic goods. We do not believe that the addition of the words "over imported" can be construed to weaken that link. Rather, we believe that they were intended simply to emphasize that such subsidies are prohibited because of their probable adverse effects on other Members.

---

893 Appellate Body Report on *Canada - Aircraft*, *supra* note 875, para. 167.

894 Ibid.

895 The New Shorter Oxford English Dictionary (Clarendon Press, 1993), *supra* note 884.

10.215 The European Communities further argues that its interpretation furthers the object and purpose of Article 3.1(b), which it considers to be to avoid that subsidies be used to discriminate between domestic and imported goods used in the manufacture of other goods. We recognize that Article 3.1(b) in some sense has its roots in Article III:4 of GATT and in certain interpretations of that provision, which relates to non-discrimination. We do not consider however that Article 3.1(b) *ipso facto* has the same scope as Article III:4. To the contrary, while Article III:4 of GATT speaks of "treatment no less favourable" and of requirements "affecting" internal sale, Article 3.1(b) speaks of subsidies "contingent upon the use of domestic over imported goods". We are unwilling to import into Article 3.1(b) legal principles derived from the interpretation of a text which differs so markedly from that of Article 3.1(b).

10.216 In applying these principles to the case at hand, we note that, while under the MVTO 1998 and SROs access to the import duty exemption is contingent upon satisfying certain CVA requirements,[896] a value-added requirement is in no sense synonymous with a condition to use domestic over imported goods. In this regard, we recall that the definition of "CVA" in the MVTO 1998 includes, in addition to parts and materials of Canadian origin, such other elements as direct labour costs, manufacturing overheads, general and administrative expenses and depreciation. Thus, and depending upon the factual circumstances, a manufacturer might well be willing and able to satisfy a CVA requirement without using any domestic goods whatsoever. Under these circumstances, it would be difficult for us to conclude that access to the import duty exemption is contingent, i.e. conditional or dependent, in law on the use of domestic over imported goods within the meaning of the SCM Agreement.

10.217 Finally, we recall the European Communities' argument that Article 3.1(b) prohibits subsidies contingent, *whether solely or as one of several other conditions*, on the use of domestic over imported goods. The European Communities concedes that this may cover the situation where a subsidy is simultaneously subject to two or more cumulative conditions (including the use of domestic over imported goods). The European Communities asserts, though, that this may also cover the situation where a subsidy is subject to two or more alternative conditions, so that compliance with any of them gives a right to the subsidy. If one of those conditions is "the use of domestic over imported goods" the subsidy must be deemed prohibited by Article 3.1(b), even if it is also possible to qualify for the subsidy by complying with other alternative non-prohibited conditions, such as using domestic labour or domestic services. Thus, the European Communities argues that the use of domestic over imported goods need not be a "necessary" condition in order for a subsidy to be prohibited under Article 3.1(b) of the SCM Agreement.

10.218 According to Canada, use of the clause "whether solely or as one of several other conditions" in Article 3.1(a) and (b) of the SCM Agreement means that the use of domestic goods or export performance does not have to be the only condition for

[896] However, with regard to the CVA requirements in the Letters of Undertaking, we recall our observation in para. 10.120 that the legal instruments adopted by Canada in connection with the implementation of the Auto Pact do not provide for the authority to withdraw the import duty exemption in case of a failure to meet the commitments contained in these Letters. Compliance with these commitments is not explicitly a factor in determining the eligibility for the import duty exemption.

the receipt of the subsidy. There may also be additional conditions to fulfil, but each condition must be mandatory. Canada contends that the clause is not satisfied simply because the use of domestic goods or export performance is among the ways to qualify for the subsidy. In the context of Article 3.1(a), for example, Canada denies that a subsidy is contingent on export performance if receipt of the subsidy depends on either exporting or selling domestically.

10.219 The basic disagreement between the parties concerns whether the phrase "several other conditions" in Article 3.1(b) of the SCM Agreement would include several *alternative* conditions (including the use of domestic over imported goods). We do not consider it necessary to resolve this disagreement, since we are not confronted with a situation where the bestowal of a subsidy is contingent in law on the fulfilment of several alternative conditions. The import duty exemption at issue is contingent in law on three clear conditions, all of which must be met: (1) manufacturing presence, (2) ratio requirements, and (3) CVA requirements. The use of domestic over imported goods is not an alternative condition, in law, for access to the import duty exemption. For that reason, the question of whether the prohibition in Article 3.1(b) applies in circumstances where the use of domestic over imported goods is one of several, alternative, conditions for the bestowal of a subsidy does not arise.

(d) Contingency in Fact

10.220 Having concluded that the import duty exemptions in this dispute are not contingent *in law* upon the use of domestic over imported goods, we must now consider the complainants' assertion in the alternative that those exemptions are contingent *in fact* upon the use of domestic over imported goods.

10.221 We note the disagreement of the parties as to whether Article 3.1(b) extends to the situation where a subsidy is contingent in fact upon the use of domestic over imported goods. In this context, we recall that Article 3.1 is, as clearly indicated by its chapeau, the provision that sets out the subsidies prohibited under the SCM Agreement. Paragraphs (a) and (b) are both part of Article 3.1 and manifestly similar. It is hard to imagine how the inclusion of the words "in law or in fact" in paragraph (a) and the absence of such words in paragraph (b) could be but a reflection of the intention of the drafters. We further recall that the Appellate Body has held in *Japan - Alcoholic Beverages* that "omission must have some meaning".[897] That two provisions so alike and juxtaposed together should differ from each other in such specific respect signals, in our view, that the omission of the words "in law or in fact" from Article 3.1(b) was deliberate and that Article 3.1(b) extends only to contingency in law.

10.222 For the reasons discussed in this section, we are unable to find that the Canadian import duty exemption is a subsidy within the meaning of Article 1 of the SCM Agreement which is "contingent ... upon the use of domestic over imported goods" within the meaning of Article 3.1(b) of the Agreement. We reject the European Communities' and Japan's claim accordingly.

---

[897] Appellate Body Report on *Japan - Alcoholic Beverages*, *supra* note 271, at 111.

D. *Claims Under the GATS*

1. *Introduction*

10.223 The complainants argue that the import duty exemption granted to some manufacturers/wholesalers of motor vehicles in Canada ("manufacturer beneficiaries") by the MVTO 1998 and by the SROs, is inconsistent with Canada's obligations under Article II of the GATS, in that it grants more favourable treatment to suppliers of the United States than to suppliers of the European Communities and Japan. Japan alone claims that the import duty exemption is inconsistent with Canada's obligations under Article XVII of the GATS in that it grants more favourable treatment to Canadian suppliers of wholesale trade services for motor vehicles, which benefit from duty-free treatment, than to Japanese suppliers, which do not.

10.224 Both complainants also claim that the CVA requirements in the MVTO 1998 and in the SROs are inconsistent with Article XVII of the GATS, in that they require manufacturers of motor vehicles to achieve a minimum of Canadian value added in order to benefit from the import duty exemption, therefore according more favourable treatment to services supplied in Canada than to services of other Members supplied through modes 1 ("cross-border supply") and 2 ("consumption abroad"). The complainants point out that the CVA requirements create an incentive for manufacturer beneficiaries to procure services from suppliers established in Canada to the detriment of services supplied through modes 1 and 2.

10.225 Canada rejects the claims of the complainants on the grounds, first, that the import duty exemption is not a measure affecting trade in services within the meaning of Article I of the GATS. With respect to the Article II claim, Canada argues that the import duty exemption does not modify the conditions of competition in favour of services and service suppliers of the United States, for two reasons: (i) there are European and Japanese wholesale trade service suppliers of motor vehicles which benefit from the import duty exemption; and (ii) due to vertical integration between manufacturers and wholesalers in the motor vehicle industry, there is no effective competition at the wholesale trade level, so that granting the import duty exemption to manufacturer beneficiaries cannot be said to affect competition. With respect to the claim by Japan that the import duty exemption also violates Article XVII of the GATS, Canada responds that it has no specific commitments in wholesale trade services for motor vehicles and that therefore it is not bound by the national treatment obligation in this sector. In addition, Canada argues that there are no "like" Canadian and Japanese suppliers of wholesale trade services for motor vehicles to whom national treatment would apply and that, as for Article II, due to vertical integration between manufacturers and wholesale trade service suppliers, there is no competition which can be affected at the wholesale trade level.

10.226 With respect to the claim that the CVA requirements in the MVTO 1998 and in the SROs violate Article XVII of the GATS, Canada responds that a series of circumstances exclude that these measures could violate any of its specific commitments: (i) Canada has inserted relevant limitations to its commitments in the relevant sectors; (ii) the supply of many of the relevant services through modes 1 and 2 is not technically feasible; (iii) where it is technically feasible, the supply of the relevant services through modes 1 and 2 suffers from a competitive disadvantage, due to the inherent foreign character of these services and not to the CVA requirements; and (iv) most manufacturer beneficiaries achieve the required proportion of Canadian value-added through their employment of Canadian labour so that the effect of the CVA requirements on their procurement of services is minimal.

10.227 In addition, if the Panel were to find that the import duty exemption was a measure affecting trade in services within the meaning of Article I of the GATS, Canada endorses the suggestion made by the United States in its third-party submission that Article V:1 would apply to any alleged violation of Article II arising from a provision of the NAFTA, such as the measures at issue in this case.

10.228 In our consideration of the claims raised under the GATS, we first examine the general issue of whether the measures, which the complainants claim to be in violation of Articles II and XVII of the GATS, constitute "measures affecting trade in services" within the meaning of Article I of the GATS. Second, we examine the consistency of the import duty exemption, granted under the MVTO 1998 and the SROs, with Article II and with Canada's specific commitments under Article XVII of the GATS in wholesale trade services. We then consider the compatibility of the CVA requirements in the MVTO 1998 and in the SROs with Canada's specific commitments under Article XVII of the GATS in various services sectors related to the production of motor vehicles, which the complainants claim to be affected by the CVA requirements. Finally, we address the role of Article V of the GATS with respect to the import duty exemption, which the complainants claim to be in violation of Article II of the GATS.

2. *Measures Affecting Trade in Services*

10.229 The complainants argue that the import duty exemption and the CVA requirements in the MTVO 1998 and in the SROs are "measures affecting trade in services" within the meaning of Article I of the GATS. They note that the panel and the Appellate Body in *EC - Bananas III*[898] found that the term "affecting" has a broad scope of application and that accordingly no measures are *a priori* excluded from the scope of application of the GATS. They also point out that the panel in *EC - Bananas III* found that the list of matters in Article XXVIII(c) in respect of which measures by Members affecting trade in services can be taken is an illustrative one and that the word "affecting" in Article XXVIII cannot be read as meaning merely "in respect of".

10.230 Canada responds that the import duty exemption is not a "measure affecting trade in services" within the meaning of Article I of the GATS, because, as a tariff measure, it affects the goods themselves and not the supply of distribution services. According to Canada, the import duty exemption does not affect a manufacturer in its capacity as a service supplier and in its supply of a service.

10.231 We note that Article I:1 of the GATS establishes that "this Agreement applies to measures by Members affecting trade in services". The panel and the Appellate Body in *EC - Bananas III* found that the term "affecting" in Article I of the GATS has a broad scope of application and that accordingly no measures are *a priori* excluded from the scope of application of the GATS. The panel in *EC - Bananas III* pointed out that:

---

[898] Panel Report on *EC - Bananas III*, *supra* note 269.

" ... the drafters [of the GATS] consciously adopted the terms 'affecting' and 'supply of a service' to ensure that the disciplines of the GATS would cover any measure bearing upon conditions of competition in supply of a service, regardless of whether the measure directly governs or indirectly affects the supply of the service."[899]

10.232 The Appellate Body upheld this finding of the panel and noted that:

" ... the use of the term 'affecting' reflects the intent of the drafters to give a broad reach to the GATS. The ordinary meaning of the word 'affecting' implies a measure that has 'an effect on', which indicates a broad scope of application."[900]

10.233 The Appellate Body also found that, in addition to measures affecting trade in goods as goods and measures affecting the supply of services as services, falling respectively and exclusively within the scope of the GATT 1994 or GATS:

"there is yet a third category of measures that could be found to fall within the scope of both the GATT 1994 and the GATS. These are measures that involve a service relating to a particular good or a service supplied in conjunction with a particular good. In all such cases in this third category, the measure in question could be scrutinized under both the GATT 1994 and the GATS."[901]

10.234 We note that Article I of the GATS does not *a priori* exclude any measure from the scope of application of the Agreement. The determination of whether a measure affects trade in services cannot be done in abstract terms in isolation from examining whether the effect of such a measure is consistent with the Member's obligations and commitments under the GATS. In this case, the determination of whether the MVTO 1998 and SROs are measures affecting trade in services within the meaning of Article I of the GATS should be done on the basis of the determination of whether these measures constitute less favourable treatment for the services and service suppliers of some Members as compared to those of others (Article II) and/or for services and service suppliers of other Members as compared to domestic ones (Article XVII).

10.235 Therefore, we do not address the issues of whether the MVTO 1998 and SROs affect trade in services in isolation from the issue of whether such measures have an effect that is inconsistent with an obligation in the Agreement.

3. *Claims Under Article II of the GATS*

10.236 The complainants claim that the import duty exemption granted by the MVTO 1998 and SROs to some manufacturers/wholesalers of motor vehicles - the manufacturer beneficiaries - violates Article II of the GATS in that it constitutes more favourable treatment accorded to services and service suppliers of the United States than that accorded to those of other Members. We note that Article II (1) of the GATS establishes that:

---

899 Panel Report on *EC - Bananas III (USA), supra* note 269, para. 7.281.

900 Appellate Body Report on *EC - Bananas III, supra* note 49, para. 220.

901 Ibid., para. 220.

> "With respect to any measure covered by this Agreement, each Member shall accord immediately and unconditionally to services and service suppliers of any other Member treatment no less favourable than that it accords to like services and service suppliers of any other country".

10.237 The complainants argue that the import duty exemption constitutes *de facto* discrimination because, although the criteria for obtaining the exemption contained in the MTVO 1998 and SROs are not based on nationality, in fact all the beneficiaries are suppliers of the United States. Japan also claims that the import duty exemption is inconsistent with the requirement in Article II that treatment no less favourable be granted "immediately and unconditionally". Canada argues that among the beneficiaries of the exemption there are companies which are suppliers of the European Communities and of Japan. It argues further that it is not possible to maintain that the measure modifies the conditions of competition among wholesale trade suppliers of motor vehicles because, due to vertical integration and exclusive distribution between manufacturers and wholesalers of motor vehicles, there is no competition to be affected at the wholesale trade level.

(a) Whether the Import Duty Exemption Affects Wholesale Trade Services

10.238 The complainants claim that the import duty exemption affects the supply of wholesale trade services, as it modifies the conditions of competition between the beneficiaries of the duty-free treatment and other wholesale trade service suppliers of imported motor vehicles which do not benefit from the same treatment. In particular, the import duty exemption would directly affect the cost of the goods being distributed and indirectly affect the cost and/or profitability of the related wholesale trade services. Canada responds that the import duty exemption is not a measure affecting trade in services within the meaning of Article I of the GATS, because, as a tariff measure, it affects the goods themselves and not the supply of distribution services. According to Canada, such measures do not affect a service supplier in its capacity as service supplier and in its supply of a service. On the basis of the Report of the Appellate Body in *EC - Bananas III*, Canada argues that the import duty exemption is a measure falling exclusively within the scope of the GATT 1994, as it affects trade in goods as goods, unlike other measures which involve a service relating to a particular good or a service supplied in conjunction with a particular good, which are subject to both the GATT 1994 and the GATS.

10.239 We note that if, on the one hand, it could be argued that the import duty exemption directly affects trade in goods and that it does not directly govern the supply of distribution services, on the other hand it cannot be maintained that it does not indirectly affect the supply of distribution services. Like the measures at issue in the *EC - Bananas III* case, the import duty exemption granted only to manufacturer beneficiaries bears upon conditions of competition in the supply of distribution services, regardless of whether it directly governs or indirectly affects the supply of such services. In our view, therefore, the import duty exemption falls in the third category of measures, identified by the Appellate Body in *EC - Bananas III*, as involving "a service relating to a particular good or a service supplied in conjunction with a particular good", which "could be scrutinized under both the GATT 1994 and the GATS".

10.240 Canada points out that potentially all tariff measures could be found to affect trade in services, and particularly distribution services. It therefore argues that, if it is found that the import duty exemption is a measure affecting trade in services, other tariff measures would have to be seen as "measures affecting trade in services", which might lead to the anomalous result that some measures which are legal under the GATT could be found to be in violation of the GATS. For example, differential tariffs which are legal under GATT Articles XXIV and VI might be found to violate Article II of the GATS.

10.241 Canada also points out that its view that tariff measures cannot be considered measures affecting trade in services is supported by Addendum 1 to the Scheduling Guidelines (*Scheduling of Initial Commitments in Trade in Services: Explanatory Note - Addendum*, MTN.GNS/W/164/Add.1) which provides the following answer to question 6 on whether it is "necessary to reserve the right to impose customs duties and regulations on the movement of goods in relation to the supply of a service":

> "There is no requirement in the GATS to schedule a limitation to the effect that the cross-border movement of goods associated with the provision of a service may be subject to customs duties or other administrative charges. Such measures are subject to the disciplines of the GATT.".

10.242 In the present case the issue of measures which maybe legal under the GATT but constitute a violation of the GATS does not arise. More importantly, the issue before us is not the effect of the differential between the MFN rate of duty and the preferential zero-duty itself, but rather, the effect of measures which reserve access to duty-free goods to a closed category of service suppliers, while excluding others.

10.243 We note that although the answer to the question on custom duties in the Addendum to the Scheduling Guidelines makes it clear that Members are not required to schedule customs duties, the measures which are claimed to be inconsistent with the GATS in this case are not "customs duties and regulations on the movement of goods in relation to the supply of a service", but regulations which reserve access to duty-free goods to a closed category of service suppliers, i.e. manufacturer beneficiaries, while excluding others. Canada would not therefore be required to schedule the differential tariff rates applied to imports of motor vehicles; it would only be required to schedule limitations and/or list MFN exemptions relating to measures which prevent certain distributors from having access to the right to import motor vehicles duty free.

10.244 The complainants argue that there is no difference in nature between the import duty exemption and the measures at issue in the *EC - Bananas III* case. The first, like the second, confers a tariff advantage on a restricted category of suppliers, which allows them to import and resell under more favourable conditions. The complainants note that the tariff quota at issue in *EC - Bananas III* did not prevent operators from obtaining licences, as licences were freely tradeable. However, importers who had been allocated licences by the European Communities would be able to retain the "tariff quota rent" (the advantage of importing in-quota goods at preferential rates), while other operators would have to buy licences at an additional cost on the market. The complainants also note that if it is the case that the measures at issue in *EC - Bananas III* and the import duty exemption are of the same type, differences in the intensity of their restrictive effect should not matter in the determination of whether the measures affect trade in services, as there is no *de minimis* rule in Article II or XVII of the GATS.

10.245 Regarding the analogy with the measures at issue in the *EC - Bananas III* case, Canada responds that the measure which determined the allocation of licences in that case directly affected the importers/distributors of bananas, while in the present case the differential duty on motor vehicles affects only trade in goods. Moreover, according to Canada, in *EC - Bananas III* the issue of the effect on distribution services of an existing differential duty was not even addressed by the panel. Canada also makes the point that, unlike differential duties such as those resulting from the import duty exemption, the quota for the allocation of licences in *EC - Bananas III* made it impossible for some distributors to obtain licences and this restrictive effect was not mitigated by the fact that the licences were freely tradeable, as the tariff quota rent charged by licence holders was substantial.

10.246 We note that both sets of measures allow some wholesale trade service suppliers to import and resell under more favourable conditions, while putting at a competitive disadvantage other suppliers, who have to pay the tariff or buy licences out of the tariff quota. Canada's claim that the tariff quota and licensing system in *EC - Bananas III*, unlike the import duty exemption under the Auto Pact, "was critical to the scope and profitability of the provision of services by the independent banana distributors and to the ability of even the integrated distributors to import at all" appears to be based on a quantitative assessment of the effect of the measures at issue, rather than on a distinction between tariff measures and import quotas: in the *EC - Bananas III* case, in spite of the quota system, licences were freely tradeable, so that the effect of the system was to put some distributors at a competitive disadvantage rather than to prevent them from selling in-quota bananas. In both cases there is an economic disadvantage. We note, therefore, that it is not relevant to distinguish between the measures at issue in *EC - Bananas III* and the measures at issue in this case on the basis of the *extent* of their effect on trade in services.

(b) Whether Service Suppliers Are "Like"

10.247 The complainants argue, and Canada does not contest, that manufacturer beneficiaries and non-manufacturer-beneficiaries provide "like" services and are "like" service suppliers, irrespective of whether their services are supplied with respect to motor vehicles imported by the manufacturer beneficiaries or with respect to motor vehicles imported by non-manufacturer-beneficiaries, and regardless of whether or not they have production facilities in Canada.

10.248 We agree that to the extent that the service suppliers concerned supply the same services, they should be considered "like" for the purpose of this case.

(c) Whether Treatment No Less Favourable Is Accorded

(i) Structure of Competition in the Wholesale Trade Services Market

10.249 Canada argues that it is not possible to establish whether treatment no less favourable has been granted or not, due to vertical integration and exclusive distribution arrangements existing in the motor vehicle industry between manufacturers and wholesale trade service suppliers, which exclude any actual or potential competition at the wholesale trade level. Canada points out that the characteristics of the motor vehicles industry also prevent vertically integrated companies from wholesaling vehicles manufactured by other companies. According to Canada, this factor should distinguish this case from *EC -- Bananas III*, where it was held that, in spite of vertical integration, the characteristics of the industry allowed even operators forming part of vertically integrated companies to enter the wholesale service market.

10.250 The complainants point out that, in spite of vertical integration and exclusive distribution agreements in the motor vehicle industry, it is possible to establish less favourable treatment of wholesale trade services suppliers because there is potential competition among wholesalers for the procurement of vehicles from manufacturers and actual competition for sales to retailers of directly competitive vehicles. They argue that the existence of potential competition for purchases from manufacturers is confirmed by the fact that in the past Chrysler, a company of United States origin, distributed in Canada vehicles manufactured by Mitsubishi, a company of Japanese origin. The complainants also rely on the ruling of the Appellate Body in *EC - Bananas III*, which held that "even if a company is vertically integrated ... to the extent that it is also engaged in providing 'wholesale trade services' ... that company is a service supplier within the scope of the GATS."[902]

10.251 Canada responds that the Chrysler-Mitsubishi relationship is not a good example of competition in the wholesale trade market, as the two companies were related through a joint venture agreement. It also contests that actual competition exists for sales to retailers, as, due to exclusive distribution arrangements between manufacturers and wholesalers, retailers will always have to address the same wholesaler for a particular brand of vehicle.

10.252 We note that in the *EC - Bananas III* case the Appellate Body found that:

> " ... even if a company is vertically integrated ... to the extent that it is also engaged in providing 'wholesale trade services' ... that company is a service supplier within the scope of the GATS". [903]

10.253 In our view, vertical integration of production and distribution does not exclude the possibility of considering the distribution operator as a service supplier, which may be affected in its capacity as a service supplier by measures such as the import duty exemption, regardless of whether actual competition exists in the wholesale trade market. We also note that vertical integration might determine the absence of actual competition among wholesalers with respect to the procurement of vehicles from manufacturers, but it neither rules out potential competition in the wholesaler-manufacturer relationship, nor actual competition in the wholesaler-retailer relationship. Although due to the existing structure of the market, wholesale trade service suppliers procure their vehicles from the same manufacturers, no government measure prevents even a vertically integrated wholesale distributor from approaching different manufacturers for the procurement of motor vehicles. Regarding competition for sales to retailers, the fact that, due to exclusive distribution arrangements between manufacturers and wholesalers, retailers have to address the same wholesaler for a particular brand of vehicle (absence of intra-brand competition), does not exclude

[902] Ibid., para. 227.
[903] Ibid., para. 227.

competition among wholesalers providing directly competitive vehicles (inter-brand competition).

10.254 We therefore **find** that vertical integration and exclusive distribution arrangements between manufacturers and wholesalers in the motor vehicle industry do not rule out the possibility that treatment less favourable may be granted to suppliers of wholesale trade services for motor vehicles. We also **find** that vertical integration and exclusive distribution arrangements do not preclude potential competition among wholesalers for the procurement of vehicles from manufacturers and actual inter-brand competition for sales to retailers.

(ii) Manufacturing presence and closed list of Auto Pact manufacturer beneficiaries

10.255 The complainants argue that although the criteria for eligibility for the import duty exemption are not expressly based on nationality, the import duty exemption constitutes *de facto* discrimination under Article II of the GATS as all or almost all services suppliers of other Members who benefit from the exemption are of the United States. Canada responds that not only is nationality not a criterion for granting the import duty exemption under the Auto Pact, but also that the measures do not *de facto* grant more favourable treatment to the suppliers of one Member, namely, the United States. Canada points out that at least two manufacturer beneficiaries are of EC origin (Volvo Canada Ltd. and DaimlerChrysler Canada Inc.), and one is a 50/50 joint venture between juridical persons of Japan and the United States (CAMI Automotive Inc.). This claim is rejected by the European Communities and Japan. In their replies to question 57 from the Panel both complainants have maintained that the import duty exemption results in *de facto* discrimination, but have also pointed out that in their view the existence of a closed list of manufacturer beneficiaries constitutes formally different treatment.

10.256 We note that Article XXVIII(m) of the GATS provides the following definition of a "juridical person of another Member":

> "'juridical person of another Member' means a juridical person which is either:
>
> (i) constituted or otherwise organized under the law of that other Member, and is engaged in substantive business operations in the territory of that Member or any other Member; or
>
> (ii) in the case of the supply of a service through commercial presence, owned or controlled by:
>
> 1. natural persons of that Member; or
> 2. juridical persons of that other Member identified under subparagraph (i)."

10.257 In our view, DaimlerChrysler Canada Inc. is a service supplier of the United States within the meaning of Article XXVIII(m)(ii)(2) of the GATS, because it is controlled by DaimlerChrysler Corporation, a juridical person of the United States according to subparagaph (i) of Article XXVIII(m). What is relevant, therefore, is that DaimlerChrysler Corporation is a juridical person of the United States. The fact that, in turn, DaimlerChrysler Corporation may be controlled by a juridical person of another Member is not relevant under Article XXVIII of the GATS. In order to define a "juridical person of another Member" Article XXVIII(m) of the GATS does not require the identification of the ultimate controlling juridical or natural person: it is sufficient to establish ownership or control by a juridical person of another Member, defined according to the criteria set out in subparagraph (i).[904]

10.258 Regarding CAMI Automotive Inc., it appears that it is a company jointly owned by Suzuki Motor Co. of Japan and by General Motors Corp. of the United States. The European Communities have argued that, although CAMI is jointly owned by juridical persons of Japan and of the United States, it should be regarded as a juridical person of the United States as it is controlled by General Motors Corp., a juridical person of the United States. The European Communities points out that General Motors Corp. is the largest single shareholder of Suzuki Motor Co. and that Japanese nationals constitute a minority in the board of directors of CAMI. In our view, however, no evidence has been presented which would allow the Panel to determine which juridical person "controls" CAMI, within the meaning of Article XXVIII(n)(ii) of the GATS.

10.259 As regards Volvo Canada Ltd., it should be noted that ownership and control of this company passed from Volvo AB of Sweden to Ford Motor Co. of the United States in January 1999, when the former agreed to sell its passenger car business to the latter. As a consequence, Volvo Canada Ltd. is now a juridical person of the United States according to Article XXVIII(m) of the GATS. Moreover, as Volvo Canada Ltd. closed its Canadian plant in December 1998, it would lose its right to import motor vehicles duty free under the import duty exemption.

10.260 The MVTO 1998 restricts eligibility for the import duty exemption to manufacturers who had operated in Canada in the base year 1963-64, while SROs allowed other individual manufacturers to qualify until 1989, subject to manufacturing presence and CVA requirements referring to different base years. Eligibility for SROs, however, ended in 1989, effectively freezing the *status quo* of the beneficiaries of the import duty exemption. This is confirmed by Canada's reply to question 37 from the Panel, which says that the list of manufacturers under the SROs cannot be expanded, but only updated to reflect a change in a company's name or to remove companies that have ceased manufacturing. The category of manufacturer beneficiaries is therefore currently a closed one, so that after 1989 it became impossible for other manufacturers/wholesalers to fulfil the criteria required in order to qualify for the import duty exemption.

10.261 Although none of the criteria for granting the import duty exemption is expressly based on nationality, the manufacturing presence requirement, referring to the period 1 August 1963 - 31 July 1964 in the MVTO 1998, has allowed only three service suppliers of the United States (Chrysler Canada Ltd., General Motors of Canada Ltd. and Ford Motor Company of Canada Ltd.) and one service supplier of Swe-

---

904 In the *EC - Bananas III* case, on the point of the determination of the origin of a juridical person, the panel stated that: "... suppliers which are commercially present within the EC territory and owned or controlled by, for example, Del Monte Mexico would be entitled to benefit from GATS rights because it would not matter under Article XXVIII(m) of GATS whether Del Monte Mexico was owned or controlled by natural or juridical persons of Jordan, i.e. a WTO non-Member, as long as Del Monte Mexico was incorporated in Mexico and engaged in substantive business operations in the territory of Mexico or any other Member." See, Panel Report on *EC - Bananas III (USA)*, *supra* note 269, footnote 493, para. 7.318.

den (Volvo Canada Ltd.) to qualify for the import duty exemption.[905] It was noted above that Volvo Canada Ltd. recently passed under the control of a juridical person of the United States (Ford Motor Co.). SROs have been used to expand the category of manufacturer beneficiaries by allowing two other manufacturers/wholesalers of automobiles (Intermeccanica of Canada and CAMI, a 50/50 joint venture between Suzuki Motor Co. of Japan and General Motors Corp. of the United States) and several manufacturers/wholesalers of buses and specified commercial vehicles to qualify for the import duty exemption.

10.262 In our view, the import duty exemption, as provided in the MVTO 1998 and SROs, results in less favourable treatment accorded to services and service suppliers of any other Member within the meaning of Article II:1 of the GATS, as such benefit is granted to a limited and identifiable group of manufacturers/wholesalers of motor vehicles of some Members, selected on the basis of criteria such as the manufacturing presence in a given base year. We also note that the manufacturing presence requirements in the MVTO 1998 and in the SROs explicitly exclude suppliers of wholesale trade services of motor vehicles, which do not manufacture vehicles in Canada, from qualifying for the import duty exemption. In addition, the fact that in 1989 the Government of Canada stopped granting SROs makes the list of the beneficiaries of the import duty exemption a closed one. As a result, manufacturers/wholesalers of motor vehicles of some Members can import vehicles into Canada duty-free, while manufacturers/wholesalers of other Members are explicitly prevented from importing vehicles duty free into Canada.

10.263 We do not address separately the claim by Japan that the import duty exemption is inconsistent with the requirement in Article II that treatment no less favourable be accorded "immediately and unconditionally", as in our view this claim is addressed by our finding relating to whether the import duty exemption constitutes "treatment less favourable" within the meaning of Article II of the GATS.

10.264 In light of the foregoing, we **find** that with respect to the import duty exemption, granted to a limited number of manufacturers/wholesalers of motor vehicles, Canada has failed to accord immediately and unconditionally to services and service suppliers of any other Member treatment no less favourable than it accords to like services and service suppliers of any other country. We **find**, therefore, that the import duty exemption accorded pursuant to the MVTO 1998 and the SROs is inconsistent with the requirements of Article II:1 of the GATS.

4. *Applicability of Article V of the GATS*

10.265 In its third-party submission the United States claims that the MVTO 1998 and SROs, to the extent that they provide more favourable treatment to service suppliers of the United States, are subject to the exception to Article II of the GATS conferred by Article V:1 of the GATS. According to the United States this is so, because the more favourable treatment the complainants are seeking to condemn is

[905] The MVTO 1965, which implemented the Canada-US Auto Pact in Canada, originally applied to six automobile producers (American Motors, Chrysler, Ford, General Motors, Studebaker and Volvo), all of North American origin with the exception of Volvo, and to a number of producers of specified commercial vehicles and buses.

being accorded by a member of an economic integration agreement of the type specified by Article V:1, the North American Free Trade Agreement (NAFTA), to the service suppliers of another Member of that agreement. The United States also points out that the services provisions of NAFTA clearly fall within the terms of GATS Article V:1. Canada does not invoke Article V, as it maintains that the MVTO 1998 and SROs are not measures affecting trade in services within the meaning of Article I of the GATS. However, if the Panel were to find that the MVTO 1998 and SROs were measures affecting trade in services inconsistent with Article II of the GATS, Canada argues that they are covered by Article V:1 of the GATS.

10.266 The complainants argue that Article V cannot apply to the facts of this case, because the MVTO 1998 and SROs are unilateral measures and cannot be considered an "agreement" within the meaning of Article V:1 of the GATS (the original Auto Pact is no longer being implemented by the United States). The complainants also point out that even if the MVTO 1998 and SROs were to be considered an agreement within the meaning of Article V:1 of the GATS, this would lack the substantial sectoral coverage required by Article V:1(a), it would fail to eliminate substantially all discrimination in the sense of Article XVII between or among the parties (Article V:1(b)) and it would raise the overall level of barriers to trade in services in the sector (Article V:4). Both complainants also point out that the MVTO 1998 and SROs cannot be considered a part of NAFTA, as NAFTA contains prohibitions on import duty exemptions and perfomance requirements. They note that NAFTA does not require, it merely allows Canada to maintain the MVTO 1998 and SROs by means of express exceptions.

10.267 We note that Article V:1 of the GATS provides in relevant part:

> "1. This Agreement shall not prevent any of its Members from being a party to or entering into an agreement liberalizing trade in services between or among the parties to such an agreement, provided that such an agreement:
>
> (a) has substantial sectoral coverage (*footnote omitted*), and
>
> (b) provides for the absence or elimination of substantially all discrimination, in the sense of Article XVII, between or among the parties, in the sectors covered under subparagraph (a), through:
>
> (i) elimination of existing discriminatory measures, and/or
>
> (ii) prohibition of new or more discriminatory measures"

10.268 We note the argument of the United States that the measures at issue in this case are covered by Article V:1 of the GATS because they are accorded by a member of NAFTA to the service suppliers of another member of the same economic integration agreement. In our view, however, the MVTO 1998 and SROs are measures which cannot be considered as part of NAFTA provisions on liberalization of trade in services; rather, NAFTA members have agreed to allow their continued implementation through specific exceptions granted to Canada. Paragraph 1 of Annex 300-A.1 of NAFTA states that "Canada and the United States may maintain the Agreement Concerning Automotive Products between the Government of Canada and the Government of the United States of America". Annex I - Canada of the NAFTA also states that "Canada may grant waivers of custom duties conditioned, explicitly or implicitly, on the fulfilment of performance requirements".

10.269 Even assuming that the MVTO 1998 and the SROs could be brought within the scope of the services liberalization provisions of NAFTA, we note that the import duty exemption under the MVTO 1998 and SROs is accorded to a small number of manufacturers/wholesalers of the United States to the exclusion of all other manufacturers/wholesalers of the United States and of Mexico. The MVTO 1998 and SROs, therefore, provide more favourable treatment to only some and not all services and service suppliers of Members of NAFTA, while, according to Article V:1(b), an economic integration agreement has to provide for "the absence or elimination of substantially all discrimination, in the sense of Article XVII", in order to be eligible for the exemption from Article II of the GATS.

10.270 Although the requirement of Article V:1(b) is to provide non-discrimination in the sense of Article XVII (National Treatment), we consider that once it is fulfilled it would also ensure non-discrimination between all service suppliers of other parties to the economic integration agreement. It is our view that the object and purpose of this provision is to eliminate all discrimination among services and service suppliers of parties to an economic integration agreement, including discrimination between suppliers of other parties to an economic integration agreement. In other words, it would be inconsistent with this provision if a party to an economic integration agreement were to extend more favourable treatment to service suppliers of one party than that which it extended to service suppliers of another party to that agreement.

10.271 Moreover, it is worth recalling that Article V provides legal coverage for measures taken pursuant to economic integration agreements, which would otherwise be inconsistent with the MFN obligation in Article II. Paragraph 1 of Article V refers to "an agreement liberalizing trade in services". Such economic integration agreements typically aim at achieving higher levels of liberalization between or among their parties than that achieved among WTO Members. Article V:1 further prescribes a certain minimum level of liberalization which such agreements must attain in order to qualify for the exemption from the general MFN obligation of Article II. In this respect, the purpose of Article V is to allow for ambitious liberalization to take place at a regional level, while at the same time guarding against undermining the MFN obligation by engaging in minor preferential arrangements. However, in our view, it is not within the object and purpose of Article V to provide legal coverage for the extension of more favourable treatment only to a few service suppliers of parties to an economic integration agreement on a selective basis, even in situations where the maintenance of such measures may explicitly be provided for in the agreement itself.

10.272 In light of the foregoing, we **find** that Article V:1 of the GATS does not exempt Canada from its obligations under Article II of the GATS with respect to the MVTO 1998 and SROs.

5. *Claims Under Article XVII of the GATS - Import Duty Exemption*

10.273 Japan alone claims that the import duty exemption also violates Article XVII of the GATS in that it constitutes more favourable treatment accorded to Canadian services and service suppliers, which have the right to import vehicles duty free, than to Japanese ones who do not.

10.274 We note that Article XVII of the GATS establishes that:

> "1. In the sectors inscribed in its Schedule, and subject to any conditions and qualifications set out therein, each Member shall accord to services and service suppliers of any other Member, in respect of all measures affecting the supply of services, treatment no less favourable than that it accords to its own like services and service suppliers. (*Footnote reads:* Specific commitments assumed under this Article shall not be considered to require any Member to compensate for any inherent competitive disadvantages which result from the foreign character of the relevant services or service suppliers.)
>
> 2. A Member may meet the requirement of paragraph 1 by according to services and service suppliers of any other Member, either formally identical treatment or formally different treatment to that it accords to its own like services and service suppliers.
>
> 3. Formally identical or formally different treatment shall be considered to be less favourable if it modifies the conditions of competition in favour of services or service suppliers of the Member compared to like services or service suppliers of any other Member."

10.275 Japan claims that the import duty exemption affects the supply of wholesale trade services, as it modifies the conditions of competition between Canadian beneficiaries of the duty-free treatment and foreign wholesale trade service suppliers of imported motor vehicles which do not benefit from the same treatment. In particular, the import duty exemption would directly affect the cost of the goods being distributed and indirectly affect the cost and/or profitability of the related wholesale trade services.

10.276 Canada argues that the import duty exemption is not a measure affecting trade in services within the meaning of Article I of the GATS, because, as a tariff measure, it affects the goods themselves and not the supply of distribution services. According to Canada, such measures do not affect a service supplier in its capacity as service supplier and in its supply of a service. Canada further argues that: (i) it has not undertaken commitments in wholesale trade services of motor vehicles; (ii) if it had undertaken commitments it did not need to schedule custom duties as national treatment limitations; (iii) there are no "like" Canadian and Japanese suppliers of wholesale trade services for motor vehicles in Canada; and (iv) as with Article II, it is not possible to argue that the import duty exemption modifies the conditions of competition among wholesale trade suppliers of motor vehicles because, due to vertical integration and exclusive distribution between manufacturers and wholesalers of motor vehicles, there is no competition to be affected at the wholesale trade level.

10.277 Our analysis with respect to the Article II claim on how the import duty exemption affects wholesale trade services of motor vehicles, within the meaning of Article I of the GATS, also applies to this claim under Article XVII of the GATS (see above, paragraphs 10.239-10.246).

(a) Whether Canada Has Undertaken Commitments on Wholesale Trade Services of Motor Vehicles

10.278 Japan argues that Canada's Schedule of Specific Commitments includes wholesale trade of motor vehicles either under the general entry "*B. Wholesale trade services*" or under the more specific entry "*Sale of motor vehicles including automo-*

biles and other road vehicles", United Nations Provisional Central Product Classification (CPC) number 6111. Japan also points out that under "*B. Wholesale trade services*", Canada lists a limitation for the state of Saskatchewan applying to "sale of motor vehicles". According to Japan, by inserting this limitation Canada is implying that its commitments on wholesale trade services also include wholesale services for motor vehicles. Canada responds that its entry "*B. Wholesale trade services*" expressly refers to CPC 622, which excludes distribution of motor vehicles and that the insertion of a limitation with respect to motor vehicles is a scheduling error. It also points out that CPC entry "6111" is inscribed under the heading "*C. Retail services*" and therefore should be read as a commitment only on retail services for motor vehicles.

10.279 We note that the CPC entry 622 (Wholesale trade services) does not have a sub-heading for motor vehicles, and that sub-heading 62282 (Wholesale trade services of transport equipment other than motor vehicles, motorcycles and bicycles) expressly excludes motor vehicles. In our view, the fact that Canada has inscribed a limitation applying to motor vehicles with respect to the entry "Wholesale trade services (622)" in its schedule does not in itself constitute sufficient evidence to conclude that it has undertaken a commitment on wholesale trade services of motor vehicles.

10.280 Nevertheless, Canada has also listed in its schedule of commitments an entry for "Sale of motor vehicles including automobiles and other road vehicles" with an explicit reference to CPC number 6111. In the United Nations Provisional Central Product Classification, the entry "6111 Sale of motor vehicles including automobiles and other road vehicles" includes two sub-headings: "61111 Wholesale trade services of motor vehicles"; and "61112 Retail sales of motor vehicles". In our view, if Canada had meant to limit this commitment only to retail services it should have inscribed entry 61112 (Retail sales of motor vehicles) in its schedule rather than 6111 (Sale of motor vehicles).

10.281 We note that there is a discrepancy between the inclusion of the whole CPC entry 6111 and the heading of the commitment ("C. Retailing services") in page 48 of Canada's schedule. However, the fact that entry 6111 has been listed under the heading *C. Retailing services* does not constitute sufficient evidence to exclude a commitment with respect to wholesale trade services of motor vehicles. If the heading were to prevail, the systemic impact would be that all unqualified CPC numbers in Members' schedules of commitments, referring to clearly and precisely defined subsectors, would be undermined, at least when their combination with headings is inconsistent. For these reasons we consider that the description of the CPC should prevail and that the commitments contained in page 48 of Canada's schedule also apply to wholesale trade of motor vehicles.

10.282 We **find** therefore that, by inscribing the CPC entry "6111 Sale of motor vehicles including automobiles and other road vehicles" in its schedule of specific commitments, Canada has undertaken a commitment also covering "61111 Wholesale trade services of motor vehicles".

(b) Whether Services Are "Like"

10.283 Japan contends that there are "like" Japanese and Canadian wholesale service suppliers of motor vehicles, including automobiles as well as buses and specified commercial vehicles. Canada contests the existence of like wholesale service suppliers. Japan points out that while some Canadian suppliers have qualified for the import duty exemption under SROs (Intermeccanica and three manufacturers of buses and specified commercial vehicles), Japanese suppliers cannot import vehicles duty-free, unless they acquire, or are acquired by, a Canadian subsidiary of one of the existing manufacturer beneficiaries.

10.284 Canada points out that Intermeccanica is "unlike" any Japanese wholesale service supplier of motor vehicles because it is not a wholesaler but only a manufacturer and even if it were a wholesaler, its size, sales volumes and the products it manufactures are vastly different from those of any of the establishments identified by Japan as suppliers of wholesale trade services of motor vehicles. According to Japan, the scale of companies and the nature of the products they supply should not affect the determination of likeness, insofar as service suppliers supply services listed in the same CPC category. In this respect Japan argues that Intermeccanica is "like" other Japanese suppliers of wholesale trade services for motor vehicles in Canada.

10.285 In our view, Intermeccanica, which manufactures and sells directly to consumers a small number of vehicles (artisanal replica racing cars) per year, should not be considered a supplier of wholesale trade services of motor vehicles, as it does not seem to be supplying "wholesale trade services of motor vehicles" as defined in CPC 6111.

10.286 With respect to wholesale trade services suppliers of buses and specified commercial vehicles, Canada argues that Japan has failed to identify any Canadian or Japanese suppliers of these services. Japan contests this allegation, arguing that there is at least one Japanese supplier operating in Canada (Hino Diesel Trucks) and that other Japanese wholesale trade service suppliers of motor vehicles have the capability to produce and distribute buses or specified commercial vehicles. Japan also points out that in response to question 2(4) from Japan, Canada has listed 15 companies which have imported and distributed vehicles other than automobiles under the MVTOs and SROs at least once in the last 10 years. According to Japan, at least three of these companies are of Canadian origin in accordance with Article XXVIII(m) of the GATS.

10.287 In response to a supplemental question from the Panel, Japan has produced supporting material to demonstrate that three companies which were granted the import duty exemption under SROs, A. Girardin Inc., Michel Corbeil Inc., and Western Star Trucks Inc., are juridical persons of Canada according to Article XXVIII(m) of the GATS. In response to another supplemental question from the Panel, Canada has confirmed that, to its knowledge A. Girardin Inc. and Michel Corbeil Inc. are Canadian-owned companies. Regarding Western Star Trucks Inc., Canada has pointed out that it is wholly owned by another Canadian incorporated company (Western Star Trucks Holding Ltd.), which in turn is controlled by a Singaporean incorporated company (Western Star International).

10.288 Canada, however, argues that Japan has failed to prove that the three Canadian companies, which have benefited from the import duty exemption, are suppliers of wholesale trade services. Canada points out that these companies may import buses or chassis for specified commercial vehicles as inputs for finished vehicles; they may re-import vehicles of their own manufacture that have been exported for modification in other countries; or they may import vehicles as retailers. Canada points out, however, that none of these activities would constitute supply of wholesale trade services, which consists principally in re-selling merchandise, according to the definition contained in Section 6 of the CPC.

10.289 Regarding wholesale trade services of buses and specified commercial vehicles, we note that Japan has identified one Japanese service supplier and argued that Japanese wholesale suppliers of automobiles could enter the market. We further note that the CPC entry "6111 sale of motor vehicles including automobiles and other road vehicles" also includes wholesale trade of buses and specified commercial vehicles. In our view, however, there is no clear evidence before the Panel that the Canadian manufacturers of buses and specified commercial vehicles, which benefit from the import duty exemption, also supply wholesale trade services of motor vehicles as defined in the CPC. Canada has contested that these companies are "like" suppliers of wholesale trade services for motor vehicles and Japan, with whom the burden of proof rests, has not produced evidence to demonstrate the contrary. We note that, in the absence of "like" domestic service suppliers, a measure by a Member cannot be found to be inconsistent with the national treatment obligation in Article XVII of the GATS.

10.290 Accordingly, we **find** that Japan has failed to demonstrate that the import duty exemption accorded pursuant to the MVTO 1998 and the SROs constitutes treatment less favourable accorded to Japanese service suppliers than that accorded to like Canadian service suppliers.

6. Claims Under Article XVII of the GATS - CVA Requirement

10.291 The CVA requirements in the MVTO 1998 and in SROs require manufacturer beneficiaries to achieve a minimum of Canadian value-added, a part of which may be made up through the purchase of services supplied in Canada, as a condition for obtaining the import duty exemption. With respect to services, Canadian value-added means the part of the following costs that is reasonably attributable to the production of motor vehicles: (i) the cost of maintenance and repair work executed in Canada on buildings, machinery and equipment used for production purposes; (ii) the cost of engineering services, experimental work and product development work executed in Canada; (iii) administrative and general expenses incurred in Canada. The European Communities notes that CVA also includes (iv) "fire and insurance premiums, in respect of production inventories and the production plant and equipment, paid to a company authorised by federal or provincial law to carry on business in Canada or a province".

(a) CVA Requirements as Affecting Services Related to the Production of Motor Vehicles

10.292 The complainants argue that the CVA requirements provide an incentive for the beneficiaries of the import duty exemption to use services supplied within the Canadian territory rather than like services supplied in or from the territory of other Members, thus modifying the conditions of competition among them. Canada does not contest the claim that CVA requirements affect the supply of services.

10.293 We note that the CVA requirements, in stipulating that only services supplied domestically may count toward CVA, affect directly the services which are supplied through modes 1 and 2. We therefore need to determine whether such effect is consistent with Canada's commitments under Article XVII.

(b) Whether Services Affected by the CVA Requirements Are Covered by Canada's Specific Commitments in Services

10.294 The complainants argue that all services affected by the CVA requirements are included in Canada's schedule of specific commitments, while none of the limitations inscribed cover the CVA requirements. Canada points out that relevant national treatment limitations have been inscribed for potentially affected services listed by the complainants.

10.295 In addition, the complainants argue that there are several services affected by the CVA requirements which can be supplied though modes 1 and 2, where Canada has scheduled no limitations and that, even in those sectors where limitations have been scheduled, such limitations do not exempt Canada from its Article XVII obligations with respect to the CVA requirements.[906] They point out that the CVA requirements are not listed as limitations in Canada's schedule of commitments and that other limitations such as nationality, residency or establishment requirements, which would impede the supply of a service cross-border, cannot be used to justify the CVA requirements. For this purpose the complainants refer to the answer to question 7 in the Addendum 1 to the Scheduling Guidelines (*Scheduling of Initial Commitments in Trade in Services: Explanatory Note - Addendum*, MTN.GNS/W/164/Add.1).[907] Canada responds that limitations which it had sched-

[906] (1) With respect to the first CVA requirement, "maintenance and repair work executed in Canada on buildings, machinery and equipment used for production purposes," the complainants note that Canada has included the following services in its schedule of specific commitments: *repair services incidental to metal products, machinery and equipment including computers and communication equipment on a fee or contract basis (CPC 8861 to 8866)*; (2) with respect to the second CVA requirement, "engineering services, experimental work and product development work executed in Canada," the complainants note that Canada's has included the following services in its schedule of specific commitments: *engineering services (CPC 8672)*; (3) With respect to the third CVA requirement, "administrative and general expenses incurred in Canada," the complainants note several services sectors included in Canada's schedule of specific commitments including: *professional services, computer related services, other business services, banking services, telecommunication services, courier services and travel services*; (4) With respect to the fourth CVA requirement, "fire and insurance premiums, in respect of production inventories and the production plant and equipment, paid to a company authorised by federal or provincial law to carry on business in Canada or a province" the European Communities notes that Canada has included the following services in its schedule of specific commitments: *non-life insurance services (CPC 8129).*

[907] "*How relevant is a reservation for a residence requirement, nationality condition or commercial presence requirement under cross-border trade: does that not rather imply that cross-border trade is not allowed and therefore the correct entry should be 'unbound'?*"

"It is correct to use the term 'unbound' for a mode of supply in a given sector where a Member wishes to remain free to introduce or maintain measures inconsistent with market access or national treatment. However, it has been pointed out by participants that in some cases there is advantage in inscribing a particular limitation (e.g., a residency requirement or a commercial presence requirement) instead of the term 'unbound' in that trading partners have the certainty that there are no other limitations with respect to the cross-border mode. (See also para. 8 of the scheduling guide on residency requirements, and para. 6 on nationality requirements.)"

uled such as nationality, residency or establishment requirements make the supply of a service through modes 1 and 2 impossible, so that where these limitations exist, the CVA requirements cannot violate Article XVII.

10.296 We note that Canada has undertaken specific commitments in all the sectors listed by the complainants as being affected by the CVA requirements and that it has inscribed some partial limitations on national treatment with respect to some of these sectors. In our view, however, even the national treatment limitations which have been scheduled, however restrictive, cannot be deemed to also cover the CVA requirements. Only a specific limitation referring to the CVA requirements or an "unbound" entry would achieve this effect, as the inscription of another specific limitation (such as a residency requirement or a commercial presence requirement) would imply that there are no other limitations than the one listed with respect to the cross-border mode.

10.297 We find, therefore, that Canada has undertaken specific commitments in those sectors which the complainants claim to be affected by the CVA requirements, and that the limitations that have been listed do not cover the CVA requirements.

(c) Technical Feasibility and Inherent Competitive Disadvantage of Modes 1 and 2 Services

10.298 Canada points out that with respect to the first CVA requirement relating to services, "maintenance and repair work executed in Canada on buildings, machinery and equipment used for production purposes", there can be no discrimination against services supplied through modes 1 and 2, as cross-border supply and consumption abroad of these services are not technically feasible. On hotel and other lodging services and food and beverages services, it argues that choices regarding these services are dictated by geography and have nothing to do with the CVA requirements. According to Canada, the competitive disadvantage in the foreign provision of many services listed by the complainants as being affected by the CVA requirements is inherent in the foreign character of these services and, as stated in footnote 10 to Article XVII, should not be regarded as a national treatment restriction.

10.299 The complainants argue that even if inherent disadvantages due to foreign character existed for some modes 1 and 2 services, the disadvantages caused by the CVA could not be considered inherent. They point out that Canada's argument that modes 1 and 2 services relating to the production of motor vehicles are already inherently disadvantaged due to their foreign character contradicts the very aim of the CVA requirements, that is, to favour services supplied in Canada. In addition the complainants note that footnote 10 to Article XVII only exempts Members from having to compensate for inherent competitive disadvantages due to foreign character, while in this case Canada would only be required to abstain from taking a measure which creates a disadvantage for modes 1 and 2 suppliers.[908]

10.300 We consider that, although the supply of some repair and maintenance services on machinery and equipment through modes 1 and 2 might not be technically

[908] Footnote to Article XVII states: "Specific commitments assumed under this Article shall not be considered to require any Member to compensate for any inherent competitive disadvantages which result from the foreign character of the relevant services or service suppliers."

feasible, as they require the physical presence of the supplier, all other services listed by the complainants as being affected by the CVA requirements, including some consulting and advisory services relating to repair and maintenance of machinery, can be supplied through modes 1 and 2. We further consider that treatment less favourable granted to services supplied outside Canada cannot be justified on the basis of inherent disadvantages due to their foreign character. Footnote 10 to Article XVII only exempts Members from having to compensate for disadvantages due to foreign character in the application of the national treatment provision; it does not provide cover for actions which might modify the conditions of competition against services and service suppliers which are already disadvantaged due to their foreign character.

10.301 We therefore find that lack of technical feasibility only excludes the supply of some repair and maintenance services on machinery and equipment through modes 1 and 2 from Canada's national treatment obligation. We also find that any eventual inherent disadvantages due to the foreign character of services supplied through modes 1 and 2 do not exempt Canada from its national treatment obligation with respect to the CVA requirements.

(d) Whether it is Relevant that CVA Requirements Might Be Met on the Basis of Labour Costs Alone

10.302 Canada argues that, considering that (1) any possible effects of the CVA requirements impinge only on services supplied through modes 1 and 2, (2) relevant limitations have been inscribed in the schedule for the services sectors at issue, (3) the supply of some services through modes 1 and 2 is not technically feasible, and (4) no compensation is due for any inherent competitive disadvantage resulting from the foreign character of services; the complainants' national treatment claims should thus be limited to certain services that constitute "general and administrative expenses". According to Canada the inclusion of this last category of services in the list of CVA eligible expenses, however, does not affect the conditions of competition between Canadian and foreign service suppliers, as there is evidence that most of the qualifying manufacturers exceed their CVA requirement on the basis of labour costs alone.

10.303 The complainants note that the national treatment obligation in Article XVII of the GATS, like that of Article II of the GATT, protects competitive opportunities, not actual trade flows. They note that, if measures such as the CVA requirements create an incentive for using locally supplied services, it is not necessary to show that they have any actual effect on trade flows. Therefore, even if the CVA requirements were met by all manufacturer beneficiaries on the basis of labour costs alone, such measure would still constitute a violation of Article XVII, so long as there was discrimination in favour of services supplied in Canada against like services supplied outside Canada. Moreover, the complainants point out that with respect to the Article XVII claim, Canada argues that *most* of the qualifying manufacturers exceed their CVA requirements on the basis of labour costs alone, thus admitting implicitly that some manufacturers might not do so.

10.304 We note that Article XVII requires each Member to accord to services and service suppliers of any other Member treatment no less favourable than it accords to its own like services and service suppliers, and that it defines treatment less favourable as formally different or formally identical treatment which modifies the conditions of competition in favour of domestic services and service suppliers. In our view, the CVA requirements may affect the conditions of competition between services supplied in Canada and services of other Members supplied from outside Canada through modes 1 and 2, even where a manufacturer meets its CVA requirements on the basis of labour costs alone. In fact, CVA requirements constitute an incentive to purchase services supplied in Canada and such incentive will be effective unless the requirements for a given period of time have already been met through labour costs. Moreover, even where for a given period of time it is clear that CVA requirements are going to be met on the basis of labour costs alone, thus rendering redundant any possible incentive to purchase services supplied in Canada, there is no evidence that the CVA requirements will also be met in the future on the basis of labour costs alone and that, consequently, there will be no discriminatory effect on trade in services.

10.305 We, therefore, find that the fact that most manufacturer beneficiaries currently exceed their CVA requirements on the basis of labour costs alone does not undermine the role of the CVA requirements as a discriminatory incentive favouring services supplied in Canada against services supplied from outside Canada through modes 1 and 2.

(e) Whether Treatment No Less Favourable Is Accorded

10.306 The complainants argue that the phrases "executed in Canada" and "incurred in Canada" prevent the inclusion in the CVA requirements of all services supplied under modes 1 and 2. The complainants therefore claim that the CVA requirements constitute less favourable treatment granted to like services and service suppliers of other Members, in that they create an economic incentive for manufacturer beneficiaries to purchase services supplied in Canada, thus modifying the conditions of competition in favour of services supplied in Canada compared to those of other Members supplied through modes 1 and 2 (from and in the territory of other Members). Canada points out that the supply of services through modes 3 ("commercial presence") and 4 ("presence of natural persons") is unaffected by the CVA requirements as all mode 3 and 4 suppliers, Canadian and non-Canadian, can benefit from the CVA requirements.

10.307 We note that the CVA requirements in the MVTO 1998 and SROs do not discriminate between domestic and foreign services and service suppliers operating in Canada under modes 3 and 4. This observation, however, does not suffice to conclude that the requirements of Article XVII are met. In our view, it is reasonable to consider for the purposes of this case that services supplied in Canada through modes 3 and 4 and those supplied from the territory of other Members through modes 1 and 2 are "like" services. In turn, this leads to the conclusion that the CVA requirements provide an incentive for the beneficiaries of the import duty exemption to use services supplied within the Canadian territory over "like" services supplied in or from the territory of other Members through modes 1 and 2, thus modifying the conditions of competition in favour of services supplied within Canada. Although this requirement does not distinguish between services supplied by service suppliers of Canada and those supplied by service suppliers of other Members present in Canada, it is bound to have a discriminatory effect against services supplied through modes 1 and 2, which are services of other Members.

10.308 In light of the foregoing, we **find** that the CVA requirements on manufacturer beneficiaries contained in the MVTO 1998 and the SROs accord less favourable treatment to services of other Members supplied though modes 1 and 2 and are therefore inconsistent with Canada's obligations under Article XVII of the GATS.

XI. CONCLUSIONS AND RECOMMENDATIONS

A. *Conclusions*

11.1 In light of the above findings, we **conclude** as follows:

(a) Canada acts inconsistently with Article I:1 of the GATT 1994 by according the advantage of an import duty exemption to motor vehicles originating in certain countries, pursuant to the MVTO 1998 and the SROs, which advantage is not accorded immediately and unconditionally to like products originating in the territories of all other WTO Members;

(b) the inconsistency of these measures with Article I:1 of the GATT 1994 cannot be justified under Article XXIV of the GATT 1994;

(c) Canada acts inconsistently with Article III:4 of the GATT 1994 by according less favourable treatment to imported parts, materials and non-permanent equipment than to like domestic products with respect to their internal sale or use, as a result of application of the CVA requirements as one of the conditions determining eligibility for the import duty exemption on motor vehicles under the MVTO 1998, the SROs and as a result of conditions concerning CVA requirements contained in certain Letters of Undertaking;

(d) the European Communities has failed to demonstrate that Canada acts inconsistently with Article III:4 of the GATT 1994 by applying ratio requirements under the MVTO 1998 and the SROs as one of the conditions determining eligibility for the import duty exemption on motor vehicles;

(e) Canada acts inconsistently with its obligations under Article 3.1(a) of the SCM Agreement by granting a subsidy which is contingent in law upon export performance, as a result of the application of the ratio requirements as one of the conditions determining eligibility for the import duty exemption on motor vehicles under the MVTO 1998 and the SROs;

(f) The European Communities and Japan have failed to demonstrate that Canada acts inconsistently with its obligations under Article 3.1(b) of the SCM Agreements by granting a subsidy which is contingent upon the use of domestic over imported goods, as a result of the application of the CVA requirements as one of the conditions determining eligibility for the import duty exemption on motor vehicles under the MVTO 1998 and the SROs;

(g) Canada acts inconsistently with Article II of the GATS by failing to accord immediately and unconditionally to services and service suppliers of any other Member treatment no less favourable than that it accords to like services and service suppliers of any other country, with respect to the granting of the import duty exemption to a limited number of manufacturers/wholesalers of motor vehicles pursuant to the MVTO 1998 and the SROs;

(h) the inconsistency of these measures with Article II of the GATS cannot be justified under Article V of the GATS;

(i) Japan has failed to demonstrate that the import duty exemption granted pursuant to the MVTO 1998 and the SROs constitutes treatment less favourable accorded to Japanese suppliers of wholesale trade services of motor vehicles than that accorded to like Canadian service suppliers, within the meaning of Article XVII of the GATS; and

(j) Canada acts inconsistently with Article XVII of the GATS by according treatment less favourable to services and service suppliers of other Members, supplied through modes 1 and 2, than it accords to its own like services and service suppliers, as a result of the application of the CVA requirements as one of the conditions determining eligibility for the import duty exemption on motor vehicles under the MVTO 1998 and the SROs.

11.2 Under Article 3.8 of the DSU, in cases where there is infringement of the obligations assumed under a covered agreement, the action is considered *prima facie* to constitute a case of nullification or impairment of benefits under that agreement. Accordingly, we conclude that to the extent that Canada has acted inconsistently with the provisions of the covered agreements, as described in the preceding paragraph, it has nullified or impaired benefits accruing to the complainants under those agreements.

B. Recommendations

11.3 With respect to our conclusions regarding Canada's obligations under Articles I:1 and III:4 of the GATT 1994, and Articles II and XVII of the GATS, the Panel *recommends* that the Dispute Settlement Body request Canada to bring its measures into conformity with its obligations under the WTO Agreement.

11.4 With respect to our conclusions regarding Canada's obligations under the SCM Agreement, we note that Article 4.7 of the SCM Agreement provides:

> "If the measure in question is found to be a prohibited subsidy, the panel shall recommend that the subsidising Member withdraw the subsidy without delay. In this regard, the panel shall specify in its recommendation the time-period within which the measure must be withdrawn."

11.5 Accordingly, we **recommend** that the Dispute Settlement Body request Canada to withdraw the export subsidy without delay.

11.6 With respect to the time-period within which the measure must be withdrawn, Article 4.7 of the SCM Agreement requires a Member to withdraw the prohibited subsidy "without delay" and it is "in this regard" that a panel must specify a time-period within which the prohibited subsidy must be withdrawn. The noun "delay" has been defined to mean, *inter alia*, "the action or process of delaying; procrastination; lingering; putting off", while the verb to "delay" has been defined, *inter alia*, as to "put off to a later time; postpone, defer".[909] Thus, in its ordinary meaning, the phrase "without delay" suggests that the Member must not put off, postpone or defer action, but must rather act as quickly as possible to withdraw the prohibited subsidy. Thus, in examining what time-period would represent withdrawal "without delay" in a particular case, we consider that we may take into account the nature of the steps necessary to withdraw the prohibited subsidy. We do not, however, agree with Canada that we should take into account the existence or absence of adverse or trade-distorting effects resulting from the prohibited subsidy, nor the time required to design replacement measures, as these factors are not related to the consideration of what time-period would represent withdrawal "without delay".

11.7 Applying these principles to the case at hand, we note that the MVTO 1998 and the SROs are both Orders-in-Council, and as such are acts of the executive, and not the legislative, branch of government. The amendment or revocation of an act of the executive branch can normally be effectuated more quickly than would be the case if legislative action were required. In light of the foregoing and of the information before the Panel, we consider that a time-period of 90 days would be appropriate.[910] We therefore **recommend** that the Dispute Settlement Body request Canada to withdraw the export subsidy within 90 days.

---

[909] The New Shorter Oxford English Dictionary (Clarendon Press, 1993), Vol. 1, 623.

[910] We note that, in those disputes involving a prohibited subsidy in which legislative action was not required, panels have specified a time-period of 90 days. See Panel Report on *Australia - Automotive Leather*, *supra* note 748; Panel Report on *Brazil - Aircraft*, *supra* note 490; Panel Report on *Canada - Aircraft*, *supra* note 495.

9 780521 828536